MW00679473

Congratulations on choosing the most comprehensive guide to Bed & Breakfast in Ireland. This year, for the first time, we now feature homes in Northern Ireland, as well as the Republic of Ireland, and this guide is all you will need to find the accommadtion you require in any part of the island of Ireland.

There are over 1,800 homes in this guide and all have been inspected and approved by the Tourist Board. Whether you are looking for accommodation in the hustle and bustle of the large cities, in quaint seaside villages or out in the quiet and peaceful countryside, this guide will give you full details of exactly the type of accommodation you are looking for throughout the entire island of Ireland. Each home is unique in it's own individual style and taste, but the one thing that is found in all our homes is a warm friendly welcome. What better way to meet the Irish than as a guest in the comfort of their home!.

We in Town & Country Homes Association Ltd. have been welcoming guests into our homes for nearly 30 years and we are committed to ensuring that you enjoy your stay with us. Our Association motto is "the personal touch" and is your guarantee of the very best hospitality and service while staying in our homes.

Bed & Breakfast in a Town & Country Home continues to be the most sought after, value for money accommodation in Ireland and the large number of guests who return year after year is proof of this. In order to maintain our high standard of accommodation and hospitality we would welcome your comments as we are constantly striving to improve the service we offer to you.

Over 50% of our homes can now be booked through email and we recommend that you book your first and last night accommodation in advance. Our members will be only too happy to assist you in making onward reservations before you leave their home, thus assuring you of the very best accommodation throughout your holiday.

We hope you enjoy your stay in Ireland and that you too will continue to return to Town & Country Homes again and again.

Fiona Byrne

Fiona Byrne, Chairperson

Tourist Regions of Ireland

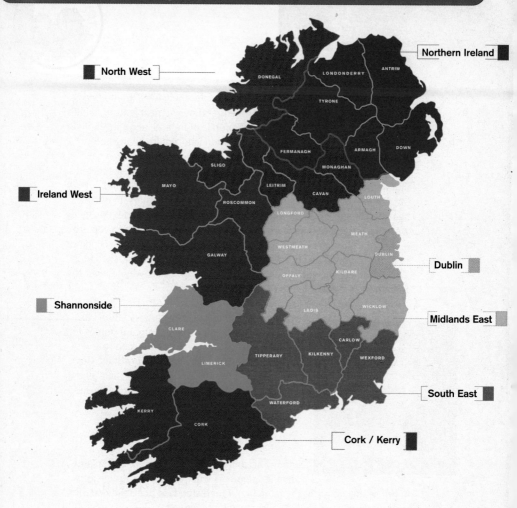

North West

Northern Ireland

DONEGAL
LONDONDERRY
ANTRIM
TYRONE
FERMANAGH
ARMAGH
DOWN
SLIGO
MONAGHAN
MAYO
LEITRIM
CAVAN
LOUTH
ROSCOMMON
LONGFORD
MEATH
WESTMEATH
DUBLIN
GALWAY
OFFALY
KILDARE
LAOIS
WICKLOW
CLARE
CARLOW
TIPPERARY
KILKENNY
WEXFORD
LIMERICK
KERRY
WATERFORD
CORK

Ireland West

Dublin

Shannonside

Midlands East

South East

Cork / Kerry

Approved Accommodation Signs
This sign will be displayed at most premises
which are approved to Irish Tourist Board
Standards.

Plakette fúr Geprúfte Unterkunft
Diese Plaketten werden an den meisten
Häusern angezeigt, die von auf die Einhaltung
der Normen der irischen
Fremdenverkehrsbehörde überprüft und
zugelassen wurden.

Borden voor goedgekeurde accommodatie
Deze borden vindt u bij de meeste huizen die
zijn goedgekeurd door voor de normen van de
Ierse Toeristenbond.

Simbolo di sistemazione approvata
Questi simboli saranno esposti nella maggior
parte delle case approvate (associazione dei
Bed & Breakfast approvati per qualità),
rispondenti agli standard dell'Ente del Turismo
Irlandese.

Símbolo de alojamiento aprobado
Estos símbolos se muestran en los
establecimientos que han sido aprobados
por bajos los estandars de la Oficina de
Turismo Irlandesa.

Skyltar för Godkänd logi
Dessa skyltar finns vid de flesta gästhus som
har godkänts (Föreningen för
kvalitetsgodkända gästhus AB), enligt irländska
turisföreningens normer.

**Panneaux d'homologation des
établissements**
Ces panneaux sont affichés dans la plupart
des établissements homologués selon les
normes de l'Office du tourisme irlandais.

Contents

HEAD OFFICE
Belleek Road, Ballyshannon, Co. Donegal.
Tel: 00353 72 22222   Fax: 00353 72 22207
(Monday-Friday 9am-5pm)
http://www.townandcountry.ie
WAP:www.bandbireland.com
e-mail:admin@townandcountry.ie

Head Office

Please forward all correspondence & enquiries to:
Mrs Margaret Storey, Chief Executive,
Town & Country Homes Association Ltd.
Belleek Road, Ballyshannon, Co. Donegal.
Tel: 00353 72 22222. Fax: 00353 72 22207.
Email: admin@townandcountry.ie
WAP: www.bandbireland.com
http://www.townandcountry.ie

Chairperson
Mrs Fiona Byrne, Glen na Smole, Ashtown Lane
Marlton Road, Wicklow, Co. Wicklow
Tel: 0404 67945, Fax: 0404 68155
Email: byrneglen@eircom.net

Vice-Chairman
Mrs Carol O'Gorman, Ashfort, Galway/Knock Rd,
Charlestown, Co. Mayo
Tel: 094 54706, Fax: 094 54706
Email: ashfort@esatclear.ie

Secretary
Mrs Noreen McBride, 3 Rossmore Grove,
off Wellington Lane, Templeogue, Dublin 6W.
Tel: 01 490 2939, Fax: 01 492 9416
Email: denismb@iol.ie

Treasurer
Mrs Tess Haughey, Rathnashee, Tessan,
Donegal Road, Sligo,
Co. Sligo
Tel: 071 43376, Fax: 071 42283

IRELAND

Bord Failte
Baggot St Bridge
Dublin 2
Tel: 01 602 4000
Fax: 01 602 4100
email:
user@irishtouristboard.ie

NORTHERN IRELAND

BELFAST

Bord Failte
53 Castle Street
Belfast BT1 1GH
Tel: 00 44 28 90327888
Fax: 00 44 28 90240201
email:info@irishtouristboardni.com

DERRY

Bord Failte
44 Foyle St.
Derry BT48 6AT
Tel: 00 44 28 71369501
Fax: 00 44 28 71369501

EUROPE

UK

Irish Tourist Board
Ireland House
150 New Bond St
London WIY OAQ
Tel: 00 44 20 7493 3201
Fax:00 44 20 7493 9065
e-mail:info@irishtouristboard.co.uk

GERMANY

Irische
Fremdenverkehrszentrale
Untermainanlage 7
D 60329 Frankfurt am
Main
Tel: 00 49 69 92 31 85 50
Fax: 00 49 69 92 31 85 88
e-mail:info@irishtouristboard.de

ITALY

Ente Nazionale del
Turismo Irlandese
via S. Maria Segreta 6
20123 Milano
Tel: 00 39 02 869 05 41
Fax:00 39 02 869 03 96
Email: info@turismo.irelandese.it

SPAIN

Turismo de Irlanda
Paseo de la Castellana
46, 3 Planta
28046 Madrid
Tel: 00 34 91 577 17 87
Fax: 00 34 91 577 69 34
e-mail: ireland@ran.es

SWEDEN

Irlandska Turistbyran
Sibyllegatan 49
PO Box 5292, 10246
Stockholm
Tel: 0046 8 662 85 10
Fax:0046 8 661 75 95
e-mail:info@irlandskaturistbyran.a.se

FINLAND

Irlannin Matkailutoimisto
Embassy of Ireland
Erottajankatu 7A, PL33
00130 Helsinki
Tel: 00 358 9608 966
Fax: 00 358 9646 022

NORWAY

Irlands Turistkontor
Karenlyst alle 9a
Postboks 295 Skoyen
0213 Oslo
Tel: 00 47 22 56 33 10
Fax:00 47 22 12 20 71

SWITZERLAND

Irland Informationsburo
Neumuhle Toss
Neumuhlestrasse 42
CH - 8406 Winterthur
Tel: 00 41 52 202 69 06
Fax: 00 41 52 202 69 08

PORTUGAL

Delegacao de Turismo
Irlandesa
Embaixada da Irlanda
Rua da Imprensa a
Estreal 1-4
1200 Lisboa
Tel: 00 351 1 392 94 40
Fax: 00 351 1 397 73 63

HOLLAND

Iers Nationaal Bureau
voor Toerisme
Spuistraat 104
1012 VA Amsterdam
Tel: 00 31 20-622 3101
Fax: 00 31 20-620 8089
e-mail: info@irishtouristboard.nl

BELGIUM

Irish Tourist Board
Avenue de Beaulieulaan
25/12, 1160 Brussels
Tel: 00 32 02 673 9940
Fax: 00 32 02 672 1066
e-mail:
info@irishtouristboard.be

FRANCE

Office National du
Tourisme Irlandais
33 rue de Miromesnil
75008 Paris
Tel: 00 33 1 53 43 12 12
Fax:00 33 1 47 42 01 64
e-mail: info@irlande-tourisme.fr

DENMARK

Det Irske Turistkontor
"Klostergaarden,"
Amagertorv 29B,3
DK1160 Copenhagen K
Tel: 0045 33 15 8045
Fax: 0045 33 93 6390
e-mail: info@irske-turistkontor.dk

JAPAN

Ireland House,
4th Floor, 2-10-7
Kojimachi
Chiyodi-ku
Tokyo 102-0083
Tel: 00 813 5275 1611
Fax: 00 813 5275 1623
Email: bfejapan@oak.ne.jp

SOUTH AFRICA

Irish Tourist Board
Everite House,
7th Floor,
20 de Korte Street
Braamfontein 2001
Johannesburg
Tel: 00 27 011 339 4865
Fax: 00 27 011 339 2474
e-mail:devprom@global.co.za

NEW ZEALAND

Irish Tourist Board
Dingwall Building
2nd Floor,
87 Queen Street
Auckland
Tel: 00 64 93 79 3720
Fax: 00 64 93 02 2420
Email: patrick.flynn@walshes.co.nz

AUSTRALIA

Irish Tourist Board
5th Level,
36 Carrington St
Sydney NSW 2000
Tel: 00 61 2 9299 6177
Fax: 00 61 2 9299 6323
e-mail: itb@bigpond.com

NORTH AMERICA

Irish Tourist Board
345 Park Avenue
New York NY 10154
Tel: 1800 22 36 470
Fax: 00 1 212 3719052
Web: www.irealndvacations.com

5

Using This Guide

The guide is divided into eight geographical regions which are subdivided into counties (see page 2 for map of regions and counties). The regions are: **Midlands East, North West, Northern Ireland, Dublin, South East, Cork/Kerry, Shannonside, Ireland West.**

Booking Procedure

It is advisable to **book first and last night's accommodation** in advance at all times.

Room Availability in Dublin

At the height of the tourist season - May to October - rooms in Dublin City and County are difficult to find unless accommodation is pre-booked. If visiting the capital city during these months, we strongly advise pre-booking all accommodation **well in advance.** Never count on finding rooms at short notice in Dublin. Always reserve in advance.

Onward Reservations:

Should problems arise finding accommodation when in Ireland, contact any Tourist Information Office, or seek advice and assistance from your host/hostess in Town and Country Homes. She/he will assist in booking subsequent night/nights for the cost of a telephone call.

Credit Card Bookings

Credit cards are accepted in homes with the cc symbol.
Telephone reservations may be guaranteed by quoting a valid credit card number. Check terms and conditions when booking.

Travel Agents Vouchers

Please present your voucher on arrival. Vouchers are only valid in homes displaying (V) .

Standard vouchers cover B&B in room without private facilities. To **upgrade to en suite** rooms the maximum charge is **£2.00 per person**. The maximum charge for 3 or more sharing should **not exceed £5 per room**.

En suite vouchers covers a room with full private facilities. No extra charge is payable.

Dublin Supplement:

A room supplement for Dublin city and county of £5 applies for the months of July & August on Travel Agency Vouchers. This charge is paid directly to the accommodation provider and is not included in the voucher.

Cancellation policy

When a reservation has been confirmed, please check cancellation policy with establishment at the time of booking. The person making the reservation is responsible for the agreed cancellation fee.

Please telephone immediately in the event of a cancellation. Should it be necessary to cancel or amend a booking without sufficient prior notice, a financial penalty applies.
- 14 days notice - no charge
- 24 hours notice/failure to show - 75% of the B&B charge for the first night.

Late Arrivals

Please note that late arrival - **after 6pm is by Special Agreement with home.**

Advance Bookings

For advance bookings, a cheque or Credit Card number may be requested to guarantee arrival. Check Terms and Conditions.

Check In/Out

Please advise of early arrival.
- Rooms available between 2pm and 6pm.
- Check out should be no later than 11am.
- Reservations should be taken up by 6pm.

Reduction for Children

Applies where children share parents room or three or more children share one room. Full rate applies when one or two children occupy separate rooms. Please check that the home is suitable for children when booking. Cots 🛏 are available in some homes – there may be a nominal charge.

Evening Meals

Book in advance preferably before 12 noon on the day. Light meals ✗ available on request.

Pets

With the exception of Guide Dogs, in the interest of hygiene pets are not allowed indoors.

Disabled Persons/Wheelchair Users

The National Disability Authority (NDA) have approved homes suitable for disabled people with a helper and these are listed by the symbol ♿.

Family Name
NAME OF TOWN OR
COUNTRY HOME
Address
Description of Town & Country Home

Colour Coded Bar for each Region

Area

TEL: FAX:
EMAIL:
WEB:
BUS NO:

			Min£/Max£	Min€/Max€	Dinner	£
B&B	#	Ensuite	Min£/Max£	Min€/Max€	Dinner	£
B&B	#	Standard	Min£/Max£	Min€/Max€	Partial Board	Min£/Max£
Single Rate			Min£/Max£	Min€/Max€	Child reduction	%

Nearest Town distance in km _(V symbol)_

Facility Symbols:

B+B PPS: Bed & Breakfast per person sharing

PARTIAL BRD: Bed & Breakfast, Evening meal for seven days.

\# No of rooms.

Open:

Child Reduction % for Children sharing parents room or where three or more children share one room

SINGLE RATE: : Single Rate for Room

Symbols

CC	Credit Cards accepted	↰	Cot available
♿	Access for disabled with helper.	✗	Light meals available
	NDA approved.	♀	Wine Licence
S	Single Room	♀	Walking
P	Private off-street parking	♣	Cycling
♣	Irish spoken	⛳	Golf within 5kms.
🐾	Facilities for Pets	▲	Horse riding within 5kms.
⊘	No smoking house	←	Facilities for Fishing
℞	No smoking bedrooms	♪ L	Lake fishing within 15km.
📺	TV in bedrooms	♪ S	Sea Fishing within 15km.
☎	Direct dial telephone in bedrooms	♪ R	River fishing within 15km.
☕	Tea/Coffee facilities in bedrooms	V	Travel Agency Vouchers Accepted.
♠	Babysitter, normally to 12 midnight	✗	Travel Agency Vouchers Not Accepted

Compliments and Comments

Complaints should always be brought to the attention of the proprietor before departure. Failing satisfaction and in the case of alleged overcharging, your receipt should be sent with your complaint to: **Customer Care, Town & Country Homes, Belleek Road, Ballyshannon, Co. Donegal.**

To maintain the high standards which the Association is renowned for, all comments on the general level of service and the standards you have experienced are welcome. All constructive criticisms will be taken seriously to ensure continued service improvement.

Errors and Omissions

Every care has been taken to ensure accuracy in this publication in compliance with the Consumer Protection Laws of Ireland. The Town & Country Homes Association Ltd. cannot accept responsibility for errors, omissions or inaccurate particulars in material supplied by members for inclusion in this publication, or for any loss or disappointment caused by dependence on information contained herein. Where such are brought to our attention, future editions will be amended accordingly. There may be changes after going to press where properties are sold, and the home changes ownership.

Page 412   Page 414   Page 416   Page 418   Page 420   Page 422   Pa 42

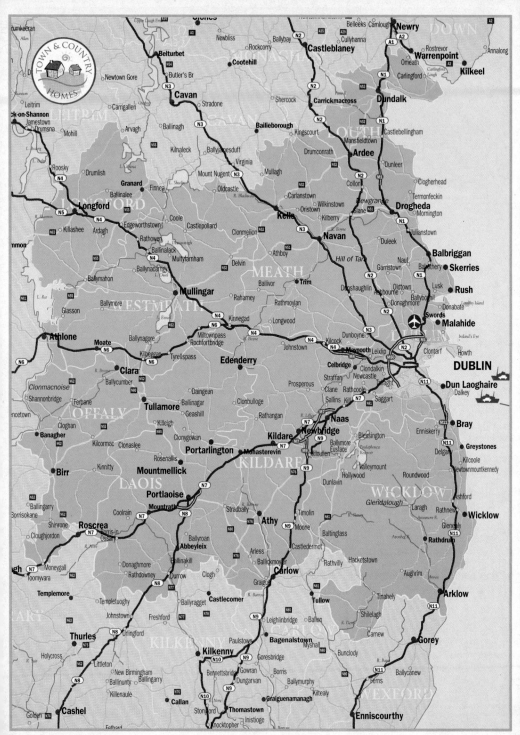

Midlands East

Where Dreams Come True......

The East Coast & Midlands Region of Ireland stretches from the golden beaches of the East Coast to the mountains of Wicklow, the Cooley Peninsula and the Slieve Blooms, to the majestic Shannon in the Midlands, this the most varied of Ireland's holiday regions.

In this part of Ireland there is something for everyone - all types of activity holidays, including some of the finest parkland and links courses in the world; outstanding angling, both freshwater and sea; superb equestrian facilities, including the Irish Racing Classics; spectacular walking terrain, relaxing cruises and exciting adventure breaks.

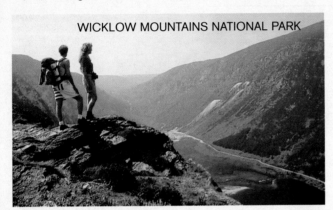

WICKLOW MOUNTAINS NATIONAL PARK

The range of visitor attractions, ancient monuments including Newgrange, heritage sites such as Clonmacnoise and Glendalough, great houses and gardens, quality restaurants and interesting comfortable affordable accommodation make the East Coast and Midlands the ideal location for that well earned holiday break.

Area Representatives

KILDARE
Mrs Tess Barrett, Lios Ciuin, Duncreevan, Kilcock, Co Kildare
Tel: 01 6287537

LAOIS
Mrs Lily Saunders, Rosedene, Limerick Road, Portlaoise, Co Laois
Tel: 0502 22345 Fax: 0502 22345

LOUTH
Mrs Marian Witherow, Krakow, 190 Ard Easmuinn, Dundalk, Co Louth
Tel: 042 9337535

MEATH
Ann Marie Russell, Sycamores, Dublin Rd, Navan, Co. Meath
Tel: 046 23719 Fax: 046 21261

OFFALY
Mrs Celine Grennan, The Bungalow, River View, Shannonbridge,
Athlone, Co Offaly   Tel: 0905 74180 Fax: 0905 74180

WESTMEATH
Mr Jim Denby, Shelmalier House, Cartrontroy, Athlone, Co Westmeath
Tel: 0902 72245/72145 Fax: 0902 73190

WICKLOW
Mrs Fiona Byrne, Glen na Smole, Ashtown Lane, Marlton Road, Wicklow,
Co Wicklow   Tel: 0404 67945 Fax: 0404 68155
Mrs Ann Griffin, Leettermore, Corballis, Rathdrum, Co. Wicklow
Tel: 0404 46506 Fax: 0404 43183
Mrs Jackie Burns, Ashdene, Knockanree Lower, Avoca, Co. Wicklow
Tel: 0402 35327 Fax: 0402 35327

i Tourist Information Offices

Mullingar
Market House
Tel: 044 48650

Dundalk
Jocelyn Street
Tel: 042 9335484

Longford Town
Market Square
Tel: 043 46566

Portlaoise
James Fintan Lawlor
Avenue
Tel: 0502 21178

Trim
Mill Street
Tel: 046 37111

Wicklow
Rialto House,
Fitzwilliam Square
Tel: 0404 69117

On Dublin's doorstep. Renowned for Horse-racing, The Curragh, Naas, Punchestown and the National Stud. Rich in history, abounding in great houses, Japanese and Arcadian gardens and Forest Park. Excellent golf clubs and Peatland Interpretative Centre, Canals, Angling and Cruising - a visitors paradise.

Castledermot 5km

Agnes Donoghue
WOODCOURTE HOUSE
Moone, Athy,
Co Kildare

Athy

Tel: **0507 24167**   Fax: **0507 24326**

Country home with extensive gardens. In woodland setting. On N9. 35 miles Dublin. Hourly bus service. Taxi available. Close to Golf courses, Race tracks, Fishing, Lovely Walks locally.

B&B	3	Ensuite	£20/£20	€25.39	Dinner	£15
B&B	1	Standard	£18/£18	€22.86	Partial Board	£200
Single Rate			£24.50/£26.50	€31.11/33.65	Child reduction	25%

Open: All Year

Celbridge 2km

Mrs Rose McCabe
GREEN ACRE
Dublin Rd, Celbridge,
Co Kildare

Celbridge

Tel: **01 6271163/6271694** Fax: **01 6271694**
Email: ptmcbe@indigo.ie
Bus No: **67 & 67A**

Bungalow on own grounds, Dublin 20 mins, 30 mins. Airport, Ferries, Bus Route, Car park. Castletown House 2km. Golf, Fishing.

B&B	6	Ensuite	£20	€25.39	Dinner	-
B&B	-	Standard	-	-	Partial Board	-
Single Rate			-	-	Child reduction	50%

Open: 1st April-31st October

Clane 3km

Mr Myles Doyle
BALLINAGAPPA COUNTRY HOUSE
Clane, Co Kildare

Clane

Tel: **045 892087**   Fax: **045 892087**

1862 period Georgian country house. Kept in original Georgian style. 2 ensuite & 1 standard. Rooms with high classed country cooking & a warm welcome on our doorstep.

B&B	2	Ensuite	£30/£30	€38.09	Dinner	-
B&B	1	Standard	-	-	Partial Board	-
Single Rate			£35/£40	€44.44/€50.79	Child reduction	-

Open: All Year

Clane 4.8km

Ms Una Healy
STRAFFAN B&B
Dublin Rd, Straffan,
Co Kildare

Clane/Straffan

Tel: **01 6272386**
Email: judj@gofree.indigo.ie
Bus No: **123, 120**

Spacious gardens, Power showers. Barberstown Castle and K club 2mins. Golf, Fishing, Mondello, Goffs nearby. Dublin 17 mins. Airport 45 mins. Exit M4 at Maynooth, Exit N7 at Kill.

B&B	3	Ensuite	£22/£25	€27.93/31.74	Dinner	-
B&B	-	Standard	-	-	Partial Board	-
Single Rate			£25.50/£25.50	€32.38	Child reduction	50%

Open: 1st January-22nd December

Mr Brian Lynch
KERRY'S
**Dublin Road, Clane,
Co Kildare**

Clane

TEL: **045 892601**

Peaceful home on Dublins doorstep. Dublin 30 min, Airport/Ferries 40 mins, Pubs/Restaurants 1 min. Curragh/Naas/Punchestown race courses, Mondello nearby. Car park.

B&B	4	Ensuite	£19/£22	€24.13/€27.93	Dinner	£16
B&B	-	Standard		-	Partial Board	-
Single Rate			£26/£30	€33.01/€38.09	Child reduction	50%

In Clane Village

Open: 2nd January-22nd December

Mrs Mary Lynch
THE LAURELS
**Dublin Road,
Clane, Co Kildare**

Clane

TEL: **045 868274**

Dublin 30 mins drive. Bus to and from City Centre. Convenient to Airport and Ferries.

B&B	3	Ensuite	£20	€25.39	Dinner	£13
B&B	-	Standard		-	Partial Board	-
Single Rate			£25.50	€32.38	Child reduction	50%

In Clane

Open: 30th April-30th September

Ms Maura Timoney
SHRIFF LODGE
**Painstown (R407)
Donadea, Co Kildare**

Clane

TEL: **045 869282**   FAX: **045 869982**
EMAIL: shrifflodge@eircom.net
WEB: http://homepage.eircom.net/~shrifflodge

On R407, Dublin 20 miles, M4 6 miles. Convenient Airport/Ferries, Curragh, Naas, Punchestown Races. Donadea Forest Park, Golf K Club, Knockanally, Pinetrees.

B&B	3	Ensuite	£20/£22	€25.39/€27.93	Dinner	-
B&B	-	Standard		-	Partial Board	-
Single Rate			£25.50/£30	€32.38/€38.09	Child reduction	33.3%

Clane 4.5km

Open: 10th February-30th November

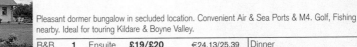

Mrs Tess Barrett
LIOS CIUIN
**Duncreevan,
Kilcock, Co Kildare**

Kilcock

TEL: **01 6287537**
EMAIL: pbarrett@eircom.net
BUS NO: **66**

Pleasant dormer bungalow in secluded location. Convenient Air & Sea Ports & M4. Golf, Fishing nearby. Ideal for touring Kildare & Boyne Valley.

B&B	1	Ensuite	£19/£20	€24.13/25.39	Dinner	-
B&B	2	Standard	£17/£17	€21.59	Partial Board	-
Single Rate			£23.50/£26.50	€29.84/33.65	Child reduction	25%

Kilcock 1km

Open: 1st May-30th September

Mrs Kathleen Farrell
BREEZY HEIGHTS
**Cappagh, Kilcock,
Co Kildare**

Kilcock

TEL: **0405 41183**

2 mins off Dublin/Galway N4 road. Dublin 30 mins. Convenient to Airport/Ferries. Quiet & peaceful. Golf, Fishing nearby.

B&B	2	Ensuite	£19/£19	€24.13	Dinner	-
B&B	2	Standard	£17/£17	€21.59	Partial Board	-
Single Rate			£23.50/£25.50	€29.84/32.38	Child reduction	25%

Kilcock 4km

Open: 31st March-30th November

11

Mrs Eileen Corcoran
MOUNT RUADHAN
**Old Road, Southgreen,
Kildare, Co Kildare**

Kildare

TEL: **045 521637**   FAX: **045 521637**

Bungalow set in landscaped garden - close to Curragh Race Course, Japanese Gardens, National Stud, Fishing, Golf, Airport, Ferries. Quiet and peaceful setting.

B&B	2	Ensuite	£20/£25	€25.39/31.74	Dinner	-
B&B	1	Standard	£18/£22.50	€22.86/28.57	Partial Board	-
Single Rate					Child reduction	25%

Kildare 1.5km

Open: 1st April-31st October

The Foran Family
HEATHERVILLE B&B
**Shaughlins Glen,
Confey, Leixlip, Co Kildare**

Leixlip

TEL: **01 6245156**
EMAIL: forans@iol.ie
BUS No: 66

Rural setting. 2 miles Leixlip, 12 miles Dublin, 30 mins Airport/Ferry. Secure parking. Exit M4/N4 Leixlip. Right at traffic lights to T junction, left 1.2 miles.

B&B	3	Ensuite	£19/£20	€24.13/25.39	Dinner	-
B&B	-	Standard			Partial Board	-
Single Rate			£25.50/£25.50	€32.38	Child reduction	50%

Leixlip 3km

Open: 1st January-22nd December

Annette Cullen
THE GABLES
**Coole, Monasterevin,
Co Kildare**

Monasterevin

TEL: **045 525564**   FAX: **045 525564**
EMAIL: thegables@eircom.net

Enjoy excellent accommodation in "The Venice of Ireland". Our home is just a short picturesque walk across the aqueduct from the town. Dublin 50 minutes.

B&B	2	Ensuite	£19/£22	€24.13/€27.93	Dinner	-
B&B	2	Standard	£17/£19	€21.59/€24.13	Partial Board	-
Single Rate			£23.50/£28	€29.84/€35.55	Child reduction	50%

Monasterevin 1km

Open: 1st April-31st October

Mrs Bridie Doherty
TWO MILE HOUSE
Naas, Co Kildare

Naas

TEL: **045 879824**

Peaceful location - 200 yds off N9 Dublin/Waterford road. Dublin 30 mins drive. Convenient to Airport and Ferries.

B&B	3	Ensuite	£19/£20	€24.13/€25.39	Dinner	-
B&B	-	Standard			Partial Board	-
Single Rate			£25.50	€32.38	Child reduction	50%

Naas 4km

Open: 1st March-31st October

Mrs Olive Hennessy
DUN AONGHUS
**Beggars End,
Naas, Co Kildare**

Naas

TEL: **045 875126**   FAX: **045 898069**
EMAIL: dunaonghus@hotmail.com

Tranquil location near town. Just off R410. 4 mins N7. Ideal for visiting Kildare, Dublin, Wicklow. Golf, Equestrian, Horseracing. 1 hour Airport and Ferryports.

B&B	4	Ensuite	£20/£25	€25.39/€31.74	Dinner	-
B&B	3	Standard	£18/£21	€22.86/€26.66	Partial Board	-
Single Rate			£24/£30	€30.47/€38.09	Child reduction	33.3%

Naas 2km

Open: 2nd January-20th December

Mrs Kathleen Garrett
SEVEN SPRINGS
**Hawkfield, Newbridge,
Co Kildare**

Newbridge

Tel: **045 431677**

Bungalow, beside Newbridge and N7. Convenient to National Stud, Japanese Gardens, Curragh, Naas. Punchestown Race Course, Boat, Airport, Dog-racing & Mondello nearby.

B&B	-	Ensuite	-	-	Dinner	£13
B&B	3	Standard	£19/£24	€24.13/€30.47	Partial Board	-
Single Rate			£25/£30	€31.74/€38.09	Child reduction	50%

Newbridge 3km

Open: March-November

Mrs Breda Kelly
BELLA VISTA
**105 Moorefield Park,
Newbridge, Co Kildare**

Newbridge

Tel: **045 431047** Fax: **045 438259**
Email: belavista@eircom.net

Long established Residence in quiet Residential Area. Convenient to Curragh, Punchestown, Japanese Gardens. Rooms en-suite, TV, Video, hairdryers, tea-making facilities.

B&B	4	Ensuite	£21/£28	€26.66/€35.55	Dinner	£12.50
B&B		Standard	-	-	Partial Board	-
Single Rate			£25.50/£30	€32.38/€38.09	Child reduction	25%

In Newbridge

Open: All Year

Mary O'Shea
KERRYHILL
**Morristown Biller,
Newbridge, Co Kildare**

Newbridge

Tel: **045 432433**

Spacious bungalow, Private Car Park, Easy Access, Japanese Gardens, National Stud, Airport, Ferries, Horse, Dog, Motor Racing.

B&B	2	Ensuite	£21/£26	€26.66/€33.01	Dinner	-
B&B	1	Standard	£19/£24	€24.13/€30.47	Partial Board	-
Single Rate			£26/£26	€33.01	Child reduction	25%

Newbridge 1km

Open: 1st March-31st October

BOOKINGS

We recommend your first and last night is pre-booked. Your hosts will make a booking for you at your next selected home for the cost of the phone call. When travelling in high season (June, July, August), it is essential to pre-book your accommodation – preferably the evening before, or the following morning to avoid disappointment.

WHEN TRAVELLING OFF-SEASON IT IS ADVISABLE TO CALL AHEAD AND GIVE A TIME OF ARRIVAL TO ENSURE YOUR HOSTS ARE AT HOME TO GREET YOU.

Laois is a picturesque inland county. Rich in historical houses and garden's, heritage sites, Museums, Golfing, Angling, Bogs, canals and rivers. Discover the Slieve Bloom mountains, their waterfalls and nature trails. The visitors relax and enjoy peace and tranquillity.

Abbeyleix 1km

Maureen Lalor
COIS NA TINE
Portlaoise Road,
Abbeyleix, Co Laois

Abbeyleix
Tel: **0502 31976**

Charming bungalow. On main Dublin Cork route, 1km from Abbeyleix Heritage Town. Adjacent to Golf, Pony/Riding, Fishing Pubs/Restaurants.

B&B	3	Ensuite	£19/£20	€24.13/€25.39	Dinner	-
B&B	-	Standard		-	Partial Board	-
Single Rate			£25.50	€32.38	Child reduction	-

Open: 3rd January-20th December

Portlaoise 20km

Mrs Janet Dooley
LANLEY B&B
Mountsalem, Coolrain,
Portlaoise, Co Laois

Coolrain/Portlaoise
Tel: **0502 35013**

Warm welcoming home at the foot of the Slieve Bloom Mountains. Situated off main Dublin Limerick Road (N7), 20km from Portlaoise, just 8km from Mountrath. Ideal touring base.

B&B	3	Ensuite	£19.50/£25	€24.76/€31.74	Dinner	-
B&B	1	Standard	£17/£23	€21.59/€29.20	Partial Board	-
Single Rate			-	-	Child reduction	25%

Open: 1st January-23rd December

Portlaoise 1km

Mrs Vera Hade
RENARD
Limerick Road, Portlaoise,
Co Laois

Portlaoise
Tel: **0502 21735**   Fax: **0502 21735**

Warm welcoming home on N7 West (R445). Relaxed atmosphere. Tea/Scones on arrival. Close to all amenities. 1 hour to Dublin.

B&B	1	Ensuite	£20	€25.39	Dinner	-
B&B	2	Standard	£18	€22.86	Partial Board	-
Single Rate			£23.50/£26	€29.84/€33.01	Child reduction	25%

Open: 1st January-23rd December

Portlaoise

Maurice & Mary Murphy
OAKVILLE
Mountrath Road,
Portlaoise, Co Laois

Portlaoise
Tel: **0502 61970**
Email: oakvillebandb@eircom.net

Situated on R445 N7 west. Crossroads of Ireland. Shops, Restaurants, Pubs, Theatre nearby. Family run. Tour guide on premises. Italian spoken. Private carpark.

B&B	3	Ensuite	£20/£20	€25.39	Dinner	-
B&B	1	Standard	£18/£18	€22.86	Partial Board	-
Single Rate			£23.50/£25.5	€29.84/€32.38	Child reduction	25%

Open: 8th January-22nd December

Mrs Lily Saunders
ROSEDENE
Limerick Road, Portlaoise,
Co Laois

Portlaoise

TEL: **0502 22345**   FAX: **0502 22345**
EMAIL: rosedene@gofree.indigo.ie

Peaceful, relaxing home. Personal attention. Bedrooms have multichannel TV, Tea/Coffee, Hairdryers. Walking distance Pubs, Restaurants. On N7 R445 West central location. Dublin 80km.

B&B	2	Ensuite	£19/£22	€24.13/€27.93	Dinner	-
B&B	1	Standard	£17/£20	€21.59/€25.39	Partial Board	-
Single Rate			£23.50/£28	€29.84/€35.55	Child reduction	33.3%

Portlaoise 1km

Open: 7th January-20th December

Abigail McEvoy
GAROON HOUSE
Birr Road, Mountmellick,
Co Laois

Mountmellick

TEL: **0502 24641**
EMAIL: abigailm@oceanfree.net
WEB: http://islandireland.com/garoonhouse

New, spacious, tastefully decorated home on large manicured grounds. Central location for touring any part of Ireland. Personally supervised breakfast menu.

B&B	5	Ensuite	£20	€25.39	Dinner	-
B&B	-	Standard			Partial Board	-
Single Rate			£25.50	€32.38	Child reduction	-

Mountmellick 1km

Open: 31st March-20th October

Noreen Murphy Ui Laighin
CONLAN HOUSE
Killanure, Mountrath,
Co Laois

Mountrath

TEL: **0502 32727**   FAX: **0502 32727**
EMAIL: conlanhouse@oceanfree.net
WEB: http://homepage.eircom.net/~conlanhouse

Spacious friendly home. Tea/Coffee/Homebaking on arrival. Personal attention assured. Extensive breakfast menu. Central for touring. Maps/Books. 1 1/2 hours Dublin and Shannon Airports.

B&B	3	Ensuite	£22.50/£22.50	€28.57	Dinner	£18
B&B	-	Standard			Partial Board	£250
Single Rate			£25.50/£30	€32.38/€38.09	Child reduction	50%

Mountrath 7km

Open: All Year

APPROVED ACCOMMODATION SIGNS

Approved Accommodation Signs
This sign will be displayed at most premises which are approved to Irish Tourist Board Standards.

Panneaux d'homologation des établissements
Ces panneaux sont affichés dans la plupart des établissements homologués selon les normes de l'Office du tourisme irlandais.

Plakette fúr Geprúfte Unterkunft
Diese Plaketten werden an den meisten Häusern angezeigt, die von auf die Einhaltung der Normen der irischen Fremdenverkehrsbehörde überprüft und zugelassen wurden.

Borden voor goedgekeurde accommodatie
Deze borden vindt u bij de meeste huizen die zijn goedgekeurd door voor de normen van de Ierse Toeristenbond.

Simbolo di sistemazione approvata
Questi simboli saranno esposti nella maggior parte delle case approvate (associazione dei Bed & Breakfast approvati per qualità), rispondenti agli standard dell'Ente del Turismo Irlandese.

Símbolo de alojamiento aprobado
Estos símbolos se muestran en los establecimientos que han sido aprobados por bajos los estandars de la Oficina de Turismo Irlandesa.

Skyltar för Godkänd logi
Dessa skyltar finns vid de flesta gästhus som har godkänts (Föreningen för kvalitetsgodkända gästhus AB), enligt irländska turisföreningens normer.

15

Longford - this inland county is approximately 80 miles from Dublin. The county is rich in literary associations. The wonderful landscape is a blend of bogland, lakeland, pastureland and Wetland. Anglers can take advantage of the excellent facilities here.

Longford Town 10km

Miss Bridie Kenny
ARDKEN
Ardagh,
Co Longford

Ardagh

TEL: **043 75029**   FAX: **043 75029**
EMAIL: ardken@iol.ie

Beautiful house in unique Estate Village. Winner of National Tidy Towns award. Identified as Heritage Village just off N4, N55.

B&B	3	Ensuite	£19/£19	€24.13	Dinner	£12.50
B&B	-	Standard	-	-	Partial Board	£185
Single Rate			£25.50/£25.50	€32.38	Child reduction	50%

Open: All Year

Longford

Mandy Etherton
OLDE SCHOOLHOUSE
Garrowhill, Newtownforbes,
Co Longford

Longford

TEL: **043 24854**

Unique old world charm, spacious in countryside. Fishing, Golf, Pitch & Putt, Trekking nearby. Take R198 towards Drumlish, at Longford bypass, at 4.8km cross-right.

B&B	3	Ensuite	£19/£19	€24.13	Dinner	£12.50
B&B	-	Standard	-	-	Partial Board	£185
Single Rate			£25.50/£25.50	€32.38	Child reduction	50%

Open: 7th January-20th December

Longford 4km

Mrs Eileen Prunty
EDEN HOUSE
Newtownforbes,
Longford, Co Longford

Longford

TEL: **043 41160**

Peaceful home in picturesque village off Newtownforbes on N4. All facilities closeby. Refreshments on arrival. Orthopaedic beds, electric blankets, TV.

B&B	4	Ensuite	£20	€25.39	Dinner	-
B&B	1	Standard	£19	€24.13	Partial Board	-
Single Rate			£26	€33.01	Child reduction	25%

Open: All Year except Christmas

SYMBOL

LOOK OUT FOR THIS SYMBOL WHICH
ALL MEMBERS OF TOWN & COUNTRY HOMES
DISPLAY

The diversity of scenery, historical/archeological sites, sporting and shopping attractions within easy access from Dublin and Belfast ports/airports.
The tranquillity of the Boyne Valley and Newgrange, to the splendour and panoramic views of Carlingford Lough at the base of the Mourne Mountains makes Louth the ideal base for all tourists.

Mrs Sheila Magennis
CARRAIG MOR
Blakestown,
Ardee, Co Louth

Ardee

Tel: **041 6853513**   Fax: **041 6853513**
Email: info@carraigmor.com
Web: www.carraigmor.com

Spacious comfortable home N2 (Dublin/Derry) 2km south Ardee. Restaurants, Golf, Fishing nearby. Central to Monasterboice, Mellifont, Newgrange. Dublin Airport 45 mins.

B&B	4	Ensuite	£19/£19	€24.13	Dinner -
B&B	1	Standard	£17/£17	€21.59	Partial Board -
Single Rate			£23.50/£25.50	€29.84/€32.38	Child reduction 50%

Open: All Year

Ardee 2km

Mrs Lyn Grills
MOURNEVIEW
Belmont, Carlingford,
Co Louth

Carlingford

Tel: **042 9373551**   Fax: **042 9373551**

Spacious family run home. Tranquil location. Panoramic views of Mourne and Cooley Mountains. TV and Tea making facilities all rooms. Sign for Carlingford. Off Dublin/Belfast road (N1).

B&B	6	Ensuite	£19/£20	€24.13/€25.39	Dinner -
B&B	-	Standard	-	-	Partial Board -
Single Rate			£25.50	€32.38	Child reduction 50%

Open: All Year

Carlingford 2km

Mrs Jackie Woods
SHALOM
Ghan Road,
Carlingford, Co Louth

Carlingford

Tel: **042 9373151**
Email: kevinwoods@eircom.net
Web: jackiewoods.com

Situated beside the Sea in the Medieval town of Carlingford. Overlooked by the Mourne mountains on one side and the Cooley Mountains on the other.

B&B	5	Ensuite	£19/£19	€24.13	Dinner -
B&B	-	Standard	-	-	Partial Board -
Single Rate			£25.50	€32.38	Child reduction 50%

Open: All Year

Carlingford

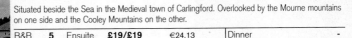

Marie McCarthy
THE HIGHLANDS
Irish Grange,
Carlingford, Co Louth

Carlingford

Tel: **042 9376104**
Email: thehighlands@eircom.net

Luxury accommodation in scenic Cooley Peninsula. Panoramic view of Carlingford Lough and Mourne Mountains. Private parking. Large gardens off R173.

B&B	3	Ensuite	£19/£20	€24.13/€25.39	Dinner -
B&B	-	Standard	-	-	Partial Board -
Single Rate			£25.50/£25.50	€32.38	Child reduction 50%

Open: 1st February-31st October

Carlingford 3km

Mrs Mary Dolores McEvoy
THE CROSS GARDEN
Ganderstown, Clogherhead
Drogheda, Route 166
Co Louth

Clogherhead
TEL: **041 9822675**

Overlooking Irish Sea, Modern dormer bungalow, on elevated site. Clogherhead one mile on Termonfeckin Road. All rooms private facilities. Warm welcome.

B&B	2	Ensuite	£19/£19	€24.13	Dinner	-
B&B	1	Standard	£19/£19	€24.13	Partial Board	-
Single Rate			£25/£25	€31.74	Child reduction	30%

Drogheda 5km

Open: All Year

Mrs Christine Dunne
LINKS VIEW
Golf Links Road, Bettystown
Drogheda, Co Louth

Drogheda
TEL: **041 9827222**
EMAIL: fergus_dunne@hotmail.com

Peaceful home beside Golf course & Beach. 30 mins Airport. Convenient to Newgrange. Facing North in Bettystown, take 3rd turn left after Golf Club.

B&B	1	Ensuite	£22	€27.93	Dinner	-
B&B	2	Standard	£20	€25.39	Partial Board	-
Single Rate			£25	€31.74	Child reduction	-

Drogheda 4km

Open: All Year

Mrs Mona Dunne
SALLYWELL HOUSE B&B
Hill-of-Rath, Tullyallen,
Drogheda, Co Louth

Drogheda
TEL: **041 9834816**   FAX: **041 9834436**
EMAIL: dunnemckeever@iegateway.net
WEB: www.dreamwater.com/sallywell

Country bungalow. Fish pond, Patio/Conservatory. Large gardens. 8km to Newgrange. 3km Monasterboice Tower and Celtic Cross. 30km from Dublin Airport. 2km Town Centre.

B&B	4	Ensuite	£20/£22	€25.39/€27.93	Dinner	£12.50
B&B	-	Standard			Partial Board	
Single Rate			£25.50/£27	€32.38/€34.29	Child reduction	25%

Drogheda 2km

Open: 5th January-23rd December

Rhona Hill
DRUMADOON
Waterunder, Collon Rd,
Drogheda, Co Louth

Drogheda
TEL: **041 9838495**

Peaceful country home ideally located on Drogheda/Collon Rd. R168 to tour Boyne Valley. Golf, Fishing, Beaches nearby. Warm welcome. Garden for guests.

B&B	2	Ensuite	£21/£23	€26.66/€29.20	Dinner	-
B&B	1	Standard	£18/£18	€22.86	Partial Board	-
Single Rate			£23.50/£25	€29.84/€31.74	Child reduction	-

Drogheda 4km

Open: April-November

Mrs Angela Kerrigan
KILLOWEN HOUSE
Woodgrange, Dublin Rd,
Drogheda, Co Louth

Drogheda
TEL: **041 9833547**   FAX: **041 9833547**
EMAIL: killowenhouse@unison.ie
WEB: http://homepage.eircom.net/~killowenhouse

Luxury home 50m off N1 near Hotels, 25 mins Airport, 40 mins City Centre. Good base touring Boyne Valley area, near Newgrange, Monasterboice, Beach, Golf. Spacious rooms. All facilities.

B&B	3	Ensuite	£22/£25	€27.93/€31.74	Dinner	-
B&B	2	Standard	£20/£22	€25.39/€27.93	Partial Board	-
Single Rate			£24/£32	€30.47/€40.63	Child reduction	25%

Drogheda 3km

Open: All Year except Christmas

Mrs Mary McCabe
SHERDARA
Beaulieu Cross,
Termonfeckin Road,
Drogheda, Co Louth

Tel: **041 9836159**

A warm welcome awaits you at our modern bungalow on Drogheda - Termonfeckin road. Conservatory diningroom. Breakfast menu. Convenient Newgrange, Golf & Airport.

				Dinner	-
B&B	3	Ensuite	£20	€25.39	Partial Board	-
B&B	1	Standard	£18	€22.86	
Single Rate			£23.50/£25	€29.84/€31.74	Child reduction	25%

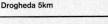
Drogheda 5km

Open: May-September

Cepta & Eobhain McDonnell
TULLYESKER COUNTRY HOUSE
Dundalk Road (N1)
Monasterboice, Drogheda,
Co Louth

Tel: **041 9830430/9832624** Fax: **041 9832624**
Email: mcdonnellfamily@ireland.com
Web: www.tullyeskerhouse.com

Official highest grade ✦✦✦✦✦ family home, 3 acres garden, panoramic view. Orthopaedic bed, Tea and Coffee, Multi TV, Gourmet breakfast menu. Parking, Airport 25 miles.

				Dinner	-
B&B	5	Ensuite	£23/£30	€29.20/€38.09	Partial Board	-
B&B	-	Standard		
Single Rate			£34/£40	€43.17/€50.79	Child reduction	-

Drogheda 4km

Open: 1st February-30th November

Tara McDonnell
BOYNE HAVEN HOUSE
Dublin Road,
Drogheda, Co Louth

Tel: **041 9836700** Fax: **041 9836700**

Truly magnificent, not to be missed. Award winning AA ✦✦✦✦. Drogheda South on N1, Airport 20 mins. Luxurious en-suite rooms, TV, Breakfast menu. Opposite Europa Hotel.

				Dinner	-
B&B	4	Ensuite	£22.50/£30	€28.57/€38.09	Partial Board	-
B&B	-	Standard		
Single Rate			£35/£40	€44.44/€50.79	Child reduction	-

Drogheda 2km

Open: All Year

Mrs Betty Nallen
ELEVENTH TEE HOUSE
Golf Links Road, Bettystown,
Drogheda, Co Louth

Tel: **041 9827613** Fax: **041 9828150**

Situated in beautiful gardens adjoining Golf Course. Large Beach 0.5km. Bettystown 1.5km. Convenient Newgrange, Mosney. Airport 30 mins. 4km off N1. Road no. R150.

				Dinner	-
B&B	3	Ensuite	£20/£23	€25.39/€29.20	Partial Board	-
B&B	1	Standard		
Single Rate			£25/£30	€31.74/€38.09	Child reduction	25%

Drogheda 5km

Open: 6th January-30th November

Peter & Mary Phillips
ORLEY HOUSE
Bryanstown, Dublin Road,
Drogheda, Co Louth

Tel: **041 9836019** Fax: **041 9836019**
Email: orleyhouse@eircom.net

Luxurious Town home off N1. Conservatory Dining Room. Airport 20 mins near Bus/Rail/Ferries/3 Golf Courses/Newgrange/Boynevalley/Hotels/Shops and Restaurants.

				Dinner	£16
B&B	4	Ensuite	£22/£25	€27.93/€31.74	Partial Board	-
B&B	-	Standard		
Single Rate			£28/£35	€35.55/€44.44	Child reduction	-

In Drogheda

Open: All Year Except Christmas

Drogheda 4km

Anne Walsh
CASTLEGADDERY
Tullyallen, Drogheda,
Co Louth

TEL: **041 9839299**   FAX: **041 9847901**
EMAIL: annesbandb@hotmail.com
WEB: www.castlegaddery.bizland.com

Luxurious B&B 4km north west of Drogheda on R168 - Collon Rd. 45mins-Dublin Airport. Close to Mellifont Abbey, Williams Glen, Bru-na, Boinne, Monasterboice.

B&B	2	Ensuite	£20/£26	€25.39/€33.01	Dinner	-
B&B	2	Standard	£19/£25	€24.13/€31.74	Partial Board	-
Single Rate			£23.50/£30	€29.84/€38.09	Child reduction	-

Open: All Year

Dundalk 4km

Mrs Evelyn Carolan
LYNOLAN
Mullaharlin Road,
Haynestown,
Dundalk, Co Louth

TEL: **042 9336553**   FAX: **042 9336553**
EMAIL: lynolan@indigo.ie

Luxury Home, in peaceful rural setting situated off new motorway, 700m from roundabout. Convenient to Fairways Hotel, Restaurants, DKIT. Signposted off N1/N52.

B&B	5	Ensuite	£19/£20	€24.13/€25.39	Dinner	£13
B&B	1	Standard	£18/£19	€22.86/€24.13	Partial Board	-
Single Rate			£25/£26	€31.74/€33.01	Child reduction	50%

Open: 15th January-15th December

Dundalk 3km

Mrs Patricia Murphy
PINEWOODS
Dublin Road, Dundalk,
Co Louth

TEL: **042 9321295**
EMAIL: olmurphy@eircom.net

Traditional Irish welcome in modern dormer bungalow just off Dublin/Belfast motorway beside Fairways Hotel. Going north, turn right at roundabout on N1, going south, turn left.

B&B	4	Ensuite	£20/£26	€25.39/€33.01	Dinner	-
B&B	1	Standard	£20/£26	€25.39/€33.01	Partial Board	-
Single Rate			£25/£35	€31.74/€44.44	Child reduction	-

Open: All Year

Dundalk 5km

Brenda Rogers
BLACKROCK HOUSE
Main Street, Blackrock Village
Blackrock, Dundalk, Co Louth

TEL: **042 9321829/9322909**   FAX: **042 9322909**
EMAIL: blackrockhsedundalk@eircom.net

Home by shore. Lounge has panoramic view Dundalk Bay. First class Bars and Restaurants. Dundalk Golf Club, Fairways Htl, Bird Sanctuary nearby. 50 mins Dublin Airport/Belfast.

B&B	6	Ensuite	£19	€24.13	Dinner	-
B&B	-	Standard			Partial Board	-
Single Rate			£25.50/£30	€32.38/€38.09	Child reduction	-

Open: All Year

In Dundalk

Mrs Marian Witherow
KRAKOW
190 Ard Easmuinn,
Dundalk, Co Louth

TEL: **042 9337535**
EMAIL: krakow@eircom.net

Modern bungalow convenient to Railway Station and Derryhale Hotel. Walking distance to Town Centre. First turn right after Railway Stn. 2 directional signs- KRAKOW B&B.

B&B	6	Ensuite	£19/£20	€24.13/€25.39	Dinner	£14
B&B	-	Standard			Partial Board	£195
Single Rate			£25.50/£27	€32.38/€34.29	Child reduction	25%

Open: All Year

Maureen & Myles Condra
BRAMBLE LODGE
**Main St, Dunleer,
Co Louth**

Dunleer
TEL: **041 6851565**
EMAIL: mcondra@esatclear.ie

Victorian house in own grounds set amid rosegardens. Furnished in period style, situated off M1. Convenient to Newgrange, Monasterboice, Mellifont, Beach & Golf courses.

B&B	3	Ensuite	£23/£23	€29.20	Dinner	£15
B&B	-	Standard			Partial Board	-
Single Rate			£29.50/£29.50	€37.46	Child reduction	33.3%

Open: 1st January-23rd December

Mrs Eileen McGeown
DELAMARE HOUSE
**Ballyoonan, Omeath,
Co Louth**

Omeath
TEL: **042 9375101**
EMAIL: eileenmcgeown@eircom.net

In peaceful rural area, overlooking Carlingford Lough and Mourne Mountains. On Carlingford/Omeath road opposite Calvary Shrine. Carlingford 3 miles.

B&B	2	Ensuite	£19	€24.13	Dinner	-
B&B	2	Standard	£17	€21.59	Partial Board	-
Single Rate			£23.50/£25.50	€29.84/€32.38	Child reduction	33.3%

Omeath 1km

Open: 15th March-15th November

Meath

Where Heritage Lives

Just stand for a few minutes on the Hill of Tara and you'll know what we mean. The sight of Trim Castle's monumental ramparts will do it to you as well. Or the mysterious neolithic wonders of Loughcrew and Newgrange at *Brú na Boinne*. Meath's heritage springs to life, grabbing the imagination with vivid images of the past. Discover Meath's living heritage.

For your free brochure and tourism inquiries contact:
Meath Tourism at Callsave: **1850 300 789** www.meathtourism.ie info@meathtourism.ie

Meath
Always a visit to treasure

Visit the stoneage passage tombs of Newgrange/Knowth, Christian sites of Kells and Hill of Tara. Navan - Capital town and Slane picturesque estate village. Trim Castle - planned opening summer 2000. Europe's largest Anglo Norman Castle, Craft shop and Visitors Centre. Activities: Golf, Equestrian, Fishing, Gardens, Fine Dining and Quaint Pubs.

Mrs Kathleen Kelly
BALTRASNA LODGE
**Baltrasna, Ashbourne,
Co Meath**

Ashbourne
TEL: 01 8350446

Luxury home on large grounds. Dublin City/Airport 20 mins. 3rd house R125 off N2. 1 single, 1 double, 2 family (2 double beds per rooms). Private guest entrances.

B&B	4	Ensuite	£20/£30	€25.39/€38.09	Dinner		-
B&B	-	Standard	-	-	Partial Board		-
Single Rate			£25/£35	€31.74€44.44	Child reduction		25%

Ashbourne 2km **Open:** 4th January-20th December

Colin & Anne Finnegan
WOODTOWN HOUSE
Athboy, Co Meath

Athboy
TEL: **046 35022**   FAX: **046 35022**
EMAIL: woodtown@iol.ie
WEB: www.iol.ie/~woodtown

Unique experience. Convenient to Trim, Kells, Dublin. Special packages;- Angling, Golf, Gardens. Take N51(Delvin road) for 2km, turn left, follow signs.

B&B	2	Ensuite	£25	€31.74	Dinner	£12.50
B&B	1	Standard	£20	€25.39	Partial Board	-
Single Rate			£25/£30	€31.74/€38.09	Child reduction	25%

Athboy 7km **Open:** 1st April-30th September

Mrs Anne Mannion
GORTKERRIN B&B
**Piercetown, Dunboyne,
Co Meath**

Dunboyne
TEL: **01 8252096**   FAX: **01 8252096**
BUS NO: **70**

Large dormer bungalow on 4 acres. Located on the Dublin/Navan road N3. Airport 15 mins. 20 mins from Dublin City. Tattersalls and Fairyhouse 3km.

B&B	3	Ensuite	£20/£20	€25.39	Dinner	-
B&B	-	Standard	-		Partial Board	-
Single Rate			£25.50/£25.50	€32.38	Child reduction	50%

Dunboyne 4km **Open:** 31st March-30th September

Valerie O' Farrell
FAIRYHOUSE RD B&B
**Dunboyne,
Co Meath**

Dunboyne
TEL: **01 8256712**   FAX: **01 8256712**
BUS NO: **70**

Country home, family run B&B located on Boyne valley Trail, 20 min from Dublin City, 15 min Dublin Airport. Convenient to Golf, Horse-riding, Restaurants, fishing.

B&B	4	Ensuite	£20	€25.39	Dinner	-
B&B	-	Standard	-		Partial Board	-
Single Rate			£30	€38.09	Child reduction	33.3%

Dunboyne 2km **Open:** 6th January-18th December

Dunshaughlin 5km

Jo Morris
KILLEENTIERNA HOUSE
Powderlough, Dunshaughlin
Co Meath

TEL: **01 8259722**　　FAX: **01 8250673**
EMAIL: imorris@clubi.ie
WEB: www.killeentierna.bizhosting.com

Welcoming residence. Direct dial, TV, Gardens, Parking. Quality lounge, Bar and Restaurant. Adjacent to N3. 5klm south of Dunshaughlin, 25 mins from Dublin Airport and City Centre.

B&B	5	Ensuite	£20/£20	€25.39	Dinner	-
B&B	-	Standard		-	Partial Board	-
Single Rate			£27/£30	€34.29/€38.09	Child reduction	25%

Open: All Year except Christmas

Drogheda 5km

Una Garvey
SMITHSTOWN LODGE
Dublin Road,
Drogheda, Co Meath

TEL: **041 9829777/9829020**
EMAIL: unagarvey@eircom.net

Luxurious home 3 miles south of Drogheda on N1. 20 mins Dublin Airport, 5 mins to Beach and Golf, 20 mins Newgrange and Boyne Valley. Breakfast menu. Routard recommended.

B&B	6	Ensuite	£19/£25	€24.13/€31.74	Dinner	-
B&B	-	Standard		-	Partial Board	-
Single Rate			£25.50/£30	€32.38/€38.09	Child reduction	50%

Open: All Year

Mrs Maureen Kington
BARDEN LODGE
Whitecross, Julianstown,
Co Meath

TEL: **041 9829369/9829910**　FAX: **041 9829369**
EMAIL: kington@eircom.net
WEB: www.dirl.com/meath/barden_lodge.htm
BUS NO: **100**

A warm welcome awaits in this quiet country house, off main N1 road north of Dublin. Close to all amenities, Newgrange, Boyne Valley. 20 mins Dublin Airport, 30 mins Dublin City.

B&B	2	Ensuite	£20/£25	€25.39/€31.74	Dinner	-
B&B	2	Standard		-	Partial Board	-
Single Rate			£25/£30	€31.74/€38.09	Child reduction	33.3%

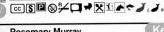

Open: 1st January-23rd December

Drogheda 5km

Tom & Marie Clarke
BIRCHWOOD
Balrath,
Kells, Co Meath

TEL: **046 40688**　　FAX: **046 40688**
EMAIL: clarket@iol.ie

Modern Country Farmhouse. Panoramic view, N52, Kells-Mullingar. Airport 1 hr. Good local Restaurants. Convenient Newgrange, Loughcrew Cairns, Kells Crosses, Golf Clubs.

B&B	4	Ensuite	£20/£20	€25.39	Dinner	-
B&B	-	Standard		-	Partial Board	-
Single Rate			£25.50/£25.50	€32.38	Child reduction	25%

Open: 1st January-23rd December

Kells 1.5km

In Kells

Rosemary Murray
WOODVIEW
Athboy Road,
Kells, Co Meath

TEL: **046 40200**
EMAIL: rosemurray@eircom.net

Quiet area, Kells Town. Tea/Coffee, TV in bedrooms. Walking distance Pubs, Restaurants. Golf, Fishing, Horseriding nearby. Convenient to Newgrange etc. 1hour Dublin Airport on R164.

B&B	2	Ensuite	£19/£20	€24.13/€25.39	Dinner	-
B&B	1	Standard	£17/£17	€21.59	Partial Board	-
Single Rate			£25	€31.74	Child reduction	50%

Open: All Year

23

Kells 3km

Peggy O'Reilly
TEACH CUAILGNE
Carlanstown,
Kells, Co Meath

TEL: **046 46621**   FAX: **046 46046**
EMAIL: pegreilly@eircom.net

Luxury home. Bedrooms on ground floor. Carlanstown Village N52. 3km from Kells, Headfort Golf Club. Convenient to Airport, Newgrange, Lough Crew. Breakfast choice, Orthapaedic beds.

B&B	2	Ensuite	£19/£20	€24.13/€25.39	Dinner	-
B&B	2	Standard	£18	€22.86	Partial Board	-
		Single Rate	£23.50/£25.50	€29.84/€32.38	Child reduction	50%

Open: 1st January-22nd December

Navan 10km

Teresa & Gerard Brennan
VILLAGE B&B
Kilmessan Village,
Navan, Co Meath

TEL: **046 25250**
EMAIL: villagebnb@eircom.net

Scenic village, off N3, beside Pubs/Hotel/Restaurant. Ideal base Hill of Tara (4km), Newgrange, Trim/Dunsany Castles, Boyne Drive. Dublin Airport/City 30 mins.

B&B	5	Ensuite	£20/£20	€25.39	Dinner	-
B&B	1	Standard	£20/£20	€25.39	Partial Board	-
		Single Rate	£25.50/£25.50	€32.38	Child reduction	50%

Open: All Year

In Navan Town

Mrs Pauline Boylan
ATHLUMNEY MANOR
Athlumney, Duleek Road,
Navan, Co Meath

TEL: **046 71388**
EMAIL: pboylan@eircom.net
WEB: http://stay.at/athlumney

Luxurious home overlooking Athlumney Castle. Rooms en-suite with TV, Coffee facilities, Phone. Minutes walk to Town Centre. Secure parking. Hourly bus to Dublin. On R153.

B&B	6	Ensuite	£19/£19	€24.13	Dinner	-
B&B	-	Standard			Partial Board	-
		Single Rate	£25.50	€32.38	Child reduction	25%

Open: All Year

Navan 2km

Mrs Louie Burke
RAHEEN
Trim Road, Navan,
Co Meath

TEL: **046 23791**

Luxury bungalow Navan/Trim road (R161), Navan 2km. Airport 30km. Mature gardens. TV in rooms. Newgrange, Tara, Trim Castle nearby. Refreshments on arrival.

B&B	2	Ensuite	£19/£20	€24.13/€25.39	Dinner	-
B&B	2	Standard	£17/£20	€21.59/€25.39	Partial Board	-
		Single Rate	£23.50/£25.50	€29.84/€32.38	Child reduction	33.3%

Open: All Year

Navan 1km

Mrs Mary Callanan
LIOS NA GREINE
Athlumney, Duleek Road (R153),
Navan, Co Meath

TEL: **046 28092**   FAX: **046 28092**
EMAIL: call@hotmail.com

Luxury home 1km off N3 on Duleek/Ashbourne/Airport (R153). Rooms Ensuite with TV, Tea/Coffee facilities. 30 mins Dublin Airport. Nearby Newgrange, Trim Castle, Tara.

B&B	3	Ensuite	£19/£19	€24.13	Dinner	£15
B&B	-	Standard	-	-	Partial Board	-
		Single Rate	£25.50/£25.50	€32.38	Child reduction	33.3%

Open: All Year

Navan 2km

Mrs Paula Casserly
BOYNE DALE
**Donaghmore, Slane Road,
Navan, Co Meath**

TEL: **046 28015**   FAX: **046 28015**
EMAIL: boynedale@iolfree.ie

Exclusive B&B on Navan-Slane road. Groundfloor bedrooms. Extensive breakfast menu. Easy accessability to Dublin, with the advantages of being in the country.

B&B	3	Ensuite	£19/£19	€24.13	Dinner	-
B&B	1	Standard	£17/£17	€21.59	Partial Board	-
Single Rate			£23.50/£25.50	€29.84/€32.38	Child reduction	25%

Open: 1st February-31st November

Navan 1km

Margaret Dunne
DUNLAIR HOUSE
**Old Road, Athlumney,
Navan, Co Meath**

TEL: **046 72551**
EMAIL: dunlair@hotmail.com

Luxury house, quiet location just off R153, 1km Navan Town, Ensuite rooms with TV/Tea/Coffee facilities, convenient to Airport.

B&B	4	Ensuite	£19/£20	€24.13/€25.39	Dinner	-
B&B	-	Standard	-	-	Partial Board	-
Single Rate			£25.50	€32.38	Child reduction	33.3%

Open: All Year

Navan 1.5km

Kathleen Keogan
HILLCREST
**Slane Rd (N51),
Navan, Co Meath**

TEL: **046 23125**
EMAIL: keogank@eircom.net

A warm friendly home on Slane Road N51. Convenient to Newgrange, Tara and other Historical sites. Close to Dublin Airport. Tea and Coffee on arrival.

B&B	3	Ensuite	£19	€24.13	Dinner	-
B&B	1	Standard	£17	€21.59	Partial Board	-
Single Rate			£23.50/£25.50	€29.84/€32.38	Child reduction	33.3%

Open: 16th January-16th December

In Navan

Mrs Nora Loughran
MEADOW VIEW
**Slane Road (N51),
Navan, Co Meath**

TEL: **046 23994/73131** FAX: **046 73131**
EMAIL: meadowview@eircom.net

Luxurious home minutes from Town Centre with award winning gardens. Rooms Ensuite with multi-channel TV, Tea facilities. Convenient to Newgrange/Airport.

B&B	2	Ensuite	£19	€24.13	Dinner	-
B&B	1	Standard	£17	€21.59	Partial Board	-
Single Rate			£23.50/£25.50	€29.84/€32.38	Child reduction	33.3%

Open: All Year Except Christmas

In Navan

Ann Marie Russell
SYCAMORES
**Dublin Road,
Navan, Co Meath**

TEL: **046 23719**   FAX: **046 21261**

Luxurious bungalow on N3 south of Navan. Private parking. Overlooking the river Boyne. Antique furnishings, Books, Paintings, Silver. Homecooking, good Restaurants.

B&B	3	Ensuite	£19/£20	€24.13/€25.39	Dinner	-
B&B	3	Standard	£19/£20	€24.13/€25.39	Partial Board	-
Single Rate			£25/£25	€31.74	Child reduction	-

Open: 6th January-20th December

Mrs Betty Gough
MATTOCK HOUSE
Newgrange, Slane, Co Meath

TEL: **041 9824592**   FAX: **041 9824592**

Bungalow situated off N51 East of Slane. Half price vouchers and tours arranged to Newgrange, Knowth and Visitors Centre. Convenient to Airport and Ferries.

B&B	2	Ensuite	£19/£19	€24.13	Dinner	-
B&B	1	Standard	£17/£17	€21.59	Partial Board	-
Single Rate			£25.50/£25.50	€32.38	Child reduction	**50%**

Drogheda 7km

Open: All Year

Mrs Lily Bagnall
HILLVIEW HOUSE
Gernonstown, Slane, Co Meath

TEL: **041 9824327**

Luxurious family home, situated on own grounds, beautiful landscaped gardens. Convenient to historic monuments and Towns. Tea and coffee facilities.

B&B	3	Ensuite	£19/£19	€24.13	Dinner	-
B&B	-	Standard	-	-	Partial Board	-
Single Rate			-	-	Child reduction	**25%**

Slane 2km

Open: 30th January-30th November

Roly Bond
BONDIQUE HOUSE
Cullen, Beauparc, Slane, Co Meath

TEL: **041 9824823**   FAX: **041 9824823**
EMAIL: bondique@iol.ie

Situated on N2, 4km south of Slane. Bru na Boinne/Newgrange 8km. Navan/Drogheda 10 mins. Dublin Airport/ City 30 mins.

B&B	2	Ensuite	£19/£20	€24.13/€25.39	Dinner	-
B&B	2	Standard	£17/£18	€21.59/€22.86	Partial Board	-
Single Rate			£23.50/£25.50	€29.84/€32.38	Child reduction	**25%**

Slane 4km

Open: All Year

Mrs Ann Curtis
WOODVIEW
Flemington, Balrath, Co Meath

TEL: **041 9825694**

Luxury bungalow 6km south of Slane, 100 metres off N2 Dublin/Derry Rd. Convenient to Newgrange Visitor Centre. Dublin Airport 30 mins. Ferries 45 mins.

B&B	2	Ensuite	£19/£19	€24.13	Dinner	-
B&B	1	Standard	£19/£19	€24.13	Partial Board	-
Single Rate			£25/£25	€31.74	Child reduction	**25%**

Slane 6km

Open: 1st March-15th October

Mrs Mary Hevey
BOYNE VIEW
Slane, Co Meath

TEL: **041 9824121**

Georgian period house overlooking scenic Boyne Valley, close to all historical monuments. N2 Dublin Road Slane Village. Dublin Airport 45 minutes.

B&B	2	Ensuite	£19	€24.13	Dinner	-
B&B	1	Standard	£17	€21.59	Partial Board	-
Single Rate			£23.50/£25.50	€29.84/€32.38	Child reduction	**25%**

In Slane Village

Open: 10th January-5th December

Slane 2km

Olive Owens
SAN GIOVANNI HOUSE
Dublin Road,
Slane, Co Meath

TEL: **041 9824147**

Large modern house on N2 in picturesque Boyne Valley, breathtaking view from house. 7km from Newgrange. 30 mins from Dublin Airport.

B&B	3	Ensuite	£19/£19	€24.13	Dinner	-
B&B	-	Standard	-	-	Partial Board	-
Single Rate			£25.50/£25.50	€32.38	Child reduction	33.3%

Open: All Year Except Christmas

In Slane Village

Mrs Marie Warren
CASTLE VIEW HOUSE
Slane, Co Meath

TEL: **041 9824510**   FAX: **041 9824510**

Modern bungalow on N51 overlooking Slane Castle Demesne. Close to historical sites, friendly atmosphere. Ideal touring base. Dublin Airport 45 mins.

B&B	4	Ensuite	£19/£19	€24.13	Dinner	-
B&B	1	Standard	£17/£17	€21.59	Partial Board	-
Single Rate			£23.50/£25.50	€29.84/€32.38	Child reduction	25%

Open: 8th January-22nd December

Navan 10km

Ms Joan Maguire
SEAMROG
Hill of Tara,
Tara, Co Meath

TEL: **046 25296**

Homely B&B located on the Hill of Tara with beautiful views, experience the awe of Tara and then relax with us in our home. 10km from Navan off the N3.

B&B	2	Ensuite	£20	€25.39	Dinner	-
B&B	1	Standard	£20	€25.39	Partial Board	-
Single Rate			£23.50	€29.84	Child reduction	50%

Open: 1st April-30th October

Navan 7km

Irene Meehan
ROYAL TARA
Castletown, Tara,
Co Meath

TEL: **046 25920**
EMAIL: royaltara@hotmail.com

Modern, spacious, peaceful home on 1 acre. Off N3 between Dunshaughlin-Navan. Beside Golf Club. Hill of Tara 1km. Near Newgrange. Dublin City/Airport 25 mins.

B&B	3	Ensuite	£19/£20	€24.13/€25.39	Dinner	-
B&B	-	Standard	-	-	Partial Board	-
Single Rate			£25.50/£25.50	€32.38	Child reduction	50%

Open: All Year

Trim 3km

Bernadette Gibbons
BOYNE LODGE B&B
Rathnally, Trim,
Co Meath

TEL: **046 81058**   FAX: **046 81059**
EMAIL: boynelodge@eircom.net
WEB: homepage.eircom.net/~boynelodge

Modern spacious country home, secludedly set on the Boyne. Trim 2km, 1km off the R161. 35 mins from Dublin Airport. Ideal for touring Boyne Valley.

B&B	2	Ensuite	£20	€25.39	Dinner	-
B&B	1	Standard	£18	€22.86	Partial Board	-
Single Rate			£26	€33.01	Child reduction	25%

Open: 1st March-1st November

Trim 1km

Marie Keane
TIGH CATHAIN
Longwood Road,
Trim, Co Meath

Trim

TEL: **046 31996**   FAX: **046 31996**
EMAIL: mariekeane@esatclear.ie

Tudor style country house on 1 acre mature gardens on R160. Large luxury ensuite rooms with Tea/Coffee, TV, Private park, Trim Castle 1km, Airport 40 mins.

B&B	3	Ensuite	£19/£20	€24.13/€25.39	Dinner	-
B&B	-	Standard	-	-	Partial Board	-
Single Rate			£25.50/£25.50	€32.38	Child reduction	33.3%

Open: 1st February-31st October

In Trim

Mrs Eliz. (Libby) O'Loughlin
WHITE LODGE B&B
New Road (Navan Road),
Trim, Co Meath

Trim

TEL: **046 36549/37697** FAX: **046 36549**
EMAIL: whitelodgetrim@eircom.net
WEB: www.whitelodgetrim.com

Town house, large ground floor bedrooms with TV/Tea in rooms. Restaurants closeby. 700m Town Centre/Trim Castle. Airport 40 mins. Frommer/Dumont recommended.

B&B	5	Ensuite	£19/£19	€24.13	Dinner	-
B&B	1	Standard	£17/£17	€21.59	Partial Board	-
Single Rate			£26	€33.01	Child reduction	-

Open: 6th January-20th December

Trim 1.5km

Anne O'Regan
CRANNMOR HOUSE
Dunderry Rd,
Trim, Co Meath

Trim

TEL: **046 31635**   FAX: **046 38087**
EMAIL: cranmor@eircom.net
WEB: www.crannmor.com

Georgian country house with gardens on the outskirts of Trim "Heritage" town. Convenient to Golf, Fishing and Boyne Valley. 35 mins Airport.

B&B	4	Ensuite	£20/£25	€25.39/€31.74	Dinner	-
B&B	-	Standard	-	-	Partial Board	-
Single Rate			£25.50/£30	€32.38/€38.09	Child reduction	25%

Open: All year

Trim Castle, Trim, Co. Meath

backdrop to "Braveheart" and largest Anglo Norman Castle in Europe.

A county of Ancient Kingdoms, Rolling Mountains, The mighty river Shannon and the most precious Irish Jewel "Clonmacnoise". Tour Castles, visit Peatlands, cruise the river Shannon and Grand canal. Play Golf and Fish and always feel welcome in the "Faithful County".

Banagher 2km

Mrs Carmel Horan
LAKYLE
Shannon Harbour Cross
Banagher, Co Offaly

TEL: **0509 51566**

Georgian style house, 3km off N62, convenient Bog-Rail Tours, Bird Watching (Corncrake), Fishing, Golf, Horse-Riding, Boating, Canoeing, Pitch-Putt. Clonmacnois.

						Dinner	-
B&B	3	Ensuite	£19/£19	€24.13		Partial Board	-
B&B	1	Standard	£17/£17	€21.59		Child reduction	25%
Single Rate			-	-			

Open: May-October

Birr 16km

Carmel Finneran
THE GABLES B&B
Castle Street, Cloghan,
Co Offaly

TEL: **0902 57355**
EMAIL: cfinneran@eircom.net

House in Village of Cloghan, 4 bedroom's ensuite. Bog tour 16km, Clonmacnoise 18km, Slieve Bloom mountains 18km. Boora Parklands 10km. Birr Castle 16km. N62 R357.

						Dinner	£12.50
B&B	4	Ensuite	£19/£19	€24.13		Partial Board	
B&B	-	Standard				Child reduction	25%
Single Rate			£25.50/£25.50	€32.38			

Open: 1st January-30th December

In Town

Catherine and Dermot Byrne
AUBURN LODGE
Colonel Perry Street,
Edenderry, Co Offaly

TEL: **0405 31319**
EMAIL: auburnlodge@eircom.net

Townhouse. Tea/Coffee, TV bedrooms. Gardens, Car park. Off N4 en route to the West. Airport, Ferryports 60 mins. Great Fishing, Golf. Central base for touring.

						Dinner	£12.50
B&B	5	Ensuite	£19	€24.13		Partial Board	
B&B	1	Standard	£17	€21.59		Child reduction	50%
Single Rate			-	-			

Open: All Year

In Kinnitty

Christina Byrne
ARDMORE HOUSE
The Walk, Kinnitty,
Co Offaly

TEL: **0509 37009**
EMAIL: ardmorehouse@eircom.net
WEB: www.kinnitty.net

Victorian House, Slieve Bloom Mountains. 2 hours Airport, Ferryports. Brass beds, turf fire, home baking. Walking, Equestrian, Irish music, Birr Castle Gardens Telescope, Clonmacnoise.

						Dinner	-
B&B	1	Ensuite	£19/£25	€24.13/€31.74		Partial Board	-
B&B	3	Standard	£17/£23	€21.59/€29.20		Child reduction	25%
Single Rate			£30/£35	€38.09/€44.44			

Open: All Year

Portarlington 4km

Liam & Marguerite Kirwan
TREASCON LODGE
Portarlington, Co Offaly

TEL: **0502 43183**   FAX: **0502 43183**
EMAIL: treasconlodgeportarlington@eircom.net

Country home on two acres. Tennis Court, Playground in quiet setting. All rooms ensuite. Golf 5 mins. Restaurant open Friday & Saturday nights.

				Dinner	-
B&B	2	Ensuite	£20	€25.39	
B&B	1	Standard	£18	€22.86	Partial Board -
Single Rate			£26	€33.01	Child reduction 33.3%

Open: All Year Except Christmas

Ballinasloe 10km

Mrs Patricia Corbett
RACHRA HOUSE (SHANNON VIEW)
Shannonbridge
via Athlone, Co Offaly

TEL: **0905 74249**

Modern house in picturesque village overlooking rivers Shannon and Suck. Clonmacnoise 6km. Bog Railtours 3km. Fishing, Golf, Horse-Riding, Tennis.

					Dinner	£12.50
B&B	2	Ensuite	£19	€24.13		
B&B	2	Standard	£17	€21.59	Partial Board £185
Single Rate			£23.50/£25.50	€29.84/€32.38	Child reduction 25%

Open: February-November

In Shannonbridge Village

Mrs Celine Grennan
THE BUNGALOW
River View, Shannonbridge,
Athlone, Co Offaly

TEL: **0905 74180**   FAX: **0905 74180**
EMAIL: shannonbungalow@eircom.net
WEB: www.infowing.ie/fishing/ac/bung.htm

In picturesque village with panoramic view of Shannon. Clonmacnoise 6km, Bog tours, Pubs, Fishing, Golf, Swimming, Tennis, Horseriding.

					Dinner	-
B&B	5	Ensuite	£19	€24.13		
B&B	1	Standard	£17	€21.59	Partial Board -
Single Rate			£23.50/£25.50	€29.84/€32.38	Child reduction 25%

Open: April-November

Tullamore 10km

Mrs Bernadette Keyes
CANAL VIEW COUNTRY HOUSE
Killina, Rahan, Tullamore
Co Offaly

TEL: **0506 55868**   FAX: **0506 55034**
WEB: canalview@tinet.ie

10km from Tullamore overlooking canal. Sauna, Steamroom, Massage, Reiki, Beauty crystal treatments available. Pedal and row boating.

					Dinner	£15
B&B	4	Ensuite	£20	€25.39		
B&B	-	Standard		-	Partial Board -
Single Rate			£25.50	€32.38	Child reduction 33.3%

Open: 1st April-31st October

Tullamore 6km

Eileen & Johann MacSweeney-Thieme
SHEPHERDS WOOD
Screggan, Tullamore, Co Offaly

TEL: **0506 21499**   FAX: **0506 21499**
EMAIL: jgott@esatclear.ie
WEB: www.dirl.com/offaly/shepherdswood.htm

Michael Scott designed home in 50 acres of forest, a wild life sanctuary. Pool, Sauna, Crocket etc., Wilderness walks. 4 miles from Tullamore (N52).

					Dinner	-
B&B	2	Ensuite	£25/£28	€31.74/€35.55		
B&B	2	Standard	£25/£28	€31.74/€35.55	Partial Board -
Single Rate			£34/£37	€43.17/€46.98	Child reduction -

Open: 1st May-30th September

Mrs Anne O'Brien
GORMAGH
Durrow, Tullamore,
Co Offaly

Tullamore
TEL: **0506 51468**

Secluded Home, 5 mins drive North of Tullamore on N52. Use of natural materials throughout the house is in harmony with wildflower gardens.

B&B	4	Ensuite	£19/£19	€24.13	Dinner	-
B&B	1	Standard		-	Partial Board	-
Single Rate			£25/£25	€31.74	Child reduction	-

Open: 1st February-15th December

Tullamore 4km

Public Holidays for 2001

New Years Day	-	Monday 1st January	(R.of Ire. & N. Ire.)
Bank Holiday	-	Monday 19th March	(R.of Ire. & N. Ire.)
Good Friday	-	Friday 13th April	(R.of Ire. & N. Ire.)
Easter Monday	-	Monday 16th April	(R.of Ire. & N. Ire.)
May Day Holiday	-	Monday 7th May	(R.of Ire. & N. Ire.)
Bank Holiday	-	Monday 28th May	(N.Ire.)
June Holiday	-	Monday 4th June	(R.of Ire)
Orangeman's Day	-	Thursday 12th July	(N.Ire.)
August Holiday	-	Monday 6th August	(R.of Ire)
Bank Holiday	-	Monday 27th August	(N.Ire.)
October Holiday	-	Monday 29th October	(R.of Ire)
Christmas Day	-	Tuesday 25th December	(R.of Ire. & N. Ire.)
St Stephen's Day	-	Wednesday 26th December	(R.of Ire. & N. Ire.)

A warm welcome awaits you in Westmeath, Ireland's undiscovered lakelands. Situated in the heart of Ireland with magnificent lakes, an anglers paradise, also Golfing, Horse-riding and Water-sports. Travel the Belvedere Fore, or Lough Ree Trails or explore the heritage sites/visitor attractions.

Athlone 8km

Pat & Teresa Byrne
BENOWN HOUSE
Glasson, Athlone,
Co Westmeath

Athlone

TEL: **0902 85406**   FAX: **0902 85776**
EMAIL: benownhouse@glasson.com
WEB: www.glasson.com

Relaxing residence in picturesque village 100m off N55 to Glasson Golf. Choice Restaurants, Pubs, Fishing, Sailing. Good food. Tea/Coffee, TV, Hairdryer in rooms.

B&B	5	Ensuite	£19/£22	€24.13/€27.93	Dinner -
B&B	1	Standard	£17/£20	€21.59/€25.39	Partial Board -
Single Rate			£25.50/£28	€32.38/€35.55	Child reduction 25%

Open: All Year

Athlone 1km

Mrs Mary Clarke
ESKER LODGE
Auburn, Dublin Road,
Athlone, Co Westmeath

Athlone

TEL: **0902 72944**

Spacious bungalow in quiet cul-de-sac. Close to Town Centre, Clonmacnoise, river Shannon. Tea/Coffee on arrival with home baking. Private garden.

B&B	3	Ensuite	£19	€24.13	Dinner -
B&B	1	Standard		-	Partial Board -
Single Rate			£23.50	€29.84	Child reduction 50%

Open: All Year

In Athlone

Mrs Joan Collins
DUN MHUIRE HOUSE
Bonavalley, Dublin Road (Town Route) Athlone, Co Westmeath

Athlone

TEL: **0902 75360**

N6 Town route. Close to town and Athlone Institute of Technology. All rooms with multi channel TV, Tea/Coffee making facilities. Vouchers accepted.

B&B	2	Ensuite	£19	€24.13	Dinner -
B&B	2	Standard	£17	€21.59	Partial Board -
Single Rate			£23.50/£25.50	€29.84/€32.38	Child reduction 50%

Open: All Year

Athlone 2km

Sean & Carmel Corbett
RIVERVIEW HOUSE
Summerhill, Galway Road (N6)
Athlone, Co Westmeath

Athlone

TEL: **0902 94532**   FAX: **0902 94532**
EMAIL: riverviewhouse@hotmail.com

Two storey red brick on N6 Galway Road. Five minutes drive from town centre. Private car park. Credit cards accepted. AA ♦♦♦♦.

B&B	4	Ensuite	£19/£20	€24.13/€25.39	Dinner -
B&B	-	Standard			Partial Board -
Single Rate			£25.50/£25.50	€32.38	Child reduction 25%

Open: 1st March-15th December

Mrs Assumpta Dempsey
LAKE BREEZE LODGE
**Ballykeeran, Athlone,
Co Westmeath**

Athlone

TEL: **0902 85087**   FAX: **0902 85087**
EMAIL: adempsey@unison.ie

In peaceful countryside. Walking distance from Lough Ree, Fishing, Golf, Restaurants. Landscaped gardens. 1km off N55 in Ballykeeran. Tea/Coffee/TV/Hairdryers.

B&B	4	Ensuite	£19		€24.13	Dinner	-
B&B		Standard			-	Partial Board	-
Single Rate			£25.50		€32.38	Child reduction	50%

Athlone 4km

Open: 1st March-31st October

Jim and Nancy Denby
SHELMALIER HOUSE
**Cartrontroy, Athlone,
Co Westmeath**

Athlone

TEL: **0902 72245/72145** FAX: **0902 73190**
EMAIL: shelmal@iol.ie

Beautiful house and gardens in quiet location. Signposted off R446 and N55. All in room services. AA ♦♦♦♦. Award winning breakfast menu. Private Parking.

B&B	7	Ensuite	£19		€24.13	Dinner	-
B&B	-	Standard			-	Partial Board	-
Single Rate			£25.50		€32.38	Child reduction	33.3%

Athlone 2km

Open: 1st February-20th December

Mrs Brigid Duffy
DE VERE HOUSE
**Retreat Road, Athlone,
Co Westmeath**

Athlone

TEL: **0902 75376**

Modern residence on own grounds. Near swimming pool. Close to Town Centre. Rail and Bus Station. Private car park.

B&B	3	Ensuite	£19		€24.13	Dinner	-
B&B	1	Standard	£17		€21.59	Partial Board	-
Single Rate			£23.50/£25.50	€29.84/€32.38		Child reduction	25%

In Athlone

Open: 1st February- 30th November

Mrs Maura Duggan
VILLA ST JOHN
**Roscommon Road, Athlone,
Co Westmeath**

Athlone

TEL: **0902 92490**   FAX: **0902 92490**
EMAIL: villastjohn@eircom.net

Ideally situated on N61 off N6. Convenient to Bars, Restaurants, Lough Ree, Clonmacnoise, 2 Golf courses. TV, Coffee, Hairdryers in bedrooms. Private secure parking at rear of house.

B&B	5	Ensuite	£19		€24.13	Dinner	-
B&B	3	Standard	£17		€21.59	Partial Board	-
Single Rate			£23.50/£25.50	€29.84/€32.38		Child reduction	33.3%

Athlone 1km

Open: 6th January-20th December

Mrs Catherine Fox
DE PORRES
**Cornamaddy, Ballykeeran,
Athlone, Co Westmeath**

Athlone

TEL: **0902 75759**
EMAIL: deporres@iol.ie

Signposted off Cavan rd N55. Quiet location with private carpark, beautiful gardens. Clonmacnoise, Restaurants, Lakes, Golf nearby. TV, Tea/Coffee in rooms. Customer Service Award winner.

B&B	3	Ensuite	£19/£19		€24.13	Dinner	-
B&B	1	Standard	£17/£17		€21.59	Partial Board	-
Single Rate			£26.50/£26.50		€33.65	Child reduction	33.3%

Athlone 2km

Open: 1st April-31st October

Roy & Rose Gandy
HEATHER VIEW
Auburn, Dublin Road,
Athlone, Co Westmeath

Athlone
TEL: **0902 72710**
EMAIL:heather.view@unison.ie

Large bungalow on 1 acre garden in quiet cul-de-sac off Dublin road, beside Regional College/ Auburn House Hotel. Large Car park. TV, Tea/Coffee, Electric Blanket, Trouser Press, Hairdryer.

B&B	4	Ensuite	£20	€25.39	Dinner	-
B&B	-	Standard	-	-	Partial Board	-
Single Rate			£25.50	€32.38	Child reduction	-

In Athlone

Open: All Year

Mrs Elizabeth Heavin
LACKAGH HOUSE
Doon, Ballinahown,
Athlone, Co Westmeath

Athlone
TEL: **0902 30156**
EMAIL: lackaghhouse@eircom.net

Country residence, Clonmacnoise 6km, Bog Tour 10km. Pub walking distance, Golf, Fishing, Rural Heritage Museum 5km. Sign posted off N62.

B&B	2	Ensuite	£19/£19	€24.13	Dinner	£12.50
B&B	2	Standard	£17/£17	€21.59	Partial Board	-
Single Rate			-	-	Child reduction	50%

Athlone 10km

Open: May-October

Jim & Eucharia King
BUSHFIELD HOUSE
Cornamaddy, Blyry, Athlone,
Co Westmeath

Athlone
TEL: **0902 75979**
WEB: http://www.dragnet_systems.ie/dira/bushfield

Signposted N6/N55. Exit Blyry off bypass. TV's, Phones, Tea/Coffee. Pub nearby. Restaurants 2Km. Clonmacnoise 20 mins. Conservatory. Customer Service Award winner.

B&B	5	Ensuite	£19	€24.13	Dinner	-
B&B	1	Standard	-	-	Partial Board	-
Single Rate			£25.50	€32.38	Child reduction	50%

Athlone 2km

Open: All Year

Mrs Mary Linnane
BURREN LODGE
Creggan, Dublin Road,
Athlone, Co Westmeath

Athlone
TEL: **0902 75157**
EMAIL: burrenlodge@ireland.com

Close to roundabout at Texaco Filling Station/Centra. Adjacent Creggan Court Hotel on N6. 15 mins to Clonmacnoise. Regular daily bus service to Dublin from door. TV, Tea/Coffee.

B&B	3	Ensuite	£19	€24.13	Dinner	-
B&B	1	Standard	£17	€21.59	Partial Board	-
Single Rate			£25.50	€32.38	Child reduction	50%

Athlone 2km

Open: All Year

Ann Meade
HARBOUR HOUSE
Ballykeeran, Athlone,
Co Westmeath

Athlone
TEL: **0902 85063**   FAX: **0902 85063**
EMAIL: ameade@indigo.ie

Luxurious quiet home on Lough Ree, 1.5km off N55 in Ballykeeran, Fishing, Golf, Restaurants locally. Tea/Coffee/TV, hairdryer facilities.

B&B	6	Ensuite	£19/£19	€24.13	Dinner	-
B&B	-	Standard	-	-	Partial Board	-
Single Rate			£25.50/£25.50	€32.38	Child reduction	25%

Athlone 5km

Open: February-November

Mrs Joanne Mulligan
MOUNT ALVERNA HOUSE
**Monksland, Athlone,
Co Westmeath**

Athlone

Tᴇʟ: **0902 94016**

Spacious bungalow. All rooms en-suite. Private grounds off N6 on R362. Near Clonmacnoise, Golf, Fishing, Open Farm, Pub and Restaurants.

B&B	4	Ensuite	£19	€24.13	Dinner	-
B&B	-	Standard	-	-	Partial Board	-
Single Rate			£25.50	€32.38	Child reduction	33.3%

Athlone 3km

Open: April-October

Mrs Audrey O'Brien
BOGGANFIN HOUSE
**Roscommon Road,
Athlone, Co Westmeath**

Athlone

Tᴇʟ: **0902 94255**   Fᴀx: **0902 94255**

Tudor style res, off N6, on N61, near roundabout opposite Renault Garage. Guide to Ireland recom, Customer Service Award. Adjacent to Town Lakes, Leisure Centre, Pubs.

B&B	5	Ensuite	£19/£19	€24.13	Dinner	-
B&B	1	Standard	£17/£17	€21.59	Partial Board	-
Single Rate			£23.50/£25.50	€29.84/€32.38	Child reduction	25%

Athlone 1.5km

Open: 10th January-20th December

Carmel & Oliver O'Neill
GLASSON STONE LODGE
**Glasson, Athlone,
Co Westmeath**

Athlone

Tᴇʟ: **0902 85004**

Beautiful house and garden in quaint village in centre of Ireland, on N55. Good breakfast. TV, Tea/Coffee in room's. Near Clonmacnoise. Excellent Restaurants, Pubs 2 min walk. Golf, Fishing.

B&B	5	Ensuite	£20	€25.39	Dinner	-
B&B	-	Standard	-	-	Partial Board	-
Single Rate			£25.50/£36	€32.38/€45.71	Child reduction	25%

Athlone 5km

Open: 1st January-4th December

Des & Mary O'Neill
AVONREE HOUSE
**Coosan, Athlone,
Co Westmeath**

Athlone

Tᴇʟ: **0902 75485**

House, Gardens. Close N6 (Exit Coosan No.3 Junction) and N55. Italian spoken. Two Golf Clubs - 10 mins. Non-smoking. Clonmacnoise 20 mins, Dublin 1 hr 20 mins.

B&B	5	Ensuite	£19/£20	€24.13/€25.39	Dinner	-
B&B	-	Standard	-	-	Partial Board	-
Single Rate			£25.50/£25.50	€32.38	Child reduction	-

Athlone 1km

Open: 1st March-31st October

Stephen & Mary O'Reilly
INNY SIDE LODGE
**Finea Village,
Co Westmeath**

Finea

Tᴇʟ: **043 81124**

Home on banks of River. Beside Lough Sheelin, Lough Kinale, Jetty & Boats, Trout Fishing, Pike, Bream & Tench, Farm attached.

B&B	3	Ensuite	£19/£19	€24.13	Dinner	£12.50
B&B	3	Standard	£17/£17	€21.59	Partial Board	£185
Single Rate			-	-	Child reduction	25%

Finea

Open: 1st January-20th December

In Village

Jimmy and Eileen Whelehan
THE VILLAGE B&B
Killucan, Co Westmeath

Kinnegad

TEL: **044 74760**   FAX: **044 74973**
EMAIL: thevillageinn@oceanfree.net

Follow B&B sign on route N4 North West of Kinnegad. Royal Canal Fishing 2 km. Golf courses 14km on route Trim, Newgrange.

B&B	2	Ensuite	£20	€25.39	Dinner	-
B&B	1	Standard	£18	€22.86	Partial Board	-
Single Rate			-	-	Child reduction	-

Open: All Year

In Moate

Mrs May Glynn
RAILWAY LODGE
**Cartronkeel, Ballymore Rd
Moate, Co Westmeath**

Moate

TEL: **0902 81596**
EMAIL: glynnj@tycohealth.com

Bungalow situated in peaceful area with landscaped Gardens, private car parking, home cooking, rooms ensuite. Knowledge of German and French.

B&B	2	Ensuite	£19/£19	€24.13	Dinner	-
B&B	1	Standard	£17/£17	€21.59	Partial Board	-
Single Rate			£23.50/£25	€29.84/€31.74	Child reduction	25%

Open: 1st January-22nd December

Moate 2km

Mrs Ethna Kelly
COOLEEN COUNTRY HOME
**Ballymore Rd,
Moate, Co Westmeath**

Moate

TEL: **0902 81044**

Picturesque bungalow set in private gardens. 2km off N6. Close to Golf, Pitch and Putt, Clonmacnoise, Heritage Centre. Home cooking, Turf fires.

B&B	3	Ensuite	£19/£19	€24.13	Dinner	-
B&B	-	Standard			Partial Board	-
Single Rate			£25.50	€32.38	Child reduction	50%

Open: 20th January-10th December

In Mullingar

Tony & Mary Barry
WOODSIDE
**Dublin Road, Mullingar,
Co Westmeath**

Mullingar

TEL: **044 41636**

Attractive family home set in peaceful location. 10 mins walking distance from Town Centre. All rooms en-suite. Residents lounge

B&B	4	Ensuite	£20	€25.39	Dinner	-
B&B	-	Standard			Partial Board	-
Single Rate			£26	€33.01	Child reduction	-

Open: All Year Except Christmas

Mullingar 1.5km

Catherine Bennet
TURNPIKE LODGE
**Dublin Road, Petits Wood,
Mullingar, Co Westmeath**

Mullingar

TEL: **044 44913**

Friendly family home. Two large family rooms, Residents lounge, relaxing atmosphere. 2 minutes drive off N4.

B&B	4	Ensuite	£20	€25.39	Dinner	-
B&B	-	Standard	-		Partial Board	-
Single Rate			£26	€33.01	Child reduction	33.3%

Open: All Year

Mullingar 2km

Pat & Elizabeth Birmingham
SOUTHFIELD COURT
Lynn Road, Mullingar,
Co Westmeath

Mullingar

Tel: **044 84666**   Fax: **044 84666**
Email: pfbirmingham@eircom.net

Spacious bungalow on N52. Convenient to Town centre, Lakes, Golf and Fishing. Belvedere House and Gardens-3km. Ideal touring base.

B&B	3	Ensuite	£20	€25.39	Dinner	-
B&B	-	Standard		-	Partial Board	-
Single Rate			£27	€34.29	Child reduction	-

Open: All Year Except Christmas

Mullingar 3km

Sean and Dympna Casey
HILLTOP
Delvin Road (N52 off N4),
Rathconnell, Mullingar,
Co Westmeath

Mullingar

Tel: **044 48958**   Fax: **044 48013**
Email: hilltopcountryhouse@eircom.net
Web: www.hilltopcountryhouse.com

Unique modern Country home, Award winning garden/breakfast. One hour from Dublin. AA selected ◆◆◆◆, Recommended Frommer, Dillard/Cousin, Sullivan guides.

B&B	5	Ensuite	£21/£22	€26.66/€27.93	Dinner	-
B&B	-	Standard		-	Partial Board	-
Single Rate			£25.50/£26	€32.38/€33.01	Child reduction	-

Open: 1st February-30th November

Mullingar 8km

Rita Fahey
BALLINAFID LAKE HOUSE
Ballinafid, Longford Road
Mullingar, Co Westmeath

Mullingar

Tel: **044 71162**
Email: rfahey@ireland.com

Spacious bungalow on the N4 Longford Rd. 8km from Mullingar beside the Covert Pub opposite Ballinafid Lake. Guest sitting room. Laundry facilities, Gardens.

B&B	4	Ensuite	£19	€24.13	Dinner	-
B&B	-	Standard		-	Partial Board	-
Single Rate			£25.50	€32.38	Child reduction	33.3%

Open: 1st April-31st October

Ms Pamela Farrell
PETIESWOOD HOUSE B&B
Dublin Road, Mullingar,
Co Westmeath

Mullingar

Tel: **044 48397**

Beautiful house, family run. Friendly atmosphere. Tree lined avenue. Beautiful gardens. Private off-road parking. 1 mile from Town Centre.

B&B	3	Ensuite	£20/£20	€25.39	Dinner	-
B&B	-	Standard		-	Partial Board	-
Single Rate			£26/£26	€33.01	Child reduction	50%

Open: All Year Except Christmas

Castletown Geog 3km

Josephine Garvey
GREENHILLS
Castletown Geog,
Mullingar, Co Westmeath

Mullingar

Tel: **044 26353**   Fax: **044 26353**
Email: josgarvey@eircom.net
Web: www.josgarvey.cjb.net

Old restored spacious country house in the heart of the Lake District. Very warm welcome assured. Pets welcome. Tea/Coffee on arrival.

B&B	3	Ensuite	£19	€24.13	Dinner	£12.50
B&B	-	Standard		-	Partial Board	£195
Single Rate			£25.50	€32.38	Child reduction	33.3%

Open: All Year

Mullingar

Mrs Regina Healy
GLENMORE HOUSE
Dublin Road, Co Westmeath

Tel: **044 48905**

Georgian house set in four acres of secluded Woodlands and Lawns. Tranquil peaceful and restful. Fishing, Golf, Tennis and Horseriding nearby.

B&B	2	Ensuite	£20/£20	€25.39	Dinner	-
B&B	2	Standard	£17.50/£17.50	€22.22	Partial Board	-
Single Rate			£25/£27	€31.74/€34.29	Child reduction	25%

Open: 1st January-16th December

Mullingar 2.5km

Mrs May McCarthy
MOORLAND
**Marlinstown, Curraghmore
(Off N4), Mullingar, Co Westmeath**

Tel: **044 40905**

House off main Dublin Road. Six rooms with private facilities. Turf Fires, Electric Blankets. Warm welcome.

B&B	6	Ensuite	£20/£20	€25.39	Dinner	-
B&B	-	Standard	-	-	Partial Board	-
Single Rate			£25.50/£25.50	€32.38	Child reduction	25%

Open: All Year

Mullingar 2km

Mrs Margaret McCormack
MC CORMACKS B&B
**Old Dublin Road,
Mullingar, Co Westmeath**

Tel: **044 41483**

On Old Dublin Road, 100 metres from Mullingar Bypass, adjacent to Roundabout. Tennis court and Pool table on grounds. Open access to farmyard and picnic area.

B&B	2	Ensuite	£19/£19	€24.13	Dinner	-
B&B	2	Standard	£17/£17	€21.59	Partial Board	-
Single Rate			£23.50/£25.50	€29.84/€32.38	Child reduction	33.3%

Open: 1st March-31st October

Mullingar 1.5km

Dolores & Anthony Quinn
MARLINSTOWN COURT
**Dublin Road, Mullingar,
Co Westmeath**

Tel: **044 40053**

Situated in a beautiful setting on own grounds. 1 mile Town Centre. All rooms ensuite, Residents lounge. Secluded parking. 2 mins off N4, 1 hour from Dublin.

B&B	5	Ensuite	£20/£20	€25.39	Dinner	-
B&B	-	Standard	-	-	Partial Board	-
Single Rate			£25.50/£25.50	€32.38	Child reduction	33.3%

Open: 1st January-20th December

Mullingar 6km

Mrs Marie Shields
SLIEVE GULLION
**Anneville, Gaybrook, Mullingar,
Co Westmeath**

Tel: **044 49465**
Email: marieshields@eircom.net

Dormer bungalow set in quiet rural area. Situated beside Bloomfield Hotel & Leisure Centre & Mullingar Golf Course. Lough Ennell 5 mins drive. Gardens for visitors use.

B&B	2	Ensuite	£19/£19	€24.13	Dinner	-
B&B	1	Standard	£17/£17	€21.59	Partial Board	-
Single Rate			£23.50/£23.50	€29.84	Child reduction	50%

Open: All Year Except Christmas

Marian Gillespie
THE SCHOOL HOUSE
Leney, Multyfarnham,
Co Westmeath

TEL: **044 71153**
EMAIL: mar.g@esatclear.ie

Tastefully converted old National School set in peaceful surroundings just off the N4, 15km Mullingar. Very spacious rooms. Excellent home cooking, close to Multyfarnham Village.

B&B	3	Ensuite	£19/£19	€24.13	
B&B	-	Standard	-	-	
Single Rate			£25.50/£25.50	€32.38	

Dinner	£13
Partial Board	
Child reduction	50%

Open: 1st January-1st December

Mullingar 15km

Hill of Tara, Co. Meath

Wicklow, the "Garden of Ireland", bounded on the east by sandy beaches and the west by lakes and mountains. Monastic site at Glendalough. Excellent facilities for Golf, Angling, Watersports and Walking. Convenient Dublin/Rosslare with easy access along N11 and N81.

Deirdre Bishop-Power
VALENTIA
Coolgreany Rd, Co Wicklow

Arklow
TEL: **0402 39200** FAX: **0402 39200**
EMAIL: valentiahouse@esatclear.ie
WEB: www.geocities.com/valentiahouse

Comfortable family home. Lovely conservatory dining room. Ideal touring base for Garden of Ireland. Good beaches. 1hr to Dublin and Wexford. Easy walk to Town.

					Dinner	-
B&B	4	Ensuite	£21/£25	€26.66/€31.74	Partial Board	-
B&B	-	Standard			Child reduction	25%
Single Rate			£25.50/£30	€32.38/€38.09		

In Arklow  **Open:** All Year

---

Mrs Margaret Connors
GLENDALE HOUSE
Wexford Road,
Arklow, Co Wicklow

Arklow
TEL: **0402 32816**

Modern friendly home, prize winning garden. Base for Dublin, Wexford, Waterford. Ballykissangel 10 mins. Sea, Golf, Leisure Centres. Excellent Pubs, Hotels nearby.

					Dinner	-
B&B	3	Ensuite	£19/£21	€24.13/€26.66	Partial Board	-
B&B	-	Standard			Child reduction	33.3%
Single Rate			£26/£26	€33.01		

Arklow 1km 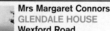 **Open:** All Year

---

Mrs Lourdes Crotty
VALE VIEW
Coolgreaney Rd,
Arklow, Co Wicklow

Arklow
TEL: **0402 32622** FAX: **0402 32622**
EMAIL: pat.crotty@ifi.ie

Edwardian hse with period furnishings on landscaped gardens. Panoramic views. Rooftop Sun Lounge. 200m off roundabout on R772 Main St. Ideal touring base.

					Dinner	-
B&B	4	Ensuite	£20/£22	€25.39/€27.93	Partial Board	-
B&B	-	Standard	-	-	Child reduction	25%
Single Rate			-	-		

In Arklow  **Open:** 1st March-1st November

---

Audrey & Joe Good
INVER DEA
Ferrybank, Arklow,
Co Wicklow

Arklow
TEL: **0402 33987**

Red Brick House at pedestrian lights on main road entering Arklow from Dublin. 5 mins. walk town Centre or Beach.

					Dinner	-
B&B	4	Ensuite	£19/£22	€24.13 /€27.93	Partial Board	-
B&B	-	Standard			Child reduction	25%
Single Rate			£25.50/£28	€32.38/€35.55		

In Arklow  **Open:** 16th February-30th November

Mrs Kathleen Hendley
SWANLAKE
Sea Road, Arklow, Co Wicklow

Arklow
Tel: **0402 32377**

Modern bungalow on coast road close to Arklow Bay Hotel and caravan park. Overlooking sea and beach. Close to Town Centre.

B&B	3	Ensuite	£19/£21	€24.13/€26.66	Dinner -
B&B		Standard	-	-	Partial Board -
Single Rate			-	-	Child reduction -

Arklow 1.5km

Open: March-November

Mrs Rita Kelly
FAIRY LAWN
Wexford Road,
Arklow, Co Wicklow

Arklow
Tel: **0402 32790**

1km from Arklow on the Wexford/Gorey Road. Tea/Coffee facilities in bedrooms. Recommended in the 300 Best B&B Guide. Credit Cards accepted.

B&B	3	Ensuite	£19	€24.13	Dinner -
B&B	1	Standard	£17	€21.59	Partial Board -
Single Rate			£23.50/£25.50	€29.84/€32.38	Child reduction 50%

Arklow 1km

Open: 1st January-20th December

Imelda Kennedy
HILL BREEZE B&B
Barniskey, Co Wicklow

Arklow
Tel: **0402 33743**
Email: hillbreeze@hotmail.com

Comfortable family home, ideal place to relax with panoramic views. 2km off N11, take Redcross Road off Roundabout.

B&B	2	Ensuite	£19/£19	€24.13	Dinner -
B&B	1	Standard	£19/£19	€24.13	Partial Board -
Single Rate			£23.50/£25.50	€29.84/€32.38	Child reduction 25%

Arklow 4km

Open: March-October

Mrs Geraldine Nicholson
PINEBROOK B&B
5 Ticknock Close,
Briggs Lane, Arklow, Co Wicklow

Arklow
Tel: **0402 31527**   Fax: **0402 23067**
Email: pinebrook@eircom.net

Modern detached townhouse within walking distance of Town Centre. Very quiet area with secure parking. Close to all amenities including beach and swimming pool.

B&B	3	Ensuite	£20	€25.39	Dinner -
B&B	-	Standard			Partial Board -
Single Rate			£25.50/£27	€32.38/€34.29	Child reduction 50%

Open: All Year

Maeve O'Connor
THE GABLES
Ballygriffin, Arklow, Co Wicklow

Arklow
Tel: **0402 33402**
Email: maeve.oconnor@oceanfree.net

Spacious country home. Landscaped gardens, Tea facilities. Electric blankets. Breakfast menu. Tennis court. Dublin/Rosslare one hour. Signposted roundabout Arklow.

B&B	4	Ensuite	£19/£20	€24.13/€25.39	Dinner -
B&B	-	Standard			Partial Board -
Single Rate			£25.50/£27	€32.38/€34.29	Child reduction 33.3%

Arklow 3km

Open: 1st March-1st November

41

Mrs Brenda Tyndall
ARKGLEN
Vale Road, Arklow,
Co Wicklow

Arklow
TEL: **0402 32454**   FAX: **0402 32454**

Luxury bungalow, in beautiful grounds five minutes walk to Pubs, Restaurants and Town Centre on Ballykissangel Road. Dublin/Rosslare 1 hr.

B&B	3	Ensuite	£19/£21	€24.13/€26.66	Dinner	-
B&B	1	Standard	£17/£19	€21.59/€24.13	Partial Board	-
Single Rate			£23.50/£25.50	€29.84/€32.38	Child reduction	25%

In Arklow

Open: March-October

Mrs Anne Brady
GORSE HAVEN
Annagolan, Ashford,
Co Wicklow

Ashford
TEL: **0404 40398**   FAX: **0404 40398**
EMAIL: gorsehaven@unison.ie

Tranquil setting on Ashford/Glendalough Rd R763. Adjacent Glendalough, Devils Glen, Usher GDS. Restaurant/Pubs, Golf course 6 minutes drive. Dunlaoghaire 35 mins.

B&B	3	Ensuite	£19/£20	€24.13/€25.39	Dinner	-
B&B	1	Standard	£17/£18	€21.59/€22.86	Partial Board	-
Single Rate			£25/£30	€31.74/€38.09	Child reduction	-

Roundwood 4km

Open: 1st May-30th September

Mrs Nancy Joynt
CARRIG LODGE
Ballylusk, Ashford, Co Wicklow

Ashford
TEL: **0404 40278**   FAX: **0404 40278**
EMAIL: carriglodge@oceanfree.net

Spacious country home. Ideal touring base. Close to Pubs, Restaurants and world famous Mount Usher Gardens. Dublin/Rosslare 1hr. Dun Laoghaire 30 mins.

B&B	3	Ensuite	£20/£22	€25.39/€27.93	Dinner	-
B&B	1	Standard	-	-	Partial Board	-
Single Rate			£28/£30	€35.55/€38.09	Child reduction	-

Ashford 2km

Open: 1st April-31st October

Mrs Phyl Long
BARTRAGH
Dublin Road, Ashford,
Co Wicklow

Ashford
TEL: **0404 40442**   FAX: **0404 49012**
EMAIL: bartragh@boinet.ie
WEB: http://homepage.eircom.net/~dlong

300 metres from Ashford village on Dublin Road (N11). Walking distance to Pubs/Restaurants. 30 Minutes Dunlaoghaire Ferryport. Rural setting.

B&B	4	Ensuite	£20/£20	€25.39	Dinner	-
B&B	-	Standard	-	-	Partial Board	-
Single Rate			-	-	Child reduction	-

In Ashford

Open: 6th January-18th December

Mrs Aine Shannon
CARRIGLEN
Ballinahinch, Ashford,
Co Wicklow

Ashford
TEL: **0404 40627**
EMAIL: carriglen@eircom.net

500 metres Ashford Village/off Main road/on Devils Glen Glendalough road. 5 min walk Pubs/Restaurants. Mount Usher Gardens. Dublin 45 min, Dunlaoghaire 35 min.

B&B	3	Ensuite	£19/£20	€24.13/€25.39	Dinner	-
B&B	-	Standard	-	-	Partial Board	-
Single Rate			£28/£29	€35.55/€36.82	Child reduction	-

Ashford 1km

Open: All Year

Aileen Synnott
Rossana
Ashford, Co Wicklow

Ashford

Tel: **0404 40163**
Email: rossana@eircom.net

150 metres off N11, 50 mins Dublin, 30 mins Dun Laoghaire. Excellent Pubs, Restaurants. Close to Mount Usher gardens, Powerscourt, Glendalough, Avoca (Ballykissangel)

B&B	3	Ensuite	£20/£22	€25.39/€27.93	Dinner -
B&B	-	Standard	-	-	Partial Board -
Single Rate			£29	€36.82	Child reduction -

Wicklow 4km

Open: All Year

Mrs Doreen Burns
GREENHILLS
Knockanree Lower,
Avoca, Co Wicklow

Avoca

Tel: **0402 35197**   Fax: **0402 35197**

Bungalow in scenic peaceful surroundings near Avoca - The location of "Ballykissangel". Ideal touring area. Convenient to Handweavers, Glendalough, Dublin, Rosslare.

B&B	3	Ensuite	£20	€25.39	Dinner -
B&B	-	Standard	-	-	Partial Board -
Single Rate			£26.50	€33.65	Child reduction -

Avoca 2km

Open: May-September

Mervyn & Jackie Burns
ASHDENE
Knockanree Lower,
Avoca, Co Wicklow

Avoca

Tel: **0402 35327**   Fax: **0402 35327**
Email: ashdene@eircom.net
Web: http://homepage.eircom.net/~ashdene

Award winning home near Handweavers and Ballykissangel. Tennis Court, Lounge with refreshments. Ideal touring base. Dublin/Rosslare 1 1/2 hrs. See homepage.

B&B	4	Ensuite	£20	€25.39	Dinner -
B&B	1	Standard	£18	€22.86	Partial Board -
Single Rate			£24/£28	€30.47/€35.55	Child reduction 25%

Avoca 2km

Open: 1st April-31st October

Mrs Rose Gilroy
KOLIBA
Beech Road, Avoca,
Co Wicklow

Avoca

Tel: **0402 32737**   Fax: **0402 32737**
Email: koliba@eircom.net
Web: www.koliba.com

Highly recommended country home. Panoramic views of Arklow Bay. Avoca location of Ballykissangel. Dublin, Rosslare 1 hour. In Avoca, turn right facing "Fitzgeralds".

B&B	3	Ensuite	£20/£20	€25.39	Dinner -
B&B	-	Standard	-	-	Partial Board -
Single Rate			-	-	Child reduction 25%

Avoca 5km

Open: 1st March-31st October

Mrs Bernie Ivers
CHERRYBROOK COUNTRY HOME
Avoca/Ballykissangel,
Co Wicklow

Avoca

Tel: **0402 35179**   Fax: **0402 35179**
Email: cherrybandb@eircom.net
Web: www.cherrybrookhouse.com

Highly recommended home in Avoca. Home of Avoca Handweavers. Minutes walk from Fitzgeralds bar of Ballykissangel. Ideal location for Golf, Walking and Touring the Garden County.

B&B	4	Ensuite	£19/£20	€24.13/€25.39	Dinner -
B&B	-	Standard	-	-	Partial Board £205
Single Rate			£30/£30	€38.09	Child reduction 50%

In Avoca

Open: All Year

43

Avoca 5km

Mrs Aine McGovern
ROCKVIEW
Beech Rd
Avoca, Co Wicklow

Avoca
TEL: **0402 39011**   FAX: **0402 39011**
EMAIL: rockview@oceanfree.net

Quiet countryside with panoramic views of Arklow Bay. All rooms ground floor. Dublin/Rosslare 1.5hrs. Take R772 off N11 facing Fitzgeralds pub, turn right.

B&B	4	Ensuite	£19	€24.13	Dinner	-
B&B	-	Standard	-	-	Partial Board	-
Single Rate			£26	€33.01	Child reduction	33.3%

Open: 1st March-31st October

Mrs Margaret McGraynor
GLENDALE HOUSE
Avoca (Ballykissangel)
Co Wicklow

Avoca
TEL: **0402 35780**   FAX: **0402 35780**

New purpose built bungalow in Avoca. 5 min walk to Fitzgeralds Pub of Ballykissangel fame. Orthopaedic beds, Hairdryers. Breakfast menu. R77 off N11 facing Fitzgeralds Pub turn right.

B&B	4	Ensuite	£20/£20	€25.39	Dinner	-
B&B	-	Standard	-	-	Partial Board	-
Single Rate			-	-	Child reduction	-

Open: 1st March-4th November

In Avoca

Blessington 6km

Mrs Andrea Begg
AVELIN
Poulaphouca, Ballymore Eustace
Near Blessington, Co Wicklow

Blessington
TEL: **045 864524**   FAX: **045 864823**
EMAIL: begg@iol.ie
WEB: avelin.hitsplc.com
BUS NO: **65**

Comfortable welcoming home by lakes and mountains. Transport to Golf, Hill walking. Ancient sites and gardens etc, also Celtic holiday retreats-see website.

B&B	4	Ensuite	£21	€26.66	Dinner	-
B&B	-	Standard	-	-	Partial Board	-
Single Rate			£27	€34.29	Child reduction	25%

Open: 8th January-15th December

Mrs Maura Byrne
ESCOMBE
Lockstown, Valleymount,
Glendalough Rd,
Blessington, Co Wicklow

Blessington
TEL: **045 867157**   FAX: **045 867450**
EMAIL: escombe@indigo.ie

By the Lakes, off N81 on R758 Glendalough, Russborough House 15 mins. Dublin, Ferries, Airport, Powerscourt, National Stud, Japanese Gardens all 45 mins

B&B	6	Ensuite	£20/£22	€25.39/€27.93	Dinner	-
B&B	-	Standard	-	-	Partial Board	-
Single Rate			£28/£35	€35.55/€44.44	Child reduction	25%

Open: 6th January-20th December

Blessington 11km

Blessington 2km

Mrs Angela Corley
SHALIMAR
Crosscool Harbour,
Blessington, Co Wicklow

Blessington
TEL: **045 865259**
EMAIL: shalimarcountryhome@hotmail.com
BUS NO: **65**

Luxurious home, scenic area, on N81. 2km North of Blessington. Dublin Airport, Ferries, Japanese Gardens, Glendalough 45 mins. Punchestown 10 mins. Golfgroups catered for.

B&B	2	Ensuite	£20/£24	€25.39/€30.47	Dinner	-
B&B	1	Standard	£18/£21	€22.86/€26.66	Partial Board	-
Single Rate			£24/£27	€30.47/€34.29	Child reduction	25%

Open: 8th January-20th December

Blessington 6km

Mrs Mary Curley
THE HEATHERS
Poulaphouca
Ballymore-Eustace,
Co Wicklow

Blessington
TEL: **045 864554**
EMAIL: theheathers@eircom.net
BUS NO: **65**

Bungalow beside Poulaphouca Lakes. 6km Blessington, 3km Russborough House. 25 min Glendalough, near National Stud, Japanese Gardens, Golf, Angling, Punchestown.

B&B	2	Ensuite	£20/£20	€25.39	Dinner	£18
B&B	2	Standard	£18/£18	€22.86	Partial Board	-
Single Rate			£26/£30	€33.01/€38.09	Child reduction	25%

Open: All Year Except Christmas

In Blessington

Mrs Patricia Gyves
HAYLANDS HOUSE
Dublin Road, Blessington,
Co Wicklow

Blessington
TEL: **045 865183**
EMAIL: haylands@eircom.net
BUS NO: **65**

AIB hospitality award winner. Spacious bungalow in quiet surroundings on N81 in scenic area. Dublin Airport and Ferries 55 mins. Ideal location for touring.

B&B	5	Ensuite	£20/£20	€25.39	Dinner	-
B&B	1	Standard	£18/£18	€22.86	Partial Board	-
Single Rate			£24/£26	€30.47/€33.01	Child reduction	25%

Open: 1st February-31st October

Adrienne Mc Cann
BEECHWOOD HOUSE
Manor Kilbride, Blessington,
Co Wicklow

Blessington
TEL: **01 4582802**   FAX: **01 4582802**
EMAIL: beechwood@iol.ie
BUS NO: **65**

Beautiful country house set in 2 acres. Mature gardens. 24 miles south of Dublin City lying between Blessington Lakes and the Wicklow Mountains.

B&B	4	Ensuite	£25/£50	€31.74/€63.49	Dinner	£18
B&B		Standard		€43.49	Partial Board	£215
Single Rate			£35/£50	€44.44/€63.49	Child reduction	-

Dublin 35km

Open: All Year

Bray 1.5km

Mrs Kay Kelly
OLD RECTORY
Herbert Road,
Bray, Co Wicklow

Bray
TEL: **01 2867515**   FAX: **01 2867515**

Gothic Victorian Rectory, picturesque setting near Bray, Bus, Ferry, Golf, Mountains, Sea. 20km Dublin (N11). Bus no145 to Rapid Rail.

B&B	3	Ensuite	£20/22	€25.39/27.93	Dinner	-
B&B	-	Standard			Partial Board	-
Single Rate			£25/£30	€31.74/€38.09	Child reduction	25%

Open: All Year Except Christmas

In Bray

Mrs Peggy Kelly
ROSSLYN HOUSE
Killarney Road,
Bray, Co Wicklow

Bray
TEL: **01 2860993**   FAX: **01 2862419**
BUS NO: **45, 45A, 84**

Elegant Victorian residence beside Bray Town Hall. Close to Rapid Rail, Bus, Car Ferry, Mountains, Sea. 20km Dublin N11 route.

B&B	4	Ensuite	£20/£22.50	€25.39 /€28.57	Dinner	-
B&B		Standard			Partial Board	-
Single Rate			£30/£35	€38.09/€44.44	Child reduction	25%

Open: March-October

In Bray

Mrs Kathleen Roseingrave
IVERAGH
44 Meath Road,
Bray, Co Wicklow

Bray
TEL: **01 2863877**
BUS NO: **84, 45**

Detached period residence beside sea. Close to Rapid Rail, Bus, Car Ferry, Sporting Amenities. Dun Laoghaire 6 mls, Dublin 12 mls.

				Dinner	-
B&B	4	Ensuite	£20/£22.50	€25.39/€28.57	
B&B	2	Standard	£18/£20	€22.86/€25.39	Partial Board —
Single Rate			£23.50/£30	€29.84/€38.09	Child reduction 25%

Open: 17th March–31st October

In Bray

Mrs Christina Smith
RATHLIN HOUSE
Killarney Road,
Bray, Co Wicklow

Bray
TEL: **01 2862655**
EMAIL: rathlinhouse@hotmail.com
BUS NO: **45, 45A, 84, 85,**

Victorian residence beside Town Hall, Close to Sea, Rapid Rail, Bus, Car Ferry, Mountains, Sporting Amenities. Dublin 20km N11 route. TV, Hairdryer, Tea, Coffee in rooms. Private parking.

				Dinner	-
B&B	4	Ensuite	£20/£22.50	€25.39/€28.57	
B&B	-	Standard	-	-	Partial Board -
Single Rate			-	-	Child reduction -

Open: March–October

In Enniskerry

Mrs Eilish Cummins
CORNER HOUSE
Enniskerry,
Co Wicklow

Enniskerry
TEL: **01 2860149** FAX: **01 2860149**
BUS NO: **44**

Old world house situated in Enniskerry Village. Close to Powerscourt Gardens and Waterfall. Convenient Car Ferries and Airport. Dublin 20km on N11. All bedrooms have own showers.

				Dinner	-
B&B	-	Ensuite	-	-	
B&B	3	Standard	£18/£20	€22.86/€25.39	Partial Board -
Single Rate			£27/£27	€34.29	Child reduction -

Open: All Year

Enniskerry 1km

Mrs Kay Lynch
CHERBURY
Monastery, Enniskerry,
Co Wicklow

Enniskerry
TEL: **01 2828679**
BUS NO: **44**

Large Bungalow, Landscaped gardens. Ideal base for touring Wicklow. Convenient Powerscourt, Glendalough, Golf, Car Ferry, Airport, Dublin 20km.

				Dinner	-
B&B	3	Ensuite	£20/£20	€25.39	
B&B	-	Standard	-	-	Partial Board -
Single Rate			-	-	Child reduction -

Open: All Year

Enniskerry 4km

Kay O'Connor
OAKLAWN
Glaskenny, Enniskerry,
Co Wicklow

Enniskerry
TEL: **01 2860493**
EMAIL: johnb@indigo.ie
WEB: www.oaklawn.20m.com
BUS NO: **185**

Delightful house. Just off Glencree Road, idyllic country setting. Beside Powerscourt and Wicklow Way. Convenient Car Ferries, Airport, Dublin 25km.

				Dinner	-
B&B	2	Ensuite	£20/£23	€25.39/€29.20	
B&B	2	Standard	£18/£20	€22.86/€25.39	Partial Board -
Single Rate			£26	€33.01	Child reduction 50%

Open: 1st March–30th November

In Enniskerry

Barry & Bernie Smyth
COILLTE
4 Enniskerry Demesne,
Enniskerry, Co Wicklow

Enniskerry
TEL: **01 2766614**   FAX: **01 2766618**
EMAIL: smyt@eircom.net
WEB: http://homepage.eircom.net/~barcoillte
BUS NO: **44, DART**

Coillte in award winning Enniskerry Demesne opposite Powerscourt and next to Summerhill Hotel, five minutes stroll from Enniskerry Village.

B&B	3	Ensuite	£27/£27	€34.29	Dinner	-
B&B	-	Standard	-		Partial Board	-
Single Rate			-		Child reduction	-

Open: 7th January-7th December

In Annamoe

Mrs Carmel Hawkins
CARMEL'S
Glendalough, Annamoe,
Co Wicklow

Glendalough
TEL: **0404 45297**   FAX: **0404 45297**
EMAIL: carmelsbandb@eircom.net

When touring Wicklow have a break at this hospitable well established country home. Set in the heart of the Wicklow Mountains. 5 mins drive Glendalough near to Airport & Ferries R755.

B&B	4	Ensuite	£19/£20	€24.13/€25.39	Dinner	-
B&B	-	Standard	-		Partial Board	-
Single Rate			-		Child reduction	-

Open: 1st March-15th November

In Laragh

Mrs Valerie Merrigan
GLENDALE
Glendalough, Co Wicklow

Glendalough
TEL: **0404 45410**   FAX: **0404 45410**
EMAIL: merrigan@eircom.ie

Country Home set in scenic Wicklow Mountains, situated 1.5km Glendalough. On Laragh to Annamoe Road, 0.5km from Shops, Restaurants and Pub.

B&B	4	Ensuite	£19/£19	€24.13	Dinner	-
B&B	-	Standard	-		Partial Board	-
Single Rate			£28/£34	€35.55/€43.17	Child reduction	25%

Open: 1st February-30th November

Laragh 1km

Martha O'Neill
GLENDALOUGH RIVER HOUSE
Derrybawn, Glendalough,
Co Wicklow

Glendalough
TEL: **0404 45577**   FAX: **0404 45577**
EMAIL: glendaloughriverhouse@hotmail.com

200 year old stone restored house. All bedrooms have beautiful river views. Located on walking trail to Glendalough. Excellent breakfast menu.

B&B	4	Ensuite	£29/£39	€36.82/€49.52	Dinner	-
B&B	-	Standard	-		Partial Board	-
Single Rate			£40/£50	€50.79/€63.49	Child reduction	25%

Open: All Year

Greystones 5km

Margaret Berkery
CULLAUN
Sea Road, Kilcoole,
Co Wicklow

Greystones
TEL: **01 2875998**
BUS NO: **84, 84A**

Dormer bungalow, private car parking, only 5km from Greystones and 30 mins drive from Car Ferry (via N11). Adjacent Glenroe/Druids Glen.

B&B	3	Ensuite	£20/£20	€25.39	Dinner	-
B&B	-	Standard	-		Partial Board	-
Single Rate			£25.50/£25.50	€32.38	Child reduction	25%

Open: 1st May-31st October

Ms Mary Doyle
LA CASA
Kilpedder Grove, Kilpedder, Greystones, Co Wicklow

Greystones
TEL: **01 2819703**
EMAIL: lacasabb@yahoo.com
BUS NO: **184**

Situated in Kilpedder village N11 route. 10 mins Greystones, Airport 1 hour, Ferries 30 mins. 184 bus Greystones/Bray, DART every 20 mins, Glendalough. 30 mins drive, Powerscourt 15 mins.

B&B	2	Ensuite	£19/£23	€24.13/€29.20	Dinner	-
B&B	1	Standard	£18/£22	€22.86/€27.93	Partial Board	-
Single Rate			£25/£28	€31.74/€35.55	Child reduction	-

Greystones 5km

Open: All Year Except Christmas

Malcolm & Penny Hall
GLANDORE
St Vincent Rd, Burnaby Estate Greystones, Co Wicklow

Greystones
TEL: **01 2874364**   FAX: **01 2874364**
BUS NO: **84**

House of great charm, set in mature gardens in beautiful old world estate. Five minutes from all amenities.

B&B	4	Ensuite	£20	€25.39	Dinner	-
B&B	-	Standard	-	-	Partial Board	-
Single Rate			£25.50	€32.38	Child reduction	33.3%

In Greystones

Open: All Year

Mary & Michael Hogan
THORNVALE
Kilpedder, Greystones, Co Wicklow

Greystones
TEL: **01 2810410**
EMAIL: hoganwicklow@eircom.net
WEB: www.wicklow.ie
BUS NO: **184**

Modern family home on 1.5 acre gardens. Exit N11 for Kilquade at Kilpedder, immediate right. Ideal for touring Wicklow & Dublin. DART at Greystones/Bray.

B&B	4	Ensuite	£20/£20	€25.39	Dinner	-
B&B	-	Standard	-	-	Partial Board	-
Single Rate			£26/£30	€33.01/€38.09	Child reduction	-

Greystones 5km

Open: All Year

Mrs Kathleen Nunan
SILLAN LODGE
Church Lane, Greystones Co Wicklow

Greystones
TEL: **01 2875535**
EMAIL: sillanlodge@ireland.com
BUS NO: **84, 84X**

Sillan Lodge is situated off a peaceful tree lined avenue, with extensive grounds, mountain and sea views. Close to City, Car Ferry and Rapid Rail service (DART). Scenic drives nearby.

B&B	2	Ensuite	£20/£22	€25.39/€27.93	Dinner	-
B&B	1	Standard	£18/£20	€22.86/€25.39	Partial Board	-
Single Rate			£27/£30	€34.29/€38.09	Child reduction	-

In Greystones

Open: March-October

Mrs Denise Toolan
PRIMROSE LODGE
Kilquade Hill, Kilquade, (Near Greystones), Co Wicklow

Greystones
TEL: **01 2877291**   FAX: **01 2873677**

Mediterranean style spacious home, overlooking Druids Glen Golf club, Snooker. Dart 5 minutes. Ferry 30 minutes. Exit N11 Kilpedder for Kilquade. Credit Cards.

B&B	2	Ensuite	£21/£25	€26.66/€31.74	Dinner	-
B&B	1	Standard	£18/£22	€22.86/€27.93	Partial Board	-
Single Rate			£24/£30	€30.47/€38.09	Child reduction	25%

Greystones 6km

Open: 1st March-31st October

Mrs Patricia Treacy
CASTANEA
Rathdown Road
Greystones, Co Wicklow

TEL: **01 2876373** FAX: **01 2878025**
EMAIL: castanea@ireland.com
BUS NO: **84, 84X, 184**

Secluded home N11 to R761/2. Lovely gardens, Patio. Safe Parking. Close to best Restaurants, Sea, Dart. Ideal base for Dublin, Golf, Heritage gardens, Mountains.

				Dinner	-
B&B	4	Ensuite	£19/£20	€24.13/€25.39	
B&B	-	Standard		-	Partial Board -
Single Rate			£25.50/£30	€32.38/€38.09	Child reduction 33.3%

Open: 1st March-31st October

In Greystones

Ms Rose Byrne
ROSANNA's
Hollywood, Co Wicklow

TEL: **045 864225**
BUS NO: **65**

Luxury residence on main N81 road, convenient to Airport/Ferries (30 mins). Glendalough, Blessington Lakes, Curragh Racecourse, Punchestown and Golf Courses.

					Dinner	£15
B&B	2	Ensuite	£19/£28	€24.13/€35.55		
B&B	1	Standard	£17/£25	€21.59/€31.74	Partial Board	
Single Rate			£25.50/£40	€32.38/€50.79	Child reduction 25%	

Open: March-November

Blessington 6km

Mrs Kathleen Healy
HOLLYWOOD LODGE
Glendalough Road,
Hollywood, Co Wicklow

TEL: **045 864230**
BUS NO: **65**

Cosy mountain home R756 near Lakes, Glendalough, National Stud, Japanese Gardens. Racing, Golf, Walking. Le Routard, Le Petit Fute Guide, Bleue Vasion recommended. Truly Irish home.

				Dinner	-
B&B	4	Ensuite	£19/£19	€24.13	
B&B	-	Standard		Partial Board -	
Single Rate			£25.50/£28.50	€32.38/€36.19 Child reduction 25%	

Open: March-November

Blessington 12km

TP and Frances MacDermott
AN T'AOIBHNEAS
Sliabhcorragh, Hollywood
Co Wicklow

TEL: **045 864577**

Pleasant tasteful home in a natural environment with exquisite mountain views. Located 3km off N81 on R756 Hollywood/Glendalough Road. Good Restaurants.

				Dinner	-
B&B	3	Ensuite	£19/£19	€24.13	
B&B	-	Standard		Partial Board -	
Single Rate			£25.50/£28	€32.38/€35.55 Child reduction 50%	

Open: 31st January-10th December

Hollywood 3km

Agnes Reilly
CHESTNUT HOUSE
Hollywood Lower, Hollywood,
Co Wicklow

TEL: **045 864661** FAX: **045 864661**

On N81 in the scenic Hollywood Glen. Convenient for visiting Russborough House, Glendalough, Powerscourt, National Stud & Japanese Gardens. Airport 45 mins.

				Dinner	-
B&B	4	Ensuite	£20/£22.50	€25.39/€28.57	
B&B	-	Standard		Partial Board -	
Single Rate			£28/£35	€35.55/€44.44 Child reduction 25%	

Open: All Year

Blessington 6km

In Newtownmountkennedy

Catherine Tierney
DRUIDS HOUSE
Kilmacullagh,
Newtownmountkennedy,
Co Wicklow

Tel: **01 2819477**

Ideal base Glendalough, Powerscourt, Mount Usher Gardens. Walking distance Druids Glen Golf Course. Bray 10 mins, Dublin 40 minutes. Breakfast menu. Tea/Coffee/TV all rooms.

B&B	3	Ensuite	£19	€24.13	Dinner	-
B&B	-	Standard	£25.50	-	Partial Board	-
Single Rate				€32.38	Child reduction	25%

Open: All Year

Rathdrum 2km

Mr Gerry Fulham
ABHAINN MOR HOUSE
Corballis, Rathdrum,
Co Wicklow

Tel: **0404 46330**   Fax: **0404 43150**
Email: abhainnmor@eircom.net
Web: http://homepage.eircom.net/~wicklowbandb/

Enjoy good food and wine in a comfortable home with spacious gardens. Family rooms. AA ♦♦♦. Close to Glendalough and Avoca. 2km south of Rathdrum R752.

B&B	6	Ensuite	£19/£20	€24.13/€25.39	Dinner	£13
B&B	-	Standard	-	-	Partial Board	£210
Single Rate			£26	€33.01	Child reduction	33.3%

Open: All Year Except Christmas

Rathdrum 2km

Mrs Ann Griffin
LETTERMORE
Corballis, Rathdrum,
Co Wicklow

Tel: **0404 46506**   Fax: **0404 43183**
Email: lettermore@eircom.ie
Web: http://homepage.eircom.net/~lettermore

Country home 2km south of Rathdrum, Avoca road (R752). Close Avondale, Meetings of the Water, Avoca, Glendalough. From Airport M50 to Blessington, Hollywood, Wicklow Gap, Laragh, Rathdrum.

B&B	4	Ensuite	£19/£20	€24.13/€25.39	Dinner	£14
B&B	1	Standard	£17/£19	€21.59/€24.13	Partial Board	£205
Single Rate			£23.50/£25.50	€29.84/€32.38	Child reduction	33.3%

Open: March-October

Rathdrum 1km

Marian Long & Sean Lyons
BEECHLAWN
Corballis, Rathdrum,
Co Wicklow

Tel: **0404 46474**   Fax: **0404 43389**
Email: caj@tinet.ie

Modern bungalow in large garden on Avoca Road. Close to Avondale, Glendalough, Town, Bus and Train. Private Parking.

B&B	3	Ensuite	£21	€26.66	Dinner	£15
B&B	1	Standard	£19	€24.13	Partial Board	£220
Single Rate			£30	€38.09	Child reduction	25%

Open: 1st February-30th November

Rathdrum 2km

Mrs Maeve Scott
ST BRIDGET'S
Corballis, Rathdrum,
Co Wicklow

Tel: **0404 46477**

Quiet countryside location. 2km south of Rathdrum town R753. Just 50 yds off Avoca road R752. All bedrooms on ground floor. Adjacent to Avondale, Avoca, Glendalough, Wicklow Mountains.

B&B	3	Ensuite	£19/£20	€24.13/€25.39	Dinner	-
B&B	-	Standard	-	-	Partial Board	-
Single Rate			£25.50/£30	€32.38/€38.09	Child reduction	25%

Open: 1st January-20th December

In Rathdrum

Mrs Eileen Sheehan
THE HAWTHORNS
Corballis, Rathdrum,
Co Wicklow

Rathdrum

TEL: **0404 46683/46217** FAX: **0404 46217**
EMAIL: thehawthorns1@eircom.net

Modern bungalow in award winning garden. 1/2 km from Rathdrum and railway station. Ideal centre for Golf, Fishing, walking. 1hr to Airport and Ferries. Lonely Planet Recommended.

B&B	1	Ensuite	£20/£20	€25.39	Dinner	-
B&B	2	Standard	£18/£18	€22.86	Partial Board	-
Single Rate			£23.50/£25	€29.84/€31.74	Child reduction	-

Open: 6th January-18th December

Wicklow 2km

Mrs Fiona Byrne
GLEN NA SMOLE
Ashtown Lane, Marlton Road,
Wicklow, Co Wicklow

Wicklow

TEL: **0404 67945**   FAX: **0404 68155**
EMAIL: byrneglen@eircom.net
WEB: http://homepage.eircom.net/~byrneglen

Comfortable family home. Award winning breakfasts. 2km Grand Hotel/Beehive Pub off Wicklow/Wexford Road. Golf, Fishing arranged. Low season discounts.

B&B	4	Ensuite	£19/£20	€24.13/€25.39	Dinner	£12.50
B&B	-	Standard	-	-	Partial Board	£185
Single Rate			£25.50/£29	€32.38/€36.82	Child reduction	50%

Open: March-October

In Wicklow

Mrs Rita Byrne
ROSITA
Dunbur Park, Wicklow Town,
Co Wicklow

Wicklow

TEL: **0404 67059**

Luxurious spacious home overlooking Wicklow Bay. Take coast road, turn into Dunbur Park at pedestrian crossing. 5 minutes walk to Town.

B&B	4	Ensuite	£20/£21	€25.39 /€26.66	Dinner	-
B&B	-	Standard	-	-	Partial Board	-
Single Rate			£25.50/£32	€32.38/€40.63	Child reduction	25%

Open: 1st March-31st October

Wicklow 2km

Catherine Doyle
DROM ARD
Ballynerrin Lr,
Wicklow Town, Co Wicklow

Wicklow

TEL: **0404 66056**   FAX: **0404 62873**
EMAIL: dromardwicklow@excite.com

Modern spilt-level home with splendid views of Mountains, Sea, Countryside within easy reach of Glendalough. Ideal base for touring South-East, Dublin-Rosslare.

B&B	3	Ensuite	£19/£20	€24.13/€25.39	Dinner	-
B&B	1	Standard	£17/£18	€21.59/€22.86	Partial Board	-
Single Rate			£24/£26	€30.47/€33.01	Child reduction	50%

Open: 3rd January-3rd December

In Wicklow

Mrs Lyla Doyle
SILVER SANDS
Dunbur Road,
Wicklow, Co Wicklow

Wicklow

TEL: **0404 68243**
EMAIL: lyladoyle@eircom.net

Overlooking Wicklow Bay. Through Wicklow Town, take coast road, 1km Town centre. Frommer recommended and Elsie Dillards "300 Best B&Bs".

B&B	4	Ensuite	£22/£22	€27.93	Dinner	-
B&B	1	Standard	£20/£20	€25.39	Partial Board	-
Single Rate			£27/£32	€34.29/€40.63	Child reduction	50%

Open: 1st March-30th November

Wicklow 1km

Mrs Helen Gorman
THOMOND HOUSE
St Patricks Road Upr, Wicklow,
Co Wicklow

Wicklow
TEL: **0404 67940**   FAX: **0404 67940**
EMAIL: thomondhouse@eircom.net

House with balcony. Wonderful views Sea, Mountains. 1km past RC Church. Frommer, Lets Go, Lonely Planet, Rough Guide recommended. Golf arranged. Warm welcome.

B&B	2	Ensuite	£20	€25.39	Dinner	-
B&B	3	Standard	£18	€22.86	Partial Board	-
Single Rate			£25	€31.74	Child reduction	-

Open: 1st April-31st October

In Wicklow Town

Ms Marion Healy
HILLCREST B&B
2 Weston Close,
Wicklow, Co Wicklow

Wicklow
TEL: **0404 67796**
EMAIL: bnb@eircom.net

Tudor style house in Town Centre. Warm welcome assured. Golf, Pubs, Restaurants, Beach a stroll away. In Town, turn right at Hopkins, uphill into cul-de-sac.

B&B	3	Ensuite	£20/£22	€25.39/€27.93	Dinner	-
B&B	-	Standard		-	Partial Board	-
Single Rate			£26/£28	€33.01/€35.55	Child reduction	33.3%

Open: February-October

Wicklow 1.5km

Mrs Hilary McGowan
ARCH HOUSE
Ballynerrin, Wicklow Town,
Co Wicklow

Wicklow
TEL: **0404 68176**
EMAIL: gerrymcgowan@tinet.ie
WEB: http://www.angiefire.com

A dormer bungalow with a panoramic view of Wicklow Bay and Mountains. Golf, Fishing, Horseriding nearby. A friendly welcome awaits you.

B&B	3	Ensuite	£19/£19	€24.13	Dinner	-
B&B	1	Standard	£17/£18	€21.59/€22.86	Partial Board	-
Single Rate			£23.50/£25	€29.84/€31.74	Child reduction	50%

Open: 1st March- 31st October

In Wicklow

Mrs Ann Mitchell
OLANDA
Dunbur Park, Wicklow,
Co Wicklow

Wicklow
TEL: **0404 67579**

Comfortable welcoming home bungalow in peaceful quiet location. 5 minutes walk to Town. Take Coast Road, turn right at pedestrian crossing into Dunbur Park.

B&B	2	Ensuite	£19	€24.13	Dinner	-
B&B	2	Standard	£17	€21.59	Partial Board	-
Single Rate			£23.50	€29.84	Child reduction	50%

Open: All Year

In Wicklow Town

Una Redmond
MAC REAMOINN TOWNHOUSE
Summerhill, Wicklow Town,
Co Wicklow

Wicklow
TEL: **0404 61113**

A warm welcome awaits you at our tastefully decorated townhouse. A stroll from many Restaurants and Pubs. Ideal touring base.

B&B	3	Ensuite	£20/£22	€25.39/€27.93	Dinner	-
B&B	-	Standard			Partial Board	-
Single Rate			£26/£28	€33.01/€35.55	Child reduction	-

Open: 7th January-31st October

Open your eyes to Ireland's exciting heritage...

Yearly ticket available!

Dúchas offers a guide-information service and visitor facilities at over 65 sites throughout Ireland.
For further information contact:

'Heritage Card'
Education and Visitor Service
Department of Arts, Heritage, Gaeltacht & the Islands
6 Ely Place Upper, Dublin 2, Ireland.

Tel: +353 1 6472461   Fax: +353 1 6616764
email: heritagecard@ealga.ie
web: www.heritageireland.ie

Dúchas The Heritage Service

An Roinn Ealaíon, Oidhreachta, Gaeltachta agus Oileán
Department of Arts, Heritage, Gaeltacht and the Islands

Please send me details about the Heritage Card and Dúchas sites

Name _____

Address _____

_____

Send to :

'Heritage Card',
Education & Visitor Service,
Department of Arts, Heritage, Gaeltacht & the Islands
6 Ely Place Upper,
Dublin 2, Ireland.

T&C 2001

North West

Discover the North West and discover the best of Ireland! This is truly the greenest part of Europe's Green Island...unspoilt, uncrowded and undiscovered.

In the counties of Cavan, Donegal, Leitrim, Monaghan and Sligo there is a wealth of scenery, heritage and hospitality. With geography that ranges from wild Atlantic coast through gentle meandering rivers to sylvan lakeland, and a history that dates from Neolithic archaeology through to modern Irish writing, every interest can be met.

Glenveagh National Park

For the active there are classic links and parkland golf courses; superb equestrian centres; hill walking and mountain climbing; summer schools of every variety; wide open beaches, some with world class surfing; and at the end of every day Irish hospitality at its best in bars and restaurants.

Area Representatives

CAVAN
Mrs Brid Myles, Halcyon, Drumalee, Cavan Town, Co Cavan
Tel: 049 4331809 Fax: 049 4362531

DONEGAL
Ms Christina Cannon, Cuan Na Mara, Ballyness, Falcarragh,
Co Donegal Tel: 074 35327
Mr John Hughes, Randwick, Bundoran Road, Ballyshannon,
Co Donegal Tel: 072 52545 Fax: 072 52545
Mrs Ann McClean, Credo House, Benroe, Killybegs, Co Donegal
Tel: 073 31364 Fax: 073 31364

LEITRIM
Mrs Valerie Rowley, Corbally Lodge, Dublin Road, Carrick on Shannon, N4
Co Leitrim Tel: 078 20228 Fax: 078 20228

SLIGO
Mrs Tess Haughey, Rathnashee, Teesan, Donegal Road N15, Sligo, Co Sligo
Tel: 071 43376 Fax: 071 42283
Mrs Maeve Walsh, Cruckawn House, Ballymote/Boyle Road, Tubbercurry,
Co Sligo Tel: 071 85188 Fax: 071 85188

Tourist Information Offices

Sligo Town
Temple Street
Tel: 071 61201

Donegal Town
The Quay
Tel: 073 21148

Carrick-on-Shannon
The Old Barrel
Store
Tel: 078 20170

Letterkenny
Derry Road
Tel: 074 21160

Cavan Town
Farnham Street
Tel: 049 4331942

Monaghan Town
Market House
Tel: 047 81122

website" www.ireland_northwesttravel.ie

Cavan, a county rich in history and culture is also a haven for the lover of the quiet outdoors. The Angler, Golfer, Horse-rider and Hill-walker are all catered for. Swimming, Tennis, River Cruising and many other activities will make your visit an unforgettable one.

Ballyconnell 2km

Patrick and Ann Duignan
HILLCREST HOUSE
Slievebricken,
Ballyconnell, Co. Cavan

Ballyconnell
TEL: **049 9526475**

2km from Ballyconnell on the Killeshandra Rd. Relax with Golfing at Slieve Russell Hotel and Country Club or cruise the Shannon, Erne waterway. all within 3km.

B&B	2	Ensuite	£20/£22	€25.39/€27.93	Dinner	-
B&B	1	Standard	£18/£20	€22.86/€25.39	Partial Board	-
Single Rate			£23.50/£25	€29.84/€31.74	Child reduction	50%

Open: All Year

Bawnboy 3km

Catherine and Joseph O'Reilly
LAKE AVENUE HOUSE
Port, Bawnboy,
Co. Cavan

Bawnboy
TEL: **049 9523298**   FAX: **049 9523298**
EMAIL: lakeave@eircom.net

Beautiful new home, quiet scenic rural setting. Ideal base for Fishing, Touring, Walking, Cycling and Golf. 3km from Bawnboy on N3. Belturbet/Swanlinbar Rd.

B&B	4	Ensuite	£19/£22	€24.13 /€27.93	Dinner	£12.50
B&B		Standard	-	-	Partial Board	-
Single Rate			£25.50/£25.50	€32.38	Child reduction	20%

Open: 8th January-16th December

Belturbet 6km

James & Susan McCauley
ROCKWOOD HOUSE
Cloverhill, Belturbet, Co Cavan

Belturbet
TEL: **047 55351**   FAX: **047 55373**
EMAIL: jbmac@eircom.net

Lovely country house situated in secluded peaceful woodlands and surrounded by lawns and gardens on the N54, 2 miles from Butlersbridge, 6 miles Cavan.

B&B	4	Ensuite	£20	€25.39	Dinner	-
B&B		Standard	-	-	Partial Board	-
Single Rate			£25.50	€32.38	Child reduction	25%

Open: All Year

In Cavan

Ms Eileen Flynn
GLENDOWN
33 Cathedral Road,
Cavan, Co Cavan

Cavan
TEL: **049 4332257**
EMAIL: tfflynn@eircom.net

Warm friendly comfortable home, residential area. Convenient to Equestrian centre/ Golf course/Sports Complex. Good Fishing and Genealogy Research centre.

B&B	3	Ensuite	£20/£20	€25.39	Dinner	-
B&B		Standard	-	-	Partial Board	-
Single Rate			£25.50/£25.50	€32.38	Child reduction	10%

Open: 20th February-20th December

In Cavan

Ann & Paddy Gaffney
OAKDENE
29 Cathedral Rd.
Cavan, Co Cavan

Cavan
Tel: **049 4331698**

Spacious comfortable home. Residential area. 10 minutes walking from Town Centre. Convenient to Equestrian Centre, Sports Complex, Golf Club, Fishing. Close to N3, Cavan by-pass.

B&B	4	Ensuite	£20	€25.39	Dinner	-
B&B	-	Standard			Partial Board	-
Single Rate			£25.50	€32.38	Child reduction	25%

Open: 1st January- 21st December

Cavan 2km

Ben & Teresa Gaffney
ROCKVILLA
Moynehall, Cavan,
Co Cavan

Cavan
Tel: **049 4361885**   Fax: **049 4361885**
Email: rockvilla@eircom.net

Situated just off the N55 approaching from N3. Left at "Shell" gas station. Help with Genealogical research in Cavan. Ideal Dublin-Donegal stopover. Parking.

B&B	4	Ensuite	£19	€24.13	Dinner	-
B&B	-	Standard		-	Partial Board	-
Single Rate			£25.50	€32.38	Child reduction	25%

Open: 1st January-20th December

In Cavan

Brid Myles
HALCYON
Drumalee, Cavan Town
Co Cavan

Cavan
Tel: **049 4331809**   Fax: **049 4362531**

Spacious highly recommended ground floor accommodation in peaceful surroundings. Sunroom, Tea/Coffee facilities. Extensive library. Help with Ancestral tracing. AA ♦♦♦.

B&B	4	Ensuite	£19/£20	€24.13/€25.39	Dinner	£12.50
B&B	1	Standard	£17/£18	€21.59/€22.86	Partial Board	-
Single Rate			£23.50/£25.50	€29.84/€32.38	Child reduction	25%

Open: April-October

Cavan 2.5km

Mrs Alacoque O'Brien
BALLYCLOONE HOUSE
Golf Links Road,
Cavan, Co Cavan

Cavan
Tel: **049 4362310**
Email: michaelobrien01@eircom.net

Luxurious friendly accommodation, quiet road. Convenient to Town Centre, Golf Club, Equestrian Centre, Sports Complex.

B&B	2	Ensuite	£20	€25.39	Dinner	-
B&B	1	Standard	-	-	Partial Board	-
Single Rate			£25	€31.74	Child reduction	25%

Open: 1st January-20th December

Cavan 2.5km

Mrs Vera Greenan
THE BEECHES
Station Road, Cootehill,
Co Cavan

Cootehill
Tel: **049 5552307**

Modern dormer bungalow, situated in cul-de-sac off Shercock Road. Prime fishing area, home cooking and warm welcome to all visitors.

B&B	2	Ensuite	£19/£19	€24.13	Dinner	£12.50
B&B	1	Standard	£17/£17	€21.59	Partial Board	-
Single Rate			£23.50/£25.50	€29.84/€32.38	Child reduction	33.3%

Open: 1st February-31st October

Killeshandra

Mrs Maura O'Reilly
CLOONEEN HOUSE
Belturbet Rd, T52/R201
Killeshandra, Co Cavan

TEL: **049 4334342**   FAX: **049 4334342**
EMAIL: clooneen_house@esatclear.ie

Turn right facing Ulster Bank. Dormer bungalow situated T52/R201. Ideal stopover between Dublin/Donegal. Help with Ancestral tracing. Killykeen Park, Walks, Fishing, Pony Trekking.

B&B	2	Ensuite	£19	€24.13	Dinner £12.50
B&B	2	Standard	£17	€21.59	Partial Board -
Single Rate			£23.50/£25.50	€29.84/€32.38	Child reduction 25%

Killeshandra 2km

Open: April-October

Virginia

Mrs Julie Mulvany Fox
LISDUFF HOUSE B & B
Lisduff, Virginia, Co Cavan

TEL: **046 45054**   FAX: **046 45054**

Renovated 18th century Farmhouse, N3, overlooking Lough Crew, Hill of Four, Lough Ramor, Blackwater River, St Killian's Heritage Centre, Mullagh.

B&B	5	Ensuite	£20/£20	€25.39	Dinner -
B&B	-	Standard	-	-	Partial Board -
Single Rate			£25.50	€32.38	Child reduction -

Virginia 3km

Open: All Year

Virginia

Mrs Emily McHugo
THE WHITE HOUSE
Oldcastle Road, Virginia,
Co Cavan

TEL: **049 8547515**   FAX: **049 8547515**
EMAIL: mchugo@esatclear.ie

Warm welcome, breakfast menu. Tea/Coffee bedrooms. Forest walks. Fish at Lough Ramor. Horseriding, Watersports. Visit Loughcrew, Newgrange, Fore Abbey.

B&B	4	Ensuite	£20	€25.39	Dinner -
B&B	-	Standard	-	-	Partial Board -
Single Rate			£25.50	€32.38	Child reduction 25%

Virginia 1km

Open: All Year

Virginia

Mrs Bernie O'Reilly
ST KYRAN'S
Dublin Road, Virginia,
Co Cavan

TEL: **049 8547087**

Luxurious, ranch-type bungalow on Lough Ramor's shore. Panoramic view, mature gardens, excellent breakfast menu, electric blankets, tea making facilities.

B&B	2	Ensuite	£20	€25.39	Dinner -
B&B	2	Standard	£18	€22.86	Partial Board -
Single Rate			£23.50/£25.50	€29.84/€32.38	Child reduction 25%

Virginia 1km

Open: 1st April-30th September

SYMBOL

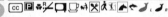

LOOK OUT FOR THIS SYMBOL WHICH
ALL MEMBERS OF TOWN & COUNTRY HOMES
DISPLAY THIS SYMBOL

Donegal is undoubtedly one of Ireland's most beautiful and rugged counties, with its spectacular scenery, rambling hills, magnificent mountains, lakes and its many blue-flag beaches, so too, has its heritage and culture. Noted for its hospitality and friendliness. Famous for it's tweed, hand knits and traditional music. Catering for all leisure and sporting activities.

In Annagry

Jackie Bonner Sharkey
BAYVIEW HOUSE
Annagry(R259)
The Rosses, Co Donegal

Annagry The Rosses
Tel: **075 48175**
Email: jns@tinet.ie

Quiet relaxing residence in Gaeltacht. Scenic views, Beaches, Hillclimbing nearby. Errigal-Dunlewey 15km. Glenveagh Park 25km. Daniel O'Donnell Hotel 8km.

B&B	3	Ensuite	£19/£19	€24.13	Dinner	-
B&B	1	Standard	£17/£17	€21.59	Partial Board	-
Single Rate			£23.50/£25.50	€29.84/€32.38	Child reduction	-

Open: 1st April-31st October

Ardara 1km

Charles & Marian Bennett
BAY VIEW COUNTRY HOUSE
Portnoo Road, Ardara,
Co Donegal

Ardara
Tel: **075 41145**   Fax: **075 41858**
Email: chbennett@eircom.net

Spacious, overlooking sea. Large gardens. Breakfast award 1994. Recommended: Frommers, AA, Real Guide, Fodors. Tea/coffee facilities. Turf fire. Credit Cards.

B&B	6	Ensuite	£19/£19	€24.13	Dinner	-
B&B	-	Standard	-		Partial Board	-
Single Rate			£25.50/£25.50	€32.38	Child reduction	25%

Open: 1st February-15th December

Ardara 5km

Mrs Eva Friel
THALASSA COUNTRY HOME
Narin - Portnoo,
Co Donegal

Ardara Portnoo
Tel: **075 45151**

Magnificent coastal region overlooking Ocean, Lake, Beaches, 18-hole Golf Course, Scenic Walks. Ancient Historic Monuments. Warm welcoming home. Recommended Guide de Routard.

B&B	4	Ensuite	£19/£20	€24.13/€25.39	Dinner	£15
B&B	-	Standard	-		Partial Board	£225
Single Rate			£25.50/£25.50	€32.38	Child reduction	25%

Open: 1st February-1st December

Ardara 1.6km

Mrs Marie Therese Haughey
IMEALL NA COILLE
Monargan, Ardara,
Co Donegal

Ardara
Tel: **075 41518**
Email: dhaughey@eircom.net

Excellent accommodation. Tranquil secluded location. Bluestack Way marked walk. Bicycle lockup. All facilities. Touring base. Experience genuine hospitality.

B&B	3	Ensuite	£19/£19	€24.13	Dinner	-
B&B	-	Standard	-		Partial Board	-
Single Rate			£25.50	€32.38	Child reduction	25%

Open: March-December

Ardara 1km

Vincent & Susan McConnell
ROSEWOOD COUNTRY HOUSE
Killybegs Road, Ardara,
Co Donegal

Ardara

TEL: **075 41168**   FAX: **075 41168**
EMAIL: jmccon@gofree.indigo.ie

Recommended by Le Guide de Routard, Ireland's best 300 B&B's. Fresh baked muffins and home-made jam served for breakfast. Tea/Coffee served in Guest lounge on arrival. Credit cards.

B&B	6	Ensuite	£19/£19	€24.13	Dinner	-
B&B	-	Standard	-		Partial Board	-
Single Rate			-		Child reduction	25%

Open: 1st January-1st December

In Ardara

Eileen Molloy
GREENHAVEN
Sea & Mountain View Hse
Portnoo Road, Ardara,
Co Donegal

Ardara

TEL: **075 41129**   FAX: **075 41129**

Frommer/Foder recommended. Quiet place to relax and enjoy excellent view of Sea & Mountain from dining room. Lounge, Patio & private garden. 3 minutes from Town.

B&B	5	Ensuite	£19/£19	€24.13	Dinner	-
B&B	-	Standard	-		Partial Board	-
Single Rate			£25.50	€32.38	Child reduction	-

Open: March-October

Stranorlar 1km

Mrs Evelyn Campbell
STRANORLAR HOUSE
Stranorlar, Co Donegal

Ballybofey Stranorlar

TEL: **074 30225**   FAX: **074 30225**

Beautiful Victorian house, antique furniture, unique breakfast menu. Extensive gardens. Ideally situated to explore the highlands and coast of Donegal.

B&B	4	Ensuite	£20/£20	€25.39	Dinner	-
B&B	-	Standard	-	-	Partial Board	-
Single Rate			£25.50/£25.50	€32.38	Child reduction	33.3%

Open: All Year

Ballybofey Stranorlar 1km

Judy McDermott
HILL TOP
Letterkenny Road,
Stranorlar, Co Donegal

Ballybofey Stranorlar

TEL: **074 31185**
EMAIL: admiran@unison.ie

Comfortable home set among the rolling hills of Donegal. Good touring base. Golf and Fishing facilities available locally. Breakfast menu with home baking.

B&B	3	Ensuite	£19	€24.13	Dinner	-
B&B	-	Standard	-		Partial Board	-
Single Rate			£25.50	€32.38	Child reduction	25%

Open: 1st April-31st October

Ballybofey 3km

Mrs Mary McGranaghan
TEEVICKMOY HOUSE
Letterkenny Road, Ballybofey,
Co Donegal

Ballybofey Stranorlar

TEL: **074 31866**   FAX: **074 31866**
EMAIL: mmcgranaghan@eircom.ie

Quiet rural location overlooking Steeple Woodlands, 0.5KM up from N13. Ideal Touring, Heritage base for NW. Sporting/Fishing/Beltony Stone Circle.

B&B	4	Ensuite	£20/£22	€25.39/€27.93	Dinner	-
B&B	-	Standard	-	-	Partial Board	-
Single Rate			£25.50/£25.50	€32.38	Child reduction	33.3%

Open: 1st April-3rd November

Ballybofey Stranorlar 1km

Mrs Gertrude Patton
FINN VIEW HOUSE
Lifford Road,
Ballybofey/Stranorlar, Co Donegal

Ballybofey Stranorlar
TEL: **074 31351**

Modern dormer bungalow. Ideal touring centre for Glenveagh National Park and Giants Causeway. Salmon Fishing, 18 hole Golf Course.

B&B	2	Ensuite	£19	€24.13	Dinner -
B&B	1	Standard	£17	€21.59	Partial Board -
Single Rate			£23.50	€29.84	Child reduction -

 **Open:** 1st April-30th September

---

Ballyshannon 1km

Mrs Mary Conlon
TEEVOGUE
Bundoran Road,
Ballyshannon, Co Donegal

Ballyshannon
TEL: **072 51386**   FAX: **072 51386**
EMAIL: teevogue@iol.ie

Bungalow overlooking Bay on N15, Spectacular view. Convenient to Donegal & Belleek China, Celtic Weave, Beaches, Horse Riding, Golf, Fishing. Rooms ensuite, TV, Hairdryer, Homebaking.

B&B	4	Ensuite	£19/£19	€24.13	Dinner £12.50
B&B	-	Standard	-		Partial Board -
Single Rate			£25.50/£25.50	€32.38	Child reduction 33.3%

Open: 1st May-31st October

Ballyshannon 1km

John & Clare Hughes
RANDWICK
Bundoran Road,
Ballyshannon, Co Donegal

Ballyshannon
TEL: **072 52545**   FAX: **072 52545**
EMAIL: randwick9@eircom.net

House on N15, magnificent views overlooking Erne Estuary. Le Guide du Routard. On parle francais. AIB Accommodation and Services Award 1998.

B&B	4	Ensuite	£19	€24.13	Dinner £13
B&B	1	Standard	£17	€21.59	Partial Board -
Single Rate			£23.50	€29.84	Child reduction 50%

Open: 1st March-31st December

Ballyshannon 1km

Mrs Deirdre Kelly
ASHBROOK HOUSE
Ashbrook Drive, Rossnowlagh Rd.
Ballyshannon, Co Donegal

Ballyshannon
TEL: **072 51171**
EMAIL: ashbrook_house@hotmail.com
WEB: ashbrookhouse.tripod.com

Newly built luxury home on scenic Rossnowlagh coast road (R231). Short walk to Town. All rooms TV, Tea/Coffee, Power Showers, Hairdryers-Smoke Free home.

B&B	3	Ensuite	£20	€25.39	Dinner -
B&B	-	Standard	-	-	Partial Board -
Single Rate			£26	€33.01	Child reduction 25%

Open: 1st April-31st October

Ballyshannon 2km

Siobain & George Luke
ASPEN
Parkhill, Ballyshannon,
Co Donegal

Ballyshannon
TEL: **072 52065**   FAX: **072 52065**
EMAIL: gluke@eircom.net

Modern dormer bungalow in quiet location on N15. Donegal Town 20kms, Belleek 8kms. Ground floor bedrooms. Non-smoking house. Power showers

B&B	3	Ensuite	£19/£19	€24.13	Dinner £12.50
B&B	-	Standard	-		Partial Board -
Single Rate			£25.50/£25.50	€32.38	Child reduction -

Open: 1st April-31st October

Ballyshannon 3km

Mrs Agnes McCaffrey
CAVANGARDEN HOUSE
Donegal Road,
Ballyshannon, Co Donegal

Ballyshannon
Tel: **072 51365**
Email: cghouse@iol.ie

Georgian house 1750, Donegal Road (route N15) on 380-acres, 0.5Km Driveway, Antique Furniture, Beach, Golf Course, Fishing, Belleek. Frommer recommended.

B&B	6	Ensuite	£20/£21	€25.39/€26.66	Dinner £13
B&B	-	Standard	-	-	Partial Board -
Single Rate			£26	€33.01	Child reduction 33.3%

Open: All Year Except Christmas

In Ballyshannon

Mrs B McCaffrey
ROCKVILLE HOUSE
Belleek Road, Ballyshannon,
Co Donegal

Ballyshannon
Tel: **072 51106**
Email: rockvillehouse@eircom.net

Late 17th century, overlooking River Erne. Convenient to Bundoran, Belleek Pottery, Rossnowlagh Beaches. Experience peace & beauty of old refurbished house.

B&B	4	Ensuite	£19/£20	€24.13/€25.39	Dinner -
B&B	2	Standard	£17/£18	€21.29/€22.86	Partial Board -
Single Rate			£25.50/£27.50	€32.38/€34.91	Child reduction 25%

Open: All Year Except Christmas

Ballyshannon 5km

Mrs Rose McCaffrey
ARDPATTON HOUSE
Cavangarden, Ballyshannon,
Co Donegal

Ballyshannon
Tel: **072 51546**

Ardpatton House is a warm comfortable family home on a large working farm on route N15. Close to Donegal Town, Belleek, with Golf, Fishing, Beaches.

B&B	6	Ensuite	£19/£19	€24.13	Dinner £12.50
B&B	-	Standard	-	-	Partial Board £185
Single Rate			£25.50	€32.38	Child reduction 50%

Open: 1st March-30th November

In Ballyshannon

Karen McGee
ELM BROOK
East Port, Ballyshannon,
Co Donegal

Ballyshannon
Tel: **072 52615**

Spacious, modern home in peaceful location, yet convenient to all amenities. 3 mins walk Town Centre. Ideal touring base.

B&B	3	Ensuite	£19	€24.13	Dinner -
B&B	-	Standard	-	-	Partial Board -
Single Rate			£25.50	€32.38	Child reduction 33.3%

Open: 1st March-31st October

In Ballyshannon

Mrs Bridget Nolan-Coyle
MULLAC NA SI
Bishop Street, Ballyshannon,
Co Donegal

Ballyshannon
Tel: **072 52702** Fax: **072 52702**
Email: www.mullacnasi.com

This home features large bright ensuite rooms with remarkable countryside views. Convenient to Beaches, Golf and Fishing. Ideal touring base for the North West.

B&B	2	Ensuite	£19/£19	€24.13	Dinner -
B&B	1	Standard	£17/£17	€21.59	Partial Board -
Single Rate			£23.50/£25.50	€29.84/€32.38	Child reduction 25%

Open: 1st April-31st October

In Bundoran

Bernie Dillon
GILLAROO LODGE
West End, Bundoran,
Co Donegal

TEL: **072 42357** FAX: **072 42172**
EMAIL: gillaroo@iol.ie
WEB: http://ireland.iol.ie/~gillaroo/

Superbly located B&B on main road. Close to Beaches, Waterworld, Golf, Hillwalking. Angling Centre with angling guides, Tackle and Boat hire. Drying and Tackle room.

B&B	4	Ensuite	£19/£20	€24.13/€25.39	Dinner	-
B&B	1	Standard	£17/£18	€21.59/€22.86	Partial Board	-
Single Rate			£23.50/£25	€29.84/€31.74	Child reduction	%

Open: 1st January-20th December

Derry City 8km

Mrs J Martin
MOUNT ROYD COUNTRY HOME
Carrigans, Co Donegal

TEL: **074 40163** FAX: **074 40400**
EMAIL: jmartin@mountroyd.com
WEB: www.mountroyd.com

Giants Causeway 1 hour. Grianan Aileach nearby. Old style home. Ground floor bedroom. Breakfast winner. Frommer Guide de Routard. AA & RAC ✦✦✦✦. Finalist AA landlady year 2000.

B&B	4	Ensuite	£19/£20	€24.13/€25.39	Dinner	-
B&B	-	Standard	-	-	Partial Board	-
Single Rate			£25.50/£25.50	€32.38	Child reduction	25%

Open: 1st February- 30th November

Carrigart 5km

Ann & Myles Gallagher
SONAS
Upper Carrick, Carrigart,
Letterkenny, Co Donegal

TEL: **074 55401** FAX: **074 55195**
EMAIL: sonas1@indigo.ie

"Sonas" Modern Dormer Bungalow overlooking Bay combining modern facilities with old style hospitality. Ideal touring base. Home baking. Power showers.

B&B	5	Ensuite	£19	€24.13	Dinner	£14
B&B	-	Standard	-	-	Partial Board	-
Single Rate			£25.50	€32.38	Child reduction	-

Open: All Year Except Christmas

Clonmany 5km

Fidelma McLaughlin
FOUR ARCHES
Urris, Clonmany,
Inishowen, Co Donegal

TEL: **077 76561/76109**

Modern bungalow surrounded by Sea and Mountains. Ideal for touring Inishowen Peninsula. Near Mamore Gap. 20km from Malin Head. 20km from Buncrana Town.

B&B	5	Ensuite	£19/£19	€24.13	Dinner	-
B&B	-	Standard	-	-	Partial Board	-
Single Rate			£25.50/£25.50	€32.38	Child reduction	50%

Open: All Year Except Christmas

Malin 6km

Mrs Anne Lynch
CEECLIFF HOUSE
Culdaff, Inishowen, Co Donegal

TEL: **077 79159** FAX: **077 79159**

Family run home. Excellent views of Beach, River & Mountains. Close to all amenities. Home cooking, A La Carte & special diets.

B&B	3	Ensuite	£19/£19	€24.13	Dinner	£12.50
B&B	-	Standard	-	-	Partial Board	£185
Single Rate			£25.50/£25.50	€32.38	Child reduction	25%

Open: All Year

Donegal Town 8km

Sile Callaghan
THE GAP LODGE
**Barnesmore Gap,
Donegal Town, Co Donegal**

Donegal Town
TEL: 073 21956

10 minutes drive from Donegal Town. Our spacious family run home is on the Letterkenny & Derry road, left side. Credit Cards accepted.

B&B	4	Ensuite	£19/£19	€24.13	Dinner	-
B&B	1	Standard	£17/£17	€21.59	Partial Board	-
Single Rate			£23.50/£23.50	€29.84	Child reduction	25%

Open: 1st April-30th October

Donegal Town 1km

Mrs Marie Campbell
LYNDALE
**Doonan, Donegal Town,
Co Donegal**

Donegal Town
TEL: 073 21873
EMAIL: lyndale@inet-sec.com
WEB: www.inet-sec.com/lyndale.htm

Luxurious home 200 metres off Coast Rd.(N56) next to Mill Park Hotel and Leisure Centre, Breakfast menu, Homebaking, TV, Electric Blankets, Hairdryers, Tea/Coffee facilities all rooms.

B&B	3	Ensuite	£19	€24.13	Dinner	-
B&B	1	Standard	£17	€21.59	Partial Board	-
Single Rate			£23.50/£25.50	€29.84/€32.38	Child reduction	25%

Open: 1st January-30th November

Donegal Town 1km

Bernadette Dowds
ISLAND VIEW HOUSE
**Tullaghcullion, Donegal Town
Co Donegal**

Donegal Town
TEL: 073 22411
EMAIL: islandview@eirbyte.com
WEB: www.eirbyte.com/islandview

New two storey Georgian style house overlooking Donegal Bay. 10 minute walk to Town Centre. Ideal base for touring North West Donegal.

B&B	4	Ensuite	£19/£21	€24.13/€26.66	Dinner	-
B&B	-	Standard	-	-	Partial Board	-
Single Rate			£26/£30	€33.01/€38.09	Child reduction	25%

Open: All Year Except Christmas

Donegal 1km

Mrs Kathleen Durcan
CRANAFORD
**Ardeskin, Donegal Town,
Co Donegal**

Donegal Town
TEL: 073 21455
EMAIL: cranaford@ireland.com

Modern family bungalow in peaceful residential area. Walking distance to town. Ideal touring base. Rooms with TV and Tea/Coffee facilities.

B&B	2	Ensuite	£19	€24.13	Dinner	-
B&B	1	Standard	£17	€21.59	Partial Board	-
Single Rate			£23.50/£25.50	€29.84/€32.38	Child reduction	25%

Open: 1st April-30th October

Donegal Town 4km

Mrs Sheila Gatins
HILLCREST COUNTRY HOME
**Ballyshannon Road, Laghey,
Donegal, Co Donegal**

Donegal Town
TEL: 073 21837   FAX: 073 21674
EMAIL: sheilagatins@unison.ie

Quiet location in small village off N15. Donegal Golf course and blue flag Beach closeby. Recommended Best 300 B&B. Tea/Coffee making facilities.

B&B	2	Ensuite	£19	€24.13	Dinner	-
B&B	1	Standard	£17	€21.59	Partial Board	-
Single Rate			£23.50/£25.50	€29.84/€32.38	Child reduction	25%

Open: 15th April-1st October

Donegal 1km

Mrs Margaret Geary
KNOCKNAGOW
**Ballydevitt, Donegal,
Co Donegal**

Donegal Town
TEL: **073 21052**

Modern bungalow situated in quiet countryside. Close to all amenities. Ideal touring base, excellent Shops, Crafts, Restaurants nearby.

B&B	1	Ensuite	£19	€24.13	Dinner	-
B&B	2	Standard	£17	€21.59	Partial Board	-
Single Rate			£23.50/£25.50	€29.84/€32.38	Child reduction	25%

Open: 15th April-30th September

Donegal 6km

Mrs Mary J Harvey
CLYBAWN
**Station Road, Mountcharles,
Co Donegal**

Donegal Mountcharles
TEL: **073 35076**

Modern bungalow in scenic location overlooking Donegal Bay. Lake, River and Sea Fishing nearby. Donegal Town 6km, Murvagh Golf Course 15km. Private car park.

B&B	3	Ensuite	£19	€24.13	Dinner	£12.50
B&B	1	Standard	£17	€21.59	Partial Board	£185
Single Rate			£23.50/£25.50	€29.84/€32.38	Child reduction	33.3%

Open: 1st April-30th September

Donegal 2.5km

Liam & Joan McCrea
THE COVE LODGE
**Drumgowan, Donegal Town
Co Donegal**

Donegal Town
TEL: **073 22302**
EMAIL: thecovelodge@ireland.com

Charming country residence overlooking Donegal Bay, just off N15 on R267. Golf Course, Beaches. Craft village. Comfort and relaxation assured.

B&B	4	Ensuite	£19/£23	€24.13/€29.20	Dinner	-
B&B	-	Standard	-	-	Partial Board	-
Single Rate			£27/£32	€34.29/€40.63	Child reduction	25%

Open: 1st March-31st October

In Donegal

Mrs Bridget McGuinness
BAY-VIEW
**Golf Course Road
Donegal Town, Co Donegal**

Donegal Town
TEL: **073 23018**

Quiet location overlooking Donegal Bay. Excellent Golfing, Fishing, sand beaches, walking trails nearby. Ten minutes walk Town Centre. R267 off N15.

B&B	4	Ensuite	£19	€24.13	Dinner	-
B&B	-	Standard	-	-	Partial Board	-
Single Rate			-	-	Child reduction	-

Open: 1st March-6th November

Donegal Town 4km

Bried McGinty
MEADOW LANE B & B
**Birchill, Donegal Town,
Co Donegal**

Donegal Town
TEL: **073 23300**

Luxurious Country House on N15. 4km North of Donegal Town. Magnificient views of Bluestack Mountain. Ideal touring base. Peaceful and quiet.

B&B	6	Ensuite	£19/£20	€24.13/€25.39	Dinner	-
B&B	-	Standard	-	-	Partial Board	-
Single Rate			£25.50/£27	€32.38/€34.29	Child reduction	-

Open: 1st January-15th December

Donegal 8km

Mrs Mary McGinty
ARDEEVIN
Lough Eske, Barnesmore,
Donegal, Co Donegal

Donegal Town Lough Eske
TEL: **073 21790**   FAX: **073 21790**
EMAIL: seanmcginty@eircom.ie
WEB: http://members.tripod.com/~Ardeevin

Charming country residence, magnificent view Lough Eske, Bluestack Mountains. Guide de Routard, Frommer recommended. AA ♦♦♦. RAC ♦♦♦♦, RAC Sparkling Diamond Award.

				Dinner	-
B&B	6	Ensuite	£20/£25	€25.39/€31.74	
B&B	-	Standard		Partial Board	-
Single Rate			£25.50/£30	€32.38/€38.09	Child reduction 25%

Open: 18th March-30th November

Donegal Town 8km

Mrs Noreen McGinty
THE ARCHES COUNTRY HOUSE
Lough Eske, Barnesmore,
Co Donegal

Donegal Town Lough Eske
TEL: **073 22029**   FAX: **073 22029 (man)**
EMAIL: archescountryhse@eircom.net

Luxurious residence, all rooms having panoramic views of Lough Eske/Bluestacks. Guide de Routard, Lonely Planet, Birrbauns, McQuillans Ireland recommended.

				Dinner	-
B&B	6	Ensuite	£20/£25	€25.39 /€31.74	
B&B	-	Standard		Partial Board	-
Single Rate			£25.50/£30	€32.38/€38.09	Child reduction 25%

Open: All Year

In Donegal

Marie McGowan
THE WATERS EDGE
Glebe, Donegal Town,
Co Donegal

Donegal Town
TEL: **073 21523**
EMAIL: thewatersedgebb2000@hotmail.com

Sligo road R267, opposite school, turn into cul-de-sac at Ballinderg House, 5th House down. Overlooking Bay/15th Century Abbey Ruins.

				Dinner	-
B&B	4	Ensuite	£19/£24	€24.13/€30.47	
B&B	-	Standard	-	-	Partial Board	-
Single Rate			-	-	Child reduction	-

Open: 15th January-15th December

Donegal Town 5km

Mrs Shona McNeice
LAKELAND B&B
Birchill, Lough Eske,
Donegal Town, Co Donegal

Donegal Town Lough Eske
TEL: **073 22481**   FAX: **073 22481**
EMAIL: mcneice@gofree.indigo.ie

Modern country residence with superb panoramic view of Lough Eske and Blue Stack Mountains. 3 miles from Donegal Town just off N15 Ballybofey road. Ideal touring base.

				Dinner	-
B&B	4	Ensuite	£20/£25	€25.39/€31.74	
B&B	-	Standard		Partial Board	-
Single Rate			£25/£30	€31.74/€38.09	Child reduction 25%

Open: 1st January-15th December

Donegal Town 6km

Mrs Mary T Martin
BAYSIDE
Mullinasole, Laghey,
Co Donegal

Donegal Town
TEL: **073 22768**

Coastal residence off N15 overlooking inlet of Donegal Bay. Golf Course and Beach 1km. Central touring location. Tea/coffee facilities.

				Dinner	-
B&B	5	Ensuite	£19/£20	€24.13/€25.39	
B&B	1	Standard	-	-	Partial Board	-
Single Rate			£23.50/£25.50	€29.84/€32.38	Child reduction 25%

Open: 1st March-31st October

Mrs Georgina Morrow
HIGHFIELD
**The Haugh, Lough Eske Road,
Donegal Town, Co Donegal**

Donegal Town
TEL: **073 22393**
EMAIL: georginamorrow@tinet.ie

Quiet elevated home with lovely view, close to Harvey's Point Country Hotel. Leave Donegal via N56, first turn right, signposted Lough Eske road for 2km

B&B	2	Ensuite	£19/£19	€24.13	Dinner	-
B&B	1	Standard	£17/£17	€21.59	Partial Board	-
Single Rate			£25/£30	€31.74/€38.09	Child reduction	-

Donegal 2km

Open: 1st February-30th November

Mrs Bernie Mulhern
MILLTOWN HOUSE
**Ardlenagh, Sligo Road,
Donegal Town, Co Donegal**

Donegal Town
TEL: **073 21985**   FAX: **073 21985**
EMAIL: milltown@oceanfree.net

Spacious home on R267 (off N15). Ideal touring base. Convenient Beaches, Golf, Fishing, Craft Village. Opposite Park Golf Driving Range.

B&B	3	Ensuite	£19/£20	€24.13/€25.39	Dinner	-
B&B	1	Standard	£17	€21.59	Partial Board	-
Single Rate			£26/£30	€33.01/€38.09	Child reduction	33.3%

Donegal 2km

Open: 1st February-30th November

Mrs Breege Mulhern
ROSEARL
**The Glebe, Donegal Town,
Co Donegal**

Donegal Town
TEL: **073 21462**
EMAIL: rosearl@indigo.ie

Modern spacious home in quiet residential area. 5 mins walk Town Centre. Golf, Beaches, Crafts nearby. Ideal touring base.

B&B	4	Ensuite	£19/£21	€24.13/€26.66	Dinner	-
B&B		Standard		-	Partial Board	-
Single Rate			£26/£35	€33.01/€44.44	Child reduction	33.3%

In Donegal

Open: All Year

Mrs Eileen Mulhern
ARDLENAGH VIEW
**Ardlenagh, Sligo Road (R267 off
N15) Donegal PO, Co Donegal**

Donegal Town
TEL: **073 21646**

Spacious, elevated home, with view of Donegal Hills and Bay, 3 mins drive from Donegal Town on R267 off N15. Quiet location. Ideal touring base.

B&B	5	Ensuite	£19/£20	€24.13/€25.39	Dinner	-
B&B		Standard		-	Partial Board	-
Single Rate			£25.50/£30	€32.38/€38.09	Child reduction	50%

Donegal 2km

Open: All Year Except Christmas

Ms Caroline Needham
INCHBURGH B & B
**Coast Road, Doonan,
Donegal Town, Co Donegal**

Donegal Town
TEL: **073 21273**

Bungalow on N56 situated 3/4 km from Donegal Town. Peaceful location off main road. TV's, Tea/Coffee facilities in rooms.

B&B	2	Ensuite	£19/£19	€24.13	Dinner	-
B&B	1	Standard	£17/£18	€21.59/€22.86	Partial Board	-
Single Rate			£23.50/£25	€29.84/€31.74	Child reduction	25%

In Donegal

Open: 1st April-30th October

In Dunfanaghy

Mrs Roisin McHugh
ROSMAN HOUSE
Dunfanaghy, Co Donegal

Dunfanaghy
TEL: **074 36273/36393** FAX: **074 36273**
EMAIL: rossman@eircom.net
WEB: http://come.to/rosmanhouse

Luxurious modern bungalow with spectacular views. 300 Best B&B's recommended. Breakfast menu, Electric blankets, Hairdryers, Radio Alarms.

B&B	6	Ensuite	£19/£22	€24.13/€27.93	Dinner	-
B&B	-	Standard	-	-	Partial Board	-
Single Rate			£25.50/£30	€32.38/€38.09	Child reduction	25%

Open: 13th March-8th November

In Dunfanaghy

Mrs Anne Marie Moore
THE WHINS
Dunfanaghy, Letterkenny,
Co Donegal

Dunfanaghy
TEL: **074 36481** FAX: **074 36481**
EMAIL: whins@hotmail.com
WEB: http://whins.ibusinessdot.com

Award winning home, with unique character. Recommended for comfort hospitality and "Fine Breakfasts" - New York Times. Opposite beach, Golf course.

B&B	4	Ensuite	£20/£21	€25.39/€26.66	Dinner	-
B&B	-	Standard	-	-	Partial Board	-
Single Rate			£25.50/£28	€32.38/€35.55	Child reduction	25%

Open: 5th January-20th December

In Dunfanaghy

Bridget Moore
CARRIGAN HOUSE
Kill, Dunfanaghy,
Co Donegal

Dunfanaghy
TEL: **074 36276** FAX: **074 36276**
EMAIL: carriganhouse@oceanfree.net

Luxurious modern home 5 min walk from village. Ideal touring base. Glenveagh National Park, Dunlewey Lakeside. Tea/Coffee facilities. Breakfast menu.

B&B	4	Ensuite	£20/£21	€25.39/€26.66	Dinner	-
B&B	-	Standard	-	-	Partial Board	-
Single Rate			£25.50/£28	€32.38/€35.55	Child reduction	25%

Open: March-October

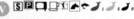

In Dungloe

Mrs Noreen Greene
SEA VIEW
Mill Road, Dungloe,
Co Donegal

Dungloe
TEL: **075 21353**

Spacious house overlooking Dungloe Bay and Mountains. Convenient to Beaches and Golf Course. Ideal for fishing enthusiasts. 5 min walk Town Centre.

B&B	6	Ensuite	£19	€24.13	Dinner	-
B&B	-	Standard	-	-	Partial Board	-
Single Rate			£25.50	€32.38	Child reduction	50%

Open: 1st March-1st November

Dungloe 2km

Mrs B McLaughlin
MARTELLO HOUSE
Meenmore, Dungloe,
Co Donegal

Dungloe
TEL: **075 21669**

Family run Bungalow, peaceful setting. Breathtaking sea view. Ideal for Fishing, Golf, Beaches, Touring Arranmore Island, Glenveagh. Clock, Radios, Hairdryers.

B&B	4	Ensuite	£19	€24.13	Dinner	-
B&B	-	Standard	-	-	Partial Board	-
Single Rate			£25.50	€32.38	Child reduction	25%

Open: 1st March-1st November

Falcarragh 1km

Christina Cannon
CUAN-NA-MARA
**Ballyness, Falcarragh,
Co Donegal**

Dormer bungalow overlooking Ballyness Bay & Tory Island. Glenveagh National Park 16km. Golf, Fishing, miles of Beach locally. Electric blankets. Guide du Routard recommended.

B&B	2	Ensuite	£19	€24.13	Dinner -
B&B	2	Standard	£17	€21.59	Partial Board -
Single Rate			£24	€30.47	Child reduction 50%

Open: 1st June-30th September

In Falcarragh

Ms Margaret Murphy
FERNDALE
**Falcarragh, Letterkenny,
Co Donegal**

Bungalow on scenic route N.W. 200m from Falcarragh. Beaches, Mountains, Fishing, Golfing nearby. Within easy reach of Glenveagh National Park.

B&B	1	Ensuite	£19/£19	€24.13	Dinner -
B&B	3	Standard	£17/£17	€21.59	Partial Board -
Single Rate			£23.50/£25.50	€29.84/€32.38	Child reduction 25%

Open: 1st May-30th September

Killybegs 28km

Mrs J P Byrne
CORNER HOUSE
**Cashel, Glencolumkille,
Co Donegal**

Situated in peaceful valley of Glencolumbkille, Ardara road, five minutes from Folk Museum, Sandy Beaches. Hill climbing & good fishing.

B&B	4	Ensuite	£19/£19	€24.13	Dinner -
B&B	-	Standard	-	-	Partial Board -
Single Rate			£25.50/£25.50	€32.38	Child reduction 25%

Open: April-30th September

Glenties 1km

Ms Jean Billingsley
LYNDALE
**Mullantyboyle, Glenties,
Co Donegal**

A warm welcome awaits you in my country home, situated on the banks of River Owenea and surrounded by Bluestacks. All home cooking. Turf Fires, Electric Blankets in all rooms.

B&B	2	Ensuite	£19	€24.13	Dinner -
B&B	1	Standard	£17	€21.59	Partial Board -
Single Rate			£25.50	€32.38	Child reduction 25%

Open: 15th April-30th September

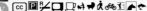

Glenties 1km

Mary Ita Boyle
AVALON
**Glen Road, Glenties,
Co Donegal**

Family run home, in a scenic location. Setting for Brian Friels play "Dancing at Lughnasa". Ideal place when touring the county. Coeliacs catered for.

B&B	3	Ensuite	£19	€24.13	Dinner £12.50
B&B	1	Standard	£17	€21.59	Partial Board £190
Single Rate			£23.50/£25.50	€29.84/€32.38	Child reduction 33.3%

Open: 1st January-30th November

In Glenties

Rosaleen Campbell & Conal Gallagher
LISDANAR HOUSE
Mill Road, Glenties, Co Donegal

Glenties
TEL: **075 51800**
EMAIL: lisadanar@eircom.net

Beautiful home country setting yet only 2 mins walk to the village on R253. Half way between Glenveagh National Park and Slieve League. Many extras.

B&B	4	Ensuite	£20/£21	€25.39/€26.66	Dinner	-
B&B	-	Standard	-	-	Partial Board	-
Single Rate			£26	€33.01	Child reduction	-

Open: 1st April-1st November

Glenties 1km

Mrs Margaret McCafferty
CLARADON COUNTRY HOUSE
Glen Road, Glenties, Co Donegal

Glenties
TEL: **075 51113**   FAX: **075 51113**
EMAIL: mccafferty@eircom.net

Scenic mountain views/walks. Local Heritage/Museum/Beach/Golf 12km. Advice/Central for touring county. Fishing. 5 Tidy Towns wins. Genealogy help. On R253.

B&B	4	Ensuite	£19	€24.13	Dinner	£12.50
B&B	-	Standard	-	-	Partial Board	£190
Single Rate			£25.50	€32.38	Child reduction	33.3%

Open: All Year Except Christmas

In Glenties

Mrs Marguerite McLoone
MARGUERITE'S
Lr Main Street, Glenties, Co Donegal

Glenties
TEL: **075 51699**

Modern new house located in Town. Ideal base for touring. Beach/Golf 8 miles, local Museum, Scenic Walks, Fishing.

B&B	4	Ensuite	£19	€24.13	Dinner	-
B&B	-	Standard	-	-	Partial Board	-
Single Rate			£25.50	€32.38	Child reduction	33.3%

Open: All Year

In Glenties

Mrs Mary Regan
ARDLANN
Mill Rd, Glenties, Co Donegal

Glenties
TEL: **075 51271**   FAX: **075 51271**

On N56. Spacious house with panoramic views from all rooms. Beside Museum, Hotel & Church. Touring base for "Highlands & Islands of Donegal". Golf/Beach 10km.

B&B	3	Ensuite	£19/£20	€24.13/€25.39	Dinner	-
B&B	1	Standard	£17/£18	€21.59/€22.86	Partial Board	-
Single Rate			£23.50/£25.50	€29.84/€32.38	Child reduction	50%

Open: March-November

Killybegs 7km

Ms Grainne Cafferty
ROOM WITH A VIEW
Coast Road, Kilcar, Co Donegal

Kilcar
TEL: **073 38018**   FAX: **073 31976**
EMAIL: grainne@donegalrefrigeration.ie

200 hundred year old refurbished house situated on scenic road to Kilcar. Overlooking Donegal Bay /Sligo Mountains. Ideal location to Sliabh League. Walking distance to Beaches/Restaurants.

B&B	2	Ensuite	£20/£22	€25.39/€27.93	Dinner	-
B&B	1	Standard	£17.50	€22.22	Partial Board	-
Single Rate			£25/£27	€31.74/€34.29	Child reduction	50%

Open: 1st March-31st October

Kilcar 1km

Mrs Mairead Byrne
HILLCREST
Cashel, Kilcar,
Co Donegal

Kilcar
Tel: **073 38243**   Fax: **073 38243**

West of Kilcar. Home baking. Rooms with TV. Near Harbour, Beach, Boat Trips, Pony Trekking, Country Walks. Slieve League 9km.

B&B	3	Ensuite	£19	€24.13	Dinner -
B&B	1	Standard	£17	€21.59	Partial Board -
Single Rate			£23.50/£25.50	€29.84/€32.38	Child reduction 33.3%

Open: All Year

Killybegs 1km

Ms Mary Anderson
CORNTON HOUSE
Old Fintra Road, Killybegs,
Co Donegal

Killybegs
Tel: **073 31588**
Email: manderson@tinet.ie
Web: http://homepage.tinet.ie/~manderson

Modern family home set in quiet scenic location. Beautiful gardens, superb views. 1km west of Killybegs(10 mins walk). Ideal touring base. Angling, Pony trekking, Beach, Restaurants nearby.

B&B	4	Ensuite	£19/£19	€24.13	Dinner -
B&B	-	Standard	-		Partial Board -
Single Rate			£25.50/£25.50	€32.38	Child reduction -

Open: 1st March-1st November

Killybegs 1km

The Cahill Family
LISMOLIN COUNTRY HOME
Fintra Road, Killybegs,
Co Donegal

Killybegs
Tel: **073 31035/32310** Fax: **073 32310**
Email: lismolincountryhome@hotmail.com

Frommer, Guide de Routard recommended. Quiet location 1km west of Killybegs. Mountain view, Scenic walks. Rooms have TV, Hairdryer, Tea/Coffee.

B&B	5	Ensuite	£19	€24.13	Dinner -
B&B	-	Standard	-		Partial Board -
Single Rate			£25.50/£30	€32.38/€38.09	Child reduction 33.3%

Open: 1st June-30th September

Killybegs 5km

Mrs Helena Cunningham
OCEAN VIEW
Largy, Killybegs,
Co Donegal

Killybegs
Tel: **073 31576**   Fax: **073 31576**

Luxurious home on elevated site 5km west of Killybegs. Spectacular views of Atlantic Ocean, Sligo Mountains. Beaches, Restaurants nearby. Slieve League 14km.

B&B	5	Ensuite	£19/£23	€24.13/€29.20	Dinner -
B&B	-	Standard	-	-	Partial Board -
Single Rate			£25.50/£30	€32.38/€38.09	Child reduction 25%

Open: 1st May-30th September

Killybegs 1km

Mrs Ann Keeney
HOLLYCREST LODGE
Donegal Road,
Killybegs, Co Donegal

Killybegs
Tel: **073 31470**
Email: hollycrest@hotmail.com

Recommended 300 Best B&B's. On main Donegal/Killybegs road, situated on right. Guests TV lounge. Bedrooms Tea/coffee facilities, Hairdryers.

B&B	3	Ensuite	£19/£20	€24.13/€25.39	Dinner -
B&B	1	Standard	£17/£18	€21.59/€22.86	Partial Board -
Single Rate			£24/£26	€30.47/€33.01	Child reduction 25%

Open: 1st February-30th November

Killybegs 3km

Frankie & Ann McClean
CREDO HOUSE
Benroe, Killybegs,
Co Donegal

Killybegs
Tel: **073 31364**   Fax: **073 31364**
Email: credohouse@eircom.net

Luxurious secluded accommodation at edge of Atlantic, magnificent sea & mountain views. Delicious cooking, friendly atmosphere (off R263). Highly recommended.

B&B	5	Ensuite	£19/£22.50	€24.13 /€28.57	Dinner £18
B&B	-	Standard	-	-	Partial Board -
Single Rate			£25.50/£27.50	€32.38/€34.91	Child reduction 25%

Open: April-October

Killybegs 1km

Mrs Sadie McKeever
LOUGH HEAD HOUSE
Donegal Road, Killybegs,
Co Donegal

Killybegs
Tel: **073 31088**

Panoramic views of Killybegs Harbour & Light House. Inside Ireland recommended. Tea or Coffee on arrival. Scenic walks nearby. Electric blankets.

B&B	2	Ensuite	£19/£20	€24.13/€25.39	Dinner -
B&B	1	Standard	£18/£18	€22.86	Partial Board -
Single Rate			£30/£30	€38.09	Child reduction -

Open: May-31st October

In Killybegs

Phyllis Melly
BANNAGH HOUSE
Fintra Road, Killybegs,
Co Donegal

Killybegs
Tel: **073 31108**

Modern bungalow on elevated site overlooking Killybegs Harbour and Fishing Fleet. Rooms ensuite. Private car park. Frommer recommended, 300 best B&B's.

B&B	4	Ensuite	£18.50/£20	€23.49/€25.39	Dinner -
B&B	-	Standard	-	-	Partial Board -
Single Rate			-	-	Child reduction 25%

Open: April-30th October

Killybegs 1km

Mrs Ellen O'Keeney
GLENLEE HOUSE
Fintra Road, Killybegs,
Co Donegal

Killybegs
Tel: **073 31026**   Fax: **073 31026**

Modern bungalow on main Killybegs - Glencolmcille Road, situated on right - hand side with fountain in garden. Beautiful Fintra Beach 1km.

B&B	5	Ensuite	£19	€24.13	Dinner -
B&B	-	Standard	-	-	Partial Board -
Single Rate			£25.50	€32.38	Child reduction 33.3%

Open: All Year

Killybegs 2km

Tully Family
TULLYCULLION HOUSE
Tullaghacullion, Killybegs,
Co Donegal

Killybegs
Tel: **073 31842**   Fax: **073 31842**
Email: tullys@gofree.indigo.ie
Web: http://www.infowing.ie/fishing/ac/tu2.htm

New luxurious country home. Conservatory. Secluded, elevated 2 acre site. Panoramic view overlooking Killybegs Port/Hills/Farmland/Donkeys. Boat shaped signs (N56).

B&B	4	Ensuite	£19/£21	€24.13/€26.66	Dinner -
B&B	-	Standard	-	-	Partial Board -
Single Rate			£25.50/£27	€32.38/€34.29	Child reduction 25%

Open: March-November

Catherine A Walsh
OILEAN ROE HOUSE
Fintra Rd, Killybegs,
Co Donegal

Killybegs
TEL: **073 31192**
EMAIL: walsh01@eircom.net

Spacious 2 storey home, near Beach & Restaurants. Convenient to Slieve League, Glencolumbkille & Killybegs Harbour. TV & Tea in lounge.

B&B	4	Ensuite	£19/£19	€24.13	Dinner	-
B&B	-	Standard	-	-	Partial Board	-
Single Rate			£25.50	€32.38	Child reduction	50%

Killybegs 1km

Open: 12th March–30th September

Daniel & Genevieve McElwee
FERN HOUSE
Lower Main Street, Kilmacrennan,
Letterkenny, Co Donegal

Kilmacrennan
TEL: **074 39218**

Bright spacious two storey town house in village on N56 to Dunfanaghy. Glenveagh National Park 16K. Bars/Restaurants walking distance.

B&B	4	Ensuite	£19/£19	€24.13	Dinner	-
B&B	-	Standard	-	-	Partial Board	-
Single Rate			£25.50/£25.50	€32.38	Child reduction	50%

Letterkenny 9km

Open: All Year Except Christmas

Mrs Sophia Boyle
BRIDGEBURN HOUSE
Trentagh, Letterkenny,
Co Donegal

Letterkenny
TEL: **074 37167**

15 mins drive from Letterkenny N56 to village of Kilmacrennan, turn left at signpost for Churchill - 5km. Ideal for Glenveagh Park, Flaxmill, Glebe Gallery.

B&B	3	Ensuite	£19/£19	€24.13	Dinner	£12.50
B&B	1	Standard	£17/£17	€21.59	Partial Board	£220
Single Rate			£23.50/£25.50	€29.84/€32.38	Child reduction	50%

Letterkenny 9km

Open: All Year

Mrs Jennie Bradley
RADHARC NA GIUISE
Kilmacrennan Road, Letterkenny,
Co Donegal

Letterkenny
TEL: **074 22090/25139** FAX: **074 25139**
EMAIL: bradleybb21@hotmail.com

Spacious home overlooking town on N56 to Glenveagh National Park and West Donegal. 0.5km above Hospital. TV, Tea/Coffee and Hairdryer in bedrooms.

B&B	6	Ensuite	£19/£20	€24.13/€25.39	Dinner	-
B&B	-	Standard	-	-	Partial Board	-
Single Rate			£25.50/£30	€32.38/€38.09	Child reduction	33.3%

Letterkenny 1km

Open: 8th January–20th December

Mrs Elizabeth Cullen
ARDLEE
Gortlee, Letterkenny,
Co Donegal

Letterkenny
TEL: **074 21943**   FAX: **074 21943**

Modern house close to town Bus Station, Theatre, Hotels. TV, Tea tray in rooms. Turn left off Ramelton road opposite Aldi store, up Gortlee road, next left at top.

B&B	5	Ensuite	£19/£20	€24.13/€25.39	Dinner	-
B&B	-	Standard	£17/£19	€21.59/€24.13	Partial Board	-
Single Rate			£23.50/£25.50	€29.84/€32.38	Child reduction	33.3%

Letterkenny 1km

Open: All Year

73

Danny & May Herrity
TOWN VIEW
**Leck Road, Letterkenny,
Co Donegal**

TEL: **074 21570/25138**
EMAIL: townview@eircom.net

Frommer & Guide du Routard listing. Food awards. 3 downstairs rooms. Teamaking, Hairdryers, Electric blankets. Cross bridge at Dunnes Stores, keep left for 1km.

B&B	6	Ensuite	£19	€24.13	Dinner	-
B&B	-	Standard	-	-	Partial Board	-
Single Rate			£30	€38.09	Child reduction	-

Letterkenny 1km

Open: All Year

Breid & Paddy Kelly
ARDGLAS
**Lurgybrack , Sligo Road,
Letterkenny, Co Donegal**

TEL: **074 22516/25140** FAX: **074 22516**
EMAIL: ardglas@yahoo.co.uk
WEB: ardglas.com

Spacious home panoramic views. 1km from Dryarch roundabout and Holiday Inn on N13 to Sligo. Ideal tour and golf base. TV, Hairdryer, Tea Facilities, Frommer.

B&B	6	Ensuite	£19/£20	€24.13 /€25.39	Dinner	-
B&B	-	Standard	-	-	Partial Board	-
Single Rate			£25.50/£28	€32.38/€35.55	Child reduction	25%

Letterkenny 3km

Open: 1st April-30th September

Mrs Mary T Lee
BELLA VISTA
**Dromore/Derry Road,
Letterkenny, Co Donegal**

TEL: **074 22529**

Secluded residence overlooking Lough Swilly off Derry/Letterkenny dual carriageway (N13). Ideal for touring Donegal and Giants Causeway. TV, Tea/Coffee, Hairdryers in bedrooms.

B&B	3	Ensuite	£19	€24.13	Dinner	-
B&B	-	Standard	-	-	Partial Board	-
Single Rate			£25.50	€32.38	Child reduction	33.3%

Letterkenny 2km

Open: 1st May-30th September

Majella Leonard
OAKLANDS B&B
**8 Oakland Park, Gortlee Road
Letterkenny, Co Donegal**

TEL: **074 25529**   FAX: **074 25205**
EMAIL: oakland@unison.ie

Family run B&B in quiet cul-de-sac opposite Aldi. 5 mins walk from Bars, Clubs, Restaurants. Ideal base for touring NW Region.

B&B	5	Ensuite	£19	€24.13	Dinner	-
B&B	1	Standard	£17	€21.59	Partial Board	-
Single Rate			£25.50	€32.38	Child reduction	50%

Letterkenny 1km

Open: 1st January-15th December

Mrs Mary McBride
RINNEEN
**Woodland, Ramelton Road,
Letterkenny, Co Donegal**

TEL: **074 24591**

Modern home situated in peaceful countryside. Warm welcome. Convenient to local amenities. Ideal base for touring Donegal. Non-smoking home.

B&B	1	Ensuite	£19	€24.13	Dinner	-
B&B	2	Standard	£17	€21.59	Partial Board	-
Single Rate			£23.50/£25.50	€29.84/€32.38	Child reduction	33.3%

Letterkenny 6km

Open: 1st May-31st October

Mrs Maureen McCleary
GLENCAIRN HOUSE
Ramelton Road, Letterkenny,
Co Donegal

Letterkenny
Tel: **074 24393/25242**
Email: glencairnbb@hotmail.com

Panoramic view from patio. On R245, near Mount Errigal Hotel/Silver Tassie and Golf. Central for touring. Guide du Routard recommended. All ground floor bedrooms, TV/Tea/Coffee/Hairdryer.

B&B	5	Ensuite	£19	€24.13	Dinner	-
B&B	1	Standard	£17	€21.59	Partial Board	-
Single Rate			£23.50/£25.50	€29.84/€32.38	Child reduction	33.3%

Open: All Year Except Christmas

Letterkenny 2km

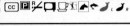

Leonie McCloskey
BLACKWOOD HOUSE
Ramelton Road, Letterkenny,
Co Donegal

Letterkenny
Tel: **074 26364**
Email: blackwoodbb@eircom.net

Warm hospitality offered in this tastefully decorated home. Well situated on main Ramelton road R245. Home baking and breakfast menu available.

B&B	4	Ensuite	£19/£20	€24.13/€25.39	Dinner	-
B&B		Standard	-	-	Partial Board	-
Single Rate			£25.50/£25.50	€32.38	Child reduction	50%

Open: 3rd January-26th December

Letterkenny 2km

Philomena McDaid
LARKFIELD B&B
Drumnahoe, Letterkenny,
Co Donegal

Letterkenny
Tel: **074 21478**

Quiet comfortable house. Secure private parking. Great view. First left past Holiday Inn on N13 towards Letterkenny. Tea on arrival. Ideal for touring Giants Causeway, Glenveagh National Park.

B&B	2	Ensuite	£19/£19	€24.13	Dinner	-
B&B	1	Standard	£17/£17	€21.59	Partial Board	-
Single Rate			£23.50/£25.50	€29.84/€32.38	Child reduction	50%

Open: All Year Except Christmas

Letterkenny 2km

Larry & Margaret Maguire
HILL CREST HOUSE
Lurgybrack, Sligo Road N13,
Letterkenny, Co Donegal

Letterkenny
Tel: **074 22300**   Fax: **074 22300**

Modern bungalow overlooking town and river on N13 to Ballybofey/Sligo. 1km from Dry Arch roundabout and Holiday Inn Hotel. Evening meals served all year.

B&B	5	Ensuite	£19/£20	€24.13 /€25.39	Dinner	£14
B&B	1	Standard	£17	€21.59	Partial Board	-
Single Rate			£24/£30	€30.47/€38.09	Child reduction	33.3%

Open: All Year

Letterkenny 3km

Mrs Sara Maguire
PARK HOUSE
Doobalagh, Sligo Road,
Letterkenny, Co Donegal

Letterkenny
Tel: **074 24492**

Frommer recommended. Panoramic view, 2 miles from Dry/Arch roundabout, on N13 to Sligo. Ideal base for touring North-West. TV, Hairdryers, Tea/Coffee.

B&B	4	Ensuite	£19/£19	€24.13	Dinner	-
B&B		Standard	-	-	Partial Board	-
Single Rate			£25.50/£27	€32.38/€34.29	Child reduction	33.3%

Open: All Year Except Christmas

Letterkenny 3km

Ms M A Murray
PINE TREES
Gortlee, Letterkenny,
Co Donegal

Quiet location off N56 to National Park. 10 mins Town, Golf, Horseriding. All rooms ground floor and garden view. TV, Hairdryer, Tea/Coffee facilities. Near all Hotels.

B&B	2	Ensuite	£19/£20	€24.13/€25.39	Dinner	-
B&B	1	Standard	£17/£19	€21.59/€24.13	Partial Board	-
Single Rate			£24/£30	€30.47/€38.09	Child reduction	33.3%

Letterkenny 1km

Open: April-October

Eugene & Ann O'Donnell
WHITE PARK B & B
Ballyraine, Letterkenny,
Co Donegal

On R245 to Ramelton. Large comfortable home. Spacious bedrooms. Superb location for touring. 30 Mins Glenveagh National Park and beach. 5 Mins walk to Mount Errigal Hotel, Pitch & Putt.

B&B	6	Ensuite	£19	€24.13	Dinner	-
B&B	-	Standard	-	-	Partial Board	-
Single Rate			£25.50	€32.38	Child reduction	50%

Letterkenny 1km

Open: 14th January-20th December

Mrs Ena Corry
CRAMMOND HOUSE
Market Square,
Ramelton, Co Donegal

Warm hospitality offered in 18th century home. Convenient to Restaurants etc. Family & triple rooms available. Le Guide du Routard recommended.

B&B	2	Ensuite	£19	€24.13	Dinner	-
B&B	2	Standard	£17	€21.59	Partial Board	-
Single Rate			£23.50/£25.50	€29.84/€32.38	Child reduction	50%

In Ramelton

Open: 1st April-30th October

Mrs Daphne Courtney
MEADOWELL
Burnside Road, Ramelton,
Co Donegal

Warm welcome. Situated off the main Letterkenny to Rathmullan Road. Ideal base for touring Fanad Peninsula and National Park.

B&B	2	Ensuite	£19	€24.13	Dinner	-
B&B	2	Standard	£17	€21.59	Partial Board	-
Single Rate			£23.50/£25.50	€29.84/€32.38	Child reduction	50%

Ramelton

Open: March-October

Mrs Shirley Chambers
STRABANE ROAD
Raphoe, Co Donegal

Modern house in peaceful location. 3 minutes walk from Raphoe, Beltony Stone Circle 4km. Tea making facilities. Ideal touring base Giants Causeway, Grianan Aileach.

B&B	4	Ensuite	£19	€24.13	Dinner	-
B&B	-	Standard	-	-	Partial Board	-
Single Rate			£25.50	€32.38	Child reduction	50%

In Raphoe

Open: 1st April-31st October

www.Donegal.ie

Take a horse for a gallop down a beach in Donegal, and you'll run out of horse long before you run out of beach.

Take a seat around the bar in any of hundreds of village bars, and don't be surprised if the evening stretches long into the night.

Take a surfboard out into the Atlantic rollers, and see what your nerves are made of. Take a walk, in any direction, and expect to want to just keep on going.

Take a look over a harbour wall, and watch fish being landed fresh from the ocean. Then find a little restaurant, and savour it.

Take a bag of golf clubs, and measure yourself against some of the world's finest links courses, if you can keep your eye off the view.

Take this number down, now, and prepare all your senses for a work out.

For Brochure
☎ **1800 621 600**

Information
☎ **074 21160**

Calling from outside Ireland dial:
00.353.74.21160

Co Leitrim with it's beautiful Lakelands, it's deep valleys and unspoiled terrain is famous for it's international coarse angling cruising and overseas tourists enjoy numerous festivals and attractions. Horse-riding, Golfing, Cycling, Hill-walking and other outdoor activities.

Ballinamore 2km

Mrs Eileen Breen
SUI MHUIRE
Cleendargen, Ballinamore, Co Leitrim

Ballinamore
TEL: **078 44189**

Situated 2.5 acres, scenic surroundings, Excellent fishing, golf, own boats. Entry/Exit drives. Situated route N202 Swanlinbar/Enniskillen Road. Highly recommended.

B&B	6	Ensuite	£20/£20	€25.39	Dinner	£12.50
B&B	-	Standard		-	Partial Board	£185
Single Rate			£26/£26	€33.01	Child reduction	33.3%

Open: April-October

Ballinamore 4.5km

Mrs Julie Curran
THE OLD RECTORY
Fenagh, Glebe, Ballinamore, Co Leitrim

Ballinamore
TEL: **078 44089**
EMAIL: theoldrectoryleitrim@eircom.net

The Old Rectory is an atmospheric 19th century Georgian Home on 50 acres of woodland overlooking Fenagh Lake and located beside Fenagh's historic Abbey's.

B&B	2	Ensuite	£22/£24	€27.93/€30.47	Dinner	£12.50
B&B	2	Standard	£18/£20	€22.86/€25.39	Partial Board	£230
Single Rate			£23.50/£30	€29.84/€38.09	Child reduction	25%

Open: 10th January-1st December

Carrick-on-Shannon 2.5km

Mrs Patricia Butler
WEIR VIEW
Jamestown,Carrick-on-Shannon N4, Co Leitrim

Carrick-on-Shannon
TEL: **078 24726**
EMAIL: donweirview@unison.ie

Just off the main N4. Family home in peaceful location. Dublin-Sligo-Donegal-Fermanagh route. Golf, Fishing nearby. Breakfast choice. Highly recommended.

B&B	2	Ensuite	£19/£19	€24.13	Dinner	-
B&B	2	Standard	£17/£17	€21.59	Partial Board	-
Single Rate			£23.50/£25.50	€29.84/€32.38	Child reduction	50%

Open: March-October

Carrick-on-Shannon 1km

Mrs Valerie Cahill
ATTYRORY LODGE
Dublin Road, Carrick-on-Shannon, Co Leitrim

Carrick-on-Shannon
TEL: **078 20955**   FAX: 078 20955
EMAIL: attyrorylodge@eircom.net

Roots dating 100 years in Leitrim. Complimentary interior capturing warmth and history in style. Rough Guide recommended. Located on N4 Dublin/Sligo/Donegal route.

B&B	5	Ensuite	£19	€24.13	Dinner	£12.50
B&B	-	Standard	-	-	Partial Board	£185
Single Rate			£25.50	€32.38	Child reduction	25%

Open: 1st January-23rd December

Gerard & Jeanette Conefrey
CANAL VIEW HOUSE
Keshcarrigan, Carrick-on-Shannon, Co Leitrim

Carrick-on-Shannon
Tel: **078 42056**   Fax: **078 42056/42261**
Email: canalviewcountryhome@eircom.net

Delightful country home and Restaurant with breathtaking view of Cruisers passing. All rooms with pleasant outlook. Quiet walks and cycle routes. Fishing on doorstep. Music in Pubs.

In Keshcarrigan

B&B	6	Ensuite	£25/£25	€31.74	Dinner	£15
B&B	-	Standard	-	-	Partial Board	£195
Single Rate			£30/£30	€38.09	Child reduction	25%

Open: All Year Except Christmas

Mrs Breedge Nolan
VILLA FLORA
Station Road, Carrick-on-Shannon Co Leitrim

Carrick-on-Shannon
Tel: **078 20338**

Modernised Georgian House, walking distance to Town Centre and Railway Station. Adjacent N4. Fishing and Boating Facilities, Pub Entertainment.

In Carrick-on-Shannon

B&B	3	Ensuite	£20/£25	€25.39/€31.74	Dinner	-
B&B	1	Standard	£19/£20	€24.13/€25.39	Partial Board	-
Single Rate			£30	€38.09	Child reduction	25%

Open: 1st April-30th October

PJ & Valerie Rowley
CORBALLY LODGE
Dublin Road, Carrick-on-Shannon N4, Co Leitrim

Carrick-on-Shannon
Tel: **078 20228**   Fax: **078 20228**
Email: valerierowley@hotmail.com

Country peacefulness on N4. Landscaped gardens, Antique furnishings. Dublin/Sligo/Donegal, Fermanagh route. Recommended Best 300 B&B's and Dillard Causin Guide. Help with Ancestral tracing.

Carrick-on-Shannon 2.5km

B&B	3	Ensuite	£19/£19	€24.13	Dinner	-
B&B	1	Standard	£17/£17	€21.59	Partial Board	-
Single Rate			£23.50/£25.50	€29.84/€32.38	Child reduction	50%

Open: March-October

Eleanor & Seamus Shortt
MOYRANE HOUSE
Dublin Road, Carrick-on-Shannon, Co Leitrim

Carrick-on-Shannon
Tel: **078 20325**
Email: eleanorshortt@eircom.net
Web: http://homepage.eircom.net/~eleanorshortt

Highly recommended. Real Irish home. Peacefully set back from N4. Dublin/Sligo/Donegal route. Breakfast choices, French spoken. Credit cards. Near lively riverside town and quiet countryside.

Carrick-on-Shannon 1km

B&B	3	Ensuite	£19/£19	€24.13	Dinner	-
B&B	1	Standard	£17/£17	€21.59	Partial Board	-
Single Rate			£23.50/£25.50	€29.84/€32.38	Child reduction	25%

Open: 1st April-31st October

Mrs Mairin Heron
FRAOCH BAN
Corlough, Drumshanbo, Co Leitrim

Drumshanbo
Tel: **078 41260**
Email: dec@iol.ie

Highly recommended country home situated on the R207. Overlooking Lough Allen. Panoramic views of Lake and Mountains. Walking, Equestrian and Canoeing Centre nearby.

Drumshanbo 1km

B&B	4	Ensuite	£19	€24.13	Dinner	£12.50
B&B	-	Standard	-	-	Partial Board	£185
Single Rate			£26	€33.01	Child reduction	25%

Open: 1st April-30th October

Manorhamilton

Tony & Mary McPartland
LAUREL LODGE
**Clooneen, Manorhamilton,
Co Leitrim**

Manorhamilton
Tel: **072 55018**

Georgian House, picturesque setting, in North Leitrim Glens area. Private developed gardens. Fishing on site. Central for Sligo, Donegal, Fermanagh.

B&B	3	Ensuite	£20/£20	€25.39	Dinner	-
B&B	2	Standard	£18/£18	€22.86	Partial Board	-
Single Rate			£25/£28	€31.74/€35.55	Child reduction	25%

Open: 1st May-31st October

Lough Melvin

'County of the Little Hills'. The constant presence of the attractive lakes - Muckno, Gasslough, Erny and Darty has a special appeal to the sportsman. The intriguing roads winding around the hills serve to portray the dignified charm of pastoral landscape.

Margaret Flanagan
SHANMULLAGH HOUSE
Killanny Rd (off Dundalk Rd)
Carrickmacross, Co Monaghan

Carrickmacross
Tel: **042 9663038**   Fax: **042 9661915**
Email: flanagan@esatclear.ie

Modern artistically decorated house in rural surroundings. Convenient to Nuremore Hotel & Country Club. Golf, Fishing, Horse Riding locally.

B&B	5	Ensuite	£19	€24.13	Dinner	-
B&B	1	Standard		-	Partial Board	-
Single Rate			£25.50	€32.38	Child reduction	33.3%

Carrickmacross 3km

Open: 1st February-5th December

Mrs Eilish McConnell
BRAEVIEW HOUSE
Toneyellida , Donaghmoyne,
Carrickmacross, Co Monaghan

Carrickmacross
Tel: **042 9663465**

Modern bungalow overlooking N2 Dublin/Derry road. Private parking. Tea/Coffee/TV/Hairdryer facilities. Close by Golf, Fishing, Equestrian. Kavanagh Country.

B&B	3	Ensuite	£19/£19	€24.13	Dinner	-
B&B	-	Standard	-	-	Partial Board	-
Single Rate			£25.50/£25.50	€32.38	Child reduction	-

Carrickmacross 4km

Open: 8th January-18th December

The Russell Family
NUREBEG HOUSE
Ardee Road, Carrickmacross,
Co Monaghan

Carrickmacross
Tel: **042 9661044**

Situated N2 Dublin/Derry Road. Beside Nuremore Hotel, 2 miles Carrickmacross. Fishing, Horse Riding, Golf locally. Central Touring, Newgrange, Carlingford.

B&B	5	Ensuite	£19	€24.13	Dinner	-
B&B	1	Standard	£17	€21.59	Partial Board	-
Single Rate			£23.50	€29.84	Child reduction	25%

Carrickmacross 3km

Open: All Year

Pat & Vera Conlon
BLITTOGUE HOUSE B & B
Dublin Road, Castleblaney,
Co Monaghan

Castleblaney
Tel: **042 9740476**
Email: blittogue.house@ireland.com

New luxury family run accommodation, situated near to scenic Lough Muckno. Walking, Fishing, Golf, Horse Riding, Bowling, Boating. Skiing. Situated on N2 road.

B&B	3	Ensuite	£19.50	€24.76	Dinner	-
B&B	2	Standard	£17.50	€22.22	Partial Board	-
Single Rate			£23.50/£25.50	€29.84/€32.38	Child reduction	25%

Castleblaney 1km

Open: All Year

Clones 1.5km

Clones

Mrs Anne Rooney
CLONKEEN COTTAGE
**Clonkeencole, Clones,
Co Monaghan**

TEL: **047 51268**
EMAIL: clonkeencottage@hotmail.com

Situated in the heart of Drumlin region, relax and enjoy warm and friendly hospitality. Ideal base for touring North, Midlands.

B&B	3	Ensuite	£19	€24.13	Dinner	£12.50
B&B	-	Standard	-	-	Partial Board	£185
Single Rate			£25.50	€32.38	Child reduction	50%

Open: 8th January-20th December

In Emyvale Village

Emyvale

Anna & Fergus Murray
AN TEACH BAN
**Main Street, Emyvale,
Co Monaghan**

TEL: **047 87198**   FAX: **047 87198**
EMAIL: anteachban@eircom.net

Modern spacious family residence situated in the picturesque village of Emyvale on the N2, 11km north of Monaghan Town.

B&B	4	Ensuite	£19	€24.13	Dinner	-
B&B	-	Standard	-	-	Partial Board	-
Single Rate			£25.50	€32.38	Child reduction	25%

Open: 10th January-20th December

APPROVED ACCOMMODATION SIGNS

Approved Accommodation Signs

This sign will be displayed at most premises which are approved to Irish Tourist Board Standards.

Panneaux d'homologation des établissements

Ces panneaux sont affichés dans la plupart des établissements homologués selon les normes de l'Office du tourisme irlandais.

Plakette fúr Geprúfte Unterkunft

Diese Plaketten werden an den meisten Häusern angezeigt, die von auf die Einhaltung der Normen der irischen Fremdenverkehrsbehörde überprüft und zugelassen wurden.

Borden voor goedgekeurde accommodatie

Deze borden vindt u bij de meeste huizen die zijn goedgekeurd door voor de normen van de Ierse Toeristenbond.

Simbolo di sistemazione approvata

Questi simboli saranno esposti nella maggior parte delle case approvate (associazione dei Bed & Breakfast approvati per qualità), rispondenti agli standard dell'Ente del Turismo Irlandese.

Símbolo de alojamiento aprobado

Estos símbolos se muestran en los establecimientos que han sido aprobados por bajos los estandars de la Oficina de Turismo Irlandesa.

Skyltar för Godkänd logi

Dessa skyltar finns vid de flesta gästhus som har godkänts (Föreningen för kvalitetsgodkända gästhus AB), enligt irländska turisföreningens normer.

Sligo has surprising contrasting landscapes, spectacular scenery, dream for painters, writers, historians, and archaeologists. Sligo has the second largest megalithic cemetery in Europe. Sandy beaches - Golf - Fishing - Theatre - Equestrian - Water Sports - Traditional music, good restaurants and a warm welcome for visitors.

Ballisodare 4.5km

Mrs Ann Campbell
SEASHORE
**Off Ballina Road (N59),
Lisduff, Ballisodare, Co Sligo**

Ballisodare
TEL: **071 67827**   FAX: **071 67827**
EMAIL: seashore@oceanfree.net
WEB: seashore.firebird.net

Country home with Conservatory/Dining room overlooking Knocknarea, Ox Mountains, Ballisodare Bay. Tennis Court, Jacuzzi. AA ♦♦♦ listed. Seashore walks, birdwatching facility.

B&B	4	Ensuite	£20/£22.50	€25.39/€28.57	Dinner	-
B&B	-	Standard	-	-	Partial Board	-
Single Rate			£25	€31.74	Child reduction	25%

Open: All Year

In Ballymote

Mrs Noreen Mullin
MILLHOUSE,
**Keenaghan, Ballymote,
Co Sligo**

Ballymote
TEL: **071 83449**

AIB "Best Overall" and Galtee breakfast award winning superb family home, peaceful location. Private tennis court. TV, Hairdryers. Megalithic tomb, Castle.

B&B	4	Ensuite	£19	€24.13	Dinner	-
B&B	1	Standard	£17	€21.59	Partial Board	-
Single Rate			£25.50/£30	€32.38/€38.09	Child reduction	33.3%

Open: 10th January-20th December

Cliffoney 2km

Mrs Beatrice McLoughlin
VILLA ROSA
**Donegal Road, Bunduff
Cliffoney PO, Co Sligo**

Bunduff/ Cliffoney
TEL: **071 66173**   FAX: **071 66173**

N15, Coastal region, Walks on Hills, Mountains, Seashore, Lakeshore, Creevykeel Megalithic Tomb, Bird sanctuary. Cycling tourists welcome.

B&B	4	Ensuite	£19/£20	€24.13/€25.39	Dinner	-
B&B	-	Standard	-	-	Partial Board	-
Single Rate			£25.50	€32.38	Child reduction	-

Open: May-September

Sligo 9km

Mrs Masie Rooney
CASTLETOWN HOUSE
Drumcliffe, Co Sligo

Drumcliffe
TEL: **071 63204**
EMAIL: f_rooney_ie@yahoo.co.uk

Situated beneath the bliss of Benbulben Mountains. Peaceful location. Hospitality, nearby W. B. Yeats grave. Glencar Waterfalls. Restaurants, Lisadell Hse.

B&B	3	Ensuite	£19	€24.13	Dinner	-
B&B	1	Standard	£17	€21.59	Partial Board	£185
Single Rate			£25.50	€32.38	Child reduction	20%

Open: March-October

In Enniscrone

Mrs Brenda Quinn
GOWAN BRAE
Pier Road, Enniscrone, Co Sligo

Enniscrone
Tel: 096 36396
Email: brenda.quinn@oceanfree.net

Georgian style home in Village. House enjoys lovely views of Killala Bay and Enniscrone Beach. Waterpoint Leisure Centre close by.

				Dinner	-
B&B	5	Ensuite	£20/£21	€25.39/€26.66	Partial Board	-
B&B		Standard	-	-	
Single Rate			£25.50/£26.50	€32.38/€33.65	Child reduction	50%

Open: 1st March-3rd December

Grange 2km

Mrs Una Brennan
ARMADA LODGE
Donegal Road N15,
Grange North, Co Sligo

Grange
Tel: 071 63250   Fax: 071 63250
Email: armadalodge@eircom.net
Web: homepage.eircom.net/~armadalodge

Peaceful tranquility ride on Beach. Climb Benbulben. Walk or Bike, Sea, Angling & Diving, Golf, Archaeology. Wonderful rooms & breakfasts, Laundry. Seaweed Baths.

				Dinner	-
B&B	6	Ensuite	£19/£21	€24.13/€26.66	Partial Board	-
B&B		Standard	-	-	
Single Rate			£25.50/£28	€32.38/€35.55	Child reduction	25%

Open: 15th March-22nd October

Grange 1km

Mattie & Patricia Hoey
ROWANVILLE LODGE
Grange, Co Sligo

Grange
Tel: 071 63958
Email: rowanville@hotmail.com

On N15, Superb scenic setting beneath Mountains/Sea. WB Yeats, Lissadell House, Horseriding nearby. Breakfast conservatory. Tea/Coffee, Hairdryers. Warm welcome.

				Dinner	£16
B&B	3	Ensuite	£19/£20	€24.13/€25.39	Partial Board	£195
B&B		Standard	-	-	
Single Rate			-	-	Child reduction	25%

Open: 12th February-12th November

Grange 2km

Mrs Maureen McGowan
MOUNT EDWARD LODGE
Off N15, Ballinfull,
Grange, Co Sligo

Grange
Tel: 071 63263   Fax: 071 63263
Email: mountedwardlodge@eircom.net

Panoramic peaceful setting off N15. Views Sea, Mountains. Midway Sligo/Donegal. Breakfast conservatory, Breakfast menu. TV, Tea/Coffee, Electric blankets. Golf, Horseriding. Credit cards.

				Dinner	-
B&B	3	Ensuite	£19/£20	€24.13/€25.39	Partial Board	-
B&B	1	Standard	£17/£17	€21.59	
Single Rate			£30	€38.09	Child reduction	25%

Open: All Year

In Grange

Mrs Kathleen Neary
ROSSWICK
Grange, Co Sligo

Grange
Tel: 071 63516
Email: rosswick@eircom.net

Family home, Personal attention. Panoramic view of Benbulben, Benwisken. Beaches, Horse riding, Hillwalking. Yeats Country closeby. TV, Hairdryer, Clock Radio all rooms. Breakfast menu.

				Dinner	-
B&B	2	Ensuite	£19/£21	€24.13/€26.66	Partial Board	-
B&B	2	Standard	£17	€21.59	
Single Rate			£24	€30.47	Child reduction	25%

Open: 1st April-31st October

Mrs Mary Conefrey
BAYVIEW
Doonierin, Cregg,
Rosses Point, Co Sligo

Rosses Point
TEL: **071 62148**

In quiet scenic countryside overlooking Drumcliffe Bay and majestic view of Benbulben. Golf, Restaurants nearby. Ideal base for touring.

B&B	3	Ensuite	£19	€24.13	Dinner	-
B&B	-	Standard	-	-	Partial Board	-
Single Rate			£25.50	€32.38	Child reduction	25%

Rosses Point 5km

Open: 1st March-30th September

Mrs Ita Connolly
IORRAS
Ballincar, Rosses Point Road,
Sligo, Co Sligo

Rosses Point
TEL: **071 44911**

Modern spacious home situated 2kms on Sligo to Rosses Point Road. TV, Tea/coffee in bedrooms. Golf, Sailing, Beach nearby.

B&B	4	Ensuite	£20	€25.39	Dinner	-
B&B	-	Standard	-	-	Partial Board	-
Single Rate			£26	€33.01	Child reduction	50%

Sligo 4km

Open: 1st April-31st October

Mrs Eithne Curran
CHANNEL BREEZE
Ballincar, Rosses Point Road,
Co Sligo

Rosses Point
TEL: **071 45542**
EMAIL: eithnecurran@eircom.ie

Bungalow with panoramic views of Sligo Bay and Mountains, ideal base in Yeats Country. Many recommendations. Beaches, Golf, Fishing.

B&B	2	Ensuite	£20	€25.39	Dinner	-
B&B	2	Standard	£17	€21.59	Partial Board	-
Single Rate			£23.50/£25.50	€29.84/€32.38	Child reduction	-

Sligo 4km

Open: May-September

Mrs I Fullerton
SEA PARK HOUSE
Rosses Point Road,
Sligo, Co Sligo

Rosses Point
TEL: **071 45556**   FAX: **071 45556**
EMAIL: ismayfullerton@eircom.net

3.5km from Sligo on R291 Rosses Point rd. 3km Beach, Sailing, Golf. Extensive b'fast menu. TV, Tea/Coffee, Hairdryers in bedrooms. Orthopaedic beds, Electric blankets. Many recommendations.

B&B	4	Ensuite	£20	€25.39	Dinner	-
B&B	2	Standard	£17	€21.59	Partial Board	-
Single Rate			£23.50/£25.50	€29.84/€32.38	Child reduction	33.3%

Sligo 3.5km

Open: 7th January-17th December

Mrs Cait Gill
KILVARNET HOUSE
Rosses Point, Co Sligo

Rosses Point
TEL: **071 77202**
EMAIL: kilvarnethouse@eircom.net
WEB: http://homepage.eircom.net/~kilvarnet

Modern comforts, traditional hospitality. In heart of Yeats Country, within walking distance of championship Golf Course, Yacht Club, Beaches, Restaurants.

B&B	4	Ensuite	£20	€25.39	Dinner	-
B&B	-	Standard	-	-	Partial Board	-
Single Rate			£25.50	€32.38	Child reduction	-

Sligo Town 8km

Open: 1st March-30th November

Rosses Point 5km

Kelly Family
SERENITY
**Doonierin, Kintogher,
Rosses Point, Co Sligo**

Rosses Point
TEL: **071 43351**

Award winner for hospitality. High quality food and accommodation. Superb Bay and Mountain views, cul-de-sac. Seaside location. You won't find a nicer place.

B&B	3	Ensuite	£20/£22	€25.39/€27.93	Dinner	-
B&B	1	Standard	£17/£19	€21.59/€24.13	Partial Board	-
Single Rate			£25/£30	€31.74/€38.09	Child reduction	-

Open: 1st April-31st October

Sligo 4km

Mrs Marian Nealon
SANIUD
**Ballincar, Rosses Point,
Co Sligo**

Rosses Point
TEL: **071 42773**

Welcoming family home. Quiet location beside Ballincar House Hotel. Convenient to Beaches, Golf, Sailing, Tennis in heart of Yeats Country.

B&B	3	Ensuite	£20/£20	€25.39	Dinner	-
B&B		Standard		-	Partial Board	-
Single Rate			£25.50	€32.38	Child reduction	-

Open: 1st April-30th September

Sligo 4km

Mrs Mary Scanlon
PHILMAR HOUSE
**Ballincar, Rosses Point Rd,
Sligo, Co Sligo**

Rosses Point
TEL: **071 45014**

Old style with modern comforts in quiet, scenic location. Large gardens for guests. Minutes from Golf course, Beaches, Sailing, Tennis.

B&B	2	Ensuite	£20/£21	€25.39/€26.66	Dinner	-
B&B	2	Standard	£18/£19	€22.86/€24.13	Partial Board	-
Single Rate			£23.50/£30	€29.84/€38.09	Child reduction	25%

Open: All Year Except Christmas

Sligo 4km

Mrs Renagh Burns
OCHILLMORE HOUSE
**Scarden-Beg, Strandhill Road,
Co Sligo**

Sligo
TEL: **071 68032**

Dormer Bungalow on Strandhill/Airport Road. TV, Hairdryers, Electric Blankets, Tea making facilities. Close Beach, Airport, Golf, Megalithic Tombs, Mountains.

B&B	4	Ensuite	£16/£17	€20.32 /€21.59	Dinner	-
B&B	-	Standard	-	-	Partial Board	-
Single Rate			£21	€26.66	Child reduction	50%

Open: All Year

In Sligo

Mary Cadden
LISSADELL
**Mailcoach Road (N15/N16)
Sligo, Co Sligo**

Sligo Town
TEL: **071 61937**

5 minute walk Town Centre. On N15/16. 200 yards off N4. TV, Hairdryers. Tea/Coffee facilities all rooms. Non-smoking.

B&B	3	Ensuite	£20/£22	€25.39/€27.93	Dinner	-
B&B		Standard			Partial Board	-
Single Rate			£25.50/£30	€32.38/€38.09	Child reduction	-

Open: 8th January-20th December

Mary & Tommy Carroll
ARD CUILINN LODGE
**Drumiskabole (R284),
Sligo, Co Sligo**

Sligo
TEL: **071 62925**
EMAIL: ardcuiln@esatclear.ie

Luxury accommodation, tranquil scenic surroundings. Home cooking. Guide de Routard, Petit Fute recommended. Near Lough Gill, 1km off N4(Carrowroe roundabout) on R284. Warm welcome.

B&B	2	Ensuite	£19/£21	€24.13/€26.66	Dinner	-
B&B	2	Standard	£17/£19	€21.59/€24.13	Partial Board	-
Single Rate			-	-	Child reduction	-

Sligo 5km

Open: 1st March-31st October

Mrs Phil Clancy
SEISNAUN
**Kintogher, off Donegal Rd,
Sligo, Co Sligo**

Sligo
TEL: **071 43948**

Beautiful country home on small farm with panoramic views overlooking Drumcliff Church/Yeats country. Situated 3 miles North of Sligo, 300 metres off Donegal road, N15. TV, Tea/Coffee.

B&B	4	Ensuite	£19/£20	€24.13/€25.39	Dinner	-
B&B	-	Standard	-	-	Partial Board	-
Single Rate			£27/£30	€34.29/€38.09	Child reduction	-

Sligo 4km

Open: 1st February-30th November

Ms Martina B Connolly
BERKANA
**Lisnalurg, Sligo,
Co Sligo**

Sligo
TEL: **071 71734**
EMAIL: berkana@gofree.indigo.ie

Bright relaxed setting overlooking Sligo Bay and Benbulben Mountain range (N15). Vegetarian food a speciality. Aromatherapy/Reflexology by appointment.

B&B	3	Ensuite	£19/£19	€24.13	Dinner	-
B&B	-	Standard	-	-	Partial Board	-
Single Rate			£25.50/£25.50	€32.38	Child reduction	25%

Sligo 3km

Open: All Year

Mrs Mary Conway
STONECROFT
**off Donegal Road N15, Kintogher,
Sligo, Co Sligo**

Sligo
TEL: **071 45667**   FAX: **071 44200**
EMAIL: stonecroft_sligo@yahoo.com

Cosy home in Yeats country 300m off N15 Donegal Road. Near Drumcliffe Church. Superb views. Credit Cards, TV, Tea facilities.

B&B	5	Ensuite	£19/£20	€24.13 /€25.39	Dinner	-
B&B	-	Standard	-	-	Partial Board	-
Single Rate			£25.50/£27	€32.38/€34.29	Child reduction	33.3%

Sligo 4km

Open: 1st February-8th December

Peter & Martha Davey
CARBURY HOUSE
Teesan, Sligo, Co Sligo

Sligo
TEL: **071 43378**   FAX: **071 47433**
EMAIL: carbury@indigo.ie

Luxurious spacious home on N15. Warm welcome. All rooms ensuite, Orthopaedic beds, Clocks, TV, Power Showers. 3 kms from Sligo. Touring base Sligo/Donegal.

B&B	6	Ensuite	£20/£22	€25.39/€27.93	Dinner	-
B&B	-	Standard	-	-	Partial Board	-
Single Rate			£25.50/£30	€32.38/€38.09	Child reduction	50%

Sligo 3km

Open: All Year

Des and Nan Faul
AISLING
Cairns Hill, Sligo, Co Sligo

Sligo Town
TEL: **071 60704**   FAX: **071 60704**
EMAIL: aislingsligo@eircom.net

Overlooking garden and sea. All rooms ground floor. Signposted 300m Sligo Park Hotel off N4. AA ♦♦♦, cosy. Listed in many Guides. Electric Blankets, TV's, Hairdryers.

B&B	3	Ensuite	£20/£22	€25.39/€27.93	Dinner	-
B&B	2	Standard	£18/£20	€22.86/€25.39	Partial Board	-
Single Rate			£24.50/£28.50	€31.11/€36.19	Child reduction	-

Open: All Year Except Christmas

Sligo 1km

Geraldine Gorman
GLENVALE
Cornageeha, Upper Pearse Road, Sligo, Co Sligo

Sligo Town
TEL: **071 61706**
EMAIL: geraldinegorman@eircom.net

Friendly family home on N4. 100 metres after Sligo Park Hotel. Private Parking. Close to Races, Sports Complex. Tea/Coffee, H/Dryer, TV, AA ♦♦♦ Award.

B&B	3	Ensuite	£19/£20	€24.13/€25.39	Dinner	-
B&B	1	Standard	-	-	Partial Board	-
Single Rate			£24/£26	€30.47/€33.01	Child reduction	50%

Open: 7th January-20th December

Sligo 3km

Tess Haughey
RATHNASHEE,
Teesan, Donegal Road N15, Sligo, Co Sligo

Sligo
TEL: **071 43376**   FAX: **071 42283**

Welcome to an Irish home. Scenic Area. Midway Sligo/Drumcliff en route Donegal. Homebaking. Many recommendations. Frommer, Guide du Routard. Lounge with extensive library. Old books.

B&B	2	Ensuite	£19/£19	€24.13	Dinner	-
B&B	1	Standard	£17/£17	€21.59	Partial Board	-
Single Rate			£23.50/£25.50	€29.84/€32.38	Child reduction	-

Open: April-October

Sligo 1.5km

Mary Hennessy
DAINGEAN
Hazelwood Rd, Ballinode, Co Sligo

Sligo
TEL: **071 45706**
EMAIL: daingeanhennessy@eircom.net

Friendly family home, situated 1.5 km from Town Centre. Close to all amenities. Spacious garden. Hazelwood Park, Lough Gill, Parkes Castle nearby.

B&B	3	Ensuite	£20	€25.39	Dinner	-
B&B	-	Standard	-	-	Partial Board	-
Single Rate			£26	€33.01	Child reduction	-

Open: 1st March-30th November

Sligo 3km

Mrs Christina Jones
CHESTNUT LAWN
Cummeen, Strandhill Road, Sligo, Co Sligo

Sligo
TEL: **071 62781**   FAX: **071 62781**

Modern spacious dormer bungalow situated 3km from Sligo on main Strandhill/Airport road. Close to Megalithic Tombs. T.V, Hairdryers.

B&B	2	Ensuite	£19/£19	€24.13	Dinner	-
B&B	1	Standard	£17/£17	€21.59	Partial Board	-
Single Rate			£23.50/£25	€29.84/€31.74	Child reduction	25%

Open: 1st February-21st December

Mrs Veronica Kane
GLENVIEW
**Cummeen, Strandhill Road,
Sligo, Co Sligo**

Sligo
TEL: **071 70401/62457** FAX: **071 62457**

Modern bungalow Strandhill Road, Megalithic Tombs. Golf, Beaches, Airport, Colour TV, Hairdryers, Electric Blankets, Tea making facilities, Lets Go recommended.

B&B	4	Ensuite	£19/£19	€24.13	Dinner	-
B&B	-	Standard			Partial Board	-
Single Rate			£25.50/£25.50	€32.38	Child reduction	50%

Sligo 2km   **Open:** January-November

Mrs Marie Kelly
ST JUDE'S
**Rathonoragh, Strandhill Road,
Sligo, Co Sligo**

Sligo
TEL: **071 60858**   FAX: **071 60858**
EMAIL: saintjudes@eircom.net

Close Airport, Bus, Railway station. Surfing, Swimming, Seaweed baths nearby. Climb Knocknarea Mountain, Megalithic Tombs, Heritage & Genealogy society. Electric blankets, Tea facilities.

B&B	2	Ensuite	£19	€24.13	Dinner	-
B&B	1	Standard	£17	€21.59	Partial Board	-
Single Rate			£23.50/£25.50	€29.84/€32.38	Child reduction	25%

Sligo 3km   **Open:** April-October

Mrs Shirley Kilfeather
LAR-EASA
**12 Kestrel Drive, Kevinsfort,
Strandhill Road, Co Sligo**

Sligo
TEL: **071 69313**   FAX: **071 69313**
EMAIL: lareasa@iolfree.ie

Situated within the parklands of Kevinsfort House. Ideally located for touring Yeats Country and Carrowmore tombs. Complimentary Fishing. Ballisodare River(on selected dates).

B&B	3	Ensuite	£19/£20	€24.13/€25.39	Dinner	-
B&B	-	Standard	-	-	Partial Board	-
Single Rate			£25.50/£25.50	€32.38	Child reduction	25%

Sligo 1km   **Open:** All Year

Mrs Ursula Leyden
RENATE HOUSE
**Upper John Street,
Sligo, Co Sligo**

Sligo
TEL: **071 62014/69093** FAX: **071 69093**

Frommer listed. Beside Bus/Train station. All amenities, Restaurants, Pubs, Tourist Office, Theatre, Hospitals, Churches. TV, Tea/Coffee, Hairdryer, Radio.

B&B	4	Ensuite	£19	€24.13	Dinner	-
B&B	2	Standard	£17	€21.59	Partial Board	-
Single Rate			£23.50/£25.50	€29.84/€32.38	Child reduction	25%

In Sligo   **Open:** 6th January-20th December

Ronan and Doreen MacEvilly
TREE TOPS
**Cleveragh Road (off Pearse Rd
N4), Sligo Town, Co Sligo**

Sligo Town
TEL: **071 60160**   FAX: **071 62301**
EMAIL: treetops@iol.ie
WEB: www.sligobandb.com

5 minutes walk Town Centre. T.V, Hairdryers, Direct Dial Telephones, Tea Facilities all rooms. Non smoking. Frommer, Guide du Routard recommended.

B&B	5	Ensuite	£20/£22	€25.39/€27.93	Dinner	-
B&B	-	Standard	-	-	Partial Board	-
Single Rate			£25.50/£30	€32.38/€38.09	Child reduction	-

In Sligo   **Open:** 8th January-15th December

89

Sligo 4km

Mary McGoldrick
ST MARTIN DE PORRES
**Drumshanbo Rd, Carraroe,
Sligo, Co Sligo**

Sligo
TEL: **071 62793**
EMAIL: stmdeporres@eircom.net

Peaceful rural setting, 1km off N4 at Carraroe roundabout on R284. Convenient to Lough Gill, Megalithic Tombs, Forest Walks. Secure parking. TV, Electric blankets.

B&B	4	Ensuite	£19/£19	€24.13	Dinner	-
B&B	-	Standard			Partial Board	-
Single Rate			£25.50/£25.5	€32.38	Child reduction	50%

Open: All Year

Sligo 2km

Evelyn and Declan McPartland
TEACH EAMAINN
**off N16, Hazelwood,
Clogherevagh, Co Sligo**

Sligo
TEL: **071 43393**   FAX: **071 43393**

Situated on two acres off N16. Tea room, over looking Knocknarae, Benbulben, Ox Mountains, Sligo Bay. T.V and Hairdryers. Parties special rate.

B&B	6	Ensuite	£19	€24.13	Dinner	-
B&B	-	Standard	-	-	Partial Board	-
Single Rate			£25.50	€32.38	Child reduction	-

Open: 9th April- 30thNovember

In Sligo

Mrs Nuala Monaghan
LOUGH GILL HOUSE
**Pearse Road, Sligo,
Co Sligo**

Sligo
TEL: **071 50045**   FAX: **071 50045**

Georgian town house on N4. 5 minutes walk town, close to Races, Golf, Sports Complex, Beach, Fishing, Rail and Bus Station. Non smoking.

B&B	4	Ensuite	£20/£22.50	€25.39/€28.57	Dinner	-
B&B	2	Standard	£19/£20	€24.13/€25.39	Partial Board	-
Single Rate			£30	€38.09	Child reduction	-

Open: All Year

Sligo 2km

Mrs Norah Mugan
MOIN NA TAOIBH
**Lisnalurg, off Donegal Rd N15,
Sligo, Co Sligo**

Sligo
TEL: **071 43584**
EMAIL: norahmugan@hotmail.com
WEB: http://members.xoom.com/countysligo/

USA "Best Guide" recommended. Guaranteed satisfaction. Architect designed. Panoramic views Mountains/Sea. Quality Beds, Tea/Coffee, H/Dryer, Peaceful Large rooms, non-smoking.

B&B	3	Ensuite	£20/£25	€25.39/€31.74	Dinner	-
B&B	-	Standard	-	-	Partial Board	-
Single Rate			£35	€44.44	Child reduction	-

Open: 1st February-30th November

Mel & Kathleen Noonan
STRADBROOK
**Cornageeha, Pearse Road,
Sligo, Co Sligo**

Sligo Town
TEL: **071 69674/50663** FAX: **071 69933**
EMAIL: stradbrook@futurenet.ie
WEB: www.stradbrook.com

Welcoming family home on N4. Sligo Park Hotel 100 metres. All facilities. Guide du Routard/AA recommended. Beaches, Golf, Fishing nearby. Ideal base for touring Yeats Country/Donegal.

B&B	4	Ensuite	£20/£22	€25.39/€27.93	Dinner	-
B&B	-	Standard			Partial Board	-
Single Rate			£25.50/£26	€32.38/€33.01	Child reduction	25%

Sligo 1.5km

Open: All Year

Sligo 1.5km

Mrs Bernie O'Connor
ALVERNO
Cairns Hill Rd, off N4,
Sligo Town, Co Sligo

Sligo Town
Tel: **071 62893**

2 storey georgian house. Modern facilities.

B&B	2	Ensuite	£20/£20	€25.39	Dinner	-
B&B	1	Standard	£18/£18	€22.86	Partial Board	-
Single Rate			-	-	Child reduction	-

Open: 1st April-30th September

In Sligo

Elma O'Halloran
ROSSCAHILL
19 Marymount, Pearse Road
Sligo, Co Sligo

Sligo Town
Tel: **071 61744**

Entering Sligo, N4, turn left into Marymount opposite ESSO station before second set of traffic lights. Located in quiet Cul-de- Sac.

B&B	3	Ensuite	£19/£21	€24.13/€26.66	Dinner	-
B&B	-	Standard	-	-	Partial Board	-
Single Rate			£25.50/£28	€32.38/€35.55	Child reduction	-

Open: 15th April-1st November

Sligo 2km

Olivia Quigley
BENWISKIN LODGE
Shannon Eighter, Off Donegal
Road N15, Sligo, Co Sligo

Sligo
Tel: **071 41088**   Fax: **071 41088**
Email: pquigley@iol.ie

Welcoming home, country setting. 2km Sligo, 50m off N15 behind "The Red Cottage". All facilities. Yeats Grave, Beach, Golf closeby.

B&B	5	Ensuite	£20/£21	€25.39/€26.66	Dinner	-
B&B	1	Standard	-	-	Partial Board	-
Single Rate			£26/£30	€33.01/€38.09	Child reduction	-

Open: All Year

Sligo 8km

Mrs Carmel Connolly
KNOCKNAREA
Shore Road, Strandhill,
Co Sligo

Strandhill
Tel: **071 68313/68810**
Email: connollyma@eircom.net

Large family home beside Beach, Seaweed Baths, Golf, Surfing, Horse Riding, Airport. Ideal for peaceful scenic walks. TV and Tea/Coffee in all rooms.

B&B	4	Ensuite	£19	€24.13	Dinner	-
B&B	-	Standard	-	-	Partial Board	-
Single Rate			£25.50	€32.38	Child reduction	25%

Open: March-October

Tubbercurry 1km

Mrs Mary Brennan
EDEN VILLA
Ballina Road, Tubbercurry,
Co Sligo

Tubbercurry
Tel: **071 85106**   Fax: **071 85106**
Email: edenvilla@ireland.com

A warm welcome awaits you at our luxurious family home. Tea/Coffee, Homebaking on arrival. Guest TV lounge with peat fire, breakfast menu. Ideal touring base. 250mtrs off N17.

B&B	2	Ensuite	£19	€24.13	Dinner	£15
B&B	1	Standard	£17	€21.59	Partial Board	-
Single Rate			£23.50/£25.50	€29.84/€32.38	Child reduction	33.3%

Open: 1st March-30th November

In Tubbercurry

Mrs Monica Brennan
ROCKVILLE
Charlestown Road, Tubbercurry,
Co Sligo

Tubbercurry
TEL: **071 85270**

Quiet, friendly Irish home on N17. Tea/Coffee, Home baking on arrival, Hairdryers, Electric blankets. Clock radios. Breakfast menu. Knock Airport 10 miles.

B&B	3	Ensuite	£19/£19	€24.13	Dinner	-
B&B	1	Standard	£17/£17	€21.59	Partial Board	-
Single Rate			£23.50/£25.50	€29.84/€ 32.38	Child reduction	33.3%

cc 🅟 ... **Open:** 1st March-30th November

Tubbercurry 1km

Mrs Joan Brett
ST ENDA'S
Charlestown Rd, Tubbercurry,
Co Sligo

Tubbercurry
TEL: **071 85100**

Friendly family home on N17. Scenic area. Home baking, Electric blankets. Gardens, Fishing and Golf nearby. Knock Airport 10 miles, Knock Shrine 22 miles.

B&B	4	Ensuite	£19	€24.13	Dinner	-
B&B	-	Standard	-	-	Partial Board	-
Single Rate			£25.50	€32.38	Child reduction	33.3%

cc 🅟 ... **Open:** 1st March-31st October

Mrs Noreen Donoghue
ROSSLI HOUSE
Doocastle, Tubbercurry,
Co Sligo

Tubbercurry
TEL: **071 85099**　　FAX: **071 85099**
EMAIL: *rossli@esatclear.ie*

Tubbercurry 6km

Rural setting. Tea/Coffee. Hairdryers, Electric blankets. Laundry facilities. Conservatory. Frommer Guide, Le Guide du Routard, Interconnections listed. Travel 6km on Ballymote road.

B&B	4	Ensuite	£19	€24.13	Dinner	£14
B&B	-	Standard	-	-	Partial Board	-
Single Rate			£25.50	€32.38	Child reduction	33%

cc Ⓢ 🅟 ... **Open:** All Year

Tubbercurry

Mrs Teresa Kelly
PINEGROVE
Ballina Road, Tubbercurry,
Co Sligo

Tubbercurry
TEL: **071 85235**

Friendly atmosphere, home-baking, evening meals, electric blankets. Gardens, Fishing, Shooting & Golf. Knock Shrine. 300 metres off N17.

B&B	5	Ensuite	£19/£20	€24.13/€25.39	Dinner	£15
B&B	-	Standard	-	-	Partial Board	-
Single Rate			£25.50/£25.50	€32.38	Child reduction	33.3%

🅟 ... **Open:** All Year

In Tubbercurry

Mrs Mary Kennedy
CINRAOI
Ballymote/Boyle Road
Tubbercurry, Co Sligo

Tubbercurry
TEL: **071 85268**　　FAX: **071 85268**

Modern bungalow on own grounds. Golf, Fishing, Horse Riding closeby. Le Guide du Routard listed.

B&B	2	Ensuite	£19/£19	€24.13	Dinner	£13
B&B	2	Standard	£17/£17	€21.59	Partial Board	-
Single Rate			-	-	Child reduction	-

🅟 ... **Open:** 9th January-10th December

Mrs Teresa O'Gorman
ANNALEA HOUSE
Tubbercurry, Co Sligo

Tubbercurry
TEL: **071 85141**

Bungalow located on N17 with Award winning gardens, viewed from conservatory. Individual attention a priority. Fishing, Golf available locally.

B&B	2	Ensuite	£19/£19	€24.13	Dinner	-
B&B	1	Standard	£17/£17	€21.59	Partial Board	-
Single Rate			£24/£24	€30.47	Child reduction	33.3%

In Tubbercurry

Open: 1st February-20th December

Mrs Maeve Walsh
CRUCKAWN HOUSE
**Ballymote/Boyle Rd,
Tubbercurry, Co Sligo**

Tubbercurry
TEL: **071 85188**   FAX: **071 85188**
EMAIL: cruckawn@esatclear.ie

Award winning family home in peaceful suburb, overlooking Golf Course. AIB "Best Hospitality". Many recommendations, Guide de Routard. AA ♦♦♦. Sunlounge, Laundry. Off N17 on R294 Rd.

B&B	5	Ensuite	£19/£20	€24.13/€25.39	Dinner	-
B&B	-	Standard	-	-	Partial Board	-
Single Rate			£25.50	€32.38	Child reduction	25%

In Tubbercurry

Open: 1st March-1st November

BOOKINGS

We recommend your first and last night is pre-booked. Your hosts will make a booking for you at your next selected home for the cost of the phone call. When travelling in high season (June, July, August), it is essential to pre-book your accommodation – preferably the evening before, or the following morning to avoid disappointment.

WHEN TRAVELLING OFF-SEASON IT IS ADVISABLE TO CALL AHEAD AND GIVE A TIME OF ARRIVAL TO ENSURE YOUR HOSTS ARE AT HOME TO GREET YOU.

Northern Ireland

Welcome to Northern Ireland! Gloriously green countryside, spectacular coast and mountains - an ancient land with a rich historical and cultural tradition and some of the friendliest people anywhere.

Visit our capital city of Belfast, famous for its industrial heritage and birthplace of the Titanic, where you can experience a unique combination of award winning restaurants, traditional pubs, history and culture. Also well worth a visit is the city of Derry, one of the finest examples of a walled city in Europe and Armagh, the ecclesiastical capital of Ireland.

Northern Ireland is perfect for a host of outdoor pursuits. A day's walking amid spectacular scenery, an exhilarating horseback gallop along a quiet beach or a relaxing game of golf on one of our many famous courses. Alternatively you might consider a breathtaking bike ride on one of our new cycle routes, a peaceful afternoon boating or fishing or a leisurely stroll through the National Trust gardens of Mount Stewart.

Carrick-a-rede

The Majestic mountains of Mourne, the uncongested waterways of Lough Erne, the breathtaking Antrim coast with its world heritage site at the Giant's Causeway. The list is endless but whatever your preference - seaside, town, city or countryside, there is a special place for you to stay.

Area Representative

NORTHERN IRELAND
Charles Kelly, Keef Halla Country House, 20 Tully Road, Nutts Corner, Crumlin, Co. Antrim, BT29 4SW. Tel: 028 9082 5491. Fax: 028 9082 5940

ℹ️ Tourist Information Offices

Armagh
40 English St.,
BT61 7BA
Tel: 028 37521800

Belfast
Belfast Welcome
Centre
Eastwood House,
35-39 Donegall Place,
BT1 5AW
Tel: 028 90246609

Derry
44 Foyle Street,
BT48 6AT
Tel: 028 7126 7284

Dungannon
Killymaddy TIC
Ballygawley Road
BT70 1TF
Tel: 028 8776 7259

Enniskillen
Wellington Road,
BT74 7EF
Tel: 028 6632 3110

Giant's Causeway
44 Causeway Road
BT57 8SU
Tel: 028 2073 1855

Larne
Narrow Gauge Road,
BT40 1XB
Tel: 028 2826 0088

Newcastle
10-14 Central
Promenade
BT33 0AA
Tel: 028 4372 2222

www.discovernorthernireland.com

NORTHERN IRELAND
FARM AND
COUNTRY
HOLIDAYS
Something Special

Thirty years ago the Northern Ireland Farm and Country Holidays Association was formed with the aim of bringing to a wider audience the best of Farm and Country Holiday accommodation. Since then thousands of holidaymakers and business people have experienced the pleasure of staying in our members' homes.

NIFCHA members are well renowned for the welcome they provide as well as the quality of their home cooking. Our properties are located in areas of outstanding beauty, some close to villages and market towns, others in more rural areas. Wherever the location, you are invited to relax in comfortable, well appointed accommodation, feast on hearty Ulster fare and sample at first hand our world renowned hospitality.

All of our properties are rigorously inspected and certified on an annual basis by the Northern Ireland Tourist Board and are open all year round unless otherwise stated.

I am personally delighted that NIFCHA members are included in this publication for the first time. We look forward to welcoming you into our homes and promise you that "something special".

Louie Reid

Louie Reid
Chairperson Northern Ireland Farm
and Country Holidays Association

Valerie Brown
GLENMORE HOUSE
White Park Road, Ballycastle,
Co Antrim
BT54 6LR

Ballycastle

Tel: **028 20763584**   Fax: **028 20763584**
Email: glenmore_house3@lineone.net

New building with panoramic sea view on the B15 and set on 90 acres for walks with fishing lake. Central for Causeway and Glens. TV and Tea making facilities in room. Tea on arrival.

B&B	6	Ensuite	Stg£16/£19.50	Dinner	Stg£12
B&B	-	Standard	-	Partial Board	-
Single Rate			Stg£20/£26	Child reduction	50%

Ballycastle 3km

Open: All Year

Mrs Valerie McFall
VALLEY VIEW COUNTRY HOUSE
6A Ballyclough Road, Bushmills
Co Antrim
BT57 8TU

Bushmills

Tel: **028 20741608/41319** Fax: **028 20742739**
Email: valerie.mcfall@btinternet.com
Web: nifcha-com/valleyview

Attractive country house. Beautiful views. Homely atmosphere, Tea on arrival. Close to Giants Causeway, Rope Bridge and Distillery. Off B17 to Coleraine.

B&B	7	Ensuite	Stg£17/£19	Dinner	-
B&B	-	Standard	-	Partial Board	-
Single Rate			Stg£23/£25	Child reduction	50%

Bushmills 6km

Open: All Year Except Christmas

Mr & Mrs C Kelly
KEEF HALLA COUNTRY HOUSE
20 Tully Road, Nutts Corner,
Crumlin, Co Antrim BT29 4SW

Crumlin

Tel: **028 90825491**   Fax: **028 90825940**
Email: info@keefhalla.com
Web: www.keefhalla.com

Nearest 4 star guesthouse to Belfast International Airport. All rooms are ensuite with satellite TV, Tea/Coffee and biscuits. A great base for visiting the North.

B&B	7	Ensuite	Stg£20/£25	Dinner	Stg£10
B&B	-	Standard	-	Partial Board	Stg£200
Single Rate			Stg£25/£35	Child reduction	50%

Crumlin 4km

Open: All Year

Anne McKavanagh
CALDHAME LODGE
102 Moira Rd, Nutts Corner,
Crumlin, Co Antrim BT29 4HG

Crumlin

Tel: **028 94423099**   Fax: **028 94423099**
Email: info@caldhamelodge.co.uk
Web: www.caldhamelodge.co.uk

Award winning house, mins Belfast International Airport. Superior luxurious accomodation, Satellite TV, Tea/Coffee facilities. Bridal suite/jacuzzi /4 poster bed. Near Pubs, Restaurants.

B&B	6	Ensuite	Stg£20/£25	Dinner	Stg£15
B&B	-	Standard	-	Partial Board	-
Single Rate			Stg20/£30	Child reduction	-

Crumlin 1.6km

Open: All Year

Mrs Olive McAuley
CULLENTRA HOUSE
16 Cloughs Road, Cushendall,
Co Antrim
BT44 0SP

Cushendall

Tel: **028 21771762**   Fax: **028 21771762**
Email: cullentra@hotmail.com
Bus No: 150

Award winning B&B nestled amidst panoramic views of Antrim Coast and Glens. Close to Giants Causeway, Rope Bridge etc. Last B&B on Cloughs road.

B&B	3	Ensuite	Stg£17/£17	Dinner	Stg£12.50
B&B	-	Standard	-	Partial Board	-
Single Rate			Stg£22/£22	Child reduction	33.3%

Cushendall 2km

Open: All Year

Mr James McHenry
DIESKIRT FARM
**104 Glen Road, Glenariffe,
Co Antrim
BT44 0RG**

Glenariffe

TEL: **028 21771308**   FAX: **028 21771308**

A working farm with its own private scenic walks just off Antrim Coast Road A2. 5 mins walk from Glenariffe Forest Park/Restaurant. Listed in Le Guide du Routard Irelande.

B&B	2	Ensuite	Stg£17/£17	Dinner	-
B&B	1	Standard	Stg£14/£14	Partial Board	-
Single Rate			Stg£22/£22	Child reduction	25%

Cushendall 8km

Open: May-December

Norman & Esther Kerr
MOURNEVIEW
**32 Drumnascamph Road,
Laurencetown, Gilford, Co Down
BT63 6DU**

Banbridge

TEL: **028 40626270/24251** FAX: **028 40624251**
EMAIL: mourneview@dial.pipex.com

Situated on A50 between Banbridge and Gilford. Ideal base to see Co Down Coast/Mourne Mountains/Linen homelands. 30 mins to Airports/Belfast. Excellent Restaurants nearby.

B&B	4	Ensuite	Stg£18/£18	Dinner	-
B&B		Standard		Partial Board	-
Single Rate			Stg£22/£22	Child reduction	-

Banbridge 5km

Open: All Year Except Christmas

John & Liz McMorris
SWAN LODGE
**30 St Patricks Road, Saul,
Downpatrick, Co Down
BT30 7JQ**

Downpatrick

TEL: **028 44615542**   FAX: **028 44615542**
EMAIL: breaks@swanldg.force9.co.uk
WEB: www.swanldg.force9.co.uk

Superbly situated overlooking Strangford Lough, St Patricks Heritage area. Ideal touring base. Luxury family home in scenic surroundings. Excellent cuisine.

B&B	3	Ensuite	Stg£20/£25	Dinner	-
B&B		Standard	-	Partial Board	-
Single Rate			Stg£25.50/£28	Child reduction	25%

Downpatrick 4km

Open: 2nd January-15th December

Rosemary Armstrong
ARCH TULLYHONA HOUSE
**59 Marble Arch Road,
Florencecourt, Enniskillen
Co Fermanagh BT92 1DE**

Enniskillen

TEL: **028 66348452**
EMAIL: tullyguest60@hotmail.com
WEB: www.archhouse.com

AA ♦♦♦. Winner-15 awards. Restaurant seats 50+. Near Marble Arch Caves/Florencecourt Hse/Belleek Pottery. Children welcome. Follow signs for caves Enniskillen Rd, left Swanlinbar Rd.

B&B	6	Ensuite	Stg£18/£21	Dinner	Stg£12.50
B&B		Standard	-	Partial Board	-
Single Rate			Stg£23.50	Child reduction	50%

Enniskillen 11km

Open: All Year

Mrs Joan Moore
THE OLDE SCHOOLHOUSE
**Tully, Killadeas, Enniskillen
Co Fermanagh
BT94 1RE**

Enniskillen

TEL: **028 68621688**   FAX: **028 68621688**
EMAIL: j.moore@swiftsoft.net

Recently renovated old school. Set in heart of the Fermanagh Lakes. Good food, home baking. Personal attention. From Enniskillen take A32 then B82, turn right at Killadeas Church.

B&B	5	Ensuite	Stg£19/£21	Dinner	Stg£13
B&B	1	Standard	Stg£18/£19	Partial Board	-
Single Rate			Stg£21/£29	Child reduction	50%

Enniskillen 10km

Open: All Year Except Christmas

Mrs Elizabeth Buchanan
ELAGH HALL
Buncrana Road, Derry
Co Londonderry
BT48 8LU

Derry
TEL: **028 71263116**
EMAIL: lizelagh@yahoo.com

Listed historic house, spacious gardens, own spring water. Views of Grianan Castle & Donegal Hills. From City take A2 Buncrana road for 2 miles, right Elagh road.

B&B	2	Ensuite	Stg£18	Dinner	-
B&B	1	Standard	Stg£17	Partial Board	-
Single Rate			Stg£22	Child reduction	50%

Derry 3km

Open: April-October

Mrs Averil Campbell
KILLENNAN HOUSE
40 Killennan Road, Drumahoe
Londonderry
BT47 3NG

Derry
TEL: **028 71301710**   FAX: **028 71301710**
EMAIL: averil@killennan.co.uk
WEB: www.killennan.co.uk

Warm welcome, 19th century country house, beautiful gardens. 10 mins from Derry, Airport. Ideal touring base. Off A6 to Belfast, take B118 Eglinton.

B&B	3	Ensuite	Stg£18/£20	Dinner	-
B&B	-	Standard	-	Partial Board	-
Single Rate			Stg£25	Child reduction	25%

Derry 8km

Open: All Year Except Christmas

Mrs J Brown
BROWNS COUNTRY HOUSE
174 Ballybogey Road, Coleraine,
Co Londonderry
BT52 2LP

Bushmills
TEL: **028 20732777**   FAX: **028 20731627**
EMAIL: brownscountryhouse@hotmail.com

Family run home near Giants Causeway. Reputation for superb food and friendly athmosphere. Convenient to beaches and Golf links. Good touring base B62.

B&B	8	Ensuite	Stg£19/£22	Dinner	-
B&B	-	Standard	-	Partial Board	-
Single Rate			Stg£25/£30	Child reduction	33.3%

Bushmills 4.5km

Open: 3rd January-19th December

Mrs Florence Sloan
DRUMCOVITT HOUSE
704 Feeny Road, Feeny,
Derry, Co Londonderry
BT47 4SU

Feeny
TEL: **028 77781224**   FAX: **028 77781224**
EMAIL: drumcovitt.feeny@btinternet.com
WEB: www.drumcovitt.com

Georgian farm house 103 hectares. Log fires, oil heating, gracious rooms. Walks, Birds, Selfcater, Visit Sperrin, Causeway, Donegal, Derry 14km. A6/B74 1km east Feeny.

B&B	-	Ensuite	-	Dinner	Stg£15
B&B	3	Standard	Stg£19/£23	Partial Board	-
Single Rate			Stg£19/£23	Child reduction	50%

Dungiven 5km

Open: All Year

ADVICE ABOUT TELEPHONING BETWEEN NORTHERN IRELAND AND REPUBLIC OF IRELAND

DIALLING FROM THE REPUBLIC OF IRELAND INTO NORTHERN IRELAND
Callers in the Republic of Ireland can dial either 048 followed by the new eight digit number or 00 44 28 followed by the new eight digit number.
DIALLING FROM NORTHERN IRELAND INTO THE REPUBLIC OF IRELAND
Callers in Northern Ireland should dial 00 353 followed by premises number (whilst always taking care to drop the zero prefix of the area code).

Mrs Mary Montgomery
CLANABOGAN HOUSE
85 Clanabogan Road, Omagh, Co Tyrone
BT78 1SL

Omagh
Tel: **028 82241171**   Fax: **028 82241171**
Email: r&m@clanaboganhouse.freeserve.co.uk
Web: www.clanaboganhouse.freeserve.co.uk

A restored period residence set in 5 acres of woodland and gardens. Bar, Golf, Driving range and Pony stables on site. Spacious rooms. Friendly relaxed atmosphere.

B&B	6	Ensuite	Stg£25	Dinner	-
B&B	2	Standard	Stg£22	Partial Board	-
Single Rate			-	Child reduction	25%

Omagh 1.5km

Open: All Year

Louie Reid
GREENMOUNT LODGE
58 Greenmount Road, Gortaclare, Omagh, Co Tyrone
BT79 0YE

Omagh
Tel: **028 82841325**   Fax: **028 82840019**
Email: greenmountlodge@lineone.net

Luxury ✦✦✦✦ guesthouse set in mature woodlands. Guest laundry facilities. Off A5 south of Omagh, turn right after Carrickkeel Pub. 1 mile on left.

B&B	8	Ensuite	Stg£20/£24	Dinner	Stg£12.50-£15
B&B	-	Standard	-	Partial Board	-
Single Rate			Stg£25	Child reduction	50%

Omagh 12km

Open: All Year

Northern Ireland Tourist Board Offices

DUBLIN
16 Nassau St, Dublin 2.
Tel: 01 671977, Fax: 01 6791863.
CallSave 1850 230230.

LONDON
24 Haymarket, London SW1Y 4DG
Tel: 08701-555 250. Fax 020-7766 9929.

GLASGOW
98 West George St, 7th Floor, Glasgow G2 1PJ
Tel: 0141-572 4030, Fax: 0141-572-4033.

USA
551 Fifth Avenue, Suite 701, New York,
NY 10176. Tel: 212 9220101 or 800 326 0036.
Fax: 212 922 0099.

CANADA
2 Bloor Street West, Suite 1501, Toronto
M4W 3E2.
Tel: 416 925 6368 or 1 800 576 8174,
Fax: 416 925 6033.

GERMANY
Westendstr. 16-22 60325 Frankfurt/Main
Tel: 069 23 45 04, Fax: 069 23 34 80.

FRANCE
Enquiries to Tourisme d'Irlande du Nord,
Centre PO 166, 23, rue Lecourbe, 75015 Paris.
Tel: 1 49390577.

AUSTRALIA
Enquiries to All Ireland Tourism, 5th Level,
36 Carrington Street, Sydney, NSW 2000.
Tel: 02 9299 6177 Fax: 02 9299 6323.

NEW ZEALAND
Enquiries to Walshes World, Dingwall Building,
87 Queen Street, Private Bag 92136, Auckland 1,
DX 69051.
Tel: 09 379 3708. Fax: 09 309 0725.

Enjoy a bigger kind of welcome...

holiday in the land of giants.

Next time you're planning your holiday, try Northern Ireland for size. The massive, mysterious Giant's Causeway will take your breath away.

There's so much to see and do in this fascinating country. Don't miss Belfast, with its classic Victorian architecture, vibrant festivals and traditional musical sessions in the city pubs. Take in a round or two of golf on our world class courses. Come horse riding in the beautiful Mountains of Mourne or cycling in the nine glens of Antrim. Enjoy a walking tour or relax with a cruise on Lough Erne in County Fermanagh.

W e can offer almost any kind of holiday – and this is only a glimpse of what's available. For an even bigger picture, give us a call.

It's easy to find out more. Call the Northern Ireland Tourist Board now on

Republic of Ireland
003531 679 1977

Great Britain
00 44 171 766 9920

United States
00 1 212-922 0101

Germany
00 49 69-234 504

Canada
00 1 416-925 6368

Northern Ireland
Tourist Board

Northern Ireland. See for yourself.

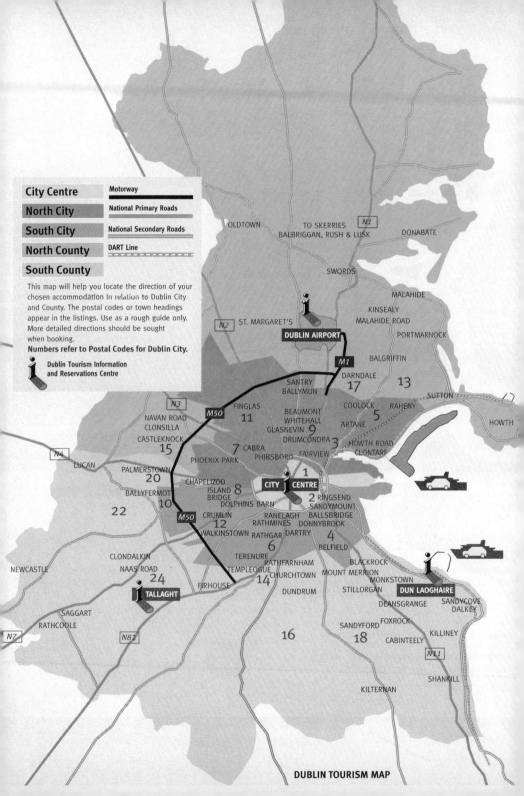

DUBLIN TOURISM MAP

Dublin, Ireland's capital, steeped in history and buzzing with youthful energy. From its gracious Georgian Squares and terraces, mountain walks and sandy beaches to the intimacy of its pub and cafe life, Dublin is a thriving centre for culture. It is home to a great literary tradition where the cosmopolitan and charming converge in an atmosphere of delightful diversity.

Fine museums and art galleries chronicle its long and colourful past while the pubs and cafes buzz with traditional entertainment. Dublin's attractions are many from castles, museums and art galleries to the lively spirit of Temple Bar within a half hour of the city centre there are mountain walks, stately homes and gardens, sandy beaches and quaint fishing villages.

During your stay with us you will sample some of the charm of Dublin and particularly the warmth and wit of its people that has never ceased to win the heart of the visitor.

St. Stephens Green, Dublin 2

Area Representatives

DUBLIN
Mrs Rita Kenny, Seaview, 166 Bettyglen, Raheny, Dublin 5
Tel: 01 831 5335

Mrs Margaret McLoughlin-O'Connell, Loyola, 18 Charleville Road, Phibsboro, Dublin 7
Tel: 01 838 9973 Fax: 01 868 6569

Mrs Noreen McBride, 3 Rossmore Grove, Off Wellington Lane, Tempelogue, Dublin 6W Tel: 01 490 2939 Fax: 01 492 9416

 ## Tourist Information Offices

Dublin

Dublin Tourism Centre
Suffolk St.,
Dublin 2
Tel: 1850 230 330

O'Connell St.,
Dublin 1

Internet:
http://www.visitdublin.com
Email: information@dublin-tourism.ie

Arrivals Hall
Dublin Airport

Dun Laoghaire Harbour
Ferry Terminal Building
Dun Laoghaire
Co Dublin

Baggot Street Bridge
Dublin 2

The Square Towncentre
Tallaght
Dublin 24

Mrs Mary O'Reilly
RATHLEEK
**13 Brookwood Rd,
Artane, Dublin 5**

Artane

TEL: **01 8310555**
BUS NO: **42, 42B, 42C, 27**

10 mins Beaumont Hospital, City Centre, Irish Ferries, Car Ferry, Connolly Station, Central Bus Station. Dart. Sea Front. Tea, TV, Radio, Hairdryer all rooms.

B&B	-	Ensuite	-	-	Dinner	-
B&B	3	Standard	£20	€25.39	Partial Board	-
Single Rate			£25	€31.74	Child reduction	-

Dublin 4km

Open: 1st March-October

Kevin & Anne Rodgers
BLAITHIN B&B
**18 St Brendans Avenue,
Artane, Dublin 5**

Artane

TEL: **01 8483817**   FAX: **01 8674029**
EMAIL: blaithin@oceanfree.net
BUS NO: **27, 42**

Luxurious family home. Excellent rooms with Tea/Coffee, TV. Close to Seafront, Golf. City 10 min. Buses at door. Airport 15 min, Ferry 10 min. Safe Parking.

B&B	3	Ensuite	£21/£24	€26.66/€30.47	Dinner	-
B&B	1	Standard	£20/£20	€25.39	Partial Board	-
Single Rate			£36/£36	€45.71	Child reduction	-

Dublin 5km

Open: 10th January-15th December

Mrs Eve Mitchell
ASHBROOK HOUSE
**River Rd, Ashtown,
Castleknock, Dublin 15**

Castleknock

TEL: **01 8385660**   FAX: **01 8385660**
BUS NO: **37, 39, 39A**

A beautiful old Georgian house, close to Phoenix Park, large Gardens & Tennis court. 10 mins City Centre, 10 mins Airport.

B&B	4	Ensuite	£30/£35	€38.09/€44.44	Dinner	-
B&B	-	Standard	-	-	Partial Board	-
Single Rate			£40/£45	€50.79/€57.14	Child reduction	25%

In Castleknock

Open: 2nd January-20th December

Mrs Marie O'Reilly
**67 The Pines
Auburn Ave, Castleknock,
Dublin 15**

Castleknock

TEL: **01 8215560**   FAX: **01 8215560**
BUS NO: **37, 39, 38**

Select area, close Phoenix Park. Adjacent M50 Motorway linking with routes North, South, West. City 15 mins. Airport 15 mins.

B&B	1	Ensuite	£22	€27.93	Dinner	-
B&B	2	Standard	£20	€25.39	Partial Board	-
Single Rate			£30	€38.09	Child reduction	-

Dublin 6km

Open: 1st March-30th September

Caroline and Paul Connolly
KINCORA LODGE
**54 Kincora Court,
Clontarf, Dublin 3**

Clontarf

TEL: **01 8330220**   FAX: **01 8330007**
BUS NO: **130**

Modern home quiet area. Parking. 15 mins Airport, City Centre, Ferry, Point Theatre, Golf Courses, Beach, Park within walking distance. TV, Hairdryers all rooms. Courtesy tray available.

B&B	3	Ensuite	£25/£27.50	€31.74/€34.91	Dinner	-
B&B	-	Standard	-	-	Partial Board	-
Single Rate			£35/£40	€44.44/€50.79	Child reduction	50%

Dublin 4km

Open: All Year Except Christmas

Dublin City 3km

Mrs Susan Delahunty
GLENBROOK
34 Howth Road, Clontarf,
Dublin 3

Clontarf

Tel: 01 8331117/8532265
Bus No: 29A, 31, 31A, 31B, 32, 32A, 32B

Victorian town house, close to City, Ferryport, Airport, Bus and Rail Terminals. Beach and Golf courses nearby.

B&B	2	Ensuite	£22.50/£35	€28.57/€44.44	Dinner	-
B&B	1	Standard	-	-	Partial Board	-
Single Rate			£25/£30	€31.74/€38.09	Child reduction	25%

Open: 1st March-31st October

Dublin 5km

Miss M Dereymont
18 Seacourt
St Gabriel's Road, Clontarf,
Dublin 3

Clontarf

Tel: 01 8333313
Bus No: 130

Georgian residence, convenient to City, Airport, Ferry, Restaurants, Point Theatre. Non smoking. Adults only. Closes 1am (opposite St Gabriel's Church). Shops nearby.

B&B	1	Ensuite	£28.50/£32	€36.19/€40.63	Dinner	-
B&B	2	Standard	£27.50/£30	€34.91/€38.09	Partial Board	-
Single Rate			£50/£55	€63.49/€69.82	Child reduction	-

Open: 1st April - 31st October

Dublin 5km

John & Delia Devlin
ANNAGH HOUSE
301 Clontarf Road, Dublin 3

Clontarf

Tel: 01 8338841   Fax: 01 8338841
Bus No: 130

Charming Victorian house, convenient to City, Airport, Ferryport, Restaurants, Pubs, Theatres, Golf, Beach. Superb location to explore culture of Dublin. Bus route.

B&B	3	Ensuite	£22.50/£25	€28.57/€31.74	Dinner	-
B&B	-	Standard	-	-	Partial Board	-
Single Rate			-	-	Child reduction	-

Open: 5th January-22nd December

Dublin 5km

Mrs Carmel Drain
BAYVIEW
265 Clontarf Rd, Clontarf,
Dublin 3

Clontarf

Tel: 01 8339870   Fax: 01 8339870
Email: carmeldrain@eircom.net
Bus No: 130

Overlooking Dublin Bay, convenient Beach, Park, Golf, Ferry, Airport, City, Point Theatre. Tea, Coffee, TV, Hairdryer, Menu, Pubs Restaurant near, frequent Bus.

B&B	2	Ensuite	£22/£25	€27.93/€31.74	Dinner	-
B&B	1	Standard	£20/£22	€25.39/€27.93	Partial Board	-
Single Rate			£32/£35	€40.63/€44.44	Child reduction	-

Open: February-October

Dublin City 3km

Mary Dunwoody
ELDAR
19 Copeland Avenue,
Clontarf, Dublin 3

Clontarf

Tel: 01 8339091
Email: cdunwoody@eircom.net
Bus No: 20, 28, 29, 31, 32, 42, DART

Situated between Malahide road/Howth road, Griffith Avenue end. Convenient all services. Tea/Coffee, Hairdryer, Ironing facilities all rooms.

B&B	2	Ensuite	£21.50	€27.30	Dinner	-
B&B	1	Standard	£19	€24.13	Partial Board	-
Single Rate			£23/£26.50	€29.20/€33.65	Child reduction	-

Open: March-October

Jackie Egan
VALENTIA HOUSE
37 Kincora Court, Clontarf
Dublin 3

Clontarf

TEL: 01 8338060   FAX: 01 8339990
EMAIL: jackie/egan@esatclear.ie
BUS No: 130

Dublin City 4km

Family run home, convenient City/Airport/Ferry/Point Theatre/Beach/Golf Clubs/Restaurants.130 Bus fom Abbey St. to Clontarf road. Left at Depot, at crossroads right, first right & first right.

B&B	4	Ensuite	£22.50/£25	€28.57/€31.74	Dinner -
B&B	-	Standard	-	-	Partial Board -
Single Rate			£30/£35	€38.09/€44.44	Child reduction 50%

Open: 5th January-20th December

Mrs Margo Harahan
JAYMARA
67 Hampton Court, Off Vernon
Avenue, Clontarf, Dublin 3

Clontarf

TEL: 01 8336992
BUS No: 130, 28, 29, 31, DART

Dublin 5km

Semi detached between Vernon Avenue, Castle Avenue in quiet residential area. 15 mins Airport, Ferry, Point Theatre, City Centre 5 mins. Clontarf Castle Hotel.

B&B	2	Ensuite	£21.50/£21.50	€27.30	Dinner -
B&B	1	Standard	£19/£19	€24.13	Partial Board -
Single Rate			£25/£27	€31.74/€34.29	Child reduction -

Open: 1st April-31st October

Mrs Moira Kavanagh
SPRINGVALE
69 Kincora Drive, Off Kincora
Grove, Clontarf, Dublin 3

Clontarf

TEL: 01 8333413
EMAIL: moira_kav@hotmail.com
BUS No: 29A, 31, 32, 130, DART

Dublin 4km

Modern house, quiet residential area. 15 mins Airport, Car Ferry, City, Point Theatre. Frommer Recommended. Tea/coffee facilities. 4 rooms with shower only.

B&B	-	Ensuite	-	-	Dinner -
B&B	4	Standard	£19	€24.13	Partial Board -
Single Rate			£24	€30.47	Child reduction -

Open: 1st January-22nd December

Mrs Eileen Cummiskey Kelly
GARRYBAWN
18 Copeland Avenue, Clontarf,
Dublin 3

Clontarf

TEL: 01 8333760
BUS No: 20, 20B, 42, 31

Dublin 3km

Near Point Theatre, Airport, Ferryport, City Centre. 2km Croke Park, 1km Buses to Centre no.'s 20, 20B, 42, 31.

B&B	2	Ensuite	£22.50	€28.57	Dinner -
B&B	1	Standard	£20	€25.39	Partial Board -
Single Rate			£25	€31.74	Child reduction -

Open: All Year Except Christmas

Mrs Eileen P Kelly
TORC HOUSE
17 Seacourt (off Seafield Road)
Clontarf, Dublin 3

Clontarf

TEL: 01 8332547
BUS No: 130

Dublin City 5km

Detached Georgian house, residential area. Convenient City, Airport, Ferry Port, Beach, Golf, Rose Gardens, Point. Frommer/RAC/Sullivan Guide recommended.

B&B	2	Ensuite	£24/£24	€30.47	Dinner -
B&B	1	Standard	£20/£20	€25.39	Partial Board -
Single Rate			£40	€50.79	Child reduction -

Open: May-October

Dublin 3km

Joseph & Mary Mooney
WILLOWBROOK
14 Strandville Ave East,
Clontarf, Dublin 3

TEL: **01 8333115**
EMAIL: willowbrook@ireland.com
BUS NO: **130, DART**

Gracious detached home on quiet street. Close to City, Ferry port, Airport, Beach, Golf Courses, Bus & Rail services. First left off Clontarf Rd coming from City.

B&B	3	Ensuite	£25/£30	€31.74/€38.09	Dinner	-
B&B	-	Standard	-	-	Partial Board	-
Single Rate			£40	€50.79	Child reduction	-

Open: All Year Except Christmas

Dublin 5km

Mrs Myra O'Flaherty
SEA BREEZE
312 Clontarf Road,
Clontarf, Dublin 3

TEL: **01 8332787**
BUS NO: **130**

On seafront close to Ferry/Airport, Golf. Frequent bus service to and from City. Beach, Pubs and Restaurants closeby.

B&B	3	Ensuite	£22.50/£25	€28.57/€31.74	Dinner	-
B&B	1	Standard	£20/£20	€25.39	Partial Board	-
Single Rate			£35/£40	€44.44/€50.79	Child reduction	25%

Open: 1st February-30th November

Dublin 2.5km

Mrs Mary Wright
LAWRENCE HOUSE
26 St Lawrence Rd, Clontarf,
Dublin 3

TEL: **01 8332539**   FAX: **01 8332539**
BUS NO: **130, 31, 32, 29A**

Lovely Victorian house. 10 minutes to City, DART, Car Ferry, Airport and Point Theatre. Private car parking. Buses 130, 31, 32, 29A to St Lawrence Rd.

B&B	5	Ensuite	£25/£30	€31.74/€38.09	Dinner	-
B&B	-	Standard	-	-	Partial Board	-
Single Rate			£35/£40	€44.44/€50.79	Child reduction	-

Open: 1st January-20th December

Dublin City 1km

Mrs Roma Gibbons
JOYVILLE
24 St Alphonsus Road,
Drumcondra, Dublin 9

TEL: **01 8303221**
BUS NO: **3, 11, 11A, 16, 16A, 41**

Victorian town house off main Airport road. Convenient to Car Ferry, Botanic Gardens, City Centre.

B&B	-	Ensuite	-	-	Dinner	-
B&B	4	Standard	£18	€22.86	Partial Board	-
Single Rate			£24	€30.47	Child reduction	-

Open: 7th January-20th December

Dublin 2km

Mrs Hilda Gibson
THE GABLES
50 Iona Crescent, off Hollybank
Road, Drumcondra, Dublin 9

TEL: **01 8300538**
BUS NO: **3, 11, 16, 33, 36, 41, 51A**

Comfortable family home off main Airport Road (N1), 10 minutes Airport, Car Ferry, City Centre, Point Theatre, Private Car Park.

B&B	3	Ensuite	£22/£22	€27.93	Dinner	-
B&B	1	Standard	-	-	Partial Board	-
Single Rate			£24/£28	€30.47/€35.55	Child reduction	25%

Open: 1st January-20th December

Dublin 1km

Mrs Ann Griffin
MUCKROSS HOUSE
Claude Road, off Whitworth Rd,
Drumcondra, Dublin 9

TEL: **01 8304888**
EMAIL: muckrosshouse01@eircom.net
BUS NO: **13, 40, 40A, 40B**

Situated off main Airport road (N1). Convenient to City Centre, Airport, Car Ferry & Point Depot. Private enclosed car parking.

				Dinner	-
B&B	5	Ensuite	£22.50/£25	€28.57/€31.74	
B&B		Standard	-	-	Partial Board	-
Single Rate			£30	€38.09	Child reduction	25%

Open: 3rd January-20th December

Dublin City 3km

Mrs Frances Hughes
WOODLANDS
326 Collins Avenue, Drumcondra,
Whitehall, Dublin 9

TEL: **01 8370754**
BUS NO: **20B, 16A, 16**

Woodlands, attractive detached modern house. Very large car parking space in front, convenient to City Centre, Airport, Buses and Dart travel.

					Dinner	-
B&B	2	Ensuite	£20/£20	€25.39		
B&B	1	Standard	£18/£18	€22.86	Partial Board	-
Single Rate			£30/£30	€38.09	Child reduction	25%

Open: 1st March-30th November

Dublin City Centre 3km

Mrs Nuala Kenny
RATHMORE
22 Walnut Rise, Courtlands off
Griffith Ave, Drumcondra
Dublin 9

TEL: **01 8370986**
BUS NO: **3, 16, 16A, 41, 13A**

Modern family home off main Airport road. City Centre, Airport, Car Ferry all within 10/15 mins. TV, Tea making facilities and Hairdryers in all rooms.

					Dinner	-
B&B	-	Ensuite	-	-		
B&B	3	Standard	£18	€22.86	Partial Board	-
Single Rate			£25	€31.74	Child reduction	-

Open: 8th January-20th December

Dublin City 1.5km

Cathy Lydon
LYDON HOUSE
200 Clonliffe Rd,
Drumcondra, Dublin 3

TEL: **01 8570192**   FAX: **01 8360045**
EMAIL: sean_lydon@hotmail.com
WEB: www.lydonhouse.com
BUS NO: **11, 11B, 41, 41C, 16A, 16, 3**

Georgian period house of great character. Recently refurbished to a high standard, decorated with antique and original furniture and fittings.

					Dinner	-
B&B	4	Ensuite	£23/£25	€29.20/€31.74		
B&B	-	Standard	-	-	Partial Board	-
Single Rate			-	-	Child reduction	50%

Open: 7th January-14th December

Dublin City 4km

Mrs Cait Cunningham Murray
30 Walnut Ave, Courtlands Estate,
off Griffith Ave, Drumcondra,
Dublin 9

TEL: **01 8379327**
BUS NO: **3, 16, 16A, 41, 41A, 13A**

Modern home, off Griffith Ave overlooking park. Off N1 convenient to Airport, City Centre and B&I Ferry. Very quiet location. Smoke free home.

					Dinner	-
B&B	2	Ensuite	£20/£20	€25.39		
B&B	1	Standard	£18/£18	€22.86	Partial Board	-
Single Rate			-	-	Child reduction	-

Open: 1st April-30th September

Mrs Gemma Rafferty
GREEN-VIEW
36 Walnut Avenue, Courtlands, Off Griffith Ave, Drumcondra Dublin 9

Drumcondra
TEL: **01 8376217**
BUS No: **3, 13A, 16, 16A, 41A, 41B**

Peaceful location opposite Park off N1. 10 mins City Centre, Airport, Car Ferry, Golf Courses.

B&B	2	Ensuite	£20	€25.39	Dinner -
B&B	1	Standard	£18	€22.86	Partial Board -
Single Rate			-	-	Child reduction -

Dublin City 4km

Open: 1st March-20th December

Irene Coyle Ryan
BLANFORD HOUSE
37 Lambay Road, off Griffith Ave, Drumcondra, Dublin 9

Drumcondra
TEL: **01 8378036**
BUS No: **11, 11A, 13A**

Town house near Airport, Ferry Port, Botanic Gardens, Forbairt, Point Theatre. Dublin City University. Bonsecours Hospital, Matter Hospital.

B&B	1	Ensuite	£21/£25	€26.66/€31.74	Dinner -
B&B	3	Standard	£18/£20	€22.86/€25.39	Partial Board -
Single Rate			£25/£25	€31.74	Child reduction -

Dublin City 3km

Open: All Year Except Christmas

Mrs Teresa Ryan
PARKNASILLA
15 Iona Drive, Drumcondra, Dublin 9

Drumcondra
TEL: **01 8305724**
BUS No: **11, 16, 16A, 41, 13, 19, 19A, 3.**

Edwardian detached residence, off main Airport Road N1, 10 minutes to City Centre, Airport, Boat Ferry, Bus & Rail Terminals.

B&B	2	Ensuite	£20/£22	€25.39/€27.93	Dinner	-
B&B	2	Standard	£18/£20	€22.86/€25.39	Partial Board	-
Single Rate			£22/£25	€27.93/€31.74	Child reduction	20%

Dublin 1.5km

Open: 1st January-21st December

Mrs Margaret McLoughlin-O'Connell
LOYOLA
18 Charleville Road, Phibsboro, Dublin 7

Phibsboro
TEL: **01 8389973**
BUS No: **10, 38, 120, 121, 122**

Victorian house convenient to Rail, Bus, Airport, Car Ferry Terminals, Zoo, Public Parks, Mater Hospital, Link Roads.

B&B	2	Ensuite	£22.50	€28.57	Dinner	-
B&B	2	Standard	£20	€25.39	Partial Board	-
Single Rate			£25/£30	€31.74/€38.09	Child reduction	20%

Dublin City 1km

Open: All Year Except Christmas

Mrs Maureen Flynn
FOUR SEASONS
15 Grange Park Green, Raheny, Dublin 5

Raheny
TEL: **01 8486612**
BUS No: **29A, 31, 32**

Convenient to City Centre, Car Ferry, Airport, DART and Bus. Private parking. Restaurants in Village. TV lounge with Tea/Coffee, Hairdryers in rooms.

B&B	4	Ensuite	£20/£22.50	€25.39/€28.57	Dinner	-
B&B	-	Standard	-	-	Partial Board	-
Single Rate			-	-	Child reduction	25%

Dublin City 7km

Open: 6th January-20th December

In Raheny

Mrs Eileen Keane	Raheny
BREIFNE	TEL: **01 8313976**
23 Bettyglen, Raheny, Dublin 5	BUS NO: **31, 31A, 32**

Large detached house overlooking sea. Private parking. 10km Dublin Airport, 6km B&I Car Ferry, 4km City Centre, Guest Lounge.

				Dinner	-
B&B	3	Ensuite	**£22/£22.50**	€27.93/€28.57	
B&B	1	Standard	**£19/£20**	€24.13/€25.39	Partial Board	-
		Single Rate	**£23.50/£25.50**	€29.84/€32.38	Child reduction	**33.3%**

Open: All Year Except Christmas

Dublin City 5km

Mrs Rita Kenny	Raheny
SEAVIEW	TEL: **01 8315335**
166 Bettyglen, Raheny, Dublin 5	BUS NO: **31, 31A, 32, 32B**

Large semi detached house overlooking Sea. Private parking. Convenient to Airport, Car Ferry, DART, Buses, Golf Courses. Orthopaedic beds, Tea in rooms. Room rate.

B&B	2	Ensuite	**£22.50**	€28.57	Dinner	-
B&B	1	Standard	**£20**	€25.39	Partial Board	-
		Single Rate	**£25**	€31.74	Child reduction	**25 %**

Open: 1st January-23rd December

Dublin 4km

Mrs Anne Brannigan	Santry
HAZELWOOD	TEL: **01 8426065** FAX: **01 8426065**
34 Lorcan Drive, Santry, Dublin 9	BUS NO: **16, 16A, 33, 33B, 41, 41A**

Comfortable family home off main Airport road (N1). 2km Airport. Beside Omni-Park shopping and Leisure Complex, convenient to City Centre.

B&B	2	Ensuite	**£20/£22.50**	€25.39/€28.57	Dinner	-
B&B	2	Standard	**£18/£20**	€22.86/€25.39	Partial Board	-
		Single Rate	**£25/£30**	€31.74/€38.09	Child reduction	-

Open: 1st January-22nd December

ROOM AVAILABILITY IN DUBLIN

At the height of the Tourist Season - May to October - rooms in Dublin City and County are difficult to find unless accommodation is pre-booked.

If visiting the capital city during these months, we strongly advise pre-booking all accommodation **well in advance.**

Never count on finding rooms at short notice in Dublin. Always reserve in advance.

Balbriggan 4km

Jacqueline Clarke
KNIGHTSWOOD B&B
**6 Knightswood, Balrothery,
Balbriggan, Co Dublin**

Tel: **01 8411621**
Email: clarketom@eircom.net

Comfortable residence. Airport 20 minutes, Golf Course & Hostelry nearby. Take N1 north from Airport, 1st exit for Balbriggan (R132) 3km.

B&B	2	Ensuite	£21/£22.50	€26.66/€28.57	Dinner	-
B&B	1	Standard	£19/£20	€24.13/€25.39	Partial Board	-
Single Rate			£28/£33	€35.55/€41.90	Child reduction	25%

cc P ⚡ 🖥 🍽 ☂ **Open:** 14th May-30th September

Swords 11km

Thomas & Mary Hoey
STELLAS REST
**Burrow Road, Portrane,
Donabate, Co Dublin**

Tel: **01 8436302**   Fax: **01 8435933**
Bus No: **33B**

Turn right 3km north of Swords. Follow signpost to Donabate, turn left at Donabate Village to Portrane. Spacious heated bungalow. Parking. Beach & Golf.

B&B	3	Ensuite	£20/£22	€25.39/€27.93	Dinner	-
B&B	1	Standard	£18/£20	€22.86/€25.39	Partial Board	-
Single Rate			£25/£27	€31.74/€34.29	Child reduction	50%

P ⚡ 🖥 🚲 🍽 **Open:** 30th April-31st October

Howth 1.5km

Mrs Rosaleen Hobbs
HAZELWOOD
**2 Thormanby Woods,
Thormanby Road,
Howth, Dublin 13**

Tel: **01 8391391**   Fax: **01 8391391**
Email: 101706.3526@compuserve.com.ie
Web: www.hazelwood.net
Bus No: **31B, DART**

Modern dormer bungalow situated in own grounds. Ample car parking. Convenient Golf, Beach, Restaurants, Scenic Cliff Walks and Fishing Village.

B&B	4	Ensuite	£22	€27.93	Dinner	-
B&B	1	Standard	-	-	Partial Board	-
Single Rate			£30	€38.09	Child reduction	50%

P ⊗ 🚲 🍽 **Open:** All Year

Swords 4km

Ms Patricia Butterly
BROOKFIELD LODGE B&B
**Blakes Cross, Belfast Road,
Lusk, Co. Dublin**

Tel: **01 8430043**   Fax: **01 8430177**
Email: trishb@indigo.ie
Bus No: **100**

Modern country home, 10 minutes north Dublin Airport N1. Ignore sign for Lusk, continue past Esso garage for 400 meters. Located on junction N1/R129.

B&B	4	Ensuite	£19/£25	€24.13/€31.74	Dinner	-
B&B	-	Standard	-	-	Partial Board	-
Single Rate			-	-	Child reduction	-

P ⊗ 🖥 ☕ 🚲 🍽 **Open:** 2nd January-30th November

Swords 9km

Freda Rigney
IVY BUNGALOW
**Ballough, Lusk,
Co. Dublin**

Tel: **01 8437031**
Email: ivybungalow.co.uk

Quaint country home off Belfast Dublin Road. 10 mins North of Dublin Airport, City Centre 30 mins. Peaceful surroundings. Ground floor accommodation. Pub 300 yards.

B&B	3	Ensuite	£22.50/£25	€28.57/€31.74	Dinner	-
B&B	1	Standard	£20/£22	€25.39/€27.93	Partial Board	-
Single Rate			£30/£35	€38.09/€44.44	Child reduction	50%

P ⊗ ⚡ 🖥 ☕ 🍽 **Open:** All Year

Malahide 3km

Christopher & Nora Duff
MEADOW VIEW
Posey Lane, Kinsealy,
Malahide, Co Dublin

Malahide

TEL: **01 8460359**   FAX: **01 8460359**
BUS NO: **42, 43**

Modern house in cul-de-sac. Private Parking. Castle/Golf/Cinema/Gym 2 miles- Airport 3 miles. Ferry 6 miles. Hairdryer, Electric blanket. M50- 1 mile /behind Top garage.

B&B	4	Ensuite	£21	€26.66	Dinner	-
B&B	-	Standard	-	-	Partial Board	-
Single Rate			£30	€38.09	Child reduction	33.3%

Open: 15th January-15th December

Malahide 3km

Mrs Monica Fitzsimons
PEBBLE MILL
Kinsealy, Malahide,
Co Dublin

Malahide

TEL: **01 8461792**
BUS NO: **42, 43**

Country home on 4 Acres. Golf, Horseriding, Yachting, Castle closeby. Airport 7mins, B&I 20 mins. Room rates, TV, Hairdryers, Tea/Coffee all rooms.

B&B	3	Ensuite	£20/£22	€25.39/€27.93	Dinner	-
B&B	-	Standard	-	-	Partial Board	-
Single Rate			£30/£30	€38.09	Child reduction	50%

Open: 1st March-31st October

Malahide 3km

Mrs Maura Halpin
HEATHER VIEW
Malahide Road, Kinsealy,
Co Dublin

Malahide

TEL: **01 8453483**   FAX: **01 8453818**
EMAIL: hview@eircom.net
BUS NO: **42, 43, AIRPORT 230**

Luxury country home on R107, Airport 6km. Castle 1km, M50 3km. Parking. All rooms TV, Clockradio, Hairdryer, Tea/Coffee. Breakfast menu.

B&B	5	Ensuite	£23.50/£25	€29.84/€31.74	Dinner	-
B&B	-	Standard	-	-	Partial Board	-
Single Rate			-	-	Child reduction	-

Open: All Year Except Christmas

Malahide 1.5km

Mrs Noreen Handley
AISHLING
59 Biscayne (off Coast Rd)
Malahide, Co Dublin

Malahide

TEL: **01 8452292**   FAX: **01 8452292**
BUS NO: **32A, 42, 102, 230 AIRPORT**

Pass Grand Hotel, 2nd turn right after Islandview Hotel. Excellent accommodation, overlooking Beach. Adjacent Golf, Yachting, Castle, Restaurants, 15 mins Airport.

B&B	2	Ensuite	£20	€25.39	Dinner	-
B&B	1	Standard	£19	€24.13	Partial Board	-
Single Rate			-	-	Child reduction	-

Open: April - September

In Malahide

Liz Dagg-Hanley
MAYWOOD HOUSE
13 St Andrews Grove, Off Church
Road, Malahide, Co Dublin

Malahide

TEL: **01 8451712**   FAX: **01 8451712**
EMAIL: maywood@indigo.ie
BUS NO: **42, 32A, 230**

In quiet cul-de-sac in Malahide with its many amenities. 3 mins walk to DART/Train and Bus to Airport and City Centre. Conservatory/Garden for guests use.

B&B	2	Ensuite	£27.50	€34.91	Dinner	-
B&B	2	Standard	£25	€31.74	Partial Board	-
Single Rate			-	-	Child reduction	50%

Open: February - October

Olive Hopkins
EVERGREEN
Kinsealy Lane, Malahide,
Co Dublin

Tel: **01 8460185**
Email: evergreendub@eircom.net
Bus No: **42**

Luxury home on 1 acre. Private parking. Malahide/Restaurants 1 mile. TV, Hairdryers all rooms. Turn right before main entrance to Malahide Castle/Park. Airport 10 mins. Ferry/City 20 mins.

B&B	4	Ensuite	£20/£22	€25.39/€27.93	Dinner	-
B&B	1	Standard	£19/£20	€24.13/€25.39	Partial Board	-
Single Rate			£28/£30	€35.55/€38.09	Child reduction	33.3%

Malahide 2km

Open: 1st February-30th November

Mrs Jane F Kiernan
LISCARA
Malahide Road, Kinsealy,
Dublin 17

Tel: **01 8483751** Fax: **01 8483751**
Bus No: **42, 43**

Private parking. Airport 10 mins, City/Ferry 20 mins. Convenient Golf, Indoor Bowling, Cinemas, Malahide Castle & Town, Swimming Pools. M50 1 mile.

B&B	6	Ensuite	£20/£22.50	€25.39/€28.57	Dinner	-
B&B	-	Standard	-	-	Partial Board	-
Single Rate			£30/£32.50	€38.09/€41.27	Child reduction	-

Malahide 4.5km

Open: 1st March-31st October

Mrs Cathy McConnell
SAN JUAN
Baskin Lane, Kinsealy,
Dublin 17

Tel: **01 8460424** Fax: **01 8460910**
Bus No: **42, 43**

Country style residence on one acre. 5 mins to Airport, close to Malahide Castle/Village, 20 mins to City Centre.

B&B	4	Ensuite	£19/£22	€24.13/€27.93	Dinner	-
B&B	-	Standard	-	-	Partial Board	-
Single Rate			£25.50/£30	€32.38/€38.09	Child reduction	50%

Malahide 2km

Open: 1st February-31st November

Mrs Brigid Mangan
CILL MUIRE HOUSE
18 Yellow Wall's Rd,
Malahide, Co Dublin

Tel: **01 8452178** Fax: **01 8453258**
Bus No: **42**

Old house with modern facilities, tea/coffee, hairdryer, TV. Airport 6km. Restaurants, Yachting, Golf, Beach within walking distance.

B&B	4	Ensuite	£20/£22.50	€25.39/€28.57	Dinner	-
B&B	-	Standard	-	-	Partial Board	-
Single Rate			-	-	Child reduction	25%

Malahide 1km

Open: 1st March-31st October

Mrs Elizabeth O'Brien
PEGASUS
56 Biscayne, Coast Rd,
Malahide, Co Dublin

Tel: **01 8451506** Fax: **01 8453288**
Bus No: **42, 32A, 102, 230**

Excellent accommodation beside Beach, Golf, Castle & Restaurants. Airport 15 mins. Pass Grand Hotel & Island View Hotel, second turn right, keep left, left again.

B&B	2	Ensuite	£21/£22	€26.66/€27.93	Dinner	-
B&B	1	Standard	£19/£19	€24.13	Partial Board	-
Single Rate			£35/£35	€44.44	Child reduction	-

Malahide 1.5km

Open: 1st March - 31st October

In Malahide

Mrs Sile O'Donovan
CASTLELAKE
**15 St Andrew's Grove,
Malahide, Co Dublin**

TEL: **01 8455042**   FAX: **01 8455042**
EMAIL: sileod@iol.ie
BUS NO: **42**

Quiet location in Malahide off Church road. Grand Hotel nearby. Off street parking. Public transport to Dublin. Airport 4 miles. Large family suite (with 2 bathrooms).

B&B	4	Ensuite	£22.50/£25	€28.57/€31.74	Dinner	-
B&B	-	Standard	-	-	Partial Board	-
Single Rate			£35/£35	€44.44	Child reduction	25%

Open: All Year

Malahide 2km

Mrs Jean O'Leary
HAZELGROVE
**Blackwood Lane, Malahide,
Co Dublin**

TEL: **01 8462629**   FAX: **01 8462629**
EMAIL: oleary@hazelgrove.iol.ie
BUS NO: **42, 102, 230**

Gracious home. Private Grounds. Dublin Airport 9km. Mairna Village off Malahide 2km. Close to 9 Golf Clubs. Ferryport, Castle. City Centre 13km. Breakfast menu.

B&B	3	Ensuite	£25/£25	€31.74	Dinner	-
B&B	-	Standard	-	-	Partial Board	-
Single Rate			£35/£35	€44.44	Child reduction	-

Open: 1st March-20th October

In Malahide Village

Mrs Mary Sweeney
SOMERTON
**The Mall, Malahide Village,
Co Dublin**

TEL: **01 8454090**
EMAIL: somerton@iol.ie
BUS NO: **32A, 42, 102, 230**

In heart of Malahide village. All social amenities within short walking distance. City Centre within easy reach by bus or train. True Irish welcome assured. Home from home comforts.

B&B	4	Ensuite	£27.50/£30	€34.91/€38.09	Dinner	-
B&B	-	Standard	-	-	Partial Board	-
Single Rate			-	-	Child reduction	25%

Open: 1st January-15th December

Malahide 3km

Mrs Anne Askew
HOWTH VIEW
**9 Beach Park on Blackberry Lane,
Portmarnock, Co Dublin**

TEL: **01 8460665**   FAX: **01 8169895**
EMAIL: howthview@oceanfree.net
WEB: www.howthview.com
BUS NO: **32, 32A, 102, 230, DART**

First right after Portmarnock Hotel. Fourth house on the right. Modern detached house. Convenient to several Golf courses, Airport, Ferryport, and Beach.

B&B	4	Ensuite	£20/£23	€25.39/€29.20	Dinner	-
B&B	-	Standard	-	-	Partial Board	-
Single Rate			£30/£35	€38.09/€44.44	Child reduction	25%

Open: All Year

Malahide 3km

Mrs Margaret Creane
ROBINIA
**452 Strand Rd, Portmarnock,
Co Dublin**

TEL: **01 8462987**
BUS NO: **32, 32A, 102, 230**

Modern home overlooking Beach. Convenient to Golf, City, Malahide Castle. On Airport and City Bus route.

B&B	2	Ensuite	£22/£25	€27.93/€31.74	Dinner	-
B&B	1	Standard	£20/£24	€25.39/€30.47	Partial Board	-
Single Rate			£35	€44.44	Child reduction	25%

Open: 1st January-20th December

Malahide 1.5km

Marie D'Emidio
SOUTHDALE
**143 Heather Walk,
Portmarnock, Co Dublin**

Portmarnock

TEL: **01 8463760**   FAX: **01 8463760**
BUS NO: **32, 32A, 32B, 102, 230**

A pleasant friendly family home. Beach and Golf within walking distance. Airport 15 mins, City 30 min. Bus and Rail service.

B&B	4	Ensuite	£20/£22.50	€25.39/€28.57	Dinner	-
B&B	-	Standard	-		Partial Board	-
Single Rate			£30/£30	€38.09	Child reduction	20%

Open: 1st January-23rd December

Malahide 2km

Ms Marie Doran
ROSMAY
**468B Strand Road,
Portmarnock, Co Dublin**

Portmarnock

TEL: **01 8463175**
BUS NO: **32, 32B, 32A, 102, 230, DART**

Modern house overlooking Beach. Golf courses nearby. Convenient to City, Airport and Ferry. Bus route to City, Airport and Malahide Castle.

B&B	2	Ensuite	£20/£24	€25.39/€30.47	Dinner	-
B&B	2	Standard	£20/£22	€25.39/€27.93	Partial Board	-
Single Rate			£25/£35	€31.74/€44.44	Child reduction	25%

Open: May-October

Portmarnock 1km

Mr Sean Keane
GREENSIDE
**47 Beach Park, Portmarnock,
Co Dublin**

Portmarnock

TEL: **01 8462360**   FAX: **01 8462360**
EMAIL: greenside@eircom.net
WEB: http://homepage.eircom.net/~greenside
BUS NO: **32, 230 (Airport)**

Large townhouse, Airport 7 miles, Bus 230. City 9 miles, Bus and Rail. Beach and Golf 200 yards. Guest lounge with patio access.

B&B	4	Ensuite	£20/£25	€25.39/€31.74	Dinner	-
B&B	-	Standard	-		Partial Board	-
Single Rate			£28/£30	€35.55/€38.09	Child reduction	33.3%

Open: 5th January-19th December

Malahide 2km

Mrs Mary Lee
TARA
**14 Portmarnock Crescent,
Portmarnock, Co Dublin**

Portmarnock

TEL: **01 8462996**
BUS NO: **32, 32A, DART, 102, 230**

First turn right after Sands Hotel then sharp left. Near Beach, City Bus Route, convenient to Golf Club, Airport, Ferryport.

B&B	1	Ensuite	£20/£22.50	€25.39/€28.57	Dinner	-
B&B	2	Standard	£19/£20	€24.13/€25.39	Partial Board	-
Single Rate			£30/£35	€38.09/€44.44	Child reduction	-

Open: 1st March-31st October

Portmarnock 1km

Aileen Lynch
OAKLEIGH
**30 Dewberry Park,
Portmarnock, Co Dublin**

Portmarnock

TEL: **01 8461628**
EMAIL: aileenlynch@eircom.net
BUS NO: **32, 32A, 102, DART (AIRPORT 230)**

Past Sands Hotel, 1st right, Wendell Ave, Then 2nd right. Beach, Restaurants, Golf. Airport 15 mins, City 30 mins. Malahide Castle 2 miles.

B&B	2	Ensuite	£20/£22.50	€25.39/€28.57	Dinner	-
B&B	2	Standard	£20	€25.39	Partial Board	-
Single Rate			£25/£30	€31.74/€38.09	Child reduction	25%

Open: All Year

Malahide 3km

Mrs Kathleen O'Brien
CLARA
22 Beach Park,
Portmarnock, Co Dublin

TEL: **01 8461936**
BUS NO: **32, 32A, 102, 230**

Comfortable family home. Second turn right after the Portmarnock Hotel and Golf links "Blackberry Lane". Next right into Beachpark and right again.

B&B	2	Ensuite	£20/£22	€25.39/€27.93	Dinner	-
B&B	1	Standard	£18/£20	€22.86/€25.39	Partial Board	-
Single Rate			-	-	Child reduction	-

Open: 1st March-31st October

Malahide 2km

Mrs Margaret Treanor
SEAGLADE HOUSE
off Coast Road, At Round Tower
Portmarnock, Co Dublin

TEL: **01 8462458/8462232**   FAX: **01 8460179**
BUS NO: **32, 32A, 102, 230**

Spacious home in secluded grounds of 3 acres, directly overlooking Irish Sea. Dublin Airport 15 mins, City Centre 30 mins.

B&B	6	Ensuite	£22/£24	€27.93/€30.47	Dinner	-
B&B	-	Standard	-	-	Partial Board	-
Single Rate			-	-	Child reduction	-

Open: January-20th December

Mrs Bridget Whelan
SAN MARINO
40 Carrickhill Road,
Portmarnock, Co Dublin

TEL: **01 8463220/8169883**
EMAIL: sanmarino@eircom.net
BUS NO: **32, 32A, 102, DART, 230** AIRPORT

Portmarnock 1km

Pass Portmarnock Golf Hotel, to traffic lights then turn right up Carrickhill Road 500 metres. Golf courses, Airport 9km. City 10km. Ferry 10km. M50 6km. Beach 500m.

B&B	2	Ensuite	£20/£22.50	€25.39/€28.57	Dinner	-
B&B	1	Standard	-	-	Partial Board	-
Single Rate			£25/£30	€31.74/€38.09	Child reduction	-

Open: 1st January-23rd December

Skerries 1km

Mrs Violet Clinton
THE REEFS
Balbriggan Coast Road, Skerries,
Co Dublin

TEL: **01 8491574**
BUS NO: **33**

Spacious comfortable home overlooking the Sea. Golf nearby. "Ireland Guide" recommended. Convenient to Dublin City and Newgrange. Airport 20 kms.

B&B	4	Ensuite	£20	€25.39	Dinner	-
B&B	-	Standard	-	-	Partial Board	-
Single Rate			-	-	Child reduction	25%

Open: 1st April-30th September

Mrs Zita Devine
BENEDA
South Strand, Skerries,
Co Dublin

TEL: **01 8491042**
EMAIL: zitadevine@esatclear.ie
BUS NO: **33**

Family Built House 1902. Overlooking Sea, Lighthouse, Islands. Beside Town Centre, Windmill, Golf Course, Sailing, etc. Airport 20 kms. Dublin 30kms.

B&B	3	Ensuite	£22/£25	€27.93/€31.74	Dinner	-
B&B	1	Standard	£22/£25	€27.93/€31.74	Partial Board	-
Single Rate			£35	€44.44	Child reduction	50%

Open: 1st March-30th November

In Skerries

Mary Halpin
GREENVALE
Holmpatrick,
Skerries, Co Dublin

Tel: **01 8490413**
Email: halpinm@indigo.ie
Bus No: **33**

Large Victorian House overlooking Sea and Islands in quiet location close to Town Centre. Dublin 30 kms, Airport 20 kms.

B&B	4	Ensuite	£22.50	€28.57	Dinner	-
B&B	-	Standard	-	-	Partial Board	-
Single Rate			£35	€44.44	Child reduction	25%

cc **Open:** 17th March-1st November

In Skerries

Margaret Swan
HILL HOUSE
Milverton, Skerries,
Co Dublin

Tel: **01 8491873**
Bus No: **33**

Luxury bungalow in quiet scenic area. Beaches, Golf, Sailing, Horse Riding, archaelogical and historic interests nearby. Dublin 25 mins. Airport 15 mins.

B&B	1	Ensuite	£20/£22.50	€25.39/€28.57	Dinner	-
B&B	2	Standard	£18/£20	€22.86/€25.39	Partial Board	-
Single Rate			£25/£30	€31.74/€38.09	Child reduction	25%

Open: 1st March-30th September

Howth 2km

Mrs Geraldine Conlan
THE MEADOWS
257 Sutton Park,
Sutton, Dublin 13

Tel: **01 8390257/2835741**
Bus No: **31, 32, DART**

Highly rated Bed & Breakfast. 15 mins from Dublin City by Dart Train. 15 mins from Airport.

B&B	-	Ensuite	-	-	Dinner	-
B&B	3	Standard	£20/£20	€25.39	Partial Board	-
Single Rate			£25/£25.50	€31.74/€32.38	Child reduction	50%

Open: 1st January-15th December

Dublin 10 km

Ms Colette Gillett
55 Glencarraig, Sutton,
Dublin 13

Tel: **01 8325553**
Email: cgillett@esatclear.ie
Bus No: **31, DART**

Family house in the heart of Sutton. Howth/Dart/Bus - 5 minutes. City Airport/Ferry 15 minutes.

B&B	2	Ensuite	£22	€27.93	Dinner	-
B&B	1	Standard	£20	€25.39	Partial Board	-
Single Rate			£25	€31.74	Child reduction	50%

Open: 31st January-31st November

Dublin City 10km

Eileen Hobbs
HILLVIEW
39 Sutton Park, Dublin Road,
Sutton, Dublin 13

Tel: **01 8324584**
Email: hillviewhouse@ireland.com
Bus No: **31, 32**

Friendly comfortable home, peaceful surroundings. 5 minutes walk to Dart/Bus. Convenient to Point Theatre, City Centre, Ferry. 10 minutes to Howth. 15 minutes to Airport.

B&B	3	Ensuite	£20/£23	€25.39/€29.20	Dinner	-
B&B	1	Standard	£18/£20	€22.86/€25.39	Partial Board	-
Single Rate			£30/£30	€38.09	Child reduction	50%

Open: 1st January-20th December

Dublin 10 km

Mrs Mary McDonnell
DUN AOIBHINN
30 Sutton Park, Sutton,
Dublin 13

Sutton
TEL: **01 8325456**   FAX: **01 8325213**
EMAIL: mary_mcdonnell@ireland.com
BUS NO: **31, 31A, 31B, 32, 32A, DART**

Luxurious detached home in quiet residential area facing amenity park. Adjacent coast road. City Centre 10km, Airport 12km. Howth 3km. Dart/Bus 3 mins walk.

B&B	3	Ensuite	£20/£22.50	€25.39/€28.57	Dinner	-
B&B	-	Standard	-	-	Partial Board	-
Single Rate			£32.50/£35	€41.27/€44.44	Child reduction	-

Open: 7th January-20th December

Howth Village 3km

Mrs Eileen Staunton
STAUNTONS
20 Offington Drive,
Sutton, Dublin 13

Sutton
TEL: **01 8324442**   FAX: **01 8324442**
EMAIL: spotta@iol.ie
BUS NO: **31, 31A, 31B**

Friendly family home in quiet area on Howth Peninsula. One mile before Howth. Restuarants, walking nearby. Close to Bus, DART. 20 mins to City, Airport & Ferry.

B&B	2	Ensuite	£22.50/£22.50	€28.57	Dinner	-
B&B	1	Standard	£22.50/£22.50	€28.57	Partial Board	-
Single Rate			£27.50/£27.50	€34.91	Child reduction	25%

Open: 10th January-10th December

Dublin 10km

Mrs Eileen Sutton
SUTTONS B&B
154 Sutton Park, Sutton,
Dublin 13

Sutton
TEL: **01 8325167**   FAX: **01 8395516**
EMAIL: rwppu@iol.ie
BUS NO: **DART, 31, 32**

Excellent accommodation close to Seafront & Dart Station. 15 mins Airport, Point Theatre, City Centre, Ferry, Golfing, Fishing, Restaurants, Amenities nearby.

B&B	2	Ensuite	£22.50	€28.57	Dinner	-
B&B	1	Standard	£20	€25.39	Partial Board	-
Single Rate			£25.50/£26	€32.38/€33.01	Child reduction	-

Open: All Year Except Christmas

In Swords

Kathleen Kenegan
CEDAR HOUSE
Jugback Lane,
Swords, Co Dublin

Swords
TEL: **01 8402757**   FAX: **01 8402041**
BUS NO: **41, 33, 41B**

Situated 5 mins walk from Swords main st. Modern town house, 5 mins drive from Airport. 30 mins from City Centre. Carpark. Home from home.

B&B	4	Ensuite	£23/£23	€29.20	Dinner	-
B&B	-	Standard	-	-	Partial Board	-
Single Rate			£30/£30	€38.09	Child reduction	33.3%

Open: All Year

Swords 1km

Mrs Rosemarie Barrett O'Neill
BLACKBRIDGE AIRPORT LODGE
Lissenhall, Swords,
Co Dublin

Swords/Airport
TEL: **01 8407276**   FAX: **01 8407276**
EMAIL: blackbridge.lodge@indigo.ie
BUS NO: **41, 41B, 41C, 33**

Situated just off Belfast/Dublin road. 5 minutes Airport, 20 mins City. Room rates, reliable transport arranged, private car park.

B&B	5	Ensuite	£16/£25	€20.32/€31.74	Dinner	-
B&B	-	Standard	-	-	Partial Board	-
Single Rate			£25/£45	€31.74/€57.14	Child reduction	33.3%

Open: 8th January-16th December

Swords 1km

Mrs Catherine Cavanagh
RIVERSDALE
Balheary Road, Swords,
Co Dublin

Swords/Airport

TEL: **01 8404802**   FAX: **01 8404802**
EMAIL: michaelc@indigo.ie
BUS NO: **41, 41B, 33, 33B, 41C**

6 mins North of Airport off N1- onto R125, to traffic lights turn right- 1km straight. Quiet location. TV, Tea/Coffee. Ground floor rooms. Guest lounge. City 20 mins.

B&B	5	Ensuite	£19/£25	€24.13/€31.74	Dinner	-
B&B	1	Standard			Partial Board	-
Single Rate			£35/£40	€44.44/€50.79	Child reduction	33.3%

Open: 16th January-16th December

Swords 1km

Mrs Sara Daniels
DAWN HOUSE
Balheary, Swords/Airport,
Co Dublin

Swords/Airport

TEL: **01 8403111**   FAX: **01 8403111**
EMAIL: sara.daniels@oceanfree.net
BUS NO: **41, 41B, 33, 33B, 41C**

Quiet location, just off Dublin/Belfast road, 8 mins Airport, 20 mins City. Room rates. Private car park. From Airport N1 bypass Swords, left at "Emmaus" sign.

B&B	5	Ensuite	£19/£22.50	€24.13/€28.57	Dinner	-
B&B		Standard	-		Partial Board	-
Single Rate			£30/£35	€38.09/€44.44	Child reduction	25%

Open: 1st March-31st October

Ballyboghil 3km

Margaret Farrell
HOLLYWOOD B&B
Hollywood, Ballyboghil,
Co Dublin

Swords/Ballyboghil

TEL: **01 8433359**   FAX: **018433359**
EMAIL: hwood@indigo.ie

Country home 15 minutes Airport, 25 minutes City. From Airport take N1 North, 2 miles past Swords turn next left after Esso Garage onto R129, follow signs for Hollywood Lakes Golf Club.

B&B	4	Ensuite	£19/£21	€24.13/€26.66	Dinner	-
B&B	-	Standard	-		Partial Board	-
Single Rate			£26/£28	€33.01/€35.55	Child reduction	-

Open: All Year

Swords 3km

Mrs Marie Jackson
OAKVIEW COUNTRY HOME
Leas Cross, Naul Road,
Swords, Co Dublin

Swords/Airport

TEL: **01 8405256**   FAX: **01 8405256**
EMAIL: oakview@esatclear.ie
WEB: http://myhome.iolfree.ie/~oakview/
BUS NO: **41B**

Country home peaceful setting, adjacent Dublin Airport (runway 2.5 miles), Carpark, 8 miles City Centre, Horse Riding, Golf. Route 108 via Naul north of Dublin Airport.

B&B	3	Ensuite	£19/£25	€24.13/€31.74	Dinner	-
B&B	-	Standard	-		Partial Board	-
Single Rate			£20/£35	€25.39/€44.44	Child reduction	50%

Open: All Year Except Christmas

Balbriggan 8km

Betty Keane
HALF ACRE
Hynestown, Naul,
Co Dublin

Swords/Balbriggan

TEL: **01 8413306**

Country home. Ideal touring base. Airport 20 mins, City 45 mins, Coast 10 mins. Tea/Coffee all rooms. Private car park.

B&B	3	Ensuite	£20/£20	€25.39	Dinner	-
B&B	-	Standard	-		Partial Board	-
Single Rate			£25.50/£25.50	€32.28	Child reduction	-

Open: 1st January-30th November

Swords 6km

Mrs Sheila White
ARD-CILL
**The Rath, Rolestown,
Swords, Co Dublin**

Swords
TEL: **01 8405172**
BUS NO: **41B**

Spacious dormer bungalow in quiet country surroundings. Large safe Car Park, 15 mins Airport, 15 mins Malahide Castle. 5 mins Golf.

B&B	1	Ensuite	£20	€25.39	Dinner	-
B&B	2	Standard	£18	€22.86	Partial Board	-
Single Rate			£25/£35	€31.74/€44.44	Child reduction	-

Open: 1st April-1st October

CASINO
OFF THE MALAHIDE ROAD, MARINO, DUBLIN 3
TEL + 353 1 833 1618

The Casino, Marino, North Dublin, designed by the famous architect Sir William Chambers in 1759 is one of the finest neo-classical buildings in Europe.

Carmel Chambers
25 Anglesea Road, Ballsbridge, Dublin 4

Ballsbridge

Tel: **01 6687346**   Fax: **01 6687346**
Bus No: **7A, 7, 8, 45, 84, 63**

Edwardian home. Located in popular Ballsbridge, close to Bus, Rail (Dart), Embassies, Art Galleries, Trinity College, Point Theatre & RDS.

B&B	1	Ensuite	£25/£30	€31.74/€38.09	Dinner —
B&B	3	Standard	£23/£25	€29.20/€31.74	Partial Board —
Single Rate			£23/£35	€29.20/€44.44	Child reduction —

City Centre 2km

Open: All Year Except Christmas

Colm Dunne
AARON HOUSE
152 Merrion Road, Ballsbridge, Dublin 4

Ballsbridge

Tel: **01 2601644**   Fax: **01 2601651**
Email: aaronhouse@indigo.ie
Bus No: **5, 7, 8, 45**

Luxurious accommodation. All rooms en-suite. Convenient to Point Theatre, RDS, Golf Clubs, all Embassies, Restaurants. Direct-dial telephones.

B&B	6	Ensuite	£25/£45	€31.74/€57.14	Dinner —
B&B	-	Standard	-	-	Partial Board —
Single Rate			£30/£90	€38.09/€114.28	Child reduction 25%

In Ballsbridge

Open: All Year

Ms Catherine Foy
20 Pembroke Park, Ballsbridge, Dublin 4

Ballsbridge

Tel: **01 6683075**

Victorian house just minutes walk from City Centre. Warm, friendly atmosphere. Close to RDS, Universities, Embassies, RTE, Lansdowne Stadium. Serviced by Aircoach.

B&B	3	Ensuite	£28/£33	€35.55/€41.90	Dinner —
B&B	-	Standard	-	-	Partial Board —
Single Rate			£40/£40	€50.79	Child reduction —

In Ballsbridge

Open: All Year

Leslie Griffin
AARON COURT
144 Merrion Road, Ballsbridge, Dublin 4

Ballsbridge

Tel: **01 2602631**
Email: aaroncourt@yahoo.com
Bus No: **5, 7, 8, 45, DART**

Elegant family residence in the heart of Ballsbridge. All rooms en-suite, direct dial phones, TV. RDS, Point, Restaurants, Embassies.

B&B	6	Ensuite	£25/£45	€31.74/€57.14	Dinner —
B&B	-	Standard	-	-	Partial Board —
Single Rate			£30/£90	€38.09/€114.28	Child reduction 25%

In Ballsbridge

Open: All Year

Teresa Muldoon
OAK LODGE
4 Pembroke Park, Off Clyde Rd, Ballsbridge, Dublin 4

Ballsbridge

Tel: **01 6606096/6681721** Fax: **01 6681721**
Email: oaklodgebandb@hotmail.com
Bus No: **10, 46A**

Victorian residence close to RDS, Universities, Embassies, Dart. Breakfast menu. Direct Air Coach from Airport. Nearest stop Jury's Hotel.

B&B	3	Ensuite	£25/£30	€31.74/€38.09	Dinner —
B&B	1	Standard	-	-	Partial Board —
Single Rate			£25/£45	€31.74/€57.14	Child reduction 50%

City Centre 1.5km

Open: 2nd January - 17th December

Dublin 2km

Mrs Therese Clifford Sanderson | **Ballsbridge**
CAMELOT
37 Pembroke Park,
Ballsbridge, Dublin 4

TEL: **01 6680331**   FAX: **01 6671916**
BUS NO: **10, 46A**

Victorian home, friendly atmosphere. Close to City Centre, RDS, American Embassy, Museums, Art Galleries, Universities. Fine Restaurants within walking distance.

B&B	3	Ensuite	£28/£30	€35.55/€38.09	Dinner	-
B&B	-	Standard	-	-	Partial Board	-
Single Rate			£40/£40	€50.79	Child reduction	-

Open: All Year

Dublin 3km

Joan Donnellan | **Donnybrook**
HAZELHURST
166 Stillorgan Rd, Donnybrook,
Dublin 4

TEL: **01 2838509**   FAX: **01 2600346**
BUS NO: **10, 46A**

Luxurious spacious residence situated on N11. Adjacent Embassies, UCD, Montrose Hotel, RTE, RDS, main route to Ferry. Private car park. AA ◆◆◆◆.

B&B	5	Ensuite	£27.50/£30	€34.91/€30.09	Dinner	-
B&B	-	Standard	-	-	Partial Board	-
Single Rate			£37.50/£45	€47.62/€57.14	Child reduction	25%

Open: 1st February-30th November

Dublin 2.2km

Mrs Mai Bird | **Ranelagh**
ST DUNSTANS
25A Oakley Rd, Ranelagh,
Dublin 6

TEL: **01 4972286**
BUS NO: **11, 11A, 11B, 13B, 44, 48**

Edwardian townhouse. Frommer recommended. Convenient City Centre, RDS, Ferry, Jurys, Universities. Laundrette, Restaurants, Banks, and Post Office in immediate vicinity.

B&B	-	Ensuite	-	-	Dinner	-
B&B	3	Standard	£20/£22	€25.39/€27.93	Partial Board	-
Single Rate			£28/£28	€35.55	Child reduction	-

Open: All Year Except Christmas

Dublin 6km

Mrs Mary Byrne | **Rathfarnham**
LITTLE SILVER
2 Fonthill Park, Rathfarnham,
Dublin 14

TEL: **01 4931677**
BUS NO: **16, 16A, 15C**

Modern house near 15C, 16, 16A Bus stops. Leisure Centre, Shops and Restaurants. Near M50 to Airport near Marley Park for start of Wicklow Way trail.

B&B	-	Ensuite	-	-	Dinner	-
B&B	3	Standard	£19/£25	€24.13/€31.74	Partial Board	-
Single Rate			£24/£27	€30.47/€34.29	Child reduction	25%

Open: 1st March-30th September

RESERVATIONS

- Confirm phone bookings in writing without delay with agreed deposit.
- To avoid misunderstandings later, check rate on booking and clarify any additional changes which may apply to your booking.
- Give details of any special requirements.
- State clearly day, date of arrival and departure date.

Mrs Monica Byrne
RICHMON HOUSE
59 Marian Crescent,
Rathfarnham, Dublin 14

Rathfarnham

TEL: **01 4947582**   FAX: **01 4947582**
EMAIL: monicabyrne@ireland.com
BUS NO: **15B**

Modern home. Quiet cul-de-sac. Beside 15B Bus to City, Shops, Restaurants, Sport Leisure Centres. Routes from Ferry and Airport. M50 to North, South and West.

B&B	-	Ensuite	-	-	Dinner	-
B&B	3	Standard	£18.50/£20.50	€23.49/€26.03	Partial Board	-
Single Rate			£23.50/£25.50	€29.84/€32.38	Child reduction	-

Dublin 6km

Open: 1st March-30th September

Mrs Beatrice O'Connor
CRANOG
15 Butterfield Avenue,
Rathfarnham, Dublin 14

Rathfarnham

TEL: **01 4943660**
EMAIL: beatriceoconnor@oceanfree.net
BUS NO: **15B, 75, 15**

Family home. 15B bus stop outside house to City Centre. Tea/Coffee maker. Near N81 M50 motorway. Restaurants, Shop, Pub, Bank nearby.

B&B	3	Ensuite	£20/£24	€25.39/€30.47	Dinner	-
B&B	1	Standard	£19/£21	€24.13/€26.66	Partial Board	-
Single Rate			£23.50/£30	€29.84/€38.09	Child reduction	25%

Dublin 6km

Open: February-30th November

Mrs Nuala Wells
35 Anne Devlin Avenue,
Rathfarnham,
Dublin 14

Rathfarnham

TEL: **01 4947403**
BUS NO: **15B**

Central heated. Adjacent 15B bus. Near Wicklow Way commencement. Convenient to Tallaght Hospital. Near M50.

B&B	-	Ensuite	-	-	Dinner	-
B&B	3	Standard	£18/£23	€22.86/€29.20	Partial Board	-
Single Rate			£23.50/£25.50	€29.84/€32.38	Child reduction	-

Dublin 6km

Open: All Year

Mrs Beda Wolfe
NEWCOURT
31 Silverwood Road,
Rathfarnham, Dublin 14

Rathfarnham

TEL: **01 4944103**
BUS NO: **15B**

Modern house, beside terminus 15B Bus. Near Badminton, Hockey, Tennis, Swimming, Golf. On route South, West, Car Ferry, M50 Airport.

B&B	1	Ensuite	£20/£22	€25.39/€27.93	Dinner	-
B&B	3	Standard	£18/£20	€22.86/€25.39	Partial Board	-
Single Rate			£23.50/£25	€29.84/€31.74	Child reduction	10%

Dublin City 5km

Open: 1st March-30th November

Mrs Aida Boyle
ST JUDES
6 Fortfield Tce,
Upper Rathmines, Dublin 6

Rathmines

TEL: **01 4972517**
BUS NO: **14A, 13**

Beautiful Victorian home, well maintained, quiet locality. Spacious bedrooms. 7 min Shops, Restaurants, Banks, Pubs, Churches, Parks, Walks, RDS, Dart, Point Theatre.

B&B	2	Ensuite	£23/£30	€29.20/€38.09	Dinner	-
B&B	3	Standard	£20/£23	€25.39/€29.20	Partial Board	-
Single Rate			-	-	Child reduction	

Dublin 3km

Open: All Year Except Christmas

Dublin City 8km

Nola Martini
PINEHILL
Sandyford Village,
Dublin 18

Tel: **01 2952061** Fax: **01 2958291**
Email: martini@indigo.ie
Web: www.martini.pair.com
Bus No: **44, 114, DART**

Charming Cottage style home with modern amenities. Close to Leopardstown Race Course (Stillorgan), Dun Laoghaire Ferry Port.

B&B	2	Ensuite	£25/£30	€31.74/€38.09	Dinner	-
B&B	2	Standard	£25/£30	€31.74/€38.09	Partial Board	-
Single Rate			£30/£35	€38.09/€44.44	Child reduction	-

Open: 4th January-14th December

Dublin 2km

Mrs Dolores Abbott Murphy
14 Sandymount Castle Park
off Gilford Road, Sandymount,
Dublin 4

Tel: **01 2698413**
Bus No: 3

Quiet safe location beside Village, Sea, Bus, Rail (DART), Embassies, Museums, Art Galleries, Point Theatre, RDS, UCD, Trinity, St Vincents Hospital.

B&B	1	Ensuite	£23/£23	€29.20	Dinner	-
B&B	2	Standard	£20/£20	€25.39	Partial Board	-
Single Rate			£30/£30	€38.09	Child reduction	-

Open: 1st May-30th September

Dublin City 2.5km

Mrs Kathleen Lee
ARDAGH HOUSE
6 St Annes Road Sth, South
Circular Road, Dublin 8

Tel: **01 4536615**
Bus No: **19, 121, 122**

Home overlooking Grand Canal. Convenient to all places of interest. Bus 19, 121, 122. Road opposite John Player and Sons. 2.5km to City Centre. Easy access to N1, N4, N7, N11, M50.

B&B	3	Ensuite	£22/£23	€27.93/€29.20	Dinner	-
B&B	1	Standard	£18/£20	€22.86/€25.39	Partial Board	-
Single Rate			£23/£28	€29.20/€35.55	Child reduction	-

Open: 6th January-30th November

Botanic Gardens, Dublin 9

Dublin 6km

Mrs Noreen Devine
CLARENDON B&B
293 Orwell Park Grove
Templeogue, Dublin 6W

Templeogue
TEL: **01 4500007**   FAX: **01 4565725**
BUS NO: **150, 54A, 15A**

Located off N81, exit at Spawell roundabout onto Wellington Lane, straight through next roundabout, see B&B sign on right.

				Dinner	-
B&B	4	Ensuite	£20/£25	€25.39/€31.74	
B&B	-	Standard			Partial Board	-
Single Rate			£25.50/£30	€32.38/€38.09	Child reduction	25%

Open: All Year Except Christmas

Dublin 6km

Ms Maura Leahy
ABBEY COURT
7 Glendown Court, Off Templeville Rd, Templeogue, Dublin 6W

Templeogue
TEL: **01 4562338**

Comfortable, friendly, smoke-free home in quiet cul-de-sac. Near M50, N4, N7 and Car Ferry. Leisure facilities locally.

					Dinner	-
B&B	2	Ensuite	£20/£22	€25.39/€27.93		
B&B	1	Standard	-	-	Partial Board	-
Single Rate			£24.50/£25.50	€31.11/€32.38	Child reduction	25%

Open: All Year

Dublin 6km

Mrs Noreen McBride
3 Rossmore Grove
Off Wellington Lane,
Templeogue, Dublin 6W

Templeogue
TEL: **01 4902939**   FAX: **01 4929416**
EMAIL: denismb@iol.ie
BUS NO: **150, 54A**

Frommer, AA recommended. 20 mins City & Airport. Bus every 10 mins to City. Near Restaurant & M50. Located off N81 at Spawell roundabout first right Rossmore Rd.

					Dinner	-
B&B	2	Ensuite	£20/£25	€25.39/€31.74		
B&B	2	Standard	£20/£25	€25.39/€31.74	Partial Board	-
Single Rate			£25.50/£30	€32.38/€38.09	Child reduction	-

Open: 1st January-15th December

Dublin City 6km

Mrs Mary McGreal
SEEFIN
28 Rossmore Grove,
Templeogue, Dublin 6W

Templeogue
TEL: **01 4907286**   FAX: **01 4907286**
EMAIL: mcgreal_28@yahoo.co.uk
BUS NO: **150, 54A**

Modern home in cul-de-sac off Wellington Lane. 1/2km from Spawell roundabout on N81. On Ferry and Bus Routes. 5 mins M50 motorway. Restaurants, Pubs, Sporting facilities locally.

					Dinner	-
B&B	2	Ensuite	£22/£25	€27.93/€31.74		
B&B	1	Standard	£19/£20	€24.13/€25.39	Partial Board	-
Single Rate			£25/£30	€31.74/€38.09	Child reduction	-

Open: 15th January-15th December

Dublin City 4km

Mrs Ellie Kiernan
LOUGHKIERN
65 Rockfield Ave, Off Kimmage Rd West, Terenure, Dublin 12

Terenure
TEL: **01 4551509**
BUS NO: **15A, 150**

Comfortable modern family home. 15 mins to City. Convenient to Restaurants, Sports Centre, Bus, Park, Links Road and Ferry Terminal.

					Dinner	-
B&B	1	Ensuite	£21/£24	€26.66/€30.47		
B&B	2	Standard	£19/£22	€24.13/€27.93	Partial Board	-
Single Rate			£24/£28	€30.47/€35.55	Child reduction	25%

Open: All Year Except Christmas

Monica & Michael Leydon
AARONA
150 Clonkeen Rd, Deansgrange, Blackrock, Co Dublin

TEL: **01 2893972** FAX: **01 2898622**
EMAIL: aarona.bandb.ireland@gmx.net
BUS NO: **45**

Exquisitely situated beside all amenities. Bus to City Centre. Dun Laoghaire, Ferry Port 5 mins. Highest standards maintained in friendly family atmosphere.

B&B	3	Ensuite	£25	€31.74	Dinner	-
B&B	-	Standard		-	Partial Board	-
Single Rate			£35	€44.44	Child reduction	-

Dun Laoghaire 2km

Open: All Year Except Christmas

Kitty McEvoy
87 Monkstown Avenue, Blackrock, Co Dublin

TEL: **01 2804004**
BUS NO: **46A, 7, 8**

Modern relaxed home, ample parking off main road. Convenient to all transport, Ferry and Restaurants. 36 years in business. Splendid food and hospitality.

B&B	-	Ensuite	-	-	Dinner	-
B&B	3	Standard	£18/£20	€22.86/€25.39	Partial Board	-
Single Rate			£23/£25	€29.20/€31.74	Child reduction	-

Dun Laoghaire 1km

Open: 1st January-31st November

Mrs Mary Corbett Monaghan
46 Windsor Park, Off Stradbrook Road, Blackrock, Co Dublin

TEL: **01 2843711**
BUS NO: **46A, 7, 8**

Bright comfortable family home, convenient to Ferry, Restaurants, Bus and Salthill DART Station. Secure car parking. Ideal touring base.

B&B	2	Ensuite	£22	€27.93	Dinner	-
B&B	2	Standard	£19	€24.13	Partial Board	-
Single Rate			£25/£35	€31.74/€44.44	Child reduction	-

Dun Laoghaire 2km

Open: April-October

Mrs Anne D'Alton
ANNESGROVE
28 Rosmeen Gardens, Dun Laoghaire, Co Dublin

TEL: **01 2809801**
BUS NO: **7, 7A, 8, 46A & DART**

Quiet Cul-de-Sac beside Dart, Buses & Ferry. Breakfast from 7am, room rates. Frommer, Europe, Cadogan Irish B&B, Dan McQuillan, Rough Guide.

B&B	2	Ensuite	£23/£25	€29.20/€31.74	Dinner	-
B&B	2	Standard	£20/£20	€25.39	Partial Board	-
Single Rate			£25/£30	€31.74/€38.09	Child reduction	25%

In Dun Laoghaire

Open: 1st February-15th December

Steve & Maria Gavin
LYNDEN
2 Mulgrave Tce, Dun Laoghaire, Co Dublin

TEL: **01 2806404** FAX: **01 2302258**
EMAIL: lynden@iol.ie
BUS NO: **7, 7A, 8, 45A, 46A, 59, 111, DART**

Georgian house. Quiet location. Adjacent Buses, Train, Shops. Car Ferry 5 mins walk. Early breakfasts, parking. TV & tea making facilities.

B&B	2	Ensuite	£19/£21	€24.13/€26.66	Dinner	-
B&B	2	Standard	£17/£18	€21.59/€22.86	Partial Board	-
Single Rate			£29/£31	€36.82/€39.36	Child reduction	50%

In Dun Laoghaire

Open: All Year

Dun Laoghaire 1km

Mrs Ann Harkin
7 Claremont Villas
(Off Adelaide Road), Glenageary,
Dun Laoghaire, Co Dublin

Dun Laoghaire

TEL: 01 2805346   FAX: 01 2805346
EMAIL: claremontvillas@yahoo.com
BUS NO: 8, 59, DART

124-year old Victorian home, near Ferry, Bus, Train. Quiet cul-de-sac. Early breakfast, tea-making facilities, own restaurant nearby. Tourist information.

B&B	4	Ensuite	£22/£24	€27.93/€30.47	Dinner	-
B&B	1	Standard	£20/£20	€25.39	Partial Board	-
Single Rate			£27/£30	€34.29/€38.09	Child reduction	50%

Open: All Year Except Christmas

Dun Laoghaire

Mrs Mary Kane
SEAVIEW HOUSE
2 Granite Hall, Rosmeen Gardens,
Dun Laoghaire, Co Dublin

Dun Laoghaire

TEL: 01 2809105   FAX: 01 2809105
BUS NO: 7, 7A, 8

Comfortable detached family home in quiet cul-de-sac within walking distance Dart, Sea Front and all amenities. Parking.

B&B	3	Ensuite	£23.50/£26	€29.84/€33.01	Dinner	-
B&B	-	Standard	-	-	Partial Board	-
Single Rate			-	-	Child reduction	-

Open: 1st January-15th December

Dun Laoghaire

Mrs Mary Lehane
CILL DARA
5 Tivoli Rd, Dun Laoghaire,
Co Dublin

Dun Laoghaire

TEL: 01 2807355   FAX: 01 2807355
BUS NO: 7, 7A, 8, 46A

Modern friendly home. Opposite Dun Laoghaire Golf Club. Very convenient for Ferries, Buses, Trains, Shops, Restaurants & Seafront.

B&B	2	Ensuite	£22/£22	€27.93	Dinner	-
B&B	1	Standard	£20/£20	€25.39	Partial Board	-
Single Rate			£30/£37	€38.09/€46.98	Child reduction	-

Open: 1st January-30th November

In Dun Laoghaire

Mrs Joan M Murphy
ROSMEEN HOUSE
Rosmeen Gardens,
Dun Laoghaire, Co Dublin

Dun Laoghaire

TEL: 01 2807613
BUS NO: 7, 8, DART

Attractive Spanish type villa. Frommer Europe and Ireland recommended. Early breakfast, walking distance Train, Bus and Ferry.

B&B	2	Ensuite	£23.50/£25	€29.84/€31.74	Dinner	-
B&B	2	Standard	£20/£20	€25.39	Partial Board	-
Single Rate			£30	€38.09	Child reduction	-

Open: 1st February-1st December

Dun Laoghaire 3km

Mrs Mary Murphy
GLENVIEW HOUSE
5 Glenview, Rochestown Avenue,
Dun Laoghaire, Co Dublin

Dun Laoghaire

TEL: 01 2855043   FAX: 01 2855043
EMAIL: glenbb@indigo.ie
WEB: www.glenviewhousebb.com
BUS NO: 7, 45A, 111, 46

Comfortable family home. Convenient to Ferries, DART, Buses, Pubs, Restaurants. Opposite Killiney Shopping Centre. Close to N11. Tea making facilities. Parking.

B&B	4	Ensuite	£25/£25	€31.74	Dinner	-
B&B	-	Standard	-	-	Partial Board	-
Single Rate			£30/£30	€38.09	Child reduction	50%

Open: 1st February-30th November

In Dun Laoghaire

Mary O'Farrell
WINDSOR LODGE
3 Islington Ave, Sandycove,
Dun Laoghaire, Co Dublin

Dun Laoghaire
TEL: **01 2846952**   FAX: **01 2846952**
EMAIL: winlodge@eircom.net
BUS NO: **7, 8, DART**

Victorian home beside Dublin Bay. Close to all amenities. 5 minutes Stena Ferry. Beside Bus/Dart. 20 minutes City Centre.

B&B	4	Ensuite	£20/£25	€25.39/€31.74	Dinner	-
B&B	-	Standard	-	-	Partial Board	-
Single Rate			-	-	Child reduction	-

Open: 1st January-23rd December

Dalkey 2km

Mrs Bridie O'Leary
ROSEMONT
51 Bellevue Road, Glenageary,
Dun Laoghaire, Co Dublin

Dun Laoghaire
TEL: **01 2851021**   FAX: **01 2851021**
BUS NO: **59, 7, 7A**

Bright comfortable home. Quiet location, convenient to Bus, Train and Ferry. Close to Fitzpatrick Castle, Killiney. Early breakfast. Private parking.

B&B	3	Ensuite	£20/£20	€25.39	Dinner	-
B&B	1	Standard	-	-	Partial Board	-
Single Rate			£26/£26	€33.01	Child reduction	25%

Open: 1st February-30th November

Mrs Connie O'Sullivan
DUNCREE
16 Northumberland Avenue,
Dun Laoghaire, Co Dublin

Dun Laoghaire
TEL: **01 2806118**
BUS NO: **7, 7A, 8, 46A**

Comfortable Georgian house, quiet location. Adjacent to Buses, Trains & Shops. Car Ferry 5 mins walk.

B&B	2	Ensuite	£20	€25.39	Dinner	-
B&B	2	Standard	£18	€22.86	Partial Board	-
Single Rate			£22.50/£25	€28.57/€31.74	Child reduction	25%

Open: 1st January-23rd December

In Dun Laoghaire

Des & Marie Power
ARIEMOND
47 Mulgrave Street,
Dun Laoghaire, Co Dublin

Dun Laoghaire
TEL: **01 2801664**   FAX: **01 2801664**
EMAIL: ariemond@hotmail.com
BUS NO: **8, 7, 46A, 45A, DART**

Geogian house Town Centre. Ferry 5 minutes walk. Beside Buses and Train. Dublin City Centre 15 minutes. Golf and Rock climbing nearby.

B&B	3	Ensuite	£20	€25.39	Dinner	-
B&B	2	Standard	£17.50	€22.22	Partial Board	-
Single Rate			£35/£40	€44.44/€50.79	Child reduction	-

Open: 1st January-20th December

Dun Laoghaire 2km

Ms Betty MacAnaney
70 Avondale Rd,
Killiney, Co Dublin

Killiney
TEL: **01 2859952**   FAX: **01 2859952**
EMAIL: mcananey@hotmail.com
WEB: http://gofree.indigo.ie/~macanany/
BUS NO: **59**

Quiet area, 4-minute drive to Car Ferry. 12-minute walk to Glenageary Dart Station. Dalkey close by. Easy reach City Centre & Co Wicklow. Private Parking.

B&B	3	Ensuite	£22/£25	€27.93/€31.74	Dinner	-
B&B	1	Standard	£20/£22	€25.39/€27.93	Partial Board	-
Single Rate			£26/£30	€33.01/€38.09	Child reduction	25%

Open: February-November

In Lucan

Colette Egan
MOAT LODGE
**Newcastle Road,
Lucan, Co Dublin**

Tel: **01 6241584**   Fax: **01 6281356**
Bus No: **66A, 67, 67A, 25, 25A, 66**

Exclusive 17th Century House convenient to Shops, Bus, City Centre. Ideal base for Golf & Fishing. Off N4. Near N7, N3, M50.

B&B	4	Ensuite	£19/£19	€24.13	Dinner	-
B&B	-	Standard			Partial Board	-
Single Rate			£25.50/£25.50	€32.38	Child reduction	25%

Open: All Year

Lucan 1km

Seamus & Patricia McCormack
BEAUMONT
**Newcastle Road,
Lucan, Co Dublin**

Tel: **01 6281956**
Bus No: **25, 25A, 66, 67**

Modern bungalow just off N4, convenient to City, Airport and Car Ferry. Private car park. Bedrooms non-smoking.

B&B	4	Ensuite	£19/£21	€24.13/€26.66	Dinner	-
B&B	-	Standard			Partial Board	-
Single Rate			£30/£35	€38.09/€44.44	Child reduction	25%

Open: All Year

Lucan

Mrs Ethna McDonald
KEW LODGE
**57 Kew Park, Lucan,
Co Dublin**

Tel: **01 6280057**   Fax: **01 6280057**
Email: kewlodge@eircom.net
Bus No: **66, 66A, 67**

Modern home, quiet area. 30 mins City, Airport. Ferries. Beside Bus Eireann stop, Spa Hotel, N4, N7, Golf, Fishing. Bedrooms non smoking.

B&B	2	Ensuite	£20	€25.39	Dinner	-
B&B	1	Standard	£18	€22.86	Partial Board	-
Single Rate			£26	€33.01	Child reduction	-

Open: 1st April-20th December

Rathcoole 2km

Brenda & Gerry Beirne
BEECHBROOK LODGE
**Kilteel Road, Rathcoole,
Co Dublin**

Tel: **01 4580827**
Email: beechbrooklodge@eircom.net
Bus No: **69**

Spacious country lodge on 2 acres. Tennis/Basketball Court. Adjoining Golf/Equestrian Centre. Ideal base touring Wicklow/Kildare. City/Airport - 25 mins.

B&B	4	Ensuite	£20/£22	€25.39/€27.93	Dinner	-
B&B	-	Standard			Partial Board	-
Single Rate			£27.50/£30	€34.91/€38.09	Child reduction	50%

Open: All Year Except Christmas

In Rathcoole

Mrs Ann Eagers
BANNER HOUSE
Main St, Rathcoole, Co Dublin

Tel: **01 4589337**   Fax: **01 4589337**
Bus No: **69**

Modern family home. 100yds off N7. Convenient to Pub/Restaurant. Golf and Horseriding nearby. Airport, City Centre, 25 Minutes. In Rathcoole village.

B&B	5	Ensuite	£20/£22.50	€25.39/€28.57	Dinner	-
B&B	-	Standard			Partial Board	-
Single Rate			£25.50/£30	€32.38/€38.09	Child reduction	-

Open: 15th January-15th December

Rathcoole 2km

Elizabeth Freeland
HILLBROOK
**Redgap, Rathcoole,
Co Dublin**

Rathcoole

TEL: **01 4580060**
EMAIL: lizfreeland@hotmail.com
BUS NO: **69**

Welcoming home in scenic countryside, adjacent to Golf, Horseriding, Pitch & Putt. Dublin City, Airport 30 minutes. Close to N7. Convenient to all main routes.

B&B	2	Ensuite	£20/£22.50	€25.39/€28.57	Dinner	-
B&B	2	Standard	-	-	Partial Board	-
Single Rate			£23.50/£27.50	€29.84/€34.91	Child reduction	25%

Open: All Year Except Christmas

Rathcoole 1.5km

Elizabeth Keogh
BEARNA RUA LODGE
Redgap, Rathcoole, Co Dublin

Rathcoole

TEL: **01 4589920/4587880**   FAX: **01 4587880**
EMAIL: bearnarualodge@hotmail.com
BUS NO: **69**

Panoramic view, peaceful rural setting yet only 30 mins from Airport/Dublin City. Adjacent to Forest walks, Horseriding, Golf. Off N7. 1.5km from Village.

B&B	3	Ensuite	£20/£22.50	€25.39/€20.57	Dinner	-
B&B	-	Standard	-	-	Partial Board	-
Single Rate			£30/£30	€38.09	Child reduction	-

Open: All Year Except Christmas

Rathcoole 3km

Mrs Mary Spillane
GREENACRES
**Kilteel Road, Rathcoole,
Co Dublin**

Rathcoole

TEL: **01 4580732**   FAX: **01 4580732**
BUS NO: **69**

Bungalow 2 miles from Rathcoole on Kilteel Rd, opposite Beech Park Golf Club. Riding Stables locally.

B&B	5	Ensuite	£19/£22	€24.13/€27.93	Dinner	-
B&B	1	Standard	£18/£20	€22.86/€25.39	Partial Board	-
Single Rate			£25/£30	€31.74/€38.09	Child reduction	-

Open: All Year Except Christmas

Bray 3km

Mrs Eileen McNamee
CORGLASS
**15 Shanganagh Grove,
Quinns Road, Shankill,
Co Dublin**

Shankill

TEL: **01 2820370**
BUS NO: **45, 45A, 84, DART**

Comfortable house, South Dublin. Quiet cul-de-sac beside Sea, Golf, Dun Laoghaire Ferry and scenic Wicklow. Off N11.

B&B	2	Ensuite	£19/£20	€24.13/€25.39	Dinner	-
B&B	1	Standard	£18/£20	€22.86/€25.39	Partial Board	-
Single Rate			£25/£30	€31.74/€38.09	Child reduction	-

Open: 1st February-30th November

TELEPHONE

- Operator assisted calls within Ireland   Dial 10
- International telephone operator   Dial 11818
- Directory Enquiries   Dial 11811

FOR TROUBLE-FREE TELEPHONE CALLS FROM PUBLIC PAY PHONES IT IS ADVISABLE TO PURCHASE A TELE-PHONE CALLCARD AVAILABLE IN POST OFFICES AND WHEREVER YOU SEE A CALLCARD SIGN.
TO DIAL IRELAND FROM ABROAD: Country Access Code + 353 + Area Code (omit first zero) + Local Number

Dublin Viking Adventure

Malahide Castle

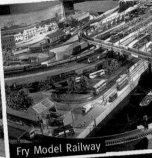
Fry Model Railway

Something to write home about

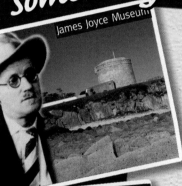
James Joyce Museum

Dear Sarah

We're having an amazing time, Dublin is even more than we expected. Our first stop was **Malahide Castle** - a magnificent place with splendid rooms and antique furnishings. In the grounds we found the **Fry Model Railway**, it's like a small boy's wildest dream and your father couldn't get enough of it. Back in town we went to **Dublin's Viking Adventure**. We didn't just meet live vikings, we smelt them as well! It was just like being in Dublin a thousand years ago.

The history here is something else, it's certainly the land of scholars (though we're not sure about the saints yet). We started our literary round-up at the **Shaw Birthplace** (where 'GBS' was born) - a real Victorian experience. Our next stop was the **Dublin Writers Museum**, in a gorgeous old Georgian house all gilt and plasterwork, full of literary memorabilia. It's astonishing how many great writers were Irish, and all with such fascinating lives! Of course the best of the lot has the **James Joyce Museum** all to himself in a great spot by the sea in Sandycove. I was so thrilled to be there where Ulysses begins that I made your father promise to read it - tonight!

We had planned to come home at the weekend but we're having such a great time we might just stay another week.

Bye for now,
Lots of love -
Mum & Dad

Shaw Birthplace

Dublin Writers Museum

For further information please contact:
Tel:+353 1 846 2184 Fax:+353 1 846 2537
enterprises@dublintourism.ie
www.visitdublin.com

Dublin Tourism Enterprises

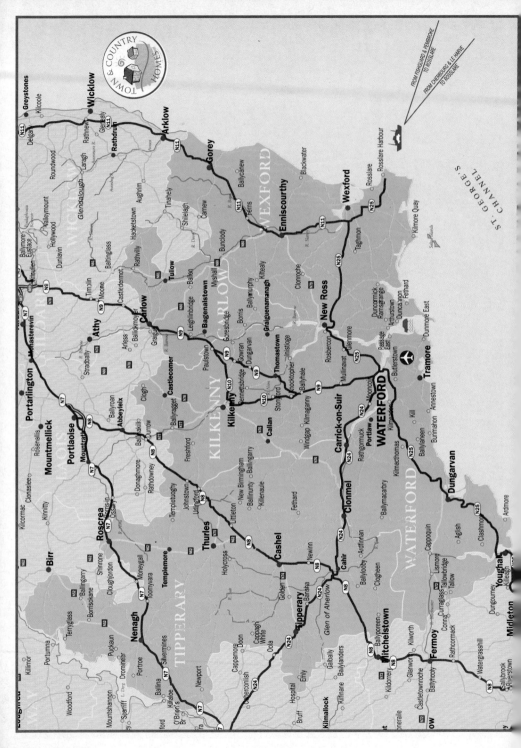

South East

The well-known term "Sunny South East" derives equally from the mildness of the climate and the warmth of the people in this lovely corner of Ireland.

There are five counties in the region - Carlow, Kilkenny, South Tipperary, Waterford and Wexford, and five major river systems - the Barrow, Blackwater, Nore, Slaney, and the Suir.

Their undulating valleys criss-cross the region as they meander peacefully through the fertile landscape which is dotted with more heritage sites than virtually any other tourism region in Ireland.

Cahir Castle

The South East is a mix of seaside and activity - the coastal resorts from Courtown to Ardmore backed by a mix of opportunities to golf, fish, horse-ride, walk and cycle. For the more leisurely, there are gardens in abundance and riverside villages where time still stands still!

Area Representatives

CARLOW
Mrs Therese O'Donovan, Cloonlara, Kilkenny Road, Carlow,
Co Carlow Tel: 0503 41863
KILKENNY
Mr Pat Banahan, Church View, Cuffesgrange, Callan Road, Kilkenny,
Co Kilkenny Tel: 056 29170 Fax: 056 29170
Mr John Cahill, Launard House, Maiden Hill, Kells Road, Kilkenny,
Co Kilkenny Tel: 056 51889 Fax: 056 71017
TIPPERARY
Ms Joan Brett Moloney, Tir Na Nog, Dualla, Cashel, Co Tipperary
Tel: 062 61350 Fax: 062 62411
Mrs Kathleen Healy, Rathnaleen House, Golf Club Road, Old Birr Road,
Nenagh, Co Tipperary Tel: 067 32508
WATERFORD
Mrs Phyllis McGovern, Ashleigh, Holy Cross, Cork Road, Waterford,
Co Waterford Tel: 051 375 171 Fax: 051 375 171
Mrs Margo Sleator, Rosebank House, Coast Road, Dungarvan,
Co Waterford Tel: 058 41561
WEXFORD
Mrs Ann Foley, Riversdale House, Lower William Street, New Ross,
Co Wexford Tel: 051 422515 Fax: 051 422800
Mrs Ann Sunderland, Hillside House, Tubberduff, Gorey, Co Wexford
Tel: 055 21726/22036 Fax: 055 22567

Tourist Information Offices

Waterford
The Granary
The Quay
Tel: 051 875823

Carlow
Bridewell Lane
Kennedy Ave.
Tel: 0503 31554

Clonmel
Sarsfield Street
Tel: 052 22960

Dungarvan
Towncentre
The Square
Tel: 058 41741

Gorey
Main Street
Tel: 055 21248

Kilkenny
Shee Alms House
Rose Inn Street
Tel: 056 51500

Rosslare
Kilcrane
Tel: 053 33232

Wexford
Crescent Quay
Tel: 053 23111

Situated in the great river valley of the Barrow and Slaney, famous for salmon and trout. This extensive waterways is renowned for cruising. Visit the Brown Hill Dolmen; Magnificent golf courses. Enjoy Cycling, Walking, Horse-riding or explore the countryside.

Bagenalstown 2km

Mairead Heffernan
ORCHARD GROVE
N9 Wells, Bagenalstown,
Co Carlow

Bagenalstown
TEL: **0503 22140**
EMAIL: orchardgrove@eircom.net
WEB: www.carlowtourism.com/orchard.html

Warm welcoming family home. Superb accommodation. Midway Carlow/Kilkenny. On N9. Breakfast Menu. Ideal base touring South East. Golf, Fishing, Walking close by. Children's play area.

B&B	3	Ensuite	£22/£24	€27.93/€30.47	Dinner £14
B&B	1	Standard	£19/£19	€24.13	Partial Board £235
Single Rate			£25.50	€32.38	Child reduction 50%

Open: 1st January-30th November

In Carlow

Pat & Noeleen Dunne
GREENLANE HOUSE
Dublin Road, Carlow Town,
Co Carlow

Carlow
TEL: **0503 42670**   FAX: **0503 30903**

Luxury town house situated N9. Ideal place to relax or use as base for exploring Historical and Architectural gems of East and South East Ireland. 1 hour from Dublin/Rosslare. Private car park.

B&B	6	Ensuite	£21/£25	€26.66/€31.74	Dinner -
B&B	1	Standard	£21	€26.66	Partial Board -
Single Rate			-		Child reduction -

Open: All Year Except Christmas

In Carlow

Mrs Mary Dwyer-Pender
BARROW LODGE
The Quay, Carlow Town,
Co Carlow

Carlow Town
TEL: **0503 41173**
EMAIL: georgepender@eircom.net

Always a popular choice with tourists due to its central riverside location. A short stroll from Carlow's excellent Restaurants, Pubs, Clubs etc.

B&B	5	Ensuite	£20/£22	€25.39/€27.93	Dinner -
B&B	-	Standard	-	-	Partial Board -
Single Rate			£25.50/£25.50	€32.38	Child reduction -

Open: February-November

Carlow 3km

Mrs Therese O'Donovan
CLOONLARA
Kilkenny Road,
Carlow, Co Carlow

Carlow
TEL: **0503 41863**
EMAIL: ntodonovan@oceanfree.net

Modern residence situated on N9 (Kilkenny Road). Landscaped gardens with River Barrow at rear. Fishing, Golf and Dolmen Hotel nearby.

B&B	3	Ensuite	£20/£22.50	€25.39/€28.57	Dinner -
B&B	-	Standard	-	-	Partial Board -
Single Rate			£28	€35.55	Child reduction 25%

Open: 1st April-31st October

In Carlow

Carmel & James O'Toole
BORLUM HOUSE
**Kilkenny Road, Carlow,
Co Carlow**

TEL: **0503 41747**

Built as a Coaching Inn in the early 1800's, Borelum House is set in secluded gardens where guests can enjoy Georgian charm & the comforts expected by discerning guests.

B&B	4	Ensuite	£19.50/£22.50	€24.76/€28.57	Dinner	-
B&B	-	Standard	-	-	Partial Board	-
Single Rate			-	-	Child reduction	25%

Open: 1st March-20th December

In Rathvilly

Mr E Tononi
THE WATERMILL
Rathvilly, Co Carlow

TEL: **0503 61392**

16th Century Watermill on river Slaney, N81 midway Dublin/Rosslare. Free fishing. Continental cuisine, Home grown vegetables. Italian, French spoken.

B&B	3	Ensuite	£20/£20	€25.39	Dinner	£14
B&B	-	Standard	£18/£18	€22.86	Partial Board	£220
Single Rate			£25/£27	€31.74/€34.29	Child reduction	-

Open: 1st February-30th November

Tullow 1km

Anne & Edward Byrne
LABURNUM LODGE
**Bunclody Road, Tullow,
Co Carlow**

TEL: **0503 51718**
EMAIL: lablodge@indigo.ie

Elegant Georgian house. Downstairs accommodation. Overlooking Mount Wolseley golf course. Altamount garden. Midway Dublin/Rosslare. Orthopaedic beds, Electric blankets, Hairdryers.

B&B	4	Ensuite	£20/£21	€25.39/€26.66	Dinner	-
B&B	-	Standard	-	-	Partial Board	-
Single Rate			£26	€33.01	Child reduction	25%

Open: All Year

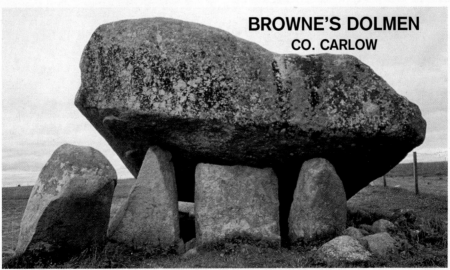

BROWNE'S DOLMEN
CO. CARLOW

Kilkenny - Medieval Capital of Ireland, its splendid castle as its centrepiece is home to Ireland's best known craft centre. County Kilkenny offers visitors an ideal base for touring the South East, a couple of days here will reward the discerning visitor.

In Bennettsbridge

Mrs Sheila Cole
NORELY THEYR
Barronsland, Bennettsbridge, Co Kilkenny

Bennettsbridge
TEL: **056 27496**

Luxurious, spacious bungalow, Rosslare/Kilkenny Road. Quiet, restful, friendly accommodation. Tea/coffee room facilities. Restaurant. Visa/Access Brochure available.

B&B	2	Ensuite	£19/£20	€24.13/€25.39	Dinner	£12.50
B&B	2	Standard	£17/£18	€21.59/€22.86	Partial Board	£185
Single Rate			£23.50/£25.50	€29.84/€32.38	Child reduction	25%

Open: All Year

Kilkenny 6km

Margaret Cullen
THE LOFT
Bennettsbridge, Co Kilkenny

Bennettsbridge
TEL: **056 27147**   FAX: **056 27147**

Large rooms. Buffet & Full Irish Breakfast. Walking distance Pubs, Restaurants, Mosse Jackson Pottery's. Close: Golf, Fishing, Pet Farm. Touring Base.

B&B	3	Ensuite	£19/£20	€24.13/€25.39	Dinner	-
B&B	2	Standard	£18/£19	€22.86/€24.13	Partial Board	-
Single Rate			£23.50/£25.50	€29.84/€32.38	Child reduction	25%

Open: All Year

Callan 6km

Mrs Mary Butler
HARTFORD HOUSE
Graigue, Kilmanagh, Co Kilkenny

Callan
TEL: **056 69215**
EMAIL: marypbutler@eircom.net

Comfortable home in tranquil location. Home baking. Traditional music. Close to woodland walk, Nature reserve and Ballykeeffe Amphitheatre on R695 Kilmanagh.

B&B	3	Ensuite	£19/£22	€24.13/€27.93	Dinner	-
B&B	-	Standard	-	-	Partial Board	-
Single Rate			£25.50	€32.38	Child reduction	33.3%

Open: 1st February-31st October

In Freshford

Mrs Priscilla Flanagan
POMADORA HOUSE
Clinstown Road, Freshford, Co Kilkenny

Freshford
TEL: **056 32256**

Home on Hunter Stud on R693 to Cashel. Gardens, Fishing, Horseriding, Hunting in Winter. Stabling for Horses, Dog Kennels, meals.

B&B	3	Ensuite	£20	€25.39	Dinner	£12.50
B&B	-	Standard	-	-	Partial Board	-
Single Rate			£26	€33.01	Child reduction	25%

Open: All Year

Freshford 3km

Mrs Bridget Nolan
CASTLE VIEW
**Balleen, Freshford,
Co Kilkenny**

Freshford

TEL: 056 32181

Bungalow, peaceful location, panoramic view of country side. Orthopaedic beds. 15 mins drive to Kilkenny City on route to Rock of Cashel.

B&B	2	Ensuite	£19/£19	€24.13	Dinner —
B&B	1	Standard	£17/£17	€21.59	Partial Board —
		Single Rate	£23.50	€29.84	Child reduction 50%

Open: All Year

Kilkenny City 4km

Pat & Monica Banahan
CHURCH VIEW
**Cuffesgrange, Callan Road,
Kilkenny, Co Kilkenny**

Kilkenny

TEL: 056 29170   FAX: 056 29170
EMAIL: churchview@eircom.net
WEB: www.churchviewkilkenny.com

Warm comfortable luxurious home on the main Clonmel/Cork/Killarney route, N76. Only 4 minutes drive from the medieval city of Kilkenny. Peaceful location. A warm welcome assured.

B&B	4	Ensuite	£19/£20	€24.13/€25.39	Dinner —
B&B	2	Standard	£17/£18	€21.59/€22.86	Partial Board —
		Single Rate	£33/£35	€41.90/€44.44	Child reduction 25%

Open: All Year

In Kilkenny

Ms Miriam Banville
BANVILLE'S B&B
**49 Walkin Street,
Kilkenny, Co Kilkenny**

Kilkenny

TEL: 056 70182
EMAIL: mbanville@eircom.net

Warm comfortable home near City Centre. Private parking. Rooms Ensuite, Multichannel TV, Hairdryers, Alarm Clocks.

B&B	4	Ensuite	£19	€24.13	Dinner —
B&B		Standard	-	-	Partial Board —
		Single Rate	£25.50	€32.38	Child reduction 50%

Open: All Year Except Christmas

In Kilkenny City

Mrs Breda Beirne
ANNA VILLA
**4 College Road, Kilkenny,
Co Kilkenny**

Kilkenny

TEL: 056 62680   FAX: 056 62680

Town house in residential area. Private parking. 5 mins walk to City Centre. Family run B&B.

B&B	4	Ensuite	£22/£25	€27.93/€31.74	Dinner —
B&B	-	Standard	-	-	Partial Board —
		Single Rate	£25.50/£28	€32.38/€35.55	Child reduction 25%

Open: 1st March-31st October

In Kilkenny City

Mrs Nuala Brennan
MELROSE HOUSE
**Circular Road, Kilkenny,
Co Kilkenny**

Kilkenny

TEL: 056 65289   FAX: 056 65289
EMAIL: brennanpn@eircom.net

Modern family run B&B. N76 opposite Hotel Kilkenny. 8 mins walk to City Centre. Private parking. Guest garden, quiet location. Multi channel TV, Hairdryers, Radio in rooms.

B&B	3	Ensuite	£20/£25	€25.39/€31.74	Dinner —
B&B	1	Standard	£19/£22	€24.13/€27.93	Partial Board —
		Single Rate	£25/£30	€31.74/€38.09	Child reduction —

Open: 4th January-20th December

In Kilkenny

Ms Angela Byrne
CELTIC HOUSE
18 Michael Street, Kilkenny City, Co Kilkenny

Kilkenny
TEL: 056 62249

Excellent location, walk everywhere. In the heart of Kilkenny City. Built 1998. Private lock-up. Parking. 4 min walk Bus and Train Station. Excellent standards. TV, Tea/Coffee facilities.

B&B	4	Ensuite	£22.50/£25	€28.57/€31.74	Dinner	-
B&B	-	Standard	-	-	Partial Board	-
Single Rate			£25.50/£30	€32.38/€38.09	Child reduction	50%

Open: All Year Except Christmas

Kilkenny 1km

Mrs Rita Byrne
MAJELLA
Waterford Road, Kilkenny, Co Kilkenny

Kilkenny
TEL: 056 21129

Modern comfortable bungalow on main Kilkenny/Waterford Road. Convenient to City and all amenities. TV lounge with Tea/Coffee. Breakfast choice.

B&B	4	Ensuite	£19/£20	€24.13/€25.39	Dinner	-
B&B	-	Standard	-	-	Partial Board	-
Single Rate			£26/£26	€33.01	Child reduction	50%

Open: 1st May-31st October

Kilkenny 1km

John & Sandra Cahill
LAUNARD HOUSE
Maiden Hill, Kells Road, Kilkenny, Co Kilkenny

Kilkenny
TEL: 056 51889   FAX: 056 71017
EMAIL: launardhouse@email.com
WEB: www.launardhouse.com

Luxurious purpose built home, overlooking ring road. TV, Hairdryers all bedrooms. Best Guides "Irish Experts" and Hidden Places recommended. "A Touch of Class".

B&B	5	Ensuite	£19/£25	€24.13/€31.74	Dinner	-
B&B	-	Standard	-	-	Partial Board	-
Single Rate					Child reduction	-

Open: 1st March-31st October

Kilkenny 1km

Mary Cahill
BREAGAGH VIEW
1 Maiden Hill, Kells Road, Kilkenny, Co Kilkenny

Kilkenny
TEL: 056 61353

Luxurious home & gardens. Purpose built B&B. Extra spacious bedrooms. TV/Hairdryers/Electric Blankets, close to Hotel, overlooking ring road.

B&B	4	Ensuite	£20/£25	€25.39/€31.74	Dinner	-
B&B	-	Standard	-	-	Partial Board	-
Single Rate					Child reduction	-

Open: 1st February-31st November

Kilkenny 2km

Mrs Marie Callan
LICHFIELD HOUSE
Bennettsbridge Rd, Kilkenny, Co Kilkenny

Kilkenny
TEL: 056 65232   FAX: 056 70614
EMAIL: lichfield2@eircom.net
WEB: www.lichfieldhouse.com

Georgian Country Home on 1 acre. Quiet location (R700). Kilkenny 5 mins drive. Breakfast menu. Spacious bedrooms with Tea/Coffee - T.V. Equestrian 1km.

B&B	3	Ensuite	£20/£20	€25.39	Dinner	-
B&B	-	Standard	-		Partial Board	-
Single Rate					Child reduction	-

Open: All Year Except Christmas

Mrs Joan Cody
OAKLAWN B & B
8 Oakwood, Kilfera,
Bennettsbridge Road, Kilkenny,
Co Kilkenny

Kilkenny
TEL: **056 61208**

Modern detached bungalow on the R700 main New Ross/Rosslare Road. Quiet area. Tastefully decorated. Set in mature lawns.

B&B	2	Ensuite	£19/£19	€24.13	Dinner	**£12.50**
B&B	1	Standard	£17/£17	€21.59	Partial Board	-
Single Rate		-	-		Child reduction	**50%**

Kilkenny 4km

Open: March-October

Mrs Mary Cody
OLINDA
Castle Road, Kilkenny,
Co Kilkenny

Kilkenny
TEL: **056 62964**

Comfortable house, quiet location. Large garden area for guests. Tea/Coffee facilities. Walking distance to Pubs and Restaurants. Private parking. Hairdryers, Alarm clocks.

B&B	2	Ensuite	£19	€24.13	Dinner	-
B&B	1	Standard	£17	€21.59	Partial Board	-
Single Rate		-	-		Child reduction	**25%**

In Kilkenny

Open: March-November

Mrs Vicky Comerford
PARK VILLA
Castlecomer Road,
Kilkenny, Co Kilkenny

Kilkenny
TEL: **056 61337**
EMAIL: vicpat@eircom.net
WEB: www.kilkennybedandbreakfast.com/parkvilla

Failte!! Modern family run home. Opposite Newpark Hotel. Prize gardens. Kettle always boiling. Warm welcome guaranteed. Rooms ensuite TV/Hairdryers. Convenient Bus, Rail, Pubs, Golf etc.

B&B	5	Ensuite	£20/£20	€25.39	Dinner	-
B&B	-	Standard	-	-	Partial Board	-
Single Rate			£25.50/£30	€32.38/€38.09	Child reduction	**25%**

In Kilkenny

Open: All Year

Ms Breda Dore
AVILA B&B
Freshford Road,
Kilkenny, Co Kilkenny

Kilkenny
TEL: **056 51072**
EMAIL: doreb@indigo.ie
WEB: www.avilakilkenny.com

Family run B&B within 15 minutes walk of City Centre. Located in quiet area. Warm welcome and best Irish breakfast guaranteed. Beside St. Lukes and Auteven Hospital R693.

B&B	3	Ensuite	£20/£25	€25.39/€31.74	Dinner	-
B&B	1	Standard	£18/£20	€22.86/€25.39	Partial Board	-
Single Rate		-	-		Child reduction	**25%**

Kilkenny City 1km

Open: All Year Except Christmas

Mrs Kitty Dowling
GLEN VIEW
Castlecomer Rd, Kilkenny,
Co Kilkenny

Kilkenny
TEL: **056 62065**   FAX: **056 62065**
EMAIL: glenvew@iol.ie

Cead Mile Failte chugat o ar dteach. Warm friendly welcome assured on N78. Medieval City, Castle, Theatre within walking distance. Adjacent Newpark Hotel and Golf Club.

B&B	3	Ensuite	£19/£22	€24.13/€27.93	Dinner	-
B&B	-	Standard	-	-	Partial Board	-
Single Rate		-	-		Child reduction	-

Kilkenny 1km

Open: 31st January-30th November

139

Mrs Margaret Drennan
HILLGROVE
Warrington, Bennettsbridge Road,
Kilkenny, Co Kilkenny

Kilkenny
TEL: 056 51453/22890 FAX: 056 51453
EMAIL: hillgrove@esatclear.ie
WEB: http://homepage.eircom.net/~hillgrove

National Breakfast Award-Winning Country Home, furnished with antiques, on R700. Orthopaedic beds, Electric blankets. Recommended Frommer, Dillard/Causin, Denver Post.

B&B	5	Ensuite	£20/£21	€25.39/€26.66	Dinner	-
B&B	-	Standard	-	-	Partial Board	-
Single Rate			£27/£27	€34.29	Child reduction	50%

Kilkenny 2km

Open: February-November

Mrs Helen Dunning
DUNBOY
10 Parkview Drive, off Freshford
Road, Kilkenny City,
Co Kilkenny

Kilkenny
TEL: 056 61460   FAX: 056 61460
EMAIL: dunboy@eircom.net
WEB: www.dunboy.com

Welcoming home in quiet cul-de-sac. Le Routard Recommended. Close to City Centre. Take Freshford road R693, turn left at second roundabout, then right.

B&B	4	Ensuite	£19/£22	€24.13/€27.93	Dinner	-
B&B	-	Standard	-	-	Partial Board	-
Single Rate					Child reduction	-

Kilkenny 1km

Open: February-December

Mrs Ella Dunphy
AUBURN LODGE
Warrington,
Bennettsbridge Road, Kilkenny,
Co Kilkenny

Kilkenny
TEL: 056 65119   FAX: 056 70008
EMAIL: patdunphy@tinet.ie

AA Recommended. Country home beside Riding School. Orthopaedic beds, electric blankets, TV, Hairdryers. Quiet area on R700. Car parking. Tennis Court.

B&B	3	Ensuite	£19/£21.50	€24.13/€27.30	Dinner	-
B&B	2	Standard	£17/£19.50	€21.59/€24.76	Partial Board	-
Single Rate			£23.50/£30	€29.84/€38.09	Child reduction	-

Kilkenny 2km

Open: 20th January-20th December

Mrs Bernadette Egan
KNOCKAVON HOUSE
Dublin/Carlow Road, Kilkenny,
Co Kilkenny

Kilkenny
TEL: 056 64294

Luxurious town house accommodation. Beside city centre. 3 Minutes to Bus and Station, Pubs, Restaurants, Theatre and Golf Club.

B&B	5	Ensuite	£19/£22	€24.13/€27.93	Dinner	-
B&B	-	Standard	-	-	Partial Board	-
Single Rate			£25.50	€32.38	Child reduction	25%

In Kilkenny City

Open: All Year

Mrs Oonagh Egan Twomey
CARRAIG RUA
Dublin Rd, Kilkenny City,
Co Kilkenny

Kilkenny City
TEL: 056 22929

Elegant two storey city house on N10. 4 mins walk to bus and rail station. Close to City Centre, Kilkenny Castle, Langtons, Hotels and Restaurants.

B&B	5	Ensuite	£19/£20	€24.13/€25.39	Dinner	-
B&B	1	Standard	£17	€21.59	Partial Board	-
Single Rate			£26/£30	€33.01/€38.09	Child reduction	25%

In Kilkenny City

Open: 5th January-15th December

Agnes & Frank Fennelly
SAN JOSE
**Baun, Castlecomer Rd,
Kilkenny, Co Kilkenny**

Kilkenny
Tel: **056 21198**

Elegant villa style residence, antique furnished. Large mature Gardens. 2km north of Newpark Hotel on N77. Breakfast menu. Tea/Coffee, Hairdryers, Orthopaedic beds, Electric blankets.

B&B	2	Ensuite	£20/£22	€25.39/€27.93	Dinner	-
B&B	1	Standard	£17/£19	€21.59/€24.13	Partial Board	-
Single Rate			£25/£30	€31.74/€38.09	Child reduction	25%

Kilkenny 2km

Open: 1st February-30th November

Mrs Marie Finnegan
ARDEE HOUSE
**Springmount, Waterford Road,
Kilkenny, Co Kilkenny**

Kilkenny
Tel: **056 62699**   Fax: **056 62699**
Email: ptf@indigo.ie
Web: ardeehouse.com

Town house N10 beside Springhill Court Hotel. Breakfast menu. Guests Lounge. Bedrooms TV, Hairdryers, Radio/Alarm Clocks. Reduction low season.

B&B	5	Ensuite	£20/£20	€25.39	Dinner	-
B&B	1	Standard	£20/£20	€25.39	Partial Board	-
Single Rate			-	-	Child reduction	-

Kilkenny 2km

Open: All Year Except Christmas

Mrs Joan Flanagan
BURWOOD
**Waterford Road, Kilkenny,
Co Kilkenny**

Kilkenny
Tel: **056 62266**

Modern bungalow on Kilkenny/Waterford Road. Enclosed car-park. "300 Best B & B's" Recommended. Convenient to City Centre.

B&B	3	Ensuite	£19/£20	€24.13/€25.39	Dinner	-
B&B	1	Standard	£17/£19	€21.59/€24.13	Partial Board	-
Single Rate			£25	€31.74	Child reduction	-

Kilkenny 1km

Open: May-October

Pauline Flannery
ASHLEIGH
**Waterford Rd, Kilkenny,
Co Kilkenny**

Kilkenny
Tel: **056 22809**

Bungalow main Waterford Rd (N10). Convenient Hotels, City. Breakfast menu. Tea/Coffee available. Reduction low season. Frommer Guide, Berkeley Europe recommended.

B&B	2	Ensuite	£19/£21	€24.13/€26.66	Dinner	-
B&B	1	Standard	£17/£19	€21.59/€24.13	Partial Board	-
Single Rate			£24/£26	€30.47/€33.01	Child reduction	25%

Kilkenny 1km

Open: All Year Except Christmas

Mrs Breda Hennessy
SILVER SPRINGS
**Waterford Road, Kilkenny,
Co Kilkenny**

Kilkenny
Tel: **056 62513**

Beautiful dormer bungalow on main Kilkenny/Waterford road (N10). Convenient to Hotels, Castle, City, Golf. Breakfast menu, Tea/Coffee making facilities.

B&B	5	Ensuite	£19/£20	€24.13/€25.39	Dinner	-
B&B	1	Standard	£18/£19	€22.86/€24.13	Partial Board	-
Single Rate			-	-	Child reduction	-

Kilkenny City 1km

Open: All Year Except Christmas

Kilkenny

Michael Hennessy
SHILLOGER HOUSE
Callan Road (N76), Kilkenny,
Co Kilkenny

Kilkenny
TEL: **056 63249**   FAX: **056 64865**
EMAIL: shillogherhouse@tinet.ie
WEB: www.shillogherhouse.com

Luxurious home. All bedrooms Tea/Coffee makers, TV, Phones. Garden Conservatory. Susan Causin recommended. RAC AA ♦♦♦♦. Breakfast menu. Ideal touring base.

B&B	6	Ensuite	£20/£25	€25.39/€31.74	Dinner	-
B&B	-	Standard	-	-	Partial Board	-
Single Rate			£25.50/£40	€32.38/€50.79	Child reduction	33.3%

Open: All Year

Mrs Teresa Holden
AUBURNDALE
Springmount, Waterford Rd,
Kilkenny, Co Kilkenny

Kilkenny
TEL: **056 62716**   FAX: **056 71238**
EMAIL: auburndale@eircom.net

On N10 adjacent Springhill Hotel. Bedrooms incl. Hairdryers, TV. Tea/Coffee in the reading lounge. Ideal touring base for the South East. Hard to leave, easy to find.

B&B	5	Ensuite	£20/£25	€25.39/€31.74	Dinner	-
B&B	-	Standard	-	-	Partial Board	-
Single Rate			-		Child reduction	-

Kilkenny 1km

Open: 15th January-20th December

Kilkenny 1km

Liam & Brigid Holohan
ALCANTRA
Maidenhill, Kells Road,
Kilkenny, Co Kilkenny

Kilkenny
TEL: **056 61058**   FAX: **056 61058**
EMAIL: alcantra@tinet.ie
WEB: homepage.eircom.net/~alcantra

Spacious comfortable home with guest lounge and conservatory, located on R697. Exactly 1km from City Centre. Numerous recommendations. AA ♦♦♦♦.

B&B	4	Ensuite	£19/£22	€24.13/€27.93	Dinner	-
B&B	-	Standard	-	-	Partial Board	-
Single Rate			£25.50/£27	€32.38/€34.29	Child reduction	-

Open: 1st January-15th December

Kilkenny 7km

Aileen Kennedy
NEWLANDS COUNTRY HOUSE
Seven Houses (off N10)
Danesfort, Kilkenny,
Co Kilkenny

Kilkenny
TEL: **056 29111**   FAX: **056 29171**
EMAIL: newlands@indigo.ie

Come enjoy an oasis, AA ♦♦♦♦♦ luxury home. Firm king & queen beds, gourmet food, varied menus, spa baths (supp). Major awards ie. "Kilkenny for Excellence", "Customer Care".

B&B	6	Ensuite	£25/£30	€31.74/€38.09	Dinner	£25
B&B	-	Standard	-	-	Partial Board	-
Single Rate			-		Child reduction	-

Open: 1st January-20th December

Kilkenny 1km

Mrs Mary Langton-Hennessy
VIEWMOUNT HOUSE
Castlecomer Road, Kilkenny City
Co Kilkenny

Kilkenny
TEL: **056 62447**   FAX: **056 62447**

Luxurious home situated between Newpark Hotel and Kilkenny Golf Club on N78. Breakfast menu. Tea/Coffee making facilities. Le Routard recommended.

B&B	6	Ensuite	£20/£22	€25.39/€27.93	Dinner	-
B&B	-	Standard	-	-	Partial Board	-
Single Rate			-		Child reduction	-

Open: 1st January-20th December

Mrs Mary Lawlor
RODINI
Waterford Road (R910 off N10), Kilkenny, Co Kilkenny

Kilkenny City
TEL: **056 21822/70836**
EMAIL: rodini@eircom.net

Comfortable home. Convenient Hotels, City Centre, Castle and other amenities. Family room. Electric blankets, Hairdryers available. Ideal base to tour the beautiful historic South East.

				Dinner	-
B&B	5	Ensuite	£19/£21	€24.13/€26.66	
B&B	-	Standard			Partial Board	-
Single Rate			£25.50/£26	€32.38/€33.01	Child reduction	50%

Kilkenny 1km

Open: All Year

Rosie & Martin Mahony
ASHGROVE B&B
Dunglen Court, Castlecomer Road, Kilkenny, Co Kilkenny

Kilkenny
TEL: **056 22604**   FAX: **056 56935**

Family run home close to Golf club, Caves, Fishing. Convenient to Newpark Hotel. Private parking.

					Dinner	-
B&B	2	Ensuite	£20/£25	€25.39/€31.74		
B&B	1	Standard	£18/£24	€22.86/€30.47	Partial Board	-
Single Rate			£23.50/£23.50	€29.84	Child reduction	-

Kilkenny 2km

Open: All Year Except Christmas

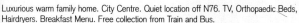

Bill & Helen McEvoy
BREFFNI
Waterford Road, Kilkenny, Co Kilkenny

Kilkenny
TEL: **056 63344**

Detached Dormer Bungalow. Easy access to Hotels, Castle, Golf Clubs, Fishing, Shops. Tea/Coffee available. Reduction low season. Kilkenny 1km.

					Dinner	-
B&B	3	Ensuite	£19/£21	€24.13/€26.66		
B&B	-	Standard	-	-	Partial Board	-
Single Rate			-	-	Child reduction	50%

Kilkenny 1km

Open: 1st February-20th December

Brian & Betty McHenry
THE LAURELS
College Road, Kilkenny, Co Kilkenny

Kilkenny
TEL: **056 61501**   FAX: **056 71334**
EMAIL: laurels@eircom.net
WEB: thelaurelskilkenny.com

Luxurious warm family home. City Centre. Quiet location off N76. TV, Orthopaedic Beds, Hairdryers. Breakfast Menu. Free collection from Train and Bus.

					Dinner	-
B&B	4	Ensuite	£18/£25	€22.86/€31.74		
B&B	-	Standard	-	-	Partial Board	-
Single Rate			-	-	Child reduction	10%

In Kilkenny

Open: All Year

Ms Katherine Molloy
MENA HOUSE
Castlecomer Road (N78), Kilkenny, Co Kilkenny

Kilkenny
TEL: **056 65362**

Antique furnished luxurious home. Prize gardens. TV all rooms. Tea making facilities. Breakfast choice, homemade preserves. Adjacent New Park Hotel, Golf, Swimming, Horse-riding.

					Dinner	-
B&B	7	Ensuite	£19/£20	€24.13/€25.39		
B&B	2	Standard	£17/£18	€21.59/€22.86	Partial Board	-
Single Rate			£23.50/£25.50	€29.84/€32.38	Child reduction	50%

In Kilkenny City

Open: All Year Except Christmas

Kilkenny City 2km

Mrs Maud Morrissey
BEECH LODGE B&B
Bennettsbridge Road,
Kilkenny, Co Kilkenny

Kilkenny
TEL: 056 64083

Warm friendly home, quiet location on main New Ross/Rosslare road. Picturesque garden. Spacious rooms. Orthopaedic beds, Electric blankets.

				Dinner	-
B&B	4	Ensuite	£19/£20 €24.13/€25.39	Partial Board	-
B&B	-	Standard	-	Child reduction	33.3%
Single Rate			£23.50/£25.50 €29.84/€32.38		

Open: 1st January-30th November

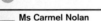

Kilkenny 2km

Ms Carmel Nolan
THE RISE
Dunmore, Kilkenny,
Co Kilkenny

Kilkenny
TEL: 056 64534
EMAIL: carmeljn@gofree.indigo.ie

A warm welcome awaits our guests at our newly renovated 19th Century family farm home. Tea/Coffee on arrival. Stroll through our fields at your leisure etc.

				Dinner	-
B&B	2	Ensuite	£19/£20 €24.13/€25.39	Partial Board	-
B&B	2	Standard	£17/£20 €21.59/€25.39	Child reduction	33.3%
Single Rate			£23.50/£23.50 €29.84		

Open: All Year

Kilkenny City 1km

Mrs Nora O'Connor
SUNDOWN
Freshford Rd, Kilkenny,
Co Kilkenny

Kilkenny City
TEL: 056 21816

Welcoming friendly home situated on Freshford road R693. Walking distance City Centre. Large car park. TV, Radio, Hairdryers all rooms. New Greyhound Stadium and Hospital nearby.

				Dinner	-
B&B	4	Ensuite	£20/£22.50 €25.39/€28.57	Partial Board	-
B&B	1	Standard	£20 €25.39	Child reduction	33.3%
Single Rate			£25 €31.74		

Open: 1st February-20th December

Kilkenny 1km

Mrs Teresa O'Neill
HILLCREST
College Gardens, Callan Rd,
Kilkenny, Co Kilkenny

Kilkenny
TEL: 056 65560
EMAIL: teresaoneill@ireland.com

Family home in quiet cul-de-sac off Callan/Cork Rd N76. Hotel Kilkenny 300m. Walking distance of City. Orthopaedic beds, Electric blankets, Hairdryers.

				Dinner	-
B&B	2	Ensuite	£19/£21 €24.13/€26.66	Partial Board	-
B&B	2	Standard	£17/£18 €21.59/€22.86	Child reduction	25%
Single Rate			£23.50/£25 €29.84/€31.74		

Open: March-November

In Kilkenny

Josephine O'Reilly
CARRIGLEA
Archers Avenue, Castle Road,
Kilkenny, Co Kilkenny

Kilkenny City
TEL: 056 61629
EMAIL: archers@iol.ie

Spacious elegant home. Five minutes walk to City Centre, Pubs, Restaurants etc. Situated in quiet residential cul-de-sac. 200m past Castle on right.

				Dinner	-
B&B	2	Ensuite	£19/£20 €24.13/€25.39	Partial Board	-
B&B	1	Standard	£18/£18 €22.86	Child reduction	33.3%
Single Rate			£25.50/£25.50 €32.38		

Open: 1st February-30th November

Mrs Ann Peters
DERDIMUS B&B
Callan Road N76, Kilkenny,
Co Kilkenny

Kilkenny
TEL: **056 65782**   FAX: **056 65782**
EMAIL: apeters@esatclear.ie

First class accommodation. Friendly luxurious (award winning), peaceful location. Garden/Patio. Cork/Clonmel (N76). Convenient Hotel Kilkenny. Low season reduction. Ideal touring South East.

B&B	2	Ensuite	£20/£20	€25.39	Dinner	-
B&B	1	Standard	£20/£20	€25.39	Partial Board	-
Single Rate			-	-	Child reduction	-

Kilkenny 3km   **Open:** January-20th December

Mrs V Rothwell
DUNROMIN
Dublin Rd, Kilkenny,
Co Kilkenny

Kilkenny
TEL: **056 61387**   FAX: **056 70736**
EMAIL: valtom@oceanfree.net

A warm welcome to our 19th Century family home (on Dublin road N10). Walking distance Medieval City Centre. Golf, Horse Riding nearby. Kettle always boiling.

B&B	4	Ensuite	£20/£21	€25.39/€26.66	Dinner	-
B&B	-	Standard	-	-	Partial Board	-
Single Rate			£25.50	€32.38	Child reduction	-

In Kilkenny City   **Open:** 1st March-20th December

Kathleen Ryan
THE MEADOWS
6 Greenfields Road
Bishops Meadows, Kilkenny City,
Co Kilkenny

Kilkenny
TEL: **056 21649**   FAX: **056 21649**
EMAIL: kryan@indigo.ie
WEB: www.themeadows.bizland.com

Quiet area off R693. Home baking. Menu. Walking distance City. Orthopaedic beds, Electric blankets, Hairdryer, Ironing facilities in room. Itinerary planned.

B&B	2	Ensuite	£19/£20	€24.13/€25.39	Dinner	-
B&B	1	Standard	-	-	Partial Board	-
Single Rate			£23.50/£25	€29.84/€31.74	Child reduction	25%

Kilkenny City 1km   **Open:** 1st January-12th December

Mrs Helen Sheehan
CNOC MHUIRE
Castle Road, Kilkenny,
Co Kilkenny

Kilkenny
TEL: **056 62161**   FAX: **056 62161**
EMAIL: cnocmhuire@eircom.net
WEB: www.cnocmhuire.com

Warm comfortable home off Rosslare Road (R700). Quiet location. Orthopaedic beds, electric blankets. Hairdryers. Parking. 10 minute walk to centre and Castle.

B&B	4	Ensuite	£20/£21	€25.39/€26.66	Dinner	-
B&B	-	Standard	-	-	Partial Board	-
Single Rate			£25.50/£30	€32.38/€38.09	Child reduction	50%

Kilkenny City 1km   **Open:** 15th January-15th December

Ms Ruby Sherwood
ASHBURY LODGE
Castlecomer Road,
Kilkenny, Co Kilkenny

Kilkenny City
TEL: **056 21572**   FAX: **056 22892**
EMAIL: rubys@esatclear.ie

Secluded home on elevated site surrounded by mature gardens. Warm friendly atmosphere near Newpark Hotel on N77. Car park. Spacious rooms, TV, Hairdryer, Visa.

B&B	3	Ensuite	£20/£20	€25.39	Dinner	-
B&B	1	Standard	£19/£19	€24.13	Partial Board	-
Single Rate			£25/£25	€31.74	Child reduction	50%

Kilkenny 2km   **Open:** All Year Except Christmas

In Kilkenny City

Jim & Joan Spratt
CHAPLINS
Castlecomer Road,
Kilkenny, Co Kilkenny

Kilkenny
TEL: 056 52236
EMAIL: chaplins@eircom.net

Spacious Town house N77. All rooms equipped with Multi-Channel TV. Hairdryers, Tea/Coffee. RAC selected AA ♦♦♦.

B&B	6	Ensuite	£20/£25	€25.39/€31.74	Dinner		-
B&B	-	Standard	-	-	Partial Board		-
Single Rate			-	-	Child reduction		-

Open: All Year Except Christmas

Kilkenny 2km

Mrs Mary Trant
BROOKFIELD
Castlecomer Road, Kilkenny,
Co Kilkenny

Kilkenny
TEL: 056 65629
EMAIL: trants@esatclear.ie

Modern bungalow 2km north of Newpark Hotel N77. Mature gardens, Quiet location. Tea on arrival. Wheelchair access. Orthopaedic beds, Electric blankets.

B&B	2	Ensuite	£19/£19	€24.13	Dinner	-
B&B	2	Standard	£17/£17	€21.59	Partial Board	-
Single Rate			£23.50/£25.50	€29.84/€32.38	Child reduction	50%

Open: January-15th December

Kilkenny 3km

Mrs Maria Witherow
WHITE OAKS
Tennypark, Callan Road N76,
Kilkenny, Co Kilkenny

Kilkenny
TEL: 056 63295
EMAIL: whiteoaks@eircom.net

Modern home situated on N76 Clonmel/Cork road. Set in peaceful landscaped gardens. Secure parking. Breakfast choice. Tea & Coffee making facilities.

B&B	3	Ensuite	£20/£22	€25.39/€27.93	Dinner	-
B&B	1	Standard	£18/£20	€22.86/€25.39	Partial Board	-
Single Rate			-	-	Child reduction	25%

Open: 1st March-31st October

In Kilkenny City

Mary & Eamonn Wogan
TIR NA NOG
Greenhill (off Castlecomer Rd),
Kilkenny, Co Kilkenny

Kilkenny City
TEL: 056 65250/62345 FAX: 056 63491
EMAIL: emw@iol.ie
WEB: homepages.iol.ie/~emw

Luxurious ensuite rooms, incl. TV/Radio, Trouserpress/Iron, Hairdryer, Breakfast menu. Convenient to Bus/Rail Station and City Centre.

B&B	4	Ensuite	£20/£22	€25.39/€27.93	Dinner	-
B&B	-	Standard	-	-	Partial Board	-
Single Rate			£25.50/£28	€32.38/€35.55	Child reduction	-

Open: All Year

Thomastown

Mrs Helen Blanchfield
ABBEY HOUSE
Jerpoint Abbey,
Thomastown, Co Kilkenny

Thomastown
TEL: 056 24166   FAX: 056 24192

Period house C1750. Standing on the banks of the little Arrigle River opposite Jerpoint Abbey. Halfway Waterford & Kilkenny. Rosslare 1hr. Mount Juliet 6 mins. Dublin 2 hrs. AA ♦♦♦♦.

B&B	7	Ensuite	£20/£30	€25.39/€38.09	Dinner	-
B&B	-	Standard	-	-	Partial Board	-
Single Rate			£25.50/£40	€32.38/€50.79	Child reduction	25%

Open: 1st January-23th December

Mrs Julie Doyle
CARRICKMOURNE HOUSE
New Ross Road,
Thomastown, Co Kilkenny

Thomastown
Tel: **056 24124**   Fax: **056 24124**

Elevated site, surrounded by scenic views peaceful country setting. Convenient Jerpoint Abbey, Mount Juliet Golf, Fishing, Restaurants. AA ♦♦♦. 2km off New Ross Rd.

B&B	5	Ensuite	£20/£25	€25.39/€31.74	Dinner	-
B&B	-	Standard	-	-	Partial Board	-
Single Rate			£25.50/£30	€32.38/€38.09	Child reduction	25%

Thomastown 3km

Ⓥ ⌂ 🅢 🅟 ⊗ ✂ ▢ ☕ ✈ 🏠 ⬥ ↝ ♪ ᵣ

Open: January-November

Public Holidays for 2001

New Years Day	-	Monday 1st January	(R.of Ire. & N. Ire.)
Bank Holiday	-	Monday 19th March	(R.of Ire. & N. Ire.)
Good Friday	-	Friday 13th April	(R.of Ire. & N. Ire.)
Easter Monday	-	Monday 16th April	(R.of Ire. & N. Ire.)
May Day Holiday	-	Monday 7th May	(R.of Ire. & N. Ire.)
Bank Holiday	-	Monday 28th May	(N.Ire.)
June Holiday	-	Monday 4th June	(R.of Ire)
Orangeman's Day	-	Thursday 12th July	(N.Ire.)
August Holiday	-	Monday 6th August	(R.of Ire)
Bank Holiday	-	Monday 27th August	(N.Ire.)
October Holiday	-	Monday 29th October	(R.of Ire)
Christmas Day	-	Tuesday 25th December	(R.of Ire. & N. Ire.)
St Stephen's Day	-	Wednesday 26th December	(R.of Ire. & N. Ire.)

The loveliest and most scenic inland county in Ireland. Known as the Golden Vale county, lends itself to a longer stopover with its rolling plains and mountains. The River Suir transverses its entire length. Visit - Abbeys, Castles, and historic moats. Pony Trekking, Golf, Fishing, Greyhound and Horse racing. Hill Walking, Birdwatching. Many walking tours available.

Carmen & Wolfgang Rodder
DANCER COTTAGE
Curraghmore,
Borrisokane, Co Tipperary

Borrisokane
Tel: **067 27414**   Fax: **067 27414**
Email: dcr@eircom.net
Web: dancercottage.cjb.net

Comfortable house, quiet rural location. Large garden for guests. Fresh seasonal home cooking/baking, children welcome, Bicycles. Golf, Lough Derg nearby.

B&B	4	Ensuite	£19/£21	€24.13/€26.66	Dinner	£17
B&B	-	Standard		-	Partial Board	-
Single Rate			£25.50	€32.38	Child reduction	33.3%

Borrisokane 1.9km   **Open:** February-November

Butler Family
CARRIGEEN CASTLE
Cahir,
Co Tipperary

Cahir
Tel: **052 41370**   Fax: **052 41370**

Manor of Cahir. Historic (prison) home. Warm, comfortable, spacious, overlooking Town. Walled garden. Walking distance Bus/Train. Ideal touring base.

B&B	3	Ensuite	£22/£22	€27.93	Dinner	-
B&B	4	Standard	£18/£18	€22.86	Partial Board	-
Single Rate			£28/£28	€35.55	Child reduction	-

Cahir 1km   **Open:** 2nd January-15th December

Ms Kay Byrne
ARBUTUS
Tipperary Road, Cahir,
Co Tipperary

Cahir
Tel: **052 41617**

Comfortable family home. Spacious en-suite bedrooms with TV, Hairdryers. Tea/Coffee making facilities. View the Galtee mountains on N24 off N8 roundabout.

B&B	2	Ensuite	£19/£20	€24.13/€25.39	Dinner	-
B&B	1	Standard	£17/£17.50	€21.59/€22.22	Partial Board	-
Single Rate			£25/£26	€31.74/€33.01	Child reduction	25%

Cahir 1km   **Open:** 1st May-30th October

Mrs Anne Devereaux
SPRINGHILL
Cashel Road (N8)
Cahir, Co Tipperary

Cahir
Tel: **052 41754**   Fax: **052 41754**

Spacious country home overlooking farmlands on the outskirts of Cahir on N8. Ideal touring centre. Tea/Coffee facilities, Golf, Horse riding, Walks nearby.

B&B	3	Ensuite	£19/£19	€24.13	Dinner	-
B&B	-	Standard	-		Partial Board	-
Single Rate			£25.50/£25.50	€32.38	Child reduction	25%

Cahir 3.5km   **Open:** 1st April-30th October

Mrs Jo Doyle
KILLAUN
Clonmel Road, Cahir,
Co Tipperary

Cahir
Tel: **052 41780**

Bungalow, bedrooms overlooking spacious gardens, 5 mins walk from town, Bus and Train Station. Golf, Fishing and Horseriding closeby. On N24

B&B	3	Ensuite	£19/£19	€24.13	Dinner	-
B&B	1	Standard	£17/£17	€21.59	Partial Board	-
Single Rate			£23.50/£25.50	€29.84/€32.38	Child reduction	25%

In Cahir

Open: All Year Except Christmas

Mrs Marian Duffy
THE HOMESTEAD
Mitchelstown Road, Cahir,
Co Tipperary

Cahir
Tel: **052 42043**

Spacious modern bungalow near Town Centre, TV bedrooms; Large private car park; Families welcome; Ideal Touring Base; Tea/Coffee on arrival.

B&B	4	Ensuite	£19	€24.13	Dinner	-
B&B	-	Standard	-	-	Partial Board	-
Single Rate			£25.50	€32.38	Child reduction	25%

In Cahir

Open: 2nd January-30th November

Mrs Mary English
BROOKFIELD HOUSE
Old Cashel Road,
Cahir, Co Tipperary

Cahir
Tel: **052 41936**

Comfortable homely residence. All rooms have TV., Hairdryers, Tea/Coffee making facilities. Private parking. Conservatory and Guest Lounge.

B&B	2	Ensuite	£19	€24.13	Dinner	-
B&B	1	Standard	£17.50	€22.22	Partial Board	-
Single Rate			£24/£25.50	€30.47/€32.38	Child reduction	25%

Cahir 1km

Open: 1st April-30th September

Mrs Breda Fitzgerald
ASHLING
Cashel Road, Cahir,
Co Tipperary

Cahir
Tel: **052 41601**

Ground level family home, smoke free. Antique furnishing. Prize winning gardens, electric blankets, Tea/Coffee making facilities. Country Inns recommended.

B&B	3	Ensuite	£20/£20	€25.39	Dinner	-
B&B	1	Standard	-	-	Partial Board	-
Single Rate			£30/£30	€38.09	Child reduction	25%

Cahir 1km

Open: All Year

Margaret Neville
HOLLYMOUNT HOUSE
Upper Cahir Abbey, Cahir,
Co Tipperary

Cahir
Tel: **052 42888**

Get away from it all! wind your way to the top of the mountain road, for peace and tranquillity. Only 5 minutes drive from town. Spectacular view. Quiet.

B&B	2	Ensuite	£19	€24.13	Dinner	-
B&B	2	Standard	£17	€21.59	Partial Board	-
Single Rate			£23.50/£25.50	€29.84/€32.38	Child reduction	25%

Cahir 2km

Open: All Year

In Cahir

Mrs Hannah-Mai O'Connor
SILVER ACRE
Clonmel Road, Cahir,
Co Tipperary

Cahir
TEL: 052 41737

Modern bungalow, Tourism award winner, in quiet cul-de-sac. Private parking. Bus, Train, Fishing, Golf nearby. Tea and Coffee facilities.

					Dinner	-
B&B	3	Ensuite	£19/£19	€24.13	Dinner	-
B&B	1	Standard	£17.50/£18	€22.22/€22.86	Partial Board	-
Single Rate			£25/£25	€31.74	Child reduction	-

Open: 1st January-10th December

In Cahir

Liam and Patricia Roche
TINSLEY HOUSE
The Square, Cahir,
Co Tipperary

Cahir
TEL: 052 41947   FAX: 052 41947

19th Century Town House. 3 Storey house with bedrooms upstairs. Separate sitting room for guests with Tea/Coffee making facilities. Period decor and Roof Garden accessible to guests.

					Dinner	-
B&B	2	Ensuite	£19/£20	€24.13/€25.39	Dinner	-
B&B	1	Standard	£18/£19	€22.86/€24.13	Partial Board	-
Single Rate			£25/£27	€31.74/€34.29	Child reduction	25%

Open: 1st February-30th November

Carrick-on-Suir 11km

Mrs Ann Coady
THE GRAND INN
Nine-Mile-House,
Carrick-On-Suir, Co Tipperary

Carrick-On-Suir
TEL: 051 647035   FAX: 051 647035

Former 17th century Bianconi Inn Family Home. In scenic Valley of Slievenamon. Spacious gardens. Antique furnishings. On Clonmel/Kilkenny Road N76.

					Dinner	-
B&B	3	Ensuite	£20	€25.39	Dinner	-
B&B	2	Standard	£18	€22.86	Partial Board	-
Single Rate			£24	€30.47	Child reduction	25%

Open: All Year

In Cashel Town

Anna & Patrick Hayes
ROCKVILLE HOUSE
Cashel, Co Tipperary

Cashel
TEL: 062 61760

Located between 12th Century Abbey and the famous Royal Historic Castle. Recommended family home, relaxing garden. Local amenities. Secure car park.

					Dinner	-
B&B	6	Ensuite	£19	€24.13	Dinner	-
B&B	-	Standard	-	-	Partial Board	-
Single Rate			£25.50	€32.38	Child reduction	25%

Open: All Year

Cashel 7km

Mrs Mary Hickey
GORT-NA-CLOC
Ardmayle, Cashel,
Co Tipperary

Cashel
TEL: 0504 42362   FAX: 0504 42002
EMAIL: gortnaclocbandb@hotmail.com

Comfortable home set in peaceful countryside. Situated L185 Ardmayle road, off N8. Fishing, Golf, Walks nearby. Private parking. Orthopaedic beds, TV all rooms.

					Dinner	-
B&B	3	Ensuite	£19/£20	€24.13/€25.39	Dinner	-
B&B	2	Standard	£17/£18	€21.59/€22.86	Partial Board	-
Single Rate			£24/£25	€30.47/€31.74	Child reduction	50%

Open: 1st March-20th November

Joan & Rem Joy
GEORGESLAND B&B
**Dualla/Kilkenny Road, Cashel,
Co Tipperary**

Cashel
TEL: **062 62788**   FAX: **062 62788**

Modern Country Home, situated R691 Dualla/Kilkenny road. Set in peaceful landscaped gardens, surrounded by scenic countryside. Secure parking. Orthopaedic beds.

B&B	6	Ensuite	£20/£20	€25.39	Dinner	-
B&B	-	Standard	-	-	Partial Board	-
Single Rate			£26/£26	€33.01	Child reduction	25%

Cashel 1km   **Open:** 16th March-31st October

Mrs Mary A Kennedy
THORNBROOK HOUSE
**Dualla/Kilkenny Rd (R691)
Cashel, Co Tipperary**

Cashel
TEL: **062 62388**   FAX: **062 61480**
EMAIL: thornbrookhouse@eircom.net

Elegant country home. Antique furnishing, Landscaped gardens. Orthopaedic beds, Hairdryers, Tea/coffee, TV in all bedrooms. Internationally acclaimed.

B&B	3	Ensuite	£21.50/£23.50	€27.30/€29.84	Dinner	-
B&B	2	Standard	£19/£21	€24.13/€26.66	Partial Board	-
Single Rate			£28/£33	€35.55/€41.90	Child reduction	25%

Cashel 1km   **Open:** April-November

Carmel & Pat Lawrence
MARYVILLE
**Bank Place, Cashel,
Co Tipperary**

Cashel
TEL: **062 61098**   FAX: **062 61098**
EMAIL: maryvill@iol.ie

Family welcome. Town Centre. Panoramic views of "Rock". 13th Century Abbey adjoining garden. Photographers delight. Private Parking. Home of World Champion Irish Dancer.

B&B	6	Ensuite	£20/£22	€25.39/€27.93	Dinner	£13
B&B	-	Standard	-	-	Partial Board	-
Single Rate			£30	€38.09	Child reduction	25%

In Cashel   **Open:** All Year

Mrs Evelyn Moloney
ROS-GUILL HOUSE
**Kilkenny/Dualla Road, Cashel,
Co Tipperary**

Cashel
TEL: **062 62699**   FAX: **062 61507**

Elegant country home, overlooking Rock of Cashel. Superbly appointed. Breakfast Award Winner. Hairdryers, Tea/Coffee in bedrooms. Recommended Internationally. Credit Cards.

B&B	4	Ensuite	£22.50/£25	€28.57/€31.74	Dinner	-
B&B	1	Standard	£20/£22.50	€25.39/€28.57	Partial Board	-
Single Rate			£30/£35	€38.09/€44.44	Child reduction	25%

Cashel 1km   **Open:** 1st May-20th October

Joan Brett Moloney
TIR NA NOG
Dualla, Cashel, Co Tipperary

Cashel
TEL: **062 61350**   FAX: **062 62411**
EMAIL: tnanog@indigo.ie
WEB: www.tipp.ie/tirnaog.htm

Warm friendly luxurious country home. Landscaped gardens. Peaceful surroundings. Home Baking, Peat Fires, Orthopaedic Beds. R691 Cashel/Kilkenny Road. Dinner/Breakfast Menu.

B&B	5	Ensuite	£19/£24	€24.13/€30.47	Dinner	£14.95
B&B	1	Standard	£17/£22	€21.59/€27.93	Partial Board	-
Single Rate			£23.50/£28	€29.84/€35.55	Child reduction	-

Cashel 5km   **Open:** All Year Except Christmas

In Cashel

Mrs Sarah Murphy
INDAVILLE
Cashel,
Co Tipperary

Cashel
TEL: 062 62075
EMAIL: indaville@eircom.net

Charming period home. Superb view of Rock of Cashel. Built in 1729 on 4 acres of Beechwood. Centrally located on N8, south of Main Street. Large comfortable rooms.

				Dinner	-
B&B	4	Ensuite	£19/£20	€24.13/€25.39	Dinner -
B&B	-	Standard	-	-	Partial Board -
Single Rate			£25.50/£30	€32.38/€38.09	Child reduction 50%

Open: 16th March-30th October

Mrs Breda O'Grady
ROCKVIEW HOUSE
Bohermore, Cashel,
Co Tipperary

Cashel
TEL: 062 62187

Modern bungalow situated in the Town of Cashel. Panoramic view of the Rock of Cashel. Tea & Coffee in Bedrooms. Breakfast Menu. Friendly hospitality.

B&B	3	Ensuite	£19	€24.13	Dinner -
B&B	-	Standard	-	-	Partial Board -
Single Rate			-	-	Child reduction 25%

Open: 17th March-31st October

In Cashel

Ellen Ryan & Paul Lawrence
ABBEY HOUSE
1 Dominic Street, Cashel,
Co Tipperary

Cashel
TEL: 062 61104   FAX: 062 61104
EMAIL: teachnamainstreach@eircom.net

Town House, opposite Dominic's Abbey. 150 metres Rock of Cashel. Television/Tea/Coffee all bedrooms. Parking. Town Centre 50 metres.

B&B	4	Ensuite	£20/£20	€25.39	Dinner -
B&B	1	Standard	£18/£18	€22.86	Partial Board -
Single Rate			£26/£30	€33.01/€38.09	Child reduction -

Open: 1st February-30th November

In Cashel

Michael & Laura Ryan
ASHMORE HOUSE
John Street, Cashel,
Co Tipperary

Cashel
TEL: 062 61286   FAX: 062 62789
EMAIL: ashmorehouse@eircom.net
WEB: www.ashmorehouse.com

Georgian Family Home, heart of Cashel, Warm Welcome, Spacious Gardens, Private Parking, Residents Lounge, Touring Base, all amenities nearby. AA ♦♦♦.

B&B	5	Ensuite	£22/£23	€27.93/€29.20	Dinner £14
B&B	-	Standard	-	-	Partial Board -
Single Rate			-	-	Child reduction -

Open: 1st January-23rd December

Cashel 1km

Mary & Matt Stapleton
PALM GROVE HOUSE
Dualla/Kilkenny Road,
Cashel, Co Tipperary

Cashel
TEL: 062 61739
EMAIL: sstapleton@eircom.net

Highly recommended family home. Scenic view in quiet location. Take R688 from Cashel, turn left after Church on R691 and "Palm Grove" 1km on right.

B&B	3	Ensuite	£19.50	€24.76	Dinner -
B&B	2	Standard	£17.50	€22.22	Partial Board -
Single Rate			£25/£30	€31.74/€38.09	Child reduction 25%

Open: 1st May-20th October

Mrs Sheila Cox
EDERMINE HOUSE
Rathronan, Fethard Rd,
Clonmel, Co Tipperary

Clonmel
TEL: **052 23048**   FAX: **052 23048**
EMAIL: spike1@esatclear.ie

Spacious dormer bungalow overlooking farm beside modern Equestrian Centre. Secure private parking. Golf, Fishing nearby.

B&B	2	Ensuite	£19	€24.13	Dinner -
B&B	2	Standard	£17	€21.59	Partial Board -
Single Rate			£23.50/£25.50	€29.84/€32.38	Child reduction 25%

Clonmel 2km

Open: 7th January-19th December

Mrs Lily Deely
BEENTEE
Ballingarrane, Cahir Road N24
Clonmel, Co Tipperary

Clonmel
TEL: **052 21313**

Comfortable family bungalow, quiet cul-de-sac on main Limerick, Rosslare, Cork, Waterford road N24. Private parking.

B&B	3	Ensuite	£20/£20	€25.39	Dinner -
B&B	1	Standard	£18	€22.86	Partial Board -
Single Rate			£23.50	€29.84	Child reduction 33.3%

Clonmel 1km

Open: All Year

Denis & Kay Fahey
FARRENWICK COUNTRY HOUSE
Poulmucka, Currantown,
Clonmel, Co Tipperary

Clonmel
TEL: **052 35130**   FAX: **052 35377**
EMAIL: kayden@clubi.ie
WEB: www.theaa.co.uk/region16/81934html

AA ♦♦♦ accommodation R687, 3km, NW off N24 and 6.5km, SE off N8. Family Rooms. Credit Cards. Tour Guide Service.

B&B	3	Ensuite	£19	€24.13	Dinner -
B&B	1	Standard	-	-	Partial Board -
Single Rate			£25.50	€32.38	Child reduction 33.3%

Clonmel 9km

Open: 1st January-18th December

Mrs Nuala Healy
OAK HILL LODGE
Kilcash, Clonmel,
Co Tipperary

Clonmel
TEL: **052 33503**   FAX: **052 33503**
EMAIL: healy@eircom.net
WEB: www.iol.ie/tipp/oakhill-lodge.htm

Country Lodge 20 acres. Under Slievenamon & Kilcash Castle on N76. Kilkenny 29kms, Clonmel 10kms. Woodlands & Gardens. Tea & Scones on arrival. Email facilities.

B&B	3	Ensuite	£19/£19	€24.13	Dinner -
B&B	-	Standard	-	-	Partial Board -
Single Rate			£25.50/£25.50	€32.38	Child reduction 33.3%

Ballypatrick 2km

Open: All Year

Ms Agnes McDonnell
CLUAIN FHIA
25 Ballingarrane, Clonmel,
Co Tipperary

Clonmel
TEL: **052 21431**

Family home, quiet cul de sac. Main Limerick, Cork, Waterford, Rosslare Rd N24. Private parking.

B&B	2	Ensuite	£19	€24.13	Dinner -
B&B	2	Standard	£17/£17	€21.59	Partial Board -
Single Rate			£23.50/£25.50	€29.84/€32.38	Child reduction 33.3%

Open: All Year

Mr Michael J Moran
LISSARDA
**Old Spa Road, Clonmel,
Co Tipperary**

Clonmel
TEL: 052 22593/22294

Spacious purpose built residence within walking distance of Town Centre. Landscaped gardens. Power showers, TV, Tea/Coffee, Hairdryers. Breakfast menu.

B&B	4	Ensuite	£20/£22.50	€25.39/€/28.57	Dinner -
B&B	-	Standard	-	-	Partial Board -
Single Rate			£25.50/£25.50	€32.38	Child reduction 33.3%

In Clonmel

Open: 1st January-23rd December

Mrs Rita Morrissey
HILLCOURT
**Marlfield, Clonmel,
Co Tipperary**

Clonmel
TEL: 052 21029/29711

Bungalow in peaceful surroundings 300 metres off main Cork/Limerick Rd (N24). Golf, Fishing within 2 miles. TV.

B&B	5	Ensuite	£19	€24.13	Dinner -
B&B	-	Standard	-	-	Partial Board -
Single Rate			£25.50	€32.38	Child reduction 50%

Clonmel 1.5km

Open: All Year

David & Jacinta Stott
KILMOLASH UPPER
**Springmount, Clonmel,
Co Tipperary**

Clonmel
TEL: 052 35152
EMAIL: kilmolash@eircom.net
WEB: www.dirl.com/tipperary/kilmolash.htm

Friendly country house in peaceful scenic surroundings overlooking the Suir Valley. Situated 2km off main Clonmel/Cahir road (N24) & only 16km from Cashel.

B&B	2	Ensuite	£19/£19	€24.13	Dinner -
B&B	1	Standard	£17/£17	€21.59	Partial Board -
Single Rate			£23.50/£25.50	€29.84/€32.38	Child reduction 25%

Clonmel 7km

Open: All Year

Mrs Margaret Whelan
AMBERVILLE
**Glenconnor Rd (off Western Rd)
Clonmel, Co Tipperary**

Clonmel
TEL: 052 21470
EMAIL: amberville@eircom.net

Spacious bungalow off Western road near Hospitals. Ideal base for touring, Hillwalking, Golf, Fishing. Guests TV lounge with Tea/Coffee facilities. Visa Cards.

B&B	3	Ensuite	£19	€24.13	Dinner -
B&B	2	Standard	£17	€21.59	Partial Board -
Single Rate			£23.50/£25.50	€29.84/€32.38	Child reduction 33.3%

In Clonmel

Open: 1st January-1st December

Mrs Mary Lynch
SHANNONVALE HOUSE
**Dromineer, Nenagh,
Co Tipperary**

Dromineer
TEL: 067 24102

Modern two storey house, close to Lough Derg. Quiet location in an idyllic setting. All the comforts of home.

B&B	3	Ensuite	£19	€24.13	Dinner -
B&B	-	Standard	-	-	Partial Board -
Single Rate			£25.50	€32.38	Child reduction 50%

Nenagh 9km

Open: 17th March-30th September

The Stanley Family
BALLINACOURTY HOUSE
Glen of Aherlow,
Co Tipperary

Glen of Aherlow
TEL: **062 56000**   FAX: **062 56230**
EMAIL: info@ballinacourtyhse.com
WEB: ballinacourtyhse.com

Situated in a beautiful valley. Our 18th Century modernised home was once a stable courtyard. Restaurant with resident Chef. Tennis, Forest walks start at gate.

B&B	4	Ensuite	£19	€24.13	Dinner	£17.50
B&B	1	Standard	£17	€21.59	Partial Board	£230
Single Rate			£23.50/£25.50	€29.84/€32.38	Child reduction	25%

Tipperary 13km

Open: 1st February-16th December

Brian & Mary Devine
WILLIAMSFERRY HOUSE
Fintan Lalor Street, Nenagh,
Co Tipperary

Nenagh
TEL: **067 31118**   FAX: **067 31256**
EMAIL: williamsferry@eircom.net

AA ♦♦♦. Elegant townhouse 1830. Private parking. Guest lounge. TV, Hairdryer, Tea/Coffee facilities in rooms. Central to Town. Very comfortable. Warm welcome.

B&B	6	Ensuite	£19/£19	€24.13	Dinner	-
B&B		Standard	-		Partial Board	-
Single Rate			£25.50/£25.50	€32.38	Child reduction	33.3%

In Nenagh

Open: 1st January-22nd December

Mary & William Hayes
MARYVILLE
Ballycommon, Near Dromineer,
Nenagh, Co Tipperary

Nenagh
TEL: **067 32531**
EMAIL: maryvilleguest@eircom.net

Comfortable home in quiet location in Ballycommon Village. On R495 to Dromineer Bay on Lough Derg, off N7 adjacent to renowned Bar/Restaurant. Home cooking.

B&B	2	Ensuite	£19/£19	€24.13	Dinner	-
B&B	1	Standard	£18/£18	€22.86	Partial Board	-
Single Rate			£23.50/£25.50	€29.84/€32.38	Child reduction	50%

Nenagh 4km

Open: All Year

Mrs Kathleen Healy
RATHNALEEN HOUSE
Golf Club Road, Old Birr Road,
Nenagh, Co Tipperary

Nenagh
TEL: **067 32508**

Neo-Georgian house, antique furniture in all rooms. Quiet location. Spacious grounds, Golf, Fishing, Horse Riding Arena nearby. Good touring base.

B&B	2	Ensuite	£19	€24.13	Dinner	-
B&B	3	Standard	£17	€21.59	Partial Board	-
Single Rate			£23.50/£25.50	€29.84/€32.38	Child reduction	25%

Nenagh 2km

Open: All Year Except Christmas

Mrs Joan Kennedy
THE COUNTRY HOUSE
Thurles Road, Kilkeary,
Nenagh, Co Tipperary

Nenagh
TEL: **067 31193**

Luxurious residence recommended Frommer Guide. Large parking. Rooms Tea/coffee facilities. Breakfast menu. Orthopaedic beds. Fishing, Golf, Horse riding nearby.

B&B	3	Ensuite	£19	€24.13	Dinner	-
B&B	2	Standard	£17	€21.59	Partial Board	-
Single Rate			£23.50	€29.84	Child reduction	33.3%

Nenagh 6km

Open: All Year

Mrs Gay McAuliffe
AVONDALE
Tyone, Nenagh,
Co Tipperary

Nenagh
TEL: **067 31084**
EMAIL: gay.mcauliffe@oceanfree.net

Comfortable, detached residence across from Hospital. Quiet location. Tea/Coffee facilities, Orthopaedic beds. Ideal for touring Midlands. Golf, Fishing, Tennis.

B&B	2	Ensuite	£19/£20	€24.13/€25.39	Dinner	-
B&B	2	Standard	£17/£18	€21.59/€22.86	Partial Board	-
Single Rate			-	-	Child reduction	25%

Nenagh 1km

Open: All Year

Mary McGeeney
COOLANGATTA
Brocka, Ballinderry, Nenagh,
Co Tipperary

Nenagh Terryglass
TEL: **067 22164**
EMAIL: lmcgeene@ie.packardbell.org

Spectacular views of Lough Derg and surrounding Countryside. Breakfast menu, Tea/Coffee, Lounge with TV/Video. Use of landscaped garden. Folk dancing classes.

B&B	3	Ensuite	£19/£19	€24.13	Dinner	£12.50
B&B	-	Standard	-	-	Partial Board	-
Single Rate			£25.50	€32.38	Child reduction	-

Nenagh 20km

Open: 1st March-31st October

Tom & Patricia McKeogh
WILLOWBROOK
Belleen, Nenagh,
Co Tipperary

Nenagh
TEL: **067 31558**   FAX: **067 41222**
EMAIL: willowbrook@oceanfree.net

Relax in a peaceful atmosphere amid landscaped surroundings. Ideal base for touring/business. Itinerary planned, Breakfast menu. R461 Nenagh/Portroe road.

B&B	6	Ensuite	£19	€24.13	Dinner	-
B&B	-	Standard	-	-	Partial Board	-
Single Rate			£25.50	€32.38	Child reduction	50%

Nenagh 2km

Open: All Year

Margaret & PJ Mounsey
ASHLEY PARK HOUSE
Ashley Park, Nenagh,
Co Tipperary

Nenagh Lough Derg
TEL: **067 38223**   FAX: **067 38013**
EMAIL: margaret@ashleypark.com

17th Century house stands on the shores of Lough Orna. Centrally located, ideal for those who love tranquillity, Fishing, Golfing.

B&B	5	Ensuite	£25/£33	€31.74/€41.90	Dinner	£23
B&B	5	Standard	£25/£33	€31.74/€41.90	Partial Board	-
Single Rate			£28/£35	€35.55/€44.44	Child reduction	25%

Nenagh

Open: All Year

Mrs Mae Fallon
CREGGANBELL
Birr Road, Roscrea,
Co Tipperary

Roscrea
TEL: **0505 21421**
EMAIL: cregganbell@eircom.net

Spacious bungalow, Electric blankets, Golf, Fishing, Forest and Mountain Walks. Ideal for touring Midlands. Tea/Coffee free. 3 mins off N7.

B&B	4	Ensuite	£19/£19	€24.13	Dinner	-
B&B	-	Standard	-	-	Partial Board	-
Single Rate			-	-	Child reduction	-

In Roscrea

Open: 15th April-30th October

In Terryglass

Sheila & Oliver Darcy
LAKE LAND LODGE
Terryglass, Nenagh,
Co Tipperary

Terryglass

Tel: **067 22069**   Fax: **067 22069**
Email: lakelandlodge@eircom.net

Luxurious accommodation in beautiful scenic area. "A home away from home" Close to all Lake amenities eg. Fishing, Water Sports, Traditional Music, Golf etc.

				Dinner	£12.50
B&B	2	Ensuite	£19/£20	€24.13/€25.39	
B&B	1	Standard	£19/£20	€24.13/€25.39	Partial Board	-
Single Rate			£25.50/£25.50	€32.38	Child reduction	33.3%

Open: 1st January-23rd December

In Thurles

Mrs Helen Buggle-Sheahan
ST JOSEPHS
The Mall,
Horse & Jockey/Cashel Rd.
N62, Thurles, Co Tipperary

Thurles

Tel: **0504 24211**

Charming bungalow. Superb location, Breakfast menu. Professional cuisine. Tea/Coffee facilities. shower robes. Genealogy discussed. Itineraries planned. le Routard recommended.

					Dinner	-
B&B	5	Ensuite	£20/£22.50	€25.39/€28.57	
B&B	1	Standard	£18/£20	€22.86/€25.39	Partial Board	-
Single Rate			£25.50/£30	€32.38/€38.09	Child reduction	25%

Open: 1st March-31st October

In Thurles

Mrs Ellen Cavanagh
CUILIN HOUSE
Templemore Road N62,
Thurles, Co Tipperary

Thurles

Tel: **0504 23237**   Fax: **0504 26075**
Email: thurlesbandb@eircom.net
Web: homepage.eircom.net~thurlesbandb/bord.html

Luxurious accommodation spacious decorative bedrooms, TV, Tea/Coffee, homebaking, breakfast menu, worldwide guest recommendations, itineraries planned, genealogy tracing assistance.

					Dinner	-
B&B	3	Ensuite	£20	€25.39	
B&B		Standard	-	-	Partial Board	-
Single Rate			£25.50/£30	€32.38/€38.09	Child reduction	50%

Open: 1st March-30th November

Thurles 3km

Ms Noreen O'Mahony
HAWTHORN VIEW
Knockroe, Thurles,
Co Tipperary

Thurles

Tel: **0504 21710**

Luxurious bungalow on own private grounds, secluded gardens. On N62 route. Ideal touring base Holycross Abbey, Rock of Cashel, 2 mins Thurles Golf club. TV, Tea/Coffee, Homebaking.

					Dinner	-
B&B	3	Ensuite	£20/£23	€25.39/€29.20	
B&B		Standard	-	-	Partial Board	-
Single Rate			£25.50/£30	€32.38/€38.09	Child reduction	25%

Open: 1st March-30th November

Thurles 6km

Anna Stakelum
BOHERNA LODGE
Clohane, Tipperary Road,
Holycross, Thurles, Co Tipperary

Thurles

Tel: **0504 43121**
Email: boherna@oceanfree.net
Web: www.dirlcom/tipperary/boherna-lodge.html

Spacious country home, peaceful surrounding. Warm professional welcome. Ideal base for touring Holycross Abbey, Rock of Cashel. Golf, Fishing, Riding nearby.

					Dinner	£12.50
B&B	3	Ensuite	£19/£19	€24.13	
B&B	1	Standard	£17/£17	€21.59	Partial Board	-
Single Rate			£23.50/£25.50	€29.84/€32.38	Child reduction	25%

Open: All Year Except Christmas

157

Tipperary 1.5km

Mrs Noreen Collins
PURT HOUSE
**Bohercrowe, Emly Road,
Tipperary Town, Co Tipperary**

Tipperary
Tel: **062 51938**
Email: purthouse@eircom.net

Warm welcome R515 to Killarney, Tea/Coffee, TV, Hairdryers in bedrooms, hot scones, Credit cards, laundry facilities, Irish Night arranged.

B&B	5	Ensuite	£19/£22	€24.13/€27.93	Dinner	£14
B&B	1	Standard	£19	€24.13	Partial Board	-
Single Rate			£25/£28.50	€31.74/€36.19	Child reduction	33.3%

Open: 1st March-31st October

In Tipperary

Mrs Kay Crowe
RIVERSIDE HOUSE
**Galbally Road, Tipperary Town,
Co Tipperary**

Tipperary
Tel: **062 51219/51245** Fax: **062 51219**
Email: riversidehouse@hotmail.com
Web: www.riversidehouse.com

Luxury modern home, main Cork route (R662). 5 mins walk Town Centre. All facilities in bedrooms. Guests Lounge, Sports Complex, Swimming Pool, Tennis & Cinema nearby, available to guests.

B&B	2	Ensuite	£20/£20	€25.39	Dinner	-
B&B	1	Standard	£18/£18	€22.86	Partial Board	-
Single Rate			£25/£27	€31.74/€34.29	Child reduction	33.3%

Open: 1st March-31st October

Tipperary Town 3km

Douglas & Angela Edinborough
BALLYKISTEEN LODGE
Monard, Co Tipperary

Tipperary
Tel: **062 33403** Fax: **062 33711**
Email: ballykisteenlodge@oceanfree.net
Web: www.tipp.ie/ballykis.htm

Luxurious residence. Adjacent to Ballykisteen Golf & Country Club, Tipperary Racecourse. 10 minutes to Tipperary. Breakfast menu. TV, Tea/Coffee facilities. TV lounge.

B&B	4	Ensuite	£20/£22	€25.39/€27.93	Dinner	-
B&B	-	Standard			Partial Board	-
Single Rate			£25.50/£25.50	€32.38	Child reduction	33.3%

Open: 1st April-30th November

Tipperary 1.5km

Mrs Margaret Merrigan
TEACH GOBNATHAN
**Glen of Aherlow, Golf Links Road,
Brookville, Tipperary, Co Tipperary**

Tipperary
Tel: **062 51645**

Suburban home in scenic location beside Golf Club. Close to all amenities. Turn down at traffic lights, centre of Tipperary town, right at roundabout, two bends past Golf Club. Failte.

B&B	3	Ensuite	£19/£19	€24.13	Dinner	-
B&B	1	Standard	£17/£17	€21.59	Partial Board	-
Single Rate			£25.50/£25.50	€32.38	Child reduction	25%

Open: 1st March-30th November

Tipperary 2km

Mrs Mary O'Neill
VILLA MARIA
**Limerick Road,
Tipperary Town, Co Tipperary**

Tipperary
Tel: **062 51557**

Modern bungalow N24 Waterford/ Limerick Road. Footpath to Tipperary. Limerick-Junction Station, Ballykisteen Golf, Tipperary Racecourse 1.5km. Tea/coffee served.

B&B	2	Ensuite	£19.50/£19.50	€24.76	Dinner	-
B&B	1	Standard	£17.50/£17.50	€22.22	Partial Board	-
Single Rate			£23.50/£25.50	€29.84/€32.38	Child reduction	25%

Open: May-September

Tipperary 3km

Mrs Nuala O'Sullivan
WOODLAWN
Galbally Road,
Tipperary Town,
Co Tipperary

Tipperary
TEL: **062 51272**
EMAIL: woodlawn_tipp@hotmail.com

Modern spacious comfortable home in peaceful surroundings on R662 to Cork /Killarney. Large landscaped gardens and ample parking. Warm welcome.

B&B	4	Ensuite	£19	€24.13	Dinner	-
B&B	-	Standard	-	-	Partial Board	-
Single Rate			£25.50	€32.38	Child reduction	33.3%

Open: April-October

In Tipperary

Mrs Mary Quinn
CLONMORE HOUSE
Cork/Galbally Rd, Tipperary Town
Co Tipperary

Tipperary
TEL: **062 51637**
EMAIL: clonmorehouse@eircom.net

Bungalow 5 mins walk town, scenic surroundings, overlooking Galtee Mountains, Frommer, Birnbaun, Best B&B Guides recommended. Ground floor bedrooms, Electric blankets.

B&B	5	Ensuite	£20/£20	€25.39	Dinner	-
B&B	-	Standard	-	-	Partial Board	-
Single Rate			£26/£26	€33.01	Child reduction	-

Open: 1st March-31st October

Tipperary 1.5km

Mrs Marian Quirke
AISLING
Glen of Aherlow Road,
Tipperary, Co Tipperary

Tipperary
TEL: **062 33307**   FAX: **062 82955**
EMAIL: ladygreg@oceanfree.net

Relaxed country location beside Golf Club. Family run homely atmosphere. Take route R664 from traffic lights Tipperary Town. Base for touring Tipp triangle. Near Castle ruins, etc.

B&B	4	Ensuite	£19/£19	€24.13	Dinner	-
B&B	-	Standard	-	-	Partial Board	-
Single Rate			£25.50	€32.38	Child reduction	50%

Open: 1st January-30th November

Tipperary 8km

Mrs Teresa Russell
BANSHA CASTLE
Bansha, Co Tipperary

Tipperary
TEL: **062 54187**   FAX: **062 54294**
EMAIL: johnrus@iol.ie
WEB: www.iol.ie/tipp/bansha-castle.htm

Historic country house. Private gardens, Mature trees. Snooker room. Superb cooking. Walking/cycling. Pre booking recommended. 10 mins south Tipperary N24.

B&B	3	Ensuite	£30	€38.09	Dinner	£18
B&B	3	Standard	£27	€34.29	Partial Board	£300
Single Rate			£35	€44.44	Child reduction	25%

Open: 1st January-20th December

RESERVATIONS

- Confirm phone bookings in writing without delay with agreed deposit.
- To avoid misunderstandings later, check rate on booking and clarify any additional changes which may apply to your booking.
- Give details of any special requirements.
- State clearly day, date of arrival and departure date.

South East | Waterford

Waterford, The Crystal County boasts of splendid scenery, mountain passes, miles of spectacular coastline with safe and sandy beaches. The city of Waterford is a bustling maritime city, with 1,000 years of History, Museums and Heritage centres to see and explore.

Mrs Mary Byron Casey
BYRON LODGE
Ardmore, Co Waterford

Ardmore
TEL: **024 94157**

Home of Nora Roberts Irish Triology books. Monastic settlement. Georgian house. Superbly situated, 150 years old. Private parking. Historic Village of Artists and Writers. Cliff Walks.

B&B	4	Ensuite	£20	€25.39	Dinner	-
B&B	2	Standard	£18	€22.86	Partial Board	-
Single Rate			£23.50	€29.84	Child reduction	50%

In Ardmore

Open: 1st April-31st October

Ms Theresa Troy
CUSH
Duffcarrick, Ardmore,
Co Waterford

Ardmore
TEL: **024 94474**

Situated adjacent picturesque Ardmore, off N25, with views of Bay, historic Ancient sites and surrounding countryside. Warm personal welcome assured.

B&B	2	Ensuite	£19/£20	€24.13/€25.39	Dinner	-
B&B	1	Standard	£17/£19	€21.59/€24.13	Partial Board	-
Single Rate			-	-	Child reduction	-

Ardmore 2 km

Open:1st April-30th September

Richard & Nora Harte
CNOC-NA-RI
Nire Valley, Ballymacarby,
Via Clonmel, Co Waterford

Ballymacarbry Nire Valley
TEL: **052 36239**
EMAIL: nharte@ireland.com
WEB: homepage.eircom.net/~cnocnari/

Friendly home, Elevated site. Exhilarating views. Rooms ensuite with every comfort for guests. Homecooking, Breakfast menu. Walking, Golf, Horseriding, Fishing, Relaxing. Off R671/R672.

B&B	3	Ensuite	£20/£22	€25.39/€27.93	Dinner	-
B&B	-	Standard	-	-	Partial Board	£250
Single Rate			£27.50/£27.50	€34.91	Child reduction	25%

Clonmel 14km

Open: 1st January-14th December

Mrs Catherine Mary Scanlan
COOLHILLA
Ballyhane, Cappoquin,
Co Waterford

Cappoquin
TEL: **058 54054**   FAX: **058 54054**
EMAIL: cscanlan@eircom.ie

'Ambassador of Tourism' winner. Home Cooking. All rooms en-suite with TV, Tea/Coffee facilities. Ideal location Walking/Fishing/Golfing. Excellent food & Irish music. Main N72. Credit cards accepted

B&B	3	Ensuite	£20	€25.39	Dinner	£15
B&B	-	Standard	-	-	Partial Board	£220
Single Rate			£25.50	€32.38	Child reduction	50%

Cappoquin 5km

Open: All Year Except Christmas

Mrs Onra Fennell
MAPLE LEAF
Windgap (Cork Rd),
Dungarvan, Co Waterford

Dungarvan
TEL: **058 41921**

Second left junction after last roundabout, West of Dungarvan, 200mts off N25. Panoramic view of Dungarvan Bay and mountains. Landscaped gardens.

B&B	3	Ensuite	£19/£19	€24.13	Dinner	£12.50
B&B	-	Standard	-	-	Partial Board	£185
Single Rate			£25.50/£25.50	€32.38	Child reduction	25%

Dungarvan 6km   **Open:** 1st March-31st October

Sheila Lane
BALLINAMORE HOUSE
Ballyduff, Dungarvan,
Co Waterford

Dungarvan
TEL: **058 42146**

Just off R672, 3km west Dungarvan. Superior accommodation, homely atmosphere in idyllic setting. Minutes from Town, Fishing, Golf, Horseriding and Walking areas. Patio, garden for guests.

B&B	3	Ensuite	£19/£19	€24.13	Dinner	-
B&B	-	Standard	-	-	Partial Board	-
Single Rate			£25.50/£25.50	€32.38	Child reduction	-

Dungarvan 3km   **Open:** All Year Except Christmas

Mrs Patricia McCarthy
BRICKEY VALLEY
Coolnagour, Dungarvan,
Co Waterford

Dungarvan
TEL: **058 45056**
EMAIL: brickeyvalleyb.b@oceanfree.net

New dormer bungalow situated in scenic peaceful location off N25. Spacious rooms, Power showers, Breakfast menu. 1.5km from 18 hole Golf course and Restaurant.

B&B	3	Ensuite	£19/£20	€24.13/€25.39	Dinner	-
B&B	-	Standard	-	-	Partial Board	-
Single Rate			£25.50/£25.50	€32.38	Child reduction	50%

Dungarvan 3km   **Open:** 1st March-31st October

Bridget Maher
HELVICK VIEW
Ring, Dungarvan,
Co Waterford

Dungarvan
TEL: **058 46297**

Modern bungalow overlooking Dungarvan Bay and Comeragh Mountains and Helvick Head. Rose garden for visitors.

B&B	4	Ensuite	£19	€24.13	Dinner	-
B&B	-	Standard	-	-	Partial Board	-
Single Rate			-	-	Child reduction	-

Dungarvan 8km   **Open:** 20th April-30th September

Sheila Norris
BAYSIDE
Gold Coast Road,
Dungarvan, Co Waterford

Dungarvan
TEL: **058 44318**
EMAIL: pnorris@gofree.indigo.ie
WEB: http://members.nbci.com/adnexal/adnexal/bayside1p.htm

Modern dormer bungalow in a rural setting, on the seafront, overlooking Dungarvan Bay. Private car park.

B&B	4	Ensuite	£19/£19	€24.13	Dinner	-
B&B	-	Standard	-	-	Partial Board	-
Single Rate			£25.50/£25.50	€32.38	Child reduction	50%

Dungarvan 5km   **Open:** 4th January-22nd December

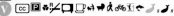

Helen O'Connell
HILLCREST
**Waterford Road,
Tarr's Bridge, Dungarvan,
Co Waterford**

Tel: 058 42262

Bungalow on Waterford/Cork Road (N25). Adjacent 18 hole Golf Course. Rosslare 1.5 hours. Electric blankets. Safe Parking. Ideal touring centre. Early breakfasts served.

B&B	2	Ensuite	£19	€24.13	Dinner	-
B&B	1	Standard	£17	€21.59	Partial Board	-
Single Rate			£23.50	€29.84	Child reduction	50%

Dungarvan 3km

Open: 1st April-31st October

Mrs Kathleen Phelan
ABBEY HOUSE
**Friars Walk, Abbeyside,
Dungarvan, Co Waterford**

Tel: 058 41669

Luxury bungalow by the sea. Stroll to town and beach. 3x18 Hole Golf Courses close by. Warm welcome assured.

B&B	4	Ensuite	£19/£22	€24.13/€27.93	Dinner	-
B&B	-	Standard	-	-	Partial Board	-
Single Rate			£25	€31.74	Child reduction	-

In Dungarvan

Open: All Year Except Christmas

Mrs R Prendergast,
THE OLD RECTORY
**Waterford Rd, Dungarvan,
Co Waterford**

Tel: 058 41394   Fax: 058 41394
Email: tournore@eircom.net
Web: homepage.eircom.net/~1108

Waterford side of town on N25, Offstreet Parking. Walking distance of Town Centre. TV, Tea/Coffee facilities in bedrooms. 3x18 Hole Golf Courses nearby.

B&B	4	Ensuite	£20/£22	€25.39/€27.93	Dinner	-
B&B	-	Standard	-	-	Partial Board	-
Single Rate			£25.50/£27.50	€32.38/€34.91	Child reduction	50%

In Dungarvan

Open: All Year

Mrs Margo Sleator
ROSEBANK HOUSE
**Coast Road, Dungarvan,
Co Waterford**

Tel: 058 41561
Email: msleator@eircom.net
Web: www.rosebankhouse.com

Take R675 from Dungarvan, following signposting for Clonea Strand, own signposting en-route, Tea/Coffee in lounge. Highly recommended. Varied Breakfast menu.

B&B	3	Ensuite	£19	€24.13	Dinner	-
B&B	1	Standard	£17	€21.59	Partial Board	-
Single Rate			£23.50/£25.50	€29.84/€32.38	Child reduction	-

Dungarvan 3km

Open: 1st March-22nd December

Mrs Breda Battles
ASHGROVE
**Dunmore East,
Co Waterford**

Tel: 051 383195
Email: battlesb@gofree.indigo.ie

Country home situated in peaceful scenic surroundings. Sign-posted in Village at junction across from "The Church". Frommer/Le Routard recommended.

B&B	4	Ensuite	£19/£20	€24.13 /€25.39	Dinner	-
B&B	-	Standard	-	-	Partial Board	-
Single Rate			£25.50/£26.50	€32.38/€33.65	Child reduction	25%

Dunmore East 1km

Open: 1st March-31st October

Winnie & Tony Brooke
SPRINGFIELD
Dunmore East,
Co Waterford

Dunmore East
TEL: **051 383448**
EMAIL: springfieldbb@esatclear.ie
WEB: www.springfield-dunmore.com

Luxurious home in beautiful peaceful surroundings yet 200 metres from Beach, Restaurants etc. Tea/Coffee facilities in Conservatory. Breakfast menu.

B&B	6	Ensuite	**£19/£22**	€24.13/€27.93	Dinner	-
B&B	-	Standard	-	-	Partial Board	-
Single Rate			-	-	Child reduction	**25%**

In Dunmore East

Open: 1st March-30th November

Kathleen Burke
CARRAIG LIATH
Harbour Road, Dunmore East,
Co Waterford

Dunmore East
TEL: **051 383273**   FAX: **051 383273**
EMAIL: beatltd@esatclear.ie

Large residence in Village centre. Overlooking Harbour, Sailing Club. Walking distance Beaches, Tennis, Swimming Pool, Restaurants. Golf 4 mins drive.

B&B	4	Ensuite	**£20/£22**	€25.39/€27.93	Dinner	-
B&B	-	Standard	-	-	Partial Board	-
Single Rate			-	-	Child reduction	-

In Dunmore East

Open: 1st April-31st October

Elizabeth Hayes
COPPER BEECH
Harbour Road, Dunmore East,
Co Waterford

Dunmore East
TEL: **051 383187/385957**
EMAIL: copperbeech25@hotmail.com

Delightful family home, Village Centre overlooking Harbour. Beside Beaches, Tennis, Sailing, Golf. Excellent Restaurants. Private parking. Frommer recommended.

B&B	4	Ensuite	**£19/£20**	€24.13/€25.39	Dinner	-
B&B	-	Standard	-	-	Partial Board	-
Single Rate			-	-	Child reduction	-

In Dunmore East

Open: March-October

Phyllis & Ed Lannon
CHURCH VILLA
Dunmore East,
Co Waterford

Dunmore East
TEL: **051 383390**   FAX: **051 383023**
EMAIL: churchvilla@eircom.net
WEB: homepage.eircom.net/~churchvilla

Victorian Town House, centre Village. Idyllic surrounds. Excellent Restaurants, Pubs walking distance. Five Golf courses nearby. Swim, Sail, Cliff walk - It's all here.

B&B	6	Ensuite	**£19/£21**	€24.13/€26.66	Dinner	-
B&B	-	Standard	-	-	Partial Board	-
Single Rate			**£24.50/£26**	€31.11/€33.01	Child reduction	**25%**

In Dunmore East

Open: All Year Except Christmas

Mrs Kathleen Martin
CREADEN VIEW
Dunmore East, Co Waterford

Dunmore East
TEL: **051 383339**   FAX: **051 383339**

Charming friendly home, centre of Village on road to Harbour/Sailing Club. Walking distance Restaurants, Bars, Beaches, Golf club 2km. Recommended Frommer/Lonely Planet. Breakfast menu.

B&B	6	Ensuite	**£20/£22**	€25.39/€27.93	Dinner	-
B&B	-	Standard	-	-	Partial Board	-
Single Rate			-	-	Child reduction	**25%**

In Dunmore East

Open: 1st March-31st October

The Sutton Family
GLOR NA MARA
**Kilmacleague, Dunmore East,
Co Waterford**

Dunmore East

Tel: **051 383361** Fax: **051 383361**
Email: tsutton@gofree.indigo.ie

Country home, peaceful scenic surroundings. Golf, Fishing, Scenic Walks. Good food locally. All rooms ensuite with TV, Tea/Coffee facilities. Dunmore East 5km.

B&B	3	Ensuite	£19/£19	€24.13	Dinner	-
B&B	-	Standard	-	-	Partial Board	-
Single Rate			£25.50/£25.50	€32.38	Child reduction	50%

Dunmore East 5km

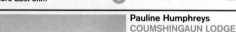 **Open:** 1st March-30th September

---

Pauline Humphreys
COUMSHINGAUN LODGE
**Kilclooney, Kilmacthomas,
Co Waterford**

Kilmacthomas Comeragh Mtns

Tel: **051 646238** Fax: **051 646238**
Email: coumshingaun@eircom.net
Web: homepage.eircom.net/~coumshingaunlodge/

Magnificent mountain setting near Lough Coumshingaun on scenic route (R676). Breakfast menu, relaxed atmosphere, open fire, traditional musicians.

B&B	4	Ensuite	£20/£20	€25.39	Dinner	-
B&B	-	Standard	-	-	Partial Board	-
Single Rate			£26/£26	€33.01	Child reduction	25%

Kilmacthomas 12km

Open: 12th April-30th September

Mrs Ann Fitzgerald
DAWN B&B
**Kildarmody, Kilmeaden,
Co Waterford**

Kilmeaden Waterford

Tel: **051 384465**
Email: dawnb.and.b@esatclear.ie

Modern bungalow in peaceful quiet area. 1/2km off N25. 12km Waterford Crystal. Restaurant and pub in walking distance. Private car park, garden for guests.

B&B	3	Ensuite	£19/£19	€24.13	Dinner	-
B&B	-	Standard	-	-	Partial Board	-
Single Rate			£25.50/£25.50	€32.38	Child reduction	33.3%

Waterford City 12km

Open: March-October

Mrs June Power
BEECHCROFT
**Deerpark Road,
Lismore, Co Waterford**

Lismore

Tel: **058 54273** Fax: **058 54273**

A warm welcome awaits you in our home. TV, Hairdryers, Electric blankets in bedrooms. Tea/Coffee facilities. Drying room. Mature Garden. Leave N72 at Lismore. Located opposite Infants School.

B&B	2	Ensuite	£19/£19	€24.13	Dinner	-
B&B	1	Standard	£18/£18	€22.86	Partial Board	-
Single Rate			£23.50/£25	€29.84/€31.74	Child reduction	25%

In Lismore

Open: All Year Except Christmas

Mrs Rosaleen Breen
SEACREST
**Pickardstown, Tramore,
Co Waterford**

Tramore

Tel: **051 381888** Fax: **051 381888**
Email: rosaleenbreen@eircom.net
Web: homepage.eircom.net/~seacrestaccomm

Peaceful secluded country home adjacent to R675 from Waterford. Algemeen Dagblad Best B&B's. Breakfast choice. Parking. Hairdryers. Triple/Family rooms.

B&B	3	Ensuite	£19/£20	€24.13/€25.39	Dinner	-
B&B	1	Standard	£18/£18	€22.86	Partial Board	-
Single Rate			£23.50/£27	€29.84/€34.29	Child reduction	50%

Tramore 1km

Open: May-October

Mrs Sheila Brennan
CLUAIN RINN
**Pickardstown, Tramore,
Co Waterford**

TEL: **051 381560**

Spacious friendly home. Large bedrooms. Quiet location. Waterford side of Tramore. Off R675. Generous breakfast menu. TV lounge. Tea/Coffee.

B&B	2	Ensuite	£19/£19	€24.13	Dinner	-
B&B	1	Standard	£17/£17	€21.59	Partial Board	-
Single Rate			£23.50/£23.50	€29.84	Child reduction	50%

Tramore 1km

Open: 1st May-30th September

Mrs Maria Byrne
KILLERIG HOUSE
**Lower Branch Rd, Tramore,
Co Waterford**

TEL: **051 381075**

200 year old town house in Tramore opposite Splashworld Amusement Park and Beach. Beside Majestic Hotel and Bus stop. 10km Waterford Crystal & City.

B&B	6	Ensuite	£20/£25	€25.39/€31.74	Dinner	-
B&B		Standard	-	-	Partial Board	-
Single Rate			£30	€38.09	Child reduction	25%

In Tramore

Open: All Year

Frances & Cyril Darcy
SEAVIEW LODGE
**Sea View Park, Tramore,
Co Waterford**

TEL: **051 381122**   FAX: **051 381122**
EMAIL: seaviewlodge@eircom.net

Spectacular seaviews, beautiful gardens. Parking. Frommer/Le Routard, AA ◆◆◆◆. TV, Hairdryer, Tea/Coffee, Jacuzzi Bath. "Menu". Waterford Crystal 10 mins R675.

B&B	4	Ensuite	£19/£23	€24.13/€29.20	Dinner	-
B&B		Standard	-	-	Partial Board	-
Single Rate			£32/£34	€40.63/€43.17	Child reduction	25%

In Tramore

Open: May-October

Mrs Lillian Delaney
WESTCLIFFE
**5 Newtown, Tramore,
Co Waterford**

TEL: **051 381365**
EMAIL: westclif@indigo.ie

Modern two storey house overlooking Tramore. 2 mins from 18 hole Golf Course. Guest sitting room.

B&B	4	Ensuite	£19/£22	€24.13/€27.93	Dinner	-
B&B	1	Standard	£17/£20	€21.59/€25.39	Partial Board	-
Single Rate			-	-	Child reduction	50%

In Tramore

Open: 1st January-1st December

Frank & Majella Heraughty
GLENART HOUSE
**Tivoli Rd, Tramore,
Co Waterford**

TEL: **051 381236**   FAX: **051 391236**
EMAIL: tourismse@eircom.net

Elegant restored 1920's detached residence. Convenient Racecourse, Splashworld, Beach & Golf. Friendly atmosphere. Breakfast menu. Tea/coffee facilities. Ideal touring base.

B&B	4	Ensuite	£20/£25	€25.39/€31.74	Dinner	-
B&B		Standard	-	-	Partial Board	-
Single Rate			£27.50	€34.91	Child reduction	50%

In Tramore

Open: 1st March-30th November

Anne Lawlor
FERN HILL
Newtown, Tramore,
Co Waterford

Tramore

TEL: 051 390829   FAX: 051 390829
EMAIL: fernhill@tramore.net

Warm and luxurious house opposite Tramore Golf Club and 1km from Beach. Beautiful views of Tramore Bay. All facilities within the area.

B&B	4	Ensuite	£20/£23	€25.39/€29.20	Dinner	-
B&B	1	Standard	£18/£20	€22.86/€25.39	Partial Board	-
Single Rate			£25/£28	€31.74/€35.55	Child reduction	50%

In Tramore

Open: 1st March-30th October

Mrs Anne McCarthy
SEAMIST
Newtown, Tramore,
Co Waterford

Tramore

TEL: 051 381533   FAX: 051 381533
EMAIL: annflor@iol.ie
WEB: www.tramore.net/seamist/

Luxurious spacious home. Renowned generous breakfast. On site parking at rear. On coastal historical walk. 250 metres from Tramore Golf club, signposted on R675.

B&B	3	Ensuite	£19/£20	€24.13/€25.39	Dinner	-
B&B	-	Standard	£17		Partial Board	-
Single Rate			£25.50/£25.50	€32.38	Child reduction	33.3%

In Tramore

Open: 1st March-31st October

Mrs Olive McCarthy
OBAN
1 Eastlands, Pond Road,
Tramore, Co Waterford

Tramore

TEL: 051 381537

"Breakfast over the Bay" in central comfortable home. Walking distance to Racecourse, Beach, Pubs, Restaurants etc. Extensive Breakfast menu. Ideal touring base.

B&B	3	Ensuite	£19	€24.13	Dinner	-
B&B	1	Standard	£17	€21.59	Partial Board	-
Single Rate			£23.50/£25.50	€29.84/€32.38	Child reduction	50%

In Tramore

Open: 8th January-16th December

Mrs Rosaleen McGrath
ARD MOR HOUSE
Doneraile Drive, Tramore,
Co Waterford

Tramore

TEL: 051 381716

Family home centrally located in quiet area overlooking the Bay. Bedrooms with sea view. Walking distance Restaurants, Pubs, Beaches, Splashworld, Golf. Lonely Planet, Lets Go Guides.

B&B	3	Ensuite	£20/£25	€25.39/€31.74	Dinner	-
B&B	-	Standard			Partial Board	-
Single Rate			£30/£32	€38.09/€40.63	Child reduction	25%

In Tramore

Open: April-October

Thomas & Elizabeth Moran
SEA COURT
Tivoli Road, Tramore,
Co Waterford

Tramore

TEL: 051 386244
EMAIL: sea-court@tramore.net
WEB: www.tramore.met-tramore

Friendly home in the heart of Tramore. All rooms with multi-channel TV, Tea/Coffee facilities. Guest lounge. Secure parking. Extensive Breakfast menu.

B&B	3	Ensuite	£20/£20	€25.39	Dinner	-
B&B	1	Standard	£18/£18	€22.86	Partial Board	-
Single Rate			£23.50/£27	€29.84/€34.29	Child reduction	50%

Open: April-October

In Tramore

Mrs Marie Murphy
GLENORNEY
Newtown, Tramore,
Co Waterford

Tel: **051 381056**   Fax: **051 381103**
Email: glenoney@iol.ie
Web: www.glenorney.com

Award winning luxurious spacious home panoramic view Tramore Bay. RAC & AA ♦♦♦♦'s selected with Sparkling Diamond award. 2 family suites. Extensive menu.

B&B	5	Ensuite	£20/£23	€25.39/€29.20	Dinner	-
B&B	1	Standard	£17/£20	€21.59/€25.39	Partial Board	-
Single Rate			£25/£35	€31.74/€44.44	Child reduction	25%

Open: AllYear

In Tramore

Niall & Penny Nordell
NORLANDS
Glen Road, Tramore,
Co Waterford

Tel: **051 391132**
Email: nordell@eircom.net
Web: www.tramore.net/tramore/norlands.

Luxurious family home beside Racecourse - 10 min drive to Waterford Crystal. Tranquil surroundings. 8 magnificent Golf courses - 30 min drive. Golfers welcome.

B&B	3	Ensuite	£19/£22	€24.13/€27.93	Dinner	-
B&B	-	Standard	-	-	Partial Board	-
Single Rate			£30/£32	€38.09/€40.63	Child reduction	33.3%

Open: 6th January-20th December

In Tramore

Anne O'Brien
TWELVE OAKS
Ard na Groi, Crobally,
Tramore, Co Waterford

Tel: **051 386938**

Luxurious family home in quiet area beside Racecourse. Convenient to all Tramore amenities. Waterford City 10km. Private parking. Breakfast menu.

B&B	3	Ensuite	£20/£25	€25.39/€31.74	Dinner	-
B&B	-	Standard	-	-	Partial Board	-
Single Rate			£25.50/£30	€32.38/€38.09	Child reduction	50%

Open: All Year Except Christmas

In Tramore

Mrs Anne O'Connor
ARDVIEW HOUSE
Lower Branch Road,
Tramore, Co Waterford

Tel: **051 381687**   Fax: **051 381687**
Email: john041@gofree.indigo.ie

Georgian house - panoramic view of bay. Satellite TV all rooms. Tea/Coffee all rooms. Breakfast menu. Credit cards, Very central. Warm welcome assured.

B&B	4	Ensuite	£20/£22	€25.39/€27.93	Dinner	-
B&B	2	Standard	£18/£20	€22.86/€25.39	Partial Board	-
Single Rate			£25/£28	€31.74/€35.55	Child reduction	33.3%

Open: All Year

Tramore 2 km

Ann & John O'Meara
KNOCKVILLE
Moonvoy, Tramore,
Co Waterford

Tel: **051 381084**
Email: knockville@iolfree.ie

Country home in rural area on R682, 7km from N25. Owner chef. Breakfast/Dinner menu. Bring your own wine. Tea/Coffee facilities. Private parking. Credit cards.

B&B	3	Ensuite	£19/£19	€24.13	Dinner	£13
B&B	2	Standard	£17/£17	€21.59	Partial Board	£190
Single Rate			£23.50/£23.50	€29.84	Child reduction	50%

Open: 1st April-1st December

Pat & Hilary O'Sullivan
CLIFF HOUSE
**Cliff Road, Tramore,
Co Waterford**

Tramore
TEL: **051 381497/391296** FAX: **051 381497**
EMAIL: hilary@cliffhouse.ie
WEB: www.cliffhouse.ie

"Simply the Best" luxurious. AA ♦♦♦♦. Panoramic view Tramore Bay. Family suites. Extensive menu. Recommended Le Routard, Dillard/Causin Fran/Frank Sullivan Guides.

B&B	6	Ensuite	£20/£23	€25.39/€29.20	Dinner -
B&B	-	Standard	-	-	Partial Board -
Single Rate			£28/£35	€35.55/€44.44	Child reduction 25%

In Tramore · cc S P ... **Open:** 1st February–15th December

Mrs Teresa O'Sullivan
TIVOLI HOUSE
**Waterford Road, Tramore,
Co Waterford**

Tramore
TEL: **051 390208**   FAX: **051 390208**

Spacious friendly home overlooking Tramore Bay. Beside Splashworld, Golf, Racecourse, Beach, Waterford Crystal. 1 hour Rosslare, 300M from roundabout. Breakfast menu.

B&B	3	Ensuite	£20/£23	€25.39/€29.20	Dinner -
B&B	-	Standard	-	-	Partial Board -
Single Rate			£25.50/£27	€32.38/€34.29	Child reduction 50%

In Tramore · cc P ... **Open:** 1st January–20th December

Neil & Maria Skedd
CLONEEN
**Love Lane, Tramore,
Co Waterford**

Tramore
TEL: **051 381264**   FAX: **051 381264**
EMAIL: cloneen@iol.ie

Family run bungalow set in landscaped gardens. Sun Lounge and Patio for guests. Quiet location with private parking. Beach, Golf and Splashworld nearby.

B&B	4	Ensuite	£20/£20	€25.39	Dinner £12.50
B&B	-	Standard	-	-	Partial Board -
Single Rate			£27/£27	€34.29	Child reduction 50%

In Tramore · cc P ... **Open:** 1st March–31st October

Mrs Jo St John
VENEZIA HOUSE
**Church Road Grove, Tramore,
Co Waterford**

Tramore
TEL: **051 381412**
EMAIL: veneziahouse@ireland.com
WEB: come.to/veneziahouse

Spacious bungalow quiet cul de sac, landscaped gardens, secure parking. 3 mins beach & amenities. Lonely Planet, Lets Go, Dillard/Causin Guides acclaimed. Breakfast menu.

B&B	3	Ensuite	£20/£20	€25.39	Dinner -
B&B	-	Standard	-	-	Partial Board -
Single Rate			-	-	Child reduction 33.3%

In Tramore · cc P ... **Open:** April–October

Frank & Margaret Walsh
SUMMERHILL LODGE
**Ballycarnane, Tramore,
Co Waterford**

Tramore
TEL: **051 381938**   FAX: **051 391333**

Quality welcoming home with private parking and gardens. 10 mins walk beach. Approach via Main Street and Summerhill-200 yards past Credit Union & Catholic Church.

B&B	6	Ensuite	£20/£22	€25.39/€27.93	Dinner -
B&B	-	Standard	-	-	Partial Board -
Single Rate			£25.50/£30	€32.38/€38.09	Child reduction -

In Tramore · cc P ... **Open:** 1st March–31st October

In Tramore

Aine & Joe Whelan
TURRET HOUSE
2 Church Road, Town Centre,
Tramore, Co Waterford

"Tramore at it's Best". Quiet home in the heart of Tramore with superb views. All facilities. Family suite. Private parking.

B&B	4	Ensuite	£19/£21	€24.13/€26.66	Dinner	-
B&B	-	Standard	£17/£19	€21.59/€24.13	Partial Board	-
Single Rate			£25.50/£30	€32.38/€38.09	Child reduction	50%

cc ☐ ☐ ☐ ⚷ ⇢ ✕ ⚷ ⬐ ⤸

Open: April-October

Waterford 5km

Susan Bailey-Daunt
SAMUELS HERITAGE
Ballymaclode, Halfway House,
Dunmore Rd, Co Waterford

Panoramic views, quiet and peaceful country surroundings, close proximity to Beaches, Golf, Angling, Walking, Horseriding and wide choice of Restaurants.

B&B	3	Ensuite	£19	€24.13	Dinner	-
B&B	-	Standard	-	-	Partial Board	-
Single Rate			£25.50	€32.38	Child reduction	50%

cc ☐ ☐ ⊘ ⚷ ⇢ 🛉 ⚷ ⬐ ⤸ J Js JR

Open: All Year

Waterford 5km

Teresa Begadon
RONCALLI
Ballynaneashagh, Cork Road,
Waterford, Co Waterford

Modern house. Spacious bedrooms. Large car park. TV, Tea/Coffee making facilities in bedrooms. Non smoking throughout. Waterford Crystal Factory 1km.

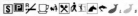

B&B	6	Ensuite	£19	€24.13	Dinner	-
B&B	-	Standard	-	-	Partial Board	-
Single Rate			£25.50	€32.38	Child reduction	25%

☐ ⊘ R ⬐ ☐ ☐ ⚷ ⬐ ⤸ J Js JR

Open: 7th January-15th December

Waterford 7km

Mrs Eithne Brennan
HILLVIEW LODGE
Kilmeaden, Co Waterford

Two storey house with large mature garden on N25. Horse Riding and Golf, Driving Range nearby. Convenient to Waterford Crystal.

B&B	4	Ensuite	£19	€24.13	Dinner	-
B&B	1	Standard	£17	€21.59	Partial Board	-
Single Rate			£23.50	€29.84	Child reduction	25%

S ☐ ⬐ ☐ ⚷ ✕ 🛉 ⚷ ⬐ ⤸ J Js

Open: 1st March-31st October

Waterford 2.5km

Miriam Corcoran
CLADDAGH
Lr Newrath, Ferrybank,
Waterford, Co Waterford

Modern home, quiet area, situated off N9/N24. Adjacent to 18 hole Golf Course. Private Car Park, Tea/Coffee in Bedrooms.

B&B	5	Ensuite	£19/£19	€24.13	Dinner	-
B&B	-	Standard	-	-	Partial Board	-
Single Rate			£25.50/£26	€32.38/€33.01	Child reduction	25%

S ☐ R ⬐ ☐ ☐ 🛉

Open: 1st March-30th November

Waterford 1km

Patrick & Noreen Dullaghan
LOUGHDAN
Newrath, Dublin Rd,
Waterford, Co Waterford

TEL: **051 876021**
EMAIL: info@loughdan.net
WEB: www.loughdan.net

Modern house Dublin/Limerick Rd. N9/N24. Convenient Golf, Bus/Train Station. Tea/Coffee facilities, TV, Hairdryers in bedrooms. Breakfast menu.

B&B	5	Ensuite	£19	€24.13	Dinner	-
B&B	1	Standard	£17	€21.59	Partial Board	-
Single Rate			£26	€33.01	Child reduction	25%

Open: 1st February-30th November

Waterford City 3km

Mrs Catherine Evans
ROSEWOOD
Slieverue, Via Waterford,
Co Waterford

TEL: **051 832233**   FAX: **051 358389**
EMAIL: mevans@waterford.ie

Family run purpose built B&B, beautiful gardens. Located in the small country village of Slieverue on the N25, 3km from Waterford City. Convenient to Waterford Crystal and Golf.

B&B	4	Ensuite	£20/£20	€25.39	Dinner	-
B&B	-	Standard	-	-	Partial Board	-
Single Rate			£26/£26	€33.01	Child reduction	25%

Open: January-October

Waterford 3.5km

Margaret C Fitzmaurice
BLENHEIM HOUSE
Blenheim Heights, Waterford,
Co Waterford

TEL: **051 874115**
EMAIL: blenheim@eircom.net
WEB: http://homepage.eircom.net/~blenheim/

Georgian residence C1763. Furnished throughout with Antiques & object d'art. Surrounded by lawns and private Deer Park. Convenient to Waterford Castle and Faithlegg Golf clubs.

B&B	6	Ensuite	£20	€25.39	Dinner	-
B&B	-	Standard	-	-	Partial Board	-
Single Rate			£25	€31.74	Child reduction	25%

Open: All Year

Waterford 3km

Phil Harrington
BROOKDALE HOUSE
Carrigrue, Ballinaneeshagh,
Waterford, Co Waterford

TEL: **051 375618**

Modern home, quiet location, landscaped surroundings 400m off Cork/Waterford Rd (N25). Spacious Car Park, Tea/Coffee rooms. Near Crystal Factory.

B&B	3	Ensuite	£19/£20	€24.13/€25.39	Dinner	-
B&B	-	Standard	-	-	Partial Board	-
Single Rate			£25.50/£25.50	€32.38	Child reduction	-

Open: 1st April-30th September

Waterford 4.5km

Mrs Margaret Hayes
ARRIVISTE
Holycross, Cork Road,
Butlerstown, Co Waterford

TEL: **051 354080**   FAX: **051 354080**
EMAIL: arriviste_bb@hotmail.com

Country house, central heated. Private car park. Lounge, TV rooms, Tea/Coffee facilities. Large relaxing Conservatory. Landscaped gardens. Situated on N25. 2km from Waterford Crystal.

B&B	5	Ensuite	£19/£19	€24.13	Dinner	-
B&B	-	Standard	-	-	Partial Board	-
Single Rate			£25.50	€32.38	Child reduction	25%

Open: All Year Except Christmas

Mrs Alice O'Sullivan-Jackman
THE PINES
Knockboy, Dunmore Road,
Waterford, Co Waterford

Waterford
TEL: **051 874452**   FAX: **051 841566**
EMAIL: bjackman@eircom.net
WEB: homepage.eircom.net/~pines/

Picturesque rural bungalow, near Hospital, Airport. Breakfast menu. Fishing, Golf, Beaches, Pubs, Seafood Restaurants locally. http://homepage.eircom.net/~pines/

				Dinner	-
B&B	5	Ensuite	£19/£20	€24.13/€25.39	Dinner	-
B&B	-	Standard			Partial Board	-
Single Rate			£25.50	€32.38	Child reduction	-

Waterford City 3km   **Open:** All Year

Antoinette & George Kavanagh
SION HILL HOUSE
Ferrybank, Waterford City,
Co Waterford

Waterford
TEL: **051 851558**   FAX: **051 851678**
EMAIL: sionhill@eircom.net

Spacious Georgian Manor on 5 acres garden. Relaxed atmosphere. AA ◆◆◆◆. 300 metres from Waterford Bridge on Waterford/Rosslare road N25. Next to Jurys Hotel.

					Dinner	-
B&B	4	Ensuite	£24/£30	€30.47/€38.09	Dinner	-
B&B	-	Standard			Partial Board	-
Single Rate			£30/£40	€38.09/€50.79	Child reduction	25%

In Waterford City   **Open:** 3rd January-22nd December

Bernadette Kiely
ASHFIELD B&B
Belmount Road, Ferrybank,
Waterford, Co Waterford

Waterford
TEL: **051 832266**

Comfortable family home on N25. Rosslare 55 mins. Close to Golf, Shops, Crystal Factory and Beaches. Ideal for touring Southeast. TV Lounge with Tea/Coffee Facilities.

					Dinner	-
B&B	3	Ensuite	£19/£20	€24.13/€25.39	Dinner	-
B&B	1	Standard			Partial Board	-
Single Rate			£23.50/£25	€29.84/€31.74	Child reduction	25%

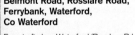

Waterford 2km   **Open:** 1st March-31st October

Mrs Eileen Landy
BELMONT HOUSE
Belmont Road, Rosslare Road,
Ferrybank, Waterford,
Co Waterford

Waterford
TEL: **051 832174**

Easy to find on Waterford/Rosslare Rd. N25. Spacious Modern house. No smoking. Private parking. AA listed. Tea/Coffee facilities. Convenient to Crystal Factory, Golf, Train & Bus City 2km.

					Dinner	-
B&B	3	Ensuite	£19/£21	€24.13/€26.66	Dinner	-
B&B	1	Standard	£17/£19	€21.59/€24.13	Partial Board	-
Single Rate			£27/£30	€34.29/€38.09	Child reduction	-

Waterford City 2km   **Open:** 1st May-31st October

Phyllis McGovern
ASHLEIGH
Holy Cross, Cork Road,
Waterford, Co Waterford

Waterford
TEL: **051 375171**   FAX: **051 375171**
EMAIL: ashleighhouse@eircom.net
WEB: www.ashleigh-house.com

Award of Excellence winner 98/99. Spacious home, gardens, carpark. On N25 close to Waterford Crystal, Pub & Restaurant. TV, Tea/Coffee in rooms. Breakfast menu.

					Dinner	-
B&B	6	Ensuite	£19/£20	€24.13/€25.39	Dinner	-
B&B	-	Standard			Partial Board	-
Single Rate			£25.50	€32.38	Child reduction	25%

Waterford 4km   **Open:** All Year Except Christmas

John & Ann Morrissey
WOODSIDE HOUSE
Whitfield, Cork Rd, Waterford,
Co Waterford

Waterford
TEL: **051 384381**   FAX: **051 384547**
EMAIL: woodsidehouse@eircom.net
WEB: www.woodsidehouse.com

Spacious country house, 5 mins drive Waterford Crystal, Main Cork road (N25). Ideal touring, Golfing base. Best Homestay Award winner. Highly recommended.

B&B	6	Ensuite	£20	€25.39	Dinner	£14
B&B	-	Standard			Partial Board	
Single Rate			£25.50/£30	€32.38/€38.09	Child reduction	25%

Kilmeaden 1.5km   **Open:** 1st January-20th December

Mrs Mary Naughton
UTOPIA B&B
Butlerstown, Co Waterford

Waterford
TEL: **051 384157**   FAX: **051 384157**

Bungalow with large mature landscaped gardens, on N25. Waterford Crystal 3km. Exclusive entrance to guests. Parking. Breakfast menu. Tea/Coffee Facilities.

B&B	3	Ensuite	£20/£20	€25.39	Dinner	£14
B&B	-	Standard			Partial Board	
Single Rate			£25.50/£25.50	€32.38	Child reduction	33.3%

Waterford 3km   **Open:** All Year

Mrs Marian O'Keeffe
ST ANTHONY'S
Ballinaneesagh, Cork Road,
Waterford, Co Waterford

Waterford
TEL: **051 375887**   FAX: **051 353063**

Spacious bungalow with landscaped garden on N25 near Waterford Crystal. Breakfast menu. Colour TV, Tea/Coffee facilities, Hairdryers, Electric Blankets. Frommer reader recommended.

B&B	6	Ensuite	£19	€24.13	Dinner	-
B&B	-	Standard		-	Partial Board	-
Single Rate			£25.50	€32.38	Child reduction	33.3%

Waterford 2km   **Open:** All Year Except Christmas

Terence & Anne O'Neill
ST. JOSEPH'S
Ballinaneeshagh, Cork Road,
Waterford, Co Waterford

Waterford
TEL: **051 376893**

Spacious friendly home. Waterford/Cork N25 2 mins. Crystal Factory. Cable TV, Tea/Coffee facilities in bedrooms. City Bus service. Breakfast menu.

B&B	3	Ensuite	£19.50/£19.50	€24.76	Dinner	-
B&B	-	Standard		-	Partial Board	-
Single Rate			£25.50	€32.38	Child reduction	25%

Waterford 1.5km   **Open:** January-30th November

Mrs Phyllis O'Reilly
ANNVILL HOUSE
1 The Orchard,
Kingsmeadow, Waterford,
Co Waterford

Waterford
TEL: **051 373617**   FAX: **051 373617**

From City, turn right at N25, roundabout near Regional Sports Centre and Waterford Crystal Factory. Frommer Recommended. Tea/Coffee facilities, Breakfast Menu, Hairdryers. City Bus.

B&B	4	Ensuite	£19	€24.13	Dinner	-
B&B	1	Standard	£17	€21.59	Partial Board	-
Single Rate			£26	€33.01	Child reduction	-

Waterford City 1km   **Open:** 1st January-22nd December

Paul & Breda Power
DUNROVEN B&B
Ballinaneesagh, Cork Rd N25,
Waterford City, Co Waterford

Waterford
TEL: **051 374743**   FAX: **051 377050**
EMAIL: dunroven@iol.ie
WEB: www.dunroven-ireland.com

Modern home. Cork/Waterford road N25. 2 minutes Crystal Factory, W.I.T. College. Cable TV, Tea/Coffee, Hairdryers. Breakfast menu. City bus IMP. No Smoking house.

B&B	6	Ensuite	£19	€24.13	Dinner	-
B&B	-	Standard	-	-	Partial Board	-
Single Rate			£26	€33.01	Child reduction	-

Waterford City 1.5km

Open: All Year

Mrs Rena Power
GLENCREE
The Sweep, Kilmeaden,
Co Waterford

Waterford
TEL: **051 384240**

Country home off Cork/Waterford (N25). Crystal Factory, Horse Riding, Pubs, Restaurants locally. Ideal for Coastal, Mountain or Heritage tours.

B&B	3	Ensuite	£19	€24.13	Dinner	-
B&B	2	Standard	£17	€21.59	Partial Board	-
Single Rate			£23.50/£25.50	€29.84/€32.38	Child reduction	25%

Waterford 9km

Open: 1st March-31st October

Mrs Marie Prendergast
TORY VIEW
Mullinavat, Co Waterford

Waterford
TEL: **051 885513**   FAX: **051 885513**

Modern house on N9 Dublin/Kilkenny Road. Tea/Coffee Facilities, TV, Hairdryers in Bedrooms. Convenient Golf & Waterford Crystal.

B&B	4	Ensuite	£19/£19	€24.13	Dinner	-
B&B	1	Standard	£17/£17	€21.59	Partial Board	-
Single Rate			£23.50/£25.50	€29.84/€32.38	Child reduction	25%

Waterford 8km

Open: 1st March-30th October

Helen Quinn
WHITE WEBBS
Ballinaneeshagh,
Waterford, Co Waterford

Waterford
TEL: **051 370696**

Modern home, quiet location 400m off Cork road (N25). Landscaped garden. Tea/Coffee, TV in all rooms. Spacious car park.

B&B	2	Ensuite	£19/£19	€24.13	Dinner	-
B&B	1	Standard	£18/£18	€22.86	Partial Board	-
Single Rate			£25	€31.74	Child reduction	-

Waterford 3km

Open: 1st March-31st October

Maureen Wall
SUNCREST
Slieverue, Ferrybank, Via
Waterford, Co Waterford

Waterford
TEL: **051 832732**   FAX: **051 851861**
EMAIL: suncrest@inet-sec.com

Split level bungalow in quiet rural location 600 metres off N25 Waterford/Rosslare road. In Slieverue village, Waterford City 3kms, Rosslare 50 mins. Ideal base for touring South East.

B&B	5	Ensuite	£20	€25.39	Dinner	-
B&B	-	Standard	-	-	Partial Board	-
Single Rate			£26	€33.01	Child reduction	25%

Waterford 3km

Open: 1st March-30th November

Mrs Patricia Wall
SAN-MARTINO
Ballinaneeshagh, Cork Rd,
Waterford, Co Waterford

Waterford
TEL: 051 374949

Modern bungalow on main Waterford/Cork road. 3 mins from Waterford Crystal Factory. Tea/Coffee facilities. Winner of Award of Excellence for 1998 and 1999.

B&B	5	Ensuite	£19	€24.13	Dinner	£12.50
B&B	-	Standard	-	-	Partial Board	-
Single Rate			£25.50	€32.38	Child reduction	25%

Waterford City 2km

Open: 1st February-31st October

Siobhan Walsh
KINARD
Adamstown, Kilmeaden,
Co Waterford

Waterford
TEL: 051 384505 FAX: 051 384505
EMAIL: kinard@eircom.net
WEB: homepage.eircom.net/~kinard

Bungalow set in mature gardens on N25. Crystal Factory, Beaches, Restaurants, Mountains nearby. TV, Tea/Coffee in all rooms.

B&B	2	Ensuite	£19/£19	€24.13	Dinner	-
B&B	1	Standard	£17/£17	€21.59	Partial Board	-
Single Rate			£23.50/£25.50	€29.84/€32.38	Child reduction	50%

Waterford 9km

Open: 1st May-30th September

Mrs Stella White
BALLYCANAVAN LODGE
Faithlegg, Half Way House,
Waterford, Co Waterford

Waterford
TEL: 051 873928 FAX: 051 873928

Country house set in mature gardens. Adjacent to Golf Courses, Restaurants. Passage East Car Ferry 4km. Ideal location for activity holiday.

B&B	2	Ensuite	£19/£20	€24.13/€25.39	Dinner	£15
B&B	1	Standard	£17/£18	€21.59/€22.86	Partial Board	£225
Single Rate			£23.50/£23.50	€29.84	Child reduction	25%

Waterford 6km

Open: 14th March-1st November

IRELAND AND THE ENVIRONMENT

Ireland is a beautiful country. Research has shown that people come to Ireland to meet the friendly local people and enjoy our unspoilt natural landscape. We try as much as we can to keep our country clean and "green" and we appreciate your co-operation in this matter.

We love to share this beauty with as many people as we can. Therefore it is in all our interests to maintain and enhance the natural splendour that Ireland is lucky enough to enjoy. Respect for natural amenities is essential in order to sustain this beautiful, unspoilt environment. By leaving the places we visit tidy we can all do our bit to help, thus ensuring that future generations will come to visit a naturally green Ireland too.

A region rich in history, landscaped with ancient Castles, Abbeys and Museums. Savor the dramatic scenery of Hook peninsula or leisurely enjoy the sunny South East's golden beaches. Gateway to Britain and Europe - Wexford is famous for its Opera Festival.

Mrs Ann Crosbie
GLENDINE HOUSE
Arthurstown, Co Wexford

Arthurstown
TEL: **051 389258**   FAX: **051 389677**
EMAIL: glendinehouse@eircom.net

We invite you to our charming 1830 Georgian home. We offer superb accommodation, bedrooms enjoy sweeping views of the Estuary. From N25, take R733.

B&B	4	Ensuite	£20/£25	€25.39/€31.74	Dinner	-
B&B	-	Standard		-	Partial Board	-
Single Rate			£30/£35	€38.09/€44.44	Child reduction	25%

Waterford 7km

Open: 1st February-30th November

Ms Peggy Murphy
ARTHUR'S REST
Arthurstown, Co Wexford

Arthurstown
TEL: **051 389192**   FAX: **051 389362**
EMAIL: arthursrest@hotmail.com

Highly recommended spacious country home in estuary village, on the R733 scenic route from Wexford to Waterford. Close to Restaurants, Pubs and Beaches.

B&B	4	Ensuite	£19/£24	€24.13/€30.47	Dinner	-
B&B	-	Standard		-	Partial Board	-
Single Rate			£25.50/£30	€32.38/€38.09	Child reduction	25%

Waterford 7km

Open: All Year

Ms Phil Kinsella
MEADOW SIDE B&B
**Ryland Street, Bunclody,
Co Wexford**

Bunclody
TEL: **054 76226/77459** FAX: **054 76226**

Elegant stone Georgian Town House ideally situated. Tea/Coffee on arrival, TV Lounge, spacious rooms ensuite. Private Car Park.

B&B	3	Ensuite	£20/£25	€25.39/€31.74	Dinner	-
B&B	1	Standard	£18	€22.86	Partial Board	-
Single Rate			£25/£28	€31.74/€35.55	Child reduction	-

In Bunclody

Open: All Year Except Christmas

Mary Parle
ARAS-MUILLINN
**Ambrosetown,
Duncormick, Co Wexford**

Duncormick
TEL: **051 563145**   FAX: **051 563245**

New refurbished modern house. Comfortable surroundings and homely atmosphere. 20 mins from Ferry Port. Early Breakfast.

B&B	2	Ensuite	£19/£19	€24.13	Dinner	-
B&B	1	Standard	£17/£17	€21.59	Partial Board	-
Single Rate			£25.50/£25.50	€32.38	Child reduction	25%

Wexford 22.4km

Open: January-20th December

Mrs A Delany
ST JUDES
Munfin, Tomnalossitt,
Enniscorthy, Co Wexford

Enniscorthy
TEL: 054 33011   FAX: 054 37831

Home located 2km off the N30 on Bree Rd. Scenic countryside. Nearest B&B to Enniscorthy Golf club. Early Breakfast. Rosslare Ferryport 38km. Bedrooms ground floor.

B&B	4	Ensuite	£19/£19	€24.13	Dinner	£14.50
B&B	1	Standard	£17/£17	€21.59	Partial Board	-
Single Rate			£23.50/£25.50	€29.84/€32.38	Child reduction	25%

Enniscorthy 4km

Open: All Year

Helen Kenny
MOYHILL
Bellefield, Enniscorthy,
Co Wexford

Enniscorthy
TEL: 054 34739
EMAIL: helenkenny@ireland.com

We are 50 metres off the Enniscorthy/Kiltealy/Kilkenny Road (R702). Signposted on N30 and at Doyles pub, above Cathedral. Rosslare 40km, Dublin 120km.

B&B	2	Ensuite	£19/£20	€24.13/€25.39	Dinner	-
B&B	1	Standard	£17/£18	€21.59/€22.86	Partial Board	-
Single Rate			£23.50/£25.50	€29.84/€32.38	Child reduction	50%

Enniscorthy 1km

Open: 1st March-31st October

Mrs Noreen Byrne
PERRYMOUNT COUNTRY HOME
Inch, Gorey, Co Wexford

Gorey
TEL: 0402 37418

Situated 50 metres off Dublin/Rosslare Road (N11) at Inch north of Gorey. TV, Tea/Coffee facilities in rooms. Breakfast menu. Pub, Restaurant 50 metres.

B&B	3	Ensuite	£20/£21	€25.39/€26.66	Dinner	£14
B&B	-	Standard	-	-	Partial Board	£230
Single Rate			£25.50/£26	€32.38/€33.01	Child reduction	50%

Gorey 8km

Open: 1st January-20th December

Mrs Martina Redmond
CARRAIG VIEW
Ballycale, Gorey,
Co Wexford

Gorey
TEL: 055 21323   FAX: 055 21323

Select accommodation, rooms ensuite with TV, Hairdryer, Tea/Coffee facilities. Breakfast menu. Situated on the R741 or turn off N11 at Clough Beach nearby.

B&B	2	Ensuite	£19/£20	€24.13/€25.39	Dinner	-
B&B	1	Standard	£17/£18	€21.59/€22.86	Partial Board	-
Single Rate			£23.50/£25.50	€29.84/€32.38	Child reduction	33.3%

Gorey 2km

Open: 1st January-20th December

Mrs Ann Sunderland
HILLSIDE HOUSE
Tubberduff, Gorey,
Co Wexford

Gorey
TEL: 055 21726/22036 FAX: 055 22567
EMAIL: hillside@eircom.net
WEB: http://hillside.virtualave.net

Spacious modern hse, ideal for touring S. East. 3km off N11, 1hr Dublin/Rosslare Ports. All rooms Tea/Coffee, TV, Hairdryers, Electric blankets. Guest lounge with open fire. AA ♦♦♦♦ Award.

B&B	6	Ensuite	£20/£25	€25.39/€31.74	Dinner	£15
B&B	-	Standard	-	-	Partial Board	£225
Single Rate			£25.50/£28	€32.38/€35.55	Child reduction	25%

Gorey 5km

Open: 1st January-18th December

Kilmore Quay 5km

Sean & Mary Cousins
GROVESIDE
**Ballyharty, Kilmore,
Co Wexford**

Kilmore Quay

TEL: 053 35305   FAX: 053 35305
EMAIL: grovesidefarmb-b@iolfree.ie
WEB: www.iolfree.ie/grovesidefarmb_b

Situated on quiet country road, Arable farm. TV, Hairdryer all rooms. Home baking, Restaurants locally. 20 mins Rosslare, Wexford, Sandy Beaches, Saltee Islands.

B&B	3	Ensuite	£19	€24.13	Dinner	-
B&B	-	Standard	-	-	Partial Board	-
Single Rate			£23.50	€29.84	Child reduction	25%

Open: 15th April-30th September

New Ross 14km

Mr Colin Campbell
WOODLANDS HOUSE
**Carrigbyrne, New Ross,
Co Wexford**

New Ross

TEL: 051 428287   FAX: 051 428287
EMAIL: woodwex@eircom.net

Beautifully situated between Wexford and Waterford (N25). 30 Minutes to Rosslare. Tastefully refurbished. Guest lounge. Country walks. Early Breakfast. AA RAC.

B&B	4	Ensuite	£19/£20	€24.13/€25.39	Dinner	£13.50
B&B	-	Standard	-	-	Partial Board	-
Single Rate			£25.50/£25.50	€32.38	Child reduction	-

Open: 1st March-31st October

Mrs Noreen Fallon S.R.N, S.C.M.
KILLARNEY HOUSE
**The Maudlins, New Ross,
Co Wexford**

New Ross

TEL: 051 421062
EMAIL: noreenfallon@eircom.net

New Ross 1km

Frommer recommended. Bedrooms ground floor. Breakfast Menu. Peaceful. Electric Blankets. Reduction for more than 1 night. Complimentary Tea/Coffee. Pub nearby. Rosslare Ferry 45 mins.

B&B	2	Ensuite	£19/£19	€24.13	Dinner	-
B&B	1	Standard	£17/£17	€21.59	Partial Board	-
Single Rate			£23.50/£25.50	€29.84/€32.38	Child reduction	33.3%

Open: 1st April-30th September

Mrs Ann Foley
RIVERSDALE HOUSE
**Lr William Street, New Ross,
Co Wexford**

New Ross

TEL: 051 422515   FAX: 051 422800
EMAIL: riversdalehse@eircom.net

In New Ross

Spacious ensuite bedrooms (one triple) with TV, Tea/Coffee, Electric blankets, Hairdryers. Parking. Sun Lounge. Gardens. Non smoking home. 5 mins walk to Town Centre.

B&B	4	Ensuite	£19/£20	€24.13/€25.39	Dinner	-
B&B	-	Standard	-	-	Partial Board	-
Single Rate			£29/£29	€36.82	Child reduction	-

Open: 1st April-1st November

New Ross 1km

Mrs Philomena Gallagher
ROSVILLE HOUSE
**Knockmullen, New Ross,
Co Wexford**

New Ross

TEL: 051 421798
EMAIL: rosvillehouse@oceanfree.net
WEB: members.tripod.com/~rosvillehouse

Modern home in peaceful surroundings. Guaranteed hospitality/comfort. Overlooking River Barrow. Rosslare Ferries 40 mins. Early breakfast. Private Parking.

B&B	4	Ensuite	£19/£19	€24.13	Dinner	-
B&B	1	Standard	£17/£17	€21.59	Partial Board	-
Single Rate			£23.50/£25.50	€29.84/€32.38	Child reduction	25%

Open: March-November

New Ross 1.5km

Ms Susan Halpin
OAKWOOD HOUSE
Ring Road, Mountgarrett,
New Ross, Co Wexford

New Ross
TEL: **051 425494**   FAX: **051 425494**
EMAIL: susan@oakwoodhouse.net
WEB: www.oakwoodhouse.net

Modern house on N30 own grounds. Private car park. Spacious en suite bedrooms with TV, Tea/Coffee facilities. Rosslare Ferries 40 mins. Early breakfast.

B&B	4	Ensuite	£19/£19	€24.13	Dinner	-
B&B	-	Standard	-	-	Partial Board	-
Single Rate			£25.50/£25.50	€32.38	Child reduction	25%

Open: 1st March-31st October

New Ross 4km

Annette Kinsella
GREENPARK
Creakan Lower, New Ross,
Co Wexford

New Ross
TEL: **051 421028**   FAX: **051 421028**

Greenpark is an Olde Worlde country house. Just off the R733, 4km from New Ross. 45 mins drive from Rosslare. Peaceful rural setting. No weddings.

B&B	2	Ensuite	£20/£20	€25.39	Dinner	-
B&B	1	Standard	£17/£17	€21.59	Partial Board	-
Single Rate			£23.50/£28	€29.84/€35.55	Child reduction	25%

Open: 1st February-30th November

In New Ross

Mrs Sadie Michels
VENROODE
off William St, Lr South Knock,
New Ross, Co Wexford

New Ross
TEL: **051 421446**   FAX: **051 421446**
EMAIL: michelstom@hotmail.com

Venroode" is set in peaceful mature gardens overlooking River Barrow. Ideal base for touring. Early breakfast. Dutch and German spoken.

B&B	2	Ensuite	£19/£19	€24.13	Dinner	-
B&B	1	Standard	£17/£17	€21.59	Partial Board	-
Single Rate			£23.50/£25.50	€29.84/€32.38	Child reduction	33.3%

Open: 5th January-20th December

Rosslare 3km

Mrs Ann Kelly
DECCA HOUSE
Rosslare, Co Wexford

Rosslare
TEL: **053 32410**
EMAIL: deccahouse@eircom.net

Early breakfast. Location R740 (1km off main N25). Quiet area. Convenient Ferries. Access/Visa.

B&B	3	Ensuite	£19	€24.13	Dinner	-
B&B	2	Standard	£17	€21.59	Partial Board	-
Single Rate			£24	€30.47	Child reduction	-

Open: January-19th December

Rosslare 1.5km

Susan & Eric Stewart
BALLYBRO LODGE
Tagoat, Killinick,
Co Wexford

Rosslare
TEL: **053 32333**   FAX: **053 32333**
EMAIL: ballybrolodge@oceanfree.net

Modern home. Peaceful landscaped gardens. Convenient - Beaches, Golf, Car Ferry. Guest Lounge. Tea/Coffee facilities. Early breakfasts. R736 Rosslare-Tagoat.

B&B	4	Ensuite	£19	€24.13	Dinner	-
B&B	-	Standard		-	Partial Board	-
Single Rate			£26	€33.01	Child reduction	50%

Open: All Year Except Christmas

Rosslare Harbour 1km

Sue & Neil Carty
MARIANELLA
Kilrane, Rosslare Harbour, Co Wexford

Rosslare Harbour
TEL: **053 33139**

Comfortable bungalow on N25. 1km Ferry Port. All rooms on ground floor with TV & Tea/Coffee facilities. Guest lounge. Early breakfast. Restaurants nearby.

B&B	4	Ensuite	**£19/£19**	€24.13	Dinner -
B&B	2	Standard	**£17/£17**	€21.59	Partial Board -
Single Rate			**£23.50/£25.50**	€29.84/€32.38	Child reduction **33.3%**

Open: All Year Except Christmas

Rosslare Harbour 1km

Kay Crean
OLD ORCHARD LODGE
Kilrane, Rosslare Harbour, Co Wexford

Rosslare Harbour
TEL: **053 33468**
EMAIL: oldorchardlodge@eircom.net
WEB: homepage.eircom.net/~oldorchardlodge/

1km Ferry. Early breakfast available. Private Parking. All rooms ensuite, Tea/Coffee & TV. Beside good Restaurants & Pubs. On quiet country road opposite Pubs in Kilrane village.

B&B	5	Ensuite	**£19/£19**	€24.13	Dinner -
B&B	-	Standard			Partial Board -
Single Rate			**£25.50/£25.50**	€32.38	reduction **50%**

Open: All Year

Rosslare Harbour 5km

Mrs Margaret Day
ASHLEY LODGE B&B
Ballycowan, Tagoat, Rosslare Harbour, Co Wexford

Rosslare Harbour
TEL: **053 31991**

The house is 400 metres off the N25 to Rosslare Harbour. Turn on to R736 at Tagoat Village, Ashley Lodge is on the Right, 400 metres off N25.

B&B	4	Ensuite	**£20/£22**	€25.39/€27.93	Dinner -
B&B	-	Standard			Partial Board -
Single Rate			**£25.50/£25.50**	€32.38	Child reduction **25%**

Open: 1st January-24th December

In Rosslare Harbour

Mrs Mary Duggan
ELMWOOD
Rosslare Harbour, Co Wexford

Rosslare Harbour
TEL: **053 33321**

Excellent recommendations. Le Guide du Routard. Peaceful location 2 mins drive from Ferry. Signposted opposite church. Hairdryer, Tea/Coffee. Early Breakfast menu.

B&B	3	Ensuite	**£19**	€24.13	Dinner -
B&B	-	Standard		-	Partial Board -
Single Rate			**£25.50**	€32.38	Child reduction **25%**

Open: 1st May-30th September

Wexford

Ms Helen Farrell
PADUA
Kilscoran, Tagoat, Co Wexford

Rosslare Harbour
TEL: **053 31373**

Modern family home, 1km from Rosslare Harbour on the main road. Early Breakfast. Private Parking. Convenient to all facilities. Hairdryers in bedrooms.

B&B	3	Ensuite	**£19**	€24.13	Dinner -
B&B	-	Standard		-	Partial Board **£185**
Single Rate			**£25.50**	€32.38	Child reduction **25%**

Open: All Year Except Christmas

Anne Gleeson
WAYSIDE HOUSE
Ballygeary, Kilrane, Rosslare Harbour, Co Wexford

Rosslare Harbour
Tel: **053 33475**

Country house on quiet road off N25. 1km Rosslare Port. Rooms with shower/toilet, TV, Tea/Coffee. Private Parking. Early breakfast.

B&B	3	Ensuite	**£19**	€24.13	Dinner	-
B&B	-	Standard	-	-	Partial Board	-
Single Rate			**£25.50**	€32.38	Child reduction	**50%**

Rosslare Harbour 1.5km

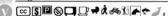

Open: 31st March-31st October

Mr Stephen Hession
ASGARD B&B
1 The Moorings, Rosslare Harbour, Co Wexford

Rosslare Harbour
Tel: **053 33602**   Fax: **053 33602**
Email: asgardbb@ireland.com
Web: www.asgardbb.com

Friendly Irish Home located 500m from the Ferry Port, Bus and Train Terminals. Close to Pubs, Hotels, Restaurants and Bank. Early Breakfast. TV, rooms en-suite.

B&B	3	Ensuite	**£19/£20**	€24.13/€25.39	Dinner	-
B&B	-	Standard	-	-	Partial Board	-
Single Rate			**£25.50/£26**	€32.38/€33.01	Child reduction	**33.3%**

In Rosslare Harbour

Open: 1st March-31st November

JFK ARBORETUM
NEW ROSS, CO. WEXFORD
TEL + 353 51 388171 FAX+ 353 51 388172

The John F. Kennedy Arboretum, on 252 hectares, contains 45,000 types of trees, and scrubs, 200 forest plots, rhododrendrons, dwarf conifers, lake, viewing point, tea room and visitor centre with an audio-visual show.

Rosslare Harbour Village 1km

Mrs Kathleen Lawlor
CARRAGH LODGE
**Station Road, Rosslare Harbour,
Co Wexford**

Tel: **053 33492**

Modern bungalow on quiet side road off N25. 3 minutes drive from Ferryport. TV, Tea & Coffee facilities.

B&B	3	Ensuite	£19/£19	€24.13	Dinner	-
B&B	1	Standard	£17/£17	€21.59	Partial Board	-
Single Rate			£23.50/£25.50	€29.84/€32.38	Child reduction	-

Open: 1st March-31st October

Rosslare Harbour 2km

Mrs Carmel Lonergan
CLOVER LAWN
**Kilrane, Rosslare Harbour,
Co Wexford**

Tel: **053 33413**
Email: cloverlawn@eircom.net
Web: homepage.eircom.net/~cloverlawn

Highly recommended comfortable home. 1km from Ferry Port. In Kilrane Village turn left between pubs 3rd house on right. Early Breakfast. Golf, Beaches, Restaurants, Bus and Rail nearby.

B&B	2	Ensuite	£19/£19	€24.13	Dinner	-
B&B	2	Standard	£17/£17	€21.59	Partial Board	-
Single Rate			£23.50/£30	€29.84/€38.09	Child reduction	33.3%

Open: 1st March-31st October

Rosslare Harbour

Mary McDonald
OLDCOURT HOUSE
Rosslare Harbour, Co Wexford

Tel: **053 33895**

Modern house overlooking Rosslare Bay. Close to Hotels & Ferryport. Early Breakfast. Golf, Beaches nearby. AA ✦✦✦✦ selected.

B&B	6	Ensuite	£19/£20	€24.13/€25.39	Dinner	-
B&B		Standard	-	-	Partial Board	-
Single Rate			£25/£25.50	€31.74/€32.38	Child reduction	33.3%

Open: All Year

Rosslare Harbour 5km

John & Catherine McHugh
BALLYCOWAN LODGE
Tagoat, Co Wexford

Tel: **053 31596**   Fax: **053 31596**

Secluded peaceful location only 150m off N25. 5 mins to Ferry. Early Breakfast. All rooms TV & Tea/Coffee making facilities.

B&B	4	Ensuite	£19/£20	€24.13/€25.39	Dinner	-
B&B		Standard	-	-	Partial Board	-
Single Rate			£25.50/£27.50	€32.38/€34.91	Child reduction	50%

Open: All Year Except Christmas

In Rosslare Harbour

Brigid Murphy
ABRAE HOUSE
**Kilrane, Rosslare Harbour,
Co Wexford**

Tel: **053 33283**   Fax: **053 33283**

Luxury home on main N25. Restaurants and Tourist Amenities within walking distance. 2 mins to Ferry. Early Breakfast.

B&B	4	Ensuite	£19/£19	€24.13	Dinner	-
B&B		Standard	-	-	Partial Board	-
Single Rate			-	-	Child reduction	-

Open: 1st January-23rd December

Rosslare Harbour 1km

Mrs Dorothy O'Brien
BORO LODGE
Kilrane, Rosslare Harbour,
Co Wexford

Rosslare Harbour
Tel: 053 33610

Modern bungalow 200ms off main N25 at Kilrane. 3 mins drive from Ferry & Rail. Convenient to Golf, Beach, Bus, Restaurant. Early breakfast. Private parking.

B&B	2	Ensuite	£19/£19	€24.13	Dinner	-
B&B	2	Standard	£17/£17	€21.59	Partial Board	-
Single Rate			£23.50/£25.50	€29.84/€32.38	Child reduction	25%

Open: 1st February-31st October

In Rosslare Harbour

Mr & Mrs D O'Donoghue
LAUREL LODGE
Rosslare Harbour,
Co Wexford

Rosslare Harbour
Tel: 053 33291

Comfortable home on quiet road off Rosslare Harbour Village. 1km from Ferry. Within walking distance of 3 Hotels.

B&B	4	Ensuite	£19	€24.13	Dinner	-
B&B	-	Standard	-	-	Partial Board	-
Single Rate			£25.50	€32.38	Child reduction	-

Open: 1st March-31st October

In Rosslare Harbour

Ann O'Dwyer
AILESBURY
5 The Moorings,
Rosslare Harbour, Co Wexford

Rosslare Harbour
Tel: 053 33185   Fax: 053 33185
Email: ailesb@eircom.net

Comfortable home. Closest B&B on N25 to Ferryport, Rail/Bus terminals. Restaurants nearby. AA listed, Orthopaedic beds, Hairdryers. Early breakfast.

B&B	3	Ensuite	£19/£20	€24.13/€25.39	Dinner	-
B&B	1	Standard	-	-	Partial Board	-
Single Rate			£25/£30	€31.74/€38.09	Child reduction	-

Open: All Year Except Christmas

In Rosslare

Ms Una Stack
DUNGARA B&B
Kilrane, Rosslare Harbour,
Co Wexford

Rosslare Harbour
Tel: 053 33391   Fax: 053 33391

Comfortable home with friendly athmosphere on N25. 1km to Ferry. TV, Electric Blankets, Tea/Coffee in rooms. Early Breakfast. Shops and Restaurants nearby.

B&B	5	Ensuite	£19/£19	€24.13	Dinner	-
B&B	1	Standard	£17/£17	€21.59	Partial Board	-
Single Rate			£23.50	€29.84	Child reduction	50%

Open: All Year Except Christmas

Rosslare Harbour 2km

Ms Siobhan Whitehead
KILRANE HOUSE
Kilrane, Rosslare Harbour,
Co Wexford

Rosslare Harbour
Tel: 053 33135   Fax: 053 33739

Period house. Many original features, superb ornate. Guest lounge. Opposite Pub, Restaurants. TV in 4 rooms. 3 mins drive from Ferry. Recommended by many guides.

B&B	6	Ensuite	£19/£20	€24.13/€25.39	Dinner	-
B&B	-	Standard	-	-	Partial Board	-
Single Rate			£25.50/£34	€32.38/€43.17	Child reduction	33.3%

Open: 2nd January-23rd December

Wexford

James F Cahill
ARD RUADH MANOR
**Spawell Road, Wexford,
Co Wexford**

Wexford

Tel: **053 23194**   Fax: **053 23194**
Email: ardruadh@hotmail.com
Web: www.ardruadh-manor.com

Luxurious Victorian house (1893). One acre private gardens. Beside all amenities. AA ♦♦♦♦ selected. Ferry 15 mins. 3 mins walk to Town Centre. Sea views.

B&B	6	Ensuite	£20/£30	€25.39/€38.09	Dinner	-
B&B	-	Standard			Partial Board	-
Single Rate			£25.50/£40	€32.38/€50.79	Child reduction	25%

cc P ☕ 🛏 ♦ ⚓ 🏃

Open: All Year Except Christmas

Peter and Mary Caulfield
NEWTOWN HOUSE
**Newtown Road, Wexford,
Co Wexford**

Wexford

Tel: **053 43253**

Luxurious family home on elevated site. Scenic view, convenient to Beaches, Golf, Fishing and Horseriding. Ideal tourists base for Wexford.

B&B	3	Ensuite	£19/£22	€24.13/€27.93	Dinner	-
B&B	1	Standard	£18/£18	€22.86	Partial Board	-
Single Rate			£25/£30	€31.74/€38.09	Child reduction	25%

cc P ♣ ⊗ ✂ 🛏 ☕ ♦ ⚓

Wexford 2.5km

Open: January-15th December

Mrs Maria Doyle-Colfer
THE ROSE
**Camross, Foulksmills,
Wexford, Co Wexford**

Wexford

Tel: **054 40524**
Email: marcol@eircom.net

Situated on the N25, easy access. Breakfast menu, Conservatory. French spoken, Refreshments on arrival. Restaurants, pleasant walks nearby, Central location.

B&B	2	Ensuite	£19	€24.13	Dinner	-
B&B	2	Standard	£17	€21.59	Partial Board	-
Single Rate			-	-	Child reduction	33.3%

S P ♣ ✂ ☕ ✕

Wexford 18km

Open: 15th April-31st October

Ms Grainne Cullen
GRANVILLE HOUSE
**Clonard Road, Wexford,
Co Wexford**

Wexford

Tel: **053 22648**

Luxury accommodation in warm friendly family home surrounded by award winning gardens. Interior designed to the highest standards. Close to N11 and N25.

B&B	6	Ensuite	£20/£25	€25.39/€31.74	Dinner	-
B&B	-	Standard			Partial Board	-
Single Rate			£25/£30	€31.74/€38.09	Child reduction	-

cc P ♣ ✂ ⊗ ✂ 🛏 ☕ ♦ ⚓ 🏃

Wexford 1.5km

Open: March-December

TELEPHONE

- Operator assisted calls within Ireland   Dial 10
- International telephone operator   Dial 11818
- Directory Enquiries   Dial 11811

FOR TROUBLE-FREE TELEPHONE CALLS FROM PUBLIC PAY PHONES IT IS ADVISABLE TO PURCHASE A TELEPHONE CALLCARD AVAILABLE IN POST OFFICES AND WHEREVER YOU SEE A CALLCARD SIGN.
TO DIAL IRELAND FROM ABROAD: Country Access Code + 353 + Area Code (omit first zero) + Local Number

---

In Wexford

Mrs Angela Doocey
TOWNPARKS HOUSE
Coolcotts, Wexford,
Co Wexford

Wexford
TEL: 053 45191

Purpose-built Georgian house off R769. 10 mins walk Town Centre. 20 mins Rosslare Ferries.
Tea/Coffee facilities, Clock Radios, Hairdryers. Early Breakfast.

B&B	4	Ensuite	£19/£21	€24.13/€26.66	Dinner	-
B&B	1	Standard	£19/£21	€24.13/€26.66	Partial Board	-
Single Rate			£25.50/£30	€32.38/€38.09	Child reduction	33.3%

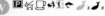

Open: All Year Except Christmas

Mrs Jackie Dooley
THE BROMLEY
Country House, Coolcotts Lane,
Wexford, Co Wexford

Wexford
TEL: 053 46222   FAX: 053 46222
EMAIL: jackie@thebromley.buyandsell.ie

Magnificent country house, spacious bedrooms tastefully decorated. Peaceful scenic surroundings.
2 mins Wexford Town, 15 mins Rosslare Harbour/Beach.

B&B	3	Ensuite	£25/£30	€31.74/€38.09	Dinner	-
B&B	-	Standard		-	Partial Board	-
Single Rate			£35/£35	€44.44	Child reduction	50%

Open: 1st January-21st December

Wexford 2km

Mrs Maureen Gurhy
LITTLE ASH
Glenville Road, Clonard,
Co Wexford

Wexford
TEL: 053 41475

Warm friendly home surrounded by 1 acre of beautiful gardens. Family rooms, Electric blankets,
Hairdryers. Ferry 15 mins. Early Breakfasts. N25/N11 roundabout (R769).

B&B	3	Ensuite	£19/£20	€24.13/€25.39	Dinner	-
B&B	1	Standard	£23.50/£25.50	€29.84/€32.38	Partial Board	-
Single Rate					Child reduction	50%

Open: 1st January-20th December

Rosslare

Dorothy Healy
LORANDA LODGE
Ballygillane, Rosslare Harbour,
Co Wexford

Wexford
TEL: 053 33804   FAX: 053 33804
EMAIL: loranda@esatclear.ie

Peaceful location 5 mins from Ferry. Early breakfast. Turn up village at Church, Supermarket on
left, Railway club on right, next turn on right, house on left.

B&B	3	Ensuite	£19	€24.13	Dinner	-
B&B	-	Standard		-	Partial Board	-
Single Rate			£25.50	€32.38	Child reduction	50%

Open: 1st March-31st October

Wexford Town

Mrs Maureen Keogh
ELMLEIGH
Coolcots, Wexford Town,
Co Wexford

Wexford
TEL: 053 44174
EMAIL: maureen.keogh@oceanfree.net

Modern home in peaceful residential area. Secure parking. Guests garden. Family rooms. 1 minute
from N11/N25. 10 mins walk to Town Centre. 20 mins to Ferry, Rosslare.

B&B	3	Ensuite	£19	€24.13	Dinner	-
B&B	1	Standard	£17	€21.59	Partial Board	-
Single Rate			£23.50	€29.84	Child reduction	50%

Open: 1st January-21st December

Ms Sarah I Lee
ROCKCLIFFE
Coolballow, Wexford,
Co Wexford

Wexford
Tel: **053 43130**
Email: sarahlee@ireland.com

Lovely landscaped garden on 1 acre. Scenic views. Frommer Recommended. N25 from Rosslare Harbour through roundabout towards Wexford. R730 Junction left after "Farmers Kitchen".

B&B	3	Ensuite	£19/£19	€24.13	Dinner	-
B&B	1	Standard	£17/£17	€21.59	Partial Board	-
Single Rate			£25.50/£25.50	€32.38	Child reduction	25%

Wexford 3km

Open: April-October

Ms Mary D Moore
ROCKVILLE
Rocklands, Wexford Town,
Co Wexford

Wexford
Tel: **053 22147**   Fax: **053 22147**
Email: marydm@indigo.ie

Comfortable home, quiet location. Southern fringe Wexford town (R730). Private parking, secluded gardens. Walking distance Town Centre. Ferry 15 minutes.

B&B	2	Ensuite	£19/£19	€24.13	Dinner	-
B&B	1	Standard	£17.50/£17.50	€22.22	Partial Board	-
Single Rate			£25/£25.50	€31.74/€32.38	Child reduction	50%

In Wexford

Open: 1st January-20th December

Mrs Fionnuala Murphy
THE GALLOPS B&B
Bettyville, Newtown Road,
Wexford, Co Wexford

Wexford
Tel: **053 44035**   Fax: **053 44950**

Beautiful home architecturally designed, excellent accommodation. Tea/Coffee, TV's, Hairdryers. Overlooking garden. Scenic views. Early breakfast. 1mile Town centre. Private Car park.

B&B	4	Ensuite	£22.50/£25	€28.57/€31.74	Dinner	-
B&B	-	Standard	-	-	Partial Board	-
Single Rate			£25.50/£30	€32.38/€38.09	Child reduction	50%

Wexford 2km

Open: 2nd January-20th December

Nicholas & Kathleen Murphy
GLENHILL
Ballygoman, Barntown,
Co Wexford

Wexford
Tel: **053 20015**

Modern home peaceful surroundings. Guaranteed hospitality. On N25 15 mins Rosslare Ferries. Early breakfast. Private car park. Ferrycarrig 2km. Wexford 4km.

B&B	3	Ensuite	£19/£20	€24.13/€25.39	Dinner	-
B&B	-	Standard	-	-	Partial Board	-
Single Rate			-	-	Child reduction	33.3%

Wexford 4km

Open: 1st January-20th December

Mrs Kathleen Nolan
DARRAL HOUSE
Spawell Road, Wexford,
Co Wexford

Wexford
Tel: **053 24264**   Fax: **053 24284**

Beautiful period house (1803). Luxury accommodation. AA ♦♦♦♦ Wexford Town centre 3 mins walk, Car Ferry 15 mins. Private car park.

B&B	4	Ensuite	£20/£27.50	€25.39/€34.91	Dinner	-
B&B	-	Standard	-	-	Partial Board	-
Single Rate			£25/£35	€31.74/€44.44	Child reduction	50%

Open: All Year Except Christmas

David & Mary O'Brien
AUBURN HOUSE
2 Auburn Tce, Redmond Road,
Wexford, Co Wexford

Wexford
TEL: **053 23605**   FAX: **053 42725**
EMAIL: mary@obriensauburnhouse.com
WEB: www.obriensauburnhouse.com

Built in 1891, our elegantly restored townhouse offers excellent accommodation. Rooms are charming and spacious, many enjoying a view of the River Slaney.

B&B	4	Ensuite	£20/£25	€25.39/€31.74	Dinner —
B&B	1	Standard	£20/£25	€25.39/€31.74	Partial Board —
Single Rate			£30/£30	€38.09	Child reduction 50%

 In Wexford

Open: 2nd January-18th December

Nick & Eleanor O'Connor
TROON LODGE
Ballycrane, Castlebridge,
Wexford, Co Wexford

Wexford
TEL: **053 59012**   FAX: **053 59200**
EMAIL: troon@iol.ie
WEB: www.troonlodge.com

Modern friendly home. Ideal for Rosslare Ferry, Curracloe/Beach. Wexford Town 3 min drive. All rooms ensuite, Power showers. Lovely gardens. Early Breakfast.

B&B	3	Ensuite	£22.50/£25	€28.57/€31.74	Dinner —
B&B	1	Standard	—	—	Partial Board —
Single Rate			£25.50/£45	€32.38/€57.14	Child reduction 20%

Wexford 3km

Open: 1st March-30th November

Mrs Breda O'Grady
VILLA MARIA
Ivy Lane, Coolcots,
Wexford, Co Wexford

Wexford
TEL: **053 45143**

Modern bungalow in private cul-de-sac. Convenient Heritage Park, Golf, Rosslare Ferry. Tea/Coffee facilities, early Breakfast.

B&B	3	Ensuite	£19	€24.13	Dinner —
B&B	1	Standard	£17	€21.59	Partial Board —
Single Rate			£25/£30	€31.74/€38.09	Child reduction 50%

 Wexford 1km

Open: 7th January-22th December

Ms Margaret Redmond
FERRYCARRIG LODGE
Park, Ferrycarrig Road,
Wexford, Co Wexford

Wexford
TEL: **053 42605**

Charming, relaxing residence, nestled on riverbank. Individually designed rooms, 10 min walk Heritage Park, Hotel, Quality Restaurants, Ferries 15 mins.

B&B	4	Ensuite	£20/£25	€25.39/€31.74	Dinner —
B&B	-	Standard	—	—	Partial Board —
Single Rate			£25.50/£30	€32.38/€38.09	Child reduction 33.3%

Wexford 2km

Open: All Year

Bernard & Anne Roche
ANBER HOUSE
Glenbrook, Newton Road,
Wexford, Co Wexford

Wexford
TEL: **053 47313**
EMAIL: anberhouse@yahoo.com

This newly built house is in an elevated position just 10 minutes walk from the Town Centre. There is a relaxing Guests Room and Sun Lounge off diningroom.

B&B	3	Ensuite	£19/£20	€24.13/€25.39	Dinner —
B&B	-	Standard	—	—	Partial Board —
Single Rate			£25.50/£25.50	€32.38	Child reduction 33.3%

In Wexford

Open: 3rd January-20th December

Mrs Catherine Saunderson
FARRANSEER HOUSE
**Coolcots, Wexford,
Co Wexford**

Wexford
TEL: 053 44042

Spacious home in Wexford Town. Landscaped grounds. Convenient to local amenities. TV bedrooms and lounge. Tea/Coffee facilities. Early Breakfast.

				Dinner	-
B&B	2	Ensuite	£19/£20	€24.13/€25.39	Dinner -
B&B	2	Standard	£17/£18	€21.59/€22.86	Partial Board -
Single Rate			£26/£30	€33.01/€38.09	Child reduction -

In Wexford   **Open:** All Year

Ms Imelda Scallan
THE BLUE DOOR B&B
**18 Lower George Street,
Wexford, Co Wexford**

Wexford
TEL: 053 21047
EMAIL: bluedoor@indigo.ie
WEB: indigo.ie/~bluedoor

Luxury accommodation in Georgian Townhouse. Views of Westgate Castle. Beside traditional music Pubs, Restaurants, Shops. Bus/Rail 2 mins. Opposite Whites Hotel.

					Dinner	-
B&B	4	Ensuite	£18/£25	€22.86/€31.74	Dinner -
B&B	-	Standard	-	-	Partial Board -
Single Rate			£25/£30	€31.74/€38.09	Child reduction 50%

In Wexford   **Open:** All Year

Ms Yvette Shovlin
TARA
**Kitestown Cross, Ferrycarrig,
Wexford, Co Wexford**

Wexford
TEL: 053 20133
EMAIL: taracountryhome@hotmail.com

Excellent accommodation, spacious rooms. On main N11. Walking distance Ferrycarrig Hotel, Pub/Restaurant, Heritage Park. 5 mins Wexford, Ferries 15 mins.

					Dinner	-
B&B	5	Ensuite	£19/£25	€24.13/€31.74	Dinner -
B&B	-	Standard	-	-	Partial Board -
Single Rate			£25.50/£30	€32.38/€38.09	Child reduction 33.3%

Wexford 4km   **Open:** 1st February-20th December

Eamonn & Margaret Sreenan
MAPLE LODGE
**Ballycrane, Castlebridge,
Co Wexford**

Wexford
TEL: 053 59195   FAX: 053 59195
EMAIL: sreenan@tinet.ie
WEB: gofree.indigo.ie/~mapleldg

Tea & Scones await you in our home on R741. 4km Wexford, 6km Curracloe Beach, 20 mins Rosslare Port. Breakfast menu. Home baking. AA ♦♦♦♦. Award Winning gardens. Golf arranged.

					Dinner	-
B&B	4	Ensuite	£20/£22.50	€25.39/€28.57	Dinner -
B&B	-	Standard	-	-	Partial Board -
Single Rate			£25.50/£30	€32.38/€38.09	Child reduction 33.3%

Wexford 4km   **Open:** 1st February-30th November

Mrs Christina Toomey
BEDFORD HOUSE
**Ballymorris, Clonard,
Wexford, Co Wexford**

Wexford
TEL: 053 45643
EMAIL: bedford@eircom.net

Situated on Duncannon New Line Road (R733) 0.5 kms off N25. 15 mins Rosslare Ferry. Early breakfast. Large family room.

					Dinner	-
B&B	4	Ensuite	£19/£19	€24.13	Dinner -
B&B	-	Standard	-	-	Partial Board -
Single Rate			£25.50/£25.50	€32.38	Child reduction 50%

Wexford 3km   **Open:** All Year Except Christmas

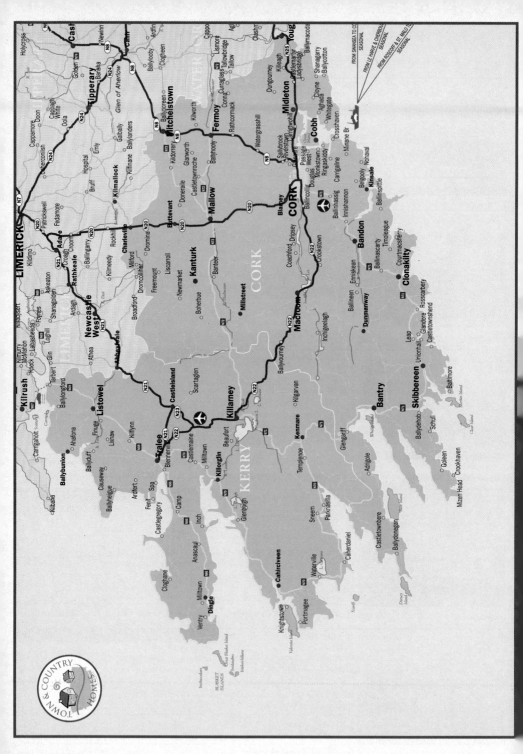

Located in the south-west corner of Ireland, the Cork and South Kerry region offers its visitors a great diversity of scenery, culture and leisure activities. The region claims some of the most varied and spectacular scenery in the country. Here you will find the full range of holiday options to ensure a memorable, refreshing and very different holiday.

The South Western coastline, sculptured by the ice-age and influenced by the warm waters of the Gulf Stream, is steeped in ancient history and folklore from the East and West Cork coasts, The Beara and Dingle Peninsulas, and from the Ring of Kerry to the Lakes of Killarney and the Bandon, Lee and Blackwater Valleys.

Ross Castle, Killarney

Some of Ireland's best international festivals are hosted in the region and attractions for all the family, guarantees a fun filled holiday.

Area Representatives

CORK
Mrs Georgina Coughlan, Glebe House, Tay Road, Cobh, Co Cork
Tel: 021 811373 Fax: 021 811373
Mrs Gillian Good, Glebe Country House, Ballinadee,
Bandon, Co Cork Tel: 021 778294 Fax: 021 778456
Mrs Anne O'Leary, Ashlee Lodge, Tower, Blarney, Co Cork
Tel: 021 385346 Fax: 021 385726

KERRY
Mrs Noreen Dineen, Manor House, 18 Whitebridge Manor,
Ballycasheen, Killarney, Co Kerry
Tel: 064 32716 Fax: 064 32716
Mrs Mary Hodnett, Silvertrees, Lansdowne Lodge, Kenmare,
Co Kerry Tel: 064 41008
Mrs Margaret Ryle, Crana-Li, Curragraigue, Blennerville,
Tralee, Co Kerry Tel: 066 7124467

 ## Tourist Information Offices

Cork
Aras Failte, Grand Parade
Tel: 021 4273251

Blarney
Tel: 021 4381624

Killarney
Beech Road
Tel: 064 31633

Skibbereen
Town Hall
Tel: 028 21766

Cork, the southern capital, Ireland's largest county. West Cork warmed by the Gulf stream with spectacular scenic beauty. Experience the tranquillity of East Cork with its sandy beaches. Get lost in nature in North Cork through rolling hills and valleys.

In Ballincollig

Mrs Rose Cotter
WESTFIELD HOUSE
West Village, Ballincollig, Co Cork

Ballincollig
TEL: **021 871824**   FAX: **021 877415**
EMAIL: rosecotter@tinet.ie

Welcoming Tea/Coffee on arrival. Modern house, adjacent Ballincollig main Cork/Killarney N22. On bus route, convenient Blarney, Airport, Ferry, Dogtrack.

B&B	2	Ensuite	£19/£22	€24.13/€27.93	Dinner -
B&B	1	Standard	£17/£20	€21.59/€25.59	Partial Board -
Single Rate			£23.50/£25.50	€29.84/€32.38	Child reduction 25%

Open: 1st January-22nd December

Ballincollig 2km

Mrs Maureen Cronin
THE MILESTONE
Ovens, Ballincollig, Co Cork

Ballincollig
TEL: **021 4872562**   FAX: **021 4872562**
EMAIL: milestone@eircom.net

AA ✦✦✦ Award. On N22 road, Ballincollig 2km. Tea/coffee/hairdryer in large rooms. Warm welcome. Highly commended. Central, Airport-Ferry-Cork-Blarney-Kinsale-Cobh.

B&B	5	Ensuite	£19/£22	€24.13/€27.93	Dinner -
B&B	-	Standard	-		Partial Board -
Single Rate			£25.50/£25.50	€32.38	Child reduction 33.3%

Open: All Year Except Christmas

Ballincollig 11.5km

John & Elizabeth Plaice
MUSKERRY HOUSE
Farnanes, Co Cork

Ballincollig
TEL: **021 7336469**   FAX: **021 7336469**

Cork/Killarney road N22. Entry from N22/R619 intersection. Ballincollig 11.5km. Spacious rooms, full bathrooms. Central - Airport, Ferry, Blarney, West Cork and Kerry. Restaurant 5 min.

B&B	6	Ensuite	£20	€25.39	Dinner -
B&B	-	Standard	-	-	Partial Board -
Single Rate			£25.50	€32.38	Child reduction 25%

Open: 16th January-20th December

Ms Patricia Blanchfield
BLANCHFIELD HOUSE
Rigsdale (Cork/Bandon N71)
Halfway, Ballinahassig, Co Cork

Ballinhassig Kinsale
TEL: **021 4885167**   FAX: **021 4885805**
EMAIL: blanchfield@eircom.net

Period country home on N71, near City Airport, Ferry Port, Kinsale. Good tour base West Cork/Kerry. Private Salmon, Trout Fishing, Restaurant. AA ✦✦, Credit Cards.

B&B	2	Ensuite	£19/£24	€24.13/€30.47	Dinner £20
B&B	4	Standard	£17/£22	€21.59/€27.93	Partial Board £240
Single Rate			£23.50/£30	€29.84/€38.09	Child reduction 33.3%

Kinsale 14km

Open: 1st January-15th December

Ms Nora Lucey
NORVILLE HOUSE
**Balymakeera, Macroom,
Co Cork**

Ballyvourney
Tel: **026 45486** Fax: **026 45486**

Luxury house with a beautiful view. 2 min off N22 situated on the Cork to Killarney road. 50 min from Cork/Blarney, 20 min from Killarney and Kenmare. Gardens with Crazy Golf and Barbecue.

B&B	5	Ensuite	£19/£19	€24.13	Dinner	-
B&B	1	Standard	£17/£17	€21.59	Partial Board	-
Single Rate			-	-	Child reduction	50%

Macroom 7km

Open: All Year

Mrs Joan Collins
LAHERN LODGE
Baltimore, Co Cork

Baltimore
Tel: **028 20429**
Email: lahernlodge@eircom.net

Welcome to an Irish family home. Tastefully decorated in peaceful location off main road to village. 5 minutes walk from Harbour and Village centre.

B&B	1	Ensuite	£19/£23	€24.13/€29.20	Dinner	-
B&B	2	Standard	£18/£20	€22.86/€25.39	Partial Board	-
Single Rate			£25/£30	€31.74/€38.09	Child reduction	25%

In Baltimore

Open: April-October

Mrs Margaret Harrington
CHANNEL VIEW
**Baltimore,
Co Cork**

Baltimore
Tel: **028 20440**
Email: channelview@eircom.net

Spacious Dormer Bungalow, private car park, spectacular views overlooking the Bay. Sailing, Fishing, Island Trips, Diving, Scenic Walks, Golf, Tea/Coffee facilities.

B&B	5	Ensuite	£19/£22.50	€24.13/€28.57	Dinner	-
B&B	-	Standard	-	-	Partial Board	-
Single Rate			£30	€38.09	Child reduction	25%

In Baltimore

Open: March-October

Mrs Anne Buckley
ST ANNE'S
**Clonakilty Road, Bandon,
Co Cork**

Bandon
Tel: **023 44239** Fax: **023 44239**
Email: stannesbandon@eircom.net

Georgian house. Walled gardens. Near Town Centre. Convenient to Golf, Beaches, Fishing and Walking. Teamaking facilities. Airport 16 miles.

B&B	6	Ensuite	£20/£21	€25.39/€26.66	Dinner	-
B&B	-	Standard	-	-	Partial Board	-
Single Rate			£25.50/£25.50	€32.38	Child reduction	33.3%

Bandon 1km

Open: All Year Except Christmas

Mrs Carmel Nash
RIVERVIEW
**7 Riverview Estate, Bandon,
Co Cork**

Bandon
Tel: **023 41080** Fax: **023 41080**
Email: nashf@indigo.ie

Friendly relaxed home edge of town. Scenic views. 30 mins to Airport, Ferry. Convenient Golf, Beaches and Kinsale. Ideal touring West Cork, Kerry.

B&B	4	Ensuite	£19/£20	€24.13/€25.39	Dinner	-
B&B	-	Standard	-	-	Partial Board	-
Single Rate			£25.50/£26.50	€32.38/€33.65	Child reduction	-

In Bandon

Open: All Year

Mrs Theresa O'Connor
ASHGROVE HOUSE
Castle Road, Bandon, Co Cork

Bandon
Tel: **023 41033**

Patio back and front, 5 minutes from Town Centre. House on Golf Club road. Beach 6km from House. Kinsale 20km.

B&B	4	Ensuite	£19/£20	€24.13/€25.39	Dinner -
B&B	-	Standard	-	-	Partial Board -
Single Rate			£25.50/£25.50	€32.38	Child reduction -

Bandon 1km   **Open:** 1st January-20th December

Ms Mary Rose O'Donovan
FLORAVILLE
Mill Place, Bandon, Co Cork

Bandon
Tel: **023 42232**

Georgian town house with beautiful gardens in centre of Bandon Town. Antique furnishings, Guest lounge. Car park. Warm welcome. Breakfast menu.

B&B	2	Ensuite	£20/£25	€25.39/€31.74	Dinner -
B&B	-	Standard	-	-	Partial Board -
Single Rate			£25.50	€32.38	Child reduction -

In Bandon   **Open:** 1st January-20th December

Mrs Eileen Andrews
FERNDEENE
4 Slip Lawn, Bantry, Co Cork

Bantry
Tel: **027 50146**   Fax: **027 50146**
Email: ferndeene@yahoo.com
Bus No: **8**

Warm hospitality in comfortable home off N71. Menu. Private car park. Bicycle garage. Tea/Coffee, TV in bedrooms. Credit Cards. Ideal touring West Cork/Kerry.

B&B	3	Ensuite	£19	€24.13	Dinner -
B&B	-	Standard	-	-	Partial Board -
Single Rate			£25.50	€32.38	Child reduction 50%

In Bantry   **Open:** 10th January-31st November

Mrs Mary Cronin
COULIN
Gurteenroe, Bantry, Co Cork

Bantry
Tel: **027 50020**
Email: coulin@indigo.ie
Web: http://indigo.ie/~coulin/

Bungalow on Bantry/Glengarriff Road N71. Fabulous views. TV, Tea making facilities in rooms. Electric blankets, hairdryers.

B&B	3	Ensuite	£19/£20	€24.13/€25.39	Dinner -
B&B	-	Standard	-	-	Partial Board -
Single Rate			£30/£30	€38.09	Child reduction 25%

Bantry 5km   **Open:** May-September

Mrs Genny Dooley
ATLANTIC VIEW
Gurteenroe, Bantry, Co Cork

Bantry
Tel: **027 51221**

Superb Sea and Mountain views, secluded and peaceful location with attractive gardens. Beside Golf club. Bantry/Glengarriff road N71. Private car parking.

B&B	3	Ensuite	£19/£20	€24.13/€25.39	Dinner -
B&B	-	Standard	-	-	Partial Board -
Single Rate			£26/£26	€33.01	Child reduction 25%

Bantry 3km   **Open:** All Year

Ms Peggie Downing
BRU NA PAIRCE
7 Slip Park, Bantry, Co Cork

Bantry

Tᴇʟ: **027 51603**

Modern home quiet locality, overlooking Caha mountains. 5 minutes walk from Town. Centre of West Cork and South Kerry.

B&B	2	Ensuite	£20/£20	€25.39	Dinner	-
B&B	1	Standard	-	-	Partial Board	-
Single Rate			£23.50/£23.50	€29.84	Child reduction	20%

Open: 1st January-21st December

Bantry 1km

Maggie Doyle
ATLANTIC SHORE
Newtown, Bantry, Co Cork

Bantry

Tᴇʟ: **027 51310**   Fᴀx: **027 52175**
Eᴍᴀɪʟ: divebantry@aol.com

A spacious purpose built bungalow with a panoramic view of Bantry Bay. 50 metres past 30mph speed sign off Bantry/Glengarriff road N71.

B&B	5	Ensuite	£20/£20	€25.39	Dinner	-
B&B	1	Standard	£17/£17	€21.59	Partial Board	-
Single Rate			£24.50/£24.50	€31.11	Child reduction	25%

Open: 1st February-30th November

Bantry 1km

Mrs Phyllis Foley
ARD NA GREINE
Newtown, Bantry, Co Cork

Bantry

Tᴇʟ: **027 51169**

Country home. Mature gardens. Peaceful rural location. One mile from Bantry. Off N71 off Glengarriff/Killarney Road. House signs on main N71 road.

B&B	4	Ensuite	£19	€24.13	Dinner	-
B&B	-	Standard	-	-	Partial Board	-
Single Rate			£25.50	€32.38	Child reduction	25%

Open: 1st April-30th November

In Bantry

Mrs Brenda Harrington
LEYTON
23 Slip Lawn, Bantry, Co Cork

Bantry

Tᴇʟ: **027 50665**

Modern home, quiet locality. Breakfast menu. Car park. Bicycle garage. Off N71. Signposted at junction Glengarriff Road end of Bantry Town. Minutes to Town Centre.

B&B	3	Ensuite	£19	€24.13	Dinner	-
B&B	1	Standard	£17	€21.59	Partial Board	-
Single Rate			£23.50	€29.84	Child reduction	25%

Open: 1st May-30th September

In Bantry

Mrs Sheila Harrington
ELMWOOD HOUSE
6 Slip Lawn, Bantry, Co Cork

Bantry

Tᴇʟ: **027 50087**

Warm friendly home off main road. Tea/Cakes on arrival, Town 5 minutes. Turf fire, Bicycle garage. Archivist. Off N71. Signposted end of Town near Peace Park.

B&B	2	Ensuite	£19	€24.13	Dinner	-
B&B	2	Standard	£17	€21.59	Partial Board	-
Single Rate			-	-	Child reduction	50%

Open: All Year

Bantry 1km

Ms Tosca Kramer
THE MILL
Newtown, Bantry, Co Cork

Bantry
TEL: **027 50278**   FAX: **027 50278**
EMAIL: bbthemill@eircom.net
BUS NO: **8**

Well established accommodation, (N71) Bantry (1km), AA✦✦✦, RAC, highly recommended. Own art on display. Satellite T.V. all bedrooms. Laundry service.

B&B	6	Ensuite	£20/£23	€25.39/€29.30	Dinner	-
B&B	-	Standard			Partial Board	-
Single Rate			£25/£30	€31.74/€38.09	Child reduction	25%

Open: 1st April-31st October

Bantry 10km

Kathleen Lynch
AVOCA HOUSE
Durrus, Bantry, Co Cork

Bantry
TEL: **027 61511**   FAX: **027 61511**

Situated in Durrus village. Avoca House offers a warm welcome and a good breakfast menu. Ideally situated for touring Sheeps Head & Mizen Head Peninsula's.

B&B	4	Ensuite	£19/£20	€24.13/€25.39	Dinner	£14
B&B	-	Standard			Partial Board	-
Single Rate			£25.50/£25.50	€32.38	Child reduction	25%

Open: 1st January-20th December

Bantry 4km

Siobhan Lynch
LA MIRAGE
Droumdaniel, Ballylickey,
Bantry, Co Cork

Bantry
TEL: **027 50688**
EMAIL: lamirage@eircom.net

Elevated spacious country home, overlooking Bantry Bay. Peaceful location, friendly atmosphere, Tea/Coffee, home baking on arrival, off N71.

B&B	2	Ensuite	£19	€24.13	Dinner	-
B&B	2	Standard	£17	€21.59	Partial Board	-
Single Rate			£23.50/£25.50	€29.84/€32.38	Child reduction	25%

Open: April-September

Bantry 4km

Ms Mary C McCarthy
TIROROA
Gurteenroe, Near Ballylickey,
Bantry, Co Cork

Bantry
TEL: **027 50287**
BUS NO: **8**

On Bantry/Glengarriff road (N71). Panoramic view Lake, Sea, Mountains. Ideal for touring Ring of Beara and Mizen Head. Tea/Coffee, TV in rooms. Credit cards.

B&B	3	Ensuite	£19	€24.13	Dinner	-
B&B	-	Standard			Partial Board	-
Single Rate			£25.50	€32.38	Child reduction	25%

Open: 9th March-31st October

Bantry 25km

194

Helen McNamee
CAHER B&B
Caher, Kilcrohane, Bantry,
Co Cork

Bantry
TEL: **027 67299**   FAX: **027 67299**
EMAIL: caherguests@hotmail.com
WEB: www.cork-guide.ie

Spacious comfortable home with views over Dunmanus Bay. Situated on the unspoilt Sheeps Head Peninsula. Perfect for Walks/Cycling. Village 3km, Bantry 25km.

B&B	2	Ensuite	£20/£20	€25.39	Dinner	£15
B&B	1	Standard	£18/£18	€22.86	Partial Board	-
Single Rate			£23.50/£25	€29.84/€31.74	Child reduction	20%

Open: 15th April-31st October

Mrs Cait Murray
ROCKLANDS
Gurteenroe, Bantry, Co Cork

Bantry
TEL: 027 50212

Modern Bungalow on Bantry/Glengarriff Rd. N71. Magnificent views Bantry Bay, Lake, Sea, Mountains. Tea/Coffee, home baking on arrival. Private parking. Close to all tourist amenities.

B&B	3	Ensuite	£19	€24.13	Dinner	-
B&B	-	Standard	-	-	Partial Board	-
Single Rate			£26	€33.01	Child reduction	25%

Bantry 4km — **Open:** March-October

Mrs Kathleen O'Donovan
ASHLING
Cahir, Bantry, Co Cork

Bantry
TEL: 027 50616

Bungalow with panoramic views of Bantry Bay and Caha Mountains. Ideally situated for touring or relaxing. Private parking. Close to 18 hole Golf course.

B&B	3	Ensuite	£19	€24.13	Dinner	-
B&B	1	Standard	£17	€21.59	Partial Board	-
Single Rate			£25.50	€32.38	Child reduction	33.3%

Bantry 3km — **Open:** 1st May-30th September

Mrs Breda O'Regan
SUNVILLE
Newtown, Bantry, Co Cork

Bantry
TEL: 027 50175

Bungalow situated in select area, 5 minutes walk to Town and Sea. Family run. Close to all tourist amenities.

B&B	3	Ensuite	£19/£20	€24.13/€25.39	Dinner	-
B&B	1	Standard	£17/£18	€21.59/€22.86	Partial Board	-
Single Rate			-	-	Child reduction	33.3%

In Bantry — **Open:** 5th May-1st October

Mrs Margaret O'Sullivan
PARK VIEW
Newtown, Bantry,
Co Cork

Bantry
TEL: 027 51174   FAX: 027 51174
BUS NO: 8

Modern home, ideal touring centre. On main Bantry Glengarriff (N71). Beaches, Golf, Fishing, Horse Riding convenient. Scenic drives. Choice of breakfast.

B&B	2	Ensuite	£19	€24.13	Dinner	-
B&B	2	Standard	£17	€21.59	Partial Board	-
Single Rate			£23.50	€29.84	Child reduction	25%

Bantry 1km — **Open:** All Year

Vincent and Margaret O'Sullivan
SONAMAR
Dromleigh South, Bantry,
Co Cork

Bantry
TEL: 027 50502
EMAIL: sonamar@iol.ie

Distinctive bungalow with extensive gardens, overlooking town, unsurpassed view of Bantry Bay, Scenic walks, quiet location. Signposted from the square.

B&B	3	Ensuite	£19/£19	€24.13	Dinner	-
B&B	2	Standard	£17/£17	€21.59	Partial Board	-
Single Rate			£23.50/£25.50	€29.84/€32.38	Child reduction	25%

Bantry 2km — **Open:** 1st May-30th September

Ursula Schiesser
SHANGRI-LA
Glengarriff Road,
Newtown/Bantry, Co Cork

Bantry
TEL: **027 50244**   FAX: **027 50244**
EMAIL: schiesserbb.eircom.net

Bungalow with spectacular views of Bantry Bay. Spacious garden. Tea/Coffee making facilities. Credit Cards welcome, Golf nearby. German/French spoken.

				Dinner	£14
B&B	6	Ensuite	£20	€25.39	
B&B	-	Standard	£25.50	-	Partial Board -
Single Rate			£25.50	€32.38	Child reduction 25%

In Bantry

Open: 15th February-15th November

Mrs Joan Sweeney
HIGHFIELD
Newtown, Bantry, Co Cork

Bantry
TEL: **027 50791**
BUS NO: **7**

Situated on main Bantry/Glengarriff Road. Overlooking Bantry Bay. Electric blankets, hairdryers available. Garage for bicycles. Close to all amenities.

					Dinner	-
B&B	3	Ensuite	£19/£19	€24.13		
B&B	-	Standard	£17/£17	€21.59	Partial Board -	
Single Rate			£23.50/£25.50	€29.84/€32.38	Child reduction 50%	

Bantry 1km

Open: 1st April-1st November

Helen Allcorn
ALLCORN'S COUNTRY HOME
Shournagh Road, Blarney,
Co Cork

Blarney
TEL: **021 4385577**   FAX: **021 4382828**
EMAIL: allcorns_blarney@hotmail.com

Really spacious country home/gardens beside Shournagh river. Surrounded by mature woods and meadows. Just off R617 Blarney/Killarney Road.

					Dinner	-
B&B	3	Ensuite	£19/£23	€24.13/€29.20		
B&B	1	Standard	£23.50	-	Partial Board -	
Single Rate			£23.50	€29.84	Child reduction 25%	

Blarney 2km

Open: April-31st October

Mrs Veronica Annis-Sisk
YVORY HOUSE
Killowen, Blarney,
Co Cork

Blarney
TEL: **021 4381128**

Modern luxury bungalow in scenic farming location. Horseriding, Golf, Music locally, TV in bedrooms, Tea/Coffee facilities. 1km off Blarney/Killarney Rd. (R617).

					Dinner	-
B&B	2	Ensuite	£19/£20	€24.13/€25.39		
B&B	1	Standard	£17/£18	€21.59/€22.86	Partial Board -	
Single Rate			£23.50/£28	€29.84/€35.55	Child reduction 25%	

Blarney 1km

Open: March-November

Mrs Mary Buckley
LAURISTON
Coolowen, Blarney,
Co Cork

Blarney
TEL: **021 4381007**

Luxury bungalow in landscaped gardens. Located on second crossroad, on Station road. All rooms with TV, Hairdryers, Tea/Coffee. Cork City 10 mins, Blarney 5 mins. Private parking.

					Dinner	-
B&B	2	Ensuite	£19/£19	€24.13		
B&B	1	Standard	£17/£17	€21.59	Partial Board -	
Single Rate			£23.50/£25.50	€29.84/€32.38	Child reduction 25%	

Blarney 2km

Open: 1st March-18th November

Blarney

Mrs Philomena Bugler
LYNVARA
Killard, Blarney, Co Cork

TEL: **021 4385429**

Modern home, bedrooms on ground floor. Private parking. Heating, Tea/Coffee, Hairdryers. Breakfast menu. Cork 5 miles, Airport 9 miles. Walking distance to Blarney.

B&B	2	Ensuite	£19/£19	€24.13	Dinner	-
B&B	1	Standard	£17/£17	€21.59	Partial Board	-
Single Rate			-	-	Child reduction	25%

Blarney 1km

Open: 1st April-14th November

Blarney

The Callaghan Family
BUENA VISTA
Station Road, Blarney, Co Cork

TEL: **021 4385035**

Well established, AA listed, bungalow & garden, tranquil location. Walking distance Castle/Town. Breakfast menu. 3rd left from Blarney, on Cork side.

B&B	5	Ensuite	£19/£20	€24.13/€25.39	Dinner	-
B&B	-	Standard	-	-	Partial Board	-
Single Rate			£26/£30	€33.01/€38.09	Child reduction	25%

In Blarney

Open: 15th January-15th December

Blarney

Tom and Breda Cashman
ROCK ISLAND B&B
Kiln Road, Killeens, Blarney, Co Cork

TEL: **021 4399761**

Modern friendly home. Private car park. Quiet. TV, Tea/Coffee facilities. Blarney 2.5 miles. Cork City 2.5 miles. Off N20 from Cork, exit at Killeens, house 300m.

B&B	3	Ensuite	£19/£19	€24.13	Dinner	-
B&B	-	Standard	-	-	Partial Board	-
Single Rate			£25.50/£25.50	€32.38	Child reduction	25%

Blarney 3km

Open: 1st March-31st October

Blarney

Colette Collins
HEATHER LODGE
Kerry Road, Tower, Blarney, Co Cork

TEL: **021 4381216**   FAX: **021 4381216**
EMAIL: chelo@iol.ie
WEB: www.iol.ie/~chelo

Highly recommended. Delightful country home with superb views in peaceful setting. 1km off Blarney/Killarney Rd. R617. Tea/Coffee, Scones on arrival.

B&B	3	Ensuite	£19/£20	€24.13/€25.39	Dinner	-
B&B	-	Standard	-	-	Partial Board	-
Single Rate			£25.50/£30	€32.38/€38.09	Child reduction	-

Blarney 4km

Open: 1st March-31st October

Blarney

Pat and Regina Coughlan
THE WHITE HOUSE
Shean Lower, Blarney, Co Cork

TEL: **021 4385338**

Well heated luxurious home, overlooking Castle. All rooms with Satellite TV, Tea/coffee facilities, hairdryers. AA ♦♦♦♦ selected. Breakfast menu.

B&B	6	Ensuite	£20/£22.50	€25.39/€28.57	Dinner	-
B&B	-	Standard	-	-	Partial Board	-
Single Rate			£32/£32	€40.63	Child reduction	25%

In Blarney

Open: 7th January-20th December

Mrs Anne Cremin
ASHCROFT
Stoneview, Blarney, Co Cork

Tel: **021 4385224**
Email: creminanne@hotmail.com

Ashcroft offers magnificent views of Blarney Castle and Golf course. All rooms with TV, Tea/Coffee, Hairdryers and Power Showers. Breakfast menu. Follow signs for Blarney Golf course.

B&B	2	Ensuite	£19	€24.13	Dinner	-
B&B	2	Standard	£17	€21.59	Partial Board	-
Single Rate			£24.50	€31.11	Child reduction	25%

Blarney 1.5km

Open: 1st February–30th November

Fran & Tony Cronin
HILLVIEW HOUSE
Killard, Blarney, Co Cork

Tel: **021 4385161**
Email: hillview_blarney@yahoo.co.uk
Web: www.blarneyaccommodation.com

Beautiful view. Ground floor rooms. Car park. Sun Lounge. Pressurised showers, Cable TV, Hairdryers. Extensive Breakfast Menu. Walking distance to Blarney.

B&B	4	Ensuite	£19/£20	€24.13/€25.39	Dinner	-
B&B	-	Standard			Partial Board	-
Single Rate			£26/£32	€33.01/€40.63	Child reduction	25%

Blarney 1km

Open: 8th January–22nd December

Mrs Margaret Cronin
ROSEMOUNT
The Square, Blarney, Co Cork

Tel: **021 4385584**

Modern two storey home in peaceful location. Landscaped garden, private car park, at main bus stop. Two minutes walk to Castle, Shops, Entertainment.

B&B	2	Ensuite	£20/£21	€25.39/€26.66	Dinner	-
B&B	3	Standard	£18/£19	€22.86/€24.13	Partial Board	-
Single Rate			£26/£30	€33.01/€38.09	Child reduction	25%

In Blarney

Open: 1st April–31st October

Mrs Mary Falvey
CUANAN HOUSE
**12 Castle Close Road,
Blarney, Co Cork**

Tel: **021 4385329**
Email: cuanan@iname.com

Family run comfortable home. Refreshments on arrival. Find us 400m east of Blarney Square. Walking distance to Castle, Restaurants, Shops, Music and Bus.

B&B	-	Ensuite	-	-	Dinner	-
B&B	3	Standard	£17	€21.59	Partial Board	-
Single Rate			-	-	Child reduction	33.3%

In Blarney

Open: 1st February–1st December

Neil & Noreen Finnegan
THAR AN UISCE
Magoola, Dripsey, Co Cork

Tel: **021 7334788**
Email: tharanuisce@eircom.net

Lakeside setting on Blarney/Killarney route R618. All rooms ensuite with TV, Tea/Coffee, Hairdryers. Fishing, Waterskiing, Riverside walk all alongside.

B&B	3	Ensuite	£19/£19	€24.13	Dinner	-
B&B	-	Standard			Partial Board	-
Single Rate			£25.50/£25.50	€32.38	Child reduction	50%

Blarney 9km

Open: May–October

Blarney 1km

Mrs Ann Fogarty
GLENMAROON HOUSE
Pauds Cross, Blarney,
Co Cork

Blarney
TEL: 021 4385821

Luxurious country home in tranquil surroundings with complimentary Tea on arrival/request. 1km from Blarney. First left off Blarney/Killarney road R617.

B&B	4	Ensuite	£20/£23	€25.39/€29.20	Dinner	-
B&B	-	Standard		-	Partial Board	-
Single Rate			£25/£30	€31.74/€38.09	Child reduction	50%

Open: 1st January-22nd December

Blarney 5km

Eucharia Hannon
WESTWOOD COUNTRY HOUSE
Dromin, Blarney,
Co Cork

Blarney
TEL: 021 4385404   FAX: 021 4385404
EMAIL: westwood.country.house@oceanfree.net

Luxurious family home. Elegantly furnished. TV's, Hairdryers. Tea, scones on arrival. Adjacent Blarney Castle, Shops, Pubs, Restaurants. Superb base for touring Killarney, Kinsale, Cobh.

B&B	3	Ensuite	£20/£20	€25.39	Dinner	-
B&B	-	Standard		-	Partial Board	-
Single Rate			£28/£30	€35.55/€38.09	Child reduction	-

Open: 15th January-15th December

In Blarney

Mrs Bridget Harrington
CURRAC BUI
30 Castle Close Drive,
Blarney, Co Cork

Blarney
TEL: 021 4385424
EMAIL: curracbui@tinet.ie
WEB: http://homepage.eircom.net/~curracbuiblarney

Personnally run modern home. 5 min walk Blarney Castle/Local amenities/Cork Bus route. Bedrooms with TV, Hairdryers, Tea/Coffee. Home baking, Breakfast choice.

B&B	3	Ensuite	£19/£20	€24.13/€25.39	Dinner	-
B&B	1	Standard	£17	€21.59	Partial Board	-
Single Rate			£23.50/£25.50	€29.84/€32.38	Child reduction	33.3%

Open: 1st April-31st October

Cork City 6km

Mrs Eileen Hempel
EDELWEISS HOUSE
Leemount, Carrigrohane,
Co Cork

Blarney
TEL: 021 4871888   FAX: 021 4871888
EMAIL: edelweisshouse@eircom.net
WEB: www.homepage.eircom.net/~edelweisshouse/

Swiss style home overlooking river Lee. Chef owner. Super meals. TV in rooms, Hairdryers. Credit cards accepted. 4.5 miles Blarney, Cork City 2 miles on N22. Killarney road signposted.

B&B	3	Ensuite	£20/£22	€25.39/€27.93	Dinner	£15
B&B	3	Standard	£17/£18	€21.59/€22.86	Partial Board	£245
Single Rate			£23.50/£28	€29.84/€35.55	Child reduction	25%

Open: 10th March-23rd December

In Blarney

Mrs Anne Hennessy
BLARNEY VALE HOUSE
Cork Road (R617)
Blarney, Co Cork

Blarney
TEL: 021 4381511
EMAIL: relax@blarneyvale.com
WEB: www.blarneyvale.com

Luxurious home on private grounds overlooking village. AA ◆◆◆◆ selected, friendly atmosphere. Bedrooms with TV, Hairdryers, Tea/Coffee facilities. Breakfast menu. Cork City 8 mins.

B&B	4	Ensuite	£20/£22.50	€25.39/€/28.57	Dinner	-
B&B	-	Standard			Partial Board	-
Single Rate			£26/£38	€33.01/€48.25	Child reduction	25%

Open: March-November

In Blarney

Mrs Margaret Kearney
SUNVILLE
**1 Castle Close Lawn,
Blarney, Co Cork**

Blarney
Tel: 021 4381325

Modern comfortable home 5 mins walk to Castle, Restaurants, Shops, Entertainment. Adjacent to bus route and beautiful country walk. Tea/Coffee facilities.

					Dinner	-
B&B	2	Ensuite	£19/£20	€24.13/€25.39	Dinner	-
B&B	1	Standard	£23.50	-	Partial Board	-
Single Rate			£23.50	€29.84	Child reduction	33.3%

Open: 1st March-1st December

Blarney 1km

Susan & Brian Kenna
LANESVILLE B&B
Killard, Blarney, Co Cork

Blarney
Tel: 021 4381813
Email: kennab@indigo.ie
Web: www.lanesvillebandb.com

Newly opened family run home. Walking distance to Blarney Castle and Shops. Rooms with TV, Tea/Coffee making facilities. Full breakfast menu. Private parking.

					Dinner	-
B&B	4	Ensuite	£19/£20	€24.13/€25.39	Dinner	-
B&B	1	Standard	-	-	Partial Board	-
Single Rate			£25.50/£25.50	€32.38	Child reduction	25%

Open: All Year Except Christmas

Blarney 5km

Mrs Cecilia Kiely
CLARAGH
**Waterloo Road, Blarney,
Co Cork**

Blarney
Tel: 021 4886308   Fax: 021 4886308
Email: claraghbandb@eircom.net
Web: www.claragh.com

Welcoming tray with hot scones. Breakfast menu includes French toast. Electric blankets, Hairdryers. Recommended McQuillan/Sullivan Guides. 10 mins drive to Castle.

					Dinner	-
B&B	4	Ensuite	£19/£20	€24.13/€25.39	Dinner	-
B&B	-	Standard	-	-	Partial Board	-
Single Rate			£25.50/£25.50	€32.38	Child reduction	-

Open: 1st April-31st October

Blarney 1km

Maura Lane
BELLEVUE HOUSE
**Station Road, Blarney,
Co Cork**

Blarney
Tel: 021 381686

Enjoy the best of Irish hospitality in friendly modern home. Close to Castle, restaurants, shops, golf and all other amenities.

					Dinner	-
B&B	2	Ensuite	£20/£23	€25.39/€29.20	Dinner	-
B&B	1	Standard	£18	€22.86	Partial Board	-
Single Rate			£26/£26	€33.01	Child reduction	25%

Open: 1st April-2nd November

Blarney 2km

Mrs Anne Lynch
THE GABLES
**Stoneview, Blarney,
Co Cork**

Blarney
Tel: 021 4385330
Email: anne@gablesblarney.com

Former Victorian Rectory on two acres, overlooking Blarney Castle. Golf course - Bar & Restaurant alongside. Home baking. Private parking. Itineraries arranged.

					Dinner	-
B&B	3	Ensuite	£19/£20	€24.13/€25.39	Dinner	-
B&B	-	Standard	-	-	Partial Board	-
Single Rate			£26/£28	€33.01/€35.55	Child reduction	25%

Open: All Year Except Christmas

Mrs Marie McLoughney S.R.N
GREENWAY'S
Woodside, Kerry Pike, Co Cork

Blarney
Tel: **021 4385383**

Spacious home offering every comfort. From Blarney direction Killarney, take 1st road to left. Cork City four miles. Blarney two miles. TV in bedrooms. Quality Breakfast.

B&B	4	Ensuite	£19/£19	€24.13	Dinner	-
B&B	-	Standard	-		Partial Board	-
Single Rate			£25.50/£25.50	€32.38	Child reduction	50%

Blarney 3km

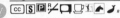 **Open:** February-November

---

Mrs Caroline Morgan
KILLARNEY HOUSE
Station Road, Blarney, Co Cork

Blarney
Tel: **021 4381841**   Fax: **021 4381841**
Email: killarneyhouseblarney@eircom.net

Purpose built luxury accommodation on 1 acre of landscaped gardens. Adjacent to Castle, Restaurants, Shops & Entertainment. Private Car park.

B&B	6	Ensuite	£20/£23	€25.39/€29.20	Dinner	-
B&B	-	Standard	-	-	Partial Board	-
Single Rate			£26/£32	€33.01/€40.63	Child reduction	25%

Blarney 1km

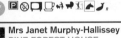 **Open:** All Year

---

Mrs Janet Murphy-Hallissey
PINE FOREST HOUSE
Elmcourt, Blarney, Co Cork

Blarney
Tel: **021 4385979**
Email: info@pineforestbb.com
Web: www.pineforestbb.com

Spacious bungalow situated in peaceful wooded area with large landscaped garden. 1km on Blarney/Killarney Road (617). Tea and Coffee on arrival. Private parking.

B&B	4	Ensuite	£19/£20	€24.13/€25.39	Dinner	-
B&B	-	Standard	-	-	Partial Board	-
Single Rate			£25.50/£30	€32.38/€38.09	Child reduction	25%

Blarney 1km

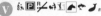 **Open:** All Year Except Christmas

---

Mrs Marian Nugent
COOLIM
Coolflugh, Tower, Blarney, Co Cork

Blarney
Tel: **021 4382848**
Email: nugent.coolim@oceanfree.net

Friendly home with large garden. Private parking. Refreshments on arrival. Home baking. Blarney Castle 4km (on R617). Muskerry Golf club 1km.

B&B	3	Ensuite	£19/£21	€24.13/€26.66	Dinner	-
B&B	-	Standard	-	-	Partial Board	-
Single Rate			£28/£30	€35.55/€38.09	Child reduction	33.3%

Blarney 4km

 **Open:** All Year

---

Mrs Mary O'Brien
FIRGROVE
1 Castle Close Villas, Blarney, Co Cork

Blarney
Tel: **021 4381403**

Well recommended quiet comfortable home. Friendly atmosphere. Mins walk Bus, Castle, Shops, Restaurants, Golf. Ideal touring base. From village square, 2nd turn left on Castle Close Road.

B&B	2	Ensuite	£20/£21	€25.39/€26.66	Dinner	-
B&B	-	Standard	£18/£19	€22.86/€24.13	Partial Board	-
Single Rate			£26/£30	€33.01/€38.09	Child reduction	20%

In Blarney

Open: 1st March-30th November

Blarney 6km

Mrs Ita O'Donovan
KNOCKAWN WOOD
Curraleigh, Inniscarra,
Co Cork

Blarney

TEL: **021 4870284** FAX: **021 4870284**
EMAIL: odknkwd@iol.ie
WEB: http://homepages.iol.ie/~odknkwd/

Picturesque, restful. Tea & scones. Electric blankets. Meal without notice. Cork, Ferry, Airport 30 mins, N22/R618, Blarney/Killarney Rd R618. Inniscarra fishing.

B&B	3	Ensuite	£19/£19	€24.13	Dinner	£12.50
B&B	1	Standard	£17/£17	€21.59	Partial Board	£185
Single Rate			£23.50/£25.50	€29.84/€32.38	Child reduction	50%

Open: All Year

Blarney 3km

Anne & John O'Leary
ASHLEE LODGE
Tower, Blarney,
Co Cork

Blarney

TEL: **021 4385346** FAX: **021 4385726**
EMAIL: info@ashleelodge.com
WEB: http://www.ashleelodge.com

Superbly appointed luxury bungalow situated in tranquil gardens. Blarney/Killarney road (R617). AA recommended. Breakfast menu. French/German spoken.

B&B	5	Ensuite	£20/£22.50	€25.39/€28.57	Dinner	-
B&B	1	Standard	£18/£20	€22.86/€25.39	Partial Board	-
Single Rate			£26/£32	€33.01/€40.63	Child reduction	25%

Open: All Year

Blarney 4km

Mrs Gertie O'Shea
TRAVELLERS JOY
Tower, Blarney, Co Cork

Blarney

TEL: **021 438554**
EMAIL: travellersjoy@iname.com

Blarney/Killarney R617. Causin/Dillard recommended. Private parking. Prizewinning gardens. Tea/Coffee in bedrooms. Quality breakfasts. Close to all amenities.

B&B	3	Ensuite	£20/£22	€25.39/€27.93	Dinner	-
B&B	-	Standard	-	-	Partial Board	-
Single Rate			£26/£26	€33.01	Child reduction	50%

Open: 1st February-20th December

Blarney 1km

Mrs Rose O'Sullivan
AVONDALE LODGE
Killowen, Blarney, Co Cork

Blarney

TEL: **021 381736**
EMAIL: avondalelodge@eircom.net

Warm friendly home in scenic farming location. Golf, Horseriding, Music locally. Tea/Coffee facilities, TV in rooms. Hairdryers. Breakfast menus. Private parking.

B&B	4	Ensuite	£19/£20	€24.13/€25.39	Dinner	-
B&B	-	Standard	-	-	Partial Board	-
Single Rate			£25.50/£28	€32.38/€35.55	Child reduction	25%

Open: 1st January-23rd December

Blarney 3km

Chef Billie & Catherine Phelan
PHELAN'S WOODVIEW HOUSE
Tweedmount, Blarney, Co Cork

Blarney

TEL: **021 4385197** FAX: **021 4385197**

Enjoy Gourmet Cooking at Phelans, Seafood a speciality. TV in bedrooms. Tea/coffee facilities, Credit Cards. Frommer & Eye Witness Guides recommended.

B&B	7	Ensuite	£20/£22.50	€25.39/€28.57	Dinner	£17
B&B	1	Standard	£18/£20	€22.86/€25.39	Partial Board	-
Single Rate			£32/£32	€40.63	Child reduction	-

Open: 1st March-31st October

Noelle and Patrick Roche
CHIRIQUI
Canons Cross, Inniscarra,
Co Cork

Blarney
TEL: 021 4871061   FAX: 021 4871930
EMAIL: chiriqui@eircom.net
WEB: http://homepage.eircom.net/~chiriqui/

Friendly & warm. Scenic Killarney R618 Rd. 30 mins Air/Ferryport. Spacious home/gardens. Pressure showers, hairdryers, orthopaedic beds, electric blankets, Satellite TV.

B&B	4	Ensuite	£19/£20	€24.13/€25.39	Dinner	-
B&B	-	Standard		-	Partial Board	-
Single Rate			£26/£30	€33.01/€38.09	Child reduction	-

Blarney 6km

Open: 1st April-31st October

Mrs Olwen Venn
MARANATHA COUNTRY HOUSE
Tower, Blarney, Co Cork

Blarney
TEL: 021 4385102   FAX: 021 4382978
EMAIL: douglasvenn@eircom.net

Stroll through the beautiful private gardens and woodlands surrounding this lovely Victorian mansion. Spacious romantic bedrooms. Beautiful historic antiques throughout.

B&B	4	Ensuite	£21/£26	€26.66/€33.01	Dinner	-
B&B	1	Standard	£21/£26	€26.66/€33.01	Partial Board	-
Single Rate			£28/£35	€35.55/€44.44	Child reduction	50%

Blarney 2km

Open: 16th March-November

Gretta O'Grady
CHESTNUT LODGE
Carrigaline, Co Cork

Carrigaline Cork Airport Ferryport
TEL: 021 4371382   FAX: 021 4372818

Spacious luxurious home, peaceful surroundings, Golf, Angling, Horseriding, Cinema, Restaurants, Beaches closeby. Sun-lounge, patio. Ferryport 5km, Airport 10km.

B&B	4	Ensuite	£19/£25	€24.13/€31.74	Dinner	£15
B&B	-	Standard		-	Partial Board	-
Single Rate			£25.50/£35	€32.38/€44.44	Child reduction	-

Carrigaline 1km

Open: All Year Except Christmas

Mrs Ann O'Leary
THE WILLOWS
Ballea Road, Carrigaline,
Co Cork

Carrigaline Cork Ferryport Airport
TEL: 021 4372669   FAX: 021 4372669

Split level house with gardens front and rear. Fishing, Golfing, Horse Riding, and Beaches 3km. Cork Airport 6km. Ringaskiddy Ferry 5km.

B&B	3	Ensuite	£19/£21	€24.13/€26.66	Dinner	-
B&B	2	Standard	£17/£19	€21.59/€24.13	Partial Board	-
Single Rate			£23.50/£26	€29.84/€33.01	Child reduction	33.3%

Carrigaline 1km

Open: All Year Except Christmas

Mrs Breda Hayes
CEDARVILLE
Carrigtwohill, Co Cork

Carrigtwohill
TEL: 021 4883246
EMAIL: cedarville@oceanfree.net

N25 Cork/Waterford road. Private parking. Frommer recommended. Restaurants nearby. Fota, Wildlife, Jameson Heritage, Trabolgan, Cobh. 20 minutes Airport.

B&B	2	Ensuite	£19	€24.13	Dinner	-
B&B	2	Standard	£17.50	€22.22	Partial Board	-
Single Rate			£23.50/£25.50	€29.84/€32.38	Child reduction	50%

In Carrigtwohill

Open: May-October

Miss Margot Seymour
DUN-VREEDA HOUSE
Carrigtwohill, Co Cork

Carrigtwohill
TEL: **021 4883169**

Off N25 Cork, Waterford/Rosslare road at Carrigtwohill. Near Fota Wildlife, Cobh, and Jameson Heritage Centre. Golf, Fishing, Riding nearby. Bus route. Church in area. Snacks, light meals.

B&B	2	Ensuite	£19/£19	€24.13	Dinner	£12.50
B&B	2	Standard	£17/£17	€21.59	Partial Board	£185
Single Rate			£23.50/£25.50	€29.84/€32.38	Child reduction	50%

In Carrigtwohill

Open: All Year

Mrs Mary Donegan
REALT-NA-MARA
Castletownbere, Co Cork

Castletownbere
TEL: **027 70101**

Friendly home big garden, overlooks sea on Glengarriff Castletownbere road. Near Beara Way walking route. Near Town, Golf, Fishing. Tea/Coffee facilities on request.

B&B	4	Ensuite	£19/£19	€24.13	Dinner	-
B&B	1	Standard	£17/£17	€21.59	Partial Board	-
Single Rate			£23.50/£25.50	€29.84/€32.38	Child reduction	33.3%

Castletownbere 1km

Open: All Year

Mrs Noralene McGurn
SEA BREEZE
**Derrymihan, Castletownbere,
Beara Peninsula, Co Cork**

Castletownbere
TEL: **027 70508**   FAX: **027 70508**
EMAIL: mcgurna@gofree.indigo.ie

Warm friendly home. Situated on seafront overlooking Bere Island. Near Beara Way walking route. Ideal base for touring. Beara a peaceful spot.

B&B	3	Ensuite	£19/£20	€24.13/€25.39	Dinner	-
B&B	-	Standard	-	-	Partial Board	-
Single Rate			£25.50	€32.38	Child reduction	25%

Castletownbere 1.5km

Open: All Year Except Christmas

Mary & John Gerard O'Sullivan
SEA VILLA
**Castletownberehaven Cst Rd,
Ardgroom Inward,
Beara Peninsula, Co Cork**

Castletownberehaven Ardgroom
TEL: **027 74369**   FAX: **027 74369**

New luxurious accommodation in tranquil scenic location on Coast Road/Beara way, surrounded by Sea, Mountains and natural unspoiled rugged landscape.

B&B	3	Ensuite	£19/£19	€24.13	Dinner	-
B&B	-	Standard	-	-	Partial Board	-
Single Rate			£25.50	€32.38	Child reduction	25%

Ardgroom Village 5km

Open: 1st April-31st October

Sean & Eileen Clancy
SEA BREEZE
Carhue, Clonakilty, Co Cork

Clonakilty
TEL: **023 34427**

Tranquility and total relaxaton in this idyllic home, just off N71, less than 1km from town. Close to all amenities. A warm welcome assured.

B&B	4	Ensuite	£20/£22	€25.39/€27.93	Dinner	-
B&B	-	Standard	-	-	Partial Board	-
Single Rate			£28	€35.55	Child reduction	25%

Clonakilty 1km

Open: All Year

Tony & Noreen Driscoll
BAY VIEW HOUSE
**Old Timoleague Road,
Clonakilty, Co Cork**

Clonakilty
TEL: **023 33539**

Enjoy affordable luxury at our beautiful home. Superb views & delightful gardens. Town 3 mins walk. Signposted at roundabout on Cork/Kinsale approach road.

B&B	5	Ensuite	£19/£21	€24.13/€26.66	Dinner	-
B&B	1	Standard		-	Partial Board	-
Single Rate			£25/£33	€31.74/€41.90	Child reduction	33.3%

In Clonakilty

Open: 1st March-31st October

Mrs Clare Hayes
WYTCHWOOD
**Emmet Square, Clonakilty,
Co Cork**

Clonakilty
TEL: **023 33525**   FAX: **023 35673**
EMAIL: wytchost@iol.ie

Georgian house with walled garden in a peaceful and tranquil setting. Breakfast choice. Bike hire. Le Guide du Routard and Lonely Planet recommended.

B&B	6	Ensuite	£20/£25	€25.39/€31.74	Dinner	-
B&B	-	Standard		-	Partial Board	-
Single Rate			£25.50/£35	€32.38/44.44	Child reduction	-

In Clonakilty

Open: 1st January-20th December

Mrs Marie Hanly
GLENDINE
**Tawnies Upper, Clonakilty,
Co Cork**

Clonakilty
TEL: **023 34824**
EMAIL: glendine@eircom.net
WEB: www.glendine.com

Panoramic views of surrounding countryside, overlooking town. Country hillside setting, 10 mins. walk from town. Signposted from Church. Breakfast menu.

B&B	3	Ensuite	£19/£22	€24.13/€27.93	Dinner	-
B&B	-	Standard		-	Partial Board	-
Single Rate			£25.50/£30	€32.38/€38.09	Child reduction	50%

In Clonakilty

Open: 1st February-1st December

Mrs Ann Lehane
BALARD HOUSE
**Ballymacowen, Clonakilty,
Co Cork**

Clonakilty
TEL: **023 33865**

Modern home in peaceful location on Kinsale/Clonakilty Road R600. Restaurants, Beaches, Sailing, Golf & Horseriding within easy reach.

B&B	3	Ensuite	£19	€24.13	Dinner	-
B&B	-	Standard		-	Partial Board	-
Single Rate			£25.50	€32.38	Child reduction	50%

Clonakilty 4km

Open: May-October

Noreen & David McMahon
NORDAV
**off Western Road,
(Fernhill Rd), Clonakilty, Co Cork**

Clonakilty
TEL: **023 33655**

Very private, 300 mts Church & Town Centre. Award winning gardens. 1 Family suite (includes 2 bedrooms & lounge). 1 suite with verandah, £25 p.p.s. Studio apartment.

B&B	4	Ensuite	£19/£20	€24.13/€25.39	Dinner	-
B&B	-	Standard		-	Partial Board	-
Single Rate			£25.50/£32	€32.38/€40.63	Child reduction	-

In Clonakilty

Open: April-September

Clonakilty 2km

Mrs Breda Moore
SHALOM
**Ballyduvane, Clonakilty,
Co Cork**

Clonakilty
TEL: 023 33473

Modern bungalow in rural setting on main Clonakilty - Skibbereen road (N71). 2km Clonakilty Town, 6km beautiful sandy Inchydoney Beach.

B&B	2	Ensuite	£18	€22.86	Dinner	-
B&B	1	Standard	£16	€20.32	Partial Board	-
Single Rate			-	-	Child reduction	50%

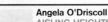

Open: March-October

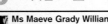

In Clonakilty

Angela O'Driscoll
AISLING HEIGHTS
**Clogheen Meadows, Clogheen,
Clonakilty, West Cork, Co Cork**

Clonakilty
TEL: 023 33491

Beautifully decorated newly built house in nice area close to all amenities and within walking distance of town.

B&B	4	Ensuite	£20	€25.39	Dinner	-
B&B	-	Standard	-	-	Partial Board	-
Single Rate			£25.50/£32	€32.38/€40.63	Child reduction	33.3%

Open: 1st February-31st October

Ms Maeve Grady Williams
MACLIAM LODGE
**Western Road, Clonakilty,
Co Cork**

Clonakilty
TEL: 023 35195
EMAIL: macliamlodge@eircom.net

Newly refurbished home. All rooms TV, Tea/Coffee, Power showers, Hairdryers. Ideal touring base. On the N71, from Cork drive through town to West side. Welcome assured.

B&B	6	Ensuite	£20/£22.50	€25.39/€28.57	Dinner	-
B&B	-	Standard	-	-	Partial Board	-
Single Rate			£25.50/£30	€32.38/€38.09	Child reduction	50%

Clonakilty

Open: All Year

Clonakilty 3km

Mrs Nora O'Regan
ASSUMPTION HOUSE
**Ballinascarthy, Clonakilty,
Co Cork**

Clonakilty
TEL: 023 39268

Situated on N71, in Ballinascarthy. Warm welcoming home. Freshly prepared wholesome food. Home baking a speciality. Ideal location to beaches & day tours

B&B	2	Ensuite	£20/£22	€25.39/€27.93	Dinner	-
B&B	1	Standard	£18/£20	€22.86/€25.39	Partial Board	-
Single Rate			£28	€35.55	Child reduction	25%

Open: 10th March-31st October

Cobh 2km

Mrs Georgina Coughlan
GLEBE HOUSE
**Tay Road, Cobh,
Co Cork**

Cobh
TEL: 021 4811373   FAX: 021 4811373
EMAIL: glebehouse@eircom.net
WEB: glebehousecobh.com

Warm spacious friendly home. Convenient Fota, Golf, Ferryport, Airport. Over bridge at Fota, turn left 2 miles to Crossroads, turn left. Breakfast menu. French spoken.

B&B	4	Ensuite	£20/£23	€25.39/€29.20	Dinner	-
B&B	-	Standard	-	-	Partial Board	-
Single Rate			£27/£33	€34.29/€41.90	Child reduction	25%

Open: All Year

In Cobh

Mrs Noreen Hickey
MOUNT VIEW
**Beechmount, Cobh,
Co Cork**

Cobh

TEL: **021 4814260**   FAX: **021 4814260**

Town house spectacular view of Cathedral and harbour. Close to International and local ferries and Queenstown Story. Private car park. Signposted at Cathedral.

B&B	4	Ensuite	£19/£20	€24.13/€25.39	Dinner -
B&B	-	Standard	-	-	Partial Board -
Single Rate			£25.50/£30	€32.38/€38.09	Child reduction 33.3%

Open: All Year Except Christmas

Cobh 1.4km

Pat & Martha Hurley
HIGHLAND
**Ballywilliam, Cobh,
Co Cork**

Cobh

TEL: **021 4813873**   FAX: **021 4813873**
EMAIL: highlandcobh@eircom.net

Modern home with panoramic views, close to Local and International Ferries. Fota Golf, Wildlife Park, Queenstown Story. Ground floor rooms on request.

B&B	5	Ensuite	£19/£21	€24.13/€26.66	Dinner -
B&B	-	Standard	-	-	Partial Board -
Single Rate			£26/£30	€33.01/€38.00	Child reduction 25%

Open: 1st March-31st October

Cobh 2km

Mrs Bernadette de Maddox
TEARMANN
Ballynoe, Cobh, Co Cork

Cobh

TEL: **021 4813182**   FAX: **021 4814011**

19th Century Traditional House. Lovely garden. Car park. Close Heritage Centres, FOTA, Golf etc. Airport and Port 25 mins. Follow R624 pass, cross river ferry, 1st left up road on left.

B&B	2	Ensuite	£19/£19	€24.13	Dinner £15
B&B	1	Standard	£17/£17	€21.59	Partial Board -
Single Rate			£25/£30	€31.74/€38.09	Child reduction -

Open: 1st March-31st October

Tallow 2km

Kevin & Joan Ryan
THE GRANGE
**Curraglass, Conna,
Near Tallow, Co Cork**

Conna

TEL: **058 56247**   FAX: **058 56247**

Large 3 storey Georgian house dating back to 1840. Set on 8 acres of mature gardens, woodlands. Ideally based. Fishing on the Blackwater 5 mile. 9 excellent Golf courses within 12 miles.

B&B	4	Ensuite	£25	€31.74	Dinner -
B&B	-	Standard	-	-	Partial Board -
Single Rate			£30	€38.09	Child reduction 33.3%

Open: 1st April-31st October

Cork City 5km

Mrs Mary Bayer
WHITE LODGE
**Airport Cross, Kinsale Road,
Cork, Co Cork**

Cork City Airport Kinsale Road

TEL: **021 4961267**

Take Airport road to roundabout at Airport gates, take Cork exit off roundabout, 100m on, turn left down side road. We are first B&B on left. City 6km.

B&B	3	Ensuite	£19	€24.13	Dinner £12.50
B&B	1	Standard	-	-	Partial Board -
Single Rate			£23.50	€29.84	Child reduction 50%

Open: 10th January-21st December

Mrs Helena Higgins
HELENA
**Kinsale Road, Ballygarvan,
Co Cork**

Cork City Airport Kinsale Road
Tel: **021 4888126**

Modern bungalow overlooking picturesque countryside on the main Cork Airport/Kinsale Road. From Cork N27=R600, 5 mins drive to Airport, Ferryport 8km.

				Dinner	-
B&B	2	Ensuite	£19	€24.13	
B&B	1	Standard	£17.50	€22.22	Partial Board -
Single Rate			£25	€31.74	Child reduction 25%

Cork 5km

Open: 1st April-31st October

Mrs Brid O'Connor
BEECHWOOD
**Curra, Riverstick,
Co Cork**

Cork City Airport Kinsale Road
Tel: **021 4771456**

Country home set in scenic and tranquil surroundings, off R600 (Airport/Kinsale Road). Convenient to Airport, Ferry Port and Kinsale.

					Dinner	-
B&B	4	Ensuite	£19/£19	€24.13		
B&B	-	Standard	-		Partial Board	-
Single Rate			£25.50/£25.50	€32.38	Child reduction	25%

Kinsale 8km

Open: 1st May-1st October

Mrs Breeda Savage
GREEN ISLE
**Ballygarvan Village, Off
Airport/Kinsale Road, Co Cork**

Cork City Airport Kinsale Road
Tel: **021 4888171**

Country Home in scenic valley off Cork/Kinsale Road. Airport 2km. Near Kinsale. Ferryport 8km. Tea/Coffee, Hairdryer in rooms. Visa.

					Dinner	-
B&B	2	Ensuite	£19/£19	€24.13		
B&B	1	Standard	£17.50/£17.50	€22.22	Partial Board	-
Single Rate			£25/£25	€31.74	Child reduction	20%

Cork City 10km

Open: 6th January-20th December

Mrs Ilona Kiely
ARBORETUM HOUSE
**Ardarostig, Bishopstown,
Cork City, Co Cork**

Cork City Bishopstown
Tel: **021 4342056**   Fax: **021 4342056**
Email: arboretumhouse@eircom.net
Bus No: **8**

Elegant country residence set in spacious gardens, just 1km off N25 on N71. Convenient to Cork Greyhound Track, Airport, Ferry, CIT and University Hospital.

					Dinner	-
B&B	3	Ensuite	£19/£21	€24.13/€26.66		
B&B	-	Standard	-		Partial Board	-
Single Rate			£25.50/£25.50	€32.38	Child reduction	25%

Cork City 8km

Open: 1st March-31st October

Mrs Kay O'Donovan
DUNDERG
**38 Westgate Road,
Bishopstown, Cork City,
Co Cork**

Cork City Bishopstown University
Tel: **021 4543078**   Fax: **021 4543078**
Email: dunderg@eircom.net
Bus No: **5 & 8**

Quiet location 400m off N71 Bishopstown Bar. Convenient to Greyhound Stadium, Leisure Centre, University Hospital, UCC, FAS, West Cork, Killarney, Ferry, Airport.

					Dinner	-
B&B	4	Ensuite	£19/£22.50	€24.13/€28.57		
B&B	-	Standard	-	-	Partial Board	-
Single Rate			£25.50/£30	€32.38/€38.09	Child reduction	25%

Cork City 2km

Open: 1st January-20th December

Mrs Eileen Stack
CAROLEVILLE
**36 Beaumont Drive,
Ballintemple, Blackrock, Co Cork**

Cork City Blackrock Area
Tel: **021 294321**
Bus No: **2**

Comfortable family home in residential area. TV/Coffee/Tea facilities in rooms. Private parking. Adjacent to Showgrounds, Airport, Car Ferry.

B&B	3	Ensuite	£19/£20	€24.13/€25.39	Dinner -
B&B	-	Standard	-	-	Partial Board -
Single Rate			-	-	Child reduction -

Cork City 2km

Open: 1st January-20th December

Mrs Barbara Ahern
BRANDON
Hillgrove Lawn, South Douglas Road, Cork City, Co Cork

Cork City Douglas Area
Tel: **021 4893859**
Bus No : **6**

Detached house in quiet cul-de-sac. Convenient to Airport, Ferry, Bus, Shopping, Restaurant, Bars, Golf. Parking. TV in bedrooms. 4km to City. Near O'Sullivans Pharmacy.

B&B	3	Ensuite	£19/£22.50	€24.13/€28.57	Dinner -
B&B	1	Standard	-	-	Partial Board -
Single Rate			£25.50/£30	€32.38/€38.09	Child reduction -

Cork City 2.5km

Open: 1st January-20th December

Mrs Catherine Edwards
RIVER VIEW
Douglas East, Cork, Co Cork

Cork City Douglas Area
Tel: **021 4893762**
Email: edwardsc@tinet.ie
Bus No: **7**

Victorian 1890 home in Douglas Village, near Barrys Pub. Convenient Restaurants Shopping Centres, Churches, Airport, Ferry. Cable TV all bedrooms. Access via tunnel to Douglas Village.

B&B	3	Ensuite	£19/£22.50	€24.13/€28.57	Dinner -
B&B	-	Standard	-	-	Partial Board -
Single Rate			£25.50/£29	€32.38/€36.82	Child reduction 25%

Cork 3km

Open: January-18th December

Mrs Betty French
GLENMALURE
Carrigaline Road, Douglas, Co Cork

Cork City Douglas Area
Tel: **021 4894324**
Bus No: **7**

Personal attention in comfortable family home. From Cork South Link Road to join N25 all routes, N25, second Douglas exit. From Ferryport Douglas exit R609.

B&B	1	Ensuite	£19/£20	€24.13/€25.39	Dinner -
B&B	2	Standard	£17/£18	€21.59/€22.86	Partial Board -
Single Rate			£25/£25	€31.74	Child reduction 33.3%

Cork 4km

Open: 10th January-10th December

Mrs Elizabeth O'Shea + Family
FATIMA HOUSE
Grange Road, Douglas, Cork City, Co Cork

Cork City Douglas Area
Tel: **021 4362536**   Fax: **021 4362536**
Email: fatimabandb@eircom.net
Bus No: **6,7**

South ring = N25. Kinsale road roundabout. Airport exit = N27 immediate left Little Chef/Touchdown Tavern. 2km. Parking. City buses. Taxi. Menu. Room rates. Visa.

B&B	4	Ensuite	£19/£25	€24.13/€31.74	Dinner -
B&B	1	Standard	-	-	Partial Board -
Single Rate			£25.50/£35	€32.38/€44.44	Child reduction -

Cork City 4km

Open: 8th January-5th December

Cork City 1km

Mrs Evelyn O'Sullivan
COOLFADDA HOUSE
**Douglas Road, Cork City,
Co Cork**

Cork City Douglas Area

Tel: **021 4363489**
Bus No: **7, 7a, 6, 10**

Spacious home in garden setting. Accessed from Douglas road up short driveway. Walking distance City Centre. Bus, Train & Airport close by. Near St. Finbars Hospital & Briar Rose Pub.

B&B	2	Ensuite	£20/£23	€25.39/€29.20	Dinner	-
B&B	3	Standard	£18/£20	€22.86/€25.39	Partial Board	-
Single Rate			£25/£30	€31.74/€38.09	Child reduction	33.3%

Open: 15th January-15th December

Cork 3km

Mrs Ann Ryan
HILLCREST HOUSE
**South Douglas Road,
Cork, Co Cork**

Cork City Douglas Area

Tel: **021 4891178**
Bus No: **6**

Detached family home. Bedrooms overlooking large garden. Walking distance City Centre, Golf, Swimming, Shops nearby.

B&B	2	Ensuite	£20	€25.39	Dinner	-
B&B	1	Standard	£18	€22.86	Partial Board	-
Single Rate			£25	€31.74	Child reduction	25%

Open: 1st April-31st October

Cork City 3km

Mrs Eleanor Tobin
BRIARVILLE
**South Douglas Road, Cork,
Co Cork**

Cork City Douglas

Tel: **021 4891597**

Midway Cork City/Douglas. Convenient to Restaurants, Ferry, Airport, Golf Courses, Cinema, Swimming. Kinsale 20km. Cork City 3km.

B&B	2	Ensuite	£20/£22.50	€25.39/€28.57	Dinner	-
B&B	1	Standard	£18/£20	€22.86/€25.39	Partial Board	-
Single Rate			£25/£30	€31.74/€38.09	Child reduction	-

Open: 1st April-31st October

In Cork City

Mr Kevin Flynn
AARAN HOUSE B&B
**49 Lower Glanmire Road,
Cork City, Co Cork**

Cork City Lower Glanmire Road

Tel: **021 4551501**
Email: aarankev@hotmail.com

Town House, adjacent to Train Station. Easy walking distance to Bus Station and City Centre 5 mins. Early Breakfast.

B&B	6	Ensuite	£19/£21	€24.13/€26.66	Dinner	-
B&B	-	Standard	-	-	Partial Board	-
Single Rate			£25.50	€32.38	Child reduction	33.3%

Open: All Year

In Cork City

Mrs Marjorie Flynn
KENT HOUSE
**47 Lower Glanmire Road,
Cork City, Co Cork**

Cork City Lower Glanmire Road

Tel: **021 4504260**
Email: kenthouse47@hotmail.com

Family run home adjacent to Railway Station and Bus Station. City Centre 5 mins walk.

B&B	4	Ensuite	£19/£21	€24.13/€26.66	Dinner	-
B&B	2	Standard	£17/£21	€21.59/€26.66	Partial Board	-
Single Rate			-	-	Child reduction	-

Open: All Year

In Cork

Ellen Murray
OAKLAND B&B
51 Lower Glanmire Road,
Cork, Co Cork

TEL: **021 4500578**
BUS No: **11**

Our house was built in the 18th Century. It is a terraced house within 5 mins walk of the Bus Station, City Centre and adjacent to the Railway Station.

B&B	5	Ensuite	£20/£22	€25.39/€27.93	Dinner	-
B&B	-	Standard	-	-	Partial Board	-
Single Rate			£28/£30	€35.55/€38.09	Child reduction	25%

Open: 1st January-21st December

In Cork

Jerry Spillane
NUMBER FORTY EIGHT
48 Lr. Glanmire Rd, Cork,
Co Cork

TEL: **021 505790**   FAX: **021 505790**

Victorian town house on Cork/Dublin road (N8). Adjacent to Railway Station. Walking distance to City Centre/Bus Station. Home baking.

B&B	6	Ensuite	£22/£28	€27.93/€35.55	Dinner	-
B&B	-	Standard	-	-	Partial Board	-
Single Rate			£25.50/£30	€32.38/€38.09	Child reduction	25%

Open: All Year

In Cork City

Mrs Mary Foley
LISADELL HOUSE
Western Road, Cork City,
Co Cork

TEL: **021 4546172**   FAX: **024 4345530**
EMAIL: mattf@indigo.ie
BUS No: **8**

Modern house on Cork's main tourist area, on the main road to Killarney & West Cork. Close to Airport, Car Ferry.

B&B	3	Ensuite	£20/£25	€25.39/€31.74	Dinner	-
B&B	2	Standard	£18/£20	€22.86/€25.39	Partial Board	-
Single Rate			£23.50/£25	€29.84/€31.74	Child reduction	-

Open: All Year

Cork City 2km

Mrs Pauline Hickey
BERKLEY LODGE B&B
Model Farm Road (R 608)
Cork, Co Cork

TEL: **021 4341755**   FAX: **021 4347522**
EMAIL: peak@esatclear.ie
WEB: www.esatclear.ie/~berkleylodgebb
BUS No: **5 & 8**

Comfortable family home R608 (City End). Western suburbs off Wilton Rd N71-N22 at Dennehys Cross near University Hospital, FAS, RTC, UCC, Airport. West Cork/Killarney rds, City 5 min.

B&B	4	Ensuite	£19/£21	€24.13/€26.66	Dinner	-
B&B	-	Standard	-	-	Partial Board	-
Single Rate			£25.50/£25.50	€32.38	Child reduction	50%

Open: 1st January-16th December

Cork City 2km

Mrs Rita O'Herlihy
55 WILTON GARDENS
off Wilton Road, Cork City,
Co Cork

TEL: **021 4541705**
BUS No: **8 & 5**

Situated quiet park, off Wilton Road, convenient to West Cork, Killarney roads, Airport, University, Hospital, College. Frommer recommended.

B&B	2	Ensuite	£19/£20	€24.13/€25.39	Dinner	-
B&B	1	Standard	£17/£18	€21.59/€22.86	Partial Board	-
Single Rate			£23.50	€29.84	Child reduction	-

Open: February-November

Cork City 2km

Michael and Patricia Flavin
ALBATROSS
Clogheen (near Clogheen Church), Blarney Road, Co Cork

Cork City
TEL: 021 392315
EMAIL: albatross@eircom.net
BUS No: 2

Situated in peaceful area. 2km City Centre, 3km Blarney. Convenient Cork City, Gaol, Tennis, Golf. Horseriding locally. An Irish welcome.

B&B	3	Ensuite	£20	€25.39	Dinner	-
B&B	-	Standard	-	-	Partial Board	-
Single Rate			-	-	Child reduction	-

Open: February-November

Cork 2km

Anne & David Lynch
ST ANTHONY'S
Clogheen, Blarney Road, Cork, Co Cork

Cork
TEL: 021 392547
BUS No: 2

Comfortable bungalow close to Cork City and Blarney Castle. Golf/Fishing nearby. Home baking, breakfast menu, nice garden & patio.

B&B	2	Ensuite	£19/£19	€24.13	Dinner	-
B&B	1	Standard	£17/£17	€21.59	Partial Board	-
Single Rate			£23.50/£25	€29.84/€31.74	Child reduction	-

Open: 1st March-1st November

Cork City 1km

Barry & Goretti Guilfoyle
MARIAVILLE HOUSE
Coolgarten Park, Off Magazine Road, Cork, Co Cork

Cork City
TEL: 021 4316508
EMAIL: barguilfoyle@eircom.net
BUS No: 10

Family run home, quiet location. Private secure parking. Convenient to Airport, University College Cork, University Hospital. Close to Restaurants, Pubs, main Bus Routes. City Centre 15 mins walk.

B&B	4	Ensuite	£19/£20	€24.13/€25.39	Dinner	-
B&B	-	Standard	-	-	Partial Board	-
Single Rate			£25.50/£25.50	€32.38	Child reduction	-

Open: 1st June-30th September

Cork City 1km

Mrs Breeda Higgins
7 FERNCLIFF
Bellevue Park, St Lukes, Cork City, Co Cork

Cork City
TEL: 021 4508963   FAX: 021 4508963 (man)
BUS No: 7 & 8

Victorian home, quiet cul-de-sac. Bus/Train Stations/City Centre 1km. Take left at T after Ambassador Hotel, then straight ahead, and on right.

B&B	2	Ensuite	£19/£19	€24.13	Dinner	-
B&B	2	Standard	£17/£17	€21.59	Partial Board	-
Single Rate			£23.50/£25.50	€29.84/€32.38	Child reduction	33.3%

Open: March-December

In Crookhaven

Maureen & James Newman
GALLEY COVE HOUSE
Crookhaven, West Cork, Co Cork

Crookhaven Mizen Head
TEL: 028 35137   FAX: 028 35137

Friendly comfortable accommodation in peaceful scenic location. Overlooking Atlantic Ocean and Fastnet lighthouse. Near Mizen Head and Barleycove. Child Reduction.

B&B	3	Ensuite	£20/£22.50	€25.39/€28.57	Dinner	-
B&B	1	Standard	£19/£21	€24.13/€26.66	Partial Board	-
Single Rate			£25.50/£30	€32.38/€38.09	Child reduction	-

Open: 1st March-31st December

Drimoleague 2km

Mrs Marian Collins
ROSELAWN HOUSE
**Derrygrea, Drimoleague,
Co Cork**

Drimoleague Skibbereen
TEL: **028 31369**

Elegant country house on Cork/Bantry R586 route. Local amenities. Skibbereen 12km. Bantry 20km. Homely atmosphere. Tea/Coffee available at all times.

B&B	2	Ensuite	£19/£19	€24.13	Dinner	£12.50
B&B	1	Standard	£17/£17	€21.59	Partial Board	£185
Single Rate			£23.50/£25.50	€29.84/€32.38	Child reduction	50%

Open: 1st March-1st November

Fermoy 1km

Mrs Patricia O'Leary
PALM RISE
**Barrys Boreen, Duntahane Road,
Fermoy, Co Cork**

Fermoy
TEL: **025 31386**

Friendly modern home in peaceful scenic surroundings. Close to fishing, horse riding, Leisure Centre and scenic walks. 1km from N8-main Dublin/Cork Road.

B&B	3	Ensuite	£19/£25	€24.13/€31.74	Dinner	-
B&B	-	Standard	£19/£25	€24.13/€31.74	Partial Board	-
Single Rate			£25.50/£30	€32.38/€38.09	Child reduction	10%

Open: 3rd January-20th December

In Glengarriff

Mrs Rita Barry-Murphy
COIS COILLE
**Glengarriff,
Co Cork**

Glengarriff
TEL: **027 63202**

Warm hospitality in comfortable home overlooking Glengarriff Harbour. Award winning garden in quiet woodland setting. Extensive breakfast menu, home baking.

B&B	6	Ensuite	£20/£21	€25.39/€26.66	Dinner	-
B&B	-	Standard	-	-	Partial Board	-
Single Rate			£30/£30	€38.09	Child reduction	25%

Open: 12th April-30th September

Glengarriff 3km

Mrs Kathleen Connolly
CARRAIG DUBH HOUSE
**Droumgarriff, Glengarriff,
Co Cork**

Glengarriff
TEL: **027 63146**
EMAIL: carraigdubhhouse@hotmail.com

Lovely family home in quiet peaceful location. 150m off main road overlooking Harbour and Golf Club. Nice walking area. Tea/Coffee and Hairdryer in bedrooms. Lovely breakfast menu.

B&B	3	Ensuite	£19	€24.13	Dinner	-
B&B	1	Standard	£17	€21.59	Partial Board	-
Single Rate			£23.50/£25.50	€29.84/€32.38	Child reduction	25%

Open: 15th March-31st October

In Glengarriff

Mrs Ann Guerin
SEA FRONT
Glengarriff, Co Cork

Glengarriff
TEL: **027 63079**

Centrally situated, comfortable home on the Waterfront. Convenient to the Ferry for Garnish Island. 4 minutes walk to Town, Shops and Restaurants.

B&B	-	Ensuite	-	-	Dinner	-
B&B	4	Standard	£17/£17	€21.59	Partial Board	-
Single Rate			£23.50/£23.50	€29.84	Child reduction	25%

Open: 1st May-31st October

In Glengarriff

Mrs Maureen MacCarthy
MAUREENS
**Glengarriff Village Home,
Glengarriff, Co Cork**

Glengarriff
Tel: 027 63201

Two storey house adjacent/picturesque village. Beside ancient Oak Forest, Sea, Mountains, Lakes and Rivers. Opposite entrance to Garinish island.

B&B	4	Ensuite	£19	€24.13	Dinner	-
B&B	2	Standard	£17	€21.59	Partial Board	-
Single Rate			£23.50	€29.84	Child reduction	25%

Open: All Year

In Glengarriff

Eileen O'Sullivan & Imelda Lyne
ISLAND VIEW HOUSE
Glengarriff, Co Cork

Glengarriff
Tel: 027 63081   Fax: 027 63600
Email: islandview@ireland.com

Comfortable family home in peaceful scenic area. 10 minutes walk to town - 150 metres off main road. Ideal touring centre. Breakfast menu.

B&B	6	Ensuite	£19/£20	€24.13/€25.39	Dinner	-
B&B	-	Standard			Partial Board	-
Single Rate			£25.50/£26.50	€32.38/€33.65	Child reduction	25%

Open: April-November

In Goleen

Mrs Sue Hill
THE HERON'S COVE
**The Harbour, Goleen,
West Cork, Co Cork**

Goleen
Tel: 028 35225   Fax: 028 35422
Email: suehill@eircom.net
Web: www.heronscove.com

Comfortable rooms, good food, wine. Near Barleycove, Mizen Head. Hairdryers, Electric blankets. Restaurant. Fresh fish/local produce. AA ♦♦♦♦.

B&B	5	Ensuite	£19.50/£25	€24.76/€31.74	Dinner	á la carte
B&B	-	Standard			Partial Board	-
Single Rate			£26/£31.50	€33.01/€40.00	Child reduction	-

Open: All Year Except Christmas

Innishannon 3km

Mrs Kathleen Cummins
ELLAMORE
**Ballymountain, Innishannon,
Co Cork**

Innishannon near Kinsale
Tel: 021 4775807
Email: ellamore@oceanfree.net
Web: ellamore.homepage.com

Country residence, convenient to Airport, Ferryport. Follow signpost for Ballymountain house off N71 at Innishannon Bridge. Next house on left.

B&B	3	Ensuite	£20/£22	€25.39/€27.93	Dinner	-
B&B	-	Standard			Partial Board	-
Single Rate			£28.50	€36.19	Child reduction	-

Open: 1st May-30th September

In Kanturk

Mrs Phyl Grace
HILLSIDE
**Millview Road, Kanturk,
Co Cork**

Kanturk
Tel: 029 50241

A mature rambling garden welcomes you to this restful house, with pictures, old furnishings & books. Local Golf & Fishing.

B&B	3	Ensuite	£20/£20	€25.39	Dinner	-
B&B	2	Standard	£18/£18	€22.86	Partial Board	-
Single Rate			£25/£30	€31.74/€38.09	Child reduction	-

Open: 25th April-30th September

Mrs Breda Ahern
JALNA
Pike Cross, Kinsale,
Co Cork

Kinsale
Tel: **021 772692**

Luxurious modern bungalow set in country pastures. Spanish style interior and exterior. Conservatory opening on to patios and garden. Jacuzzi.

B&B	3	Ensuite	£20/£23	€25.39/€29.20	Dinner	-
B&B	-	Standard	-	-	Partial Board	-
Single Rate			-	-	Child reduction	-

Kinsale 2km

Open: 1st January-21st December

John & Eleanor Bateman
ROCKLANDS HOUSE
Compass Hill, Kinsale,
Co Cork

Kinsale
Tel: **021 4772609**   Fax: **021 4772609**
Email: rocklandshouse@eircom.net
Web: www.kinsaletown.com

Set in 3 acres of woodland on a scenic walking trail, 3 minutes drive from Town Centre. Rooms with Balconies overlooking the inner Harbour. Guest Lounge.

B&B	6	Ensuite	£20/£30	€25.39/€38.09	Dinner	-
B&B	-	Standard	-	-	Partial Board	-
Single Rate			£35/£50	€44.44/€63.49	Child reduction	-

Kinsale 1km

Open: 1st March-5th November

Mrs Ita Carey
ORCHARD COTTAGE
Farrangalway, Kinsale,
Co Cork

Kinsale
Tel: **021 4772693**
Email: orchardcottage@eircom.net

Quiet Country Home adjacent to Kinsale's 18-hole Golf course. All rooms TV, Clock Radios, Hairdryers, Tea/Coffee, AA ✦✦✦. Airport Ferry 20km. 500 mts off R607.

B&B	4	Ensuite	£20/£23	€25.39/€29.20	Dinner	-
B&B	-	Standard	-	-	Partial Board	-
Single Rate			£28/£30	€35.55/€38.09	Child reduction	25%

Kinsale 3km

Open: 7th January-20th December

Mrs Joan Collins
WATERLANDS
Cork Road, Kinsale,
Co Cork

Kinsale
Tel: **021 4772318**   Fax: **021 4774873**
Email: info@collinsbb.com
Web: www.collinsbb.com

Luxury accommodation, Breakfast Conservatory, Electric Blankets, Tea/Coffee, Hairdryers, Extensive breakfast menu. Highly recommended, AA ✦✦✦✦, Ideal touring base. Airport 20 mins.

B&B	4	Ensuite	£20/£23	€25.39/€29.20	Dinner	-
B&B	-	Standard	-	-	Partial Board	-
Single Rate			£30/£35	€38.09/€44.44	Child reduction	25%

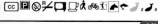

Kinsale 1km

Open: 1st March-31st October

Phyllis & PJ Crowe
WATERSIDE HOUSE
Dromderrig, Kinsale, Co Cork

Kinsale
Tel: **021 774196**   Fax: **021 774196**

Picturesque setting in spacious seaside garden. View of inner Harbour. Kinsale is a pleasant 1km waterside walk. Golf courses, Beaches nearby. R600 from Kinsale, right by Big Bridge.

B&B	3	Ensuite	£22/£28	€27.93/€35.55	Dinner	-
B&B	1	Standard	£20/£23	€25.39/€29.20	Partial Board	-
Single Rate			£30/£35	€38.09/€44.44	Child reduction	-

Kinsale 1km

Open: 1st February-1st December

Kinsale 1km

Mrs Kathleen Cummins
BAY VIEW
Clasheen, Kinsale, Co Cork

Kinsale
TEL: **021 4774054**
EMAIL: bayviewbb@indigo.ie
WEB: www.cork-guide.ie/kinsale/bayview/welcome.html

Comfortable modern spacious home. Panoramic views overlooking Bay and countryside from dining room. Breakfast menu. "Le guide du Routard" recommended.

B&B	3	Ensuite	£19/£21	€24.13/€26.66	Dinner	-
B&B	-	Standard	-	-	Partial Board	-
Single Rate			£27.50	€34.91	Child reduction	-

Open: 1st April-30th September

In Kinsale

Marian Fitzpatrick
SPRING COTTAGE
Barrick Hill, Kinsale,
Co Cork

Kinsale
TEL: **021 4774785**

Award winning traditional Irish Cottage overlooking Kinsale Town. 3 mins walk to Town Centre. Adjacent to all amenities. Fishing & Yachting.

B&B	3	Ensuite	£20/£24	€25.39/€30.47	Dinner	-
B&B	-	Standard	-	-	Partial Board	-
Single Rate					Child reduction	-

Open: 1st March-31st October

Kinsale 4km

Peggy & Eamonn Foley
FERNVILLE
Lower Cove, Kinsale,
Co Cork

Kinsale
TEL: **021 4774874**
EMAIL: fernville@oceanfree.net
WEB: www.dirl.com/cork/fernville.htm

Luxury B&B with Sea views on Kinsales outer Harbour. 1 min to Beach/Fishing. 10 mins drive to Kinsale, signs from Charles Fort. Airport/Ferry 30 mins.

B&B	3	Ensuite	£20/£25	€25.39/€31.74	Dinner	-
B&B	-	Standard	-	-	Partial Board	-
Single Rate			£30/£35	€38.09/€44.44	Child reduction	25%

Open: 17th March-31st October

Kinsale

Mrs Bernie Ryan Godkin
GOLDEN GARDEN
Cappagh, Kinsale,
Co Cork

Kinsale
TEL: **021 772490**

Luxury accommodation with old world charm, in secluded garden overlooking Harbour. Tastefully decorated, antique furniture. Victorian style sittingroom. Power showers.

B&B	4	Ensuite	£20/£35	€25.39/€44.44	Dinner	-
B&B	-	Standard	-	-	Partial Board	-
Single Rate			£35	€44.44	Child reduction	-

Open: 1st March-31st October

Kinsale 10km

Mrs Gillian Good
GLEBE COUNTRY HOUSE
Ballinadee, Nr Kinsale,
Bandon, Co Cork

Kinsale
TEL: **021 4778294**   FAX: **021 4778456**
EMAIL: glebehse@indigo.ie
WEB: http://indigo.ie/~glebehse/

Charming family run Georgian Rectory close to Beaches, Bandon & Kinsale. Take N71 to Innishannon Bridge, follow signs for Ballinadee. AA ♦♦♦♦.

B&B	4	Ensuite	£22.50/£35	€28.57/€44.44	Dinner	£20
B&B	-	Standard	-	-	Partial Board	-
Single Rate			£30/£45	€38.09/€57.14	Child reduction	50%

Open: 4th January-21st December

Mrs Teresa Gray
ROCKVILLE
The Rock, Kinsale,
Co Cork

Kinsale
TEL: **021 772791**

Modern well appointed split level home overlooking Kinsale Town and Harbour and within five minutes walk of Town Centre.

B&B	3	Ensuite	£20/£23	€25.39/€29.20	Dinner	-
B&B	-	Standard	-	-	Partial Board	-
Single Rate			£25.50/£30	€32.38/€38.09	Child reduction	-

In Kinsale

Open: March-November

Mrs M Griffin
HILLSIDE HOUSE
Camp Hill, Kinsale,
Co Cork

Kinsale
TEL: **021 4772315**   FAX: **021 4772315**
EMAIL: hillside@oceanfree.net

Beautiful spacious home. Award winning gardens. On 1601 battle site, overlooks Town. Frommer recommended. Car park. Guests conservatory. 10-15 mins walk Town. Menu.

B&B	6	Ensuite	£19/£22.50	€24.13/€28.57	Dinner	-
B&B	-	Standard	-	-	Partial Board	-
Single Rate			-	-	Child reduction	25%

Kinsale 1km

Open: All Year

Orla Griffin
GRIFFIN'S RIVERSIDE HOUSE
Kippagh, Kinsale,
Co Cork

Kinsale
TEL: **021 4774917**
EMAIL: riversidehouse@esatclear.ie

Panoramic ocean view. Luxury accommodation. TV's, Hairdryers, Tea/Coffee, Private Gardens, Car Park. All amenities walking distance. Golf, fishing arranged. Power showers.

B&B	6	Ensuite	£19/£22	€24.13/€27.93	Dinner	-
B&B	-	Standard	-	-	Partial Board	-
Single Rate			£27/£33	€34.29/€41.90	Child reduction	25%

Kinsale 1km

Open: All Year Except Christmas

Brian & Valerie Hosford
WOODLANDS HOUSE
Cappagh, Kinsale,
Co Cork

Kinsale
TEL: **021 4772633**   FAX: **021 4772649**
EMAIL: woodlandskinsale@eircom.net
WEB: homepage.eircom.net/~woodlandskinsale/

Modern luxurious accommodation with lovely views of Kinsale Town and Harbour. 7 mins walk from Kinsale Town Centre. En suite. Private parking. TV, direct dial Telephone.

B&B	3	Ensuite	£19/£35	€24.13/€44.44	Dinner	-
B&B	-	Standard	-	-	Partial Board	-
Single Rate			£25.50/£40	€32.38/€50.79	Child reduction	25%

In Kinsale

Open: 1st March-12th November

Ms Brita Hurley
AMARACH
The Glen, Kinsale,
Co Cork

Kinsale
TEL: **021 4774633**

Townhouse tastefully decorated. En-suite, TV, Tea/Coffee, Hairdryer. Credit Cards accepted. Adjacent Restaurants, Museums, right at White House, Airport/Ferry 20 mins.

B&B	3	Ensuite	£20/£25	€25.39/€31.74	Dinner	-
B&B	-	Standard	-	-	Partial Board	-
Single Rate			£25/£40	€31.74/€50.79	Child reduction	-

In Kinsale

Open: 1st March-1st December

Kinsale 3km

Mrs Joan Hurley
FOYLE
Acres, Kinsale,
Co Cork

Kinsale
TEL: **021 4772363**

Modern bungalow in rural setting with conservatory/patio for guests use. On R600 Coast Road. Old Head Golf course, Beaches nearby. Airport/Ferryport 20km.

B&B	4	Ensuite	£20/£22.50	€25.39/€28.57	Dinner	-
B&B	-	Standard		-	Partial Board	-
Single Rate			£30/£35	€38.09/€44.44	Child reduction	25%

Open: 1st March-31st October

In Kinsale

Mrs Mary Hurley
SCEILIG HOUSE
Ard Brack, Scilly, Kinsale,
Co Cork

Kinsale
TEL: **021 4772832**   FAX: **021 4772832**
EMAIL: hurleyfamily@eircom.net

Town house set in layered gardens overlooking Kinsale Harbour. Seaview from bedrooms with private patio/balcony. Frommer and "La Guide" recommended. Follow Scilly sign on entry to town.

B&B	3	Ensuite	£18.50/£25	€23.49/€31.74	Dinner	-
B&B	-	Standard		-	Partial Board	-
Single Rate			£25/£50	€31.74/€63.49	Child reduction	25%

Open: All Year

In Kinsale

Mrs Teresa Hurley
CEPHAS HOUSE
Compass Hill, Kinsale,
Co Cork

Kinsale
TEL: **021 4772689**   FAX: **021 4772689**
EMAIL: thurley@boinet.ie

Town house, beautiful private garden. Magnificent seaviews from bedrooms with balcony. Breakfast Conservatory. Scenic walk to town. Guide du Routard recommended.

B&B	3	Ensuite	£19/£25	€24.13/€31.74	Dinner	-
B&B	-	Standard		-	Partial Board	-
Single Rate			£30/£50	€38.09/€63.49	Child reduction	25%

Open: 1st March-31st October

Kinsale 2km

Mrs Nora Kelly
VALLEY-VIEW
Hospital Road, Coolvalanane,
Kinsale, Co Cork

Kinsale
TEL: **021 4772842**
EMAIL: valleyview@iol.ie

Spacious bungalow in scenic farming area. Overlooking open countryside, close to Beaches, Golf and Fishing. Airport, Ferry, half hour drive.

B&B	2	Ensuite	£19/£19	€24.13	Dinner	-
B&B	2	Standard	£17/£17	€21.59	Partial Board	-
Single Rate			£25/£28	€31.74/€35.55	Child reduction	50%

Open: All Year

Kinsale 2km

Mrs Myrtle Levis
WALYUNGA
Sandycove,
Kinsale, Co Cork

Kinsale
TEL: **021 4774126**   FAX: **021 4774126**
EMAIL: walyunga@eircom.net

Bright spacious modern bungalow. Unique design, landscaped gardens, outstanding ocean & valley views, Sandy Beaches, Scenic Coastal walks. Internationally acclaimed.

B&B	4	Ensuite	£20/£23	€25.39/€29.20	Dinner	-
B&B	1	Standard	£19/£21	€24.13/€26.66	Partial Board	-
Single Rate					Child reduction	25%

Open: 1st March-29th October

Anthony & Fiona McCarthy
SEA BREEZE
**Featherbed Lane, Kinsale,
Co Cork**

Kinsale

Tel: **021 4774854**

Dormer bungalow with view of harbour from some bedrooms. 3 mins walk town Centre, private carpark, sailing, fishing and beaches nearby.

B&B	4	Ensuite	£20/£25	€25.39/€31.74	Dinner	-
B&B	-	Standard	-	-	Partial Board	-
Single Rate			£25/£30	€31.74/€38.09	Child reduction	25%

In Kinsale

Open: All Year Except Christmas

Brian & Ann McCarthy
ROCK VIEW
**The Glen, Kinsale,
Co Cork**

Kinsale

Tel: **021 4773162**
Web: www.dragnet-system's.ie/dira/rockview.htm

Award winning attractive comfortable home located in the heart of Kinsale Town Centre. Car park and bicycle lockup behind house. Adjacent Church, Shop, Pubs.

B&B	4	Ensuite	£20/£23.50	€25.39/€29.84	Dinner	-
B&B	-	Standard	-	-	Partial Board	-
Single Rate			£25/£30	€31.74/€38.09	Child reduction	25%

In Kinsale

Open: 1st January-29th December

Mr & Mrs Michael McCarthy
HILL TOP B&B
**Sleaveen Heights, Kinsale,
Co Cork**

Kinsale

Tel: **021 4772612**

Modern spacious bungalow, conservatory overlooking Kinsale Harbour and James's Fort. Close Museum, Beaches, Golf, Yachting, Marina, Fishing. 3 mins walk Town.

B&B	6	Ensuite	£20/£23	€25.39/€29.20	Dinner	-
B&B	-	Standard	-	-	Partial Board	-
Single Rate			£25.50/£30	€32.38/€38.09	Child reduction	25%

In Kinsale

Open: All Year

Ena Murphy
RISING SUN LODGE
**Bawnleigh, Ballinhassig PO,
Kinsale, Co Cork**

Kinsale

Tel: **021 4771573**

Modern bungalow, tastefully decorated, in a country setting. Breakfast conservatory. Home baking. Warm welcome. Situated on the R607 close to Kinsale and off the N71.

B&B	2	Ensuite	£19/£21	€24.13/€26.66	Dinner	-
B&B	1	Standard	£19/£20	€24.13/€25.39	Partial Board	-
Single Rate			£23.50/£25.50	€29.84/€32.38	Child reduction	50%

Kinsale 5km

Open: 1st January-17th December

CHARLES FORT
SUMMER COVE, KINSALE, CO. CORK
TEL + 353 21 772263 FAX+ 353 21 774347

A 17th century star-shaped fort, designed by William Robinson. Together with James Fort (1602) across the estuary, Charles Fort protected the trading town of Kinsale. It continued to develop in the 18th and 19th centuries and was in use until 1921.

Kinsale 1km

Martina Murphy
FOUR WINDS
Watersland, Kinsale,
Co Cork

Kinsale
TEL: **021 4774822**

Luxury new accommodation set in peaceful area on 1 acre of beautiful garden. Kinsale 1km/Airport 20 mins/Ferry 30 mins.

B&B	3	Ensuite	£19/£22	€24.13/€27.93	Dinner	-
B&B	1	Standard	£18/£20	€22.86/€25.39	Partial Board	-
Single Rate			£25/£25	€31.74	Child reduction	50%

 Open: 1st March-1st November

Kinsale 5km

Mrs Theresa Murphy
TESBEN HOUSE
Old Head/Golf Links Road,
Barrells Cross, Kinsale,
Co Cork

Kinsale
TEL: **021 4778354**   FAX: **021 4778354**
EMAIL: tesbenhouse@eircom.net
WEB: http://homepage.eircom.net/~tesbenhouse

Tranquil surroundings unrivalled. Picturesque view R600 West Cork/Kerry. "Old Head" Golf Links 4km. "Le Guide du Routard" recommended. Ferryport 20km.

B&B	2	Ensuite	£19/£22	€24.13/€27.93	Dinner	-
B&B	2	Standard	£17/£19	€21.59/€24.13	Partial Board	-
Single Rate			£25/£33	€31.74/€41.90	Child reduction	25%

Open: 1st March-15th November

In Kinsale

Mrs Eileen O'Connell
DOONEEN
Ardcarrig, Bandon Road,
Kinsale, Co Cork

Kinsale
TEL: **021 4772024**
EMAIL: dooneenbandb@esatclear.ie
WEB: www.ireland-discover.com/dooneen.htm

Modern house in peaceful setting with views of inner and outer Harbour, TV lounge, private parking, secluded gardens. Town area.

B&B	3	Ensuite	£20	€25.39	Dinner	-
B&B	1	Standard	£18	€22.86	Partial Board	-
Single Rate			£30	€38.09	Child reduction	25%

Open: All Year Except Christmas

In Kinsale

Mrs Phil O'Donovan
ROSSBRIN
Harbour Heights, Cappagh,
Kinsale, Co Cork

Kinsale
TEL: **021 4772112**

Luxury bungalow, quiet residential park. Panoramic views, gardens. Convenient all amenities. Breakfast menu. From St Multose Church on Bandon rd, drive 630m, turn left as signposted.

B&B	3	Ensuite	£19/£20	€24.13/€25.39	Dinner	-
B&B		Standard	-	-	Partial Board	-
Single Rate			-	-	Child reduction	25%

Open: February-November

In Kinsale

Betty & Pat O'Farrell
15 Main Street,
Kinsale,
Co Cork

Kinsale
TEL: **021 4774169**   FAX: **021 4774169**
EMAIL: bettyofarrell@eircom.net
WEB: http://homepage.eircom.net/~patofarrell/

Town centre historical building, comfortable family home. French/German spoken. Convenient Sailing, Golfing, Fishing, Beaches, Restaurants, Historical sites, Bicycle lock-up.

B&B	3	Ensuite	£19/£25	€24.13/€31.74	Dinner	-
B&B	1	Standard	£17/£20	€21.59/€25.39	Partial Board	-
Single Rate			-	-	Child reduction	-

Open: All Year Except Christmas

In Kinsale

Mrs Mary O'Neill
SEA GULL HOUSE
**Cork Street, Kinsale,
Co Cork**

Kinsale
Tel: **021 4772240**
Email: marytap@iol.ie
Web: seagullhouse.com

Next door to "Desmond Castle", wine museum built 1500. Near Beach, Fishing & Golf. Kinsale Gourmet Town. Groups welcome.

B&B	5	Ensuite	£19/£22.50	€24.13/€28.57	Dinner	-
B&B	1	Standard	-	-	Partial Board	-
Single Rate			£25/£30	€31.74/€38.09	Child reduction	-

Open: March-November

Kinsale 5km

Mrs Sheila O'Regan
SIROCO
**Ballyregan, Kinsale,
Co Cork**

Kinsale
Tel: **021 775129**

Country bungalow in scenic surroundings. Car Park. Right at white house - past Kinsale Hospital 400m to SIROCO signpost- past through 4 crossroads - next 4th house on left.

B&B	-	Ensuite	-	-	Dinner	-
B&B	3	Standard	£18	€22.86	Partial Board	-
Single Rate			-	-	Child reduction	-

Open: May-September

Kinsale 4km

Mrs Claire O'Sullivan
RIVERMOUNT HOUSE
**Barrells Cross, Old Head Rd,
Kinsale, Co Cork**

Kinsale
Tel: **021 4778033**   Fax: **021 4778225**
Email: rivermnt@iol.ie
Web: www.rivermount.com

Award winning luxurious home overlooking the river. AA & RAC ✦✦✦✦ with Sparkling Diamond Award. Extensive Breakfast menu. Recommended by many guides. Just off R600.

B&B	6	Ensuite	£20/£23	€25.39/€29.20	Dinner	-
B&B	-	Standard	-	-	Partial Board	-
Single Rate			£25.50/£35	€32.38/€44.44	Child reduction	25%

Open: 1st January-20th December

Mrs Phil Price
DANABEL
**Sleaveen, Kinsale,
Co Cork**

Kinsale
Tel: **021 4774087**
Email: info@danabel.com
Web: www.danabel.com

Modern house, quiet area. Town 3 mins walk. Orthopaedic beds. Hairdryers, Tea making. Airport/Ferry 20 mins. Harbour view some bedrooms. Frommer recommended/Star Rating.

B&B	5	Ensuite	£19/£25	€24.13/€31.74	Dinner	-
B&B	-	Standard	-	-	Partial Board	-
Single Rate			£30/£46	€38.09/€58.41	Child reduction	25%

Open: All Year Except Christmas

In Kinsale

Mrs Ann Salter
CROSSWAYS
**Ardbrack, Kinsale,
Co Cork**

Kinsale
Tel: **021 4772460**   Fax: **021 4772460**

Modern spacious home overlooking inner Harbour. Adjacent to Scenic Walks, Fishing, Golfing, Pub Entertainment & Gourmet Restaurants.

B&B	5	Ensuite	£20/£25	€25.39/€31.74	Dinner	-
B&B	-	Standard	-	-	Partial Board	-
Single Rate			-	-	Child reduction	25%

Open: All Year Except Christmas

In Kinsale

Margo Searls
LANDFALL HOUSE
**Cappagh, Kinsale,
Co Cork**

TEL: **021 4772575**   FAX: **021 4772575**
EMAIL: landfallhouse@eircom.net

Luxury spacious home and gardens. Panoramic views over River, Harbour and Town. Ideal touring base. Private parking. Breakfast menu. Minutes to Town. Power showers, Hairdryers etc.

B&B	4	Ensuite	£20/£23	€25.39/€29.20	Dinner	-
B&B	-	Standard	-	-	Partial Board	-
Single Rate			£30/£35	€38.09/€44.44	Child reduction	25%

Open: 1st February-30th November

June & Jack Sheehan
VILLA MARIA
**Cork Road, Kinsale,
Co Cork**

TEL: **021 4772627**

Comfortable Villa, Scenic views, Conservatory, Garden. Cork-Kinsale Bus route. Quiet 3 mins walk Town. On R600 near Music, Pubs, Restaurants, Golf, Beaches, Airport, Ferryport.

B&B	6	Ensuite	£19/£23	€24.13/€29.20	Dinner	-
B&B	-	Standard	-	-	Partial Board	-
Single Rate			-	-	Child reduction	50%

Open: March-November

Macroom 9km

Sean & Margaret Moynihan
AN CUASAN
**Coolavokig, Macroom,
Co Cork**

TEL: **026 40018**
EMAIL: cuasan@eircom.net
WEB: www.welcome.to/cuasan

Tranquil setting on N22, Blarney/Killarney. Dilliard/Causin recommended. Landscaped gardens, Walking, Golf, Traditional music family. Downstairs rooms. Bicycle shed.

B&B	5	Ensuite	£19	€24.13	Dinner	-
B&B	1	Standard	£17	€21.59	Partial Board	-
Single Rate			£23.50/£25.50	€29.84/€32.38	Child reduction	50%

Open: April-October

Macroom 5km

Kathleen & Brendan Mulcahy
FOUNTAIN HOUSE
**Cork Road, Macroom,
Co Cork**

TEL: **026 41424**   FAX: **026 41425**

Lakeside N22 landscaped gardens. Ground floor rooms. Private parking. Warm hospitality. Breakfast menu, Home baking. Touring base Blarney, Killarney, Bantry.

B&B	6	Ensuite	£20/£20	€25.39	Dinner	-
B&B	-	Standard	-	-	Partial Board	-
Single Rate			£28/£28	€35.55	Child reduction	50%

Open: 1st March-30th November

Mrs Peggy Twomey
WESTON HEIGHTS
**The Mills, Ballyvourney,
Macroom, Co Cork**

TEL: **026 45097**   FAX: **026 45097**

Charming family run 18th Century Georgian house on N22. Cead Mile Failte. Prize winning gardens. Close to all local amenities, Golf, Fishing, Walking, Horse Riding, Pubs and Restaurants.

B&B	5	Ensuite	£20/£20	€25.39	Dinner	£15
B&B	-	Standard	-	-	Partial Board	£185
Single Rate			£25.50/£25.50	€32.38	Child reduction	25%

Open: All Year

In Mallow

Mrs Sheila Clifford
ARD-NA-LAOI
**Opp Convent of Mercy,
Bathview, Mallow, Co Cork**

Mallow

TEL: **022 22317**   FAX: **022 22317**

Period residence, opposite Convent of Mercy. Mature gardens in centre of Town. Very private. Ideally situated for Fishing, Golfing, Swimming.

B&B	4	Ensuite	£19	€24.13	Dinner -
B&B	-	Standard	-	-	Partial Board -
Single Rate			£25.50	€32.38	Child reduction 50%

Open: 1st March-31st October

Mallow 2km

Mrs B Courtney
RATHMORE HOUSE
**Fermoy Road, Mallow,
Co Cork**

Mallow

TEL: **022 21688**

Peaceful setting beside Fermoy/Waterford Mitchelstown/Dublin road. Rosslare Ferryport route. Spacious grounds, parking. Home baking. Tea/coffee in rooms.

B&B	3	Ensuite	£19	€24.13	Dinner -
B&B	2	Standard	£17	€21.59	Partial Board -
Single Rate			-	-	Child reduction -

Open: 1st June-1st November

In Mallow

Mrs Mary Kiely
HILL TOP VIEW
**Navigation Road, Mallow,
Co Cork**

Mallow

TEL: **022 21491**   FAX: **022 21491**
EMAIL: mkhilltopview@eircom.net

Country residence adjacent Racecourse/Fishing, Golf, Horseriding nearby. Touring centre. TV, Tea/Coffee facilities, Hairdryers, Breakfast menu, Conservatory, Secluded gardens.

B&B	6	Ensuite	£19/£20	€24.13/€25.39	Dinner -
B&B	-	Standard	-	-	Partial Board -
Single Rate			£26/£28	€33.01/€35.55	Child reduction 25%

Open: 1st March-31st October

Mallow 15km

Mrs Eva Lane
PARK SOUTH
**Doneraile, Mallow,
Co Cork**

Mallow

TEL: **022 25296**
EMAIL: parksouth@eircom.net
WEB: parksouth.foundmark.com

Situated 1km off N73. Dublin, Killarney, Cork, Ringaskiddy, Rosslare, Ferry. Fishing, Golf, Racecourse, Parks, Gardens (Ann's Grove). Bicycle shed. Qualified Cert cook. Hot scones on arrival.

B&B	3	Ensuite	£19/£19	€24.13	Dinner £15
B&B	1	Standard	£17/£19	€21.59/€24.13	Partial Board £210
Single Rate			£23.50/£25.50	€29.84/€32.38	Child reduction 33.3%

Open: All Year

In Mallow

Mrs Winifred O'Donovan
OAKLANDS
**Springwood, Off Killarney Road,
Mallow, Co Cork**

Mallow

TEL: **022 21127**   FAX: **022 21127**
EMAIL: oaklands@eircom.net

AA ♦♦♦ Peaceful location, minutes walk to Town, Train, Racecourse. 150 yards from N20/N72 roundabout. Signposted. Tea/Coffee facilities. Breakfast menu. Luxury home.

B&B	4	Ensuite	£19/£19	€24.13	Dinner -
B&B	-	Standard	-	-	Partial Board -
Single Rate			£26/£26	€33.01	Child reduction 25%

Open: 1st April-1st November

Sean & Margaret O'Shea
ANNABELLA LODGE
Mallow, Co Cork

Mallow
Tel: **022 43991**
Email: moshea@esatclear.ie
Web: http://www.esatclear.ie/~moshea/

Purpose built luxury accommodation. Hairdryers, Electric Blankets. Ideally situated 5 mins walk Town Centre, Railway Station. Adjacent Race Course, Golf. On N72.

B&B	6	Ensuite	£20/£23	€25.39/€29.20	Dinner -
B&B	-	Standard		-	Partial Board -
Single Rate			£25.50/£28	€32.38/€35.55	Child reduction 25%

In Mallow cc P ✎ ⌂ ☎ ☕ ⚘ ♿ 🚶 🐾 ⚓ 🏊
Open: All Year

Mrs M Walsh
RIVERSIDE HOUSE
Navigation Road, Mallow, Co Cork

Mallow
Tel: **022 42761**

Country house set in scenic area overlooking River Blackwater on N72. Ideal base for touring. Convenient Town Centre, Racecourse, Railway Station.

B&B	6	Ensuite	£19	€24.13	Dinner -
B&B	-	Standard		-	Partial Board -
Single Rate			£25.50	€32.38	Child reduction 25%

In Mallow cc P ⌂ ☕ ⚓ 🐾 J_R
Open: All Year

Mrs Eileen Dowling
AMANDA
Cahermone, Midleton, Co Cork

Midleton
Tel: **021 4631135**   Fax: **021 4631135**

Situated on the (N25). Waterford side of Midleton Town, near Jameson and Cobh Heritage Centre, Ballymaloe House, Fishing and Golf nearby.

B&B	4	Ensuite	£19	€24.13	Dinner -
B&B	-	Standard		-	Partial Board -
Single Rate			£25.50	€32.38	Child reduction 50%

Midleton 1km cc P ⌂ 🐾 ⚓ J_L J_S J_R
Open: 1st April-1st November

Mrs Margaret Harty
SWAN LAKE
Loughaderra, Castlemartyr, Midleton, Co Cork

Midleton
Tel: **021 4667261**

Overlooking Loughaderra Lake, 400m off N 25, between Midleton and Castlemartyr. Convenient Midleton & Cobh, Heritage Centre, Ballymaloe Hse, Fota Wildlife.

B&B	2	Ensuite	£19/£19	€24.13	Dinner -
B&B	1	Standard	£17/£17	€21.59	Partial Board -
Single Rate			£23.50/£25.50	€29.84/€32.38	Child reduction 50%

Midleton 4km S P ✎ ⌂ ⚘ 🐾 ⚓ J_L J_S
Open: 17th March-31st October

Mrs Mary Quinlan
SUNDOWN HOUSE
Kilmountain, Castlemartyr, Midleton, Co Cork

Midleton
Tel: **021 4667375**

0.5km off Midleton to Waterford N 25, near Jameson Heritage Centre. Ballymaloe House, Blarney Castle, Deep Sea Angling/Lake Fishing, Golf nearby.

B&B	3	Ensuite	£19	€24.13	Dinner -
B&B	2	Standard	£17	€21.59	Partial Board -
Single Rate			£23.50/£25.50	€29.84/€32.38	Child reduction 50%

Midleton 5km cc P ⊗ ✎ ⌂ ⚘ 🚲 ⚓ 🐾 J_L J_S J_R
Open: 1st April-1st November

Mrs Margaret Tobin
DECIES B&B
**Castleredmond, Midleton,
Co Cork**

Midleton
TEL: 021 4632645

Family home off N25, 15 minutes walk to Midleton Town & Jameson Heritage Centre. Restaurants, Traditional music. Near Blarney Castle, Fota, Cobh, Golf, Fishing, Ballycotton.

B&B	3	Ensuite	£20	€25.39	Dinner	-
B&B	1	Standard	£20	€25.39	Partial Board	-
Single Rate			£26	€33.01	Child reduction	-

In Midleton

Open: April-November

Mrs Margaret Kiely
COOLACUNNA
**Fermoy Road,
Mitchelstown, Co Cork**

Mitchelstown
TEL: 025 24170

Modern bungalow on own grounds on main Cork/Dublin Road, overlooking Galtee Mountains. Mitchelstown Caves nearby. 3 mins walk from Town.

B&B	2	Ensuite	£19/£25.50	€24.13/€32.38	Dinner	-
B&B	1	Standard	£17	€21.59	Partial Board	-
Single Rate			£23.50	€29.84	Child reduction	25%

In Mitchelstown

Open: 1st April-31st October

Mrs Betty Luddy
RIVERSDALE
**Limerick Road R513,
Mitchelstown, Co Cork**

Mitchelstown
TEL: 025 24717

Situated just off N8 (Dublin/Cork Rd.) Golf Course at rear. Fishing rivers. Parks/Gardens. Convenient to Mitchelstown Caves.

B&B	2	Ensuite	£19/£19	€24.13	Dinner	-
B&B	1	Standard	£17/£17	€21.59	Partial Board	-
Single Rate			£23.50/£25.50	€29.84/€32.38	Child reduction	-

Mitchelstown 1km

Open: 1st March-1st November

Mrs Mary O'Connell
PALM LODGE
**Limerick Road R513,
Mitchelstown, Co Cork**

Mitchelstown
TEL: 025 24687   FAX: 025 85599
EMAIL: palmlodgebb@hotmail.com

Peaceful scenic home and gardens overlooking Golf Course/Mountains/Fishing. At centre of South via Dublin-Kerry-Rosslare. TV lounge. Restaurants nearby.

B&B	2	Ensuite	£19/£19	€24.13	Dinner	£13
B&B	1	Standard	£17/£17	€21.59	Partial Board	£185
Single Rate			£23.50/£25.50	€29.84 /€32.38	Child reduction	33.3%

Mitchelstown 1km

Open: 1st March-1st November

Ms Anne O'Rahilly
ASHDALE HOUSE
**Lower Shanbally,
Ringaskiddy, Co Cork**

Ringaskiddy
TEL: 021 4378681   FAX: 021 4378681
EMAIL: ashdalebandb@eircom.net

Spacious welcoming family home, on Cork/Ringaskiddy route N28. Ferryport (3 mins). Surrounded by Golf courses, Angling. An ideal touring base for West Cork.

B&B	5	Ensuite	£20/£25	€25.39/€31.74	Dinner	-
B&B	-	Standard	-	-	Partial Board	-
Single Rate			£25.50/£30	€32.38/€38.09	Child reduction	25%

Carrigaline 5km

Open: All Year Except Christmas

Schull 1km

Mrs Nancy Brosnan
STANLEY HOUSE
Schull,
Co Cork

TEL: **028 28425**

Modernised house, providing every comfort with spectacular views of sea and mountains. Set in beautiful garden, 1km from Schull.

B&B	4	Ensuite	£20	€25.39	Dinner	-
B&B	-	Standard	-	-	Partial Board	-
Single Rate			£27	€34.29	Child reduction	-

Open: 1st March-31st October

In Skibbereen

Mrs Cathy Gill
SUNNYSIDE
42 Mardyke Street, Skibbereen,
Co Cork

TEL: **028 21365**
EMAIL: sunnysideskibb@eircom.net

Highly recommended, excellent breakfasts hospitality and comfort. Very peaceful, in Town. Orthopaedic beds. Electric blankets. Bicycle storage. Signposted on R595.

B&B	3	Ensuite	£19/£23	€24.13/€29.20	Dinner	-
B&B	1	Standard	£18/£20	€22.86/€25.39	Partial Board	-
Single Rate			£25/£35	€31.74/€44.44	Child reduction	50%

Open: All Year

In Skibbereen

Fiona Sheane
LITTLE ACRE
Cork Road, Skibbereen,
Co Cork

TEL: **028 22528**　　FAX: **028 22528**
EMAIL: littleacre@indigo.ie
WEB: www.cork-guide.ie/laughton.htm

On N71. Spacious comfortable home. Easy stroll from Town Centre. Excellent touring base. Lovely atmosphere. Francais. Espanol.

B&B	5	Ensuite	£20/£20	€25.39	Dinner	-
B&B	-	Standard	-	-	Partial Board	-
Single Rate			£27.50/£30	€34.91/€38.09	Child reduction	10%

Open: All Year

Skibbereen 1km

Mrs Marguerite McCarthy
MARGUERITES
Baltimore Road, Coronea,
Skibbereen, Co Cork

TEL: **028 21166**
EMAIL: marguerites@eircom.net

Luxury accommodation in landscaped private grounds. Very peaceful, highly recommended. Ideal base for touring West Cork. Signposted on R595.

B&B	2	Ensuite	£19	€24.13	Dinner	-
B&B	2	Standard	£17	€21.59	Partial Board	-
Single Rate			£23.50/£30	€29.84/€38.09	Child reduction	25%

Open: All Year

Skibbereen 4km

Mrs Hannah Murnane
LAKE VIEW
Shepperton, Skibbereen,
Co Cork

TEL: **028 33301**

Comfortable home on N71 overlooking beautiful Shepperton Lakes. All amenities locally. Bicycle shed, Electric blankets, Hairdryers, Breakfast menu.

B&B	3	Ensuite	£19/£19	€24.13	Dinner	£15
B&B	-	Standard	£17/£17	€21.59	Partial Board	-
Single Rate			£25.50/£25.50	€32.38	Child reduction	50%

Open: 10th April-1st November

In Skibbereen

Mrs Hannah O'Cinneide
WOODVIEW
**Off Baltimore Road,
Skibbereen, Co Cork**

Skibbereen
Tel: 028 21740

Luxury spacious bungalow, large garden having unique position of rural setting in Skibbereen. Beaches close by. Bicycle storage. Breakfast menu. Golf arranged. Signposted on R595.

B&B	3	Ensuite	£19/£20	€24.13/€25.39	Dinner	-
B&B	1	Standard	£17/£18	€21.59/€22.86	Partial Board	-
Single Rate			£25.50/£35	€32.38/€44.44	Child reduction	50%

Open: 1st May- 30th September

Skibbereen 7km

Breda O'Driscoll
SANDYCOVE HOUSE
**Castletownend,
Skibbereen, Co Cork**

Skibbereen
Tel: 028 36223

Seaside location with superb view of Cliffs and Ocean. Beautiful sandy Beach adjacent (100m). Ideal for Rock Fishing, Swimming, Windsurfing, Cliffwalking.

B&B	4	Ensuite	£19/£20	€24.13/€25.39	Dinner	-
B&B		Standard			Partial Board	-
Single Rate			£25.50/£25.50	€32.38	Child reduction	50%

Open: 1st March-1st November

Skibbereen 1.5km

Mrs Eileen O'Driscoll
PALM GROVE
**Coolnagurrane, Bantry Road,
Skibbereen, Co Cork**

Skibbereen
Tel: 028 21703   Fax: 028 21703
Email: info@palmgrovebb.com
Web: www.palmgrovebb.com

Spacious bungalow overlooking open countryside, 1km off N71 on R593/R594 Bantry/Drimoleague Road, close to Hospital. Frommer recommended.

B&B	2	Ensuite	£20/£22	€25.39/€27.93	Dinner	-
B&B	2	Standard	£18/£20	€22.86/€25.39	Partial Board	-
Single Rate			£25/£35	€31.74/€44.44	Child reduction	25%

Open: February-December

Skibbereen 3km

Mrs Carolyn O'Neill
FERN LODGE
**Baltimore Road, Skibbereen,
Co Cork**

Skibbereen Baltimore
Tel: 028 22327
Email: cneill@oceanfree.net

Comfortable, family run. Peaceful rural setting Skibbereen/Baltimore road. Lough Ine 2km, Creagh Gardens 1km, Baltimore 7km. All amenities locally.

B&B	6	Ensuite	£19	€24.13	Dinner	-
B&B		Standard	-	-	Partial Board	-
Single Rate			£25.50	€32.38	Child reduction	50%

Open: January-30th November

In Skibbereen

Mrs K O'Sullivan
WHISPERING TREES
**Baltimore Road, Skibbereen,
Co Cork**

Skibbereen
Tel: 028 21376   Fax: 028 21376

Modern comfortable home set in scenic and tranquil surroundings in suburbs of Town. Tea/Coffee making facilities in Conservatory.

B&B	5	Ensuite	£19	€24.13	Dinner	-
B&B		Standard	-	-	Partial Board	-
Single Rate			£25.50	€32.38	Child reduction	33.3%

Open: 1st February-31st October

Mrs Sheila Poillot
WHITETHORN LODGE
**Schull Road, Skibbereen,
Co Cork**

Skibbereen

TEL: **028 22372**   FAX: **028 22372**
EMAIL: whitethornlodge@eircom.net
WEB: www.cork-guide.ie/skibbereen/whitethorn

Luxury home & large garden on N71 town suburbs. Extensive breakfast menu, complimentary tea/coffee. Electric blankets in winter. Golf arranged. Warm welcome.

B&B	5	Ensuite	£19/£22	€24.13/€27.93	Dinner	-
B&B	-	Standard		-	Partial Board	-
Single Rate			£26/£32	€33.01/€40.63	Child reduction	-

In Skibbereen

Open: All Year

Mrs Mary Holland
ATLANTIC SUNSET
**Kilsillagh, Butlerstown,
Bandon, Co Cork**

Timoleague

TEL: **023 40115**
EMAIL: atlanticsunset@hotmail.com

First class accommodation overlooking Atlantic. Dunworley sandy beaches 1km. Golf, Tennis, Fishing locally. Coastal walks. Leisure Centre 6km.

B&B	2	Ensuite	£19/£19	€24.13	Dinner	-
B&B	2	Standard	£17/£17	€21.59	Partial Board	-
Single Rate			£23.50/£25.50	€29.84/€32.38	Child reduction	33.3%

Butlerstown 1km

Open: 1st January-20th December

Pat & Jo O'Donovan
HARBOUR HEIGHTS
**Timoleague, Bandon,
Co Cork**

Timoleague

TEL: **023 46232**   FAX: **023 46232**

Modern bungalow in tranquil surroundings overlooking Timoleague Abbey & Courtmacsherry. Guest Lounge, Conservatory. Private Car Park. On R600 between Kinsale & Clonakilty.

B&B	3	Ensuite	£19/£19	€24.13	Dinner	-
B&B	1	Standard	£18/£18	€22.86	Partial Board	-
Single Rate			-	-	Child reduction	33%

Clonakilty 8 km

Open: 1st January-12th December

Mrs Catherine Ryan
PANORAMA B&B
**Chapel Hill, Timoleague (Near
Kinsale), West Cork, Co Cork**

Timoleague

TEL: **023 46248**   FAX: **023 46248**
EMAIL: panoramabb@eircom.net
WEB: www.dirl.com/cork/panorama.htm

On R600. Traditional village with unique Pub/Restaurants. Hair salon, Sun lounge - Patio, panoramic view of Abbey and Bay. Unspoilt Nature Reserve, Walks/ Beaches.

B&B	4	Ensuite	£19/£22	€24.13/€27.93	Dinner	-
B&B	-	Standard		-	Partial Board	-
Single Rate			£25.50	€32.38	Child reduction	33.3%

In Timoleague

Open: All Year Except Christmas

Adela A Nugent
SHEARWATER
**Keelbeg, Union Hall,
Skibbereen, Co Cork**

Union Hall Glandore

TEL: **028 33178**   FAX: **028 34020**
EMAIL: shearwater@esatclear.ie

"Shearwater" is situated overlooking Glandore Harbour and surrounding countryside. All bedrooms have sea views, the patio area offers outstanding scenery.

B&B	4	Ensuite	£19/£20	€24.13/€25.39	Dinner	-
B&B	-	Standard		-	Partial Board	-
Single Rate			£25.50/£30	€32.38/€38.09	Child reduction	50%

In Union Hall

Open: 1st April-31st October

D & A O'Connell
ARDAGH HOUSE
Union Hall, West Cork,
Co Cork

TEL: **028 33571**   FAX: **028 33571**
EMAIL: info@ardaghhouse.com
WEB: www.ardaghhouse.com

Beautiful 100 yr old authentically restored Farmhouse set within village. Extensive Breakfast Menu, Hairdryers, TV, Electric Blankets. Ideal touring base.

B&B	3	Ensuite	£20	€25.39	Dinner	£16.20
B&B	-	Standard	-	-	Partial Board	-
Single Rate			£25.50	€32.38	Child reduction	-

Skibbereen 8km

Open: 1st January-20th December

Mrs Therese Cliffe
THE GABLES
Kinsalebeg, Youghal,
Co Cork

TEL: **024 92739**

Two storey building on 1.25 acres site off the N25 with Tennis Court. Close to sandy Beaches, Fishing, Golf, Fota, Jameson Heritage Centre. Ardmore, Youghal, Lismore.

B&B	1	Ensuite	£19/£19	€24.13	Dinner	-
B&B	4	Standard	£17/£17	€21.59	Partial Board	-
Single Rate			£23.50/£25.50	€29.84/€32.38	Child reduction	50%

Youghal 8km

Open: March-November

Mrs Nuala Connor
LAGILE LODGE
Killeagh, Youghal,
Co Cork

TEL: **024 95323**   FAX: **024 95323**
EMAIL: lagilelodge@eircom.net

Relax among animals, wildlife and mature gardens on 10-acres, 200m off N25, beside Village with pub food. Warm spacious bedrooms. Breakfast menu.

B&B	4	Ensuite	£19/£22	€24.13/€27.93	Dinner	-
B&B	-	Standard	-	-	Partial Board	-
Single Rate			-	-	Child reduction	25%

Youghal 8km

Open: 1st May-30th September

Maura Coughlin
CARN NA RADHARC
Ardsallagh, Youghal,
Co Cork

TEL: **024 92703**

2km off N25, Youghal Bridge. Magnificent views river, mountains, quiet cul-de-sac. Locally Beaches, Heritage Centres, Fota. Comfortable bedrooms, TV lounge.

B&B	2	Ensuite	£19/£20	€24.13/€25.39	Dinner	-
B&B	1	Standard	£17/£17	€21.59	Partial Board	-
Single Rate			-	-	Child reduction	50%

Youghal 6km

Open: 1st March-31st October

Mrs Eileen Fogarty
BROMLEY HOUSE
Killeagh, Youghal,
Co Cork

TEL: **024 95235**

N25 Cork-Rosslare road. Golf, Fishing, Beaches nearby. Convenient Cobh, Midleton Heritage Centres, Blarney. Pub food nearby. Private parking.

B&B	5	Ensuite	£19/£20	€24.13/€25.39	Dinner	-
B&B	-	Standard	-	-	Partial Board	-
Single Rate			£25.50	€32.38	Child reduction	-

Youghal 9km

Open: 1st March-31st October

In Youghal

Mrs Phyllis Foley
ROSEVILLE
**New Catherine St., Youghal,
Co Cork**

Youghal
TEL: 024 92571
EMAIL: rosevillebandb@eircom.net

Attractive detached residence situated within the "Olde Town" on the N25 Rosslare/Cork route. Within easy access to all amenities. Extensive breakfast menu. A warm welcome awaits you.

B&B	5	Ensuite	£19/£20	€24.13/€25.39	Dinner	-
B&B	-	Standard	-	-	Partial Board	-
Single Rate			£25/£30	€31.74/€38.09	Child reduction	33.3%

Open: 20th January-20th December

Paddy, Mary & Esther Forde
DEVON VIEW
**Pearse Square, Youghal,
Co Cork**

Youghal
TEL: 024 92298

Charming well preserved Georgian house with antique furniture and modern house. Centrally located to all amenities. Car park.

B&B	6	Ensuite	£19	€24.13	Dinner	-
B&B	-	Standard	-	-	Partial Board	-
Single Rate			£25.50	€32.38	Child reduction	25%

Open: All Year

Mrs Eileen Gaine
AVONMORE HOUSE
**South Abbey, Youghal,
Co Cork**

Youghal
TEL: 024 92617   FAX: 024 92617
EMAIL: avonmoreyoughal@eircom.net

Elegant 18th Century Georgian House at the entrance to Youghal Harbour within 3 min walk of Youghal's famous clock tower.

B&B	6	Ensuite	£19/£25	€24.13/€31.74	Dinner	-
B&B	-	Standard	-	-	Partial Board	-
Single Rate			£25.50/£30	€32.38/€38.09	Child reduction	25%

Open: 10th January-20th December

In Youghal

Mrs Angela Leahy
LEE HOUSE
**29 Friar Street, Youghal,
Co Cork**

Youghal
TEL: 024 92292

N25 Cork/Rosslare. Charming, comfortable townhouse, small garden. Town Centre 2 mins. Beach 5 mins. Secure private parking. Visa.

B&B	4	Ensuite	£19/£21	€24.13/€26.66	Dinner	-
B&B	-	Standard	-	-	Partial Board	-
Single Rate			£25.50	€32.38	Child reduction	33.3%

Open: All Year

Youghal 2km

Mrs Mary Scanlon
GREENLAWN
**Summerfield, Youghal,
Co Cork**

Youghal
TEL: 024 93177

Modern 2 storey home, 2km from Town Centre on the N25. Blue Flag Beach within 5 mins walk. Friendly welcome.

B&B	5	Ensuite	£19/£20	€24.13/€25.39	Dinner	-
B&B	-	Standard	-	-	Partial Board	-
Single Rate			£25.50/£25.50	€32.38	Child reduction	25%

Open: 1st February-31st October

Discover the magic of Kerry, with its enthralling mountain and coastal scenery and wide diversity of culture and leisure activities. Enjoy the superb hospitality and friendliness of its people in a county that is rich in heritage and history.

Mrs Kathleen O'Connor
FOUR WINDS
Annascaul, Co Kerry

Annascaul
Tel: **066 9157168**   Fax: **066 9157174**

Recommended Dillard Causin Guide. Outstanding views, Walks, Mountain Climbing, Beaches, Fishing, Lake/River. Golfing.

B&B	3	Ensuite	£19/£19	€24.13	Dinner	-
B&B	1	Standard	£17/£17	€21.59	Partial Board	-
Single Rate			£23.50/£25.50	€29.84/€32.38	Child reduction	-

In Annascaul   **Open:** 2nd January-23rd December

Katherine Higgins
ARDKEEL HOUSE
Ardfert, Co Kerry

Ardfert
Tel: **066 7134288**   Fax: **066 7134288**
Email: ardkeelhouse@oceanfree.net

Warm welcoming hospitality. Luxurious home, quiet location off Ardfert/Fenit Road. Walking distance Bars, Restaurants, Tralee Golf Course 4km, Banna Beach 3km.

B&B	3	Ensuite	£20/£21	€25.39/€26.66	Dinner	£13
B&B	-	Standard	-	-	Partial Board	£200
Single Rate			£26/£27	€33.01/€34.29	Child reduction	25%

In Ardfert   **Open:** All Year

Mrs Bridie Sweeney
FAILTE
Tralee Road, Ardfert, Co Kerry

Ardfert
Tel: **066 7134278**
Email: bridiesweeney@eircom.net

Luxurious Bungalow on Tralee/Banna/Ballyheigue road (R551) in historical Ardfert village near Tralee Golf course. Banna beach 3km. Restaurant 2 min walk.

B&B	4	Ensuite	£19/£20	€24.13/€25.39	Dinner	-
B&B	-	Standard	-	-	Partial Board	-
Single Rate			£25/£25	€31.74	Child reduction	50%

In Ardfert   **Open:** March-November

Lillian Morgan
RASCALS THE OLD SCHOOL HOUSE
Barrys Cross, Ballinskelligs, Co Kerry

Ballinskelligs
Tel: **066 9479340**   Fax: **066 9479340**
Email: oshmb@iol.ie
Web: www.iol.ie/kerry-insight/old-school

The Old School House, family run home. All home cooked food. Close to Blue Flag Beach. Open turf fire and a song or two each evening. The Kettle is on !!

B&B	4	Ensuite	£19/£28	€24.13/€35.55	Dinner	£12.50
B&B	-	Standard	-	-	Partial Board	£185
Single Rate			£25.50/£26	€32.38/€33.01	Child reduction	50%

Waterville 7km   **Open:** All Year

Ballybunion 1km

Mrs Mary Beasley
THE 19TH GREEN
Golf Links Rd, Ballybunion,
Co Kerry

Ballybunion
TEL: **068 27592**   FAX: **068 27830**
EMAIL: the19thgreen@eircom.net

"Golfers Paradise". Directly opposite Golf course. Luxurious purpose built accommodation. Good Seven - Iron to club, Green fee reduction. Early Breakfast. Golf storage and Drying room.

				Dinner	-
B&B	4	Ensuite	£20/£35	€25.39/€44.44	
B&B	-	Standard	-	-	Partial Board	-
Single Rate			£30/£50	€38.09/€63.49	Child reduction	-

Open: 1st April-20th December

In Ballybunion

Maurice & Patricia Boyle
THE OLD COURSE
Golf Links Road, Ballybunion,
Co Kerry

Ballybunion
TEL: **068 27171**   FAX: **068 27171**
EMAIL: oldcourse@eircom.net

Warm welcoming hospitality in luxurious, spacious new home at Ballybunions old course. Green fee reduction. Early Breakfasts. Car Park. Drying facilities.

				Dinner	-
B&B	3	Ensuite	£20/£35	€25.39/€44.44	
B&B	-	Standard	-	-	Partial Board	-
Single Rate			£25/£40	€31.74/€50.79	Child reduction	-

Open: 11th April-20th October

In Ballybunion

Ms Ann Kissane
SEASHORE
Doon East, Ballybunion,
Co Kerry

Ballybunion
TEL: **068 27986**

Modern spacious home with sea views. Car park, early Breakfast, Power Showers. Near Beach and Golf. Tarbert Car Ferry 20 mins drive. Green fee reduction.

				Dinner	-
B&B	3	Ensuite	£20/£30	€25.39/€38.09	
B&B	1	Standard	-	-	Partial Board	-
Single Rate			£25.50/£30	€32.38/€38.09	Child reduction	50%

Open: 1st April-1st November

In Ballybunion

Mrs Anne McCaughey
DOON HOUSE
Doon Road, Ballybunion,
Co Kerry

Ballybunion
TEL: **068 27411/27073** FAX: **068 27411**
EMAIL: doonhouse@eircom.net

Overlooking Ballybunion and Atlantic Ocean. Beautiful panoramic Sea/Mountain view. (Golfers home away from home). Green fee reductions. Early Breakfasts.

				Dinner	-
B&B	3	Ensuite	£20/£30	€25.39/€38.09	
B&B	-	Standard	-	-	Partial Board	-
Single Rate			£25.50/£35	€32.38/€44.44	Child reduction	-

Open: 1st April-31st October

Ballybunion 3km

Nora Quane
KILCONLY HOUSE
Coast Rd, Ballybunion,
Co Kerry

Ballybunion
TEL: **068 27633**
EMAIL: kilconlyhouse@eircom.net

Peaceful coastal location off R551. North of Town. Breakfast menu, Home baking, Drying room, Patio with sea view. Ideal for touring, Golf, 15 min to Car Ferry.

				Dinner	-
B&B	3	Ensuite	£20/£30	€25.39/€38.09	
B&B	-	Standard	-	-	Partial Board	-
Single Rate			£25.50/£35	€32.38/€44.44	Child reduction	50%

Open: 1st May-1st October

Ballybunion 1km

Sean & Nora Stack
SEANOR HOUSE
**Listowel Rd, Ballybunion,
Co Kerry**

Tel: **068 27055**   Fax: **068 27055**
Email: bed@eircom.net

Luxurious welcoming family home 5 mins from Golf & Beach. Early breakfast. Green fee reduction. Tea/Coffee on arrival. Ballybunion/Listowel Rd. (553).

B&B	3	Ensuite	£20/£30	€25.39/€38.09	Dinner	-
B&B	-	Standard	-	-	Partial Board	-
Single Rate			£25.50/£30	€32.38/€38.09	Child reduction	50%

Open: 1st April-1st November

In Ballyheigue

Mrs Anne Leen
WAVE CREST
**Cliff Road, Old Mill,
Ballyheigue, Co Kerry**

Tel: **066 7133177**

Peaceful country setting. Spectacular scenery. Bedrooms overlooking Bay on edge of Atlantic Ocean with Dingle Mountain range on background.

B&B	2	Ensuite	£19/£19	€24.13	Dinner	-
B&B	1	Standard	£17/£17	€21.59	Partial Board	-
Single Rate			£23.50	€29.84	Child reduction	50%

Open: 1st April-30th September

Ballylongford 2.5km

Patricia & Garrett Dee
CASTLE VIEW HOUSE
**Carrig Island, Ballylongford,
Co Kerry**

Tel: **068 43304**   Fax: **068 43304**
Email: castleviewhouse@eircom.net
Web: www.kerry-insight.com/castleview

Relax in peaceful setting on scenic Island (entry by bridge). Facing Carrigafoyle Castle. Tarbert - Killimer Ferry. Ballybunion Golf course nearby. Scenic walks. Good food, Warm welcome.

B&B	6	Ensuite	£19	€24.13	Dinner	£12.50
B&B	-	Standard	-	-	Partial Board	-
Single Rate			£25.50	€32.38	Child reduction	50%

Open: All Year Except Christmas

In Ballylongford

Mrs Noreen Heaphy
GLEBE HOUSE
**Rushy Park, Ballylongford,
Co Kerry**

Tel: **068 43555**   Fax: **068 43229**
Email: glebeh@iol.ie
Web: www.glebehouse.ie

Period residence, beautifully restored, blending modern convenience with olde world ambiance. Tarbert - Killimer Car Ferry, 10km Ballybunion Golf Course & Beaches 15km.

B&B	4	Ensuite	£20	€25.39	Dinner	£12.50
B&B	-	Standard	-	-	Partial Board	-
Single Rate			£25.50	€32.38	Child reduction	50%

Open: All Year Except Christmas

Caherdaniel 1km

Mrs Cathy Fitzmaurice
THE OLDE FORGE
**Caherdaniel, Ring of Kerry,
Co Kerry**

Tel: **066 9475140**   Fax: **066 9475170**
Email: fitzmaue@indigo.com

Family run, overlooking Kenmare Bay. Access to Sea. Breakfast menu. Dillard, Causin Guide. Horseriding, Hill walking, Sea sport, Golf, Fishing, Diving, Kerry Way.

B&B	6	Ensuite	£19/£19	€24.13	Dinner	-
B&B	-	Standard	-	-	Partial Board	-
Single Rate			£25.50/£25.50	€32.38	Child reduction	50%

Open: All Year

Donal & Monica Hunt
DERRYNANE BAY HOUSE
Caherdaniel,
Co Kerry

Caherdaniel Ring of Kerry

TEL: **066 9475404**   FAX: **066 9475436**
EMAIL: derrynanebayhouse@eircom.net
WEB: www.ringofkerry.net

Superb accommodation, overlooking Derrynane Bay. Breakfast menu. Golf, Horse-riding, Fishing, Diving, Beaches nearby. Adjacent Kerry Way. AA & Michelin listed.

B&B	5	Ensuite	£20/£22	€25.39/€27.93	Dinner	£16
B&B	-	Standard	-	-	Partial Board	-
Single Rate			£25.50/£27.50	€32.38/€34.91	Child reduction	25%

Caherdaniel 1km   **Open:** 15th March-23rd December

Mrs Irene Curran
HARBOUR HILL
Knockeens, Cahirciveen,
Co Kerry

Cahirciveen

TEL: **066 9472844**   FAX: **066 9472844**
EMAIL: harbour_hill@hotmail.com
WEB: www.harbourhill.main-page.com

Luxurious home. Panoramic sea views. Close to all amenities. Skeilig trips. Suitable for allergy sufferers. Single and Family rooms. Special low season rates.

B&B	2	Ensuite	£19/£19	€24.13	Dinner	£13
B&B	2	Standard	£17/£17	€21.59	Partial Board	£190
Single Rate			£23.50/£25.50	€29.84/€32.38	Child reduction	33.3%

Cahirciveen 3km   **Open:** 1st April-30th September

Mrs Eilis Dennehy
SEA BREEZE
Renard Road, Cahirciveen,
Co Kerry

Cahirciveen

TEL: **066 9472609**   FAX: **066 9473275**
EMAIL: seabreezebandb@eircom.net
WEB: homepage.eircom.net/~seabreezebandb

Friendly atmosphere, spectacular views, Sea, Islands, Castle, Forts. Skellig trips. Recommended Routard, Michelin, Dillard Causin Guides; Breakfast menu. Orthopaedic beds.

B&B	4	Ensuite	£19/£19	€24.13	Dinner	-
B&B	2	Standard	£17/£17	€21.59	Partial Board	-
Single Rate			£25/£30	€31.74/€38.09	Child reduction	25%

Cahirciveen 1km   **Open:** 1st January-30th November

Mary Guirey
FERRYVIEW
Reenard, Cahirciveen,
Co Kerry

Cahirciveen

TEL: **066 9472052**
EMAIL: info@ferryview-cahersiveen.com
WEB: www.ferryview-cahersiveen.com

Luxury country home. Peaceful setting, spacious rooms. Panoramic sea, Mountain view. Skellig trips. Jacuzzi and Steamroom facility. Tea/Coffee on arrival.

B&B	3	Ensuite	£20	€25.39	Dinner	£14
B&B	-	Standard	-	-	Partial Board	-
Single Rate			£26	€33.01	Child reduction	25%

Cahirciveen 2.5km   **Open:** All Year

Mrs B Landers
SAN ANTOINE
Valentia Rd, Cahirciveen,
Co Kerry

Cahirciveen

TEL: **066 9472521**   FAX: **066 9472521**
EMAIL: sanantoine@eircom.net

Set in peaceful landscaped gardens overlooking the Bay. Sea Sports, Golf, Angling, Horse-riding, sandy beaches, scenic walks locally. Breakfast menu.

B&B	6	Ensuite	£19/£20	€24.13/€25.39	Dinner	-
B&B	-	Standard	-	-	Partial Board	-
Single Rate			£25.50/£30	€32.38/€38.09	Child reduction	25%

In Cahirciveen   **Open:** March-20th October

Ian & Ann Nugent
CUL DRAIOCHTA
Points Cross, Cahirciveen,
Co Kerry

Cahirciveen

TEL: **066 9473141**   FAX: **066 9473141**
EMAIL: inugent@esatclear.ie
WEB: www.esatclear.ie/~culdraiochta

Charming family home with panoramic scenery. Excellent location on N70. Highly recommended. Tea/Coffee on arrival. Extensive breakfast menu.

B&B	4	Ensuite	£19	€24.13	Dinner	£13
B&B	-	Standard	-	-	Partial Board	£190
Single Rate			£25.50	€32.38	Child reduction	50%

Cahirciveen 1km   **Open:** All Year

Marie O'Mahony
CASTLEVIEW
Valentia Road, Cahirciveen,
Co Kerry

Cahirciveen

TEL: **066 9472252**

On Ring of Kerry. Access to Sea, Fishing, Golf, Horse-riding, Trips to Skelligs, Coastal Walks, Scenic view from bedrooms. Tea/Coffee on arrival.

B&B	1	Ensuite	£17/£17	€21.59	Dinner	-
B&B	2	Standard	£15/£15	€19.05	Partial Board	-
Single Rate			£21.50/£21.50	€27.30	Child reduction	25%

In Cahirciveen   **Open:** May-October

Mrs Christina O'Neill
IVERAGH HEIGHTS
Carhan Rd, Cahirciveen,
Co Kerry

Cahirciveen

TEL: **066 9472545**   FAX: **066 9472545**

Luxury spacious rooms overlooking Atlantic Ocean. Trip to Skellig Michael arranged. Ideal for exploring Iveragh Peninsula, Archaeological sites. Recommended Routard, Michelin Guide.

B&B	4	Ensuite	£19/£19	€24.13	Dinner	£12.50
B&B	-	Standard	£17/£17	€21.59	Partial Board	£185
Single Rate			-	-	Child reduction	33.3%

In Cahirciveen   **Open:** All Year

Eileen O'Shea
O'SHEAS B&B
Church St, Cahirciveen,
Co Kerry

Cahirciveen

TEL: **066 9472402**

Friendly family run home. Relax in quiet peaceful location with breathtaking view of Mountain and Sea. Group and Low season reduction. Blue flag Beaches.

B&B	4	Ensuite	£19	€24.13	Dinner	-
B&B	-	Standard	-	-	Partial Board	-
Single Rate			£25.50	€32.38	Child reduction	25%

In Cahirciveen   **Open:** All Year

Mrs Fionnuala Fitzgerald
SUAN NA MARA
Lisnagree, Castlegregory Rd,
Camp, Co Kerry

Camp Castlegregory

TEL: **066 7139258**   FAX: **066 7139258**
EMAIL: suanmara@eircom.net
WEB: www.kerryweb.ie/suanmara

Peaceful accommodation. Highly recommended Laura Ashley style home. AA ♦♦♦♦. Write up in San Francisco Chronicle. Superb Breakfast menu. Private walk to Golden Beach. Pitch & Putt.

B&B	6	Ensuite	£20/£23	€25.39/€29.20	Dinner	-
B&B	-	Standard	-	-	Partial Board	-
Single Rate			£26/£46	€33.01/€58.41	Child reduction	-

Camp 4.5km   **Open:** 15th March-31st October

Stradbally 1km

Mrs Mary Ferriter
BEENOSKEE
Cappateige, Conor Pass Road, Castlegregory, Co Kerry

Castlegregory Dingle Peninsula
TEL: **066 7139263**   FAX: **066 7139263**
EMAIL: beenoskee@eircom.net
WEB: www.kerry-insight.com/beenoskee/

Tastefully decorated rooms overlooking ocean. Spectacular views - Mountains, Islands, Lake. Warm hospitality, Breakfast menu. Homebaking. "Routard" recommended. 1km West Stradbally.

					Dinner	£15
B&B	3	Ensuite	£19/£20	€24.13/€25.39	Partial Board	£220
B&B	1	Standard	£18/£18	€22.86	Child reduction	50%
Single Rate			£25.50/£26	€32.38/€33.01		

Open: All Year

Castlegregory 2.5km

Mrs Mary Ellen Flynn
BEDROCK
Stradbally, Conor Pass Road, Castlegregory, Co Kerry

Castlegregory Dingle Peninsula
TEL: **066 7139401**
EMAIL: bedrockbandb@eircom.net

Family run, overlooking Brandon Bay, Maharees Islands, Golf course, Restaurant, Beaches, Fishing, Water Sports, Horse Riding, Mountain Climbing. Breakfast menu.

					Dinner	-
B&B	4	Ensuite	£19/£20	€24.13/€25.39	Partial Board	-
B&B	-	Standard	-	-	Child reduction	50%
Single Rate			£25.50/£25.50	€32.38		

Open: All Year Except Christmas

Castlegregory

Ms Mary Kelliher
KELLIHERS
The Station, Castlegregory, Co Kerry

Castlegregory
TEL: **066 7139295**
EMAIL: kellihers@hotmail.com

Luxurious accommodation with spacious ensuite rooms on Dingle Way. Ideal touring base for Dingle Peninsula. Tea/Coffee facilities & TV in bedrooms.

					Dinner	-
B&B	4	Ensuite	£19/£20	€24.13/€25.39	Partial Board	-
B&B	-	Standard	-	-	Child reduction	25%
Single Rate			£25.50/£25.50	€32.38		

Open: All Year

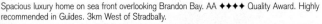

Stradbally 3km

Mrs Mary Lynch
STRAND VIEW HOUSE
Kilcummin, Conor Pass Road, Castlegregory, Co Kerry

Castlegregory Dingle Peninsula
TEL: **066 7138131**   FAX: **066 7138386**
EMAIL: strandview@eircom.net

Spacious luxury home on sea front overlooking Brandon Bay. AA ◆◆◆◆ Quality Award. Highly recommended in Guides. 3km West of Stradbally.

					Dinner	-
B&B	4	Ensuite	£19/£22	€24.13/€27.93	Partial Board	-
B&B	-	Standard	-	-	Child reduction	50%
Single Rate			£25.50/£28	€32.38/€35.55		

Open: All Year

In Castlegregory

Mrs Catherine Lyons
ORCHARD HOUSE
Castlegregory, Co Kerry

Castlegregory
TEL: **066 7139164**
EMAIL: orchardh@gofree.indigo.ie

Family home in idyllic village - on Dingle Way walk route. Convenient to all cultural, sporting and leisure amenities. Beach 5 minutes walk. Home baking.

					Dinner	-
B&B	3	Ensuite	£19/£20	€24.13/€25.39	Partial Board	-
B&B	1	Standard	£19	€24.13	Child reduction	50%
Single Rate			£25.50	€32.38		

Open: 1st March-31st October

Mrs Maura Moriarty
THE FUCHSIA HOUSE
West Main Street,
Castlegregory, Co Kerry

Castlegregory
Tel: **066 7139508**   Fax: **066 7138386**
Email: fucia@gofree.indigo.ie

New home with old Irish charm. Previous trainee Chef of the year. Home baking, Excellent Breakfast menu. On Dingle Way. Private parking. All amenities nearby.

B&B	4	Ensuite	£19/£20	€24.13/€25.39	Dinner	£15
B&B	-	Standard			Partial Board	£220
Single Rate			£25.50/£25.50	€32.38	Child reduction	50%

In Castlegregory

Open: All Year

Mrs Annette O'Mahony
THE SHORES COUNTRY HOUSE
Cappatigue, Conor Pass Road,
Castlegregory, Co Kerry

Castlegregory Dingle Peninsula
Tel: **066 7139196**   Fax: **066 7139196**
Email: theshores@eircom.net
Web: shores.main-page.com

Award winning AA ◆◆◆◆◆, luxurious spacious "Laura Ashley" style rooms all panoramic Seaview. Breakfast/Dinner menu. Highly recommended. 1 mile west Stradbally.

B&B	6	Ensuite	£19/£23	€24.13/€29.20	Dinner	£18
B&B	-	Standard	-	-	Partial Board	£280
Single Rate			£25.50/£35	€32.38/€44.44	Child reduction	25%

Dingle 14km

Open: 1st February-30th November

Mrs Agnes Reidy
GOULANE HOUSE
Stradbally, Conor Pass Road,
Castlegregory, Co Kerry

Castlegregory Dingle Peninsula
Tel: **066 7139174**

Outstanding Irish hospitality, beautiful views overlooking Brandon Bay/Mountains. 5 min walk Pub/Restaurant. 2 triples, luxury Orthopaedic beds, Tea/Coffee. Numerous recommendations.

B&B	4	Ensuite	£19/£20	€24.13/€25.39	Dinner	-
B&B	-	Standard			Partial Board	-
Single Rate			£25.50/£25.50	€32.38	Child reduction	50%

In Stradbally

Open: All Year

Mrs Sheila Rohan
CAISLEAN TI
Castlegregory,
Co Kerry

Castlegregory Dingle Peninsula
Tel: **066 7139183**
Email: caisleanti@unison.ie
Web: www.dingle-insight.com/caisleanti/

Stylish house on Dingle-way. Peaceful surroundings with sea view. Comfort assured. Home Baking. Former Calor Housewife of the year.

B&B	6	Ensuite	£19/£20	€24.13/€25.39	Dinner	-
B&B	-	Standard			Partial Board	-
Single Rate			£25.50/£25.50	€32.38	Child reduction	50%

In Castlegregory

Open: All Year

Mrs Paula Walsh
SEA-MOUNT HOUSE
Cappatigue, Conor Pass Road,
Castlegregory, Co Kerry

Castlegregory Dingle Peninsula
Tel: **066 7139229**   Fax: **066 7139229**
Email: seamount@unison.ie
Web: www.kerry-insight.com/sea-mount

AA ◆◆◆ Quality Award. Highly recommended. This charming home boast outstanding Sea views. Stylishly decorated rooms. Near Restaurant, 1km West Stradbally.

B&B	3	Ensuite	£19/£20	€24.13/€25.39	Dinner	-
B&B	-	Standard			Partial Board	-
Single Rate			£25.50/£26	€32.38/€33.01	Child reduction	50%

Dingle 14km

Open: 1st March-30th November

Mrs Eileen Cronin
GROTTO VIEW
**Currow Village, Killarney,
Co Kerry**

Castleisland
TEL: **066 9764646**   FAX: **066 9764646**

Welcoming modern family home in award winning village off N23. Airport 2km. Ideal for touring Kerry. Spacious ensuite rooms, TV, Tea/Coffee facilities.

B&B	3	Ensuite	£19	€24.13	Dinner	£13
B&B	-	Standard	-	-	Partial Board	£185
Single Rate			£25.50	€32.38	Child reduction	50%

Castleisland 4km   **Open:** April-October

Lilian Dillon
THE GABLES
**Dooneen, Limerick Road,
Castleisland, Co Kerry**

Castleisland
TEL: **066 7141060**   FAX: **066 7141060**
EMAIL: gablesdillon@eircom.net

High standard of accommodation in spacious, comfortable, country residence. Two triple rooms. Panoramic view, warm welcome, great breakfast, wonderful hospitality.

B&B	3	Ensuite	£19	€24.13	Dinner	-
B&B	1	Standard	£17/£19	€21.59/€24.13	Partial Board	-
Single Rate			£23.50/£25.50	€29.84/€32.38	Child reduction	50%

Castleisland 3km   **Open:** 1st March-30th November

Mrs Eileen O'Connor
GLENBROOK HOUSE
**Airport Road, Currow Village,
Castleisland, Killarney, Co Kerry**

Castleisland
TEL: **066 9764488**   FAX: **066 9764488**
EMAIL: glenbrookhouse@eircom.net

Highly recommended home. Ideal for touring Kerry. Home cooking a speciality. Signposted off N23. Airport 1km. Visa/Access/Mastercard accepted.

B&B	3	Ensuite	£19	€24.13	Dinner	£13
B&B	1	Standard	£17	€21.59	Partial Board	£200
Single Rate			£23.50/£25.50	€29.84/€32.38	Child reduction	

Castleisland 3km   **Open:** All Year

Breda O'Sullivan
TAILORS LODGE
**Killegane, Castleisland,
Co Kerry**

Castleisland
TEL: **066 7142170**

Luxurious new purpose built house on the R577 Castleisland/Scartaglen road. Power showers, hairdryers, guest lounge, breakfast menu. Airport 8km. Ideal touring base for Kerry.

B&B	4	Ensuite	£19/£19	€24.13	Dinner	-
B&B	-	Standard	-	-	Partial Board	-
Single Rate			£25.50/£25.50	€32.38	Child reduction	33.3%

In Castleisland   **Open:** All Year

Mrs Joan Burke
MOUNTAIN VIEW
**Ballinamona, Castlemaine,
Co Kerry**

Castlemaine
TEL: **066 9767249**

Modern two storey new house with panoramic view. Central for touring Ring of Kerry and Dingle Peninsula. Access/Visa/Euro.

B&B	4	Ensuite	£19/£19	€24.13	Dinner	£12.50
B&B	1	Standard	£17/£17	€21.59	Partial Board	-
Single Rate			£23.50/£25.50	€29.84/€32.38	Child reduction	50%

Castlemaine 1km   **Open:** 1st April-30th October

Mrs Elizabeth O'Sullivan
CAHER HOUSE
**Caherfilane, Keel,
Castlemaine, Co Kerry**

Castlemaine

Tel: 066 9766126
Email: caherf1@eircom.net

Comfortable residence overlooking Dingle Bay. Central for Dingle, Ring of Kerry, Killarney, Kerry Airport, 15kms, between Castlemaine & Inch, Scenic Walks.

B&B	5	Ensuite	£19/£19	€24.13	Dinner	£12.50
B&B	1	Standard	£17/£17	€21.59	Partial Board	£185
Single Rate			£23.50/£25.50	€29.84/€32.38	Child reduction	50%

Castlemaine 4km

Open: 1st April-31st October

Mrs Mary Barrett
BAY VIEW HOUSE
**Ballybowler, Dingle,
Co Kerry**

Dingle

Tel: 066 9151704
Email: bayhouse@indigo.ie

Magnificent views of Dingle Bay and countryside from bedrooms and conservatory. All rooms TV, Tea/Coffee. On the N86 you take a right turn at Henegans Garage.

B&B	2	Ensuite	£19/£19	€24.13	Dinner	-
B&B	1	Standard	£18/£18	€22.86	Partial Board	-
Single Rate			£25/£30	€31.74/€38.09	Child reduction	33.3%

Dingle 3.5km

Open: 1st April-31st October

Mrs Eleanor Begley
CLOOSHMORE HOUSE
**Clooshmore, Dingle,
Co Kerry**

Dingle

Tel: 066 9151117

Luxury home on the edge of Dingle Harbour. Spectacular views of Dingle Harbour from each bedroom. Featured in many guides American and Japanese.

B&B	3	Ensuite	£19/£22	€24.13/€27.93	Dinner	-
B&B		Standard	-	-	Partial Board	-
Single Rate			£25	€31.74	Child reduction	-

Dingle 2km

Open: 1st March-1st November

Mrs Kitty Brosnan
ABHAINN MHOR
**Cloghane,
Co Kerry**

Dingle

Tel: 066 7138211
Email: brosnankitty@hotmail.com
Web: www.kerryweb.ie

Beside village. On Dingle way, foot of Brandon Mountain. Near Dingle, Beaches, Hill walking, Fishing, Archaeology. Coeliacs welcome.

B&B	3	Ensuite	£19	€24.13	Dinner	£12.50
B&B	1	Standard	-	-	Partial Board	£200
Single Rate			£23.50	€29.84	Child reduction	33.3%

Dingle 10km

Open: March-November

Mrs Rita Brosnan
DROM HOUSE
**Coumgaugh, Dingle,
Co Kerry**

Dingle

Tel: 066 9151134

Situated 4.5km from Dingle Town on Ballyferriter Road. All bedrooms ensuite with TV, Clock/Radio, hairdryer & tea/coffee facilities. Breakfast menu.

B&B	3	Ensuite	£19	€24.13	Dinner	-
B&B	-	Standard	-	-	Partial Board	-
Single Rate			-	-	Child reduction	50%

Dingle 4.5km

Open: 1st May-1st October

Kerry

Mrs Camilla Browne
BROWNES
Ladies Cross,
Dingle, Co Kerry

Dingle
TEL: **066 9151259**
EMAIL: jbrownes@iol.ie

Luxurious peaceful country home on Ventry Slea Head Road, overlooking Dingle Bay and Mountains. Tea/Coffee, TV, Hairdryers, Extensive Breakfast menu.

B&B	4	Ensuite	£19/£21	€24.13/€26.66	Dinner	-
B&B	-	Standard		-	Partial Board	-
Single Rate			£25.50/£27	€32.38/€34.29	Child reduction	-

Dingle 1km

Open: 15th March-1st November

Mrs Eileen Carroll
MILESTONE
Milltown, Dingle,
Co Kerry

Dingle
TEL: **066 9151831**
EMAIL: milstone@iol.ie

Quiet home overlooking Dingle Bay, Mount Brandon. All rooms with phone, TV, Clock radio, Hairdryer, Tea/Coffee facilities. Breakfast menu, Private car park.

B&B	6	Ensuite	£19/£21	€24.13/€26.66	Dinner	-
B&B	-	Standard		-	Partial Board	-
Single Rate			£27	€34.29	Child reduction	25%

Dingle 1km

Open: 12th March-31st October

Mrs Mary Carroll
CEANN TRA HEIGHTS
Ventry, Dingle,
Co Kerry

Dingle
TEL: **066 9159866**
EMAIL: ventry@iol.ie
WEB: www.dinglewest.com/ventry/bandb/mcarroll/index.html

Quiet country home in peaceful scenic area overlooking Ventry Harbour/Dingle Bay. Seaview from rooms. In Ventry village. 5 minutes walk to blue flag Beach. Breakfast menu. Tea making facilities.

B&B	4	Ensuite	£19/£20	€24.13/€25.39	Dinner	-
B&B	-	Standard		-	Partial Board	-
Single Rate			£25.50/£30	€32.38/€38.09	Child reduction	33.3%

Dingle 4km

Open: March-November

Mrs Mary B Ui Chiobhain
ARD NA CARRAIGE
Carraig, Ballydavid,
Dingle, Co Kerry

Dingle
TEL: **066 9155295**

Scenic Gaelic area. Close to Beach, Pubs, Restaurants, Dingle Way Walk, Gallarus Oratory, Kilmaolceadar. Tea/Coffee facilities. Breakfast menu.

B&B	4	Ensuite	£19	€24.13	Dinner	-
B&B	-	Standard	-	-	Partial Board	-
Single Rate			£26	€33.01	Child reduction	-

Dingle 10km

Open: 1st May-30th September

Eileen Collins
KIRRARY
Avondale, Dingle,
Co Kerry

Dingle
TEL: **066 9151606**
EMAIL: collinskirrary@eircom.net

Personal touch, nice atmosphere. In centre of Town, scenic gardens. Ideal base Walkers/Cyclists. Sciuird Archaeology, Rent-A-Bike.

B&B	2	Ensuite	£19/£22	€24.13/€27.93	Dinner	-
B&B	1	Standard	£18/£22	€22.86/€27.93	Partial Board	-
Single Rate			£25/£28	€31.74/€35.55	Child reduction	-

In Dingle

Open: All Year Except Christmas

In Dingle

Geraldine and Kevin Devane
Goat Street, Dingle,
Co Kerry

Dingle

Tel: **066 9151193**

Townhouse, family run, overlooking Dingle Bay. Within walking distance to all amenities. Ideal touring base. TV, clock-radios, hairdryers, Tea/Coffee in bedrooms. Quiet location.

B&B	5	Ensuite	£20	€25.39	Dinner	-
B&B	1	Standard	£19	€24.13	Partial Board	-
Single Rate			-	-	Child reduction	33.3%

Open: 15th March-31st October

Ballyferriter 3km

Mrs Breda Ferris
COIS CORRAIGH
Emila, Ballyferriter,
Dingle Peninsula, Co Kerry

Dingle

Tel: **066 9156282**   Fax: **066 9156005**
Email: coiscorraigh@hotmail.com

Family home convenient to Beaches, Golf Course, Restaurants. Archaeological sites nearby, Gallarus Oratory, Riase, Kilmaoulceadar.

B&B	5	Ensuite	£19/£20	€24.13/€25.39	Dinner	-
B&B		Standard	-	-	Partial Board	-
Single Rate			£25.50/£26.50	€32.38/€33.65	Child reduction	33.3%

Open: 1st May-30th September

In Dingle

Mrs Bridie Fitzgerald
DINGLE HEIGHTS
Ballinboula, High Road,
Dingle, Co Kerry

Dingle

Tel: **066 9151543**   Fax: **066 9152445**
Email: dingleheights@hotmail.com

Warm friendly home overlooking Dingle Bay and Harbour. Private parking, Walking distance to Town and all amenities. Quiet location.

B&B	4	Ensuite	£19/£20	€24.13/€25.39	Dinner	-
B&B		Standard	-	-	Partial Board	-
Single Rate			£30	€38.09	Child reduction	-

Open: March-November

Dingle 1km

Eleanor & Eamonn Fitzgerald
DINGLE VIEW
Conor Pass Road, Dingle,
Co Kerry

Dingle

Tel: **066 9151662**   Fax: **066 9151662**
Email: dinglev@iol.ie
Web: www.iol.ie/~dinglev/

New home. Spectacular views. Conor Pass, Dingle Bay. Warm friendly hospitality. Superb location. Golf, Horse riding close by. Orhopaedic beds. Luxury TV lounge. Reduction low season.

B&B	4	Ensuite	£19/£20	€24.13/€25.39	Dinner	-
B&B		Standard	-	-	Partial Board	-
Single Rate			-	-	Child reduction	-

Open: 1st January-22nd December

Dingle 11km

Marie Dolores Nic Gearailt
NIC GEARAILTS B&B
Bothar Bui, Ballydavid,
Dingle, Co Kerry

Dingle

Tel: **066 9155142**   Fax: **066 9155142**
Email: mnicgear@indigo.ie
Web: www.nicgearailt.main-page.com

Warm friendly home, Gaelic area. Breakfast menu, Home baking. Walkers & hill climbers paradise. Pubs, Restaurants, Beach, Gallarus Oratory, Dingle Way nearby.

B&B	5	Ensuite	£19	€24.13	Dinner	£14
B&B		Standard	-	-	Partial Board	£200
Single Rate			£25.50	€32.38	Child reduction	-

Open: 15th April-15th October

Beatrice Flannery
THE PLOUGH
Ventry, Dingle, Co Kerry

TEL: **066 9159727**
EMAIL: plough@oceanfree.net
WEB: www.ireland-discover.com/plough.htm

Warm friendly home in Ventry Village. Walking distance to all amenities, Panoramic Sea/Mountain views. Tea making facilities, Breakfast menu. Restaurant nearby.

B&B	4	Ensuite	£19/£20	€24.13/€25.39	Dinner	-
B&B	-	Standard	£25.50	-	Partial Board	-
Single Rate			£25.50	€32.38	Child reduction	-

Dingle 4km

Open: All Year

Robbie & Mary Griffin
TOWER VIEW
Farranredmond, Dingle, Co Kerry

TEL: **066 9152990**   FAX: **066 9152989**
EMAIL: towerview@hotmail.com

New home, overlooking Dingle harbour, quiet location. Parking. Mins walk to Town Centre, close to all local amenities. Guest lounge, multi-channel TV, Tea/Coffee. Breakfast menu.

B&B	5	Ensuite	£20/£23	€25.39/€29.20	Dinner	-
B&B	-	Standard	-	-	Partial Board	-
Single Rate			£25.50/£28	€32.38/€35.55	Child reduction	33.3%

In Dingle

Open: March-October

Mrs Alice Hannafin
AN SPEICE
Ballyferriter West, Dingle, Co Kerry

TEL: **066 9156254**

A warm welcome awaits you at our family run B&B. Tea/Coffee on arrival. Home baking & Breakfast menu. On Slea Head Drive. Sea & Mountain views. Close, Village, Golf, Sea and Walks.

B&B	2	Ensuite	£19	€24.13	Dinner	-
B&B	1	Standard	£17	€21.59	Partial Board	-
Single Rate			£25.50	€32.38	Child reduction	50%

In Ballyferriter

Open: March-November

Mary & Michael Houlihan
ARD NA GREINE HOUSE
Spa Road, Dingle, Co Kerry

TEL: **066 9151113**   FAX: **066 9151898**
EMAIL: maryhoul@indigo.ie

AA RAC ◆◆◆◆ Award, Sparkling Diamond Award. Recommended 300 Best B&B, Ricks Steve's nationwide. Spacious rooms, Orthopaedic beds, Electric blankets, Fullbaths.

B&B	4	Ensuite	£19/£23	€24.13/€29.20	Dinner	-
B&B	-	Standard	-	-	Partial Board	-
Single Rate			-	-	Child reduction	-

In Dingle

Open: 1st February-15th December

Ms Marguerite Kavanagh
KAVANAGH'S B&B
Garfinny, Dingle, Co Kerry

TEL: **066 9151326**
EMAIL: mkavan@iol.ie
WEB: www.iol.ie/~mkavan/

Country family run home on main Tralee/Killarney Road. 5 minutes drive to Dingle. Spacious bedrooms, Hairdryers, TV, Tea/Coffee, Electric Blankets in rooms.

B&B	3	Ensuite	£19/£20	€24.13/€25.39	Dinner	£15
B&B	1	Standard	£17/£18	€21.59/€22.86	Partial Board	-
Single Rate			£23.50/£25.50	€29.84/€32.38	Child reduction	33.3%

Dingle 3km

Open: April-September

In Dingle

James & Hannah Kelliher
BALLYEGAN HOUSE
Upper John Street, Dingle,
Co Kerry

Dingle
TEL: **066 9151702**

Luxury home, magnificent views overlooking Dingle Harbour. Car parking. Minutes walk to Town. Guest lounge. AA recommended. Pass Doyles Restaurant. We are at top of Johns Street on left.

B&B	6	Ensuite	£20/£21	€25.39/€26.66	Dinner -
B&B	-	Standard			Partial Board -
Single Rate			£40/£40	€50.79	Child reduction 25%

Open: All Year

Dingle 8km

Angela Long
TIGH AN DUNA
Fahan, Slea Head, Ventry,
Dingle, Co Kerry

Dingle
TEL: **066 9159822**
EMAIL: ventrysleahead@hotmail.com

Peaceful home at Dunbeg Fort, near spectacular Slea Head. Atlantic Ocean views from bedrooms/diningroom. Near Beehives, Blasket Ferry, Restaurants, Beaches. On Dingle Way walk route.

B&B	2	Ensuite	£19/£20	€24.13/€25.39	Dinner -
B&B	1	Standard	£17/£18	€21.59/€22.86	Partial Board -
Single Rate			£25/£26	€31.74/€33.01	Child reduction 50%

Open: 8th April-14th October

Dingle 1km

Mrs Angela McCarthy
CILL BHREAC
Milltown, Dingle,
Co Kerry

Dingle
TEL: **066 9151358**
EMAIL: cbhreac@iol.ie
WEB: www.iol.ie/~cbhreac/index.htm

Spacious home overlooking Dingle Bay, Mount Bandon. All rooms with radio, hairdryer, electric blankets. Tea facilities, Satellite TV. Breakfast menu.

B&B	6	Ensuite	£19/£20	€24.13/€25.39	Dinner -
B&B	-	Standard			Partial Board -
Single Rate			£26	€33.01	Child reduction 33.3%

Open: March-November

Dingle 1 km

Tricia & Jim McCarthy
BALLYBEG HOUSE
Conor Pass Road, Dingle,
Co Kerry

Dingle
TEL: **066 9151569**
EMAIL: info@ballybeghouse.com

Warm peaceful home with breathtaking views. Rooms with Cable TV, Orthopaedic beds, Tea/Coffee, Electric blankets. Extensive Breakfast with view of Harbour.

B&B	4	Ensuite	£19/£21	€24.13/€26.66	Dinner -
B&B	-	Standard	-	-	Partial Board -
Single Rate			-	-	Child reduction -

Open: March-November

Dingle 4km

Mrs Ann Murphy
ARD-NA-MARA COUNTRY HOUSE
Ballymore, Ventry,
Dingle, Co Kerry

Dingle
TEL: **066 9159072**
EMAIL: annmurphybnb@hotmail.com

Elevated peaceful country home beside the sea overlooking Ventry Harbour. Rooms en-suite, Breakfast menu. Complimentary Tea/Coffee.

B&B	4	Ensuite	£19/£20	€24.13/€25.39	Dinner -
B&B	-	Standard			Partial Board -
Single Rate			£26/£26	€33.01	Child reduction 50%

Open: 1st March-31st October

Mrs Mary Murphy
THE LIGHTHOUSE
The High Road, Ballinaboula, Dingle, Co Kerry

Dingle
TEL: **066 9151829**
EMAIL: lighthousebandb@eircom.net
WEB: homepage.eircom.net/~murphydenis/index.html

Magnificent harbour views. 10 mins walk to town. Recommended "300 Best B&B's". Drive straight up Main St to outskirts of Town, we're third B&B on right.

				Dinner	-
B&B	6	Ensuite	£20/£23	€25.39/€29.20	
B&B	-	Standard			Partial Board	-
Single Rate			£25.50/£30	€32.38/€38.09	Child reduction	50%

In Dingle

Open: 15th February-15th November

Anne & Pat Neligan
DUININ HOUSE
Conor Pass Road, Dingle, Co Kerry

Dingle
TEL: **066 9151335**   FAX: **066 9151335**
EMAIL: pandaneligan@eircom.net

Award winning B&B. Superb location with magnificent views. Recommended by Frommer, Berlitz and 300 Best B&B's. Extensive Breakfast menu. Luxurious Guest conservatory - lounge.

					Dinner	-
B&B	5	Ensuite	£19/£21	€24.13/€26.66		
B&B	-	Standard	-	-	Partial Board	-
Single Rate			-	-	Child reduction	-

Dingle 1km

Open: February-November

Mrs Margaret Noonan
CLUAIN MHUIRE HOUSE
Spa Road, Dingle, Co Kerry

Dingle
TEL: **066 9151291**

4 Bedrooms with satellite TV. Tea/Coffee facilities, electric blankets, hairdryer. Private large car park. Credit Cards. House well signposted.

					Dinner	-
B&B	4	Ensuite	£20/£20	€25.39		
B&B	-	Standard	-	-	Partial Board	-
Single Rate			-	-	Child reduction	-

In Dingle

Open: All Year

Brid & Karl O'Connell
GORT NA GREINE
Ballymore, Ventry, Dingle, Co Kerry

Dingle
TEL: **066 9159783**

Modern home, spectacular sea views of Ventry Bay/Skellig Rocks. Guest lounge. Tea/Coffee making facilities. Breakfast choice, home baking.

					Dinner	-
B&B	4	Ensuite	£20	€25.39		
B&B	-	Standard	-	-	Partial Board	-
Single Rate			£25.50	€32.38	Child reduction	50%

Dingle 4km

Open: 1st June-31st August

Mrs Kathleen O'Connor
SRAID EOIN HOUSE
John Street, Dingle, Co Kerry

Dingle
TEL: **066 9151409**   FAX: **066 9152156**

Refurbished town house with spacious rooms, quiet location, within walking distance of all Restaurants & Bars. Family atmosphere.

					Dinner	-
B&B	4	Ensuite	£20/£22	€25.39/€27.93		
B&B	-	Standard	-	-	Partial Board	-
Single Rate			£30/£35	€38.09/€44.44	Child reduction	33.3%

In Dingle

Open: 15th March-15th October

Dingle 4km

Mrs Maureen O'Connor
ANGLERS REST
**Ventry, Dingle Peninsula,
Co Kerry**

TEL: **066 9159947**   FAX: **066 9159947**
EMAIL: avalon@iol.ie

Family run bungalow on Slea Head drive in Ventry village. Fishing on our own boat. Complimentary Tea/Coffee. Breakfast menu.

B&B	3	Ensuite	£20/£20	€25.39	Dinner	-
B&B	2	Standard	£18/£18	€22.86	Partial Board	-
Single Rate			£24/£28	€30.47/€35.55	Child reduction	25%

Open: 17th March-10th November

Dingle 2km

Mrs Helen O'Neill
DOONSHEAN VIEW
**High Road, Garfinny,
Dingle, Co Kerry**

TEL: **066 9151032**
EMAIL: doonsheanview@eircom.net
WEB: homepage.eircom.net/~doonsheanview

Bungalow with fire safety certificate. Tranquil location, scenic views, close to beaches and popular walks. Ideal for touring Dingle Peninsula.

B&B	4	Ensuite	£19/£20	€24.13/€25.39	Dinner	-
B&B	-	Standard	-		Partial Board	-
Single Rate			£25.50/£27	€32.38/€34.29	Child reduction	33.3%

Open: 15th April-October

In Dingle

Mrs Mary O'Neill
**John Street, Dingle,
Co Kerry**

TEL: **066 9151639**

Purpose built home. Quiet location. 2 minutes walk to Town Centre. Tea/Coffee making facilities, TV, Clock radio, Hairdryer. Guest TV Lounge, choice of Breakfast.

B&B	6	Ensuite	£19/£20	€24.13/€25.39	Dinner	-
B&B	-	Standard	-		Partial Board	-
Single Rate			£25.50/£30	€32.38/€38.09	Child reduction	-

Open: 1st March-30th October

Dingle 4km

Mrs Jacqueline O'Shea
TORANN NA DTONN
Ventry, Dingle, Co Kerry

TEL: **066 9159952**
EMAIL: torann@iol.ie
WEB: www.iol.ie/~torann/

Country Home beside Ventry village, on Slea Head drive. Magnificent Sea view overlooking Bay. 5 mins walk sandy beach. Fishing, Watersports, Scenic walks, Golf, Horse-riding. Breakfast menu.

B&B	5	Ensuite	£19/£20	€24.13/€25.39	Dinner	-
B&B	-	Standard	-		Partial Board	-
Single Rate			£25.50/£30	€32.38/€38.09	Child reduction	25%

Open: March-November

Dingle 3km

Maurice & Therese O'Shea
BALLYMORE HOUSE
**Ballymore, Ventry,
Dingle, Co Kerry**

TEL: **066 9159050**
EMAIL: ballyhse@iol.ie
WEB: www.dinglewest.com/ventry/bandb/ballyhse/index.html

Spacious Country Home with Sea view, tranquil location. Guest TV & reading room. Open coal fire. Extensive Breakfast & Dinner menu. Home cooking our speciality. Numerous recommendations.

B&B	5	Ensuite	£20/£22	€25.39/€27.93	Dinner	£16-£18
B&B	1	Standard	£18/£20	€22.86/€25.39	Partial Board	£230
Single Rate			£28/£30	€35.55/€38.09	Child reduction	-

Open: All Year

Eric and Eleanor Prestage
MOUNT EAGLE LODGE
Ventry, Dingle, Co Kerry

Dingle
Tel: **066 9159754**   Fax: **066 9159754**
Email: lodging@iol.ie
Web: www.dinglelodging.com

Modern home AA ◆◆◆◆. Acclaimed Breakfasts. Spectacular views of Ventry Bay from bedrooms, sun lounge, dining room. Local maps and guide books. Spacious, Tranquil.

					Dinner	-
B&B	4	Ensuite	£19/£26	€24.13/€33.01	Partial Board	-
B&B	-	Standard			Child reduction	-
Single Rate			£25.50/£32	€32.38/€40.63		

Dingle 5km   **Open:** 15th April-October

Mrs Mary Russell
RUSSELL'S B&B
**The Mall, Dingle,
Co Kerry**

Dingle
Tel: **066 9151747**   Fax: **066 9152331**
Email: maryr@iol.ie

Detached house in Town Centre. Private parking, 2 minute walk to bus stop, Restaurants etc. Recommended by Guide du Routard, Reise, Fodors close up.

					Dinner	-
B&B	6	Ensuite	£17/£21	€21.59/€26.66	Partial Board	-
B&B	-	Standard			Child reduction	-
Single Rate			£25/£31	€31.74/€39.36		

Open: 1st January-20th December

Brid Bowler Sheehy
BALLINVOUNIG HOUSE
**Ballinvounig, Dingle,
Co Kerry**

Dingle
Tel: **066 9152104**
Email: dbsheehy@hotmail.com

Excellent accommodation in quiet scenic location off main Tralee-Dingle Road. Convenient to all local amenities.

					Dinner	-
B&B	4	Ensuite	£19/£20	€24.13/€25.39	Partial Board	-
B&B	-	Standard			Child reduction	33.3%
Single Rate			£25.50/£28	€32.38/€35.55		

Dingle 1.5km   **Open:** March-October

Mrs Mary Sheehy
SHEEHY'S
**Milltown, Dingle,
Co Kerry**

Dingle
Tel: **066 9151453**

Peaceful home on the Cuas - Feoghanach road. Dingle 1km. Close to all amenities. Private parking. Choices of Breakfast. Irish speaking.

					Dinner	-
B&B	2	Ensuite	£19/£20	€24.13/€25.39	Partial Board	-
B&B	2	Standard	£17/£17	€21.59	Child reduction	50%
Single Rate			£24/£26	€30.47/€33.01		

Dingle 1km   **Open:** 1st March-1st December

Mrs Josephine Walsh
WALSHS TOWNHOUSE B&B
Main Street, Dingle, Co Kerry

Dingle
Tel: **066 9151147**   Fax: **066 9152975**
Email: walsthbb@iol.ie
Web: www.iol.ie/~walsthbb/

Luxury Town house in Town centre. Close to Shops, Restaurants & Bus. Ideal location for touring Dingle Peninsula. Breakfast menu. Low season reductions.

					Dinner	-
B&B	5	Ensuite	£19/£22.50	€24.13/€28.57	Partial Board	-
B&B	1	Standard			Child reduction	-
Single Rate			£25/£30	€31.74/€38.09		

In Dingle   **Open:** All Year Except Christmas

Doreen Caulfield
FOREST VIEW
Glenbeigh, Co Kerry

Glenbeigh
TEL: **066 9768140**

A friendly family run B&B set in a superb scenic location, on the Ring of Kerry. Adjacent to Golf Links, Forest walks, Beaches, Horseriding.

B&B	4	Ensuite	£19	€24.13	Dinner	-
B&B	-	Standard		-	Partial Board	-
Single Rate			£26	€33.01	Child reduction	33.3%

Glenbeigh 1.2km

Open: 15th April-October

Della Doyle
GLENCURRAH HOUSE
Curraheen, Glenbeigh, Co Kerry

Glenbeigh
TEL: **066 9768133**   FAX: **066 9768691**

Delightful country house with picturesque gardens overlooking Dingle Bay on the Ring of Kerry route N70. 1km from Glenbeigh village, Dooks Golf Links nearby.

B&B	5	Ensuite	£20	€25.39	Dinner	-
B&B	-	Standard		-	Partial Board	-
Single Rate			£26	€33.01	Child reduction	-

Glenbeigh 1km

Open: 1st March-31st October

Mrs Helena Fox
THE FOXTROT
Mountain Stage, Glenbeigh, Co Kerry

Glenbeigh
TEL: **066 9768417**   FAX: **066 9768552**
EMAIL: foxtrot@indigo.ie

Tranquil, luxurious, country accommodation. 4km west of Glenbeigh Village. Ideally located base for touring Ring of Kerry and Dingle Peninsula. Adjacent to Beach, Golf and Kerryway.

B&B	4	Ensuite	£20/£20	€25.39	Dinner	-
B&B	-	Standard		-	Partial Board	-
Single Rate			£25.50/£28	€32.38/€35.55	Child reduction	-

Glenbeigh 4km

Open: 15th March-31st October

Mrs Bridget McSweeney
HILLCREST HOUSE
Ballycleave, Glenbeigh, Co Kerry

Glenbeigh
TEL: **066 9769165**   FAX: **066 9769165**

On Glenbeigh Killorglin Road in peaceful scenic area. Close to Lake, Beaches, Dooks Golf, Fishing. Red Fox Restaurant/Bar, Irish music. Bog Museum walking distance. 200m off Main Rd.

B&B	3	Ensuite	£19/£19	€24.13	Dinner	-
B&B	1	Standard	£17/£17	€21.59	Partial Board	-
Single Rate			£23.50/£25.50	€29.84/€32.38	Child reduction	50%

Glenbeigh 4km

Open: 1st April-31st October

Ms Gretta Murphy
BARR VIEW LODGE
Rossbeigh, Glenbeigh, Co Kerry

Glenbeigh
TEL: **066 9768359**   FAX: **066 9768359**
EMAIL: barrviewlodge@tinet.ie

Excellent accommodation in our tastefully decorated home. Magnificent Sea views of Rossbeigh and Dingle Peninsula. Take road to Rossbeigh, go over bridge, two storey house on right.

B&B	5	Ensuite	£19/£20	€24.13/€25.39	Dinner	-
B&B	-	Standard		-	Partial Board	-
Single Rate			£25.50	€32.38	Child reduction	50%

Glenbeigh 2km

Open: All Year Except Christmas

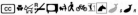

247

Glenbeigh 4.2km

Mrs Anne O'Riordan
MOUNTAIN VIEW
Mountain Stage, Glenbeigh,
Co Kerry

Glenbeigh
TEL: **066 9768541**   FAX: **066 9768541**
EMAIL: mountainstage@eircom.net

Quiet peaceful location with breathtaking views. 200 mtrs off Ring of Kerry. Adjacent to Beaches, Fishing - "Kerry Way". Low season reductions.

B&B	4	Ensuite	£19/£19	€24.13	Dinner	£12.50
B&B	-	Standard			Partial Board	£185
Single Rate			£25.50/£25.50	€32.38	Child reduction	50%

Open: 1st April-31st October

Glenbeigh 1km

Mrs Noreen O'Toole
OCEAN WAVE
Glenbeigh, Co Kerry

Glenbeigh Ring of Kerry
TEL: **066 9768249**   FAX: **066 9768412**
EMAIL: oceanwave@iol.ie
WEB: www.kerry-insight.com/oceanwave/

Enjoy the elegance of an earlier age in Frommer Recommended home overlooking Dingle Bay/Dooks Golf Links. Jacuzzi baths. Extensive breakfast menu. AA ♦♦♦♦.

B&B	6	Ensuite	£20/£25	€25.39/€31.74	Dinner	-
B&B	-	Standard	-	-	Partial Board	-
Single Rate			£25.50/£30	€32.38/€38.09	Child reduction	-

Open: 1st March-31st October

In Glenbeigh

Mrs Mary Riordan
BIRCHWOOD HOUSE
Station Road, Glenbeigh,
Co Kerry

Glenbeigh
TEL: **066 9768592**   FAX: **066 9768592**

Comfortable home in scenic village area, 70m off main Ring of Kerry road & Kerry Way. Adjacent to Blue Flag Beach. Scenic Walks & Views. Golf Dooks, Killorglin.

B&B	3	Ensuite	£19/£19	€24.13	Dinner	-
B&B	-	Standard	-	-	Partial Board	-
Single Rate			£25.50	€32.38	Child reduction	50%

Open: 1st May-31st October

Inch 1km

Mrs Bunny Ashe
LOCH EALA
Inch, Annascaul,
Co Kerry

Inch Dingle Peninsula
TEL: **066 9158135**   FAX: **066 9158001**
EMAIL: locheala@esatclear.ie

Luxurious family residence with magnificent Sea and Mountain views from all rooms. Ideal touring base. 2km from Inch Beach. On the main Killarney/Dingle road. Warm welcome assured.

B&B	3	Ensuite	£19/£19	€24.13	Dinner	-
B&B	1	Standard	£17/£19	€21.59/€24.13	Partial Board	-
Single Rate			-	-	Child reduction	25%

Open: 1st May-1st October

Mrs Eileen Kennedy
WATERSIDE
Inch, Annascaul,
Co Kerry

Inch Dingle Peninsula
TEL: **066 9158129**

Modern, spacious, friendly, quality accommodation. Adjacent to Beach, Pub, Restaurant. Guest Lounge. Superb, central, scenic seaside setting. Ideal touring base. Private shoreline.

B&B	4	Ensuite	£19/£20	€24.13/€25.39	Dinner	-
B&B	-	Standard	-	-	Partial Board	-
Single Rate			-	-	Child reduction	25%

Open: 1st March-1st November

Kenmare

Mrs Hannah Boland
MUXNAW LODGE
Castletownbere Rd, Kenmare,
Co Kerry

TEL: 064 41252

Enchanting house built in 1801. Furnished throughout with antiques. Overlooking Kenmare Bay. All weather Tennis Court. Breakfast menu. Many recommendations.

B&B	5	Ensuite	£22/£25	€27.93/€31.74	Dinner	£15
B&B	-	Standard	-	-	Partial Board	-
Single Rate			-	-	Child reduction	-

Kenmare 1km

Open: All Year

Kenmare

Dan Carraher O'Sullivan
ANNAGRY HOUSE
Sneem Road (N70), Kenmare,
Co Kerry

TEL: 064 41283
EMAIL: danscottage@eircom.net
WEB: http://homepage.eircom.net/~inkenmare/index.html

Ideal location on Ring of Kerry road (N70). Kenmare centre 6 mins walk. Peaceful. Spacious ensuite rooms. Bathtubs/Showers. Extensive menu. Fresh ground coffee. Home baking.

B&B	6	Ensuite	£20/£20	€25.39	Dinner	-
B&B	-	Standard	-	-	Partial Board	-
Single Rate			£27/£27	€34.29	Child reduction	25%

Kenmare 1km

Open: All Year

Kenmare

Mrs Anne Clifford
CHERRY HILL
Killowen, Kenmare,
Co Kerry

TEL: 064 41715
EMAIL: cherryhill@eircom.net

Located on Cork/Kilgarvan road off N22 on R569. Beautiful view of Kenmare river. Near Town, Golf course. Ideal base for touring Ring of Kerry, Beara.

B&B	2	Ensuite	£19	€24.13	Dinner	-
B&B	1	Standard	£17	€21.59	Partial Board	-
Single Rate			-	-	Child reduction	50%

Kenmare 1km

Open: 1st May-16th September

Kenmare

Tom Connor
ARDMORE HOUSE
Killarney Road, Kenmare,
Co Kerry

TEL: 064 41406   FAX: 064 41406

Spacious home in quiet location adjoining farmlands. RAC acclaimed. Frommer recommended. Town Centre 5 mins walk. Central touring base Ring of Kerry, Beara Peninsula etc.

B&B	5	Ensuite	£19/£20	€24.13/€25.39	Dinner	-
B&B	-	Standard	-	-	Partial Board	-
Single Rate			£26/£28	€33.01/€35.55	Child reduction	50%

In Kenmare

Open: 1st March-30th November

Kenmare

Mrs Edel Dahm
ARD NA MARA
Pier Road, Kenmare, Co Kerry

TEL: 064 41399   FAX: 064 41399

Family home with garden overlooking Kenmare Bay at the front & MacGillycuddy Reeks at the back on the N71 road to Bantry. 5 mins walk into Town.

B&B	4	Ensuite	£19/£20	€24.13/€25.39	Dinner	-
B&B	-	Standard	-	-	Partial Board	-
Single Rate			£25/£25	€31.74	Child reduction	33.3%

In Kenmare

Open: All Year

Mrs B Dinneen
LEEBROOK HOUSE
**Killarney Road, Kenmare,
Co Kerry**

Kenmare
TEL: **064 41521**
EMAIL: leebrookhouse@eircom.net

Experience genuine hospitality in elegant family home. Located on N71 convenient to Kenmare Town. Ideal touring base Ring of Kerry/Beara.

B&B	4	Ensuite	£19/£21	€24.13/€26.66	Dinner	-
B&B	-	Standard	-	-	Partial Board	-
Single Rate		-		-	Child reduction	25%

Kenmare 1km    **Open:** March-November

---

Mrs Marian Dwyer
ROCKCREST HOUSE
**Gortamullen, Kenmare,
Co Kerry**

Kenmare
TEL: **064 41248**
EMAIL: dodwy@eircom.net

Elegant home, spacious rooms, quiet rd. Off N71 Killarney Rd. Scenic location overlooking Druid Circle & Kenmare Town/Mts./Valley, 5 min. walk to Town Centre.

B&B	6	Ensuite	£19/£21	€24.13/€26.66	Dinner	-
B&B	-	Standard	-	-	Partial Board	-
Single Rate		£25.50/£30		€32.38/€38.09	Child reduction	33.3%

In Kenmare   **Open:** All Year

Ian Eccles
FERN HEIGHT
**Lohart, Castletownbere Road,
Kenmare, Co Kerry**

Kenmare
TEL: **064 84248**   FAX: **064 84248**
EMAIL: fernheight@eircom.net

Situated on R571. Some 15 mins drive towards Castletown Bearhaven. Rural location with views of the Bay, Mountains & Castle. Good food comes as standard.

B&B	3	Ensuite	£20/£22	€25.39/€27.93	Dinner	£15
B&B	1	Standard	£18/£20	€22.86/€25.39	Partial Board	£215
Single Rate		£24/£27		€30.47/€34.29	Child reduction	20%

Kenmare 11km 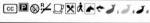   **Open:** 1st May-30th October

---

Tony & Sheila Fahy
ROCKVILLA
**Templenoe, Kenmare,
Co Kerry**

Kenmare
TEL: **064 41331**
EMAIL: rockvilla@esatclear.ie
WEB: www.esatclear.ie/~rockvilla

Rural setting near Templenoe pier. Relaxed friendly atmosphere. Ring of Kerry, Golf club, Coss Strand, Water Sports, Kerryway. Meals by request. Pool Room.

B&B	4	Ensuite	£19/£20	€24.13/€25.39	Dinner	£15
B&B	1	Standard	£17/£17	€21.59	Partial Board	£200
Single Rate		£23.50/£25.50	€29.84/€32.38	Child reduction	25%

Kenmare 5km   **Open:** 10th March-30th October

Mrs Mary Fitzgerald
WHISPERING PINES
**Glengarriff Road, Kenmare,
Co Kerry**

Kenmare
TEL: **064 41194**   FAX: **064 41194**
EMAIL: wpines@indigo.ie

Modernised period home. Spacious gardens, 3 minutes walk to Town, Golf course and Kenmare Bay. Recommended Dillard Causin/Sullivan Guide. Breakfast menu.

B&B	4	Ensuite	£20/£24	€25.39/€30.47	Dinner	-
B&B	-	Standard	-	-	Partial Board	-
Single Rate		-		-	Child reduction	-

In Kenmare   **Open:** All Year Except Christmas

In Kenmare

Mrs Gretta Gleeson-O'Byrne
WILLOW LODGE
**Convent Garden, Kenmare,
Co Kerry**

Kenmare
TEL: **064 42301**
EMAIL: willowlodgekenmare@yahoo.com

Quietly located, 2 minutes from Town Centre. Ideal base to tour Ring of Kerry & Beara Peninsula. Full facilities and jacuzzi, bath. Good Restaurants, Golf, Walking, Horse Riding & Fishing.

B&B	5	Ensuite	£22/£30	€27.93/€38.09	Dinner	-
B&B	-	Standard		-	Partial Board	-
Single Rate			£22/£44	€27.93/€55.87	Child reduction	-

Open: All Year

Kenmare 1km

Mrs Bernadette Goldrick
DRUID COTTAGE
**Sneem Road, Kenmare,
Co Kerry**

Kenmare
TEL: **064 41803**

19th Century Classic stone residence, luxuriously renovated without losing olde world charm. Complimentary tea/coffee. Hill walking enthusiast.

B&B	2	Ensuite	£19/£20	€24.13/€25.39	Dinner	-
B&B	1	Standard	£17/£18	€21.59/€22.86	Partial Board	-
Single Rate			£23.50/£25.50	€29.84/€32.38	Child reduction	25%

Open: All Year

In Kenmare

Mrs Mary Hodnett
SILVERTREES
**Lansdowne Lodge, Kenmare,
Co Kerry**

Kenmare
TEL: **064 41008**
EMAIL: hodnettc@eircom.net

Elegant home set in Rock garden, opposite Golf Course. Spacious rooms, extensive breakfast menu. Ring of Kerry/Beara/Killarney lakes.

B&B	4	Ensuite	£20/£22	€25.39/€27.93	Dinner	-
B&B	-	Standard		-	Partial Board	-
Single Rate			£30/£30	€38.09	Child reduction	-

Open: 1st March-1st November

Kenmare 1km

Mrs Anne Kelly-Murphy
MURPHYS LABURNUM HOUSE
Gortamullen, Kenmare, Co Kerry

Kenmare
TEL: **064 41034**   FAX: **064 42168**
EMAIL: murphyma@iol.ie

Charming comfortable home. Scenic surroundings on Ring of Kerry N70 Road. Convenient to all amenities. Walkers paradise. Host experienced guide.

B&B	5	Ensuite	£19/£20	€24.13/€25.39	Dinner	-
B&B	-	Standard		-	Partial Board	-
Single Rate			£25.50/£25.50	€32.38	Child reduction	-

Open: March-October

Kenmare 5km

Janet & Aiden McCabe
THE WHITE HOUSE
**Cappamore, Killarney Road,
Kenmare, Co Kerry**

Kenmare
TEL: **064 42372**   FAX: **064 42372**
EMAIL: whitehousekenmare@eircom.net
WEB: www.kerry-insight.com/white-house

Idyllic friendly, on Ring. Central Kerry/West Cork/Lakes. Panoramic mountain views. Sky TV, Sunlounge. Relaxing beds.

B&B	2	Ensuite	£19/£19	€24.13	Dinner	£13
B&B	1	Standard	£17/£17	€21.59	Partial Board	£200
Single Rate			£23.50/£25.50	€29.84/€32.38	Child reduction	33.3%

Open: All Year

Mrs Maureen McCarthy
HARBOUR VIEW
Castletownbere Haven Road,
Dauros, Kenmare, Co Kerry

Kenmare
TEL: **064 41755**   FAX: **064 42611**
EMAIL: maureenmccarthy@eircom.net
WEB: www.kenmare.com/harbourview

Award winning luxurious seashore home, panoramic views Kenmare Bay R571. AA ♦♦♦ award. Conservatory Breakfast room. Seafood. Satellite TV/Video, Trouserpress, Iron, Tea/Coffee.

B&B	4	Ensuite	£22/£23	€27.93/€29.20	Dinner	-
B&B	2	Standard	£22/£23	€27.93/€29.20	Partial Board	-
Single Rate			£30/£30	€38.09	Child reduction	20%

Kenmare 6km   (V)   **Open:** 1st March-31st October

Mrs Rosita McCarthy
ARBUTUS HOUSE
Gortamullen Heights, Killarney
Road, Kenmare, Co Kerry

Kenmare
TEL: **064 41059**

Peaceful scenic setting overlooking green pastures. Ideal touring base Ring of Kerry/Beara. All rooms TV, Tea/Coffee facilities, Breakfast menu.

B&B	3	Ensuite	£20/£20	€25.39	Dinner	-
B&B	-	Standard	-	-	Partial Board	-
Single Rate			-	-	Child reduction	-

In Kenmare   (V)   **Open:** 1st May-30th September

Ms Helen McGonigle
OLDCHURCH HOUSE
Killowen, Kenmare,
Co Kerry

Kenmare
TEL: **064 42054**
EMAIL: oldchurchkenmare@hotmail.com
WEB: www.kenmare.com/oldchurch

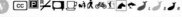

Luxury house situated on Kenmare-Cork road R569. Ideal place to relax surrounded by mountains, golf course and old church ruin. Excellent Breakfast.

B&B	3	Ensuite	£19/£22	€24.13/€27.93	Dinner	-
B&B	-	Standard	-	-	Partial Board	-
Single Rate			£30/£30	€38.09	Child reduction	33.3%

In Kenmare   (V)   **Open:** March-October

Margaret Moore
RIVERVILLE HOUSE
Gortamullen, Kenmare,
Co Kerry

Kenmare
TEL: **064 41775**
EMAIL: info@rivervillehousekenmare.com
WEB: www.rivervillehousekenmare.com

Comfortable Home, Pine Interior, overlooking Kenmare Town/Mountains. Non smoking. Ring Beara/Kerry touring base.

B&B	3	Ensuite	£18/£20	€22.86/€25.39	Dinner	-
B&B	-	Standard	-	-	Partial Board	-
Single Rate			£30/£30	€38.09	Child reduction	-

In Kenmare   (X)   **Open:** 1st February-30th November

Mrs Maura Murphy
ROSE COTTAGE
The Square, Kenmare,
Co Kerry

Kenmare
TEL: **064 41330**   FAX: **064 41355**
EMAIL: cleomurphy@eircom.net

Old World Cottage with private Gardens, having unique position of rural setting in Kenmare Town.

B&B	3	Ensuite	£19/£24	€24.13/€30.47	Dinner	-
B&B	-	Standard	-	-	Partial Board	-
Single Rate			-	-	Child reduction	-

In Kenmare   (X)   **Open:** All Year

Mrs Lisa O'Brien
THE FORD
Glengarriff Road, Bonane,
Kenmare, Co Kerry

Kenmare
TEL: 064 42431

Nestled in Caha mountains off N71. Bank of Sheen river. Unique family home. Hospitality assured. Base for Ring of Kerry, Beara Peninsula. Walkers haven.

					Dinner	-
B&B	3	Ensuite	£19/£20	€24.13/€25.39	Partial Board	-
B&B	-	Standard	-	-	Child reduction	25%
Single Rate			£30	€38.09		

Kenmare 8km

Open: 15th March-30th September

Tina O'Brien
CARA
Gort Na Dullagh, Glengarriff
Road, Kenmare, Co Kerry

Kenmare
TEL: 064 41634   FAX: 064 41634

Modern bungalow in quiet scenic surroundings. 3 km from Kenmare. Ideal touring Beara Peninsula/Ring of Kerry. Complimentary Tea/Coffee.

					Dinner	-
B&B	2	Ensuite	£19/£19	€24.13	Partial Board	-
B&B	1	Standard	£17/£17	€21.59	Child reduction	33.3%
Single Rate			£23.50/£25.50	€29.84/€32.38		

Kenmare 3km

Open: May-September

Mrs Julia O'Connor
AN BRUACHAN
Killarney Road, Kenmare,
Co Kerry

Kenmare
TEL: 064 41682   FAX: 064 41682
EMAIL: bruachan@esatclear.ie
WEB: www.esatclear.ie/~bruachan

Friendly home in 1acre of mature gardens on N71, own Riverfront, very quiet. Minutes from Town Centre. Hill walking enthusiast. Breakfast choice offered.

					Dinner	-
B&B	4	Ensuite	£19/£21	€24.13/€26.66	Partial Board	-
B&B	-	Standard	-	-	Child reduction	50%
Single Rate			£25.50	€32.38		

Kenmare 1km

Open: 1st June-September

Anne O'Doherty
BRANDYLOUGHS
Lodge Wood, Kenmare,
Co Kerry

Kenmare
TEL: 064 42147
EMAIL: brandyloughs@kenmare.com
WEB: www.kenmare.com/brandyloughs

Spacious quality country house overlooking 18 hole Golf club with scenic mountain backdrop - 2 minutes walk to award winning quality Restaurants in town of Kenmare.

					Dinner	-
B&B	4	Ensuite	£20/£24	€25.39/€30.47	Partial Board	-
B&B	-	Standard	-	-	Child reduction	-
Single Rate			£35/£35	€44.44		

In Kenmare

Open: 1st April-31st October

Mrs Lynne O'Donnell
O'DONNELLS OF ASHGROVE
Ashgrove, Kenmare,
Co Kerry

Kenmare
TEL: 064 41228   FAX: 064 41228

Beautiful home in peaceful setting. Many antiques. Mature garden. Guests welcomed as friends. German spoken. Angling enthusiast. Recommended Dillard/Causin.

					Dinner	-
B&B	3	Ensuite	£20/£22	€25.39/€27.93	Partial Board	-
B&B	1	Standard	-	-	Child reduction	-
Single Rate			£26.50/£28.50	€33.65/€36.19		

Kenmare 5km

Open: 15th April-31st October

Eilish & Pat O'Shea
THE CAHA'S
**Hospital Road, Kenmare,
Co Kerry**

Kenmare

Tel: **064 41271**   Fax: **064 41271**
Email: osheacahas@eircom.net
Web: www.kenmare.com/caha

Spacious family home in peaceful location with landscaped garden. Extensive Breakfast menu. Just 7 minutes walk from Town past Catholic Church.

B&B	3	Ensuite	£19/£22.50	€24.13/€28.57	Dinner -
B&B	-	Standard	-	-	Partial Board -
Single Rate			-	-	Child reduction 25%

In Kenmare

Open: 1st April-1st November

Mrs Kathleen Downing O'Shea
MELROSE
**Gortamullen, Kenmare,
Co Kerry**

Kenmare

Tel: **064 41020**
Email: kathleenmelrose@eircom.net

Bungalow situated off N71 Killarney road. 5 mins walk to Town Centre. Located in a scenic country area overlooking the Town. Central to all amenities.

B&B	3	Ensuite	£19/£22	€24.13/€27.93	Dinner -
B&B	1	Standard	£18/£20	€22.86/€25.39	Partial Board -
Single Rate			-	-	Child reduction -

In Kenmare

Open: 1st April-October

Bernie O'Sullivan
CARRIGMORE HOUSE
**Hospital Road, Kenmare,
Co Kerry**

Kenmare

Tel: **064 41563**

Comfortable home, spacious rooms. Scenic balcony views. Semi orthopaedic beds, Hairdryers. 5 minutes walk Town Centre. Location haven of rest. Non smoking.

B&B	3	Ensuite	£19/£20	€24.13/€25.39	Dinner -
B&B	-	Standard	-	-	Partial Board -
Single Rate			-	-	Child reduction 25%

In Kenmare

Open: All Year Except Christmas

Mrs Edna O'Sullivan
MARINO HOUSE
**Reen, Kenmare,
Co Kerry**

Kenmare

Tel: **064 41154/41501** Fax: **064 41232**

Modernised 18th century residence, sea shore setting on Ring of Kerry Road. Boating, Fishing for guests. Frommer recommended.

B&B	1	Ensuite	£19	€24.13	Dinner -
B&B	5	Standard	£17	€21.59	Partial Board -
Single Rate			£23.50	€29.84	Child reduction 25%

Kenmare 3km

Open: 15th May-1st September

Fiona & John O'Sullivan
MYLESTONE HOUSE
**Killowen Road, Kenmare,
Co Kerry**

Kenmare

Tel: **064 41753**
Email: mylestonehouse@eircom.net
Web: www.kenmare-insight.com/mylestone

Excellent spacious accommodation, friendly hospitality. Extensive Breakfast menu. Opposite Golf Course. Ideal Touring base, Ring of Kerry/ Beara Peninsula.

B&B	5	Ensuite	£20/£22	€25.39/€27.93	Dinner -
B&B	-	Standard	-	-	Partial Board -
Single Rate			£26/£30	€33.01/€38.09	Child reduction 25%

In Kenmare

Open: 15th February-10th November

Mrs Marian O'Sullivan
OAKFIELD
Castletownberehaven Rd R571
Dauros, Kenmare, Co Kerry

Kenmare
TEL: **064 41262**   FAX: **064 42888**
EMAIL: oakfield@eircom.net

Luxury country home, spacious warm bedrooms with spectacular views of Kenmare Bay. Breakfast choice. Evening meals, seafood speciality. Home from home.

B&B	4	Ensuite	£19/£20	€24.13/€25.39	Dinner	£15
B&B	1	Standard	£17/£20	€21.59/€25.39	Partial Board	£210
Single Rate			£26/£30	€33.01/€38.09	Child reduction	25%

Kenmare 5km

Open: 1st April-15th October

Mrs Ann Power
THE BRAMBLES
Gortamullen, Kenmare,
Co Kerry

Kenmare
TEL: **064 41712**
EMAIL: brambles@eircom.net
WEB: www.kenmare-insight.com/brambles

Luxury purpose built B&B, extra spacious rooms, 20 inch TV, Hairdryers, Tea/Coffee, Orthopaedic beds. Off N71. Quiet scenic location.

B&B	4	Ensuite	£19/£22	€24.13/€27.93	Dinner	-
B&B	-	Standard	-	-	Partial Board	-
Single Rate			-		Child reduction	25%

In Kenmare

Open: 1st February-30th November

Mrs Eileen M Ryan
RIVER MEADOWS
Sneem Road, Kenmare,
Co Kerry

Kenmare
TEL: **064 41306**   FAX: **064 41306**

Enjoy breakfast in our garden room against a magnificent mountain backdrop. Uniquely rustic area close to Town. Private road leading to seashore. Off N70 Ring of Kerry road.

B&B	4	Ensuite	£19/£19	€24.13	Dinner	-
B&B	-	Standard	-		Partial Board	-
Single Rate			£25.50/£25.50	€32.38	Child reduction	25%

Kenmare 2km

Open: 1st March-30th November

Mrs Maureen Sayers
GREENVILLE
The Lodge, Kenmare,
Co Kerry

Kenmare
TEL: **064 41769**

Superb residence overlooking Golf course. Full central heating. Town Centre 1 mins walk. Private parking. Extensive breakfast menu. TV in rooms.

B&B	4	Ensuite	£20/£24	€25.39/€30.47	Dinner	-
B&B	-	Standard	-	-	Partial Board	-
Single Rate			-		Child reduction	33.3%

In Kenmare

Open: All Year Except Christmas

Mrs Agnes Thornhill
FINNIHY LODGE
Killarney Road, Kenmare,
Co Kerry

Kenmare
TEL: **064 41198**
EMAIL: finnihylodge@esatclear.ie

House in scenic woodland setting overlooking Finnihy River, ideally situated for touring West Cork and Kerry. Convenient to Golf & Fishing.

B&B	3	Ensuite	£19/£21	€24.13/€26.66	Dinner	-
B&B	1	Standard	-		Partial Board	-
Single Rate			£23.50/£24	€29.84/€30.47	Child reduction	25%

Kenmare 1km

Open: All Year Except Christmas

Kenmare 4km

Mrs Geraldine Topham
GRENANE HEIGHTS
**Greenane, Ring of Kerry Road,
Kenmare, Co Kerry**

Kenmare
Tel: **064 41760** Fax: **064 41760**
Email: topham@iol.ie
Web: www.kerry-insight.com/grenaneheights

Uniquely designed home with spectacular views of Kenmare Bay & Beara. Ideal base for Ring of Kerry/Beara. Avail of laundry facilities, Email, Fax etc.

B&B	5	Ensuite	£20	€25.39	Dinner	£13
B&B	-	Standard	-	-	Partial Board	-
Single Rate			-	-	Child reduction	25%

Open: 1st May -30th September

Kilgarvan 1km

Mrs Mary MacDonnell
BIRCHWOOD
**Churchground, Kilgarvan,
Co Kerry**

Kilgarvan
Tel: **064 85473** Fax: **064 85570**
Email: birchwood@eircom.net

Home set in one acre garden in peaceful natural surroundings off R569. AA ♦♦♦♦ Approved. Ideal for touring Ring of Kerry/Beara. Golf, Fishing arranged.

B&B	5	Ensuite	£19/£19	€24.13	Dinner	£12.50
B&B	-	Standard	-	-	Partial Board	-
Single Rate			£25.50/£25.50	€32.38	Child reduction	33.3%

Open: All Year Except Christmas

In Killarney

Anne Aherne
WINDWAY HOUSE
**New Road, Killarney,
Co Kerry**

Killarney
Tel: **064 32835** Fax: **064 37887**

New Luxurious Bungalow. Ideally located 3 minutes walk from Town Centre. Recommended in all best guides.

B&B	6	Ensuite	£20/£22	€25.39/€27.93	Dinner	-
B&B	-	Standard	-	-	Partial Board	-
Single Rate			£27/£30	€34.29/€38.09	Child reduction	25%

Open: All Year Except Christmas

Killarney 2km

Mrs Delia Adams
BRIDGE HOUSE
**Coolgarrive, Tralee Road,
Killarney, Co Kerry**

Killarney Tralee Road
Tel: **064 31425**

200 metres off Killarney-Limerick road. All credit cards accepted and vouchers. Riding Stables and Golf Course nearby. Golfers welcome.

B&B	3	Ensuite	£19/£19	€24.13	Dinner	-
B&B	-	Standard	-	-	Partial Board	-
Single Rate			£25.50	€32.38	Child reduction	-

Open: 14th May-September

Killarney 8km

Mrs Margaret Blake
CHARLWOOD TOMIES
**Beaufort, Killarney,
Co Kerry**

Killarney Beaufort
Tel: **064 44117**

Just off Gap of Dunloe Road Lake District- Fishing, Golf, Horse Riding, Scenic woodland and Hill walks. Tours Dingle, Ring of Kerry. Restaurant, Music 2km.

B&B	2	Ensuite	£19	€24.13	Dinner	-
B&B	1	Standard	£17	€21.59	Partial Board	-
Single Rate					Child reduction	50%

Open: 15th March-31st October

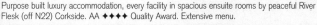

Mrs Eileen Brosnan
CRYSTAL SPRINGS
**Ballycasheen Cross
(Off Cork Road), Killarney,
Co Kerry**

Killarney Ballycasheen
TEL: **064 33272/35518** FAX: **064 35518**
EMAIL: crystalsprings@eircom.net
WEB: homepage.eircom.net/~doors/

Purpose built luxury accommodation, every facility in spacious ensuite rooms by peaceful River Flesk (off N22) Corkside. AA ✦✦✦✦ Quality Award. Extensive menu.

B&B	6	Ensuite	£20/£25	€25.39/€31.74	Dinner	-
B&B	-	Standard	-	-	Partial Board	-
Single Rate			£25/£35	€31.74/€44.44	Child reduction	25%

Killarney 1km   CC S P ... Open: 1st January-21st December

Kathy Brosnan
APPLECROFT HOUSE
**Woodlawn Road, Killarney,
Co Kerry**

Killarney Town
TEL: **064 32782**
EMAIL: applecroft@eircom.net
WEB: homepage.eircom.net/~applecroft/

Luxury accommodation off N71, peaceful country setting. 12 min walk Killarney Town. Winner of Killarney Looking Good Competition. AA -✦✦✦✦.

B&B	5	Ensuite	£20/£25	€25.39/€31.74	Dinner	-
B&B	-	Standard	-	-	Partial Board	-
Single Rate			£25.50/£30	€32.38/€38.09	Child reduction	25%

Killarney 1km   CC ...   **Open:** 1st January-12th December

Padraig & Margaret Brosnan
CLOGHROE
**14 Scrahan Court, Killarney,
Co Kerry**

Killarney
TEL: **064 34818**
EMAIL: cloghroe@gofree.indigo.ie

Enjoy warm friendly hospitality in our beautiful home. Quiet location 2 mins walk Town/Bus/Rail. Near Ross Castle/National Park/Lakes/Golf. Tours arranged.

B&B	3	Ensuite	£19/£19	€24.13	Dinner	-
B&B	-	Standard	-	-	Partial Board	-
Single Rate			£25.50/£25.50	€32.38	Child reduction	50%

In Killarney   P ...   **Open:** All Year Except Christmas

Danny & Bridie Buckley
NABRODA HOUSE
**Muckross Road, Killarney,
Co Kerry**

Killarney Muckross Road
TEL: **064 31688**

Quality Accommodation. Rooms ensuite, TV and Hairdryers. Multi-channel - Guest lounge. 5 mins walk to Town Centre on main Muckross Road. Tea/Coffee facilities.

B&B	5	Ensuite	£19/£20	€24.13/€25.39	Dinner	-
B&B	-	Standard	-	-	Partial Board	-
Single Rate			£25.50/£25.50	€32.38	Child reduction	-

In Killarney   CC P ...   **Open:** March-October

Mrs Colleen Burke
BEENOSKEE
**Tralee Rd, Killarney,
Co Kerry**

Killarney Tralee Road
TEL: **064 32435** FAX: **064 32435**
EMAIL: scoolick@iol.ie

Country home on Limerick Rd/N22. Twice National Award of Excellence winner. All rooms TV/Video, Hairdryer, Tea/Coffee. Credit Cards accepted. Landscaped garden. Home Baking.

B&B	4	Ensuite	£19/£19	€24.13	Dinner	£12.50
B&B	-	Standard	-	-	Partial Board	£185
Single Rate			£25.50/£25.50	€32.38	Child reduction	50%

Killarney 5km   CC P ...   **Open:** 1st April-31st October

Killarney 2km

Mrs Veronica Caesar
CAESAR'S
**Lissyvigeen, Cork Road,
Killarney, Co Kerry**

Killarney Cork Road Area
TEL: **064 31821**

Picturesque residence on N22. Superb location. Chosen and recommended by Irish Times Special Travel Correspondent on South West Ireland.

B&B	4	Ensuite	£20/£22	€25.39/€27.93	Dinner -
B&B	-	Standard	-	-	Partial Board -
Single Rate			£26/£26	€33.01	Child reduction 25%

Open: 1st June-30th September

Killarney 2km

Michael & Cathryn Carmody
RYEBROOK HOUSE
**3 Whitebridge Manor,
Ballycasheen, Killarney, Co Kerry**

Killarney Cork Road Area
TEL: **064 37878**
EMAIL: ryebrook@eircom.net

Situated just off the N22. This modern family home is the gateway to touring the Southwest. Peaceful scenic surroundings. Ideal for Walks, Cycling, Golf.

B&B	3	Ensuite	£19/£20	€24.13/€25.39	Dinner -
B&B	3	Standard	£17/£18	€21.59/€22.86	Partial Board -
Single Rate			£24/£26	€30.47/€33.01	Child reduction -

Open: April-October

In Killarney

Mrs Eileen Carroll
THE MOUNTAIN DEW
**3 Ross Road, Killarney,
Co Kerry**

Killarney Town
TEL: **064 33892**   FAX: **064 31332**
EMAIL: mountain.dew@oceanfree.net

Modern house in quiet area, 2 mins walk Town, Rail/Bus. Private Car Park. Tours arranged. Breakfast menu. In Killarney. Low season reductions.

B&B	6	Ensuite	£19/£20	€24.13/€25.39	Dinner -
B&B	-	Standard	-	-	Partial Board -
Single Rate			£25.50/£30	€32.38/€38.09	Child reduction -

Open: All Year

Killarney 3km

Mrs Marie Carroll
CEDAR HOUSE
**Loreto Road (off Muckross Rd),
Killarney, Co Kerry**

Killarney Muckross Road
TEL: **064 32342**   FAX: **064 35156**

House adjacent to Lakes, Gleneagle Complex, National Event Centre, Ross Golf Club. Spacious bedrooms some with Hairdryers. Tea facilities in rooms. Tours arranged.

B&B	4	Ensuite	£22/£22	€27.93	Dinner -
B&B	1	Standard	£20/£20	€25.39	Partial Board -
Single Rate			£27/£27	€34.29	Child reduction 25%

Open: 17th March-30th November

Killarney 5km

Mrs Eileen Casey
CASEYS HOMEDALE
**Dunrine, Tralee Road,
Killarney, Co Kerry**

Killarney Tralee Road
TEL: **064 33855**   FAX: **064 33855**
EMAIL: homedale@gofree.indigo.ie
WEB: gofree.indigo.ie/~homedale

Friendly welcome assured, Family run. Ground floor ensuite bedrooms. Panoramic views. Complementary Tea/Coffee. On N22. Ideal touring base. All tours arranged.

B&B	3	Ensuite	£19/£21	€24.13/€26.66	Dinner -
B&B	-	Standard	-	-	Partial Board -
Single Rate			-	-	Child reduction 50%

Open: March-October

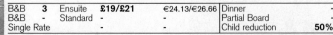

Killarney 5km

Mrs Mary Casey
DIRREEN HOUSE
Tralee/Limerick Road N22
Killarney, Co Kerry

Killarney Tralee Road

TEL: **064 31676**   FAX: **064 31676**
EMAIL: dirreenh@gofree.indigo.ie
WEB: gofree.indigo.ie/~dirreenh

Comfortable ground floor bedrooms. TV, Tea making facilities. Breakfast menu, Golf/Tours arranged. Coach pick up/drop off from premises. Expanding views of Countryside and Mountains.

B&B	4	Ensuite	£19/£21	€24.13/€26.66	Dinner	£12.50
B&B	-	Standard	-	-	Partial Board	-
Single Rate			-	-	Child reduction	33.3%

Open: 15th March-1st November

In Killarney

Liam & Anne Chute
CHUTEHALL
Lower Park Road, Killarney,
Co Kerry

Killarney Town

TEL: **064 37177**   FAX: **064 37178**
EMAIL: chutehall@eircom.net
WEB: www.killarneyaccomodation.net

New quality accommodation, quiet location. 3 min walk Town Centre. Spacious rooms/Bath & Shower. Rail/Bus. Private Car Park. Golf/Tours arranged. Lakes nearby.

B&B	5	Ensuite	£20/£30	€25.39/€38.09	Dinner	-
B&B	-	Standard	-	-	Partial Board	-
Single Rate			-	-	Child reduction	-

Open: 1st May-31st October

Killarney 9km

Mrs Peggy Coffey
HOLLY GROVE
Gap of Dunloe, Beaufort,
Killarney, Co Kerry

Killarney Gap of Dunloe

TEL: **064 44326**   FAX: **064 44326**
EMAIL: dunloe@eircom.net

Killorglin N72 road. Spacious bedrooms, 1 with 3 beds. Tea/Coffee facilities, Electric blankets. Pony riding, Golf, Fishing, Climbing, Music nearby. Ideal for touring Kerry Ring/Dingle.

B&B	3	Ensuite	£19/£19	€24.13	Dinner	£14
B&B	1	Standard	£17/£17	€21.59	Partial Board	£190
Single Rate			£23.50/£25.50	€29.84/€32.38	Child reduction	50%

Open: 15th March-31st October

In Killarney

Mary & Avril Connell
ST ANTHONYS VILLA
Cork Road, Killarney,
Co Kerry

Killarney Cork Road Area

TEL: **064 31534**

On Cork Road, walking distance town. Recommended in "Ireland on $45 a day". Ensuite rooms. Private Parking. Breakfast Menu, Peat Fires.

B&B	4	Ensuite	£19/£23	€24.13/€29.20	Dinner	-
B&B	-	Standard	-	-	Partial Board	-
Single Rate			£25.50/£30	€32.38/€38.09	Child reduction	25%

Open: 1st January-22nd December

Killarney 3km

Mrs Mary Counihan
VILLA MARIAS HOUSE
Aghadoe, Killarney,
Co Kerry

Killarney Aghadoe

TEL: **064 32307**

Situated in panoramic tranquil setting. Excellent touring area. Golf, Fishing and other amenities close by. Recommended by Dillard Causin guide.

B&B	2	Ensuite	£20/£20	€25.39	Dinner	-
B&B	1	Standard	£18/£18	€22.86	Partial Board	-
Single Rate			£23.50/£25.50	€29.84/€32.38	Child reduction	25%

Open: 1st April -31st October

Mrs Eileen Cremin
MOUNTAIN VIEW
**Gap of Dunloe, Beaufort,
Co Kerry**

Killarney Gap of Dunloe
Tel: 064 44212

Scenic area. 4km west of Killarney on N72. Turn left for Gap of Dunloe. Continue for 4km more.
Golf, Lakes, Hill walking, Horse riding, Restaurant, Music locally.

B&B	2	Ensuite	£19/£19	€24.13	Dinner	-
B&B	1	Standard	£17/£17	€21.59	Partial Board	-
Single Rate			£23.50/£25.50	€29.84/€32.38	Child reduction	50%

Killarney 8km

Open: 1st May- 30th September

Mrs Betty Cronin
DUNROSS HOUSE
**Tralee Road, Killarney,
Co Kerry**

Killarney Tralee Road
Tel: 064 36322

Luxurious home, Killarney 5km (N22). Rooms TV/Tea-making. Adjacent to National Parks,
Lakes/Golfing. Excellent location Ring Of Kerry/Dingle.

B&B	4	Ensuite	£19/£19	€24.13	Dinner	£13
B&B	-	Standard	-	-	Partial Board	£185
Single Rate			£23.50	€29.84	Child reduction	50%

Killarney 5km

Open: 1st March-31st October

Mrs Lily Cronin
CRAB TREE COTTAGE AND
GARDENS
**Mangerton Road, Muckross,
Killarney, Co Kerry**

Killarney Muckross Road
Tel: 064 33169
Email: crabtree@eircom.net

Picturesque cottage in the heart of Killarney, National Park, Lakes. Award winning landscaped
gardens. Prime location for hillwalking, mountain climbing. On route of "Kerry Way"

B&B	3	Ensuite	£19	€24.13	Dinner	£15
B&B	1	Standard	£17	€21.59	Partial Board	-
Single Rate			£23.50/£25.50	€29.84/€32.38	Child reduction	-

Killarney 4km

Open: 1st April-30th September

Paula Cronin
CILL IDE
**Muckross, Church Rd, Muckross,
Killarney, Co Kerry**

Killarney Muckross Road
Tel: 064 33339

Spacious bungalow, Scenic, Tranquil. Guest sun lounge - TV, Tea/Coffee making facilities.
Breakfast menu. Adjacent to Muckross House/Gardens, Lakes.

B&B	2	Ensuite	£19/£20	€24.13/€25.39	Dinner	-
B&B	2	Standard	£17/£18	€21.59/€22.86	Partial Board	-
Single Rate			£23.50/£25.50	€29.84/€32.38	Child reduction	25%

Killarney 4km

Open: May-October

Mrs Noreen Cudden
THE AMBER LANTERN
**Fossa, Killarney,
Co Kerry**

Killarney Fossa
Tel: 064 31921
Email: cudden@eircom.net

Well appointed home with balconies, opposite Golf Club, Lakes. Ring of Kerry/Dingle road. Horse
riding, Hill walking. Tours arranged.

B&B	5	Ensuite	£20	€25.39	Dinner	-
B&B	1	Standard	£18	€22.86	Partial Board	-
Single Rate			£24/£26	€30.47/€33.01	Child reduction	25%

Killarney 2km

Open: April-October

Killarney 5km

Mrs Agnes Curran
ARBOUR VILLA
**Golf Course Road, Fossa,
Killarney, Co Kerry**

Killarney Fossa

TEL: **064 44334**
EMAIL: curran_agnes@hotmail.com

Ring Kerry/Golf Course road, near Lakes, Gap of Dunloe, Fishing, Horse Riding, Golf 2km. Ideal Walkers/Climbers. Tours arranged.

						Dinner	**£17**
B&B	4	Ensuite	£20/£25	€25.39/€31.74		Dinner	**£17**
B&B	-	Standard	-	-		Partial Board	-
Single Rate			£25.50/£30.50	€32.38/€38.73		Child reduction	50%

Open: June-September

Killarney 2km

Hannah Daly
BROOKFIELD HOUSE
**Coolgarrive, Aghadoe,
Killarney, Co Kerry**

Killarney Aghadoe

TEL: **064 32077**

Country residence. Signposted 1km Killarney/Tralee/Limerick Road N22. Convenient for touring Ring of Kerry, Dingle, Killarney. Best guides recommended.

B&B	6	Ensuite	£19	€24.13	Dinner	**£13**
B&B	-	Standard	-	-	Partial Board	-
Single Rate			£25.50	€32.38	Child reduction	25%

Open: 1st March-1st December

Killarney 3km

Mrs K Lloyd-Davies
HAVENS REST
**Tralee Road N22, Killarney,
Co Kerry**

Killarney Tralee Road

TEL: **064 32733**   FAX: **064 32237**
EMAIL: havensrest@oceanfree.net
WEB: gofree.indigo.ie/~haverest

Lake Zurich Travel (USA) recommended - Luxury accommodation with antique furniture. Highly recommended. Real Irish welcome. On N22, 3 mins from Town Centre.

B&B	3	Ensuite	£20/£22.50	€25.39/€28.57	Dinner	-
B&B	-	Standard	-	-	Partial Board	-
Single Rate			-	-	Child reduction	33.3%

Open: 1st April-31st October

Killarney 3km

Mrs Deborah Devane
GLENMILL HOUSE
**Nunstown, Aghadoe,
Killarney, Co Kerry**

Killarney Aghadoe

TEL: **064 34391**
EMAIL: glenmillhouse@eircom.net

Luxurious home with panoramic views Lakes, Golf Course, McGillicuddy Reeks, National Park. Orthopaedic beds. Airport 15km. Adjacent to Aghadoe Heights Hotel. Tours arranged.

B&B	4	Ensuite	£19/£22	€24.13/€27.93	Dinner	-
B&B	-	Standard	-	-	Partial Board	-
Single Rate			£25.50/£25.50	€32.38	Child reduction	-

Open: 15th March-1st October

Killarney 2km

Mrs Mary Devane
REEKS VIEW
**Spa, Killarney,
Co Kerry**

Killarney Cork Road Area

TEL: **064 33910**   FAX: **064 33910**
EMAIL: devane@eircom.net
WEB: www.kerry-insight.com/reeksview

Luxurious bungalow off Killarney/Cork road. Signposted at Parkroad roundabout. N22 Cork/Killarney road, take industrial estate exit off roundabout.

B&B	5	Ensuite	£19/£19	€24.13	Dinner	**£12.50**
B&B	-	Standard	-	-	Partial Board	**£185**
Single Rate			£25.50/£25.50	€32.38	Child reduction	50%

Open: 1st April-November

Killarney 2km

Mrs Noreen Dineen
MANOR HOUSE
18 Whitebridge Manor
Ballycasheen, Killarney,
Co Kerry

Killarney Cork Road Area
Tel: **064 32716**　　Fax: **064 32716**

Modern Georgian Style house in peaceful area. Fishing, Golfing, Swimming. National Park and Lakes, Cabaret and Local Tours arranged.

B&B	4	Ensuite	£19/£20	€24.13/€25.39	Dinner	-
B&B	-	Standard	-	-	Partial Board	-
Single Rate			£25.50/£25.50	€32.38	Child reduction	25%

Open: May-September

Killarney

Mrs Aileen Doherty
BEECHWOOD HOUSE
Cahernane Meadows, Muckross
Road, Killarney, Co Kerry

Killarney Muckross Road
Tel: **064 34606**
Email: jdoh1@gofree.indigo.ie

Luxurious home. 5 mins walk from Town Centre, Rail, Bus. Adjacent to Muckross House National Park. Lakes, Mountains, Leisure Centre, Golf. Private Parking.

B&B	3	Ensuite	£19/£21	€24.13/€26.66	Dinner	-
B&B	-	Standard	-	-	Partial Board	-
Single Rate			£26/£28	€33.01/€35.55	Child reduction	25%

Open: 1st February-14th December

Killarney 2km

Mrs Kathleen Doherty
WHITE HOUSE
Lissivigeen Cross, Killarney,
Co Kerry

Killarney Cork Road Area
Tel: **064 32207**

Warm country home, family run, on 2-acres. Peaceful scenic surroundings. Horse riding, Golf, Fishing locally. Tours arranged.

B&B	5	Ensuite	£19/£20	€24.13/€25.39	Dinner	-
B&B	-	Standard	-	-	Partial Board	-
Single Rate			£25.50/£25.50	€32.38	Child reduction	33.3%

Open: May-October

In Killarney

Mrs Rita Donoghue
KYLEBEG
98 Countess Grove, Killarney,
Co Kerry

Killarney Countess Road Area
Tel: **064 37694**　　Fax: **064 37694**
Email: kylebeg@yahoo.co.uk

Bungalow in pleasant restful area off Countess Road, linking N22/N71. 7 minutes walk Town Centre, bus/rail. Hairdryers available. Tours arranged. Cab service available.

B&B	4	Ensuite	£19/£21	€24.13/€26.66	Dinner	-
B&B	-	Standard	-	-	Partial Board	-
Single Rate			£26/£29	€33.01/€36.82	Child reduction	25%

Open: All Year Except Christmas

Killorglin 8km

Mrs Tess Doona
HOLLYBOUGH HOUSE
Cappagh, Kilgobnet, Beaufort,
Co Kerry

Killarney Beaufort
Tel: **064 44255**

Quiet scenic location central for Ring of Kerry, near Ireland's highest and most majestic mountains, The McGillycuddy Reeks. Visa accepted.

B&B	3	Ensuite	£19/£19	€24.13	Dinner	£15
B&B	1	Standard	£17/£17	€21.59	Partial Board	-
Single Rate			£23.50/£25.50	€29.84/€32.38	Child reduction	25%

Open: 15th April-30th October

Killarney 4km

Mrs Carmel Dore-O'Brien

TARA

Gap of Dunloe Road, Fossa, Killarney, Co Kerry

Killarney Aghadoe/Fossa

Tel: **064 44355**
Email: tarabnb@iol.ie
Web: www.iol.ie/~tarabnb/tara.htm

Guide Routard & Hachette. Visa. AA ◆◆◆. Quiet & relaxing home off main road. Tea/Coffee, Breakfast menu, Hairdryers. Beautiful gardens N72 West, left Gap Dunloe.

B&B	4	Ensuite	£20/£20	€25.39	Dinner	-
B&B	1	Standard	£18/£18	€22.86	Partial Board	-
Single Rate			£25/£25	€31.74	Child reduction	25%

Open: June-October

In Killarney

Mrs Noreen Downing

ARDFALLEN HOUSE

Ross Road, Killarney, Co Kerry

Killarney Town

Tel: **064 33632**

Comfortable family home. Quiet scenic location, 4 mins walk to Town, Bus/Rail. Guest lounge. Private Parking. Breakfast choice. Fishing, Golfing, Lakes nearby. Tours arranged.

B&B	3	Ensuite	£20	€25.39	Dinner	-
B&B	1	Standard	-	-	Partial Board	-
Single Rate			-	-	Child reduction	-

Open: June-October

Killarney 3km

Mrs Bridie Doyle

CLONFERT

Fossa, Killarney, Co Kerry

Killarney

Tel: **064 31459**

Spacious family home. Ring of Kerry/Dingle road. Golf, Fishing, Riding 1km. Orthopaedic beds. Golf and tours arranged. Ideal for walkers/cyclists.

B&B	4	Ensuite	£19/£19	€24.13	Dinner	-
B&B	-	Standard	-	-	Partial Board	-
Single Rate			£25.50/£25.50	€32.38	Child reduction	25%

Open: 15th March-31st October

In Killarney

Mrs Greta Doyle

ALGRET HOUSE

80 Countess Grove, Off Countess Rd, Killarney, Co Kerry

Killarney Countess Road Area

Tel: **064 32337**   Fax: **064 30936**
Email: gretad@gofree.indigo.ie

Friendly home, quiet area. Town 5 min walk. All rooms have multi-channel TV, Tea/Coffee facilities and Hairdryers. Breakfast menu. N71 Muckross road, 1st left, 2nd right.

B&B	6	Ensuite	£19/£22	€24.13/€27.93	Dinner	-
B&B	-	Standard	-	-	Partial Board	-
Single Rate			£25.50/£28.50	€32.38/€36.19	Child reduction	25%

Open: 1st March-31st October

In Killarney

Mary Theresa & Derry Doyle

ELYOD HOUSE

Ross Road, Killarney, Co Kerry

Killarney Town

Tel: **064 36544/31510**

Luxurious friendly home situated verge of National Park, Golf, Fishing, Horse-riding nearby. Tours arranged. Breakfast menu. Tea/Coffee facilities available.

B&B	3	Ensuite	£20/£21	€25.39/€26.66	Dinner	-
B&B	1	Standard	£17/£17	€21.59	Partial Board	-
Single Rate			£30/£30	€38.09	Child reduction	10%

Open: 1st March-1st December

Mrs Sheila Falvey
FALSHEA HOUSE
**Tralee Road, Killarney,
Co Kerry**

Killarney Tralee Road
TEL: **064 34871**
EMAIL: falsheahouse@eircom.net

Purpose built luxury home in scenic peaceful surroundings. All rooms with TV, Tea/Coffee making facilities, Hairdryers. National Award of Excellence Winner. Tours arranged.

B&B	4	Ensuite	£20/£21	€25.39/€26.66	Dinner	£15
B&B	-	Standard	-	-	Partial Board	-
Single Rate			£26/£28	€33.01/€35.55	Child reduction	50%

Killarney 4km

Open: All Year

Mrs Theresa Ferris
WAYSIDE
**Gap of Dunloe, Killarney,
Co Kerry**

Killarney Gap of Dunloe
TEL: **064 44284**   FAX: **064 44284**
EMAIL: www.wayside@hotmail.com
WEB: www.dirl.com/kerry/wayside.htm

Peaceful lake/mountain district. Restaurants, Irish music & dancing 1km. Horse riding, Fishing & Golf Courses 1km. Dingle & Ring of Kerry 2km. Breakfast Menu. Off R562.

B&B	1	Ensuite	£20/£20	€25.39	Dinner	-
B&B	3	Standard	£18/£20	€22.86/€25.39	Partial Board	-
Single Rate			£23.50/£25.50	€29.84/€32.38	Child reduction	50%

Killarney 8km

Open: All Year Except Christmas

Mrs Anne Fleming
GLENDALE HOUSE
**Dromadeesirt, Tralee Road,
Killarney, Co Kerry**

Killarney Tralee Road
TEL: **064 32152/34952**   FAX: **064 32152**
EMAIL: aflem@gofree.indigo.ie

Luxurious house on Tralee road (N22). Killarney 6km. Kerry Airport 5 mins drive. All rooms with TV, Tea/Coffee making facilities, Hairdryers. Tours arranged.

B&B	6	Ensuite	£19	€24.13	Dinner	-
B&B	-	Standard	-	-	Partial Board	-
Single Rate			£25.50	€32.38	Child reduction	33.3%

Killarney 6km

Open: 1st May-30th September

Mrs Maureen Fleming
SHRAHEEN HOUSE
**Ballycasheen (off N22)
Killarney, Co Kerry**

Killarney Cork Road Area
TEL: **064 31286/37959**   FAX: **064 37959**
EMAIL: info@shraheenhouse.com
WEB: www.shraheenhouse.com

Luxurious home set in 2.5 acres. Satellite TV, Tea/Coffee, Hairdryer all rooms. Breakfast menu, AA ◆◆◆◆ selected. Tours arranged. Off N22 at Whitebridge sign.

B&B	6	Ensuite	£20/£22.50	€25.39/€28.57	Dinner	-
B&B	-	Standard	-	-	Partial Board	-
Single Rate			£26/£34	€33.01/€43.17	Child reduction	25%

Killarney 2km

Open: 10th January-10th December

Mrs Philomena Fleming
WHITE OAKS
**16 Scrahan Court, Ross Road,
Killarney, Co Kerry**

Killarney Town
TEL: **064 31348**

Luxurious townhouse in unrivaled locale. 7 min walk from Town, Rail facilities & Bus. TV, Tea making facilities. Tours arranged.

B&B	3	Ensuite	£18/£19	€22.86/€24.13	Dinner	-
B&B	-	Standard	-	-	Partial Board	-
Single Rate			£25	€31.74	Child reduction	25%

Killarney 1km

Open: All Year

Killarney 5km

Maureen & Gene Fogarty
OSPREY
Lough Guitane Road, Muckross
Killarney, Co Kerry

Killarney Muckross Road

TEL: **064 33213**
EMAIL: osprey3@indigo.ie

Overlooking Lakes/Mountains. National Park/Muckross House 2km. Landscaped Gardens, tranquil area. Off N71. Home baking, Frommer Guide recommended, Private parking, Tours arranged.

B&B	2	Ensuite	£19/£19	€24.13	Dinner	-
B&B	1	Standard	£19/£19	€24.13	Partial Board	-
Single Rate			£25.50/£25.50	€32.38	Child reduction	25%

Open: 1st May-15th October

Killarney 1km

Mr Denis Geaney
PINE CREST
Woodlawn Road, Killarney,
Co Kerry

Killarney Muckross Road

TEL: **064 31721**   FAX: **064 31721**

Luxurious bungalow in scenic area, convenient to Lakes, National Park, Golf Course, Airport, Ring of Kerry, Dingle, Bus. Taxi from house. 1km from the Glenagle National Events Centre.

B&B	6	Ensuite	£19/£20	€24.13/€25.39	Dinner	-
B&B	-	Standard	-		Partial Board	-
Single Rate			£25.50/£25.50	€32.38	Child reduction	-

Open: 1st March-30th October

Killarney 5km

Mrs Moira Gorman
GORMAN'S
Tralee Road, Killarney,
Co Kerry

Killarney Tralee Road

TEL: **064 33149**   FAX: **064 33149**
EMAIL: mgormans@eircom.net
WEB: www.eircom.net/~mgormans

No smoking house, smoking room available. Former B.F. garden prize winners. Low season reductions. Afternoon tea free on arrival. Visa & Vouchers welcome.

B&B	4	Ensuite	£19/£20	€24.13/€25.39	Dinner	£13.50
B&B	-	Standard	-		Partial Board	-
Single Rate			£25.50/£30	€32.38/€38.09	Child reduction	33.3%

Open: 1st January-23rd December

In Killarney

Louise Griffin
CHELMSFORD HOUSE
Muckross View, Countess Grove,
Killarney, Co Kerry

Killarney Town

TEL: **064 36402**   FAX: **064 33806**
EMAIL: info@chelmsfordhouse.com
WEB: www.chelmsfordhouse.com

Luxurious friendly home 5 mins walk to Town. Awaken to magnificent view of Lakes/Mountains. All tours arranged. TV Lounge, Breakfast Menu, Pancakes etc.

B&B	3	Ensuite	£19/£23	€24.13/€29.20	Dinner	-
B&B	-	Standard	-	-	Partial Board	-
Single Rate			-	-	Child reduction	-

Open: 10th January-20th December

Killarney 1.5km

Mary Guerin
BELLEVUE
1 Gortroe, Fossa,
Killarney, Co Kerry

Killarney

TEL: **064 34621**

Dormer style, 1.5km West of Killarney, Ring Kerry Rd, Golf, Horseriding, Tours Arranged, Rooms Ensuite, TV, Hairdryers, Private Parking.

B&B	3	Ensuite	£20	€25.39	Dinner	-
B&B	-	Standard	-	-	Partial Board	-
Single Rate			£30	€38.09	Child reduction	50%

Open: April-September

Mrs Mary Howard
COMERAGH HOUSE
Tralee Road, Dunrine,
Killarney, Co Kerry

Killarney Tralee Road
TEL: 064 34435

Modern home situated on N22. National Award of Excellence winner. Convenient base for Ring of Kerry/Dingle. Kerry Airport 10 mins.

B&B	4	Ensuite	£19/£19	€24.13	Dinner	-
B&B	-	Standard			Partial Board	-
Single Rate			£25.50/£25.50	€32.38	Child reduction	50%

Killarney 5km

Open: 1st April-31st October

Catherine Howe
DUN-A-RI HOUSE
Ross Road, Killarney,
Co Kerry

Killarney Ross Road
TEL: 064 36629
EMAIL: dunari@eircom.net

Located in scenic peaceful area. Opposite Ross Castle Holiday Homes adjacent to Ross Golf Club, National Park. Breakfast Menu, Hairdryers.

B&B	4	Ensuite	£20	€25.39	Dinner	-
B&B	-	Standard	-	-	Partial Board	-
Single Rate			£27.50	€34.91	Child reduction	-

In Killarney

Open: 1st March-1st November

Mr Tom Kearney
CILLCEARN HOUSE
Ballycasheen Road,
Killarney, Co Kerry

Killarney Cork Road Area
TEL: 064 35670   FAX: 064 34127

New luxurious home off N22, set in picturesque surroundings. Forest and river walks. Warm homely atmosphere, cable T.V lounge. Breakfast menu. Golf locally. Tours arranged.

B&B	3	Ensuite	£19/£19	€24.13	Dinner	£12.50
B&B	1	Standard	£17/£17	€21.59	Partial Board	-
Single Rate			£25.50	€32.38	Child reduction	25%

Killarney 2km

Open: 1st April-31st October

Mrs Nora Kelliher
HAZELWOOD
Park Rd, Upper Ballyspillane,
Killarney, Co Kerry

Killarney Cork Road Area
TEL: 064 34363   FAX: 064 34363
EMAIL: hazel@tinet.ie

Comfortable bungalow, 300m from Park Road roundabout on N22, walking distance from Town. Ideal touring base. Refreshments available. Tours arranged.

B&B	6	Ensuite	£20	€25.39	Dinner	£14
B&B	-	Standard	-	-	Partial Board	-
Single Rate			£25.50	€32.38	Child reduction	50%

Killarney 1km

Open: 1st May-1st November

Mr & Mrs William Kenny
SLIABH LAUCHRA HOUSE
Castlelough, Loretto Road,
Killarney, Co Kerry

Killarney Muckross Road
TEL: 064 32012

Family run house. Landscaped Gardens. 5 mins walk from Lakes, Parklands, Leisure Centre. TV. Guest room, Hairdryers, Tea/Coffee facilities. Award winner AA ♦♦♦.

B&B	6	Ensuite	£19/£20	€24.13/€25.39	Dinner	-
B&B	-	Standard	-	-	Partial Board	-
Single Rate			£27	€34.29	Child reduction	-

Killarney 1.6km

Open: April-30th September

In Killarney

Mrs Margaret Lanigan
CARAGH HOUSE
**Scrahan Court, Ross Road,
Killarney, Co Kerry**

Killarney Town
TEL: **064 34637**
EMAIL: caraghhouse@yahoo.com
WEB: www.geocities.com/caraghhouse/ireland.html

Friendly home 2 mins walk Town, Rail, Bus. Ideal touring centre. Beaches, Golf, Fishing, National Park, Pony trekking, Lakes. Tea/Coffee on arrival. Quiet cul de sac.

B&B	3	Ensuite	£17/£19	€21.59/€24.13	Dinner	-
B&B	-	Standard	-	-	Partial Board	-
Single Rate			-	-	Child reduction	-

Open: May-September

In Killarney

Mrs Josephine Lawlor
NORTHWOOD HOUSE
**Muckross View, Killarney,
Co Kerry**

Killarney Town
TEL: **064 37181**   FAX: **064 37181**
EMAIL: info@northwoodhouse.com
WEB: www.northwoodhouse.com

Newly built luxurious town house on quiet residential road with panoramic views of Killarney National Park, Lakes, Mountains, yet only a 5 minute walk to Town. Tours arranged.

B&B	4	Ensuite	£19/£23	€24.13/€29.20	Dinner	-
B&B	-	Standard	-	-	Partial Board	-
Single Rate			-	-	Child reduction	-

Open: All Year Except Christmas

Killarney 3km

Mrs Anne Leahy
AVONDALE HOUSE
**Tralee Road, Killarney,
Co Kerry**

Killarney Tralee Road
TEL: **064 35579**   FAX: **064 35197**
EMAIL: avondalehouse@eircom.net
WEB: www.kerry-insight.com/avondale

Modern new family run home. Large bedrooms, Scenic views, TV, Tea/Coffee facilities, Hairdryers, Electric blankets. Large gardens. Breakfast menu. AA listed.

B&B	5	Ensuite	£19.50/£20	€24.76/€25.39	Dinner	-
B&B	-	Standard	-	-	Partial Board	-
Single Rate			£28/£30	€35.55/€38.09	Child reduction	33.3%

Open: 20th January-30th November

In Killarney

Siobhan Leen
LEENS
**22 Marian Terrace, Killarney,
Co Kerry**

Killarney Town
TEL: **064 32819**

Modern house in residential area. At Lewis Rd go straight at roundabout, take 1st left, sign for house on right.

B&B	4	Ensuite	£19/£20	€24.13/€25.39	Dinner	-
B&B	-	Standard	-	-	Partial Board	-
Single Rate			£25.50/£26	€32.38/€33.01	Child reduction	25%

Open: 1st January-20th December

Killarney 1km

Mrs Julie Leonard
CASSARD HOUSE
**Rookery Road, Ballycasheen,
Killarney, Co Kerry**

Killarney Town
TEL: **064 35993**   FAX: **064 35993**
EMAIL: cassard@indigo.ie
WEB: www.dirl.com/kerry/cassard-house.htm

Modern family home in quiet residential area, walking distance to Town. TV's, Hairdryers, Tea/Coffee available. Off N22. Bus and Train Station nearby.

B&B	4	Ensuite	£20	€25.39	Dinner	-
B&B	-	Standard	-	-	Partial Board	-
Single Rate			£30	€38.09	Child reduction	25%

Open: March-October

267

Cathy & Mike Lohan
LOHAN'S LODGE
Tralee Road, Killarney,
Co Kerry

Killarney Tralee Road
TEL: 064 33871   FAX: 064 33871

No smoking house. Quality Awards AA ♦♦♦♦, RAC Highly Acclaimed. Recommended by Dillard/Causin and Michele Erdvigs Guides. Extensive breakfast menu.

B&B	5	Ensuite	£19.50/£20	€24.76/€25.39	Dinner	-
B&B	-	Standard	-	-	Partial Board	-
Single Rate		-		-	Child reduction	25%

Killarney 5km   cc 🅿   **Open:** 1st March-5th November

Mrs Eileen Lucey
MARIAN HOUSE
Woodlawn Road, Killarney,
Co Kerry

Killarney Muckross Road
TEL: 064 31275   FAX: 064 31275

Adjacent to Lakes, Mountains and National Park. Walking distance from Town, quiet area. Spacious Parking. Beyond Shell Filling Station on Kenmare road take left for Marian House.

B&B	6	Ensuite	£19/£20	€24.13/€25.39	Dinner	-
B&B	-	Standard	-	-	Partial Board	-
Single Rate		-		-	Child reduction	50%

In Killarney   🅿   **Open:** All Year Except Christmas

Mrs Joan Lucey
THE CASCADES
Muckross Rd, Killarney,
Co Kerry

Killarney Muckross Road
TEL: 064 34306
EMAIL: thecascades@eircom.net

Luxurious home, 5 minutes walk from Town Centre, Rail/Bus. Cabaret, Swimming, Golf nearby. Tours arranged. Private parking.

B&B	4	Ensuite	£20/£24	€25.39/€30.47	Dinner	-
B&B	-	Standard	-	-	Partial Board	-
Single Rate		-		-	Child reduction	-

In Killarney   cc 🅿   **Open:** 1st April-31st October

Mrs Kathleen McAuliffe
CARROWMORE HOUSE
Knockasarnett, Aghadoe,
Killarney, Co Kerry

Killarney Aghadoe
TEL: 064 33520
EMAIL: carrowmorehouse@eircom.net

A home from home in peaceful area. Panoramic views from TV lounge and bedrooms. Off N22 (Killarney-Tralee road), take first left after Cleeney roundabout.

B&B	4	Ensuite	£19/£20	€24.13/€25.39	Dinner	-
B&B	-	Standard	-	-	Partial Board	-
Single Rate		£25.50/£26.50		€32.38/€33.65	Child reduction	25%

Killarney 2km   cc 🅿   **Open:** May-October

Joan McCarthy
THE HARP
Muckross Road, Killarney,
Co Kerry

Killarney
TEL: 064 31272
EMAIL: ourhomeinkillarney@eircom.ie
WEB: www.kerryweb.ie/destination/kerry/killarney/harp/harp.ht

On N71 walking distance from Town. All room ensuite TV, hairdryers. Tea/Coffee facilities in Lounge. Breakfast Menu. Private Parking.

B&B	4	Ensuite	£19/£20	€24.13/€25.39	Dinner	£15
B&B	-	Standard	-	-	Partial Board	-
Single Rate		-		-	Child reduction	33.3%

In Killarney   cc 🅿   **Open:** All Year

In Killarney

Mrs Kathleen McCarthy
SANCTA MARIA
53 Park Drive, Off Park Road
Killarney, Co Kerry

Killarney Town
TEL: **064 32447**   FAX: **064 32447**

Comfortable house in residential area. Walking distance of Town, close to all amenities. Private parking. Tours arranged. Complimentary tea arrival.

B&B	3	Ensuite	£19.50/£21	€24.76/€26.66	Dinner	-
B&B	1	Standard	£17.50/£19	€22.22/€24.13	Partial Board	-
Single Rate			£24.50/£26.50	€31.11/€33.65	Child reduction	25%

Open: All Year

Killarney 1km

Mrs Margaret McCarthy
CRICKET VIEW
7 Muckross Grove, Killarney,
Co Kerry

Killarney Town
TEL: **064 32245**   FAX: **064 32245**

Modern two storey house in quiet area, 10 min walk to Town Centre. Family run, Tours arranged. Near Gleneagle Hotel.

B&B	1	Ensuite	£19	€24.13	Dinner	-
B&B	2	Standard	£17	€21.59	Partial Board	-
Single Rate			£23.50/£25.50	€29.84/€32.38	Child reduction	33.3%

Open: April-September

In Killarney

Mrs Peggy McCarthy
DROMHALL HEIGHTS
Off Countess Road, Killarney,
Co Kerry

Killarney Countess Road Area
TEL: **064 32662**
EMAIL: peggymccarthy@eircom.net

Family home, quiet private location. View mountains, Lakes. Only minutes walk to Town from Countess road through Countess Grove, to top of Hill, then left road.

B&B	2	Ensuite	£19/£21	€24.13/€26.66	Dinner	-
B&B	1	Standard	£17/£19	€21.59/€24.13	Partial Board	-
Single Rate			£23.50/£25.50	€29.84/€32.38	Child reduction	-

Open: March-November

In Killarney

Elizabeth McEnteggart
ARMAGH HOUSE
Park House, Killarney,
Co Kerry

Killarney
TEL: **064 34346**

Purpose builtt B&B. 2 minutes walk from Town Centre. Adjacent to Bus and Rail services. Convenient to National Park and surrounding Lakes and Mountains.

B&B	6	Ensuite	£19/£20	€24.13/€25.39	Dinner	-
B&B	-	Standard			Partial Board	-
Single Rate			£25.50/£25.50	€32.38	Child reduction	50%

Open: All Year

Killarney 7km

Mrs Betty McSweeney
HILTON HEIGHTS
Glebe, Tralee Road,
Killarney, Co Kerry

Killarney Tralee Road
TEL: **064 33364**

Bungalow in pleasant restful area. All ensuite rooms, Hairdryers, TV, Tea/Coffee facilities. Sign for Hilton Heights on left on Tralee road. 7km from Killarney, turn right.

B&B	4	Ensuite	£19	€24.13	Dinner	-
B&B	-	Standard	-	-	Partial Board	-
Single Rate			£25.50	€32.38	Child reduction	50%

Open: 1st April-1st October

In Killarney Town

Miss Christine McSweeney
EMMERVILLE HOUSE
Muckross Drive, Off Muckross Rd
(town end), Killarney, Co Kerry

Killarney Muckross Road
Tel: 064 33342

Comfortable home quiet cul-de-sac. Mins walk Town Centre/Bus/Rail. Tours arranged (Reduction low season). Personal attention. Entertainment closeby. Hairdryers all rooms.

B&B	4	Ensuite	£19/£20	€24.13/€25.39	Dinner -
B&B	-	Standard	-	-	Partial Board -
Single Rate			£25.50/£25.50	€32.38	Child reduction 25%

Open: All Year

In Killarney

Mrs Chriss Mannix
FLESK LODGE
Muckross Road, Killarney,
Co Kerry

Killarney Muckross Road
Tel: 064 32135   Fax: 064 32135
Email: fleskldg@gofree.indigo.ie

Luxury bungalow walking distance from Town. Close to all amenities. Beside Gleneagle Hotel Complex. Landscaped garden.

B&B	6	Ensuite	£20/£21	€25.39/€26.66	Dinner £13
B&B	-	Standard	-	-	Partial Board -
Single Rate			£26/£27	€33.01/€34.29	Child reduction 25%

Open: All Year

Killarney 6km

Anne & Neilius Moriarty
BROOKSIDE
Gortacollopa, Fossa,
Killarney, Co Kerry

Killarney Fossa
Tel: 064 44187
Email: moriartybrookside@eircom.net
Web: homepage.eircom.net/~brookside

Award winning family home, farmland setting, on Ring of Kerry/Killarney/Killorglin road near river Laune. Pastoral view, Breakfast menu, advice on tours.

B&B	5	Ensuite	£20/£20	€25.39	Dinner -
B&B	1	Standard	£18/£19	€22.86/€24.13	Partial Board -
Single Rate			£25.50/£26.50	€32.38/€33.65	Child reduction 25%

Open: 10th March-3rd November

Killarney 4km

Margaret Moriarty
BENISKA HOUSE
Lackbane, Fossa,
Killarney, Co Kerry

Killarney
Tel: 064 32200

New luxurious home on Ring of Kerry/Dingle road. Take N72 West 2.5 miles. Adjacent Killarney 3 Golf Courses and 5* Hotel Europe. Next to Pub and Restaurant.

B&B	4	Ensuite	£20/£25	€25.39/€31.74	Dinner -
B&B	-	Standard	-	-	Partial Board -
Single Rate			-	-	Child reduction -

Open: March-October

Killarney 8km

Tim & Nora Moriarty
THE PURPLE HEATHER
Glencar Rd, Gap of Dunloe,
Beaufort, Killarney, Co Kerry

Killarney Gap of Dunloe
Tel: 064 44266   Fax: 064 44266
Email: purpleheather@eircom.net
Web: homepage.eircom.net/~purpleheather

Breakfast Consevatory panoramic view. Breakfast menu. Rooms with TV, Electric Blanket, Hairdryer, Tea/Coffee, Pool Room, Irish Music, Restaurant, Golf 1km.

B&B	5	Ensuite	£19/£19	€24.13	Dinner -
B&B	1	Standard	£17/£17	€21.59	Partial Board -
Single Rate			£23.50/£25.50	€29.84/€32.38	Child reduction 50%

Open: March-October

In Killarney

Mrs Maura Moynihan
KELARE LODGE
**Muckross Drive, Off Muckross Rd,
Killarney, Co Kerry**

Killarney Muckross Road
TEL: 064 32895

Luxury B&B. Minutes walk from Town Centre. National Park, Bus, Rail station. Quiet location off Muckross road. Tours arranged.

				Dinner	-
B&B	5	Ensuite	£19/£21	€24.13/€26.66	
B&B	-	Standard	-	-	Partial Board	-
Single Rate		-		-	Child reduction	33.3%

Open: 6th January-20th December

Killarney 1km

Michael & Oonagh Moynihan
KYLEMORE
**Ballydowney, Killarney,
Co Kerry**

Killarney
TEL: **064 31771**   FAX: **064 31771**
EMAIL: kylemorehousekillarney@eircom.net

Friendly home on route N72 (Ring of Kerry and Dingle Road). Adjacent to Killarney, Golf and Fishing club, Riding stables and National Park.

					Dinner	-
B&B	6	Ensuite	£19	€24.13		
B&B	-	Standard	-	-	Partial Board	-
Single Rate			£25.50	€32.38	Child reduction	50%

Open: 1st May-31st October

Killarney 2km

Mrs Eileen Murphy
GREEN ACRES
**Fossa, Killarney,
Co Kerry**

Killarney Fossa
TEL: **064 31454**   FAX: **064 31454**

Modern family home 2km from Killarney on the main Ring of Kerry road. In the midst of three famous Golf courses, Horse riding, Fishing, 1km Walks. AA listed.

					Dinner	-
B&B	4	Ensuite	£19/£20	€24.13/€25.39		
B&B	2	Standard	£17/£18	€21.59/€22.86	Partial Board	-
Single Rate			£23.50/£25.50	€29.84/€32.38	Child reduction	25%

Open: 1st April-30th September

Killarney 3km

Mrs Evelyn Murphy
REDWOOD
**Rockfield, Tralee Road,
Killarney, Co Kerry**

Killarney Tralee Road Area
TEL: **064 34754**   FAX: **064 34178**
EMAIL: redwd@indigo.ie
WEB: www.kerry-insight.com/redwood

Surrounded by 15 acres. Large bedrooms include bath power showers, Multi-channel, Hairdryer, Teamakers, some with Kingsize beds, Extensive Menu. From Killarney take N22 towards Tralee.

					Dinner	-
B&B	6	Ensuite	£20/£22.50	€25.39/€28.57		
B&B	-	Standard	-	-	Partial Board	-
Single Rate			£25.50/£34	€32.38/€43.17	Child reduction	50%

Open: All Year

Killarney 2km

Mrs Sheila Murphy
SERENIC VIEW
**Coolcorcoran, Killarney,
Co Kerry**

Killarney Tralee Road
TEL: **064 33434**   FAX: **064 33578**
EMAIL: serenic@eircom.net
WEB: homepage.eircom.net/~serenic

Luxury ground floor accomodation. 5 min drive from Town on Ring of Kerry. Signposted on Killarney/Limerick road. Quiet scenic area. Breakfast menu. Satellite TV. Tours arranged.

					Dinner	-
B&B	4	Ensuite	£19	€24.13		
B&B	-	Standard	-	-	Partial Board	-
Single Rate			£25.50	€32.38	Child reduction	25%

Open: 1st March-31st October

Kerry

Killarney 3.5km

Vincent & Maureen Murphy
LAKELAND HAVEN
Fossa, Killarney,
Co Kerry

Killarney

Tel: **064 35322**   Fax: **064 35322**
Email: lakelandhaven@eircom.net

Luxurious home. Ring of Kerry road. Rooms with private verandahs overlooking Lakes/Mountains. Golf, Riding stables. Fishing. National Park nearby. Tours arranged.

B&B	6	Ensuite	£20.50/£22.50	€26.03/€28.57	Dinner	-
B&B		Standard	-	-	Partial Board	-
Single Rate			£25.50/£27	€32.38/€34.29	Child reduction	33.3%

Open: All Year

Killarney 3km

Ann & David Nash
NASHVILLE
Tralee Road, Killarney,
Co Kerry

Killarney Tralee Road

Tel: **064 32924**   Fax: **064 32924**
Email: nashville@tinet.ie
Web: www.kerry-insight.com/nashville

Modern family home on Tralee N22 road. Colour TV's, Hairdryers, Tea/Coffee facilities. Payphone for guests. Ideal centre for touring Kerry - all tours arranged. AA listed.

B&B	6	Ensuite	£19/£22	€24.13/€27.93	Dinner	-
B&B		Standard	-	-	Partial Board	-
Single Rate			£25.50/£28	€32.38/€35.55	Child reduction	33.3%

Open: 15th March-1st December

In Killarney

Mrs Triona Neilan
ROSSARNEY HOUSE
St Margaret's Road, Killarney,
Co Kerry

Killarney Town

Tel: **064 34630**

Award winning family home. Quiet area. 8 minutes walk Town. Guest TV, reading room with Tea/Coffee facilities. Golf, Riding stables, Park nearby. Itinerary planned. Reduction low season.

B&B	4	Ensuite	£19/£20	€24.13/€25.39	Dinner	-
B&B		Standard	-	-	Partial Board	-
Single Rate			-	-	Child reduction	-

Open: 1st January-20th December

In Killarney

Ms Maria Ní Cheallaigh
RATH BEAG
Scrahan Court, Ross Road,
Killarney, Co Kerry

Killarney Town

Tel: **064 37868**

Purpose built, centrally located in quiet residential area. 2 mins walk Town, Bus, Railway stations. Tours arranged. Tea/Coffee on arrival.

B&B	5	Ensuite	£18/£20	€22.86/€25.39	Dinner	-
B&B		Standard	-	-	Partial Board	-
Single Rate			£25/£28	€31.74/€35.55	Child reduction	-

Open: 1st May-30th September

Killarney

Maria O Carroll
TENTH GREEN
39 Demense, Ross Road,
Killarney, Co Kerry

Killarney Ross Road

Tel: **064 37369**   Fax: **064 37369**

Luxury dormer bungalow. Award winning gardens. Walking distance Town centre, Golf course, Ross Castle, National Park. All types of tours arranged.

B&B	3	Ensuite	£19/£30	€24.13/€38.09	Dinner	-
B&B		Standard	-	-	Partial Board	-
Single Rate			£25.50/£30	€32.38/€38.09	Child reduction	25%

Open: All Year

In Killarney

Mrs Rosemary O'Connell
OAKLAWN HOUSE
Muckross Drive, Off Muckross Road, Killarney, Co Kerry

Killarney Muckross Road
TEL: **064 32616**
EMAIL: oaklawnhouse@eircom.net

Award winning house. Winner of prestigious Killarney looking and best Town & Country Home '95-'98. Golden Circle Award '99. Two minutes to Town Centre.

B&B	3	Ensuite	£19/£22	€24.13/€27.93	Dinner	-
B&B	-	Standard	-	-	Partial Board	-
Single Rate			£30	€38.09	Child reduction	33.3%

Open: All Year

Killarney 1km

Mrs Anne O'Connor
CLONALIS HOUSE
Countess Road, Killarney, Co Kerry

Killarney Countess Road Area
TEL: **064 31043**   FAX: **064 31043**

Recommended Dillard Causin Guide. Luxurious home, select residential location off Muckross road and off N22. Near Town, Lakes, Golf. Tours arranged.

B&B	6	Ensuite	£20/£22	€25.39/€27.93	Dinner	-
B&B	-	Standard	-	-	Partial Board	-
Single Rate			£28/£30	€35.55/€38.09	Child reduction	-

Open: May-September

Killarney 3km

Mrs Hannah O'Connor
TORC FALLS
Lough Guitane Road, Muckross, Killarney, Co Kerry

Killarney Muckross Road
TEL: **064 33566**

Spacious modern house. Quiet location, Private Parking. Central to National Park, Muckross House/Gardens, Mountains, Lakes, all amenities. Tours arranged.

B&B	5	Ensuite	£19/£21	€24.13/€26.66	Dinner	-
B&B	-	Standard	-	-	Partial Board	-
Single Rate			-	-	Child reduction	25%

Open: 1st April-31st October

Killarney 2km

Mrs Julianne O'Donnell
HYLANDS
Coolgarrive, Aghadoe, Killarney, Co Kerry

Killarney Aghadoe
TEL: **064 34370**   FAX: **064 34370**

Modern home, quiet, scenic location, guest TV lounge, complimentary Tea/Coffee. Leaving Killarney, 1st left after roundabout off Tralee Road (N22).

B&B	4	Ensuite	£19/£20	€24.13/€25.39	Dinner	-
B&B	-	Standard	-	-	Partial Board	-
Single Rate			£26/£27	€33.01/€34.29	Child reduction	33.3%

Open: 15th March-31st October

In Killarney

Mrs Bridie O'Donoghue
MUCKROSS DRIVE HOUSE
Muckross Drive, Off Muckross Road, Killarney, Co Kerry

Killarney Muckross Road
TEL: **064 34290**   FAX: **064 39818**
EMAIL: muckrossdrive@eircom.net

Award-winning purpose built B&B. Minutes walk Town Centre. Bus/Rail. Situated in a quiet cul-de-sac. Overlooking mountains & National Park. All tours arranged.

B&B	5	Ensuite	£19/£20	€24.13/€25.39	Dinner	-
B&B	-	Standard	-	-	Partial Board	-
Single Rate			£25.50/£25.50	€32.38	Child reduction	25%

Open: All Year

Patrick & Julia O'Donoghue
WOODLANDS
**Ballydowney, Killarney,
Co Kerry**

Tel: **064 31467**   Fax: **064 31467**
Email: stayatwoodlands@eircom.net
Web: stayatwoodlands.com

Friendly home walking distance Town. Ring of Kerry road N72. Riding stables, Golf, Fishing, Lakes/National Park nearby. Ideal walkers/climbers/cycling.

B&B	3	Ensuite	£20	€25.39	Dinner	-
B&B	2	Standard	£17	€21.59	Partial Board	-
Single Rate			£25	€31.74	Child reduction	33.3%

Killarney 1km    **Open:** January-20th December

---

Mrs Phil O'Donohoe
MAYWOOD
**Mill Road, Killarney,
Co Kerry**

Tel: **064 31263**

Spacious, modern bungalow in scenic area near National Park. Golf, Fishing, Mountains, Lakes nearby. Tours arranged.

B&B	3	Ensuite	£19/£19	€24.13	Dinner	-
B&B	2	Standard	£17/£17	€21.59	Partial Board	-
Single Rate			£23.50/£25.50	€29.84/€32.38	Child reduction	25%

Killarney 1.5km    **Open:** 1st March-30th October

---

Mrs Betty O'Donovan
TIVOLI
**Cork Road, Killarney,
Co Kerry**

Tel: **064 31450**

Attractive modern home within walking distance of Town Centre, Church, Railway and Bus Station. Tours arranged. Convenient to all amenities.

B&B	3	Ensuite	£19/£19	€24.13	Dinner	-
B&B	1	Standard	£17/£17	€21.59	Partial Board	-
Single Rate			£23.50/£25.50	€29.84/€32.38	Child reduction	-

In Killarney   **Open:** 1st May-20th September

Mrs Eileen O'Grady
FORREST HILLS
**Muckross Road, Killarney,
Co Kerry**

Tel: **064 31844**

Modern, well-heated home in scenic area, a few hundred yards from Town Centre. Spacious Parking. Home cooking.

B&B	4	Ensuite	£19/£20	€24.13/€25.39	Dinner	-
B&B	2	Standard	£17.50/£17.50	€22.22	Partial Board	-
Single Rate			£25/£25	€31.74	Child reduction	50%

Killarney 1km    **Open:** February-November

---

Denis & Rosaleen O'Leary
ROSS CASTLE LODGE
**Ross Road, Killarney,
Co Kerry**

Tel: **064 36942**   Fax: **064 36942**
Email: rosscastlelodge@killarneyb-and-b.com
Web: killarneyb-and-b.com

Luxurious house, edge of town amidst magical woodland and lakeshore walks. Golf, Lake cruising, Fishing 10 mins walk. Spacious bedrooms. RAC ♦♦♦♦ Award Winner.

B&B	4	Ensuite	£20/£25	€25.39/€31.74	Dinner	-
B&B	-	Standard	-	-	Partial Board	-
Single Rate			£39	€49.52	Child reduction	-

In Killarney   **Open:** 10th March-15th November

Killarney 4km

Mrs Eileen O'Leary
THE SHADY NOOK
Crohane, Fossa,
Killarney, Co Kerry

Killarney Fossa
TEL: **064 33351**
EMAIL: the-shady-nook@unison.ie

Family home in a peaceful scenic area. 4km west of Killarney, off the N72. Ideal base for touring Ring of Kerry, Dingle, Lakes. Golf, Fishing .5km arranged.

B&B	3	Ensuite	£19	€24.13	Dinner	£12.50
B&B	-	Standard	-	-	Partial Board	£185
Single Rate			£30	€38.09	Child reduction	50%

Open: 1st May-30th September

Killarney 1km

Mrs Evelyn O'Leary
KILBROGAN HOUSE
Muckross Road, Killarney,
Co Kerry

Killarney Muckross Road
TEL: **064 31444**
EMAIL: kilbrog@indigo.ie

Family home on Ring of Kerry road adjacent National Park/Gleneagle Hotel. Log fire, home baking, spacious parking. Tours arranged. 2 single rooms.

B&B	4	Ensuite	£19/£19	€24.13	Dinner	-
B&B	-	Standard	-	-	Partial Board	-
Single Rate			£25.50/£25.50	€32.38	Child reduction	50%

Open: April-31st October

Killarney 2km

Miss Noreen O'Mahoney
MYSTICAL ROSE
Woodlawn Road, Killarney,
Co Kerry

Killarney Town
TEL: **064 31453**   FAX: **064 35846**
EMAIL: mysticalr@eircom.net

Award winning guest home. Frommer Guide recommended. Beautiful country home convenient to Mountain, Lake District. All tours arranged.

B&B	6	Ensuite	£19/£22.50	€24.13/€28.57	Dinner	£12.50
B&B	-	Standard	-	-	Partial Board	-
Single Rate			£27/£30	€34.29/€38.09	Child reduction	33.3%

Open: All Year

Killarney 1km

Sean and Sheila O'Mahony
O'MAHONY'S
Cork Road, Killarney,
Co Kerry

Killarney Town
TEL: **064 32861**

Warm comfortable family run home opposite Ryan Hotel. TV, Hairdryers, Breakfast menu, Private parking. Walking distance town centre. Tours arranged. Tea/Coffee facilities.

B&B	6	Ensuite	£19/£19	€24.13	Dinner	-
B&B	-	Standard	-	-	Partial Board	-
Single Rate			£25.50	€32.38	Child reduction	50%

Open: 1st January-1st December

Killarney 2km

Mrs Norrie O'Neill
ALDERHAVEN COUNTRY HOME
Ballycasheen, Cork Road,
Killarney, Co Kerry

Killarney Ballycasheen
TEL: **064 31982**   FAX: **064 31982**
EMAIL: alderhaven@eircom.net
WEB: www.alderhaven.com

Secluded Tudor style house off N22 at Whitebridge. 5 acres woodlands, Private avenue. Tranquil setting. Breakfast conservatory, Menu, Hairdryers. Tours arranged.

B&B	6	Ensuite	£20/£21	€25.39/€26.66	Dinner	-
B&B	-	Standard	-	-	Partial Board	-
Single Rate			£26/£28	€33.01/€35.55	Child reduction	25%

Open: 15th March-1st December

In Killarney

Killarney 5km

Mrs Patricia O'Neill
LORENZO HOUSE
Lewis Road, Killarney Town, Killarney, Co Kerry

Killarney Town
Tel: 064 31869

Modern town house, 3 minutes walk to Town centre, Bus and Railway, National Park, Golf, Riding stables nearby. Tours arranged.

B&B	4	Ensuite	£19/£20	€24.13/€25.39	Dinner	-
B&B	-	Standard	-	-	Partial Board	-
Single Rate			-	-	Child reduction	-

Open: 1st April-31st October

Sheila O'Neill
ALRAN HEIGHTS
Lough Guitane Road, Muckross, Killarney, Co Kerry

Killarney Muckross Road
Tel: 064 32071
Email: oneillsheila@eircom.net

Set in quiet tranquil location with view of Mangerton Mountain. Adjacent to Killarney National Park, 1km off the N71.

B&B	2	Ensuite	£19	€24.13	Dinner	-
B&B	1	Standard	£17	€21.59	Partial Board	-
Single Rate			-	-	Child reduction	50%

Open: 1st May-30th September

Killarney 1km

Joan and Patrick O'Riordan
ST RITAS VILLA
Mill Road, Killarney, Co Kerry

Killarney Muckross Road
Tel: 064 31517   Fax: 064 37631

House adjacent to Lakes, Muckross House, Gleneagle Hotel. Tea/Coffee served, Orthopaedic beds, Hairdryers available. Tours arranged. Private parking.

B&B	4	Ensuite	£19/£20	€24.13/€25.39	Dinner	-
B&B	1	Standard	£17/£18	€21.59/€22.86	Partial Board	-
Single Rate			£24.50/£26.50	€31.11/€33.65	Child reduction	25%

Open: 12th March-31st October

Killarney 3km

Mrs Anne O'Rourke
SILVER SPRINGS
Tralee Road, Killarney, Co Kerry

Killarney Tralee Road
Tel: 064 31016

Country home. 3km Killarney on Tralee-Limerick road N22. Bedrooms ensuite, with TV, Coffee and Tea making facilities. Tours, Golf, Horse riding and Cycling near.

B&B	3	Ensuite	£19/£19	€24.13	Dinner	£12.50
B&B	1	Standard	£17	€21.59	Partial Board	-
Single Rate			£23.50/£23.50	€29.84	Child reduction	33.3%

Open: March-December

Killarney 1km

Mrs Kay O'Shea
SPRINGFIELD LODGE
Rookery Rd, Ballycasheen, Killarney, Co Kerry

Killarney Cork Road Area
Tel: 064 32944
Email: springfieldlodge@eircom.net
Web: homepage.eircom.net/~springfieldlodge

Modern, comfortable, welcoming home. Tranquil setting, adjacent to woodlands. Central location, private parking off N22. All tours arranged.

B&B	4	Ensuite	£19/£20	€24.13/€25.39	Dinner	-
B&B	-	Standard	-	-	Partial Board	-
Single Rate			-	-	Child reduction	25%

Open: 1st March-1st October

Killarney 2km

Mrs Bernadette O'Sullivan
MUCKROSS LODGE
Muckross Road
Killarney, Co Kerry

TEL: **064 32660**   FAX: **064 32660**
EMAIL: muckrosslodge@eircom.net
WEB: www.muckrosslodge@killarneyb-and-b.com

Spacious modern home adjacent to Muckross House, National Park and Lakes. Views of Kerrys highest mountains. Ideal base for walkers/cyclists. Hairdryers, Home baking. Tours arranged.

B&B	4	Ensuite	£20/£22.50	€25.39/€28.57	Dinner	-
B&B	-	Standard	-	-	Partial Board	-
Single Rate			£30/£30	€38.09	Child reduction	-

Open: 1st April-31st October

Killorglin 8km

Mrs Eileen O'Sullivan
KINGDOM VIEW
Glencar Road, Kilgobnet,
Beaufort, Killarney, Co Kerry

TEL: **064 44343**
EMAIL: jos@iol.ie

On Killarney/Glencar Road, Slopes of McGillucuddy Mountains. Spectacular Countryside. Seafood speciality. Turf Fire. Cot available. Traditional musicians in family.

B&B	5	Ensuite	£19/£19	€24.13	Dinner	£13
B&B	1	Standard	£17/£17	€21.59	Partial Board	£185
Single Rate			£23.50/£25.50	€29.84/€32.38	Child reduction	50%

Open: 1st February-30th November

In Killarney

Mr Eugene A O'Sullivan
NORAVILLE HOUSE
St Margarets Road, Killarney,
Co Kerry

TEL: **064 36053**   FAX: **064 37446**

Highly recommended modern townhouse. Select residential location. Tea/Coffee facilities and Hairdryers in all rooms. Tours arranged. Reduction low season. Personal attention.

B&B	5	Ensuite	£19/£20	€24.13/€25.39	Dinner	-
B&B	-	Standard	-	-	Partial Board	-
Single Rate			£25.50/£30	€32.38/€38.09	Child reduction	25%

Open: All Year

Killarney 7km

Mrs Mary O'Sullivan
LIOS-A-DUN
Pallas, Beaufort,
Killarney, Co Kerry

TEL: **064 44119**
EMAIL: liosadun@hotmail.com

Christian family home warm welcome "home from home feeling". Peaceful scenic area. On main Killarney/Killorgin road N72 West. Near Golf, Fishing. Gap of Dunloe.

B&B	2	Ensuite	£19/£19	€24.13	Dinner	£12.50
B&B	1	Standard	£18/£18	€22.86	Partial Board	£190
Single Rate			£24.50/£25.50	€31.11/€32.38	Child reduction	25%

Open: May-20th September

Killarney 5km

Mrs Phyl Perlman
ASHBROOK
Tralee Road, Dunrine,
Killarney, Co Kerry

TEL: **064 39053**   FAX: **064 39053**

Luxurious home on N22. Breakfast menu and orthopaedic beds. Airport 10 mins. Ideal base for touring Killarney Lakes, Ring of Kerry and Dingle Peninsula.

B&B	4	Ensuite	£20	€25.39	Dinner	-
B&B	-	Standard	-	-	Partial Board	-
Single Rate			£25.50	€32.38	Child reduction	-

Open: 1st March-31st October

Killarney 2km

Joan & Jerry Ryan
THE GROTTO
Fossa, Killarney,
Co Kerry

Killarney

Tel: **064 33283**
Email: the_grotto@hotmail.com

On Ring of Kerry/Dingle, opposite Lake and Killarney Golf & Fishing Club. Tea facilities. Riding stables nearby. Near Castlerosse Hotel. Tours arranged.

B&B	6	Ensuite	£19/£20	€24.13/€25.39	Dinner	-
B&B	-	Standard	-	-	Partial Board	-
Single Rate			£26	€33.01	Child reduction	25%

Open: 1st March-5th November

Killarney 2km

Mrs Hazel Scott
HAZELBROOK HEIGHTS
Aghadoe, Killarney,
Co Kerry

Killarney Aghadoe

Tel: **064 34309**   Fax: **064 34309**
Email: hazelbrookheights@tinet.ie

Modern bungalow in scenic, peaceful area (off N22). Guest lounge, Tea/Coffee facilities, Breakfast menu. Tours arranged, Parking. Personal service.

B&B	4	Ensuite	£20/£20	€25.39	Dinner	-
B&B	-	Standard	-	-	Partial Board	-
Single Rate			£25.50/£27	€32.38/€34.29	Child reduction	50%

Open: 1st April-31st December

Killarney 4km

Mrs Carmella Sheehy
LINN DUBH
Aghadoe, Killarney,
Co Kerry

Killarney Aghadoe

Tel: **064 33828**
Email: ecsheehy@eircom.net

Overlooking Killarney's Lakes and Mountains. Quiet scenic area. Causin/Dillard, Hachette Visa guide recommended. Orthopaedic beds. Breakfast menu. Tours arranged.

B&B	5	Ensuite	£19/£20	€24.13/€25.39	Dinner	-
B&B	-	Standard	-	-	Partial Board	-
Single Rate			£25.50/£30	€32.38/€38.09	Child reduction	50%

Open: March-November

Killarney 1km

Mrs Catherine Spillane
BEAUTY'S HOME
Cleeney, Tralee Road,
Killarney, Co Kerry

Killarney Town

Tel: **064 31567/31836** Fax: **064 34077**
Email: deroscoachtours@eircom.net

Luxurious Bungalow. TV, Video, Movie Channel, Tea/Coffee Facilities. Electric Blankets in winter months, Orthopaedic Beds. Collection Rail/Bus Station

B&B	3	Ensuite	£19/£26	€24.13/€33.01	Dinner	-
B&B	3	Standard	£17/£22	€21.59/€27.93	Partial Board	-
Single Rate			£25/£35	€31.74/€44.44	Child reduction	25%

Open: 1st January-24th December

Killarney 1km

Mrs Eileen Tarrant
MULBERRY HOUSE
(Off Countess Road)
Rookery Road, Killarney, Co Kerry

Killarney Cork Road Area

Tel: **064 34112**   Fax: **064 32534**
Email: mulberry@eircom.net
Web: www.kerry-insight.com/mulberry

Luxurious country house backing on to Farmland. Unspoilt views Killarneys Mountain range off N22. Superb peaceful location. Tours arranged. Parking.

B&B	5	Ensuite	£19/£25	€24.13/€31.74	Dinner	-
B&B	-	Standard	-	-	Partial Board	-
Single Rate			£27/£38	€34.29/€48.25	Child reduction	25%

Open: 1st March-20th November

Killarney 4km

Mrs Anne Teahan
FAIR HAVEN
Lissivigeen (N22), Cork Road, Killarney, Co Kerry

Killarney Cork Road Area

Tel: **064 32542**
Email: fairhavenbb@eircom.net

Dillard/Causin Guide recommended. Warm country home on 2 acres. Golf, Fishing locally. Tea/Coffee facilities in TV lounge. Breakfast menu. Collection point for Ring of Kerry tours.

B&B	4	Ensuite	£19/£19	€24.13	Dinner	-
B&B	1	Standard	£17/£17	€21.59	Partial Board	-
Single Rate			£25/£25	€31.74	Child reduction	25%

Open: May-October

In Killarney

Mrs Mary Tuohy
FRIARY VIEW
Dennehy's, Bohereen, Killarney, Co Kerry

Killarney Town

Tel: **064 32996**

Peaceful home in secluded area off main road. Walking distance to Town, Bus, Rail. Tours arranged. Breakfast Menu. Small road beside Friary Church.

B&B	4	Ensuite	£19/£19	€24.13	Dinner	-
B&B	-	Standard	-	-	Partial Board	-
Single Rate			-	-	Child reduction	-

Open: 1st May-30th September

In Killarney

Mrs Eileen Twomey
GOLDEN OAKES
Dromhale (Off Countess Grove), Killarney, Co Kerry

Killarney

Tel: **064 32737**

Excellent accommodation on private grounds. Superb view of Lakes and Mountains. 5 min from Town Centre. Tea/Coffee provided on request.

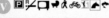

B&B	3	Ensuite	£19/£20	€24.13/€25.39	Dinner	-
B&B	-	Standard	-	-	Partial Board	-
Single Rate			£25.50/£25.50	€32.38	Child reduction	25%

Open: 1st April-30th September

Killarney 2km

Mrs Agnes Walsh
WUTHERING HEIGHTS
Knockeenduff, Killarney, Co Kerry

Killarney

Tel: **064 32756**
Email: wutheringheights_@hotmail.com

Bungalow in peaceful location signposted on Killarney/ Limerick road (N22). Tea/Coffee making facilities, Orthopaedic beds, Electric blankets, hairdryer. Low season reduction.

B&B	4	Ensuite	£19/£20	€24.13/€25.39	Dinner	£14
B&B	-	Standard	-	-	Partial Board	-
Single Rate			£25.50	€32.38	Child reduction	25%

Open: 31st January-15th December

Killarney 1km

Patricia Wright
SUNFLOWER COTTAGE
Cleeney, Tralee Road, Killarney, Co Kerry

Killarney Town

Tel: **064 32101**

First class accommodation close to Town. Ideal for touring Ring of Kerry, Dingle and Lakes. A warm welcome to be expected. Situated on N22.

B&B	4	Ensuite	£20/£26	€25.39/€33.01	Dinner	-
B&B	-	Standard	-	-	Partial Board	-
Single Rate			£25.50/£35.00	€32.38/€44.44	Child reduction	50%

Open: March-October

Mrs Irma Clifford
FERN ROCK
Tinnahalla N70, Milltown,
Co Kerry

Killorglin
TEL: 066 9761848   FAX: 066 9761848
EMAIL: fernrock@eircom.net

Excellent accommodation (on N70 Tralee Rd) superb view. Tours arranged. Golf .5km. Also 10 Golf courses within 1 hour drive. Central for Ring of Kerry/Dingle/Killarney. Beaches close by.

B&B	4	Ensuite	£19/£20	€24.13/€25.39	Dinner	-
B&B	-	Standard	-	-	Partial Board	-
Single Rate			£25.50	€32.38	Child reduction	-

Killorglin 3km   **Open:** 2nd January-15th December

Mrs Marie Clifford
HILLCREST
Killarney Road, Killorglin,
Co Kerry

Killorglin Ring Of Kerry
TEL: 066 9761552
EMAIL: hillcrest_clifford@hotmail.com

Georgian styled residence on N72, spectacular views Irelands Highest Mountain and countryside. Orthopaedic Beds, Hairdryers. Frommer Recommended.

B&B	5	Ensuite	£19/£19	€24.13	Dinner	-
B&B	-	Standard	-	-	Partial Board	-
Single Rate			£25.50/£25.50	€32.38	Child reduction	50%

Killorglin   **Open:** 1st April-30th September

Mrs Bridie Evans
ORGLAN HOUSE
Killarney Road N72, Killorglin,
Co Kerry

Killorglin Ring of Kerry
TEL: 066 9761540

Peaceful hilltop residence with magnificent mountain views, overlooking River and Town. 5 mins walk from Town. Golf, Fishing, Beaches, Hillwalking all within 20 mins of Town centre.

B&B	3	Ensuite	£19/£20	€24.13/€25.39	Dinner	-
B&B	1	Standard	£17/£18	€21.59/€22.86	Partial Board	-
Single Rate			£25.50/£30	€32.38/€38.09	Child reduction	25%

In Killorglin   **Open:** April-October

Noreen Evans
LAUNE BRIDGE HOUSE
Killarney Rd, Killorglin,
Co Kerry

Killorglin Ring Of Kerry
TEL: 066 9761161

At the Bridge of Killorglin scenic location overlooking River. Purpose built on the Ring of Kerry. Walking distance from high class Restaurants.

B&B	6	Ensuite	£19/£20	€24.13/€25.39	Dinner	-
B&B	-	Standard	-	-	Partial Board	-
Single Rate			£25/£30	€31.74/€38.09	Child reduction	-

In Killorglin   **Open:** 1st March-1st December

Mrs Christine Griffin
ARDRAHAN HOUSE
Ownagarry, Killorglin,
Co Kerry

Killorglin
TEL: 066 9762219

Family run peaceful homely accommodation, quiet location. 2km from Town. Central for Mountain and Hill walking, Cycling, Fishing, Ring of Kerry, Dingle, Killarney, Seaside, Caragh Lake.

B&B	2	Ensuite	£19/£19	€24.13	Dinner	-
B&B	1	Standard	£17/£17	€21.59	Partial Board	-
Single Rate			£23.50/£23.50	€29.84	Child reduction	50%

Killorglin 2km   **Open:** 1st April-31st October

Killorglin

Mrs Catherine Lyons
TORINE HOUSE
Sunhill Road, Killorglin, Ring of Kerry, Co Kerry

Killorglin Ring of Kerry
TEL: **066 9761352**   FAX: **066 9761352**
EMAIL: torinehouse@tinet.ie

Comfortable accommodation. Base for Ring of Kerry, Dingle, Killarney. Golf & Fishing nearby. Tea/Coffee, TV in rooms. Orthopaedic beds. Guide du Routard recommended.

B&B	5	Ensuite	£19/£19	€24.13	Dinner	£15
B&B	1	Standard	£17/£17	€21.59	Partial Board	£185
Single Rate			£25.50/£25.50	€32.38	Child reduction	50%

Open: 1st March-31st October

In Killorglin

Mrs Geraldine Mangan
RIVERSIDE HOUSE
Killorglin, Ring of Kerry, Co Kerry

Killorglin Ring Of Kerry
TEL: **066 9761184**   FAX: **066 9761184**
EMAIL: riversidehousebnb@eircom.net

Comfortable family home, superb view from rooms overlooking river. Golfing, Walking. Ideal touring base. Killarney, Ring/Kerry, Dingle. Information route N70.

B&B	3	Ensuite	£19	€24.13	Dinner	-
B&B	3	Standard	£17	€21.59	Partial Board	-
Single Rate			-	-	Child reduction	50%

Open: 10th March-1st December

In Killorglin

Christina & Jerome O'Regan
O'REGANS COUNTRY HOME & GARDENS
Bansha, Killorglin, Co Kerry

Killorglin Ring of Kerry
TEL: **066 9761200**   TEL: **066 9761200**
EMAIL: jeromeoregan@eircom.net

Luxurious modern home on award winning gardens. Golf, Fishing nearby. Ideal touring base. Home baking. AA◆◆◆ Award. Tea/Coffee facilities. TV, Hairdryer in rooms.

B&B	3	Ensuite	£19/£19.50	€24.13/€24.76	Dinner	£18
B&B	1	Standard	£17/£17.50	€21.59/€22.22	Partial Board	-
Single Rate			£23.50/£25.50	€29.84/€32.38	Child reduction	50%

Open: 1st February-30th November

Killorglin 2km

Jacinta Sheehan
THE FAIRWAYS
Tinnahalla, Killorglin, Co Kerry

Killorglin Ring of Kerry
TEL: **066 9762391**
EMAIL: fairways@gofree.indigo.ie

Luxurious friendly B&B. Refreshments on arrival. Adjacent to Golf course. Tee times arranged. Ideal base for Ring of Kerry/Dingle/Tralee/Killarney.

B&B	4	Ensuite	£19/£20	€24.13/€25.39	Dinner	-
B&B	-	Standard	-	-	Partial Board	-
Single Rate			£25.50/£30	€32.38/€38.09	Child reduction	33.3%

Open: 1st February-30th November

Listowel 2.5km

Mrs Joan Carmody
PALMGROVE HOUSE
Tarbert Rd, Listowel, Co Kerry

Listowel
TEL: **068 21857**
EMAIL: palmgrove@indigo.ie

Comfortable home on Tarbert N69 Car Ferry road. Tarbert Ferry 10 min. Spacious bedrooms, laundry service, Tea/Coffee. Fishing and Golfing nearby. Permits available. Private Car park.

B&B	3	Ensuite	£19	€24.13	Dinner	-
B&B	2	Standard	£17	€21.59	Partial Board	-
Single Rate			£23.50/£25.50	€29.84/€32.38	Child reduction	50%

Open: 1st April-31st October

Mrs Mary Costello
ARAS MHUIRE
**Ballybunion Road, Listowel,
Co Kerry**

Listowel
TEL: **068 21515/23612**
EMAIL: marycos@eircom.net
WEB: http://homepage.eircom.net/~doniec

Near Town Centre on R553 opposite Convent primary school. Ideal for Ballybunion Beach and Golf and Tarbert Car Ferry. Reduction for more than 1 night. Irish Independent recommended.

B&B	4	Ensuite	£19/£25	€24.13/€31.74	Dinner	-
B&B	-	Standard	-	-	Partial Board	-
Single Rate			£25.50/£26	€32.38/€33.01	Child reduction	50%

In Listowel   Ⓥ   cc Ⓢ Ⓟ ⚡️/⛳🍵♿️✕🚴🏊⛵️🎣ℝ   **Open:** All Year

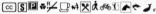

Mrs Carmel Harnett
OAKWOOD
**Cahirdown, Tarbert Road,
Listowel, Co Kerry**

Listowel
TEL: **068 22020**   FAX: **068 22020**

On N69 Tarbert Car Ferry Road. Walking distance to Town. Rooms with TV, Tea facilities, Hairdryers, Electric Blankets. Golf nearby.

B&B	3	Ensuite	£19/£23	€24.13/€29.20	Dinner	-
B&B	1	Standard	£17/£23	€21.59/€29.20	Partial Board	-
Single Rate			£23.50/£26	€29.84/€33.01	Child reduction	50%

Listowel 1km   Ⓥ   cc Ⓟ 🍵♿️🎣ℝ   **Open:** All Year

Mrs Teresa Keane
WHISPERING PINES
**Bedford, Listowel,
Co Kerry**

Listowel
TEL: **068 21503**

Comfort assured in luxurious home in peaceful location on Ballylongford Road. Ballybunion and Listowel Golf Courses, Tarbert Ferry, Beaches 10 mins.

B&B	3	Ensuite	£19/£21	€24.13/€26.66	Dinner	-
B&B	1	Standard	£17/£19	€21.59/€24.13	Partial Board	-
Single Rate			£23.50/£25	€29.84/€31.74	Child reduction	25%

Listowel 1.5km   Ⓥ   Ⓟ♿️🎣ℝ   **Open:** All Year

The Lyons Family
THE HAVEN
**Car Ferry Road, Cahirdown,
Listowel, Co Kerry**

Listowel
TEL: **068 21992**

Purpose built to fire safety standards. Walking distance Town Centre. Breakfast menu, TV, Hairdryers, Tea making facilities in bedrooms. Laundry facilities.

B&B	5	Ensuite	£19	€24.13	Dinner	-
B&B	-	Standard	-	-	Partial Board	-
Single Rate			£25.50	€32.38	Child reduction	50%

In Listowel   Ⓥ   cc Ⓟ♿️🎣ℝ   **Open:** All Year

Vera and John McDermott
Clareville (Skehenerin)
**Tarbert Road, Listowel,
Co Kerry**

Listowel
TEL: **068 23723**   FAX: **068 23723**

Dormer bungalow. Landscaped garden. Situated 2km from Listowel Town. Main N69 Tarbert Ferry Rd. Ferry 15 mins away. Golf, Salmon-Trout fishing nearby.

B&B	4	Ensuite	£19/£20	€24.13/€25.39	Dinner	-
B&B	-	Standard	-	-	Partial Board	-
Single Rate			£25.50/£25.50	€32.38	Child reduction	50%

Listowel 2km   Ⓥ   cc Ⓟ/🍵🚴♿️🎣ℝ   **Open:** 1st January-24th December

---

Mrs Breda Mahony
ASHFORD LODGE
**Tarbert Road, Listowel,
Co Kerry**

Listowel
TEL: **068 21280**
EMAIL: ashfordlodge@unison.ie

On N69 Tarbert Car Ferry road. Nearest B&B to town centre on Tarbert road. Tea/Coffee - TV - Hairdryers all rooms. Private parking. Breakfast choice. Warm welcome.

B&B	3	Ensuite	£19/£20	€24.13/€25.39	Dinner	-
B&B		Standard	£17/£18	€21.59/€22.86	Partial Board	-
Single Rate			£23.50/£25.50	€29.84/€32.38	Child reduction	50%

In Listowel

Open: All Year

Mrs Anne Moloney
GURTENARD HOUSE
Listowel, Co Kerry

Listowel
TEL: **068 21137**   FAX: **068 21206**

Georgian town house, built by Lord Listowel 1801. "Le Guide du Routard" recommended. Adjacent to Town square. Private Parking.

B&B	3	Ensuite	£19	€24.13	Dinner	-
B&B	1	Standard	£17	€21.59	Partial Board	-
Single Rate			£24	€30.47	Child reduction	50%

In Listowel

Open: All Year Except Christmas

Mrs Nancy O'Neill
ASHGROVE HOUSE
**Ballybunion Road, Listowel,
Co Kerry**

Listowel
TEL: **068 21268/23668** FAX: **068 21268**
EMAIL: nancy.oneill@ireland.com
WEB: www.dirl.com/kerry/ashgrove_house

Luxury home near Town R553. Frommer/Sullivan Guide recommended. TV-Tea-Coffee all rooms. Golf - Car Ferry 15 mins. See www.dirl.com

B&B	3	Ensuite	£20/£23	€25.39/€29.20	Dinner	-
B&B	1	Standard	£20/£23	€25.39/€29.20	Partial Board	-
Single Rate			£30/£30	€38.09	Child reduction	33.3%

Listowel 1km

Open: 1st April-31st October

Mrs Monica Quille
NORTH COUNTY HOUSE
**67 Church St, Listowel,
Co Kerry**

Listowel
TEL: **068 21238**

Centre of Town. Luxurious family run home. Convenient to Ballybunion Golf Courses (fee reduction). Tarbert Car Ferry. Ideal touring base.

B&B	6	Ensuite	£19/£23	€24.13/€29.20	Dinner	-
B&B	2	Standard	£17/£21	€21.59/€26.66	Partial Board	-
Single Rate			£23.50/£29	€29.84/€36.82	Child reduction	50%

In Listowel

Open: All Year

Mrs Kathleen Stack
CEOL NA HABHANN
**Tralee Road, Listowel,
Co Kerry**

Listowel
TEL: **068 21345**   FAX: **068 21345**
EMAIL: knstack@eircom.net

Irish National Trust Award Winner. Thatched house on wooded River bank. Frommer Guide. Elsie Dillard recommended. Superior balcony room £25 pps.

B&B	4	Ensuite	£19/£25	€24.13/€31.74	Dinner	-
B&B	-	Standard	-	-	Partial Board	-
Single Rate			£27/£35	€34.29/€44.44	Child reduction	-

Listowel 1km

Open: April-31st October

Mrs Majella Mangan
MANGAN'S COUNTRY HOME
Miltown, Killarney,
Co Kerry

Miltown Killarney
TEL: **066 9767502**   FAX: **066 9767502**
EMAIL: mangansmiltown@eircom.net

Modern comfortable welcoming home. Great location for touring Ring of Kerry, Killarney, Dingle (R563). Enjoy Pubs, Golf, Fishing, Beaches and Horse riding.

B&B	2	Ensuite	£19/£20	€24.13/€25.39	Dinner	-
B&B	1	Standard	£17/£18	€21.59/€22.86	Partial Board	-
Single Rate			£25.50	€32.38	Child reduction	33.3%

Killarney 17km   **Open:** 1st March-31st October

Ms Agnes Shortt
SHORTCLIFF HOUSE
Lyre, Milltown,
Co Kerry

Milltown
TEL: **066 9767106**   FAX: **066 9767106**

Peaceful country location 1km off N70. Ring of Kerry route. Mature gardens, Riding stables on site, Golf 5 mins. Ideal for Golf, Walking, Touring & Horse riding.

B&B	3	Ensuite	£19/£20	€24.13/€25.39	Dinner	-
B&B	-	Standard	-	-	Partial Board	-
Single Rate			£26/£26	€33.01	Child reduction	25%

Milltown 1km   **Open:** 1st April-30th September

Christina Murphy
THE WATERFRONT
Portmagee,
Co Kerry

Portmagee
TEL: **066 9477208**
EMAIL: thewaterfront@eircom.net

At entrance Portmagee village on scenic Skellig Ring near bridge linking Valentia Island to mainland. Adjacent to Skellig Heritage Centre.

B&B	6	Ensuite	£19	€24.13	Dinner	-
B&B	-	Standard	-	-	Partial Board	-
Single Rate			£25.50	€32.38	Child reduction	50%

In Portmagee   **Open:** April-October

Ann Cronin
SNEEM RIVER LODGE
Sneem,
Co Kerry

Sneem Ring of Kerry
TEL: **064 45578**   FAX: **064 45277**
EMAIL: sneemriverlodge@eircom.net

Newly built guesthouse with magnificent mountain views, overlooking Sneem river. Every comfort provided for our guests. Close to all amenities. Private parking.

B&B	4	Ensuite	£19/£19	€24.13	Dinner	£12.50
B&B	-	Standard	-	-	Partial Board	-
Single Rate			£25.50/£25.50	€32.38	Child reduction	50%

In Sneem   **Open:** All Year Except Christmas

Mrs Gretta Drummond
ROCKVILLE HOUSE
Sneem,
Co Kerry

Sneem Ring of Kerry
TEL: **064 45135**

Luxurious dormer bungalow set in private grounds. Kerry Way walking route, Golf, Fishing nearby. Bicycle shed. Breakfast menu.

B&B	4	Ensuite	£19	€24.13	Dinner	-
B&B	-	Standard	-	-	Partial Board	-
Single Rate			£25.50	€32.38	Child reduction	25%

Sneem   **Open:** 1st March-1st November

In Sneem

Mrs Noreen Drummond
BELLVIEW
**Pier Road, Sneem,
Co Kerry**

Tel: **064 45389**

Hospitable, friendly and tranquil residence situated on the Ring Of Kerry. Beaches, Scenic Walks, Fishing, Golfing and Tennis located nearby.

B&B	2	Ensuite	£19	€24.13	Dinner	-
B&B	1	Standard	£18	€22.86	Partial Board	-
Single Rate			£23.50/£25.50	€29.84/€32.38	Child reduction	33.3%

Open: 2nd January-21st December

Sneem 9km

Mrs Helen Foley
HILLSIDE HAVEN
**Doon, Tahilla, Sneem,
Killarney, Co Kerry**

Tel: **064 82065**   Fax: **064 82065**
Email: hillsidehaven@eircom.net

Spacious tastefully decorated bungalow in tranquil location with mature gardens overlooking Kenmare Bay. Caha Mountain adjacent Kerry Way walking route on N70. Sneem/Kenmare Road.

B&B	4	Ensuite	£19/£19	€24.13	Dinner	£14
B&B	-	Standard			Partial Board	£195
Single Rate			£25.50/£25.50	€32.38	Child reduction	25%

Open: 1st March-30th October

In Sneem

Mrs Margaret Harrington
BANK HOUSE
**North Square, Sneem,
Killarney, Co Kerry**

Tel: **064 45226**

Georgian house with antiques and charm situated in the heart of Ireland's most picturesque Village. Frommer and French Guide recommended. Breakfast menu.

B&B	3	Ensuite	£19/£19	€24.13	Dinner	-
B&B	2	Standard	£17	€21.59	Partial Board	-
Single Rate			£25.50/£25.50	€32.38	Child reduction	-

Open: March-November

IRELAND AND THE ENVIRONMENT

Ireland is a beautiful country. Research has shown that people come to Ireland to meet the friendly local people and enjoy our unspoilt natural landscape. We try as much as we can to keep our country clean and "green" and we appreciate your co-operation in this matter.

We love to share this beauty with as many people as we can. Therefore it is in all our interests to maintain and enhance the natural splendour that Ireland is lucky enough to enjoy. Respect for natural amenities is essential in order to sustain this beautiful, unspoilt environment. By leaving the places we visit tidy we can all do our bit to help, thus ensuring that future generations will come to visit a naturally green Ireland too.

Mrs Maura Hussey
AVONLEA HOUSE
Sportsfield Road, Sneem,
Ring of Kerry, Co Kerry

Sneem Ring of Kerry
Tel: **064 45221**
Web: www.sneem/com/avonlea

Perfect location, secluded spot beside village. Signposted. Mountain/Woodland surroundings.
Frommer, Dillard/Causin, Routard recommended. Walks, Golf, Fishing, Restaurants/Pubs.

B&B	4	Ensuite	£19	€24.13	Dinner	-
B&B	1	Standard	-	-	Partial Board	-
Single Rate			£23.50/£25	€29.84/€31.74	Child reduction	-

In Sneem

Open: April-October

Mrs Alice O'Sullivan
OLD CONVENT HOUSE
(Woodvale), Pier Road,
Sneem, Co Kerry

Sneem Ring of Kerry
Tel: **064 45181**   Fax: **064 45181**
Email: conventhouse@oceanfree.net

Old world stone house uniquely situated private grounds overlooking Estuary, Mountains. Access to
Fishing River. Numerous recommendations. Walking enthusiasts.

B&B	6	Ensuite	£20	€25.39	Dinner	-
B&B	-	Standard	-	-	Partial Board	-
Single Rate			-	-	Child reduction	25%

In Sneem

Open: All Year Except Christmas

Mrs Phil Walsh
OAKHAVEN
Sallowglen, Tarbert,
Co Kerry

Tarbert
Tel: **068 43208**   Fax: **068 43208**
Email: oakhaven@unison.ie
Web: www.oakhavenhouse.com

Situated in peaceful scenic surroundings on R551. Tarbert Car Ferry, Tarbert Woodland walk.
Ballybunion Golf and Beach, Angling, Bird watching, Horse riding. Warm welcome assured.

B&B	2	Ensuite	£19/£20	€24.13/€25.39	Dinner	-
B&B	1	Standard	£17/£18	€21.59/€22.86	Partial Board	-
Single Rate			-	-	Child reduction	50%

Tarbert 6km

Open: 1st April-31st October

Mrs Marion Barry
THE FAIRWAYS
Kerries, Fenit Road,
Tralee, Co Kerry

Tralee
Tel: **066 7127691**   Fax: **066 7127691**
Email: fairways@tinet.ie

Luxurious home, quiet peaceful location off R558. Tralee/Fenit Road. Views of Tralee
Bay/Mountains. Nearby Tralee Golf Club, Restaurants. Ideal Golf/Touring base.

B&B	4	Ensuite	£19	€24.13	Dinner	-
B&B	-	Standard	-	-	Partial Board	-
Single Rate			£25.50	€32.38	Child reduction	50%

Tralee 2km

Open: April-October

Mrs Patricia Canning
BRICRIU
20 Old Golf Links Road,
Oakpark, Tralee, Co Kerry

Tralee
Tel: **066 7126347**

Quiet area off N69 pass Railway. Take 1st right, left, right again (10 mins walk). Adjacent Sports
Complex. Convenient Golf, Beaches.

B&B	3	Ensuite	£19	€24.13	Dinner	£12.50
B&B	-	Standard	-	-	Partial Board	-
Single Rate			£25.50	€32.38	Child reduction	25%

In Tralee

Open: June-October

Hazel Costello
ARDROE HOUSE
**Oakpark Road, Tralee,
Co Kerry**

Tralee
TEL: **066 7126050**

Period town house on N69. 5 minutes walk Bus/Train depot. Close to beach, golf, mountains and all local amenities. Ideal touring base. Recommended by Rough Guide To Ireland.

B&B	2	Ensuite	£19/£20	€24.13/€25.39	Dinner -
B&B	2	Standard	£17	€21.59	Partial Board -
Single Rate			-	-	Child reduction 50%

Open: May-September

In Tralee

Mrs Eileen Curley
MOUNTAIN VIEW HOUSE
**Ballinorig West, Tralee,
Co Kerry**

Tralee
TEL: **066 7122226**

Own grounds. Close all amenities. Ideal Golf/Touring base. Approaching Tralee on N21, turn right just before roundabout. Frommer recommended.

B&B	3	Ensuite	£19	€24.13	Dinner -
B&B	1	Standard	£17	€21.59	Partial Board -
Single Rate			£23.50/£25.50	€29.84/€32.38	Child reduction 25%

Open: 1st April-31st October

Tralee 2km

Mrs Gail Daly
ASHDALE
**Fenit Road, Tralee,
Co Kerry**

Tralee Fenit Road
TEL: **066 7128927**   FAX: **066 7128927**
EMAIL: gaildaly@eircom.net
WEB: www.ashdalehouse.com

Frommer recommended. Luxurious home on R558 overlooking Slieve Mish Mountains. Enroute to Tralee Golf club. Excellent Restaurants nearby - Ideal Touring base.

B&B	3	Ensuite	£19/£24	€24.13/€30.47	Dinner -
B&B	-	Standard			Partial Board -
Single Rate			£25.50/£30.50	€32.38/€38.73	Child reduction 33.3%

Open: 15th March-1st November

Tralee 2km

Mrs Gertie Deady
GURRANE
**50 Derrylea, Tralee,
Co Kerry**

Tralee
TEL: **066 7124734**

Modern two storey house on N69 Listowel Tarbert Car Ferry road. Convenient to Rail, Bus, Town, Golf, Greyhound Track, Hotel, Restaurant, Sports complex.

B&B	2	Ensuite	£19/£19	€24.13	Dinner £12.50
B&B	2	Standard	£17/£17	€21.59	Partial Board -
Single Rate			£23.50/£23.50	€29.84	Child reduction -

Open: 6th January-23rd December

Tralee 1.5km

Mrs Hannah Devane
EASTCOTE
**34 Oakpark Demesne,
Tralee, Co Kerry**

Tralee
TEL: **066 7125942**

Select accommodation in peaceful location. All facilities in rooms. Ideal touring base. 200 metres off N69 route, Tarbert Car ferry road. Warm welcome.

B&B	2	Ensuite	£19	€24.13	Dinner -
B&B	1	Standard	£17	€21.59	Partial Board -
Single Rate			£23.50/£25.50	€29.84/€32.38	Child reduction -

Open: 1st January-20th December

Tralee 1km

Mrs Maura Dowling
LEESIDE
**Oakpark, Tralee,
Co Kerry**

In Tralee

Tralee
TEL: **066 7126475**   FAX: 066 7126475
EMAIL: dowlingsbandb@hotmail.com

On N69 Ferry route. Near Bus/Rail. Antique Irish Furniture recommended. Lets Go Ireland 2000. Orthopaedic beds. TV's, Power showers. Breakfast menu, Home baking. Tea/Coffee facilities.

B&B	3	Ensuite	£19/£19	€24.13		Dinner	-
B&B	-	Standard	-	-		Partial Board	-
Single Rate			£25.50/£25.50	€32.38		Child reduction	25%

Open: 1st March-30th November

Mrs K Dunne
OAKDENE
**53 Derrylea, Oakpark Road,
Tralee, Co Kerry**

Tralee 1.5km

Tralee
TEL: **066 7125934**

Situated on Tralee/Listowel Road N69. Convenient to Train, Bus, Airport, Pitch & Putt, Golf, Beaches.

B&B	3	Ensuite	£19	€24.13		Dinner	-
B&B	1	Standard	£17	€21.59		Partial Board	-
Single Rate			£23.50/£25.50	€29.84/€32.38		Child reduction	25%

Open: 7th January-17th December

Mrs Noreen Galvin
WEST SEVEN
**Tonevane, Blennerville,
Tralee, Co Kerry**

Tralee 3km

Tralee Dingle Road Area
TEL: **066 7129932**

Country Home on N86. Breathtaking view of Mountains. 5 minutes walk to village. Old Ship Canal, Steam Train, Horse riding, Golf, Aqua Dome, Siamsa, Theatre, Beach, Tea/Coffee at all times.

B&B	3	Ensuite	£19/£19	€24.13		Dinner	-
B&B	-	Standard	-	-		Partial Board	-
Single Rate			£25.50/£25.50	€32.38		Child reduction	33.3%

Open: 31st March-31st October

Mrs Ann Gleeson
ROSEDALE LODGE
**Oakpark Road, Tralee,
Co Kerry**

In Tralee

Tralee
TEL: **066 7125320**

On N69 Listowel (Car Ferry) Road. Luxury accommodation. Spacious bedrooms. Excellent Beaches & Restaurants nearby. Personal supervision.

B&B	3	Ensuite	£19/£20	€24.13/€25.39		Dinner	-
B&B	-	Standard	-	-		Partial Board	-
Single Rate			£25.50	€32.38		Child reduction	-

Open: March-November

Mrs Catherine Gleeson
BROOKDALE
**Castlemaine Rd, Tralee,
Co Kerry**

Tralee 1km

Tralee
TEL: **066 7125063**

Dormer bungalow on Killorglin/Ring of Kerry Rd (N70). Ideally located for Beaches, Golf, Fishing and Horse Riding. Complimentary Tea/Coffee. TV in all rooms.

B&B	3	Ensuite	£19/£19	€24.13		Dinner	-
B&B	-	Standard	-	-		Partial Board	-
Single Rate			£25.50/£25.50	€32.38		Child reduction	25%

Open: 1st May-1st October

Mrs Mary Hannafin
SHANGRI-LA
The Spa, Tralee,
Co Kerry

Tralee Fenit Road Area
TEL: **066 7136214**

Secluded country residence overlooking Tralee Bay. Walk to Beach, Pub & Restaurant. Golf Courses nearby. Ideal Golfing/Touring base. Walking route locally. On R558.

B&B	3	Ensuite	£19	€24.13	Dinner	£12.50
B&B	2	Standard	£17	€21.59	Partial Board	-
Single Rate			£23.50	€29.84	Child reduction	25%

Tralee 4km

Open: 31st January-31st November

Mrs Mary Healy
ASHMOOR
Mounthawk, Caherslee,
Tralee, Co Kerry

Tralee
TEL: **066 7124471**
EMAIL: ashmoor@eircom.net

Warm hospitality in comfortable home. 10 min walk town centre. Ideal touring base, with Golf, Sailing, Beaches, excellent Restaurants nearby. Before R558. TV, Tea/Coffee in bedrooms.

B&B	2	Ensuite	£19	€24.13	Dinner	-
B&B	1	Standard	-	-	Partial Board	-
Single Rate			£27	€34.29	Child reduction	40%

Tralee 1km

Open: April-October

Mrs Sheila Horgan
ALVERNA
26 Liosdara, Oakpark,
Tralee, Co Kerry

Tralee
TEL: **066 7126970**

Off N69. First turn right after Swimming pool and Sports Centre. Fourth house on left. Convenient to many Golf clubs. 10 mins walk Town Centre, 5 mins walk Railway/Bus depot.

B&B	2	Ensuite	£19/£22	€24.13/€27.93	Dinner	-
B&B	2	Standard	£17/£20	€21.59/€25.39	Partial Board	-
Single Rate			£23.50/£25	€29.84/€31.74	Child reduction	50%

Tralee 1km

Open: 7th January-22nd December

BOOKINGS

We recommend your first and last night is pre-booked. Your hosts will make a booking for you at your next selected home for the cost of the phone call. When travelling in high season (June, July, August), it is essential to pre-book your accommodation – preferably the evening before, or the following morning to avoid disappointment.

> **WHEN TRAVELLING OFF-SEASON IT IS ADVISABLE TO CALL AHEAD AND GIVE A TIME OF ARRIVAL TO ENSURE YOUR HOSTS ARE AT HOME TO GREET YOU.**

Mrs Jane Hurley
SINEADS
**Lios Carraig Court, Caherslee,
Tralee, Co Kerry**

Tralee
Tel: **066 7123500**   Fax: **066 7123500**

A warm welcome awaits you at Sineads. Ideal Touring/Golfing base. Excellent Beaches and Restaurants nearby. Power showers. Complimentary Tea/Coffee.

B&B	3	Ensuite	£19/£22	€24.13/€27.93	Dinner	-
B&B	-	Standard	-	-	Partial Board	-
Single Rate			£25.50/£30	€32.38/€38.09	Child reduction	25%

In Tralee

Open: March-October

Mrs Sheila Kerins
BALLINGOWAN HOUSE
**Mile Height, Killarney Road,
Tralee, Co Kerry**

Tralee Killarney Road Area
Tel: **066 7127150**   Fax: **066 7120325**
Email: ballingowan@eircom.net

All rooms with TV, Tea/Coffee facilities. Private parking. Approaching Tralee on N21/N22 on left before McDonalds.

B&B	4	Ensuite	£19/£19	€24.13	Dinner	-
B&B	-	Standard	-	-	Partial Board	-
Single Rate			£25.50/£25.50	€32.38	Child reduction	33.3%

Tralee 1km

Open: 1st April-30th September

Mrs Eileen Lynch
ST ENDAS
**Oakpark, Tralee,
Co Kerry**

Tralee
Tel: **066 7126494**   Fax: **066 7126494**

Town house convenient Sports Complex, Aqua Dome, Golf, Beaches, Greyhound Racing. 5 mins Bus and Train Depot. Private parking. Ideal touring base. N69.

B&B	4	Ensuite	£19/£19	€24.13	Dinner	-
B&B	-	Standard	-	-	Partial Board	-
Single Rate			£25.50	€32.38	Child reduction	50%

In Tralee

Open: 1st January-12th December

Helen Lyons
KNOCKBRACK
**Oakpark Road, Tralee,
Co Kerry**

Tralee
Tel: **066 7127375**
Email: knockbrackguests@eircom.net
Web: www.dirl.com/kerry/knockbrack.htm

Family home in residential area. Convenient to town centre. TV in bedrooms. Tea making facilities. Private parking. Situated on Listowel (Car Ferry) road N69.

B&B	3	Ensuite	£19/£22	€24.13/€27.93	Dinner	-
B&B	-	Standard	-	-	Partial Board	-
Single Rate			£25.50/£28	€32.38/€35.55	Child reduction	25%

In Tralee

Open: 17th March-31st October

Mrs Juliette O'Callaghan
GREEN GABLES
**1 Clonmore Villas, Ballymullen
Road, Tralee, Co Kerry**

Tralee
Tel: **066 7123354**   Fax: **066 7123354**

Listed Victorian period town house. Town Centre location adjacent County Library, Town park, on N70. 5 min walk Bus/Train station.

B&B	3	Ensuite	£19/£20	€24.13/€25.39	Dinner	-
B&B	1	Standard	£17/£19	€21.59/€24.13	Partial Board	-
Single Rate			£25/£26	€31.74/€33.01	Child reduction	-

In Tralee

Open: 1st February-15th December

Tralee 1km

Mrs Noreen O'Callaghan
ST ANNE'S
**11 Caherwisheen, Ballyard,
Tralee, Co Kerry**

TEL: 066 7122029

Spacious peaceful home 400 metres off Dingle/Ring of Kerry (N70). 3 mins drive Town Centre. TV, Tea/coffee making facilities.

B&B	4	Ensuite	£19/£20	€24.13/€25.39	Dinner	-
B&B	1	Standard	£17/£17	€21.59	Partial Board	-
Single Rate			£23.50/£25.50	€29.84/€32.38	Child reduction	25%

Open: March-November

Tralee 2km

Mrs Rose O'Connell
BARNAKYLE
**Clogherbrien, Tralee,
Co Kerry**

TEL: 066 7125048   FAX: 066 7181259
EMAIL: barnakyl@iol.ie

Situated on R551 Ardfert/Ballyheigue Road. Convenient to Beaches, Sailing, Horse-Riding, Golf, Siamsa Tire, Aqua Dome, Caves and Restaurants.

B&B	5	Ensuite	£19/£20	€24.13/€25.39	Dinner	-
B&B	-	Standard	-	-	Partial Board	-
Single Rate			£25.50	€32.38	Child reduction	50%

Open: 1st April-31st October

Tralee 1km

Mrs Joan O'Connor
SKEHANAGH LODGE
**Skehanagh,
Castlemaine Road,
Tralee, Co Kerry**

TEL: 066 7124782   FAX: 066 7124782

Bright spacious comfortable bungalow on Killorglin/Ring of Kerry road N70. Tea/Coffee facilities, TV in bedrooms. Guide de Routard recommended. Two large family rooms. Touring base.

B&B	4	Ensuite	£19/£20	€24.13/€25.39	Dinner	-
B&B	1	Standard	£17/£17	€21.59	Partial Board	-
Single Rate			£23.50/£25.50	€29.84/€32.38	Child reduction	25%

Open: 1st April-1st November

In Tralee

Philomena O'Connor
ROSELAWN LODGE
**Rathass, Tralee,
Co Kerry**

TEL: 066 7124875

Comfortable suburban bungalow, spacious car park. Central base for touring Kerry. Convenient to all tourist attractions. Situated on N21.

B&B	4	Ensuite	£19	€24.13	Dinner	-
B&B	-	Standard	-	-	Partial Board	-
Single Rate			£25.50	€32.38	Child reduction	25%

Open: 1st January-20th December

Blennerville

Ita O'Donnell
AHAROE
**Blennerville, Tralee,
Co Kerry**

TEL: 066 7123108

1 mile from Tralee towards Dingle. Right turn at T junction onto Swing bridge over canal. Quiet location. Overlooking Blennerville Village, Windmill, Steam Train, Old Ship Canal.

B&B	4	Ensuite	£19/£19	€24.13	Dinner	-
B&B	-	Standard	-	-	Partial Board	-
Single Rate			£23.50	€29.84	Child reduction	-

Open: March-October

Rose O'Keeffe
ASHVILLE HOUSE
Ballyard, Tralee,
Co Kerry

Tralee Ballyard
TEL: **066 7123717**   FAX: **066 7123898**
EMAIL: ashville@eircom.net

Architect designed, country setting off Dingle Road (N86). Tralee 2 minutes drive, TV, Hairdryers, Power Showers, Breakfast Menu, Drying Room.

					Dinner	-
B&B	6	Ensuite	£20/£21	€25.39/€26.66		
B&B	-	Standard	-		Partial Board	-
Single Rate			£25.50/£26.50	€32.38/€33.65	Child reduction	-

Tralee 1km

Open: All Year

Mrs Mary O'Neill
BEECH GROVE
Oakpark, Tralee,
Co Kerry

Tralee
TEL: **066 7126788**   FAX: **066 7180971**

On Car Ferry Rd N69. Near Railway/Bus Station, Sports Complex, Town Centre. Secure car park. Siamsa tickets. Tours arranged.

					Dinner	-
B&B	3	Ensuite	£19	€24.13		
B&B	1	Standard	£17	€21.59	Partial Board	-
Single Rate			£23.50/£25.50	€29.84/€32.38	Child reduction	50%

Tralee 1km

Open: All Year Except Christmas

Mrs Helen O'Shea
CLUAIN MOR HOUSE
Boherbee, Tralee,
Co Kerry

Tralee
TEL: **066 7125545**

On 1 acre garden. 5 mins Rail Station, Aqua Dome. Golf, Angling, Beaches 5 miles. Kerry Airport 20 mins. 5 mins walk to Tralee Town. Private Car parking.

					Dinner	-
B&B	5	Ensuite	£19	€24.13		
B&B	-	Standard	£17	€21.59	Partial Board	-
Single Rate			£25.50	€32.38	Child reduction	25%

In Tralee

Open: 1st January-20th December

Mrs Catherine O'Sullivan
MARINA LODGE
Cloherbrien, Tralee,
Co Kerry

Tralee
TEL: **066 7123565**

Warm welcome awaits you. Family run B&B. Scenic location. Complimentary Tea/Coffee. Golf, Seafood Restaurants nearby. Private parking. Tours arranged.

					Dinner	-
B&B	4	Ensuite	£19/£20	€24.13/€25.39		
B&B	-	Standard	-		Partial Board	-
Single Rate			£25.50/£25.50	€32.38	Child reduction	25%

Tralee 2.5km

Open: 1st March-30th September

Mrs Lena O'Sullivan
KNOCKANISH HOUSE
The Spa, Tralee, Co Kerry

Tralee Fenit Road Area
TEL: **066 7136268**

Luxurious home overlooking Tralee Bay. Golfing groups welcome. Nearby Tralee 18 hole Golf Course, Restaurants & Beaches. Ideal Golfing/Touring base.

					Dinner	-
B&B	5	Ensuite	£20/£25	€25.39/€31.74		
B&B	-	Standard	-		Partial Board	-
Single Rate			£30/£35	€38.09/€44.44	Child reduction	-

Tralee 3km

Open: April-1st November

In Tralee

Mrs Colette Quinn
VILLA DE LOURDES
**Brewery Road, Oakview,
Tralee, Co Kerry**

Tralee
Tel: **066 7126278**

Modern house opposite Greyhound Track, convenient to Rail/Bus station, Town Centre, Churches & Sports Complex.

B&B	-	Ensuite	-	-	Dinner	-
B&B	4	Standard	£17/£17	€21.59	Partial Board	-
Single Rate			£23.50/£23.50	€29.84	Child reduction	-

Open: 1st February-30th October

Blennerville 1.5km

Mrs Margaret Ryle
CRANA-LI
**Curragraigue, Blennerville,
Tralee, Co Kerry**

Tralee Dingle Road Area
Tel: **066 7124467**
Email: cranali@eircom.net

Looking for a quiet and scenic place? B&B off N86 at Blennerville. Gateway to Dingle/Ring of Kerry. Landscaped gardens - Nature at its best! Only 5 mins from Tralee.

B&B	2	Ensuite	£19	€24.13	Dinner	-
B&B	2	Standard	£17	€21.59	Partial Board	-
Single Rate			-	-	Child reduction	25%

Open: 1st May-30th September

Tralee 1.5km

Mrs Joan Smith
BRIANVILLE
**Clogherbrien, Fenit Road Area,
Tralee, Co Kerry**

Tralee Fenit Road Area
Tel: **066 7126645**   Fax: **066 7126645**
Email: michsmit@gofree.indigo.ie

Luxurious bungalow. AA ♦♦♦♦. Frommer guide recommended, Best B&B in Ireland. Tea/Coffee, Hairdryers, TV in rooms, all on ground floor. 18 hole Golf Links. Seafood Restaurants nearby.

B&B	5	Ensuite	£20/£25	€25.39/€31.74	Dinner	-
B&B	-	Standard	-	-	Partial Board	-
Single Rate			-	-	Child reduction	50%

Open: All Year

Tralee 3km

Paddy & Deirdre Stack
WOODBROOK HOUSE
**Laharn, Listowel Road(N69),
Tralee, Co Kerry**

Tralee
Tel: **066 7180078**
Email: woodbrookhouse@esatclear.ie
Web: www.esatclear.ie/~woodbrookhouse

Luxurious hillside residence with breathtaking views of Slieve Mish Mountains. Ideal base for Touring, Golfing, Hillwalking with excellent restaurants nearby. Groundfloor rooms.

B&B	4	Ensuite	£20/£25	€25.39/€31.74	Dinner	-
B&B	-	Standard	-	-	Partial Board	-
Single Rate			£25.50/£30	€32.38/€38.09	Child reduction	33.3%

Open: All Year

In Tralee

Tim & Mary Walshe
THE WILLOWS
**5 Clonmore Terrace, Moyderwell,
Tralee, Co Kerry**

Tralee
Tel: **066 7123779**   Fax: **066 7123779**
Email: thewillows2@eircom.net

Friendly Victorian townhouse - Olde world charm - On N70. 5 mins walk Town/Bus/Train. Breakfast menu. TV, Tea/Coffee, Hairdryers in rooms. Ideal touring base.

B&B	3	Ensuite	£19/£20	€24.13/€25.39	Dinner	-
B&B	1	Standard	£18/£19	€22.86/€24.13	Partial Board	-
Single Rate			£23.50/£25	€29.84/€31.74	Child reduction	50%

Open: 22nd January-22nd December

Mary Lane
SHEALANE COUNTRY HOUSE
Corha-Mor, Valentia Island,
Co Kerry

Valentia Island
TEL: **066 9476354**
EMAIL: marylane@eircom.net
WEB: www.kerryweb

Peaceful setting on Road bridge entrance adjacent to Skellig Experience Centre. Skellig trips, Fishing, Walking arranged. Restaurants, Traditional music nearby.

B&B	3	Ensuite	£20/£25	€25.39/€31.74	Dinner	-
B&B	-	Standard	-	-	Partial Board	-
Single Rate			£25.50/£30	€32.38/€38.09	Child reduction	25%

Portmagee 1km

Open: 1st March-1st November

Mrs Julie O'Sullivan
GLENREEN HEIGHTS
Knightstown Road,
Valentia Island, Co Kerry

Valentia Island
TEL: **066 9476241**   FAX: **066 9476241**
EMAIL: glenreen@eircom.net

Spectacular view Sea/Mountains. Orthopaedic beds. Breakfast Menu, local Seafood. Scenic walks, Pitch & Putt, Fishing and trips to Skellig arranged.

B&B	2	Ensuite	£19	€24.13	Dinner	£13
B&B	1	Standard	£17	€21.59	Partial Board	£185
Single Rate			£23.50	€29.84	Child reduction	50%

Knightstown 2km

Open: 1st February-1st November

Mrs Breda Barry
GOLF LINKS VIEW
Murreigh, Waterville,
Co Kerry

Waterville
TEL: **066 9474623**   FAX: **066 9474623**
EMAIL: jbar@eircom.net
WEB: homepage.eircom.net/~golflinksview/

AA ♦♦♦ recommended, luxury home downstairs bedrooms. Power showers, Hairdryers, TV, open peat fire. Golf Course, Fishing, Horse Riding, Beach, trips to Skelligs.

B&B	6	Ensuite	£19	€24.13	Dinner	£13
B&B	-	Standard	-	-	Partial Board	£195
Single Rate			£25.50	€32.38	Child reduction	25%

Waterville 1km

Open: 1st March-31st October

Ms Margaret Brown
OLD CABLE HOUSE
Cable Station, Waterville,
Co Kerry

Waterville
TEL: **066 9474233**   FAX: **066 9474869**
EMAIL: mbrownn@iol.ie
WEB: www.old-cable-house.com

Interesting stay, Century Old House/Milestone Site. Origins - First Transatlantic Telegraph Cable (1856). Rooms of character. Waterville Golf Links, Free Salmon Trout Fishing Lough Currane.

B&B	4	Ensuite	£19/£36	€24.13/€45.71	Dinner	-
B&B	2	Standard	£17/£26	€21.59/€33.01	Partial Board	-
Single Rate			£26/£45	€33.01/€57.14	Child reduction	25%

In Waterville

Open: All Year Except Christmas

Mrs Abbie Clifford
CLIFFORDS B&B
Waterville,
Co Kerry

Waterville
TEL: **066 9474283**   FAX: **066 9474283**

Comfortable home in Waterville village, southern end. Overlooking the Atlantic Ocean. Restaurants, Pubs, Shops walking distance. Private parking.

B&B	5	Ensuite	£19/£20	€24.13/€25.39	Dinner	-
B&B	2	Standard	£17/£19	€21.59/€24.13	Partial Board	-
Single Rate			£25.50	€32.38	Child reduction	25%

In Waterville

Open: 1st March-30th November

Waterville 4km

Mrs Patricia Curran
ATLANTIC VIEW
Toor, Waterville,
Co Kerry

Waterville

TEL: **066 9474335**   FAX: **066 9474335**
EMAIL: joecurranelect@tinet.ie

Family run country home overlooking picturesque Ballinskelligs Bay and the Atlantic Ocean. Enjoy quiet country walks. Fishing, Golf, Horseriding locally.

B&B	3	Ensuite	£19/£21	€24.13/€26.66	Dinner	-
B&B	1	Standard	£17	€21.59	Partial Board	-
Single Rate			£23.50	€32.38	Child reduction	-

Open: May-September

In Waterville

Mrs Angela Grady
O'GRADYS TOWNHOUSE
Spunkane, Waterville, Co Kerry

Waterville

TEL: **066 9474350**   FAX: **066 9474730**
EMAIL: angelao@eircom.net
WEB: www.stayatogradys.com

Ideally located B&B. Close to all amenities, Golf, Fishing, trips to Skellig Rock arranged. Spacious ensuite rooms, Visitors lounge, Breakfast Menu.

B&B	6	Ensuite	£19	€24.13	Dinner	-
B&B	-	Standard	-	-	Partial Board	-
Single Rate			£25.50	€32.38	Child reduction	25%

Open: 1st March-31st October

Mrs Cirean Morris
KLONDYKE HOUSE
New Line Road, Waterville,
Co Kerry

Waterville

TEL: **066 9474119**   FAX: **066 9474666**
EMAIL: klondykehouse@eircom.net
WEB: homepage.eircom.net/~klondykehouse

Luxurious home on Ring of Kerry road N70. Bedrooms with satellite TV, Direct dial phones, Power showers. Skellig trips/Golf arranged. Baggage transfers.

B&B	5	Ensuite	£19	€24.13	Dinner	-
B&B	1	Standard	£17	€21.59	Partial Board	-
Single Rate			£23.50/£25.50	€29.84/€32.38	Child reduction	25%

In Waterville   **Open:** All Year Except Christmas

In Waterville

Nora Murphy
ASHLING HOUSE
Main Street, Waterville,
Co Kerry

Waterville

TEL: **066 9474247**

Modern two-storey house situated on Main street overlooking Ballinskellig Bay. Sandy Beaches, Golf, Fishing, Trips to Skellig Rock, Mountain climbing.

B&B	4	Ensuite	£19/£19	€24.13	Dinner	-
B&B	1	Standard	£17/£17	€21.59	Partial Board	-
Single Rate			£23.50/£25	€29.84/€31.74	Child reduction	25%

Open: 13th March-15th October

TELEPHONE

- Operator assisted calls within Ireland   Dial 10
- International telephone operator   Dial 11818
- Directory Enquiries   Dial 11811

FOR TROUBLE-FREE TELEPHONE CALLS FROM PUBLIC PAY PHONES IT IS ADVISABLE TO PURCHASE A TELEPHONE CALLCARD AVAILABLE IN POST OFFICES AND WHEREVER YOU SEE A CALLCARD SIGN.
TO DIAL IRELAND FROM ABROAD: Country Access Code + 353 + Area Code (omit first zero) + Local Number

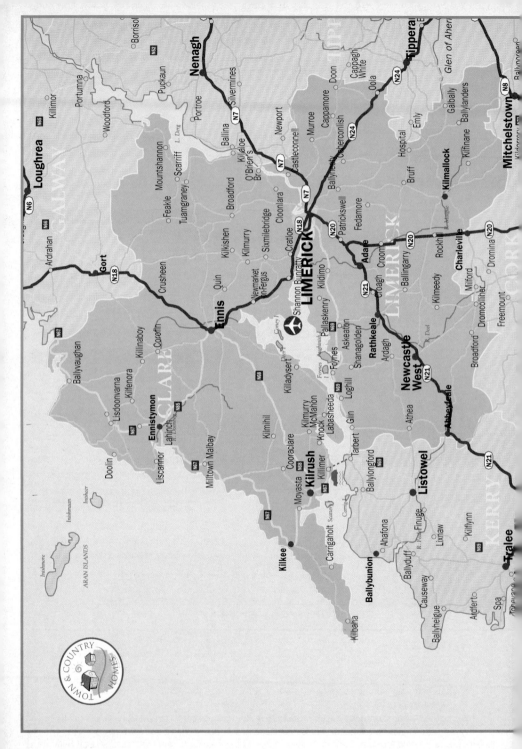

Ireland's Shannonside

The Shannon Region comprise counties Clare Limerick, North Tipperary, North Kerry and South Offaly. It is a particularly beautiful part of Ireland and is dominated by water. The Shannon river, the longest river in Ireland or the UK flows through its centre and gives the Region its name. Shannon's Lough Derg - Ireland's pleasure lake - touches on three counties, Clare, Tipperary and Galway. The Region also boasts hundreds of smaller lakes and many rivers.

The Shannon Region has a dramatic Atlantic coastline, with beautiful beaches and a purity of air that refreshes the Region and invigorates the visitor.

Though the Shannon Region is compact, only 100 miles (166 Kms), from end to end, there is tremendous diversity in its scenery from the Slieve Bloom mountains to lakelands, golden beaches, the awesome Cliffs of Moher and the Burren District.

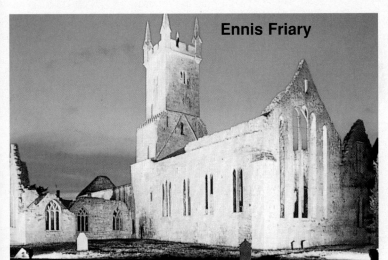

Ennis Friary

The Region offers great visitor attractions and night-time entertainment options and is also perfect for the activity enthusiast interested in Golfing, Angling, Horse Riding, Walking, Cycling or water based activities.

Area Representatives

Clare
Mrs Bernie Cosgrove, St Judes, Coast Road, Lisdoonvarna,
Tel: 065 7074108
Mr Sean Grogan, St Patricks, Corebeg, Doora, Ennis, Co Clare
Tel: 065 6840122 Fax: 065 6840122
Mrs Teresa Petty, Sunville, Off Doolin Road, Lisdoonvarna, Co.
Clare. Tel: 065 7074065 Fax: 065 7074065

Limerick
Mrs Mary Dundon, Acacia Cottage, 2 Foxfield, Dooradoyle Road,
Dooradoyle, Limerick, Co Limerick
Tel: 061 304757 Fax: 061 304757
Mrs Joan McSweeney, Trebor, Ennis Road, Limerick City,
Co Limerick Tel: 061 454632 Fax: 061 454632

 ## Tourist Information Offices

Ennis
Arthurs Road
Tel: 065 6828366

Limerick City
Arthur's Quay
Tel: 061 317522

Tralee
Ashe Hall
Denny Street
Tel: 066 7121288

Shannon Airport
Arrivals Hall
Tel: 061 471664

Clare is renowned for traditional music, its rugged beauty with Shannon Airport at its gateway.
Attractions: Bunratty Folk Park, Ennis, The famous Burren, Cliffs of Moher, Lisdoonvarna Spa Wells & Doolin. Championship Golf at Lahinch. Great fishing, excellent beaches, walks & trails.

Ballyvaughan

Hilde & Donal O'Connell
COOLSHINE B&B
**Green Road, Ballyvaughan,
Co Clare**

Ballyvaughan
TEL: **065 7077163**
EMAIL: dburren@eircom.net
WEB: homepage.eircom.net/~dburren

Beautiful, quiet, friendly home. 0.1km off Galway Road. Maps & Books for your use. German & French spoken. Organic homemade bread & jams. Family & 3 bedded room.

B&B	3	Ensuite	£19/£20	€24.13/€25.39	Dinner	-
B&B	-	Standard		-	Partial Board	-
Single Rate			£30/£35	€38.09/€44.44	Child reduction	33.3%

Open: 16th March-30th October

Bunratty 1km

Mairead Bateman
PARK HOUSE
**Low Road, Bunratty,
Co Clare**

Bunratty
TEL: **061 369902** FAX: **061 369903**
EMAIL: parkhouse@eircom.net
WEB: homepage.eircom.net/~parkhouse

Luxurious peaceful home. Full menu. Home baking. Afternoon tea. Bunratty Castle 1km. Airport 10 minutes drive. Orthopaedic beds, TV, Tea/Coffee, Curling tongs, Hairdryer. AA ♦♦♦

B&B	6	Ensuite	£22/£22	€27.93	Dinner	-
B&B	-	Standard		-	Partial Board	-
Single Rate			£30/£30	€38.09	Child reduction	25%

Open: 1st February-15th December

Bunratty

Mrs Mary Browne
BUNRATTY LODGE
**Bunratty,
Co Clare**

Bunratty
TEL: **061 369402** FAX: **061 369363**
EMAIL: reservations@bunrattylodge.com
WEB: www.bunrattylodge.com

Luxurious, well heated rooms on ground floor with every convenience. Award winning breakfast. Recommended by all leading guides. Airport 10 minutes.

B&B	6	Ensuite	£25	€31.74	Dinner	-
B&B	-	Standard	-	-	Partial Board	-
Single Rate			-	-	Child reduction	-

Open: March-November

Shannon 6km

Mrs Jackie Burns
BUNRATTY VILLA
**Bunratty East,
Co Clare**

Bunratty
TEL: **061 369241** FAX: **061 369947**
EMAIL: bunrattyvilla@eircom.net

First house on the right on the road between Durty Nelly's/Castle. TV's, Hairdryers, Clock Radios all rooms. Guest Lounge.

B&B	6	Ensuite	£20/£22.50	€25.39/€28.57	Dinner	-
B&B	-	Standard		-	Partial Board	-
Single Rate			£30/£35	€38.09/€44.44	Child reduction	25%

Open: February-November

Mrs Trish Cronin
BRIAR LODGE
Hill Road, Bunratty,
Co Clare

Bunratty
TEL: **061 363388**   FAX: **061 363161**
EMAIL: briarlodge@eircom.net
WEB: www.bb-house.com/briarlodge.htm

Turn left at corner Fitzpatricks Hotel, 1 mile on right. Tea/Coffee, Hairdryers, Curling Irons all rooms. Guest lounge. Breakfast menu. AM arrivals welcome.

					Dinner	-
B&B	6	Ensuite	£19/£20	€24.13/€25.39	Dinner	-
B&B	-	Standard	-	-	Partial Board	-
Single Rate			£28/£30	€35.55/€38.09	Child reduction	25%

Bunratty 1.5km   **Open:** 1st March-31st October

Mrs Patricia Darcy
BUNRATTY HEIGHTS
Low Road, Bunratty,
Co Clare

Bunratty
TEL: **061 369324**   FAX: **061 369324**
EMAIL: bunrattyheights@eircom.net
WEB: www.bb-house.com/bunrattyheights.htm

Morning guests welcome. Situated on Low Road 1 mile from Bunratty Castle/Durty Nellies. Airport 10 minutes. TV's, Hairdryers, Tea/Coffee facilities all rooms

B&B	4	Ensuite	£19/£20	€24.13/€25.39	Dinner	-
B&B	-	Standard	-	-	Partial Board	-
Single Rate			£26/£26	€33.01	Child reduction	50%

Bunratty 1.5km   **Open:** All Year Except Christmas

T. M. Dennehy
TUDOR LODGE
Hill Road, Bunratty,
Co Clare

Bunratty
TEL: **061 362248**   FAX: **061 362569**

Tudor style residence, Sylvan setting. All rooms have private facilities, TVs, Hairdryers. Bunratty Castle 5 mins walk. Shannon Airport 10 mins drive.

B&B	5	Ensuite	£20/£22.50	€25.39/€28.57	Dinner	-
B&B	-	Standard	-	-	Partial Board	-
Single Rate			£30/£35	€38.09/€44.44	Child reduction	25%

In Bunratty   **Open:** February-November

Mrs Anne Fuller
LEAVALE
Bunratty, Moyhill,
Cratloe, Co Clare

Bunratty
TEL: **061 357439**
EMAIL: leavale@eircom.net

South of Bunratty on N18. Airport 10 mins. Inside Ireland recommended. Ground floor rooms. Orthopaedic beds, Clock Radio, Tea/Coffee in rooms. Guest garden.

B&B	2	Ensuite	£19/£20	€24.13/€25.39	Dinner	-
B&B	1	Standard	£17	€21.59	Partial Board	-
Single Rate			£23.50/£25.50	€29.84/€32.38	Child reduction	25%

Bunratty 1km   **Open:** 1st March-31st October

Mrs Margaret Garry
ROCKFIELD HOUSE
Hill Road, Bunratty,
Co Clare

Bunratty
TEL: **061 364391**   FAX: **061 364391**

Overlooking river. Surrounded by Folk Park. 2 minutes Bunratty Castle & Durty Nelly's. Televisions, Hairdryers,Tea/Coffee, Recommended; Dillard Causin/Sullivan/Stilwell's.

B&B	6	Ensuite	£19/£22	€24.13/€27.93	Dinner	-
B&B	-	Standard	-	-	Partial Board	-
Single Rate			£28/£32	€35.55/€40.63	Child reduction	-

In Bunratty   **Open:** 1st January-20th December

Denis Hegarty
DUNEDIN LODGE
Low Road, Bunratty,
Co Clare

Bunratty

TEL: **061 369966**   FAX: **061 369953**

Purpose built luxury accommodation. Rooms ensuite, Multi channel TV rooms. 1 min drive Bunratty Castle and Folk Park. 10 mins Shannon Airport.

B&B	5	Ensuite	£22.50/£22.50	€28.57	Dinner	-
B&B	-	Standard	-	-	Partial Board	-
Single Rate			£28/£28	€35.55	Child reduction	25%

Shannon 8km

Open: All Year Except Christmas

Mrs Maureen McCabe
BUNRATTY HILLSIDE
Clonmoney North (R 471 Rd)
Bunratty, Co Clare

Bunratty

TEL: **061 364330**   FAX: **061 364330**
EMAIL: mccabe@irishtourismboard.com

Morning guests welcome. Dillard/Causin Recommended. Tea/coffee facilities. Airport 10 mins, Bunratty 2km, off N18 at Sixmilebridge R471.

B&B	5	Ensuite	£20	€25.39	Dinner	-
B&B	1	Standard	£18	€22.86	Partial Board	-
Single Rate			£28/£30	€35.55/€38.09	Child reduction	25%

Shannon 2km

Open: 1st March-1st November

Mrs Imelda McCarthy
INNISFREE
Low Road, Bunratty,
Co Clare

Bunratty

TEL: **061 369773**   FAX: **061 369926**
EMAIL: innisfree@unison.ie
WEB: www.shannonheartland.ie

Airport 10 mins. Road between Castle/Durty Nelly's. Tea/Coffee facilities, Hairdryers. Frommer Readers recommended. Breakfast menu, morning guests welcome.

B&B	4	Ensuite	£19/£20	€24.13/€25.39	Dinner	-
B&B	-	Standard	-	-	Partial Board	-
Single Rate			£27/£30	€34.29/€38.09	Child reduction	25%

Bunratty 1km

Open: 1st February-30th November

Freddie & Deirdre McInerney
AVAREST B&B
Hurlers Cross, Bunratty,
Co Clare

Bunratty

TEL: **061 360278**   FAX: **061 360535**
EMAIL: avarest@eircom.net
WEB: www.avarest.ie

New luxurious purpose-built home. Spacious rooms. Orthopaedic beds. Off N18 at Hurlers Cross. Bunratty/Airport 2 miles. Ideal touring base.

B&B	4	Ensuite	£19/£25	€24.13/€31.74	Dinner	-
B&B	-	Standard	-	-	Partial Board	-
Single Rate			£25.50/£30	€32.38/€38.09	Child reduction	25%

Shannon 3km

Open: All Year

Paula McInerney
RIVERSIDE B&B
Clonmoney West, Bunratty,
Co Clare

Bunratty

TEL: **061 364148**   FAX: **061 364148**

Custom built luxurious B&B. Spacious bedrooms with TV. Breakfast menu. Early Breakfast available. Situated on N18. Airport 10 mins, Bunratty 5 mins.

B&B	4	Ensuite	£19/£19	€24.13	Dinner	-
B&B	-	Standard	£17/£17	€21.59	Partial Board	-
Single Rate			£25/£28	€31.74/€35.55	Child reduction	33.3%

In Bunratty

Open: All Year Except Christmas

Mrs Mary McKenna
GALLOW'S VIEW
**Bunratty East,
Co Clare**

Bunratty

Tel: **061 369125**   Fax: **061 369125**
Email: gallowsview@unison.ie

Warm and friendly home. Frommer Recommended. Airport 10 mins. Breakfast Menu. TV, Hairdryers, Tea/Coffee. Road between Castle/Durty Nellies, through carpark, 7th house on right.

					Dinner	-
B&B	5	Ensuite	£19/£20	€24.13/€25.39		
B&B	-	Standard		-	Partial Board	-
Single Rate			£30	€38.09	Child reduction	25%

Shannon 6km

Open: March-October

Mrs Catherine McNamara
DEERFIELD HOUSE
**Deerpark, Sixmilebridge,
Co Clare**

Bunratty

Tel: **061 369262**   Fax: **061 369262**

Situated peaceful country setting. Road between Bunratty Castle, Durty Nelly's. Airport 10 mins. Right at end road, first left, 5th house.

					Dinner	-
B&B	4	Ensuite	£19/£20	€24.13/€25.39		
B&B	-	Standard		-	Partial Board	-
Single Rate			£25.50	€32.38	Child reduction	50%

Bunratty 1.5km

Open: 1st May-1st October

Mrs Majella Mullane
ASHFORD HOUSE
**Cloghlea, Bunratty,
Sixmilebridge, Co Clare**

Bunratty

Tel: **061 369600**   Fax: **061 369907**
Email: mullanej@iol.ie
Web: www.iol.ie/~mullanej

Luxurious home. All downstairs rooms have separate exit door. TV, Hairdryer, Clock radio. Take road between Castle and Durty Nellies.

					Dinner	-
B&B	4	Ensuite	£22.50/£22.50	€28.57		
B&B	-	Standard		-	Partial Board	-
Single Rate			£28/£30	€35.55/€38.09	Child reduction	-

Shannon Town 8km

Open: 20th March-31st October

Mrs Penny O'Connor
DUNAREE
**Low Road, Bunratty,
Co Clare**

Bunratty

Tel: **061 369131**
Email: dunaree@eircom.net
Web: www.dunaree.net

New hillside residence with panoramic views, adjacent to Bunratty Castle. Luxurious bedrooms, all en-suite. Shannon Airport 10 minutes.

					Dinner	-
B&B	5	Ensuite	£22	€27.93		
B&B	-	Standard		-	Partial Board	-
Single Rate			£30	€38.09	Child reduction	25%

Bunratty Village 1km

Open: 15th March-15th October

Mrs Kathleen O'Shea
MANDERLEY
**Deer Park, Bunratty,
Sixmilebridge, Co Clare**

Bunratty

Tel: **061 369572**
Email: manderley@oceanfree.net

Two storey country home with mature gardens. Take road between Durty Nellys and Castle, turn right at end of road, third house on left handside.

					Dinner	-
B&B	4	Ensuite	£20/£22	€25.39/€27.93		
B&B	-	Standard		-	Partial Board	-
Single Rate			£29/£30	€36.82/€38.09	Child reduction	25%

Shannon 8km

Open: 1st January- 31st November

Bunratty 1.5km

Sheila Tiernan
ASHGROVE HOUSE
Lowroad, Bunratty,
Co Clare

Bunratty
TEL: **061 369332**
EMAIL: frashe@eircom.net
WEB: www.ashgrovehouse.com

Take low road between Bunratty Castle and Durty Nellies. 10 min drive to Airport. Free carpark. Private entrances. 3 min drive to Bunratty. Warm rooms. Good beds. All facilities.

B&B	4	Ensuite	£19/£20	€24.13/€25.39	Dinner	-
B&B	-	Standard			Partial Board	-
Single Rate			£25.50/£30	€32.38/€38.09	Child reduction	25%

Open: All Year Except Christmas

Bunratty 1km

Mrs Eileen Woulfe
SHANNON VIEW
Bunratty,
Co Clare

Bunratty
TEL: **061 364056**   FAX: **061 364056**

Bungalow on N18 Shannon - Limerick road. Galtee breakfast winner.Tea/coffee making facilities in all rooms. Guests lounge.

B&B	4	Ensuite	£20	€25.39	Dinner	-
B&B	-	Standard	-	-	Partial Board	-
Single Rate			£25.50	€32.38	Child reduction	-

Open: 1st April-31st October

Kinvara 4km

Mrs Anne Martin
VILLA MARIA
Leagh South, Burren,
Co Clare

Burren
TEL: **065 7078019**
EMAIL: vmaria@eircom.net
WEB: homepage.eircom.net/~vmaria

Overlooking Galway Bay. Quiet area. Panoramic Burren setting. Information on Burren available. Irish Music. Excellent seafood locally. Smoke free home.

B&B	3	Ensuite	£19	€24.13	Dinner	£12.50
B&B	2	Standard	£17	€21.59	Partial Board	£185
Single Rate			£23.50/£25.50	€29.84/€32.38	Child reduction	25%

Open: 15th April-31st October

In Corofin

Mrs Mary Cleary
LAKEFIELD LODGE
Ennis Road, Corofin,
Co Clare

Corofin
TEL: **065 6837675**   FAX: **065 6837299**
EMAIL: mcleary.ennis@eircom.net

Recommended by "Le Guide du Routard". On periphery of Burren National Park. Cliffs of Moher, Shannon Airport 40 mins. Fishing locally. Tea/Coffee facilities.

B&B	4	Ensuite	£19/£20	€24.13/€25.39	Dinner	-
B&B	-	Standard			Partial Board	-
Single Rate			£26/£28	€33.01/€35.55	Child reduction	33.3%

Open: 1st April-31st October

Corofin 2km

Mrs Anne Connole
CONNOLES
Killeen, Corofin,
Co Clare

Corofin
TEL: **065 6837773**

A luxury family run home by Ballycullian Lake. The gateway to the Burren. 10 mins from Ennis. Leisurely activities closeby. Breakfast menu.

B&B	4	Ensuite	£19	€24.13	Dinner	-
B&B	-	Standard			Partial Board	-
Single Rate			£25.50/£25.50	€32.38	Child reduction	33.3%

Open: 1st March-30th November

Mary & Michael Corbett
KILLEEN HOUSE
Killeen, Corofin,
Co Clare

Tᴇʟ: **065 6837329**
Eᴍᴀɪʟ: killeenbnb@eircom.net
Wᴇʙ: www.bb-house.com/killeenhouse.htm

Luxury accommodation. Route R476. Tea/Coffee on arrival. Private TV lounge. Close to Burren National Park, Ailwee Cave, Cliffs of Moher. Golf and Fishing locally. 30 minutes Shannon Airport.

B&B	3	Ensuite	£19	€24.13	Dinner	-
B&B	2	Standard	£17	€21.59	Partial Board	-
Single Rate			£23.50/£25.50	€29.84/€32.38	Child reduction	33.3%

Corofin 1.5km

Open: 1st April-31st October

Mr Brendan Kearney
SHAMROCK & HEATHER
Station Road, Corofin,
Co Clare

Tᴇʟ: **065 6837061**
Eᴍᴀɪʟ: bmkearney@eircom.net

Shannon Airport 50 minutes. Lake District, Cliffs of Moher, Burren National Park, Traditional Music, Clare Heritage Centre, Museum. Hairdryer, Tea/Coffee.

B&B	2	Ensuite	£19/£19	€24.13	Dinner	-
B&B	1	Standard	£17/£17	€21.59	Partial Board	-
Single Rate			£23.50/£24.50	€29.84/€31.11	Child reduction	33.3%

Corofin

Open: 1st March-31st October

Thomas and Rita Kierce
BURREN HOUSE
Kilnaboy, Corofin,
Co Clare

Tᴇʟ: **065 6837143**

Spacious house with Burren countryside views on R476 route. Close Burren National Park, Lake District, Heritage Centre. Airport 40 mins. Tea/Coffee facilities.

B&B	3	Ensuite	£19	€24.13	Dinner	£15
B&B	1	Standard	£17	€21.59	Partial Board	-
Single Rate			£23.50/£25.50	€29.84/€32.38	Child reduction	-

Corofin 3km

Open: 17th March-31st October

Mrs Mary Corcoran
GRANGE
Wood Road, Cratloe,
Co Clare

Tᴇʟ: **061 357389**   Fᴀx: **061 357389**
Eᴍᴀɪʟ: alfie@iol.ie

Off N18 at Limerick Inn Hotel. Spacious house, all rooms ground floor. Shannon/Airport 15 minutes, Bunratty 5 minutes. Frommer, Lonely Planet recommended. Electric blankets. Family run.

B&B	3	Ensuite	£19/£20	€24.13/€25.39	Dinner	£12.50
B&B	2	Standard	£17/£18	€21.59/€22.86	Partial Board	£185
Single Rate			£23.50/£25.50	€29.84/€32.38	Child reduction	50%

Limerick 6km

Open: All Year

Jan & Jim Moloney
HUNTING LODGE B&B
Wood Road, Cratloe,
Co Clare

Tᴇʟ: **061 357216**   Fᴀx: **061 357549**
Eᴍᴀɪʟ: moloneyjj@eircom.net

Spacious house, scenic views, quiet location, Bunratty 5 minutes, Limerick 10 minutes, Airport 15 minutes. 1 mile off N18 at Limerick Inn.

B&B	2	Ensuite	£19	€24.13	Dinner	£12.50
B&B	2	Standard	£17	€21.59	Partial Board	£185
Single Rate			£23.50/£25.50	€29.84/€32.38	Child reduction	50%

Limerick 6km

Open: All Year

Mrs Rosemary Ormston
HIGHBURY HOUSE
Ballymorris, Cratloe,
Co Clare

Cratloe Near Bunratty
TEL: **061 357212**
EMAIL: cormston@iol.ie

Tudor style Country Home on N18. 2 miles from Bunratty Castle travelling south towards Limerick or 6 miles from Limerick City travelling north. Hairdryers, Electric Blankets.

B&B	4	Ensuite	£19	€24.13	Dinner	-
B&B	-	Standard	-	-	Partial Board	-
Single Rate			£25.50	€32.38	Child reduction	50%

Bunratty 1.5km

Open: 1st January-15th December

Mrs Carmel O'Ryan
SUNNYBANK
Ballymorris, Cratloe,
Co Clare

Cratloe Near Bunratty
TEL: **061 357108**

Quiet house 400 yards Limerick-Shannon (N18) at Ballymorris. Comfortable lounge. Traditional music, Bunratty 1.5 miles. Shannon Airport 5 miles. Limerick City 6 miles.

B&B	2	Ensuite	£19	€24.13	Dinner	-
B&B	1	Standard	£17	€21.59	Partial Board	-
Single Rate			-	-	Child reduction	25%

Bunratty 2km

Open: 1st April-30th September

Mrs Kathleen Cullinan
HARBOUR VIEW
Doolin,
Co Clare

Doolin
TEL: **065 7074154**   FAX: **065 7074935**
EMAIL: kathlen@eircom.net
WEB: www.clarenet.ie/harbourview

Spacious ground floor bedrooms. Breathtaking views - Cliffs of Moher, Burren, Aran Islands. Airport 1 hour. Hairdryers, Electric blankets. Rick Steeves.

B&B	4	Ensuite	£19/£19	€24.13	Dinner	-
B&B	-	Standard	-	-	Partial Board	-
Single Rate			£30/£30	€38.09	Child reduction	25%

Doolin 2km

Open: 15th February-5th November

Susan Daly
DALY'S HOUSE
Doolin,
Co Clare

Doolin
TEL: **065 7074242**   FAX: **065 7074668**
EMAIL: susan.daly@esatlink.com
WEB: www.dalys-house.com

Situated 150 yards from Doolin Village-home of Traditional Music. Panoramic views of the Sea, Cliffs of Moher, Burren. Family run.

B&B	5	Ensuite	£20/£22	€25.39/€27.93	Dinner	-
B&B	-	Standard	-	-	Partial Board	-
Single Rate			-	-	Child reduction	25%

In Doolin

Open: 1st February-30th November

Ms Olive Dowling
TOOMULLIN HOUSE
Doolin Village,
Co Clare

Doolin
TEL: **065 7074723**
EMAIL: toomullin@eircom.net

Lovely country cottage in Doolin Village. 1 mins walk to traditional music Pubs and Restaurants. Tea/Coffee. Breakfast menu. Cliffs, Burren, Aran Ferry nearby.

B&B	2	Ensuite	£20/£20	€25.39	Dinner	-
B&B	1	Standard	£18/£18	€22.86	Partial Board	-
Single Rate			£30/£35	€38.09/€44.44	Child reduction	50%

In Doolin

Open: All Year Except Christmas

Brid and Val Egan
ATLANTIC SUNSET HOUSE
Cliffs of Moher Road,
Doolin, Co Clare

Doolin
TEL: **065 7074080**   FAX: **065 7074922**
EMAIL: sunsethouse@esatclear.ie

Warm hospitable home conveniently located on R478. Near Cliffs of Moher, Aran Ferry, Burren, Music, Pubs. Breakfast Menu. Airport 1 hour. Highly recommended by Travel Guides.

B&B	6	Ensuite	£19/£20	€24.13 /€25.39	Dinner	-
B&B	-	Standard	-	-	Partial Board	-
Single Rate			£25.50/£30	€32.38/€38.09	Child reduction	-

Doolin 2km

Open: 15th January-15th December

Mrs Maeve Fitzgerald
CHURCHFIELD
Doolin,
Co Clare

Doolin
TEL: **065 7074209**   FAX: **065 7074622**
EMAIL: churchfield@eircom.net
WEB: homepage.eircom.net/~churchfield

House at Doolin P.O. View - Cliffs Moher, Sea/Countryside. Traditional music. Burren. Frommer recommended. Breakfast menu. Tea/Coffee. At bus stop.

B&B	5	Ensuite	£19/£20	€24.13/€25.39	Dinner	£12.50
B&B	1	Standard	£17/£18	€21.59/€22.86	Partial Board	-
Single Rate			£25/£30	€31.74/€38.09	Child reduction	33.3%

Doolin Village

Open: All Year Except Christmas

John D Flanagan
BALLYVARA HOUSE
Ballyvara, Doolin,
Co Clare

Doolin
TEL: **065 7074467**   FAX: **065 7074868**
EMAIL: bvara@iol.ie
WEB: www.ballyvarahouse.com

19th Century Farm Cottage remodeled by owner. Panoramic Countryside views. Music, Burren. Cliffs Moher, Aran Ferry. Quiet setting on R479. Airport 1 hour.

B&B	6	Ensuite	£19/£20	€24.13/€25.39	Dinner	-
B&B	-	Standard	-	-	Partial Board	-
Single Rate			£25.50	€32.38	Child reduction	25%

In Doolin

Open: March-October

Mrs Caitriona J Garrahy
RIVERFIELD HOUSE
Doolin,
Co Clare

Doolin
TEL: **065 7074113**   FAX: **065 7074113**
EMAIL: riverfield@eircom.net

Century-old reconstructed home. Five minutes walking to all Pubs and Restaurants. Family room. Credit Cards. Airport 1 hour.

B&B	3	Ensuite	£19/£21	€24.13/€26.66	Dinner	-
B&B	1	Standard	£17/£19	€21.59/€24.13	Partial Board	-
Single Rate			£23.50/£27	€29.84/€34.29	Child reduction	33.3%

In Doolin

Open: All Year

Darra Hughes
SEA VIEW HOUSE
Fisher Street, Doolin,
Co Clare

Doolin
TEL: **065 7074826**   FAX: **065 7074849**
EMAIL: seaviewhouse@netscape.net
WEB: www.kingsway.ie/seaviewhouse

Luxury accommodation in the Village of Doolin overlooking the Atlantic Ocean. Extensive breakfast menu. Minutes walk music pubs, restaurants, Aran Ferry.

B&B	4	Ensuite	£20/£24	€25.39 /€30.47	Dinner	-
B&B	-	Standard	-	-	Partial Board	-
Single Rate			-	-	Child reduction	20%

In Doolin

Open: 3rd January-20th December

Marian & Martin McDonagh
GLASHA MEADOWS
**Glasha, Doolin,
Co Clare**

Doolin
TEL: **065 7074443**
EMAIL: glameadows@tinet.ie

Family bungalow 1.5km from Doolin Village. Quiet location R479. Cliffs of Moher, Aran Ferries, Airport 1 hour. Breakfast menu. All guests bedrooms on ground floor.

B&B	6	Ensuite	£19/£20	€24.13/€25.39	Dinner	-
B&B	-	Standard	-	-	Partial Board	-
Single Rate			-	-	Child reduction	25%

Lisdoonvarna 6km

Open: All Year Except Christmas

Cecilia O'Callaghan
BALLINALACKAN LODGE
**Ballinalacken, Doolin,
Co Clare**

Doolin
TEL: **065 7074926**

Tranquil hillside residence, panoramic views of Aran Islands, Connemara Hills, Burren landscape. Spectacular sunsets. Near Cliffs of Moher, R477 Coast road.

B&B	4	Ensuite	£19/£22	€24.13/€27.93	Dinner	-
B&B	-	Standard	-	-	Partial Board	-
Single Rate			£25.50/£37	€32.38/€46.98	Child reduction	33.3%

Doolin 3km

Open: 1st June-31st August

Mary Jo O'Connell
SEASCAPE B&B
**Roadford, Doolin,
Co Clare**

Doolin
TEL: **065 7074451**   FAX: **065 7074451**
EMAIL: seascape@eircom.net

Located on a quiet cul-de-sac in the heart of Doolin village. Close to Pubs, Burren, Cliffs of Moher, Aran Islands Ferries.

B&B	4	Ensuite	£19/£19	€24.13	Dinner	-
B&B	-	Standard	-	-	Partial Board	-
Single Rate			£25.50/£35.00	€32.38/€44.44	Child reduction	25%

In Doolin

Open: All Year

Adrian & Bev O'Connor
CRAGGY ISLAND B&B
**Ardeamush, Doolin,
Co Clare**

Doolin
TEL: **065 7074595**
EMAIL: cragisle@gofree.indigo.ie
WEB: www.irelandaccommodation.org

Peaceful, scenic location off R477 Lisdoonvarna/Ballyvaughan Coast road. Near Cliffs of Moher, Burren, Traditional music pubs. Traditional/Vegetarian breakfasts.

B&B	5	Ensuite	£19/£19	€24.13	Dinner	-
B&B	-	Standard	-	-	Partial Board	-
Single Rate			£25.50/£25.50	€32.38	Child reduction	33.3%

Doolin 4km

Open: All Year

John and Anne Sims
ISLAND VIEW
**Cliffs of Moher Road (R478)
Doolin, Co Clare**

Doolin
TEL: **065 7074346**   FAX: **065 7074844**
EMAIL: sims@iol.ie
WEB: sites.netscape.net/islandviewdoolin/doolin

"Lonely Planet", "Le Guide du Routard" recommended. Warm welcome. Breakfast Menu. Orthopaedic Beds. Tea, scones on arrival. Transport to pubs. Cliffs 8km.

B&B	3	Ensuite	£19/£19	€24.13	Dinner	£15
B&B	1	Standard	£17/£17	€21.59	Partial Board	£200
Single Rate			£24/£30	€30.47/€38.09	Child reduction	50%

Doolin 3km

Open: 1st April-30th October

In Ennis Town

Mrs Martina Brennan
CLONEEN
Clonroad, Ennis,
Co Clare

Tel: **065 6829681**

Hiking, biking, driving ideal stop. Town Centre, Station 5 minutes walk. Airport, Burren, Cliffs, Castles 30 mins drive. Spacious gardens. Bicycle shed.

B&B	1	Ensuite	£19/£19	€24.13	Dinner	-
B&B	2	Standard	£17/£18	€21.59/€22.86	Partial Board	-
Single Rate			£25/£25	€31.74	Child reduction	-

Open: 1st April-31st October

Ennis 2km

Mrs Anne Burke
CASA MARIA
Loughville, Lahinch Road,
Ennis, Co Clare

Tel: **065 6820395**

Warm, friendly, ground floor rooms. Lovely peaceful location on N85 opposite Statoil Station. Ennis 3 minutes drive. Extensive parking.

B&B	2	Ensuite	£19/£19	€24.13	Dinner	-
B&B	1	Standard	£17/£17	€21.59	Partial Board	-
Single Rate			£23.50/£25.50	€29.84/€32.38	Child reduction	25%

Open: 15th April-31st October

Denis & Kathleen Cahill
RAILWAY VIEW HOUSE
Tulla Road, Ennis,
Co Clare

Tel: **065 6821646**

Very secluded premises, 8 mins walk from Town Centre. Large private car park. No traffic noise. Shannon Airport 30 mins. Convenient to Cliffs of Moher, Burren & Castles.

B&B	3	Ensuite	£19/£21	€24.13/€26.66	Dinner	-
B&B		Standard	-	-	Partial Board	-
Single Rate			£25.50	€32.38	Child reduction	50%

Open: March-November

Ennis 1.5km

Mrs Mary Connole
SHANLEE
Lahinch Road, Ennis,
Co Clare

Tel: **065 6840270**
Email: mac.ennis@eircom.net
Web: www.dirl.com/clare/shanlee.htm

Comfortable home with ground floor rooms on N85 to the Burren, Cliffs of Moher, Bunratty Castle, Golf, Fishing. Traditional music. Morning guests welcome.

B&B	2	Ensuite	£19/£19	€24.13	Dinner	-
B&B	2	Standard	£17/£17	€21.59	Partial Board	-
Single Rate			£23.50/£25.50	€29.84/€32.38	Child reduction	50%

Open: All Year

Ennis 3km

Natalie Crowe
GORT NA MBLATH
Ballaghboy, Doora,
Ennis, Co Clare

Tel: **065 6822204**   Fax: **065 6822204**
Email: crowe.ennis@tinet.ie

Peaceful comfortable family run home. Warm welcome. Ideal starting point for exploring the Burren. Detailed help in planning itinerary. Shannon Airport 15 mins.

B&B	2	Ensuite	£19	€24.13	Dinner	-
B&B	2	Standard	£17	€21.59	Partial Board	-
Single Rate			£23.50/£25.50	€29.84/€32.38	Child reduction	-

Open: All Year

Ennis

Teresa & Tom Crowe
SHALOM
Ballybeg, Killadysert Road, Ennis, Co Clare

Tel: **065 6829494**

Comfortable, warm, hospitable home. All rooms ground floor. Spacious bathrooms. Quiet location on R473 route, 2km to Ennis Town Centre. Spacious private parking. Shannon Airport 18km.

B&B	3	Ensuite	£19	€24.13	Dinner	-
B&B	1	Standard	£17	€21.59	Partial Board	-
Single Rate			£25	€31.74	Child reduction	-

Ennis 2km

Open: 1st May-30th September

Ennis

Judy Dowling
SYCAMORE
Tulla Road, Ennis, Co Clare

Tel: **065 6821343**

Quality accommodation 6 mins walk Town Centre.TV/Radio/Tea/Coffee in bedrooms. 20 mins Shannon Airport. Ideal touring base.

B&B	3	Ensuite	£19	€24.13	Dinner	-
B&B	-	Standard		-	Partial Board	-
Single Rate			£25.50	€32.38	Child reduction	-

In Ennis

Open: 1st March-30th November

Ennis

The Finn Family
DRUIMIN
Golf Links Road, Ennis, Co Clare

Tel: **065 6824183** Fax: **065 6843331**
Email: golfinn.ennis@tinet.ie

Tranquil setting beside Ennis Golf club on R474, with peat fire and award winning Breakfasts. We like it here, so will you.

B&B	4	Ensuite	£20/£21	€25.39/€26.66	Dinner	-
B&B	-	Standard		-	Partial Board	-
Single Rate			£28/£29	€35.55/€36.82	Child reduction	-

Ennis 1km

Open: 1st April-30th September

Ennis

Mrs Mary Finucane
MOYVILLE
Lahinch Road, Ennis, Co Clare

Tel: **065 6828278**
Email: moyville.ennis@eircom.net

Spacious comfortable home on N85 to the Burren. Cliffs of Moher. Golf, Fishing, Entertainment locally. Electric Blankets, Hairdryers in rooms.

B&B	4	Ensuite	£19	€24.13	Dinner	£12.50
B&B	-	Standard		-	Partial Board	-
Single Rate			£25.50	€32.38	Child reduction	33.3%

Ennis 1km

Open: 1st February-31st October

Ennis

Sean & Teresa Grogan
ST PATRICK'S
Corebeg, Doora, Ennis, Co Clare

Tel: **065 6840122** Fax: **065 6840122 (man)**

Quiet scenic area. Ideal location for Knappogue, Bunratty, Cragganowen, Burren, Cliffs of Moher, Golfing, Fishing, Traditional Music. Morning visitors welcome.

B&B	2	Ensuite	£19	€24.13	Dinner	£12.50
B&B	1	Standard	£17	€21.59	Partial Board	£185
Single Rate			£23.50/£25.50	€29.84/€32.38	Child reduction	20%

Ennis 4km

Open: All Year

Mrs Maura Healy
BROOKVILLE HOUSE
Tobartaoscan, Off Limerick Road, Ennis, Co Clare

Ennis
TEL: **065 6829802**

Tranquil location, garden. Bus station, Town 10 mins walk, adjacent West Co. Hotel, Golf Courses. Airport, Cliffs, Castles 30 mins.

B&B	3	Ensuite	£20/£21	€25.39/€26.66	Dinner	-
B&B	-	Standard	-	-	Partial Board	-
Single Rate			£25.50	€32.38	Child reduction	25%

In Ennis

Open: 1st February-31st November

Mrs Helen Holohan
CLONRUSH
Lahinch Road, Ennis, Co Clare

Ennis
TEL: **065 6829692**
EMAIL: clonrushennis@eircom.net

Easy to find, on N85, hard to leave. Ideal touring base, Cliffs of Moher, Bunratty Castle, Golf, Beaches, Burren. Restaurant and Bar 2 mins walk. 20 mins Airport.

B&B	4	Ensuite	£19/£20	€24.13/€25.39	Dinner	-
B&B	-	Standard	-	-	Partial Board	-
Single Rate			£25.50/£30	€32.38/€38.09	Child reduction	-

Ennis 1.5km

Open: 1st March-31st October

Fintan & Alma Kelly
KELLY'S
Teach Ui Cheallaigh, Gort Road, Ennis, Co Clare

Ennis
TEL: **065 6822114**   FAX: **065 6822114**
EMAIL: teachu.ennis@eircom.net
WEB: homepage.eircom.net/~fikel/

Spacious bungalow opposite Ennis General Hospital on main Galway road (N18). 5 minutes walk from Ennis Town Centre. Large car park at rear.

B&B	6	Ensuite	£19/£22.50	€24.13/€28.57	Dinner	-
B&B	-	Standard	-	-	Partial Board	-
Single Rate			£25.50/£30	€32.38/€38.09	Child reduction	25%

In Ennis

Open: All Year

John & Kathleen Kenneally
WILLBROOK HOUSE
Tulla Road, Ennis, Co Clare

Ennis
TEL: **065 6820782**

A warm double glazed two storey residence within walking distance of Town Centre with central heating. Close to all amenities. Great touring base for South and West.

B&B	3	Ensuite	£19/£20	€24.13/€25.39	Dinner	-
B&B	-	Standard	-	-	Partial Board	-
Single Rate			-	-	Child reduction	50%

In Ennis

Open: All Year

Mrs Maureen Langan
ST ANNES
Limerick Road, Ennis, Co Clare

Ennis
TEL: **065 6828501**

On N18, Airport 20 mins. Adjacent to West County Hotel. Convenient to Cliffs of Moher, Burren, Golf. Tea/facilities, TV, Hairdryers in bedrooms.

B&B	3	Ensuite	£19/£22	€24.13/€27.93	Dinner	-
B&B	-	Standard	-	-	Partial Board	-
Single Rate			£25.50	€32.38	Child reduction	-

Ennis 1km

Open: 1st February-12th December

Tom & Rita Meaney
ASHLEIGH HOUSE
Barefield, Ennis,
Co Clare

Ennis
TEL: **065 6827187**   FAX: **065 6827331**
EMAIL: tommeaney@eircom.net

Ennis/Galway road. Shannon Airport 30 mins. Ideal touring base. Convenient to Burren, Cliffs of Moher, Castle banquets, Golf & Fishing.

B&B	5	Ensuite	£19/£19	€24.13	Dinner	£12.50
B&B	-	Standard	£17/£17	€21.59	Partial Board	£185
Single Rate			£25.50/£25.50	€32.38	Child reduction	33.3%

Ennis 5km

Open: All Year

The Meere Family
FOUR WINDS
Limerick Road, Ennis,
Co Clare

Ennis
TEL: **065 6829831**
EMAIL: fourwinds.ennis@eircom.net

Large home on main Airport road (N18). Private Car park at rear. Golf, Pitch/Putt nearby. 5 mins walk Town centre.

B&B	5	Ensuite	£19/£22	€24.13/€27.93	Dinner	-
B&B	-	Standard	-	-	Partial Board	-
Single Rate			£25.50/£30	€32.38/€38.09	Child reduction	33.3%

In Ennis

Open: 15th March-15th October

Mrs Valerie Morris
CARRAIG MHUIRE
Barefield, Ennis,
Co Clare

Ennis
TEL: **065 6827106**   FAX: **065 6827375**

Country Home. Ennis/Galway Road. Airport 30 minutes. Convenient to Cliffs of Moher/Burren. T.V., Hairdryers, Tea/Coffee all rooms.

B&B	3	Ensuite	£19	€24.13	Dinner	-
B&B	1	Standard	£17	€21.59	Partial Board	-
Single Rate			£23.50/£25	€29.84/€31.74	Child reduction	50%

Ennis 5km

Open: 3rd January-20th December

Mrs Mareaid O'Connor
VILLA NOVA
1 Woodlawn, Lahinch Road,
Ennis, Co Clare

Ennis
TEL: **065 6828570**
EMAIL: villanova77@hotmail.com

Bungalow on N85. Big Garden. Shannon 25 mins. Restaurant, Pub with music 2 mins walk. Golf, Pitch & Putt, Swimming, Cliffs of Moher, Bunratty Castle, Aillwee Caves nearby.

B&B	2	Ensuite	£19/£19	€24.13	Dinner	£13
B&B	3	Standard	£17/£17	€21.59	Partial Board	-
Single Rate			£23.50/£25.50	€29.84/€32.38	Child reduction	33.3%

Ennis 1.5km

Open: 1st February-31st October

Mr Hugh O'Donnell
RYE HILL B&B
Tulla Road, Ennis,
Co Clare

Ennis
TEL: **065 6824313**   FAX: **065 6824313**
EMAIL: ryehillbandb@eircom.net

Easy to find R352. Town Centre 3-4 mins. Ideal touring base. Golf, Fishing, Horse riding nearby. Limerick 40 minutes. Shannon 25 minutes. Pub and Restaurant 5 minutes walk.

B&B	6	Ensuite	£19/£20	€24.13/€25.39	Dinner	-
B&B	-	Standard	-	-	Partial Board	-
Single Rate			£25.50/£29	€32.38/€36.82	Child reduction	50%

Open: January-15th December

Mrs Teresa O'Donohue
SANBORN HOUSE
Edenvale, Kilrush Road,
Ennis, Co Clare

Ennis
TEL: **065 6824959**
EMAIL: sanbornbandb@eircom.net
WEB: www.bb-house.com/sanborn.htm

Spacious neo-Georgian house in peaceful scenic setting on Kilrush/Car Ferry Road (N68).
Convenient Airport, Cliffs of Moher, Burren, Castles. Early guests welcome.

B&B	4	Ensuite	£19/£19	€24.13	Dinner	-
B&B	-	Standard	-	-	Partial Board	-
Single Rate			£25.50	€32.38	Child reduction	33.3%

Ennis 2km

Open: All Year except Christmas

Mrs Monica O'Loughlin
MASSABIELLE
Off Quin Road, Ennis,
Co Clare

Ennis
TEL: **065 6829363**   FAX: **065 6829363**

Recommended by "Frommer," "Sullivan", "Best B&B's" Guides. Friendly, relaxed family home in
peaceful rural setting with landscaped gardens, Tennis Court.

B&B	4	Ensuite	£20/£20	€25.39	Dinner	-
B&B	-	Standard	-	-	Partial Board	-
Single Rate			£25.50/£25.50	€32.38	Child reduction	25%

Ennis 3km

Open: 21st May-20th September

Mary O'Sullivan
OGHAM HOUSE
3 Abbey Court, Clare Road,
Ennis, Co Clare

Ennis
TEL: **065 6824878**
EMAIL: oghamhouseennis@eircom.net

On N18 opposite West County Hotel. Enjoy our warm hospitality in comfortable home. Bus/Train
10 mins walk. Shannon 20 mins drive. Ideal touring base.

B&B	2	Ensuite	£20/£22	€25.39/€27.93	Dinner	-
B&B	1	Standard	£19/£20	€24.13/€25.39	Partial Board	-
Single Rate			£25.50/£28	€32.38/€35.55	Child reduction	25%

Ennis 1km

Open: All Year

Mrs Brigid Pyne
KILMOON HOUSE
Kildysart Road, Off Limerick Rd,
Ennis, Co Clare

Ennis
TEL: **065 6828529**

Spacious home in peaceful environment, 20 mins from Shannon Airport. Convenient to Bunratty
Castle, Knappogue, Burren and Cliffs of Moher.

B&B	2	Ensuite	£19/£19	€24.13	Dinner	-
B&B	1	Standard	£17/£17	€21.59	Partial Board	-
Single Rate			£23.50/£25.50	€29.84/€32.38	Child reduction	50%

Ennis 1km

Open: 1st April-30th September

Joan & George Quinn
LAKESIDE COUNTRY LODGE
Barntick, Clarecastle,
Ennis, Co Clare

Ennis
TEL: **065 6838488**
EMAIL: lakesidecountry@eircom.net

Spacious home on 3 acres. Overlooking Killone Lake and Abbey, on coast road (R473) to Car
Ferry. Convenient Airport. Hairdryers. Conservatory overlooking lake.

B&B	4	Ensuite	£19/£20	€24.13/€25.39	Dinner	-
B&B	-	Standard	-	-	Partial Board	-
Single Rate			£25.50	€32.38	Child reduction	50%

Ennis 3km

Open: 1st January-21st December

Ennis

Ms Nuala Ryan
ADOBE
**21 Fernhill, Galway Road,
Ennis, Co Clare**

Ennis
TEL: **065 6823919**
EMAIL: johnryan.ennis@eircom.net

Modern detached house in quiet cul-de-sac. Breakfast menu. 5 mins walk to Town Centre, 100 metres off N18.

					Dinner	-
B&B	2	Ensuite	£19/£22.50	€24.13/€28.57	Dinner	-
B&B	2	Standard	£17/£20	€21.59/€25.39	Partial Board	-
Single Rate			£25/£30	€31.74/€38.09	Child reduction	25%

Open: All Year Except Christmas

In Ennis

T J & Pauline Roberts
CARBERY HOUSE
**Kilrush Road/Car Ferry Rd
Ennis, Co Clare**

Ennis
TEL: **065 6824046**   FAX: **065 6824046**

Route 68, morning visitors welcome. Orthopaedic beds, Electric blankets, Hospitality trays, Hairdryers. Continental breakfast reduced rate. Convenient Airport.

					Dinner	-
B&B	4	Ensuite	£19/£22	€24.13/€27.93	Dinner	-
B&B	-	Standard	-	-	Partial Board	-
Single Rate			£25.50/£25.50	€32.38	Child reduction	-

Open: 1st April-20th October

Ennis 5km

Mrs Ina Troy
HAZELDENE
**Barefield, Ennis,
Co Clare**

Ennis
TEL: **065 6827212**   FAX: **065 6827212**

Ennis/Galway Road. Morning guests welcome. Airport 30 mins distance. TV in bedrooms. Convenient Cliffs of Moher. Banquets, Golf, Fishing.

					Dinner	-
B&B	5	Ensuite	£19/£20	€24.13/€25.39	Dinner	-
B&B	-	Standard	-	-	Partial Board	-
Single Rate			£25.50/£28	€32.38/€35.55	Child reduction	25%

Open: 15th January-30th November

In Ennistymon

Mrs Kathleen Cahill
STATION HOUSE
**Ennis Road, Ennistymon,
Co Clare**

Ennistymon
TEL: **065 7071149**   FAX: **065 7071709**
EMAIL: cahilka@indigo.ie

Route 85. Spacious home. Hospitality tray, Hairdryer, Telephone, TV in bedrooms. Breakfast menu. Horse riding, Fishing, Golf, Cliffs of Moher, Burren nearby. Guide du Routard recommended.

					Dinner	-
B&B	6	Ensuite	£19/£19	€24.13	Dinner	-
B&B	-	Standard	-	-	Partial Board	-
Single Rate			-	-	Child reduction	-

Open: 1st January-22nd December

Ennistymon 1.5km

Maureen Scales
CALLURA LODGE
**Callura East, Kilfenora Road,
Ennistymon, Co Clare**

Ennistymon
TEL: **065 7071640**
EMAIL: ura@eircom.net
WEB: www.bb_house.com/calluralodge.htm

Quiet home on R481. Nearby are Kilfenora, Cliffs of Moher, the Burren, Golf and Fishing. Tea/Coffee with home baking on arrival. TV lounge. Ideal touring base.

					Dinner	-
B&B	2	Ensuite	£19	€24.13	Dinner	-
B&B	2	Standard	£17	€21.59	Partial Board	-
Single Rate			£25.50	€32.38	Child reduction	25%

Open: 1st May-1st November

Mrs Patsy Flanagan
HARBOUR LODGE
6 Marine Parade, Kilkee,
Co Clare

Kilkee
TEL: 065 9056090

Town Home across road from Beach in scenic area, adjacent all amenities. Recommended by "The Irish Bed & Breakfast Book".

B&B	4	Ensuite	£19	€24.13	Dinner	-
B&B	1	Standard	£17	€21.59	Partial Board	-
Single Rate			£25.50	€32.38	Child reduction	-

In Kilkee   **Open:** 15th March-31st October

Mrs Maureen Haugh
DUGGERNA HOUSE
West End, Kilkee,
Co Clare

Kilkee
TEL: 065 9056152

On seafront overlooking the Duggerna rocks. Scenic surroundings. Golf, Fishing, Scuba Diving, Pitch and Putt. Ideal Touring Centre.

B&B	4	Ensuite	£20/£20	€25.39	Dinner	-
B&B		Standard	-	-	Partial Board	-
Single Rate			£25.50/£25.50	€32.38	Child reduction	-

In Kilkee   **Open:** 1st May-30th September

Mary Hickie
BAYVIEW
O'Connell Street, Kilkee,
Co Clare

Kilkee
TEL: 065 9056058
EMAIL: bayview3@eircom.net
WEB: www.bb.house.com/hickiesbayview.htm

Enjoy warm friendly hospitality in our tastefully decorated home. Magnificent view of Kilkee Bay, Cliffs. Central all amenities, Breakfast menu.

B&B	8	Ensuite	£19/£21	€24.13/€26.66	Dinner	-
B&B		Standard	-	-	Partial Board	-
Single Rate			£25.50/£26	€32.38/€33.01	Child reduction	50%

In Kilkee   **Open:** All Year Except Christmas

Diana Martin
WESTCLIFF HOUSE
West End, Kilkee,
Co Clare

Kilkee
TEL: 065 9056108
EMAIL: dianamartin@eircom.net
WEB: www.bb-house.com/westcliffhouse.htm

Modernised seafront home, spacious rooms. Scenic area - Cork, Kerry, Galway within touring distance.

B&B	5	Ensuite	£19/£21	€24.13/€26.66	Dinner	-
B&B	1	Standard	£17/£19	€21.59/€24.13	Partial Board	-
Single Rate			£23.50/£25.50	€29.84/€32.38	Child reduction	25%

In Kilkee   **Open:** 15th April-31st October

Mrs Ann Nolan
NOLANS B&B
Kilrush Road, Kilkee,
Co Clare

Kilkee
TEL: 065 9060100

Spacious family run accommodation in comfortable new dormer house. Breakfast menu. Private parking. Ideal touring base. Tea and Coffee available at all times.

B&B	6	Ensuite	£19/£20	€24.13/€25.39	Dinner	-
B&B		Standard	-	-	Partial Board	-
Single Rate			£20/£25	€25.39/€31.74	Child reduction	33.3%

In Kilkee   **Open:** All Year Except Christmas

In Killaloe

Eileen Brennan
CARRAMORE LODGE
Roolagh, Ballina,
Killaloe, Co Clare

Tel: **061 376704**
Email: carramorelodge@oceanfree.net
Web: www.dirl.com/clare/carramore_lodge.htm

Spacious family home on 1.5 acres mature gardens overlooking River Shannon on Lough Derg. 5 min walk from Village, Pubs, Restaurants, Church.

B&B	2	Ensuite	£20	€25.39	Dinner	-
B&B	2	Standard	£17.50	€22.22	Partial Board	-
Single Rate			£25/£27	€31.74/€34.29	Child reduction	33.3%

Open: 1st March-31st October

Killaloe 2km

Mrs Patricia Byrnes
RATHMORE HOUSE
Ballina, Killaloe,
Co Clare

Tel: **061 379296**
Email: rathmorebb@oceanfree.net
Web: www.dirl.com/clare/rathmore-house.htm

Family home R494, close river Shannon on Lough Derg. Scenic area, Fishing, walking, cycling, water sports. Convenient Limerick City, Bunratty, Shannon Airport.

B&B	5	Ensuite	£20	€25.39	Dinner	-
B&B	1	Standard	£17.50	€22.22	Partial Board	-
Single Rate			£25/£27	€31.74/€34.29	Child reduction	25%

Open: 1st March-31st October

In O'Gonnelloe

Ms Kathleen Flannery
LIG DO SCITH
O'Gonnelloe, Scarriff,
Co Clare

Tel: **061 923172**

New home with panoramic view of Lough Derg. Convenient to Shannon Airport. Timber floors throughout. Hill walking, Fishing, Water Sports, Horse Riding 5km.

B&B	4	Ensuite	£19/£22	€24.13/€27.93	Dinner	-
B&B	-	Standard	-	-	Partial Board	-
Single Rate			£25.50/£28	€32.38/€35.55	Child reduction	33.3%

Open: 2nd January-30th November

Killaloe 7km

Celine King
SHANNARRA
Killaloe,
Co Clare

Tel: **061 376548**
Email: celineking@hotmail.com

Comfortable family run accommodation 7km north of Killaloe on Scarriff road. Scenic views. Convenient to music Pubs, Restaurants, Water Sport & Hillwalking.

B&B	4	Ensuite	£19/£19	€24.13	Dinner	-
B&B	-	Standard	-	-	Partial Board	-
Single Rate			-	-	Child reduction	-

Open: 1st February-30th November

In Killimer

314

Imy Kerrigan
COIS-NA-SIONNA
Ferry Junction, Killimer,
Kilrush, Co Clare

Tel: **065 9053073**   Fax: **065 9053073**
Email: coisnasionna@eircom.net
Web: www.bb-house.com/cois-na-sionna.htm

Spectacularly located, overlooking the beautiful Shannon Estuary and just 50 mins Shannon Airport. On the N67. Ideal touring base to tour the West of Ireland.

B&B	4	Ensuite	£19	€24.13	Dinner	-
B&B	-	Standard	-	-	Partial Board	-
Single Rate			£25.50	€32.38	Child reduction	50%

Open: All Year Except Christmas

Michael & Mary Clarke
BRUACH NA COILLE
Killimer Road - N67
Kilrush, Co Clare

Kilrush

Tel: **065 9052250**   Fax: **065 9052250**
Email: clarkekilrush@hotmail.com
Web: www.clarkekilrush.com

On N67 opposite Vandeleur walled gardens. Rooms with views. Family run. Frommer reader recommended & AA listed. Tea/Coffee on arrival, ice available. Comprehensive Breakfast menu.

B&B	2	Ensuite	£19/£22	€24.13/€27.93	Dinner	-
B&B	2	Standard	£17/£20	€21.59/€25.39	Partial Board	-
Single Rate			£24/£30	€30.47/€38.09	Child reduction	50%

Kilrush 1km   **Open:** All Year

Austin & Eithna Hynes
HILLCREST VIEW
Doonbeg Road (off N67)
Kilrush, Co Clare

Kilrush

Tel: **065 9051986**   Fax: **065 9051986**
Email: ethnahynes@hotmail.com

Luxurious purpose built B&B. Spacious rooms. AA listed. Off N67. 5 mins walk Kilrush, Killimer Ferry 8km, Airport 1 hour drive. Guest conservatory. Quiet area.

B&B	6	Ensuite	£19/£21	€24.13/€26.66	Dinner	-
B&B	-	Standard	-	-	Partial Board	-
Single Rate			£26/£30	€33.01/€38.09	Child reduction	50%

Kilrush 1km   **Open:** All Year

Mary B Nolan
DOLPHINS PASS
Jemes, Cappa, Kilrush,
Co Clare

Kilrush

Tel: **065 9051822**
Email: jemesbandb@esatclear.ie

On the Shannon Estuary. Enjoy spectacular views to Loop Head. Historic Scattery Island, our Bottle Nosed Dolphins can be seen as they pass by. Fishing, Swimming, Walking at the door step.

B&B	3	Ensuite	£19	€24.13	Dinner	-
B&B	-	Standard	-	-	Partial Board	-
Single Rate			£25.50	€32.38	Child reduction	-

Kilrush 3km   **Open:** 1st April-31st October

Mrs Alyson O'Neill
OLD PAROCHIAL HOUSE
Cooraclare, Kilrush,
Co Clare

Kilrush

Tel: **065 9059059**   Fax: **065 9059059**
Email: oldparochialhouse@eircom.net
Web: www.oldparochialhouse.com

A place to do nothing! Restored rectory (C1872) on R483. Antiques, spacious. Quiet, unspoilt, rural views. Village (400m). Seafood, Pubs/Coast nearby.

B&B	2	Ensuite	£20/£30	€25.39/€38.09	Dinner	-
B&B	2	Standard	£18/£22.50	€22.86/€28.57	Partial Board	-
Single Rate			£25/£37	€31.74/€46.98	Child reduction	33.3%

In Cooraclare   **Open:** March-November

Mrs Joanne Barrett
EDENLANDIA
School Road, Lahinch,
Co Clare

Lahinch

Tel: **065 7081361**   Fax: **065 7081361**
Email: xbarrett@iol.ie

Set with panoramic views off main Lahinch - Killimer Ferry road. Golfers' 19th, tee-times arranged. Tea/Coffee, Hairdryer all rooms. Golf Course 2 mins. Shannon Airport 50 mins.

B&B	3	Ensuite	£20	€25.39	Dinner	-
B&B	-	Standard	-	-	Partial Board	-
Single Rate			£30	€38.09	Child reduction	-

Lahinch 1km   **Open:** 1st February-15th December

Ms Rosemary Donohue
COIS FARRAIGE
Milton Malbay Road,
Cregg, Lahinch, Co Clare

Lahinch

TEL: **065 7081580**   FAX: **065 7081580**
WEB: www.bb-house.com/coisfarraige.htm

Family run magnificant ocean views. Large family room (sleeps 5). Rooms with Electric Blankets and Hairdryers. Routard, Dillard Causin recommended.

B&B	6	Ensuite	£19	€24.13	Dinner	-
B&B	-	Standard	-	-	Partial Board	-
Single Rate			£26	€33.01	Child reduction	50%

Lahinch 1km

Open: 1st March-10th November

Mrs Brid Fawl
MULCARR HOUSE
Ennistymon Road, Lahinch,
Co Clare

Lahinch

TEL: **065 7081123**   FAX: **065 7081123**
EMAIL: mulcarrhouse@esatclear.ie
WEB: www.esatclear.ie/~mulcarrhouse

Smoke free home, walking distance to Beach, Golf Course. Convenient Cliffs of Moher, Doolin, Burren. Tea making facilities. Hair Dryers. On N67.

B&B	4	Ensuite	£19/£20	€24.13/€25.39	Dinner	-
B&B	-	Standard	-	-	Partial Board	-
Single Rate			£25.50/£26	€32.38/€33.01	Child reduction	25%

In Lahinch

Open: 17th April-31st October

Mrs Anita Gallery
TUDOR LODGE
Ennistymon Road, Lahinch,
Co Clare

Lahinch

TEL: **065 7081270**

Comfortable home, personally run. Adjacent to Golf Courses. Early breakfasts if required. Rooms with electric blankets. Special rate single room.

B&B	4	Ensuite	£19	€24.13	Dinner	-
B&B	-	Standard	-	-	Partial Board	-
Single Rate			£25.50	€32.38	Child reduction	33.3%

In Lahinch

Open: 15th March-1st December

Annie O'Brien
LE BORD DE MER
Milltown Malbay Rd.,
Lahinch, Co Clare

Lahinch

TEL: **065 7081454**   FAX: **065 7081454**
EMAIL: annieobrien@boinet.ie
WEB: http://homepage.eircom.net/~annieobrien

Breathtaking Ocean View, Lahinch Championship Golf, French speaking, beside Beach. Ideal base Cliffs of Moher, Burren, Aran Islands, Routard recommended.

B&B	4	Ensuite	£19	€24.13	Dinner	-
B&B	-	Standard	-	-	Partial Board	-
Single Rate			£26	€33.01	Child reduction	25%

Lahinch 1km

Open: March-October

Mrs Frances Sarma
NAZIRA
School Road, Lahinch,
Co Clare

Lahinch

TEL: **065 7081362**

Architect designed, magnificent views of Bay, Golf Courses. Peaceful setting. Warm welcome. Recommended in Dillard Causin Best Bed Breakfast Guide.

B&B	4	Ensuite	£19/£19	€24.13	Dinner	-
B&B	-	Standard	-	-	Partial Board	-
Single Rate			£26/£26	€33.01	Child reduction	-

Lahinch 1km

Open: March-November

Lahinch 1km

Mrs Margaret Skerritt
MOHER VIEW
Ennistymon Road, Lahinch,
Co Clare

Lahinch

TEL: **065 7081206**   FAX: **065 7081206**
EMAIL: moherview@esatclear.ie

Elevated dormer bungalow overlooking golf course. Convenient to Cliffs of Moher, Doolin, Burren, Tea/Coffee making facilities. Route N85.

B&B	4	Ensuite	£19/£19	€24.13	Dinner	-
B&B	-	Standard	-	-	Partial Board	-
Single Rate			£25.50/£25.50	€32.38	Child reduction	25%

Open: 1st April-31st October

In Lahinch

Ita Slattery
SEAFIELD LODGE
Ennistymon Road, Lahinch,
Co Clare

Lahinch

TEL: **065 7081594**

Elevated dormer bungalow on N67, 5 mins walk Lahinch Beach, Golf Course. All rooms TV, Radio, & Electric Bankets, Hairdryers.

B&B	4	Ensuite	£19	€24.13	Dinner	-
B&B	-	Standard	-	-	Partial Board	-
Single Rate			£25.50	€32.38	Child reduction	25%

Open: 15th April- 31st October

Lahinch 2km

Mrs Marian White
SEA BREEZE
Carrowgar, Miltown Malbay Road,
Lahinch, Co Clare

Lahinch

TEL: **065 7081073**
EMAIL: mariantwhite@eircom.net

Family run bungalow on N67 in rural setting. 2km Lahinch. Convenient Beach, Cliffs of Moher, Burren, trips to Aran Islands, Golf Courses, Pony Trekking, Swimming Pools, Sauna, Jacuzzi.

B&B	3	Ensuite	£19/£20	€24.13/€25.39	Dinner	-
B&B	-	Standard	-	-	Partial Board	-
Single Rate			-	-	Child reduction	-

Open: 1st May-30th September

In Liscannor

Noel & Agnes Andrews
CARRAIG HOUSE
Liscannor,
Co Clare

Liscannor

TEL: **065 7081260**   FAX: **065 7081260**

Modern spacious comfortable home. Rural setting close to Village near Cliffs of Moher, Burren, trips to Aran, Golf. Sign at Village Church on R478.

B&B	6	Ensuite	£19/£19	€24.13	Dinner	-
B&B	-	Standard	-	-	Partial Board	-
Single Rate			£25.50/£25.50	€32.38	Child reduction	25%

Open: 1st January-23rd December

Liscannor 2km

Ms Marie Dowling
CLIFF VIEW LODGE
Lislarkin, Liscannor,
Co Clare

Liscannor

TEL: **065 7081783**

Modern family run home, set in rural country surround. Adjacent to Cliffs of Moher, Burren. Doolin - Aran Islands Ferry.

B&B	3	Ensuite	£19/£19	€24.13	Dinner	-
B&B	-	Standard	-	-	Partial Board	-
Single Rate			£25.50	€32.38	Child reduction	-

Open: All Year

James & Sheila Lees
SEA HAVEN
Liscannor,
Co Clare

Liscannor
TEL: **065 7081385**   FAX: **065 7081474**

Sea-Haven with sea views. On main Lahinch - Cliffs of Moher road. Orthopaedic beds. 5 minutes walk to Liscannor Village.

B&B	6	Ensuite	£19	€24.13	Dinner	-
B&B	-	Standard	-	-	Partial Board	-
Single Rate			£25.50	€32.38	Child reduction	25%

Open: January-November

In Liscannor

Kevin & Ann Thynne
SEAMOUNT
Liscannor, Co Clare

Liscannor
TEL: **065 7081367**

Family run home on road to Cliffs of Moher. In quiet secluded garden. 5 minutes walk from Liscannor Village. Close to Golf, Fishing, Pubs & Restaurants.

B&B	3	Ensuite	£19/£19	€24.13	Dinner	-
B&B	-	Standard	-	-	Partial Board	-
Single Rate			£25.50/£25.50	€32.38	Child reduction	50%

Open: 17th March-31st October

Mrs Eileen Barrett
MARCHMONT
Lisdoonvarna,
Co Clare

Lisdoonvarna
TEL: **065 7074050**

In Lisdoonvarna

Town House, Car Park. TV Lounge. Hairdryers in rooms. Bicycle lock-up. Rick Steves recommended.

B&B	5	Ensuite	£19/£20	€24.13/€25.39	Dinner	-
B&B	-	Standard	-	-	Partial Board	-
Single Rate			£25.50/£25.50	€32.38	Child reduction	25%

Open: 1st February-30th November

Mrs Bernie Cosgrove
ST JUDES
Coast Road, Lisdoonvarna,
Co Clare

Lisdoonvarna
TEL: **065 7074108**

Lisdoonvarna 1km

Elevated site overlooking countryside on N67 Doolin Road. Cliffs of Moher, Burren, Doolin, closeby. Hairdryer, Bicycle Shed, Electric Blankets, (1) three bedded room. Homebaking. Failte.

B&B	4	Ensuite	£19/£20	€24.13/€25.39	Dinner	-
B&B	-	Standard	-	-	Partial Board	-
Single Rate			£26	€33.01	Child reduction	50%

Open: 1st May-7th October

Lisdoonvarna 2km

Mrs Monica Droney
CROSSWINDS
Lisdoonvarna,
Co Clare

Lisdoonvarna
TEL: **065 7074469**
EMAIL: crwinds@mail.com
WEB: crwinds.cjb.net

Situated on Cliffs of Moher Rd, (R478). 10 mins drive Doolin, Island Ferries, Burren & Lisdoonvarna. Walking distance to nightly entertainment.

B&B	2	Ensuite	£19	€24.13	Dinner	-
B&B	1	Standard	£17	€21.59	Partial Board	-
Single Rate			£23.50/£25.50	€29.84/€32.38	Child reduction	33.3%

Open: April-October

Mrs Mary Finn
ST ENDA'S
Church Street, Lisdoonvarna,
Co Clare

Lisdoonvarna
TEL: **065 7074066**

Five minutes walk to Town Centre. Two storey house with sun lounge. Leading to main Galway Road. Welcoming tea/coffee and home baking. Bicycle lock up. Ideal base Burren, Cliffs of Moher.

B&B	3	Ensuite	£19	€24.13	Dinner	-
B&B	-	Standard	-		Partial Board	-
Single Rate			-	-	Child reduction	50%

In Lisdoonvarna

Open: 15th March-1st November

Vera Fitzpatrick
FERMONA HOUSE
Bog Road, Lisdoonvarna,
Co Clare

Lisdoonvarna
TEL: **065 7074243**

Modern bungalow 10 mins from Town Centre. Doolin, Cliffs of Moher and Burren Centre. 1hour drive to Shannon Airport and Galway. Home comfort and good breakfast.

B&B	5	Ensuite	£19/£20	€24.13/€25.39	Dinner	-
B&B	-	Standard	-		Partial Board	-
Single Rate			£25.50	€32.38	Child reduction	-

In Lisdoonvarna

Open: 1st April-7th October

Joseph & Michelle Garrihy
LIMESTONE LODGE
Ardeamush, Lisdoonvarna,
Co Clare

Lisdoonvarna
TEL: **065 7074345**   FAX: **065 7074345**
EMAIL: michelle_vaug85@hotmail.com

Family home, 5kms from the Spa town of Lisdoonvarna. Ideal base for touring the Burren, Cliffs of Moher, Doolin and the Alliwee Caves. All rooms ensuite/TV's.

B&B	4	Ensuite	£19/£22	€24.13/€27.93	Dinner	-
B&B	-	Standard	-		Partial Board	-
Single Rate			£25.50/£25.50	€32.38	Child reduction	33.3%

Lisdoonvarna 4km

Open: 1st May-1st October

Mrs Ann Green
HILLTOP
Doolin Road, Lisdoonvarna,
Co Clare

Lisdoonvarna
TEL: **065 7074134**

Elevated site on N67, quiet location. 7 minutes walk to Village. One large family room. Convenient to Cliffs of Moher, Doolin and the Burren. Traditional music locally. Boat trips to Aran.

B&B	3	Ensuite	£19/£19	€24.13	Dinner	-
B&B	-	Standard	-		Partial Board	-
Single Rate			-	-	Child reduction	33.3%

Lisdoonvarna 1km

Open: 15th May-1st November

Oliver & Deirdre McNamara
DEISE
Bog Road, Lisdoonvarna,
Co Clare

Lisdoonvarna
TEL: **065 7074360**   FAX: **065 7074360**
EMAIL: olde@iol.ie

19th Century cottage renovated to high standard, maintaining the traditional home with 21st Century conveniences! Beidh Failte romhat anseo.

B&B	4	Ensuite	£19/£22	€24.13/€27.93	Dinner	-
B&B	-	Standard	-		Partial Board	-
Single Rate			£25.50/£25.50	€32.38	Child reduction	50%

In Lisdoonvarna

Open: 1st July-30th September

Lisdoonvarna 1km

Mrs Cathleen O'Connor
RONCALLI
**Doolin Road, Lisdoonvarna,
Co Clare**

Lisdoonvarna
TEL: **065 7074115**
WEB: www.bb-house.com/roncalli.html

7 mins walk to village on N67. 5 houses from Burmah Filling Station. Quiet location. "Lets Go" recommended. Close to Burren, Cliffs of Moher, Aran Ferry, Traditional Music. TV, Hairdryer,

B&B	3	Ensuite	£19/£19	€24.13	Dinner	-
B&B	-	Standard	-	-	Partial Board	-
Single Rate			£25.50	€32.38	Child reduction	33.3%

Open: 6th April-1st November

In Lisdoonvarna

Mrs Joan O'Flaherty
GOWLAUN
**St Brendan's Road,
Lisdoonvarna,
Co Clare**

Lisdoonvarna
TEL: **065 7074369**
EMAIL: gowlaun@eircom.net

Situated on a quiet location off N67. 5 mins walk from Town Centre and bus stop. One hour drive from Shannon Airport, Burren and Cliffs of Moher closeby.

B&B	3	Ensuite	£19/£20	€24.13/€25.39	Dinner	-
B&B	-	Standard	-	-	Partial Board	-
Single Rate			£25.50/£25.50	€32.38	Child reduction	33.3%

Open: 13th April-31st October

Lisdoonvarna 1km

Anne & Denis O'Loughlin
BURREN BREEZE
**The Wood Cross,
Lisdoonvarna, Co Clare**

Lisdoonvarna
TEL: **065 7074263** FAX: **065 7074820**
EMAIL: burrenbb@iol.ie
WEB: www.iol.ie/~burrenbb

Rooms with Bath & Shower, Tea/Coffee, TV, Hairdryers. 2/3/4 night offers. Off season rates. Internet access. Information. Junction N67/R477 Doolin/Coast rd.

B&B	5	Ensuite	£13/£17	€16.51/€21.59	Dinner	£11
B&B	1	Standard	£12/£16	€15.24/€20.32	Partial Board	£175
Single Rate			£18/£32	€22.86/€40.63	Child reduction	50%

Open: 15th January-15th December

The Petty Family
SUNVILLE
**Off Doolin Road,
Lisdoonvarna, Co Clare**

Lisdoonvarna
TEL: **065 7074065** FAX: **065 7074065**
EMAIL: thepettyfamily@indigo.ie
WEB: indigo.ie/~petty/

Situated off N67, quiet area with private parking. Near Cliffs of Moher, Burren, Golf at Lahinch, Trips to Aran Island. Frommer recommended. Electric blankets, Hairdryers. Off season rates.

B&B	4	Ensuite	£19/£20	€24.13/€25.39	Dinner	-
B&B	-	Standard	-	-	Partial Board	-
Single Rate			£25.50/£27	€32.38/€34.29	Child reduction	33.3%

In Lisdoonvarna

Open: All Year

Mrs Helen Stack
ORE-A-TAVA HOUSE
Lisdoonvarna, Co Clare

Lisdoonvarna
TEL: **065 7074086** FAX: **065 7074547**
EMAIL: oreatava@eircom.net

House in quiet area on landscaped gardens with patio for visitiors use. Cliffs of Moher, Burren, Aran Islands nearby. Shannon-Galway 1 hour. Breakfast menu available. Credit cards accepted.

B&B	6	Ensuite	£19/£20	€24.13/€25.39	Dinner	-
B&B	-	Standard	-	-	Partial Board	-
Single Rate			£25.50	€32.38	Child reduction	33.3%

Lisdoonvarna 1km

Open: 20th March-31st October

Lisdoonvarna 1km

Mrs Irene Vaughan
WOODHAVEN
**Doolin Coast Road,
Lisdoonvarna, Co Clare**

Tᴇʟ: **065 7074017**

Junction off N67/R477 scenic, peaceful surroundings. Near Doolin ferry. Traditional music. Cliffs of Moher. Electric Blankets, Homebaking, Private car park, Bicycle shed, Hairdryers.

B&B	4	Ensuite	£19/£20	€24.13/€25.39	Dinner	-
B&B	1	Standard	£17	€21.59	Partial Board	-
Single Rate			£25/£25	€31.74	Child reduction	25%

Open: All Year Except Christmas

Miltown Malbay 1km

Mary Hughes
AN GLEANN
**Ennis Road, Miltown Malbay,
Co Clare**

Tᴇʟ: **065 7084281**
Eᴍᴀɪʟ: angleann@oceanfree.net
Wᴇʙ: members.xoom.com/anglean/

Friendly family run home, rooms ensuite, TV, Tea/Coffee. Located 1km Ennis Road. Recommended "New York Times". Close to all amenities. All credit cards welcome.

B&B	4	Ensuite	£19/£20	€24.13/€25.39	Dinner	-
B&B	-	Standard	-	-	Partial Board	-
Single Rate			£25.50/£25.50	€32.38	Child reduction	33.3%

Open: All Year

Miltown Malbay 4.5km

Mrs Maura Keane
SEA CREST
**Rineen, Milltown Malbay,
Co Clare**

Tᴇʟ: **065 7084429**   Fᴀx: **065 7084429**
Eᴍᴀɪʟ: seacrestguesthouse@eircom.net

On N67 overlooking Cliffs of Moher, Golf Courses and Beaches nearby. Rooms ensuite. TV Lounge for guests, use of kitchen for Tea/Coffee facilities.

B&B	5	Ensuite	£19	€24.13	Dinner	-
B&B	-	Standard	-	-	Partial Board	-
Single Rate			£25.50	€32.38	Child reduction	50%

Open: All Year

Miltown Malbay 1km

Katie & John McInerney
ATLANTIC STAR
**Spanish Point, Miltown Malbay,
Co Clare**

Tᴇʟ: **065 7084782**   Fᴀx: **065 6844889**
Eᴍᴀɪʟ: atlanticstar@eircom.net
Wᴇʙ: homepage.eircom.net/~atlanticstar

Modern spacious house on main N67 road to/from Killimer Car Ferry. Opposite Golf course. 400 metres from sandy Beach.

B&B	6	Ensuite	£20/£20	€25.39	Dinner	-
B&B	-	Standard	-	-	Partial Board	-
Single Rate			£26/£26	€33.01	Child reduction	25%

Open: All Year

In Mountshannon

Howe Family
OAK HOUSE
Mountshannon, Co Clare

Tᴇʟ: **061 927185**   Fᴀx: **061 927185**

Country home, panoramic view, overlooking Lough Derg. Private Beach, Boats, excellent facilities for Fishermen. Ideal base for touring. 200m village.

B&B	2	Ensuite	£19/£19	€24.13	Dinner	-
B&B	1	Standard	£17/£17	€21.59	Partial Board	-
Single Rate			£23.50/£25.50	€29.84/€32.38	Child reduction	25%

Open: 1st April-1st October

Shannonside · Clare

In Newmarket on Fergus

Colette Gilbert
FERGUS LODGE
Ennis Road,
Newmarket-on-Fergus,
Co Clare

Newmarket-on-Fergus
TEL: **061 368351**   FAX: **061 368351**

On N18, beside Texaco Station. Shannon Airport, Bunratty, Knappogue, 10 minutes. Dromoland Castle and Clare Inn Hotel 2 minutes drive. Walking distance to Pubs, Restaurants.

B&B	5	Ensuite	£20/£20	€25.39	Dinner	-
B&B	-	Standard	-	-	Partial Board	-
Single Rate			£25.50/£25.50	€32.38	Child reduction	25%

cc S P ... **Open:** All Year

Newmarket-on-Fergus 2km

Mrs Sheila Ryan
THE DORMER
Lisduff, Newmarket-On-Fergus,
Co Clare

Newmarket-on-Fergus
TEL: **061 368354**   FAX: **061 368354**
EMAIL: gerandsheilaryan@eircom.net
WEB: www.web-ie.com/thedormer/

Peaceful rural setting, Airport side of Newmarket-on-Fergus off N18. Shannon Airport, Bunratty 15 mins. Dromoland Castle 5 mins. Fine Restaurants locally.

B&B	2	Ensuite	£19	€24.13	Dinner	-
B&B	1	Standard	£17	€21.59	Partial Board	-
Single Rate			£25	€31.74	Child reduction	50%

cc P ... **Open:** 1st March-31st October

Killaloe 8km

Anne & Dave Hyland
SHANNON COTTAGE
O'Brien's Bridge,
Co Clare

O'Brien's Bridge
TEL: **061 377118**   FAX: **061 377966**
EMAIL: bandb@shannoncottage.com
WEB: www.shannoncottage.com

Traditional 200 year old refurbished Cottage, on the banks of the River Shannon at O'Brien's Bridge Village. Restaurants, Fishing, Walking, Golf nearby.

B&B	6	Ensuite	£19/£25	€24.13/€31.74	Dinner	-
B&B	-	Standard	-	-	Partial Board	-
Single Rate			£25.50/£35	€32.38/€44.44	Child reduction	25%

cc P ... **Open:** 15th January-15th December

In Quin

Mrs Joan Murphy
ROOSKA HOUSE
Quin, Co Clare

Quin
TEL: **065 6825661**

Modern house in village. Convenient Quin Abbey, Knappogue & Craggaunowen. Shannon Airport 30 mins, Ennis 15 mins, Limerick 30 mins.

B&B	2	Ensuite	£19	€24.13	Dinner	-
B&B	2	Standard	£17	€21.59	Partial Board	£200
Single Rate			£23.50	€29.84	Child reduction	33.3%

cc P ... **Open:** 1st May-31st October

Mr John Boland
FORT LACH
Drumline, Newmarket-on-Fergus,
Co Clare

Shannon
TEL: **061 364003**   FAX: **061 364059**
EMAIL: johnboland@eircom.net
WEB: homepage.eircom.net/~johnboland

Modern house, rural setting, 600 yds off N18. Shannon Airport, Bunratty, Golf, Horse Riding, Fishing all 10 mins. Ideal touring centre.

B&B	6	Ensuite	£19	€24.13	Dinner	-
B&B	-	Standard	-	-	Partial Board	-
Single Rate			£25.50	€32.38	Child reduction	25%

cc P ... **Open:** 1st February-30th November

Shannon 7km

Shannon 4km

Mrs Kathleen Collins
VALHALLA
Urlanbeg, Newmarket-on-Fergus,
Shannon, Co Clare

Shannon
TEL: **061 368293**   FAX: **061 368660**
EMAIL: valhalla@esatclear.ie
WEB: shannonheartland.ie

Situated on Newmarket-on-Fergus/Shannon Road R472. 1km off N18. Ideal first last stop. Morning guests welcome. Bunratty/Shannon 10 minutes. Hairdryers.

B&B	3	Ensuite	£19/£19	€24.13	Dinner	-
B&B	-	Standard	-	-	Partial Board	-
Single Rate			£25.50/£25.50	€32.38	Child reduction	33.3%

Open: 1st January-22nd December

Shannon 4km

Mrs Geraldine Enright
TRADAREE
Drumline, Newmarket-on-Fergus,
Co Clare

Shannon
TEL: **061 364386**

Old style dormer house 100m off N18 to Ennis. Bunratty Castle, Shannon Airport 5 mins. Morning guests welcome. Visitors Garden.

B&B	1	Ensuite	£19	€24.13	Dinner	-
B&B	2	Standard	£17	€21.59	Partial Board	-
Single Rate			£23.50	€29.84	Child reduction	25%

Open: 1st April-1st October

Shannon 5km

Mrs Phil Fleming
KNOCKNAGOW
Leimaneighmore,
Newmarket-on-Fergus,
Co Clare

Shannon
TEL: **061 368685**   FAX: **061 368685**
EMAIL: knocknagowbandb@eircom.net
WEB: homepage.eircom.net/~knocknagow

Purpose built B&B. 8km from Shannon Airport on R472 Shannon/Newmarket-on-Fergus Road. Convenient to Bunratty & Knappogue Castles. Early guests welcome.

B&B	4	Ensuite	£19	€24.13	Dinner	-
B&B	-	Standard	-	-	Partial Board	-
Single Rate			£25.50	€32.38	Child reduction	25%

Open: 2nd January-22nd December

Shannon 3km

Mrs Sheila Hanrahan
THE CROOKED CHIMNEY
Hurlers Cross, Shannon,
Co Clare

Shannon
TEL: **061 364696**   FAX: **061 364696**
EMAIL: thecrookedchimney@eircom.net

Off main road N18 (Exit Hurlers Cross). 3 miles Shannon, 2 miles Bunratty. Private gardens for guest viewing. Tea/Coffee facilities.

B&B	5	Ensuite	£19/£19	€24.13	Dinner	-
B&B	-	Standard	-	-	Partial Board	-
Single Rate			£25.50	€32.38	Child reduction	-

Open: January-November

In Shannon

Mrs Brede Lohan
35 Tullyglass Crescent,
Shannon, Co Clare

Shannon
TEL: **061 364268**

Home overlooking River Shannon. Cul-de-sac. Airport Terminal 1.5 miles. Leisure Centre, Swimming Pool, Sauna 200 yds. Take Tullyglass Rd off Roundabout N19.

B&B	6	Ensuite	£19	€24.13	Dinner	£19
B&B	-	Standard	-	-	Partial Board	-
Single Rate			£25.50	€32.38	Child reduction	25%

Open: All Year

In Shannon

Mrs Kay Moloney
MOLONEY'S B&B
**21 Coill Mhara, Shannon,
Co Clare**

TEL: **061 364185**

Home situated 5 mins from Airport Terminal. Shannon Town Centre 400 yds. Third road on left after Texaco filling station.

B&B	2	Ensuite	£19/£19	€24.13	Dinner	-
B&B	2	Standard	£17/£17	€21.59	Partial Board	-
Single Rate			-	-	Child reduction	33.3%

Open: 8th January-20th December

Shannon Town 2km

Mrs Mary Mooney
THE KYRENIA
**Drumline,
Newmarket-on-Fergus,
Co Clare**

TEL: **061 364137**
EMAIL: kyrenia@eircom.net

Spacious modern home off N18. 12 mins Shannon Airport, Bunratty Castle 5 mins. Morning guests welcome. Early breakfast.

B&B	2	Ensuite	£19/£19	€24.13	Dinner	-
B&B	2	Standard	£17/£17	€21.59	Partial Board	-
Single Rate			-	-	Child reduction	25%

Open: 1st March-31st October

Shannon 2km

Mrs Betty Nally
IVORY LODGE
**Drumline, Newmarket-on-Fergus,
Co Clare**

TEL: **061 364039**
EMAIL: nallyivorylodge@eircom.net

Purpose built home in Drumline, 100m off N18. Airport 12 mins, Bunratty 5 mins. TV, Hairdryer, Tea/Coffee in rooms. Morning guests welcome. Ideal base for touring.

B&B	3	Ensuite	£19/£19	€24.13	Dinner	-
B&B	1	Standard	£19/£19	€24.13	Partial Board	-
Single Rate			-	-	Child reduction	33.3%

Open: 2nd January-20th December

Shannon 2km

Mrs Wiestawa O'Brien
TARA GREEN
**Ballycally/Aerospace Rd,
Newmarket-on-Fergus, Co Clare**

TEL: **061 363789**
EMAIL: tarag@iol.ie
WEB: www.iol.ie/~tarag

3 miles Shannon Airport. Welcome to Irish/Polish home. Organic garden. Home cooking. www.iol.ie/~tarag

B&B	4	Ensuite	£19/£19	€24.13	Dinner	£15
B&B	1	Standard	-		Partial Board	-
Single Rate			£23.50/£30	€29.84/€38.09	Child reduction	-

Open: All Year

In Shannon

Mary O'Loughlin
AVALON
**11 Ballycaseymore Hill,
Shannon Town, Co Clare**

TEL: **061 362032**   FAX: **061 362032**
EMAIL: avalonbnb@eircom.net
WEB: www.avalonbnb.net

Spacious modern home in quiet cul-de-sac overlooking Shannon. 5 min drive to Airport. Near Bunratty. Turn off N19 at Shannon Court Hotel.

B&B	2	Ensuite	£19/£19	€24.13	Dinner	-
B&B	2	Standard	£17/£17	€21.59	Partial Board	-
Single Rate			£28/£32	€35.55/€40.63	Child reduction	25%

Open: 2nd January-22nd December

Mrs Fidelma Ryan
MAPLE VIEW
Urlanmore,
Newmarket-on-Fergus,
Shannon, Co Clare

Shannon
TEL: **061 368062**

Morning guests welcome. Off Shannon/Newmarket road R472. 10 mins drive Shannon Airport. Shops & Restaurants 2km. Bunratty Castle 5 mins drive. Safe parking. Scenic area.

B&B	2	Ensuite	£19/£19	€24.13	Dinner	-
B&B	2	Standard	£17/£17	€21.59	Partial Board	-
Single Rate			£23.50/£25.50	€29.84/€32.38	Child reduction	33.3%

Shannon 5km

Open: 1st February-15th November

Geraldine E Ryan
HILLCREST
Clonlohan, Shannon/Newmarket
Road, Newmarket-On-Fergus,
Co Clare

Shannon
TEL: **061 364158**   FAX: **061 360582**
EMAIL: ryanhillcrest@broker.assurelink.ie

Family home. R472 back road Shannon to Newmarket-on-Fergus. Rural setting. Overlooking Airport. Morning guests, Golf, Restaurants 2km, Bunratty 4km.

B&B	2	Ensuite	£19/£19	€24.13	Dinner	-
B&B	2	Standard	£17/£17	€21.59	Partial Board	-
Single Rate			£23.50/£23.50	€29.84	Child reduction	50%

Shannon 2km

Open: 6th January-20th December

Mrs Kathleen Ryan
ARDREE
Monument Cross,
Newmarket-on-Fergus, Co Clare

Shannon
TEL: **061 368256**   FAX: **061 368846**
EMAIL: ardree@indigo.ie
WEB: indigo.ie/~ardree

Off Shannon/Newmarket Road R472, 2km from N18. Morning guests welcome. Golf, Horse Riding, Fishing. Bunratty & Shannon 10 mins.

B&B	1	Ensuite	£19/£19	€24.13	Dinner	-
B&B	2	Standard	£17/£17	€21.59	Partial Board	-
Single Rate			£23.50/£25.50	€29.84 /€32.38	Child reduction	25%

Shannon 4km

Open: 1st April-15th October

Mrs Mary Tobin
SHANNONSIDE
Clonlohan, Shannon/Newmarket
Rd, R472 Newmarket-on-Fergus,
Co Clare

Shannon
TEL: **061 364191**   FAX: **061 362069**
EMAIL: tobins.shannonside@oceanfree.net

Morning guests welcome, Highly recommended home offering warm hospitality for over 30 years on R472, 5 mins from Airport. Scenic area. Bunratty 10 mins.

B&B	6	Ensuite	£19	€24.13	Dinner	-
B&B	1	Standard	£17	€21.59	Partial Board	-
Single Rate			£25	€31.74	Child reduction	33.3%

Shannon 1km

Open: 7th January-23rd December

RESERVATIONS

- Confirm phone bookings in writing without delay with agreed deposit.
- To avoid misunderstandings later, check rate on booking and clarify any additional changes which may apply to your booking.
- Give details of any special requirements.
- State clearly day, date of arrival and departure date.

A pleasant county of lush green pastures, bordered by the Shannon. Adare, where you will find quaint cottages nestling in the prettiest village in Ireland.
Experience the welcome in historic Limerick. Visit King John's Castle, St. Mary's Cathedral, Hunt Museum and Georgian Pery Square. Partake of the many attractions including golf, horse-riding, fishing, festivals and evening entertainment.

Ann Abbott
MURPHY'S CROSS
Adare,
Co Limerick

Adare
Tel: **061 396042**   Fax: **061 396042**

160 year old renovated Cottage on main Killarney Road. Last house on left at T Junction. All rooms upstairs. Lift for luggage.

B&B	2	Ensuite	£19/£21	€24.13/€26.66	Dinner	-
B&B	3	Standard	£17/£19	€21.59/€24.13	Partial Board	-
Single Rate			£23.50/£30	€29.84/€38.09	Child reduction	-

In Adare

Open: 18th January-15th December

Mrs Ann Benson
RIVERSDALE
Station Road, Adare,
Co Limerick

Adare
Tel: **061 396751**

Select modern house. 4 minutes walk to Town Centre. Tea making facilities in bedrooms. Automatic Hairdryers. Shannon Airport 30 minutes. Ideal touring base.

B&B	3	Ensuite	£19/£20	€24.13/€25.39	Dinner	-
B&B	1	Standard	-	-	Partial Board	-
Single Rate			£23.50	€29.84	Child reduction	50%

In Adare

Open: 17th March-20th December

Mary Boyle
KNOCKREAD HOUSE
Croom Road, Adare,
Co Limerick

Adare
Tel: **061 396935**
Email: knockreadadare@eircom.net
Web: www.eircom.net/~knockreadadare

Friendly inviting home, lovely scenic countryside. Off N21, Shannon 35 mins, Adare 5 mins. Breakfast menu. Private parking, Woodland Hotel 1.5km. Near Golf, Fishing.

B&B	1	Ensuite	£19/£20	€24.13/€25.39	Dinner	-
B&B	2	Standard	£17/£17	€21.59	Partial Board	-
Single Rate			£25/£28	€31.74/€35.55	Child reduction	33.3%

Adare 3km

Open: 1st April-1st November

May Browne
ABBEY VILLA
Kildimo Road, Adare,
Co Limerick

Adare
Tel: **061 396113**   Fax: **061 396969**
Email: abbeyvilla@esatclear.ie

Warm friendly house. Electric Blankets, Hairdryers, Satellite TV, Laundry service. Ground floor bedrooms. Walking distance to Pubs, Restaurants and Hotels.

B&B	6	Ensuite	£22.50/£25	€28.57/€31.74	Dinner	-
B&B	-	Standard	-	-	Partial Board	-
Single Rate			£35/£40	€44.44/€50.79	Child reduction	50%

In Adare

Open: 1st January-18th December

Ms Deirdre Buckley
ROSSBEIGH
Ballingarry Road, Adare,
Co Limerick

Adare
TEL: 061 395141

Elegant Tudor-style home. Tranquil surroundings. Hairdryers, breakfast menu and orthopaedic beds. Convenient Hotels and Restaurants. Shannon Airport 30 mins.

B&B	3	Ensuite	£20/£25	€25.39/€31.74	Dinner	-
B&B	-	Standard	-	-	Partial Board	-
Single Rate			£25.50/£28	€32.38/€35.55	Child reduction	-

Adare 1km

Open: 5th January-23rd December

Mrs Patsy Davis
CLONSHIRE MILL
Croagh,
Co Limerick

Adare
TEL: 069 64200
EMAIL: paddydavis@eircom.net

Comfortable 19th Century house. Warm welcome. Gardens, Donkeys. Stables available. Equestrian Centre close, Golf, Fishing, Restaurants nearby. French spoken.

B&B	-	Ensuite	-	-	Dinner	£12.50
B&B	3	Standard	£17	€21.59	Partial Board	-
Single Rate			£23.50	€29.84	Child reduction	50%

Croagh 1.5km

Open: 1st May-30th September

Mrs Anne Donegan
WESTFIELD HOUSE
Ballingarry Rd R519, Graigue,
Adare, Co Limerick

Adare
TEL: 061 396539
EMAIL: westfieldhouse@eircom.net
WEB: www.adareaccommodation.com

Purpose built home in wooded area. Mature gardens. Just off busy N21. Airport 30 minutes. Golfers haven, touring base. Spacious rooms. Extensive menu. Highly recommended.

B&B	3	Ensuite	£20/£22	€25.39/€27.93	Dinner	-
B&B	-	Standard	-	-	Partial Board	-
Single Rate			£30/£30	€38.09	Child reduction	25%

Adare 1km

Open: 1st April-30th September

Bridie & Pat Donegan
BERKELEY LODGE
Station Road, Adare,
Co Limerick

Adare
TEL: 061 396857   FAX: 061 396857
EMAIL: berlodge@iol.ie
WEB: www.adare.org

Superb warm spacious home away from home. AA ♦♦♦♦, RAC♦♦♦♦ Awards. Breakfast menu. Near Hotels/Churches/Golf/Tour base. Turn at roundabout. Shannon 30 mins. Early arrivals welcome.

B&B	5	Ensuite	£22/£25	€27.93/€31.74	Dinner	-
B&B	1	Standard	£22/£25	€27.93/€31.74	Partial Board	-
Single Rate			£30/£40	€38.09/€50.79	Child reduction	25%

In Adare

Open: All Year

Mrs Geraldine Fitzgerald
SCEILIG HOUSE
Killarney Road, Adare,
Co Limerick

Adare
TEL: 061 396627
EMAIL: sceilig_house@ireland.com

Welcoming family home in Adare. Convenient Hotels, Restaurants, Leisure amenities, Pitch and Putt at rear. Ideal touring base. Shannon 30 minutes.

B&B	4	Ensuite	£20/£20	€25.39	Dinner	-
B&B	1	Standard	£18/£18	€22.86	Partial Board	-
Single Rate			£25/£27	€31.74/€34.29	Child reduction	33.3%

In Adare

Open: All Year

Mrs Agnes Fitzpatrick
ADARE LODGE
Kildimo Road, Adare,
Co Limerick

Adare
TEL: **061 396629**   FAX: **061 395060**
EMAIL: adarelodge@tinet.ie

In Adare

Highly recommended AA ♦♦♦♦ award. TV, Tea & Coffee in rooms. Adjacent Dunraven Arm's Hotel. Golf, Horseriding, Churches. Shannon Airport 30 mins.

				Dinner	-
B&B	6	Ensuite	£20/£25	€25.39/€31.74	
B&B	-	Standard		-	Partial Board	-
Single Rate			£30/£45	€38.09/€57.14	Child reduction	50%

Open: All Year

Kathleen Glavin
CASTLEVIEW HOUSE
Clonshire, Adare,
Co Limerick

Adare
TEL: **061 396394**   FAX: **061 396394**
EMAIL: castleview@eircom.net

Adare 2km

"Sullivans B&B Guide" recommended. Beautiful warm restful country home. Award winning gardens. Tea/Coffee. Excellent breakfasts including pancakes. Electric blankets. Hairdryers.

					Dinner	£15
B&B	3	Ensuite	£20/£20	€25.39		
B&B	1	Standard	£18/£18	€22.86	Partial Board	
Single Rate			£27/£27	€34.29	Child reduction	50%

Open: All Year

Mrs Anna Harrington
AVONA
Kildimo Rd, Adare,
Co Limerick

Adare
TEL: **061 396323**   FAX: **061 396323**
EMAIL: avona@eircom.net

In Adare

Adjacent to Hotels, Restaurants. Highly Recommended. AA ♦♦♦. Tea/Coffee facilities in guest lounge. Separate breakfast room which offers a wide ranging menu. Exit N21 at roundabout.

					Dinner	-
B&B	4	Ensuite	£20	€25.39		
B&B	-	Standard		-	Partial Board	-
Single Rate			£30	€38.09	Child reduction	-

Open: 1st March-31st October

Mrs Pauline Hedderman
ELM HOUSE
Clounanna Road, Mondellihy,
Adare, Co Limerick

Adare
TEL: **061 396306**

Adare Village 1km

Elegant restored 1892 Georgian Home with character, enjoying sheltered garden. "Lonely Planet" recommended. Welcoming Tea/Coffee. Shannon Airport 30 mins.

					Dinner	-
B&B	1	Ensuite	£20/£20	€25.39		
B&B	2	Standard	£18/£18	€22.86	Partial Board	-
Single Rate			£25	€31.74	Child reduction	33.3%

Open: 1st January-15th December

Betty Hickey
IVY HOUSE
Craigue N21, Adare,
Co Limerick

Adare
TEL: **061 396270**   FAX: **061 396270**

Adare 1km

Beautifully restored 18th century country home, surrounded by Gardens, Lawns, Shrubbery, furnished with Antiques and "objects D'Art". Homely atmosphere.

					Dinner	-
B&B	3	Ensuite	£20/£23	€25.39/€29.20		
B&B	-	Standard		-	Partial Board	-
Single Rate			£32	€40.63	Child reduction	25%

Open: 1st April-31st October

Adare Village 1km

Florence and Donal Hogan
COATESLAND HOUSE B&B
Tralee/Killarney Road, Adare,
N21 Co Limerick

Adare

TEL: **061 396372**   FAX: **061 396833**
EMAIL: coatesfd@indigo.ie
WEB: http://indigo.ie/~coatesfd/

Modern warm home, RAC & AA ◆◆◆◆ awards. Friendly atmosphere. Nice gardens adjacent to Village centre and good Restaurants. Many extras. On line facilities for guests.

B&B	6	Ensuite	£20/£22	€25.39/€27.93	Dinner	-
B&B	-	Standard	-	-	Partial Board	-
Single Rate			£25.50/£30	€32.38/€38.09	Child reduction	25%

Open: 1st January-22nd December

Adare 2km

Mrs Maura Linnane
CARRIGANE HOUSE
Reinroe, Adare,
Co Limerick

Adare

TEL: **061 396778**
EMAIL: carrigane.house@oceanfree.net
WEB: www.adareaccommodation.com

Luxurious and spacious country home just off main road. Morning guests welcome. Extensive breakfast menu. Near Woodlands Hotel.

B&B	6	Ensuite	£20/£22	€25.39/€27.93	Dinner	-
B&B	-	Standard	-	-	Partial Board	-
Single Rate			£25.50/£30	€32.38/€38.09	Child reduction	33.3%

Open: 1st February-16th December

Adare 2km

Mrs Margaret Liston
GLENELG
Mondellihy, Adare,
Co Limerick

Adare

TEL: **061 396077**

Luxurious superwarm home. Tranquil location. Highly recommended Karen Brown Erdvig. Airport 30 mins, Adare 4 mins. Tea/Coffee/Scones, TV, Hairdryers.

B&B	2	Ensuite	£20/£23	€25.39/€29.20	Dinner	-
B&B	1	Standard	£20/£23	€25.39/€29.20	Partial Board	-
Single Rate			£27	€34.29	Child reduction	50%

Open: 1st February-20th December

Adare 1km

Mrs Nora Hennessy-O'Keeffe
DUHALLOW HOUSE
Ballingarry Road (R519)
Adare, Co Limerick

Adare

TEL: **061 395030**
EMAIL: duhallow@adare-ireland.com
WEB: www.adare-ireland.com

Charming Rustic Family home at edge of Village. Warm friendly atmosphere. Satellite TV's, Hairdryers in rooms. First on right after N21/R519 junction.

B&B	3	Ensuite	£19/£21	€24.13/€26.66	Dinner	-
B&B	-	Standard	-	-	Partial Board	-
Single Rate			£25.50/£30	€32.38/€38.09	Child reduction	50%

Open: 1st April-1st November

Adare 5km

Michael and Jennie Power
HILLCREST COUNTRY HOME
Clonshire, Croagh,
Adare, Co Limerick

Adare

TEL: **061 396534**   FAX: **061 396534**
EMAIL: hillcrest_irl@hotmail.com
WEB: www.dirl.com/limerick/hillcrest.htm

Hospitable, relaxed home. Amidst beautiful, tranquil pastures where nature abounds. Traditional farming. Forest and nature trails. Medieval ruins. Frommer recommended.

B&B	3	Ensuite	£19.50/£20.50	€24.76/€26.03	Dinner	-
B&B	1	Standard	£17.50/£18.50	€22.22/€23.49	Partial Board	-
Single Rate			£28/£30	€35.55/€38.09	Child reduction	25%

Open: 1st March-31st October

Adare

Mrs Bridie Riordan
CHURCHVIEW HOUSE
Adare,
Co Limerick

TEL: **061 396371** FAX: **061 396371**

Warm, friendly home in Ireland's prettiest village. Tea facilities in lounge, sun lounge for guests. Adjacent Dunraven Arms Hotel, Church, Golf, Shannon, Airport 45 mins.

B&B	4	Ensuite	£19/£20	€24.13/€25.39	Dinner	-
B&B	2	Standard	£17/£19	€21.59/€24.13	Partial Board	-
Single Rate			£23.50/£25.50	€29.84/€32.38	Child reduction	25%

Open: All Year

Askeaton Pallaskenry

Phil Clancy
DRUMINACLARA HOUSE
Pallaskenry,
Co Limerick

TEL: **061 393148**

2km from Kilcornan House off N69, scenic route. Country setting, peaceful surroundings. 3km Curragh Chase Forest Park, Celtic Park, Animal Farm. Golf and Fishing locally. 40 mins Airport.

B&B	4	Ensuite	£19/£19	€24.13	Dinner	£14
B&B	-	Standard	-	-	Partial Board	-
Single Rate			£25.50/£25.50	€32.38	Child reduction	25%

Open: 3rd January-20th December

Askeaton 6km

Askeaton

Mrs Marie Keran
KILLEEN HOUSE
Cow Park, Kilcornan,
Palaskenry, Co Limerick

TEL: **061 393023**

Spacious friendly home, lovely gardens on N69 scenic route. Beside Curragh Caravan Forest Park, Celtic Park. Shannon Airport 40 mins. Limerick City 15 min, Askeaton 5 min.

B&B	5	Ensuite	£19/£19	€24.13	Dinner	£15
B&B	1	Standard	£17/£17	€21.59	Partial Board	-
Single Rate			£23.50/£23.50	€29.84	Child reduction	25%

Open: 1st January-23rd December

Askeaton 5km

Ballyneety

Mrs Mary Conway Ryan
FOUR SEASONS
Boherlode, Ballyneety,
Co Limerick

TEL: **061 351365** FAX: **061 351643**

Relaxing home, landscaped gardens, sandwiched between Limerick (Ballyclough) R511 & Limerick. County Golf Clubs. R512, off N20, N21, N24, N7, N18. TV, hairdryers, tea coffee in rooms.

B&B	3	Ensuite	£19/£19	€24.13	Dinner	-
B&B	-	Standard	-	-	Partial Board	-
Single Rate			£25.50/£25.50	€32.38	Child reduction	50%

Open: 1st January-21st December

Ballyneety 2km

Ballyneety

Mrs Margaret Ryan
GLENGROVE
Glen, Ballyneety,
Co Limerick

TEL: **061 351399** FAX: **061 351399**

Warm welcoming elegant home. Extensive breakfasts. Walking distance Golf, Restaurant, Pubs. On R512, parallel with N7, N24. Turn at Kilmallock roundabout on Childers Road. Ideal Shannon etc.

B&B	3	Ensuite	£19/£20	€24.13/€25.39	Dinner	-
B&B	1	Standard	£19	€24.13	Partial Board	-
Single Rate			£25.50	€32.38	Child reduction	50%

Open: 10th January-18th December

Limerick 7km

William & Deirdre Guiry
SUNVILLE B&B
**Woodpark, Castleconnell,
on N7, Co Limerick**

Castleconnell

TEL: **061 377735**   FAX: **061 377735**

Modern bungalow situated on N7 with pleasant gardens, tennis court. Convenient to village, Fishing, Restaurants, Walks. University, Airport 40mins.

B&B	6	Ensuite	£19/£19	€24.13	Dinner	-
B&B	-	Standard	-		Partial Board	-
Single Rate			£25.50/£25.50	€32.38	Child reduction	25%

Limerick City 9km

Open: 1st January-20th December

Siobhan Moloney
BARKER HOUSE
Glin, Co Limerick

Glin

TEL: **068 34027**
EMAIL: wmoloney@iol.ie

Elegant Town House on 3 acres, near Glin Castle. Offers luxury ensuite accommodation. Ideal touring base. Shannon Airport 1hr drive. Tarbert Car Ferry 6km.

B&B	3	Ensuite	£19/£20	€24.13/€25.39	Dinner	-
B&B	3	Standard	-	-	Partial Board	-
Single Rate			£26	€33.01	Child reduction	50%

In Glin

Open: 1st January-20th December

Estelle O'Driscoll
O'DRISCOLL'S B&B
**Main Street, Glin,
Co Limerick**

Glin

TEL: **068 34101**

Town house, welcoming and friendly. Glin is a picturesque Villlage on the N69. Near to Tarbert Car Ferry. Ballybunion Golf course 20 min.

B&B	3	Ensuite	£19/£20	€24.13/€25.39	Dinner	-
B&B	1	Standard	£18/£20	€22.86/€25.39	Partial Board	-
Single Rate			£23.50/£25	€29.84/€31.74	Child reduction	50%

Open: All Year Except Christmas

Mrs Catherine Sweeney
SCENIC VIEW HOUSE
**Ballyculhane, Glin,
Co Limerick**

Glin Tarbert

TEL: **068 34242**

Bungalow, 7 mins Tarbert Car Ferry. Panoramic view of Shannon Estuary. Enroute from Shannon to Ring of Kerry on N69.

B&B	3	Ensuite	£19/£23.50	€24.13/€29.84	Dinner	£12.50
B&B	3	Standard	£18/£21	€22.86/€26.66	Partial Board	-
Single Rate			-	-	Child reduction	25%

Tarbert 4km

Open: All Year

Mrs Patricia Nunan
ST ANDREW'S VILLA
**Kilfinane, Kilmallock,
Co Limerick**

Kilfinane

TEL: **063 91008**

Georgian Style house with interesting history. Formerly a school in rural village accessible via R517/N8/R512/N20. Organic garden, lawns, shrubs. Warm welcome.

B&B	-	Ensuite	-	-	Dinner	-
B&B	4	Standard	£17	€21.59	Partial Board	-
Single Rate			£23.50	€29.84	Child reduction	33.3%

Kilmallock 9km

Open: 10th April-31st October

Mrs Anne O'Sullivan
DEEBERT HOUSE
Kilmallock,
Co Limerick

Kilmallock
TEL: **063 98106**   FAX: **063 82002**

Splendid Georgian residence, award winning gardens. Ideal touring centre. Adjacent to historic sites, golf, hill walking, horse riding. Loughgur Heritage Centre. On R515.

B&B	4	Ensuite	£19/£19	€24.13	Dinner	£15
B&B	1	Standard	£17/£17	€21.59	Partial Board	£220
Single Rate			£23.50/£25.50	€29.84/€32.38	Child reduction	25%

In Kilmallock

Open: 1st March-30th November

Agnes Callinan
MOYRHEE
Phares Road, Meelick,
Co Limerick

Limerick City
TEL: **061 326300**

Situated on elevated site 1/2 mile off N18 North overlooking Clare Hills. Pets welcome by arrangement. Chiropractic clinic on premises

B&B	3	Ensuite	£20/£21	€25.39/€26.66	Dinner	£18
B&B	-	Standard	-	-	Partial Board	-
Single Rate			£25.50/£25.50	€32.38	Child reduction	-

Limerick 5km

Open: 1st January-1st December

Mrs Mary Dundon
ACACIA COTTAGE
2 Foxfield, Dooradoyle Road off
N20, Dooradoyle, Limerick
Co Limerick

Limerick City
TEL: **061 304757**   FAX: **061 304757**
EMAIL: acaciacottage@iolfree.ie

Warm, welcoming, cosy, friendly home, nice garden. Highly recommended. Great Breakfasts. All rooms with cable TV, Tea/Coffee, Hairdryer. 1km off N20 at Crescent Shopping Centre roundabout.

B&B	3	Ensuite	£20/£22	€25.39/€27.93	Dinner	-
B&B	1	Standard	£25/£30	-	Partial Board	-
Single Rate			£25/£30	€31.74/€38.09	Child reduction	33.3%

Limerick 3km

Open: All Year

Lelia & Bernard Hanly
SANDVILLA
Monaleen Road, Castletroy,
Co Limerick

Limerick City Castleroy
TEL: **061 336484**   FAX: **061 336484**
EMAIL: sandvilla@indigo.ie

A warm welcoming haven off N7 and N24. Landscaped gardens. Award winning breakfast menu. Orthopaedic beds, Tea/Coffee, TV in rooms. Near Castletroy, Kilmurry Hotels, University, Golf.

B&B	2	Ensuite	£19	€24.13	Dinner	£13
B&B	2	Standard	£17	€21.59	Partial Board	£185
Single Rate			£23.50/£25.50	€29.84/€32.38	Child reduction	25%

Limerick 5km

Open: All Year

Liam & Antoinette Fitzgibbon
WHITE HOUSE B & B
St Annes, Raheen,
Co Limerick

Limerick City
TEL: **061 301709**   FAX: **061 301709**

On N20 direction Cork/Kerry. Beside Raheen roundabout. 20 mins Shannon Airport. Restaurants, Pubs walking distance. Also Regional Hospital. Bus stop to City at front gate. Guest lounge.

B&B	5	Ensuite	£20/£25	€25.39/€31.74	Dinner	-
B&B	-	Standard	-	-	Partial Board	-
Single Rate			£28/£36	€35.55/€45.71	Child reduction	33.3%

Limerick 2km

Open: All Year Except Christmas

Limerick City 3km

Mrs Bergie Carroll
COONAGH LODGE
Coonagh, Off Ennis Rd,
Limerick, Co Limerick

Limerick City Ennis Road
Tel: **061 327050**
Email: coonagh@iol.ie
Web: www.ireland-discover.com/coonaghlodge.htm

Family run home. 10 minutes drive Shannon Airport, 5 minutes to Bunratty and Limerick City. Off Ennis Road roundabout at Travel Lodge Hotel.

B&B	6	Ensuite	£19/£20	€24.13/€25.39	Dinner	-
B&B	-	Standard	-	-	Partial Board	-
Single Rate			£25.50/£28	€32.38/€35.55	Child reduction	50%

Open: 1st January-21st December

Limerick 3km

Martin & Patricia Keane
SANTOLINA
Coonagh, Ennis Road,
Limerick, Co Limerick

Limerick City Ennis Road
Tel: **061 451590/328321**
Email: patriciackeane@eircom.net
Web: homepage.eircom.net/~santolina

Spacious country home. Ground floor accommodation. Coonagh is off N18 roundabout between Travelodge and Elm Garage. Convenient for City, Bunratty, Shannon.

B&B	6	Ensuite	£19/£20	€24.13/€25.39	Dinner	-
B&B	-	Standard	-	-	Partial Board	-
Single Rate			£25.50/£25.50	€32.38	Child reduction	50%

Open: 15th January-15th December

In Limerick

Mrs Joan McSweeney
TREBOR
Ennis Road, Limerick City,
Co Limerick

Limerick City Ennis Road
Tel: **061 454632**   Fax: **061 454632**
Email: treborhouse@eircom.net

Old fashioned Town House, short walk City Centre on Bunratty Castle/Shannon Airport road. Tea/Coffee.

B&B	5	Ensuite	£19/£20	€24.13/€25.39	Dinner	-
B&B	-	Standard	-	-	Partial Board	£200
Single Rate			£25.50/£30	€32.38/€38.09	Child reduction	20%

Open: 1st April-1st November

Limerick City 3km

Mrs Evelyn Moore
AVONDOYLE COUNTRYHOME
Dooradoyle Road,
Limerick, Co Limerick

Limerick City
Tel: **061 301590/301501** Fax: **061 301501**
Email: avondoyl@iol.ie
Web: welcome.to/avondoyle

Warm welcome, 2km off N20, Crescent Shopping Centre roundabout, extensive breakfast menu. Orthopaedic beds, Peaceful surroundings, TV, Coffee/Tea in rooms.

B&B	2	Ensuite	£19	€24.13	Dinner	-
B&B	2	Standard	£17	€21.59	Partial Board	-
Single Rate			£23.50/£25.50	€29.84/€32.38	Child reduction	-

Open: All Year

Limerick 5km

Noreen O'Farrell
DOONEEN LODGE
Caher Road, Mungret,
Near Limerick, Co Limerick

Limerick
Tel: **061 301332**   Fax: **061 301332**
Email: dooneenlodge@eircom.net

0.5 km off N20/21 between Limerick, Patricswell, Sign-posted. Tea/Coffee facilities, TV in all rooms. Convenient Adare, Bunratty, Shannon. Limerick 5km.

B&B	2	Ensuite	£19/£20	€24.13/€25.39	Dinner	-
B&B	1	Standard	£17/£18	€21.59/€22.86	Partial Board	-
Single Rate			£23.50/£25.50	€29.84/€32.38	Child reduction	33.3%

Open: 1st April-31st October

333

John and Betty O'Shea
LISHEEN
Coonagh, Ennis Road,
Limerick, Co Limerick

Limerick City Ennis Road
Tel: **061 455393**

Quiet rural setting, off Ennis road roundabout. Convenient to Shannon Airport, Bunratty and the West. Le Guide Du Routard recommended.

B&B	-	Ensuite	-	-	Dinner	-
B&B	4	Standard	£17	€21.59	Partial Board	-
Single Rate			£23.50	€29.84	Child reduction	25%

Limerick 3km

Open: 1st March-30th September

Carole O'Toole
GLEN EAGLES
12 Vereker Gardens, Ennis Road,
Limerick, Co Limerick

Limerick City Ennis Road
Tel: **061 455521**   Fax: **061 455521**

Quiet cul-de-sac. Nearest B&B to the City Centre, Train/Bus/Tourist Office. Off N18 beside Jurys Hotel. Frommer recommended. Hairdryers.

B&B	4	Ensuite	£20	€25.39	Dinner	-
B&B	-	Standard	-	-	Partial Board	-
Single Rate			£26	€33.01	Child reduction	25%

In Limerick City

Open: March-November

Mrs Helen Quinn
ASHGROVE HOUSE
42 Rossroe Avenue, Caherdavin,
Ennis Road, Limerick, Co Limerick

Limerick City Ennis Road
Tel: **061 453338**

Comfortable town house, 5 mins to City, RTC College. Convenient to Shannon Airport, Bunratty, off Ennis Road at Ivans Cross to N7W.

B&B	4	Ensuite	£19/£21	€24.13/€26.66	Dinner	-
B&B	-	Standard	-	-	Partial Board	-
Single Rate			£25.50/£25.50	€32.38	Child reduction	25%

Limerick City 2km

Open: All Year

Mr Ken Ryan
ARMADA LODGE
1 Elm Drive, Caherdavin,
Ennis Road, Limerick, Co Limerick

Limerick City Ennis Road
Tel: **061 326993**

Modern town house, convenient to Shannon Airport, City Centre, Bunratty and King Johns Castle. Opposite Greenhills Hotel. Private car parking.

B&B	4	Ensuite	£19	€24.13	Dinner	£12.50
B&B	-	Standard	-	-	Partial Board	£200
Single Rate			£25.50/£25.50	€32.38	Child reduction	50%

Limerick 2km

Open: All Year

Dermot Walsh
SANTA CRUZ
10 Coolraine Terrace, Ennis Road,
Limerick, Co Limerick

Limerick City Ennis Road
Tel: **061 454500**

Spacious town house, adjacent to Ryan Hotel, Shannon bus stop. City Centre bus stop. 15 minutes to Shannon/Bunratty. 5 minutes Town. Tea/Coffee facilities.

B&B	2	Ensuite	£19/£20	€24.13/€25.39	Dinner	£14
B&B	3	Standard	£17/£18	€21.59/€22.86	Partial Board	£185
Single Rate			£23.50/£25	€29.84/€31.74	Child reduction	50%

Limerick 1km

Open: All Year

Mrs Mary Walsh-Seaver
RINNAKNOCK
**Glenstal, Murroe,
Co Limerick**

TEL: **061 386189**   FAX: **061 386189**
EMAIL: walshseaver@hotmail.com

Spacious bungalow beside Glenstal Abbey. Off N7 and N24. On Slieve Felim Cycling and Walking Trails.

B&B	3	Ensuite	£20/£20	€25.39	Dinner	£12.50
B&B	2	Standard	£18/£18	€22.86	Partial Board	£185
Single Rate			£23.50/£25.50	€29.84/€32.38	Child reduction	25%

Murroe 2km

Open: 1st April-31st October

Mrs Joan King
RANCH HOUSE
**Cork Road, Newcastle West,
Co Limerick**

TEL: **069 62313**

Luxurious home on large landscape gardens, quiet peaceful setting halfway between Shannon/Killarney/Tralee, adjacent to 18 hole Golf Course.

B&B	5	Ensuite	£19/£19	€24.13	Dinner	-
B&B	-	Standard			Partial Board	-
Single Rate			£25.50/£25.50	€32.38	Child reduction	50%

Newcastle West 1km

Open: All Year Except Christmas

Mrs Eileen Murphy
THE ORCHARD
**Limerick Road,
Newcastle West, Co Limerick**

TEL: **069 61029**   FAX: **069 61029**
EMAIL: eileen_theorchard@yahoo.co.uk

Century old home with spacious rooms. Own farm produce. Breakfast menu. Homemade Breads/Jams. Near speed limit sign, on N21. Tea/Coffee on arrival.

B&B	5	Ensuite	£19	€24.13	Dinner	£15
B&B	-	Standard	-	-	Partial Board	-
Single Rate			£25.50	€32.38	Child reduction	50%

Newcastle West 1km

Open: All Year

Mrs Carmel O'Brien
BALLINGOWAN HOUSE
**Limerick Road, Newcastle West,
Co Limerick**

TEL: **069 62341**   FAX: **069 62457**
EMAIL: ballingowanhouse@tinet.ie

Luxurious pink Georgian house with distinctive features. Dillard Causin recommended. Landscaped gardens. N21 half way stop between Shannon/Killarney. 18 hole Golf course nearby.

B&B	5	Ensuite	£19	€24.13	Dinner	-
B&B	-	Standard	-	-	Partial Board	-
Single Rate			£25.50	€32.38	Child reduction	25%

Newcastle West 2km

Open: All Year

Eilish Buckley
LAUREL LODGE
**Adare Road, Newboro,
Patrickswell, Co Limerick**

TEL: **061 355059**   FAX: **061 355059**
EMAIL: buckleyhome@yahoo.com
WEB: www.laurellodge.tourguide.net

Pamper yourself in our secluded luxurious country home. Award winning gardens between Limerick and Adare. 1.5km off N21 after Patrickswell. Limerick City 15 mins, Shannon Airport 25 mins.

B&B	3	Ensuite	£20/£20	€25.39	Dinner	-
B&B	1	Standard	£18/£18	€22.86	Partial Board	-
Single Rate			£25	€31.74	Child reduction	33.3%

Patrickswell 3km

Open: 1st April-31st October

Patrickswell 3km

The Geary Family
CARNLEA HOUSE
Caher Road, Cloughkeating,
Patrickswell, Co Limerick

TEL: **061 302902**

Spacious bungalow situated midway between Limerick City and Patrickswell (N20). Ideal stopover, Cork/Kerry/Bunratty/Shannon. Friendly atmosphere. Highly recommended.

B&B	2	Ensuite	£19/£19	€24.13	Dinner	-
B&B	2	Standard	£17/£17	€21.59	Partial Board	-
Single Rate			£25	€31.74	Child reduction	**50%**

Open: 1st March-31st October

Patrickswell

Mrs Margaret Kearney
BEECH GROVE
Barnakyle, Patrickswell,
Co Limerick

TEL: **061 355493**

Bungalow on N20/N21, off R526 Limerick/Adare. Walking distance Patrickswell. Airport 20 mins. Horse racing, Golf, Greyhound Track. Warm welcome. Ideal stopover Cork/Kerry. Visa accepted.

B&B	1	Ensuite	£19/£19	€24.13	Dinner	-
B&B	3	Standard	£17/£17	€21.59	Partial Board	-
Single Rate			£23.50/£25.50	€29.84/€32.38	Child reduction	**33.3%**

Open: 1st May-31st September

Limerick 2km

Mrs Deirdre O'Grady
IROKO
Caher Road, Cloughkeating,
Patrickswell, Co Limerick

TEL: **061 227861**   FAX: **061 227869**
EMAIL: iroko@eircom.net
WEB: homepage.eircom.net/~iroko/index.htm

First class accommodation, 1/2 way between Limerick and Patrickswell. 2nd house off N20/21. TV, Tea/Coffee facilities, Hairdryers. Convenient Adare, Bunratty, Shannon, Golf, Cork, Kerry.

B&B	5	Ensuite	£19/£22	€24.13/€27.93	Dinner	-
B&B		Standard	-	-	Partial Board	-
Single Rate			£25.50/£29	€32.38/€36.82	Child reduction	**33.3%**

Open: 1st January-18th December

Patrickswell 2km

Noreen O'Leary
CEDAR LODGE
Patrickswell,
Co Limerick

TEL: **061 355137**

Situated between Limerick and Patrickswell on N20/21. Experience quality and comfort in our friendly family-run home.

B&B	4	Ensuite	£19/£20	€24.13/€25.39	Dinner	-
B&B		Standard	-	-	Partial Board	-
Single Rate			£25.50/£30	€32.38/€38.09	Child reduction	-

Open: 1st March- 31st October

Patrickswell Village 1km

Mrs Lily Woulfe
LURRIGA LODGE
Patrickswell, Co Limerick

TEL: **061 355411**   FAX: **061 355411**
EMAIL: woulfe@esatclear.ie

Award winning luxurious country home, landscaped gardens. Between Limerick/Adare. 0.25km off N21 after Patrickswell. Shannon Airport 25 mins. Adare 6 mins.

B&B	4	Ensuite	£20	€25.39	Dinner	-
B&B		Standard	-	-	Partial Board	-
Single Rate			£25.50	€32.38	Child reduction	**25%**

Open: 1st May-30th October

Theresa Fitzgerald
THE WILLOWS
**Castlematrix, Rathkeale,
Co Limerick**

Rathkeale

TEL: **069 63157**

Luxurious, spacious home. Beautiful Antique furniture. Large Conservatory. Award winning, spacious gardens, patio. Ideal touring base Cork/Kerry/Clare. N21 route.

B&B	4	Ensuite	£25/£27.50	€31.74/€34.91	Dinner	-
B&B	-	Standard	-	-	Partial Board	-
Single Rate			£30/£30	€38.09	Child reduction	**50%**

In Rathkeale

Open: 1st April-30th September

Roscrea Castle

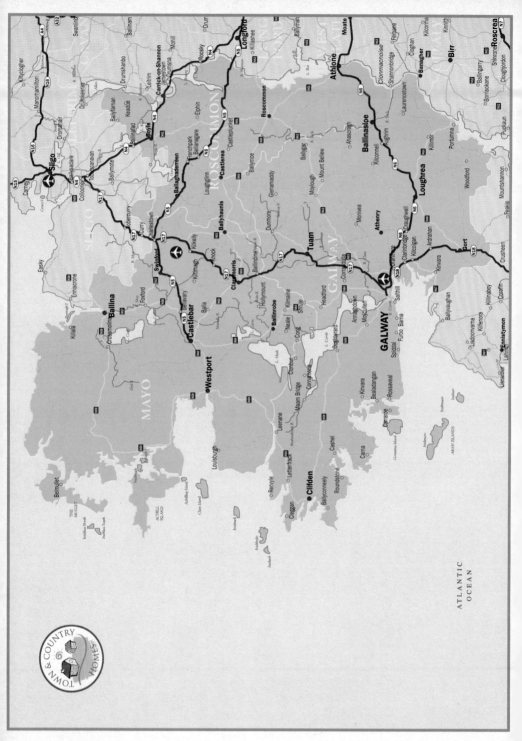

Ireland West

There is a special quality about these three beautiful Counties in the West of Ireland that is unique in Europe. The welcome is heartwarming, the quality of life, people and land-scape is all there for our visitor to share.

The spectacularly beautiful countryside, the coast that has been etched by the Atlantic, rambling hills and mountains and the lovely lakes and bays that mirror that special light from the clear skies over the countryside. Each County has its own special attractions and rich in all that is best in Irish folklore, music and song. There is something here for everyone, you will not be disappointed.

Connemara National Park

Area Representatives

GALWAY
Mrs Vera Feeney, Ardmor Country House, Greenhill, Spiddal,
Co Galway Tel: 091 553145 Fax: 091 553596
Mrs Patricia Greaney, High Tide, 9 Grattan Park, Coast Road,
Galway City, Co Galway Tel: 091 584324/589470 Fax: 091 584324
Mrs Mary Noone, Ashbrook House, Dublin Road, Oranmore,
Co Galway Tel: 091 794196 Fax: 091 794196
MAYO
Mr Robert Kilkelly, St Anthony's, Distillery Road, Westport,
Co Mayo Tel: 098 28887 Fax: 098 25172
Mrs Carol O'Gorman, Ashfort, Galway/Knock Road, Charlestown,
Co Mayo Tel: 094 54706 Fax: 094 54706
Mrs Eileen Pierce, Four Winds, Maryland, Breaffy Road, Castlebar,
Co Mayo Tel: 094 21767 Fax: 094 21767
ROSCOMMON
Mr Martin Mitchell, Abbey House, Boyle, Co Roscommon
Tel: 079 62385 Fax: 079 62385

 ## Tourist Information Offices

Galway City
Eyre Square
Tel: 091 563081

Oughterard
Main Street
Tel: 091 552808

Westport
James St
Tel: 098 25711

Galway - A vibrant University City renowned for its Festivals, Music and Theatre. Archeological sites, Golf courses, Rivers, Lakes and the Aran Islands combine to make this county a magical place. Connemara dominated by the Twelve Pins is a delight to explore.

Galway City 9km

Mrs Veronica Marley
SILVER BIRCH
Clonboo, Annaghdown, Co Galway

Annaghdown
TEL: **091 791036**
EMAIL: jmarley@eircom.net

Friendly home. Main route Cong/Connemara on N84. Walking distance Pub/Restaurant - Clonboo Riding School, Galway City 9km, Lough Corrib 4km.

B&B	4	Ensuite	£19	€24.13	Dinner	-
B&B		Standard		-	Partial Board	-
Single Rate			£25.50	€32.38	Child reduction	-

Open: 1st April-31st October

Kilronan 4.5km

Mrs Bridie Conneely
BEACH VIEW HOUSE
Oatquarter, Kilronan, Inis Mor, Aran Islands, Co Galway

Aran Islands (Inismore)
TEL: **099 61141**   FAX: **099 61141**
EMAIL: beachviewhouse@eircom.net

Situated in middle of island near Dun Aengus. Scenic and tranquil surroundings. Ideal for Cliff walk's with views of Cliff's of Moher. Blue flag Beach, Restaurants and Pubs nearby.

B&B		Ensuite	-	-	Dinner	-
B&B	6	Standard	£18	€22.86	Partial Board	-
Single Rate			£24	€30.47	Child reduction	-

Open: 15th April-30th September

Kilronan 6km

Mrs Margaret Conneely
CREGMOUNT HOUSE
Creig-An-Cheirin, Kilronan, Inis Mor, Aran Islands, Co Galway

Aran Islands (Inismore)
TEL: **099 61139**

Spectacular sea panorama from house set in unspoilt location. Historic monuments easily accessible. Qualified Cook/London City and Guilds Diploma.

B&B	2	Ensuite	£20/£21	€25.39/€26.66	Dinner	£16
B&B		Standard	£18/£19	€22.86/€24.13	Partial Board	-
Single Rate			-	-	Child reduction	-

Open: April-31th October

Kilronan

Cait Flaherty
ARD MHUIRIS
Kilronan, Aran Islands, Co Galway

Aran Islands
TEL: **099 61208**   FAX: **099 61333**
EMAIL: ardmhuiris@eircom.net

5-7 minutes from Ferry - turn right, then left. View of Galway Bay, peaceful area. Walking distance from Restaurants, Pubs, Beaches.

B&B	6	Ensuite	£20	€25.39	Dinner	-
B&B		Standard	-	-	Partial Board	-
Single Rate			-	-	Child reduction	50%

Open: March-November

In Kilronan

Bridie and Patrick McDonagh
AN CRUGAN
Kilronan, Inis Mor,
Aran Islands, Co Galway

Aran Islands (Inismore)
TEL: **099 61150**   FAX: **099 61468**
EMAIL: ancrugan@eircom.net

Situated in Kilronan, the principal port and village of Inishmore. Convenient to Restaurants, Pubs, Beaches. Visa accepted. Hairdryers in bedrooms.

B&B	5	Ensuite	£20	€25.39	Dinner	-
B&B	1	Standard	£17	€21.59	Partial Board	-
Single Rate			£30	€38.09	Child reduction	50%

Open: March-October

Kilronan 6.5km

Joe & Maura Wolfe
MAN OF ARAN COTTAGES
Kilmurvey, Inish Mor,
Aran Islands, Co Galway

Aran Islands
TEL: **099 61301**   FAX: **099 61324**
EMAIL: manofaran@eircom.net

This historic thatched cottage on an acre of organically grown vegetables and herbs was built by Robert Flaherty as a set for his film "The Man of Aran".

B&B	1	Ensuite	£25/£25	€31.74	Dinner	£17
B&B	1	Standard	£22/£22	€27.93	Partial Board	-
Single Rate			£29/£32	€36.82/€40.63	Child reduction	-

Open: 1st March-31st October

Gort 12km

Kathleen Healy
ST JUDES MEADOW
Ardrahan,
Co Galway

Ardrahan
TEL: **091 635010**
EMAIL: stjudesmeadow@hotmail.com

Spacious home on N18. Gateway to scenic West, Cliffs of Moher, etc. Famous restaurants nearby. Comfortable rooms. Excellent home-cooked food.

B&B	3	Ensuite	£19/£19	€24.13	Dinner	-
B&B	-	Standard	-		Partial Board	-
Single Rate			£25.50/£25.50	€32.38	Child reduction	33.3%

Open: 1st March-31st December

In Athenry

Ms Marion E McDonagh
TEACH AN GHARRAIN
Ballygarraun, South Athenry,
Co Galway

Athenry
TEL: **091 844579**   FAX: **091 845390**
EMAIL: mcdhaus@eircom.net
WEB: www.bb-house.com/mcdonagh.htm

Hotel Quality, B&B prices. Heritage town, Galway City-15 minutes. Ideal base for touring the west. Visit the green fields of Athenry. Take N6 to R348 Athenry. Payphone available.

B&B	4	Ensuite	£19/£20	€24.13/€25.39	Dinner	-
B&B	-	Standard	-		Partial Board	-
Single Rate			£26/£26	€33.01	Child reduction	33.3%

Open: All Year

In Athenry

Ms Mary Thompson
ARD RI
Swangate, Athenry,
Co Galway

Athenry
TEL: **091 844050**

Galway City 12km. Train station Dublin-Galway line. Ideal for touring Connemara, Burren, Aran Islands, Heritage Town. Fishing, Golfing.

B&B	4	Ensuite	£19/£20	€24.13/€25.39	Dinner	-
B&B	-	Standard	-		Partial Board	-
Single Rate			£25.50/£25.50	€32.38	Child reduction	50%

Open: All Year Except Christmas

Ballinasloe 3km

Angela Lyons
NEPHIN
Portumna Road, Kellygrove,
Ballinasloe, Co Galway

Ballinasloe
TEL: 0905 42685

Spacious house on landscaped gardens overlooking Golf Course. Complimentary Tea/Coffee. Hairdryers. Le Guide du Routard recommended. 1 mile off N6.

					Dinner	-
B&B	2	Ensuite	£19	€24.13	Dinner	-
B&B	1	Standard	£17	€21.59	Partial Board	-
Single Rate			£23.50	€29.84	Child reduction	25%

Open: 2nd April-5th November

Clifden 8km

Ms Bernadette Keogh
MURLACH LODGE
Ballyconneely Village, Clifden,
Co Galway

Ballyconneely Connemara Area
TEL: 095 23921 FAX: 095 23748
EMAIL: murlachlodge@eircom.net
WEB: www.keoghs-murlachlodge.com

Modern family home in quiet location. 1 min walk to local Pub, Restaurants and Shops etc. Convenient to Connemara, Golf Club, Beaches, Fishing, Horse Riding.

					Dinner	-
B&B	6	Ensuite	£19	€24.13	Dinner	-
B&B	-	Standard		-	Partial Board	-
Single Rate			£25.50	€32.38	Child reduction	25%

Open: All Year

Ballyconneely 1km

Bernie O'Neill
MANNIN LODGE
Mannin Road, Ballyconneely,
Co Galway

Ballyconneely Connemara Area
TEL: 095 23586 FAX: 095 23586

Family run home. Convenient to Beaches, Golf Club, Pony Trekking. All with TV and Hairdryers. Clifden 10 minutes drive. Near Restaurants.

					Dinner	-
B&B	6	Ensuite	£19/£19	€24.13	Dinner	-
B&B	-	Standard		-	Partial Board	-
Single Rate			£25.50/£25.50	€32.38	Child reduction	25%

Open: 1st April-31st October

Galway 8km

Mrs Irene Carr
VILLA DE PORRES
Barna, Galway,
Co Galway

Barna
TEL: 091 592239 FAX: 091 592239

Off Coast Road. Close to sea food Restaurants. Beaches, Fishing, Barna Golf Club, Pony trekking. Private carpark. All rooms with TV, Hairdryers, Electric blankets. Tea/Coffee facilities.

					Dinner	-
B&B	4	Ensuite	£20/£22	€25.39/€27.93	Dinner	-
B&B	1	Standard	£19/£20	€24.13/€25.39	Partial Board	-
Single Rate				-	Child reduction	25%

Open: 17th March-31st October

Galway City 8km

Mrs Joan Codyre
FREEPORT HOUSE
Barna, Co Galway

Barna
TEL: 091 592199 FAX: 091 592199

Coast road R336. Seafront in Village. Overlooking Galway Bay. Breakfast menu, Home baking. Beside village Restaurants, Pubs, Barna Golf Club, Connemara, Aran Islands.

					Dinner	-
B&B	5	Ensuite	£20/£22	€25.39/€27.93	Dinner	-
B&B	1	Standard	£19/£20	€24.13/€25.39	Partial Board	-
Single Rate				-	Child reduction	25%

Open: 17th March-1st November

Galway 7km

Mrs Geraldine Folan
AN FAOILEAN
**Freeport, Barna Village,
Co Galway**

Barna
TEL: **091 592498**   FAX: **091 592498**
EMAIL: efolan@iol.ie
WEB: www.galway-guide.com/pages/faoilean/

50m from seashore. Modern comforts. Excellent Restaurants within walking distance and Pubs.

B&B	4	Ensuite	£20/£22	€25.39/€27.93	Dinner	-
B&B	-	Standard	-	-	Partial Board	-
Single Rate			£27/£27	€34.29	Child reduction	50%

Open: 1st April-30th September

Galway City 6km

Bernadette Ryan
ABBEYVILLE
**Freeport, Barna,
Co Galway**

Barna
TEL: **091 592430**

Attractive modern home. TV, Orthopaedic beds. Private Car parking. 200 meters Restaurants, Pubs. Located off the R336 to Barna and Connemara. Also Barna Golf Club.

B&B	4	Ensuite	£20/£22	€25.39/€27.93	Dinner	-
B&B	-	Standard	-	-	Partial Board	-
Single Rate			£25.50	€32.38	Child reduction	33.3%

Open: All Year

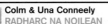

Bealadangan 1km

Colm & Una Conneely
RADHARC NA NOILEAN
**Annaghvane, Bealadangan,
Co Galway**

Beal A Daingin Connemara
TEL: **091 572137**

A friendly family home with sea and mountain views. Tea/Coffee, Scones on arrival. Aran Islands nearby, also Fishing, Walks, Golf.

B&B	3	Ensuite	£19/£19	€24.13	Dinner	-
B&B	-	Standard	-	-	Partial Board	-
Single Rate			£25.50/£25.50	€32.38	Child reduction	33.3%

Open: All Year Except Christmas

Lettermore 3km

Padraic & Angela O'Conghaile
TEACH ANACH MHEAIN
**Anach Mheain, Beal a Daingin,
Connemara, Co Galway**

Beal A Daingin Connemara
TEL: **091 572348/572212** FAX: **091 572214**
EMAIL: padraicoc@eircom.net

Modern family house. All bedrooms with Sea and Mountain view. Convenient to Aran Islands, Ferry, Golf, Fishing ,Walks, Beaches etc.

B&B	4	Ensuite	£19/£19	€24.13	Dinner	-
B&B	-	Standard	-	-	Partial Board	-
Single Rate			£25.50/£25.50	€32.38	Child reduction	33.3%

Open: 1st May-31st October

Carna 3km

Aine Collins
SANDY BEACH B&B
**Mweenish Island, Carna,
Connemara, Co Galway**

Carna
TEL: **095 32870**

3km over bridge from Carna. Luxury home 50m to Beach. Spectacular views. Nature unspoilt- wild flowers, birds, shore life. Relaxing and very quiet.

B&B	3	Ensuite	£19	€24.13	Dinner	-
B&B	-	Standard	-	-	Partial Board	-
Single Rate			£25.50	€32.38	Child reduction	33.3%

Open: 1st June-31st August

Carna 15km

Mrs Barbara Madden
HILLSIDE HOUSE
Kylesalia, Kilkieran, Carna, Connemara, Co Galway

Carna Connemara	
TEL: **095 33420**	FAX: **095 33624**
EMAIL: hillsidehouse@oceanfree.net	

Modern home tucked between the mountains and the sea. Off main road R340 to Kilkieran/Carna. Stunning views, Coastal drives, Hill walks, Beaches, Aran Islands nearby. Good food/comfort.

B&B	4	Ensuite	£19/£20	€24.13/€25.39	Dinner	-
B&B	-	Standard	-	-	Partial Board	-
Single Rate			£28/£30	€35.55/€38.09	Child reduction	-

Open: 1st February-1st December

Carraroe 1km

Mrs Tina Donoghue
DONOGHUE'S
Carraroe, Connemara, Co Galway

Carraroe	
TEL: **091 595174**	FAX: **091 595174**
EMAIL: donoghuec@esatclear.ie	

Comfortable family home on spacious grounds. Beaches and Country Walks; daily trips to Aran Islands nearby. Credit Cards accepted.

B&B	2	Ensuite	£19/£19	€24.13	Dinner	-
B&B	1	Standard	£17/£17	€21.59	Partial Board	-
Single Rate			£23.50/£25.50	€29.84/€32.38	Child reduction	50%

Open: 17th March-1st December

Galway 40km

Mrs Mary Lydon
CARRAROE HOUSE
Carraroe, Connemara, Co Galway

Carraroe Connemara
TEL: **091 595188**
EMAIL: carraroehouse@oceanfree.net

Modern family home on outskirts of village. Ideal for touring Connemara, Aran Islands, near Beaches-Coral Beach. R336 from Galway to Casla, R343 to Carraroe.

B&B	4	Ensuite	£19	€24.13	Dinner	-
B&B	1	Standard	£17	€21.59	Partial Board	-
Single Rate			-	-	Child reduction	50%

Open: All Year Except Christmas

Clifden 18km

Mrs Margaret McDonagh
GLEN-VIEW
Cashel Bay, Connemara, Co Galway

Cashel Bay Connemara Area
TEL: **095 31054**

A tranquil setting overlooking Mountains in the heart of Connemara. Ideal for Walking, Cycling, Fishing. Tea/Coffee and Homemade scones, beside the turf fire on arrival. Breakfast menu.

B&B	-	Ensuite	-	-	Dinner	£15
B&B	3	Standard	£17	€21.59	Partial Board	£195
Single Rate			£23.50	€29.84	Child reduction	25%

Open: 1st February-20th December

Galway 7km

Maura Campbell
AVONDALE
Cregboy, Claregalway, Co Galway

Claregalway
TEL: **091 798349**

Comfortable home on N17 Galway/Sligo road. Fishing and Horse riding nearby. 5km from Galway Airport. Ideal for touring Connemara/Clare.

B&B	2	Ensuite	£19	€24.13	Dinner	-
B&B	2	Standard	£17	€21.59	Partial Board	-
Single Rate			£23.50	€29.84	Child reduction	33.3%

Open: May-October

Galway City 10km

Mrs Mary McNulty
CREG LODGE
Claregalway,
Co Galway

Claregalway
TEL: **091 798862**
EMAIL: creglodge@eircom.net

Luxury family home on the N17 Galway/Sligo Road. 10km from Galway City and 5km from Airport. Restaurants/Pubs within walking distance.

				Dinner	-
B&B	4	Ensuite	£19/£21	€24.13/€26.66	
B&B	-	Standard			Partial Board	-
Single Rate			£25.50/£30	€32.38/€38.09	Child reduction	25%

Open: 1st January-20th December

Galway 12km

Mr Niall Stewart
GARMISCH
Loughgeorge, Claregalway,
Co Galway

Claregalway
TEL: **091 798606**
EMAIL: garmisch@eircom.net

Luxury dormer bungalow on N17. Adjacent to Central Tavern Bar and Restaurant. Convenient for Fishing, Golfing and Touring. Galway Airport 6km.

					Dinner	-
B&B	4	Ensuite	£20/£20	€25.39		
B&B	-	Standard	-	-	Partial Board	-
Single Rate			£25.50/£25.50	€32.38	Child reduction	50%

Open: All Year

In Clarinbridge

Mrs Dympna Callinan
CLAREVILLE
Stradbally North,
Clarinbridge, Co Galway

Clarinbridge
TEL: **091 796248**

Luxurious spacious dormer home situated in the heart of Oyster Country. 0.5km off N18, within walking distance of Village, Sea. Central to Burren, Connemara.

					Dinner	-
B&B	4	Ensuite	£19/£20	€24.13/€25.39		
B&B	-	Standard	-		Partial Board	-
Single Rate			£25.50/£28	€32.38/€35.55	Child reduction	25%

Open: March-November

Clarinbridge 1km

Mrs Bernie Diskin
ROCK LODGE
Stradbally Nth,
Clarinbridge, Co Galway

Clarinbridge
TEL: **091 796071**
EMAIL: johndiskin@eircom.net

Home in quiet area, .5km off N18. Private walkway to seashore. Tea/Coffee facilities. Breakfast choice. Near Burren/Connemara. Guide du Routard recommended.

					Dinner	-
B&B	2	Ensuite	£19	€24.13		
B&B	1	Standard	£17	€21.59	Partial Board	-
Single Rate			£23.50/£25.50	€29.84/€32.38	Child reduction	33.3%

Open: 1st March-November

In Clarinbridge

K Geraghty
INISFREE B&B
Slievaun, Clarinbridge,
Galway, Co Galway

Clarinbridge
TEL: **091 796655**

Conveniently located on the main N18. Within walking distance of Village and Restaurants. In the heart of Oyster Country and only 12 mins Galway.

					Dinner	-
B&B	3	Ensuite	£19/£19	€24.13		
B&B	-	Standard	-		Partial Board	-
Single Rate			£25.50/£25.50	€32.38	Child reduction	25%

Open: All Year

Clarinbridge 1km

Mrs Maura McNamara
SPRING LAWN
Stradbally, Clarinbridge,
Co Galway

Clarinbridge
TEL: **091 796045**   FAX: **091 796045**
EMAIL: springlawn2@hotmail.com
WEB: www.surf.to/springlawn2

Luxury family home on mature landscaped gardens. Located just off N18 near Village and Sea. Ideal base to visit Connemara, Aran Islands, Burren. Dillard Causin Guide recommended.

B&B	3	Ensuite	£19/£19	€24.13	Dinner	-
B&B	-	Standard			Partial Board	-
Single Rate			£26/£28	€33.01/€35.55	Child reduction	25%

Open: 1st March-30th November

Clarinbridge 1km

Mrs Bernie Morrissy
RAHONA
Stradbally North, Clarinbridge,
Co Galway

Clarinbridge
TEL: **091 796080**
EMAIL: rahona@gofree.indigo.ie

Conveniently located off N18 in Clarinbridge, south of Galway City. This luxuriously appointed Guest House guarantees great Irish welcome.

B&B	4	Ensuite	£20	€25.39	Dinner	-
B&B	-	Standard	-	-	Partial Board	-
Single Rate					Child reduction	-

Open: May-October

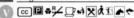

Clarinbridge 1km

Mrs Teresa O'Dea
KARAUN HOUSE
Stradbally, Clarinbridge,
Co Galway

Clarinbridge
TEL: **091 796182**
EMAIL: tod_karaun@ireland.com
WEB: http://go.to/karaun

Irish Times Recommended. 1km off N18. Walk to Sea. AA listed. Near Burren, Connemara, Aran Islands. Tea/Coffee, Hairdryers, Electric blankets. Visa, Master Cards accepted.

B&B	2	Ensuite	£19	€24.13	Dinner	-
B&B	1	Standard	£17	€21.59	Partial Board	-
Single Rate			£25	€31.74	Child reduction	-

Open: 1st March-31st October

Clarinbridge 1.5km

Mary Rodgers
OYSTER CATCHER
Weir Rd, Clarinbridge,
Kilcolgan PO, Co Galway

Clarinbridge
TEL: **091 796744**

Country home 1.5km from Clarinbridge central to the Burren, Connemara and Galway City. Superb Restaurants locally and countryside. Breakfast menu available.

B&B	4	Ensuite	£19/£20	€24.13/€25.39	Dinner	-
B&B	-	Standard	-	-	Partial Board	-
Single Rate			£25.50	€32.38	Child reduction	33.3%

Open: January-November

Cleggan 1km

William & Bernie Hughes
COIS NA MARA
Cleggan, Clifden,
Co Galway

Cleggan Connemara Area
TEL: **095 44647**   FAX: **095 44016**
EMAIL: coisnamara@hotmail.com

Family home in scenic area. Daily boat trips to Inishbofin. Safe sandy Beaches and Pony trekking within walking distance. Access/Visa accepted.

B&B	4	Ensuite	£19/£19	€24.13	Dinner	-
B&B	2	Standard	£17/£17	€21.59	Partial Board	-
Single Rate			£23.50/£25.50	€29.84/€32.38	Child reduction	33.3%

Open: 15th April-15th September

Mrs Mary King
CNOC BREAC
Cleggan,
Co Galway

Cleggan Connemara Area

TEL: **095 44688**
EMAIL: tking@gofree.indigo.ie

Family home. Peaceful, scenic area. Beside sandy Beach. Fishing, Pony Riding. Bay Cruises arranged. Convenient for Inishbofin Ferry. Village 1km.

B&B	4	Ensuite	£19	€24.13	Dinner	-
B&B	-	Standard	-	-	Partial Board	-
Single Rate			£25.50	€32.38	Child reduction	25%

Clifden 10km

Open: 1st May-30th September

Mrs Loretta O'Malley
HARBOUR HOUSE
Cleggan, Co Galway

Cleggan Connemara Area

TEL: **095 44702**
EMAIL: harbour.house@oceanfree.net

Spacious family run home situated in pretty fishing Village of Cleggan from which to explore the wonderful land and seascapes.

B&B	4	Ensuite	£19	€24.13	Dinner	-
B&B	-	Standard	-	-	Partial Board	-
Single Rate			£25.50	€32.38	Child reduction	25%

Clifden 9km

Open: 1st January- 30th November

Ms Mary O'Malley
WILD HEATHER
Cloon, Cleggan,
Co Galway

Cleggan Connemara Area

TEL: **095 44617**   FAX: **095 44790**
EMAIL: cloon@oceanfree.net
WEB: homepage.eircom.net/~omalley

Dine in scenic splendour in conservatory overlooking Bay and Islands. Relax by peat fires. Rest well and enjoy Connemara. Information provided, Village 1.5km.

B&B	4	Ensuite	£19	€24.13	Dinner	£15
B&B	-	Standard	-	-	Partial Board	-
Single Rate			£25.50	€32.38	Child reduction	25%

Cleggan 1.5km

Open: 1st April-31st October

Mrs Christina Botham
LIGHTHOUSE VIEW
Sky Road, Clifden,
Co Galway

Clifden Connemara Area

TEL: **095 22113**
EMAIL: cbotham@lighthouseview.buyandsell.ie

Friendly home on scenic Sky Road, opposite Clifden Castle. Ideal base for touring Connemara or just relaxing. Home baking. Warm welcome assured.

B&B	4	Ensuite	£19	€24.13	Dinner	-
B&B	-	Standard	-	-	Partial Board	-
Single Rate			£25.50	€32.38	Child reduction	25%

Clifden 1.5km

Open: All Year

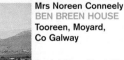

Mrs Noreen Conneely
BEN BREEN HOUSE
Tooreen, Moyard,
Co Galway

Clifden Connemara Area

TEL: **095 41171**

Comfortable well heated home. Peat fires. Magnificent view sea/mountain. Peaceful and tranquil location. Convenient to Connemara National Park.

B&B	6	Ensuite	£19	€24.13	Dinner	£15
B&B	-	Standard	-	-	Partial Board	-
Single Rate			£25.50	€32.38	Child reduction	25%

Clifden 7km

Open: 1st April-31st October

Mrs Anne Conroy
ROCKMOUNT HOUSE
Bayleek, Sky Road,
Clifden, Co Galway

Clifden Connemara Area
Tel: **095 21763**

Breathtaking views of scenic Sky Road. Convenient to Sandy Beaches, Fishing, Cliff Walks and Golf. Peaceful location, ideal touring base. Breakfast menu. Warm welcome assured.

B&B	3	Ensuite	£19/£19	€24.13	Dinner	£14
B&B	1	Standard	£17/£17	€21.59	Partial Board	£185
Single Rate			£23.50/£25.50	€29.84/€32.38	Child reduction	25%

Clifden 5km   **Open:** April-September

John & Joan Coyne
SEA VIEW
Westport Road, Clifden,
Co Galway

Clifden Connemara Area
Tel: **095 21394**   Fax: **095 21394**

Modern bungalow in peaceful surroundings. Panoramic view of Streamstown Bay and Sky Road. Electric blankets, Orthopaedic beds. Ideal touring centre for Connemara. (N59).

B&B	5	Ensuite	£19	€24.13	Dinner	-
B&B	-	Standard	-	-	Partial Board	-
Single Rate			-	-	Child reduction	25%

Clifden 2km   **Open:** All Year

Michael & Jane Delapp
HEATHER LODGE
Westport Road, Clifden,
Co Galway

Clifden Connemara Area
Tel: **095 21331**   Fax: **095 22041**
Email: 231@tinet.ie

Warm friendly home. Breakfast menu, Home baking. Comfortable rooms and Guest lounge overlooking Lake and Mountains. Great touring base for Connemara.

B&B	5	Ensuite	£20/£22	€25.39/€27.93	Dinner	-
B&B	1	Standard	-	-	Partial Board	-
Single Rate			£25	€31.74	Child reduction	25%

Clifden 1.5km   **Open:** 30th March-30th October

Mrs Breege Feneran
LOUGH FADDA HOUSE
Ballyconneely Road, Clifden,
Co Galway

Clifden Connemara Area
Tel: **095 21165**
Email: feneran@gofree.indigo.ie

Spacious, well heated country home. Lovely quiet country walks in scenic area. Peat fires, Fishing & Pony Riding arranged. Credit Cards accepted.

B&B	6	Ensuite	£19/£19	€24.13	Dinner	-
B&B	-	Standard	-	-	Partial Board	-
Single Rate			-	-	Child reduction	25%

Clifden 3km   **Open:** April-October

Brendan & Ursula Flynn
WOODWINDS
Ardbear, Clifden,
Co Galway

Clifden Connemara Area
Tel: **095 21295**   Fax: **095 21295**

Very private lakefront. All ensuite, TV, Car Park. Close to Lake, Beaches, Golf. Homely peaceful place to read, create and relax.

B&B	4	Ensuite	£19/£22	€24.13/€27.93	Dinner	-
B&B	-	Standard	-	-	Partial Board	-
Single Rate			£25.50/£25.50	€32.38	Child reduction	25%

Clifden 1.5km   **Open:** 1st May-30th November

In Clifden

Mrs Carmel Gaughan
ARD AOIBHINN
**Ardbear, Ballyconneely Road,
Clifden, Co Galway**

Clifden Connemara Area

Tel: 095 21339
Email: ardbear@eircom.net

Modern bungalow in scenic surroundings on Clifden - Ballyconneely Road convenient to safe Beaches and Golf Links. Excellent touring base.

B&B	2	Ensuite	£19	€24.13	Dinner	-
B&B	1	Standard	£17	€21.59	Partial Board	-
Single Rate			-	-	Child reduction	25%

Open: 1st April-31st October

Clifden 1km

Mrs Maureen Geoghegan
ROSSFIELD HOUSE
**Westport Road, Clifden,
Co Galway**

Clifden Connemara Area

Tel: 095 21392

Family run home. Warm welcome. Convenient to safe Beaches & Golf Links. Excellent touring base. Orthopaedic beds and peaceful location.

B&B	2	Ensuite	£19/£19	€24.13	Dinner	£14
B&B	2	Standard	£17/£17	€21.59	Partial Board	-
Single Rate			£23.50/£25.50	€29.84/€32.38	Child reduction	25%

Open: 1st April-30th October

Clifden 1.5km

Mrs Kathleen Hardman
MALLMORE HOUSE
**Ballyconneely Road, Clifden,
Co Galway**

Clifden Connemara Area

Tel: 095 21460
Email: mallmore@indigo.ie
Web: www.mallmorecountryhouse.com

Lovingly restored Georgian home. 35 acre woodland grounds, spacious rooms, superb views, open fires and award-winning breakfasts. AA ◆◆◆◆.

B&B	6	Ensuite	£19/£21	€24.13/€26.66	Dinner	-
B&B	-	Standard	-	-	Partial Board	-
Single Rate			-	-	Child reduction	25%

Open: 1st April-1st October

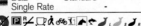

Clifden 2km

Mrs Bridie Hyland
BAY VIEW
**Westport Road, Clifden,
Co Galway**

Clifden Connemara Area

Tel: 095 21286   Fax: 095 21286
Email: bridiehyland@yahoo.com

Frommer recommended. Overlooking Streamstown Bay. View from house described "most spectacular view in Ireland". Orthopaedic Beds, Electric Blankets. Taxi.

B&B	4	Ensuite	£19/£20	€24.13/€25.39	Dinner	-
B&B	-	Standard	-	-	Partial Board	-
Single Rate			-	-	Child reduction	50%

Open: 1st February-1st December

Clifden 8km

Oliver Joyce
THE WILDERNESS
**Emloughmore,
Clifden, Co Galway**

Clifden Connemara Area

Tel: 095 21641
Email: thewilderness_b_b@hotmail.com

Modern home located in peaceful scenic wilds of Connemara with mountain views, Turf fires. Warm friendly atmosphere. 8km from Clifden on N59 route.

B&B	4	Ensuite	£19/£20	€24.13/€25.39	Dinner	-
B&B	-	Standard	-	-	Partial Board	-
Single Rate			£25.50	€32.38	Child reduction	33.3%

Open: February-November

Mrs Margaret Kelly
WINNOWING HILL
**Ballyconneely Road, Clifden,
Co Galway**

Clifden Connemara Area

Tel: **095 21281**   Fax: **095 21281**

Situated on a tranquil hill overlooking the Twelve Bens, Clifden Town and Salt Lake. Views can also be enjoyed with a cup of tea from glass conservatory.

				Dinner	-
B&B	3	Ensuite	£19/£20	€24.13/€25.39	
B&B	1	Standard	£17/£19	€21.59/€24.13	Partial Board	-
Single Rate			-	-	Child reduction	33.3%

Clifden 1km

Open: 10th March-10th November

Mrs Maureen Kelly
FAILTE
**Ardbear, off Ballyconneely Road,
Clifden, Co Galway**

Clifden Connemara Area

Tel: **095 21159**   Fax: **095 21159**
Email: kelly-failte@iol.ie

Modern home overlooking Town and Bay. Breakfast award winner. AA ✦✦✦. "Le Guide du Routard" recommended.

					Dinner	-
B&B	2	Ensuite	£19	€24.13		
B&B	3	Standard	£17	€21.59	Partial Board	-
Single Rate			£23.50/£25.50	€29.84/€32.38	Child reduction	50%

Clifden 2km

Open: April-September

Mrs Vera Kilkenny
WEST COAST HOUSE
**Westport Road, Clifden,
Co Galway**

Clifden Connemara Area

Tel: **095 21261**

Modern family run home N59. Good views, spacious en-suite bedrooms. Ideal touring base. Convenient to Beaches, Golf, Fishing, Horse Riding, Sports Centre.

					Dinner	-
B&B	4	Ensuite	£19/£20	€24.13/€25.39		
B&B	-	Standard	-		Partial Board	-
Single Rate			£25.50/£25.50	€32.38	Child reduction	25%

In Clifden

Open: 31st March-31st October

Mrs Mary King
KINGSTOWN HOUSE
**Bridge Street, Clifden,
Co Galway**

Clifden Connemara Area

Tel: **095 21470**   Fax: **095 21530**

AA, RAC registered. Long established home in Town. Convenient to Beaches, Golf, Fishing, Riding. 2 mins walk Bus, 5 mins to Sea.

					Dinner	-
B&B	6	Ensuite	£19/£20	€24.13/€25.39		
B&B	2	Standard	£17/£18	€21.59/€22.86	Partial Board	-
Single Rate			-	-	Child reduction	25%

Open: All Year Except Christmas

Martin & Mary Kirby
LAKESIDE B&B
**Goulane, Galway Road,
Clifden, Co Galway**

Clifden Connemara Area

Tel: **095 21168**

Spacious modern bungalow in quiet scenic surroundings on Galway/Clifden Rd (N59). Lake in front with views of the 12 Ben Mountains, Golf, Beaches nearby.

					Dinner	-
B&B	3	Ensuite	£19/£19	€24.13		
B&B	1	Standard	£17/£17	€21.59	Partial Board	-
Single Rate			£23.50/£25.50	€29.84/€32.38	Child reduction	-

Clifden 3km

Open: April-September

Odile LeDorven
KER MOR
Claddaghduff, Clifden, Connemara, Co Galway

Clifden Connemara Area
TEL: **095 44954/44698** FAX: **095 44773**
EMAIL: kermor@eircom.net

Peaceful and friendly house on Streamstown Bay. Large bedrooms en-suite. Surprising healthy breakfast. Something special and different, Walking, Angling etc.

B&B	3	Ensuite	£19/£22	€24.13/€27.93	Dinner	-
B&B	-	Standard	-	-	Partial Board	-
Single Rate			£25.50/£30	€32.38/€38.09	Child reduction	-

Clifden 8km   **Open: All Year**

Miss Catherine Lowry
AVE MARIA
Ballinaboy, Clifden, Co Galway

Clifden Connemara Area
TEL: **095 21368**

Spacious 2 storey house located on the Clifden to Ballyconneely/ Roundstone Coast Road. 3km from Clifden. Scenic, tranquil location. Walks, Beaches, Horse riding, Golf, Fishing nearby.

B&B	1	Ensuite	£19	€24.13	Dinner	-
B&B	4	Standard	£17	€21.59	Partial Board	-
Single Rate			£23.50	€29.84	Child reduction	25%

Clifden 3km   **Open: 1st June-30th September**

Tina McDonagh
DOONHILL LODGE
Aillebrack, Ballyconneely, Clifden, Co Galway

Clifden Connemara Area
TEL: **095 23726**   FAX: **095 23586**

Warm comfortable home, situated 0.5km from Connemara Golf Club. Walking distance to Beaches and Pony Trekking. Hairdryer, Tea/Coffee facilities and TV in rooms. Ballyconneely 2km.

B&B	4	Ensuite	£19/£19	€24.13	Dinner	£15
B&B	-	Standard	-	-	Partial Board	-
Single Rate			£25.50/£25.50	€32.38	Child reduction	25%

Clifden 7.5km   **Open: 1st April-31st October**

The McEvaddy Family
BAYMOUNT HOUSE
Seaview, Clifden, Co Galway

Clifden Connemara Area
TEL: **095 21459**   FAX: **095 21639**
EMAIL: baymounthouse@eircom.net
WEB: www.baymount-connemara.itgo.com

Spacious family home overlooking Clifden Bay. Magnificent Sea Views. Peaceful location. Hairdryers, Tea/coffee making facilities and TV in bedrooms.

B&B	10	Ensuite	£17/£18	€21.59/€22.86	Dinner	-
B&B	-	Standard	-	-	Partial Board	-
Single Rate					Child reduction	33.3%

Clifden   **Open: March-October**

Mrs Carmel Murray
OCEAN VILLA
Kingstown, Sky Road, Clifden, Co Galway

Clifden Connemara Area
TEL: **095 21357**   FAX: **095 21137**
EMAIL: oceanvilla@eircom.net
WEB: www.connemara-tourism.org/oceanvilla

Modern bungalow overlooking sea with panoramic hill and sea views. Tranquil location on famous Sky Road. All outdoor activities arranged. Recommended.

B&B	4	Ensuite	£19/£20	€24.13/€25.39	Dinner	£15
B&B	2	Standard	£17/£18	€21.59/€22.86	Partial Board	£210
Single Rate			£25/£25.50	€31.74/€32.38	Child reduction	25%

Clifden 8km   **Open: 1st March-31st October**

Mrs Mary O'Donnell
CREGG HOUSE
**Galway Road, Clifden,
Co Galway**

Clifden Connemara Area
TEL: **095 21326**   FAX: **095 21326**
EMAIL: cregghouse1@eircom.net

On N59 landscaped garden. Spacious rooms, Breakfast menu. Owenglen River nearby. Ideal touring base. Recommended Elsie Dillard, Best B&B's Ireland.

				Dinner	-
B&B	5	Ensuite	£19/£19	€24.13	
B&B	1	Standard	£17/£17	€21.59	Partial Board	-
Single Rate			£23.50/£25.50	€29.84/€32.38	Child reduction	25%

Clifden 2km

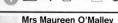

Open: 20th March-1st November

Mrs Maureen O'Malley
HILLSIDE LODGE
**Sky Road, Clifden,
Co Galway**

Clifden Connemara Area
TEL: **095 21463**

Modern family home located on scenic Sky Road. Beside entrance to Clifden Castle. "Le Guide du Routard" recommended. Tea/coffee facilities. Hairdryers.

				Dinner	-
B&B	6	Ensuite	£19/£20	€24.13/€25.39	
B&B	-	Standard			Partial Board	-
Single Rate			£25.50/£25.50	€32.38	Child reduction	33.3%

Clifden 1.5km

Open: 1st March-30th November

Mrs Pauline O'Neill
CROFDEN HOUSE
**Westport Road, Clifden,
Co Galway**

Clifden Connemara Area
TEL: **095 21444**

Modern family home on elevated site in peaceful location. Convenient to Beaches, Golf, and Fishing. Ideal touring base for Connemara.

				Dinner	-
B&B	3	Ensuite	£17/£18	€21.59/€22.86	
B&B	1	Standard	£16/£17	€20.32/€21.59	Partial Board	-
Single Rate			£22/£25	€27.93/€31.74	Child reduction	25%

In Clifden

Open: April-October

Mrs Margaret Pryce
ATLANTIC VIEW
**Letternoosh, Westport Road,
Clifden, Co Galway**

Clifden Connemara Area
TEL: **095 21291**   FAX: **095 22051**
EMAIL: atlanticview@indigo.ie
WEB: indigo.ie/~aview

From home to home. All rooms with orthopaedic beds, Tea/Coffee, TV in rooms. Wonderful views of Atlantic. Turn right at Esso located on N59/Westport Road. Ideal touring base.

				Dinner	£14
B&B	4	Ensuite	£19/£20	€24.13/€25.39	
B&B	-	Standard	-	-	Partial Board	-
Single Rate			£25.50	€32.38	Child reduction	33.3%

Clifden 2km

Open: All Year

Mrs Mary Ryan
DUN AENGUS HOUSE
**Sky Road, Clifden,
Connemara, Co Galway**

Clifden Connemara Area
TEL: **095 21069**   FAX: **095 21069**

Elegant country home superbly located. 5 min walk to Town Centre. This house has "Best view in Ireland". Cosy, all ensuite bedrooms. Hairdryers/Tea making. Own Sea Angling charter boat.

				Dinner	-
B&B	6	Ensuite	£18/£20	€22.86/€25.39	
B&B	-	Standard			Partial Board	-
Single Rate			£25/£30	€31.74/€38.09	Child reduction	25%

In Clifden

Open: All Year

Clonbur 1km

Mrs Mary G Morrin
ISLAND VIEW HOUSE
Dooroy, Clonbur/Cong,
Co Galway

Clonbur Cong Connemara Area
TEL: 092 46302   FAX: 092 46302

Scenic setting overlooking Lough Corrib. Touring base for Connemara, West Mayo. Central to Restaurants, Angling Hill, Walking. Own Boats/Engines for hire.

B&B	4	Ensuite	£18.50	€23.49	Dinner	-
B&B	-	Standard	-	-	Partial Board	-
Single Rate			£25	€31.74	Child reduction	25%

Open: April-October

Cornamona 3km

Mrs Sorcha Peirce
GRASSHOPPER COTTAGE
Dooras, Cornamona,
Co Galway

Cornamona Connemara Area
TEL: 092 48165   FAX: 092 48165
EMAIL: grasshopper@indigo.ie
WEB: www.troutfishingireland.com

Lodge on shore of Lough Corrib off R345. Superb scenery. Angling centre (boat/tackle hire). Ideal base for walking/touring Joyce Country and Connemara.

B&B	3	Ensuite	£19	€24.13	Dinner	£15
B&B	1	Standard	£17	€21.59	Partial Board	£215
Single Rate			£24/£26	€30.47/€33.01	Child reduction	25%

Open: 24th March-29th October

In Craughwell

Mrs Peggy Gilligan
AHAVEEN HOUSE
Cappanraheen, Craughwell,
Co Galway

Craughwell
TEL: 091 846147

Comfortable home on spacious grounds, just off N6 Galway - Dublin road. Excellent Restaurants, Hunting, Golf. Ideal touring base, Burren, Connemara.

B&B	4	Ensuite	£19	€24.13	Dinner	-
B&B	1	Standard	£17	€21.59	Partial Board	-
Single Rate			£23.50	€29.84	Child reduction	-

Open: All Year

Galway 3km

Mrs Bridie Leonard
THE GABLES
Castlegar, Galway,
Co Galway

Galway City Castlegar Area
TEL: 091 755375

Attractive peaceful home on 1 acre on N17. Personally run. Golf, Tennis, Beaches nearby. Electric blankets.

B&B	2	Ensuite	£20/£25	€25.39/€31.74	Dinner	-
B&B	1	Standard	£20/£25	€25.39/€31.74	Partial Board	-
Single Rate			£25.50/£25.50	€32.38	Child reduction	25%

Open: 1st January-20th December

Galway City 3km

Mrs Colette Cawley
DUNGUAIRE
8 Lurgan Park, Murrough,
Dublin Road, Galway City (East)
Co Galway

Galway City
TEL: 091 757043
EMAIL: ccawley@eircom.net
Bus No: 4E, 2E

Warm friendly home. Convenient for touring Connemara, Burren and Aran Islands. Take Galway City east exit. House opposite Corrib Great Southern Hotel, GMIT, Merlin Park Hospital on N6.

B&B	2	Ensuite	£19/£23	€24.13/€29.20	Dinner	-
B&B	2	Standard	£17/£21	€21.59/€26.66	Partial Board	-
Single Rate			£23.50/£28	€29.84/€35.55	Child reduction	50%

Open: All Year

Mrs Noreen Collins
ST ANTHONY'S
Terryland Cross, Headford Road,
Galway, Co Galway

Galway City
TEL: **091 766477**

Family run home. Warm welcome. Beside Shopping Centre. Cinema & Restaurants. Tea/Coffee facilities. Rooms ensuite. Private car park.

B&B	4	Ensuite	**£19/£20**	€24.13/€25.39	Dinner	-
B&B	-	Standard	-	-	Partial Board	-
Single Rate			**£25.50/£25.50**	€32.38	Child reduction	-

Galway City 1km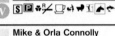

Open: 1st January-20th December

Mike & Orla Connolly
TARA LODGE
1 Barr Aille, Glenanail,
Galway City, Co Galway

Galway City
TEL: **091 771797**
EMAIL: taralodge@eircom.net
WEB: homepage.eircom.net/~taralodge/
Bus No: **3**

New luxurious home, personally run. 3 mins drive, City Centre. Tea/Coffee, TV all rooms. From Galway City take N17 at 2nd roundabout take left and sharp right.

B&B	4	Ensuite	**£19/£27.50**	€24.13/€34.91	Dinner	-
B&B	-	Standard	-	-	Partial Board	-
Single Rate			**£25.50/£30**	€32.38/€38.09	Child reduction	25%

Galway City 2km

Open: All Year

Ms Rita Conway
MOYTURA
4 Ballybane Road, Ballybane,
Galway, Co Galway

Galway City
TEL: **091 757755**
BUS NO: **20, 51**

Welcome to Moytura ideally situated beside Corrib Great Southern Hotel and GMIT. Take route to "Galway City", east off N6. Lovely view of Galway Bay and the Burren. Warm welcome assured.

B&B	3	Ensuite	**£20/£25**	€25.39/€31.74	Dinner	-
B&B	-	Standard	-	-	Partial Board	-
Single Rate			**£25.50/£25.50**	€32.38	Child reduction	25%

Galway 2km

Open: All Year

Mrs Mary Corless
COOLAVALLA
22 Newcastle Road,
Galway, Co Galway

Galway City
TEL: **091 522415**

Family house beside Hospital and University, opposite Presentation School. 6 mins walk City, 15 mins Salthill. Close to all amenities. Ideal touring base.

B&B	1	Ensuite	**£19/£21**	€24.13/€26.66	Dinner	-
B&B	3	Standard	**£17/£19**	€21.59/€24.13	Partial Board	-
Single Rate			**£23.50/£25.50**	€29.84/€32.38	Child reduction	-

Galway City

Open: 1st February-30th November

Sean & Kathryn Cummins
COIS NA TINE
2 Barr Aille , Glenanail,
Galway City, Co Galway

Galway City
TEL: **091 758787**   FAX: **091 758048**
EMAIL: scummins@indigo.ie
BUS NO: **3**

Luxurious family run home. Minutes to City Centre. Highly Recommended. Coming from Galway City take N17 route, on second roundabout take N59 route, then immediate sharp right turn.

B&B	4	Ensuite	**£19/£27.50**	€24.13/€34.91	Dinner	-
B&B	-	Standard	-	-	Partial Board	-
Single Rate			**£25.50/£30**	€32.38/€38.09	Child reduction	25%

Galway City 2km

Open: All Year

Galway City

Helen Kathleen Hanlon
CLOCHARD
4 Spires Gardens, Shantalla
Road, Galway, Co Galway

Galway City
TEL: **091 521533**   FAX: **091 522536**

Warm friendly home. Quiet Historic Site within walking distance of City Centre and Beach. Close to University, Hospital and Shops. Hairdryers.

B&B	4	Ensuite	£20/£24	€25.39/€30.47	Dinner —
B&B	-	Standard	-	-	Partial Board —
Single Rate			£27/£35	€34.29/€44.44	Child reduction —

Open: All Year Except Christmas

Galway 2km

Mrs Elizabeth Hassell
IVERNIA
41 Maunsells Park, Taylors Hill,
Galway, Co Galway

Galway City
TEL: **091 523307**
EMAIL: hasselle@indigo.ie
BUS NO: 2

Family home quiet area. 1km UCG and Hospital. Follow sign to Salthill. Right at Londis shop on Fr. Griffin Rd. Through next lights. Right into Maunsells Rd. 1st left.

B&B	1	Ensuite	£19/£22	€24.13/€27.93	Dinner —
B&B	2	Standard	£17/£20	€21.59/€25.39	Partial Board —
Single Rate			£23.50/£27	€29.84/€34.29	Child reduction 25%

Open: May-October

Galway 2km

Margaret Laffey
BREDAGH HOUSE
Ballybane Road, Galway,
Co Galway

Galway City
TEL: **091 770936**   FAX: **091 770056**
EMAIL: bredaghhouse@hotmail.com
BUS NO: 5

A recently constructed luxurious home to ensure comfort located at the East side of Galway City. Beside the Corrib Great Southern Hotel.

B&B	5	Ensuite	£20/£32	€25.39/€40.63	Dinner £14
B&B	-	Standard	-	-	Partial Board —
Single Rate			£26/£50	€33.01/€63.49	Child reduction —

Open: All Year Except Christmas

Mrs Maureen McCallion
VILLA NOVA
40 Newcastle Road, Galway,
Co Galway

Galway City
TEL: **091 524849**

Quiet bungalow off the main road. Beside Hospital & University & convenient to City Centre. Private car park.

B&B	4	Ensuite	£20/£25	€25.39/€31.74	Dinner —
B&B	-	Standard	-	-	Partial Board —
Single Rate			£25.50/£35	€32.38/€44.44	Child reduction —

Open: All Year Except Christmas

Galway 2km

Miss Bridget Phil McCarthy
PETRA
201 Laurel Park, Newcastle,
Galway City, Co Galway

Galway City
TEL: **091 521844**
BUS NO: 4, 5

Convenient to City Bus. Train/Aran Ferry, University, Hospital. Adjacent to Oughterard/Clifden Road N59. Organic wheat grass and juices available on request.

B&B	3	Ensuite	£19/£20	€24.13/€25.39	Dinner —
B&B	2	Standard	£17/£19	€21.59/€24.13	Partial Board —
Single Rate			£23.50/£25.50	€29.84/€32.38	Child reduction —

Open: 1st January-30th November

In Galway

Mrs Marcella Mitchell
LIMA
**Tuam Road, Galway City,
Co Galway**

Galway City
TEL: **091 757986**
BUS NO: **3**

Detached bungalow adjacent to City Centre, close to all amenities of a vibrant City. Private parking. TV, Tea/Coffee facilities all bedrooms. Beside AIB bank.

B&B	2	Ensuite	£19/£20	€24.13/€25.39	Dinner	-
B&B	1	Standard		-	Partial Board	-
Single Rate			£23.50	€29.84	Child reduction	50%

Open: 1st January-20th December

In Galway

Mrs Mary McLaughlin-Tobin
ARAS MHUIRE
**28 Mansells Road, Taylor's Hill,
Galway, Co Galway**

Galway City
TEL: **091 526210**   FAX: **091 526210**
EMAIL: mmtobin@eircom.net
BUS NO: **2**

Peaceful setting with a view of Galway's beautiful Cathedral. No.2 Bus. Recommended "Happy, homely warm atmosphere." Car park, walking distance Salthill and City.

B&B	2	Ensuite	£19/£25	€24.13/€31.74	Dinner	-
B&B	1	Standard	£17/£24	€21.59/€30.47	Partial Board	-
Single Rate			£23.50/£25.50	€29.84/€32.38	Child reduction	-

Open: 1st January-10th December

Galway City 1.25km

Mary O'Brien
ANACH-CUIN HOUSE
**36 Wellpark Grove,
Galway City, Co Galway**

Galway City
TEL: **091 755120**
BUS NO: **2**

Town House, quiet and peaceful location as you enter City Centre, close to Restaurants and all amenities.

B&B	4	Ensuite	£19/£20	€24.13/€25.39	Dinner	-
B&B	-	Standard		-	Partial Board	-
Single Rate			£25.50	€32.38	Child reduction	50%

Open: 1st March-30th November

In Town

Mrs Margaret Walsh
DE SOTA
**54 Newcastle Road,
Galway, Co Galway**

Galway City
TEL: **091 585064/526900**

Warm comfortable home. Convenient to Bus, Train, Aran Ferry, University and City Centre. Lock up car park.

B&B	3	Ensuite	£20/£25	€25.39/€31.74	Dinner	-
B&B	2	Standard	£20/£25	€25.39/€31.74	Partial Board	-
Single Rate			£25/£35	€31.74/€44.44	Child reduction	-

Open: 1st January-20th December

Galway 3km

Mrs Phil Concannon
WINACRE LODGE
**Bushy Park, Galway,
Co Galway**

Galway City Dangan Area
TEL: **091 523459**
EMAIL: winacrelodge@eircom.net

Modern friendly home, spectacular views of River Corrib on N59. Near Glenlo Abbey and Westwood Hotels. Private parking. TV, Tea/Coffee in bedrooms. Visa.

B&B	5	Ensuite	£19/£23	€24.13/€29.20	Dinner	£17
B&B	-	Standard		-	Partial Board	£185
Single Rate			£25.50/£30	€32.38/€38.09	Child reduction	50%

Open: All Year

Mrs Brenda Kelehan
LAKELAND HOUSE
Bushy Park, Galway,
Co Galway

Galway City Dangan Area
TEL: **091 524964**

Spectacular views of River Corrib/Glenlo Abbey, Golf Club. Adjacent to excellent Restaurants and Bars. On main route to Connemara.

B&B	5	Ensuite	£19/£23	€24.13/€29.20	Dinner	£14
B&B	1	Standard	£18/£20	€22.86/€25.39	Partial Board	£185
Single Rate			£25/£30	€31.74/€38.09	Child reduction	50%

Galway 4km   **Open:** All Year

Mrs Bernie McTigue
ABBEY VIEW
Bushy Park, Galway,
Co Galway

Galway City Dangan Area
TEL: **091 524488**

Frommer recommended. A warm welcome awaits you. View overlooks Glenlo Abbey Golf Course. Adjacent to Restaurants. Ideal for touring Connemara.

B&B	3	Ensuite	£19/£22	€24.13/€27.93	Dinner	£14
B&B	1	Standard	£17/£17	€21.59	Partial Board	£185
Single Rate			£25/£30	€31.74/€38.09	Child reduction	50%

Galway 4km   **Open:** All Year

Mrs Annette O'Grady
KILBREE HOUSE
Circular Road, Dangan Upper,
Galway, Co Galway

Galway City Dangan Area
TEL: **091 527177**   FAX: **091 520404**
EMAIL: info@kilbree.com
WEB: www.kilbree.com

Welcoming luxurious home N59 with excellent food. En route Connemara. Overlooks City and Lake near Hotels and Pubs. TV, Tea/Coffee and Hairdryer in all rooms.

B&B	6	Ensuite	£20/£25	€25.39/€31.74	Dinner	£14
B&B		Standard	-	-	Partial Board	-
Single Rate			£26/£32	€33.01/€40.63	Child reduction	-

Galway 3km   **Open:** All Year

Mrs Bridie Ward
THE ARCHES
Woodstock, Bushy Park,
Galway, Co Galway

Galway City Dangan Area
TEL: **091 527815**
EMAIL: thearches@oceanfree.net

Dormer style home on N59 enroute to Connemara. 3km from Glenlo Abbey Hotel. Golf, Fishing, Horse riding nearby. Private parking. Ideal touring base.

B&B	4	Ensuite	£19/£20	€24.13/€25.39	Dinner	-
B&B	1	Standard	£17/£18	€21.59/€22.86	Partial Board	-
Single Rate			£27/£30	€34.29/€38.09	Child reduction	50%

Galway 6km   **Open:** 1st January-20th December

Mary Beatty
SNAEFELL
6 Glenina Heights, Galway,
Co Galway

Galway City Glenina Heights
TEL: **091 751643**
BUS NO: **2, 5, 6**

Comfortable welcoming home with superb beds. Home made brown bread. Situated on N6 and main bus routes. Close to all amenities including Dog and Race Tracks.

B&B	3	Ensuite	£19/£25	€24.13/€31.74	Dinner	-
B&B		Standard	-	-	Partial Board	-
Single Rate			£25.50/£25.50	€32.38	Child reduction	-

Galway 1.5km   **Open:** January-November

Galway 1.5km

Anne Smyth
10 Glenina Heights
Dublin Road, Galway,
Co Galway

Galway City Glenina Heights
TEL: **091 753327**
BUS NO: **2, 5, 6**

Friendly family modern home. Ideally beside Hotels, Leisure centres, Beach, Golf Clubs and main Bus routes. 1.5km east of City close to Galway Ryan Hotel.

B&B	2	Ensuite	£19/£25	€24.13/€31.74	Dinner	-
B&B	1	Standard	£17/£20	€21.59/€25.39	Partial Board	-
Single Rate			£23.50/£25	€29.84/€31.74	Child reduction	25%

Open: January-November

Galway City 1km

Mrs Kathleen Burke
LISCARNA
22 Grattan Park, Coast Road,
Galway, Co Galway

Galway City Grattan Park Area
TEL: **091 585086**

Modern detached home beside Beach on Coast Road, walking distance of City Centre, Leisureland. All rooms with shower/toilet, TV.

B&B	4	Ensuite	£19/£20	€24.13/€25.39	Dinner	-
B&B	-	Standard	-	-	Partial Board	-
Single Rate			-	-	Child reduction	25%

Open: 1st February-1st November

Galway City 1km

Mrs Freda Cunningham
KYLE NA SHEE
37 Grattan Park, Galway City,
Co Galway

Galway City Grattan Park Area
TEL: **091 583505**
EMAIL: kylenashee@eircom.net
WEB: homepage.eircom.net/~kylenashee

Detached home beside Beach on Coast road to Salthill. Quiet and close to all amenities. Walking distance of City Centre. Tea/Coffee & TV in all rooms.

B&B	3	Ensuite	£19/£20	€24.13/€25.39	Dinner	-
B&B	1	Standard	-	-	Partial Board	-
Single Rate			£25.50/£26.50	€32.38/€33.65	Child reduction	-

Open: April-September

Galway City 1km

Mrs Mary B Curran
CILL CUANA
16 Grattan Park, Via Coast Road,
Galway, Co Galway

Galway City Grattan Park Area
TEL: **091 585979**   FAX: **091 581772**
EMAIL: mbanecurran@hotmail.com

Off coast road to Salthill. Beside Beach, walking distance to City, Salthill, Aran Ferry. All rooms en-suite, cable TV, Hairdryer, Tea/coffee facilities

B&B	5	Ensuite	£19/£20	€24.13/€25.39	Dinner	-
B&B	-	Standard	-	-	Partial Board	-
Single Rate			£25.50/£26.50	€32.38/€33.65	Child reduction	25%

Open: All Year

Galway City 1km

Bernadette Donoghue
KILTEVNA
24 Grattan Park, Coast Road,
Galway, Co Galway

Galway City Grattan Park Area
TEL: **091 588477**   FAX: **091 581173**

Modern detached home beside Beach, off Coast road. Within walking distance City, Leisureland. All rooms with bathrooms, TV, Hairdryers.

B&B	4	Ensuite	£19/£20	€24.13/€25.39	Dinner	-
B&B	-	Standard	-	-	Partial Board	-
Single Rate			-	-	Child reduction	25%

Open: 1st February-31st November

Mrs Pat Greaney
HIGH TIDE
9 Grattan Park, Coast Road,
Galway City, Co Galway

Galway City Grattan Park Area
TEL: 091 584324/589470 FAX: 091 584324 (man)
EMAIL: hightide@iol.ie

Panoramic views of Galway Bay. Frommer/Inside Ireland/Sullivan Guides recommended. 10 min. walk to City Centre. Also local Bus. Breakfast menu. Tours arranged.

				Dinner	-
B&B	4	Ensuite	£19/£20	€24.13/€25.39	
B&B	-	Standard	-	-	Partial Board	-
Single Rate		-	-	Child reduction	25%

Galway City

Open: 1st February-1st December

Mrs Maureen Loughnane
DUNKELLIN HOUSE
4 Grattan Park, Salthill,
Galway, Co Galway

Galway City Grattan Park Area
TEL: 091 589037

Panoramic views of Galway Bay. Walking distance of City & Salthill. Safe parking. Tours arranged. All rooms with TV, Hairdryers, Tea/Coffee. Breakfast menu.

					Dinner	-
B&B	3	Ensuite	£19/£20	€24.13/€25.39		
B&B	1	Standard	-	-	Partial Board	-
Single Rate			£26/£26	€33.01	Child reduction	25%

Galway City 1km

Open: 1st January-21st December

Mrs Mary Murphy
WATERDALE
40 Grattan Park, Coast Road,
Galway, Co Galway

Galway City Grattan Park Area
TEL: 091 586501 FAX: 091 586501
EMAIL: mary_murphy@ireland.com

Modern detached home in quiet cul-de-sac. Beside Beach off Coast Road. Within walking distance of City Centre and Salthill. All rooms with TV.

					Dinner	-
B&B	2	Ensuite	£19/£20	€24.13/€25.39		
B&B	1	Standard	-	-	Partial Board	-
Single Rate			£23.50/£23.50	€29.84	Child reduction	-

Galway City 1km

Open: May-September

Mrs Dolores Bane
THE BRANCHES
13 Woodhaven, Merlin Park,
Galway, Co Galway

Galway City Merlin Park Area
TEL: 091 752712

New luxury accomodation 5 min City Centre beside Corrib Great Southern Hotel. Cable TV, Hairdryers all rooms. Car park. Enjoy Mike's Irish breakfast.

					Dinner	-
B&B	3	Ensuite	£19/£25	€24.13/€31.74		
B&B	1	Standard	£17.50/£20	€22.22/€25.39	Partial Board	-
Single Rate			£23.50/£30	€29.84/€38.09	Child reduction	-

Galway City 2km

Open: All Year

Mrs Olive Connolly
SEACREST
Coast Road, Roscam,
Merlin Park, Galway, Co Galway

Galway City Merlin Park Area
TEL: 091 757975 FAX: 091 756531
EMAIL: djcon@iol.ie
WEB: www.iol.ie/~djcon/

Overlooking Galway Bay, Indoor Pool. Hairdryers, Radios, Bedrooms ground floor level, New York Times, Boston Globe, Le Guide du Routard recommended.

					Dinner	-
B&B	5	Ensuite	£19/£21	€24.13/€26.66		
B&B	1	Standard	£17/£19	€21.59/€24.13	Partial Board	-
Single Rate			£25/£25	€31.74	Child reduction	-

Galway City 5km

Open: 9th February-11th November

Mrs Phil Fahy
LARCHILL
14 Woodhaven, Merlin Park,
Galway, Co Galway

Galway City Merlin Park Area
TEL: **091 770915**   FAX: **091 770915**
EMAIL: fahyfamily@eircom.net

Modern spacious residence in quiet residential area adjacent Corrib Great Southern Hotel. On N6 Galway City East, Galway Crystal Heritage Centre.

B&B	4	Ensuite	£19/£25	€24.13/€31.74	Dinner	-
B&B	-	Standard	-	-	Partial Board	-
Single Rate			£25.50/£30	€32.38/€38.09	Child reduction	-

Galway 3km
Open: All Year

Mrs Millie Forde
BAYSIDE
Coast Road, Curragreen,
Merlin Park, Galway, Co Galway

Galway City Merlin Park Area
TEL: **091 794310**   FAX: **091 794310**
EMAIL: mford@indigo.ie
WEB: indigo.ie/~mford

Modern bungalow on Galway/Oranmore Coast Road, 5km from Galway. 1km from Galway Crystal, overlooking the Bay. No smoking.

B&B	4	Ensuite	£19/£21	€24.13/€26.66	Dinner	-
B&B	-	Standard	-	-	Partial Board	-
Single Rate			£25.50/£25.50	€32.38	Child reduction	-

Galway 5km
Open: 1st May-30th September

Ms Peggy Kenny
CLOONIFF HOUSE
16 Woodhaven, Merlin Park,
Galway, Co Galway

Galway City Merlin Park Area
TEL: **091 758815/582465**

Luxurious family run house beside Corrib Southern Hotel. City Centre 5 mins drive, private parking. Close to Beach and all amenities. Ideal touring base.

B&B	3	Ensuite	£19/£28	€24.13/€35.55	Dinner	-
B&B	1	Standard	-	-	Partial Board	-
Single Rate			£25/£30	€31.74/€38.09	Child reduction	-

Galway City 2km
Open: All Year Except Christmas

Matt & Marie Kiernan
ALMARA HOUSE
2 Merlin Gate, Merlin Park,
Dublin Road, Galway, Co Galway

Galway City Merlin Park Area
TEL: **091 755345**   FAX: **091 771585**
EMAIL: matthewtkiernan@eircom.net
WEB: homepage.eircom.net/~matthewkiernan
BUS NO: **4**

Situated on N6 & off N18. Tastefully appointed bedrooms furnished to highest standards. Hospitality tray, Radio alarms, Irons, Hairdryers. Extensive Breakfast menu.

B&B	4	Ensuite	£20/£30	€25.39/€38.09	Dinner	-
B&B	-	Standard	-	-	Partial Board	-
Single Rate			-	-	Child reduction	50%

Galway 3km
Open: All Year

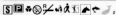

Mrs Ann McDonagh
AMBERVILLE
Coast Road, Roscam, Merlin Park,
Galway, Co Galway

Galway City Merlin Park Area
TEL: **091 757135**

Panoramic views of Galway Bay, Clare Hills and Championship Golf course. 1km from Galway Heritage. Coast Road N6. No Smoking.

B&B	4	Ensuite	£19/£25	€24.13/€31.74	Dinner	-
B&B	-	Standard	-	-	Partial Board	-
Single Rate			£25.50	€32.38	Child reduction	25%

Galway City 4km
Open: April-October

Galway City 4km

Mrs Una McNulty
BEAUPRE
Coast Road (Oranmore),
Roscam, Galway, Co Galway

Galway City Merlin Park Area
Tel: **091 753858**

Overlooking Galway Bay, Burren Golf Course. Coast Rd N6. 1km Galway Crystal. Heritage Centre, Electric Blankets, Hairdryers. Reduction low season.

B&B	4	Ensuite	£19/£23	€24.13/€29.20	Dinner	-
B&B	-	Standard	-	-	Partial Board	-
Single Rate			£25.50	€32.38	Child reduction	33.3%

Open: 15th April-31st October

Galway 3km

Declan & Juliet Manton
WOODVIEW B&B
10 Woodhaven, Merlin Park,
Galway, Co Galway

Galway City Merlin Park
Tel: **091 756843**
Bus No: 4

One of Galway City's finest B&B's, family run. Luxurious home, quiet cul de sac. Adjacent to Corrib Great Southern Hotel.

B&B	4	Ensuite	£19/£30	€24.13/€38.09	Dinner	-
B&B	-	Standard	-	-	Partial Board	-
Single Rate			£25.50/£35	€32.38/€44.44	Child reduction	-

Open: All Year Except Christmas

Galway City 3km

Liam & Yvonne O'Reilly
CORRIB VIEW B&B
12 Woodhaven, Merlin Park,
Galway, Co Galway

Galway City Merlin Park Area
Tel: **091 755667**

Luxurious residence, quiet cul-de-sac. Recommended as one of the Best B&B in the West. Bus route. City Centre 3km. Adjacent Corrib Great Southern Hotel, GMIT.

B&B	3	Ensuite	£20/£30	€25.39/€38.09	Dinner	-
B&B	-	Standard	-	-	Partial Board	-
Single Rate			£25.50/£40	€32.38/€50.79	Child reduction	-

Open: 1st January-20th December

Galway City 3km

Maria Rabbitte
GRANGE HOUSE
15 Woodhaven, Merlin Park
Galway, Co Galway

Galway Merlin Park Area
Tel: **091 755470**   Fax: **091 755470**
Email: mrabbitte@eircom.net
Bus No: 4

Luxurious home, personally run, quiet cul-de-sac. Convenient to City Bus Route. Adjacent Corrib Great Southern Hotel. Ideal touring base. Highly recommended.

B&B	4	Ensuite	£19/£30	€24.13/€38.09	Dinner	-
B&B	-	Standard	-	-	Partial Board	-
Single Rate			£25.50/£35	€32.38/€44.44	Child reduction	25%

Open: All Year Except Christmas

Galway City 3km

Ms Mary Sweeney
CORRIGEEN B&B
4 Woodhaven, Merlin Park,
Dublin Road, Galway, Co Galway

Galway City Merlin Park Area
Tel: **091 756226**   Fax: **091 756255**
Email: dess@eircom.net
Web: www.galway.net/pages/corrigeen/

Delightful purpose built B&B on main approach road to Galway City, adjacent Corrib Great Southern Hotel. One of the Best B&B's in the West.

B&B	4	Ensuite	£19/£30	€24.13/€38.09	Dinner	-
B&B	-	Standard	-	-	Partial Board	-
Single Rate			£25.50/£35	€32.38/€44.44	Child reduction	-

Open: All Year Except Christmas

Mrs Teresa Burke
LYNBURGH
Whitestrand Road, Lower Salthill,
Galway, Co Galway

Galway City Whitestrand Area
TEL: **091 581555**　　FAX: **091 581823**
EMAIL: tburke@iol.ie

Spacious residence overlooking Galway Bay. Beside Beach, walking distance to City Centre, Leisureland, University & Aran Ferry. TV, Hairdryers and Tea/Coffee facilities.

B&B	6	Ensuite	£19/£20	€24.13/€25.39	Dinner	-
B&B	-	Standard	-	-	Partial Board	-
Single Rate			-	-	Child reduction	25%

Galway 1km

Open: All Year

Mrs Esther Daly
GLENCAR
6 Beach Court, Off Grattan Road,
Lower Salthill, Galway, Co Galway

Galway City Whitestrand Area
TEL: **091 581431**

Panoramic view Galway Bay beside Beach. Walking distance to Town, Aran Ferry, Restaurants. All rooms ensuite, TV, Tea facilities, Hairdryer. Warm quiet home.

B&B	4	Ensuite	£19/£20	€24.13/€25.39	Dinner	-
B&B	-	Standard	-	-	Partial Board	-
Single Rate			£25.50/£35	€32.38/€44.44	Child reduction	25%

Galway City 1km

Open: All Year

Mrs Sara Davy
ROSS HOUSE
14 Whitestrand Avenue,
Lower Salthill, Galway, Co Galway

Galway City Whitestrand Area
TEL: **091 587431**　　FAX: **091 581970**
EMAIL: rosshousebb@eircom.net

Beside Galway Bay. All rooms en-suite, TV, Hairdryer, Hospitality tray. Ample safe offstreet parking. Ten minutes walking to City Centre. 5 minutes to Beach.

B&B	4	Ensuite	£19/£20	€24.13/€25.39	Dinner	-
B&B	-	Standard	-	-	Partial Board	-
Single Rate			-	-	Child reduction	-

Galway 1km

Open: All Year

Carmel Donoghue
ACHILL HOUSE
9 Whitestrand Road, Galway,
Co Galway

Galway City Whitestrand Area
TEL: **091 589149**

Family run home, 5 mins walk to City Centre and Beach. Ensuite rooms, Cable TV, Private Car Park. Complimentary Tea/Coffee available.

B&B	4	Ensuite	£19/£20	€24.13/€25.39	Dinner	-
B&B	-	Standard	-	-	Partial Board	-
Single Rate			-	-	Child reduction	25%

Galway City

Open: 1st January-20th December

Stella Faherty
CONSILIO
4 Whitestrand Avenue,
Lower Salthill, Galway,
Co Galway

Galway City Whitestrand Area
TEL: **091 586450**　　FAX: **091 586450**
BUS NO: 1

Friendly and comfortable home in quiet area between Galway and Salthill. Beside Beach and convenient to all City entertainment. No smoking house.

B&B	4	Ensuite	£20/£20	€25.39	Dinner	-
B&B	-	Standard	-	-	Partial Board	-
Single Rate			£28/£28	€35.55	Child reduction	-

Galway 1km

Open: All Year

Galway City 1km

Kathleen Melvin
LISKEA
**16 Whitestrand Avenue,
Lower Salthill, Galway,
Co Galway**

TEL: **091 584318**   FAX: **091 584319**

Beside Galway Bay. Beach 100 yds. Short walk to City Centre. All rooms ensuite, Television, Hairdryer, Tea/Coffee.

B&B	4	Ensuite	£19/£20	€24.13/€25.39	Dinner	-
B&B	-	Standard	-	-	Partial Board	-
Single Rate			£25.50/£29.50	€32.38/€37.46	Child reduction	25%

Open: All Year

Galway City 1km

Mrs Maureen Nolan
GLENCREE
**20 Whitestrand Avenue,
Lr Salthill, Galway City,
Co Galway**

TEL: **091 581061**   FAX: **091 581061**

Beside Galway Bay. All rooms shower & toilet, TV, Hairdryers. Short walking distance City Centre, University, Aran Ferry etc. Beach 100 yds.

B&B	4	Ensuite	£19/£20	€24.13/€25.39	Dinner	-
B&B	-	Standard	-	-	Partial Board	-
Single Rate			-	-	Child reduction	25%

Open: 1st January-23rd December

Galway 1km

Tim and Carmel O'Halloran
RONCALLI HOUSE
**24 Whitestrand Avenue,
Lower Salthill, Galway, Co Galway**

TEL: **091 584159/589013** FAX: **091 584159**

Warm comfortable home beside Galway Bay. AA listed. Walking distance City Centre. Frommer, Lonely Planet, Ireland Guide, Birnbaum recommended. Breakfast Award.

B&B	6	Ensuite	£19/£20	€24.13/€25.39	Dinner	-
B&B	-	Standard	-	-	Partial Board	-
Single Rate			£25.50/£29.50	€32.38/€37.46	Child reduction	25%

Open: All Year

In Galway

Niamh Pender
NIDER HOUSE
**37 Whitestrand Road,
Galway, Co Galway**

TEL: **091 582313**   FAX: **091 582313**
EMAIL: derek_pender@yahoo.co.uk

Warm welcoming luxurious family run accommodation walking distance. 10 mins to City, 5 mins to Beach. Ensuite rooms, TV, Hairdryer, Tea/Coffee facilities.

B&B	4	Ensuite	£19/£20	€24.13/€25.39	Dinner	-
B&B	-	Standard	-	-	Partial Board	-
Single Rate			£25.50/£29.50	€32.38/€37.46	Child reduction	25%

Open: February-November

Galway 1km

Ms Maureen Tarpey
THE DORMERS
**Whitestrand Road, Lr Salthill,
Galway, Co Galway**

TEL: **091 585034**   FAX: **091 585034**

Bungalow, conveniently situated within walking distance to City/Beach. All rooms with shower/toilet/TV/hairdryers. Some rooms on ground floor.

B&B	6	Ensuite	£19/£20	€24.13/€25.39	Dinner	-
B&B	-	Standard	-	-	Partial Board	-
Single Rate			-	-	Child reduction	33.3%

Open: All Year

In Galway

Mrs Bridie Thomson
ROCK LODGE
Whitestrand Road, Galway, Co Galway

Galway City Whitestrand Area
TEL: 091 583789   FAX: 091 583789
EMAIL: rocklodgeguests@eircom.net

Spacious residence beside Galway Bay. TV, Hairdryers, Tea/Coffee facilities. Private parking. 10 minutes walk City Centre. Beach 100 yds.

B&B	6	Ensuite	£19/£20	€24.13/€25.39	Dinner	-
B&B	-	Standard	-	-	Partial Board	-
Single Rate			£25.50/£30	€32.38/€38.09	Child reduction	25%

Open: All Year

Galway 1km

Mrs Margaret Walsh
LAWNDALE
5 Beach Court, off Grattan Road, Lower Salthill, Galway, Co Galway

Galway City Whitestrand Area
TEL: 091 586676

Warm, quiet hospitable home. Walking distance to city. Overlooking Galway Bay. Frommer, Best Guides recommended. TV. Tea-coffee facilities ensuite rooms.

B&B	5	Ensuite	£19/£20	€24.13/€25.39	Dinner	-
B&B	-	Standard	-	-	Partial Board	-
Single Rate			£26/£30	€33.01/€38.09	Child reduction	25%

Open: All Year

In Galway

Kathleen Fahy
ABHOG
28 Grattan Court, Fr Griffin Road, Galway, Co Galway

Lower Salthill
TEL: 091 589528   FAX: 091 589528
EMAIL: abhog@eircom.net

Newly refurbished home centrally located in quiet residential area. Ensuite, TV, Tea/Coffee, Hairdryers in all rooms. Ground floor bedroom. Warm friendly atmosphere.

B&B	3	Ensuite	£19/£22.50	€24.13/€28.57	Dinner	-
B&B	1	Standard	-	-	Partial Board	-
Single Rate			£23.50/£25	€29.84/€31.74	Child reduction	25%

Open: All Year

Galway 2km

Mrs Berna Kelly
DEVONDELL
47 Devon Park, Lower Salthill, Co Galway

Lower Salthill
TEL: 091 528306
EMAIL: devondel@iol.ie
WEB: www.iol.ie/~devondel
BUS NO: 1

Relaxed friendly home. Extensive Breakfast menu. Recommended by Lonely Planet and Bridgestone 100 Best B &B. Overall Winner Galway AIB Awards 1998.

B&B	4	Ensuite	£22.50/£25	€28.57/€31.74	Dinner	-
B&B	-	Standard	-	-	Partial Board	-
Single Rate			£25.50/£25.50	€32.38	Child reduction	-

Open: 1st February-31st October

Galway 1.5km

Ita Johnstone
ST JUDES
110 Lower Salthill, Galway, Co Galway

Lower Salthill
TEL: 091 521619
EMAIL: stjudes@indigo.ie
WEB: www.celtic-holidays.com/stjudes
BUS NO: 1

Distinguished family residence, elegantly furnished. Private parking on City Bus route, short walk to Beach and all amenities. Breakfast menu.

B&B	6	Ensuite	£22.50/£25	€28.57/€31.74	Dinner	-
B&B	-	Standard	-	-	Partial Board	-
Single Rate			£26/£30	€33.01/€38.09	Child reduction	25%

Open: 20th January-30th November

Galway City

Mrs Christina Ruane
25 Grattan Court
Fr Griffin Road, Lower Salthill,
Galway, Co Galway

Lower Salthill
TEL: **091 586513**

Modern detached house, quiet residential area. 10 mins walk Salthill, 5 mins Beach, Golf Club, 10 mins Hospital & University.

				Dinner	-
B&B	4	Ensuite	£19/£20	€24.13/€25.39	
B&B	1	Standard	£17/£18	€21.59/€22.86	Partial Board	-
Single Rate			£25	€31.74	Child reduction	25%

Open: All Year

Galway 1km

Mrs Frances Tiernan
VILLA MARIA
94 Fr Griffin Rd, Lower Salthill,
Galway, Co Galway

Lower Salthill
TEL: **091 589033**

Spacious home. Frommer Guide recommended. 10 mins walk City Centre, Salthill, University & Hospital, 5 mins beach. Sign for City via docks over Wolfe Tone Bridge. Past 3 traffic lights, house on right.

					Dinner	-
B&B	4	Ensuite	£19/£21	€24.13/€26.66	
B&B		Standard		-	Partial Board	-
Single Rate			£23/£25	€29.20/€31.74	Child reduction	33.3%

Open: All Year Except Christmas

In Salthill

Mrs Mary Barry
TRIESTE
12 Forster Park, Off Dalysfort
Road, Salthill, Co Galway

Salthill
TEL: **091 521014**   FAX: **091 521014**
EMAIL: maryba@indigo.ie
BUS NO: 1

Bungalow, quiet cul-de-sac. Near Beach, Golf, Leisureland. Follow Salthill sign, turn first after roundabout/Rockland Hotel, up hill and 2nd turn right.

					Dinner	-
B&B	3	Ensuite	£19/£22	€24.13/€27.93	
B&B	1	Standard	£17/£20	€21.59/€25.39	Partial Board	-
Single Rate			£23.50/£27	€29.84/€34.29	Child reduction	25%

Open: May-October

Mrs Ann Brady
CARRICKVALE
20 Dr Mannix Road,
Salthill, Co Galway

Salthill
TEL: **091 522317**

Modern home convenient to Beach and Leisureland, on bus route to City Centre. Private car park.

					Dinner	-
B&B	4	Ensuite	£19/£20	€24.13/€25.39	
B&B	-	Standard	-	-	Partial Board	-
Single Rate			£25.50/£25.50	€32.38	Child reduction	25%

Open: March-November

Galway 2km

Mrs Brenda Brennan
OCEAN VILLA
7 Cashelmara, Knocknacarra
Cross, Salthill, Galway, Co Galway

Salthill
TEL: **091 529549**   FAX: **091 529549**
EMAIL: oceanvilla@oceanfree.net
WEB: www.galway.net/pages/ocean-villa/

New luxury B&B overlooking Galway Bay. All bedrooms ensuite, Cable TV, Tea/Coffee, Hairdryers, Phone. Parking. Guests lounge. Delicious Breakfast. Galway City 2km.

					Dinner	-
B&B	6	Ensuite	£19/£30	€24.13/€38.09	
B&B	-	Standard	-	-	Partial Board	-
Single Rate			£30/£50	€38.09/€63.43	Child reduction	25%

Open: All Year Except Christmas

Mrs Catherine Carey
THE GREENWAYS
9 Glenard Crescent,
Off Dr Mannix Road, Salthill,
Galway, Co Galway

Salthill
TEL: 091 522308

Comfortable warm home. View of Galway Bay. Private parking. Close to Leisureland, Golf, Tennis & Beach.

B&B	4	Ensuite	£19/£22.50	€24.13/€28.57	Dinner	-
B&B	-	Standard	-	-	Partial Board	-
Single Rate			£25.50/£27	€32.38/€34.29	Child reduction	25%

Galway 2km

Open: 1st March-31st October

Mrs Christina Connolly
CLARE VILLA
38 Threadneedle Road,
Salthill, Co Galway

Salthill
TEL: 091 522520
EMAIL: clarevilla@yahoo.com

Spacious residence close to Beach, Tennis, Golf, Leisureland. On bus route. Complimentary Tea/Coffee 24 hours. Hairdryers. Lonely Planet recommended.

B&B	6	Ensuite	£20/£22.50	€25.39/€28.57	Dinner	-
B&B	-	Standard	-	-	Partial Board	-
Single Rate			£25.50/£30	€32.38/€38.09	Child reduction	25%

Galway 2km

Open: 1st February-31st October

Noreen Cosgrove
MAPLE HOUSE
Dr Mannix Road, Salthill,
Co Galway

Salthill
TEL: 091 526136

Purpose built luxury home. Peaceful location. Power showers. Adjacent Hotels, Golf, Tennis, Leisureland. Parking. Hairdryers. On bus route. Open all year.

B&B	4	Ensuite	£19/£20	€24.13/€25.39	Dinner	-
B&B	-	Standard	-	-	Partial Board	-
Single Rate			£25.50/£27.50	€32.38/€34.91	Child reduction	25%

In Salthill

Open: All Year Except Christmas

Ms Marie Cotter
BAYBERRY HOUSE
9 Cuan Glas, Bishop O'Donnell
Road, Taylors Hill, Galway
Co Galway

Salthill
TEL: 091 525171/525212
EMAIL: tcotter@iol.ie
WEB: www.galway.net/pages/bayberry
BUS NO: 2

A charming purpose built B&B conveniently located at the top of Taylors Hill. A stay at Bayberry combines a Georgian style elegance with a warm welcome.

B&B	4	Ensuite	£22.50/£25	€28.57/€31.74	Dinner	-
B&B	-	Standard	-	-	Partial Board	-
Single Rate			£25.50/£30	€32.38/€38.09	Child reduction	50%

Galway 2km

Open: All Year Except Christmas

Mrs Marian Coyne
COOLIN HOUSE
11 Seamount, Threadneedle Road,
Salthill, Co Galway

Salthill
TEL: 091 523411

Modern home. Beside Beach, Tennis Club, Leisureland. On bus route. Private parking. Tea/Coffee making, TV in all rooms.

B&B	4	Ensuite	£20/£22.50	€25.39/€28.57	Dinner	-
B&B	-	Standard	-	-	Partial Board	-
Single Rate			£25.50/£30	€32.38/€38.09	Child reduction	25%

Galway City 2km

Open: 1st April-31st October

Phil Flannery
FLANNERY'S
54 Dalysfort Road, Salthill,
Galway, Co Galway

Salthill

Tᴇʟ: **091 522048**   Fᴀx: **091 522048**
Eᴍᴀɪʟ: phil.flannery@iol.ie
Wᴇʙ: www.flannerysbedandbreakfast.com
Bᴜs Nᴏ: **1**

Award winning house with nice garden. German spoken. Follow signs to Salthill. On seafront between Waterfront Hotel and Leisureland, turn into Dalysfort Road.

B&B	3	Ensuite	£19/£21	€24.13/€26.66	Dinner	-
B&B	1	Standard	£17/£19	€21.59/€24.13	Partial Board	-
Single Rate			£24/£30	€30.47/€38.09	Child reduction	-

Galway 2km

Open: 1st January-19th December

Mrs Mary Geraghty
MARLESS HOUSE
Threadneedle Road, Salthill,
Galway, Co Galway

Salthill

Tᴇʟ: **091 523931**   Fᴀx: **091 529810**
Eᴍᴀɪʟ: marlesshouse@eircom.net
Wᴇʙ: www.marlesshouse.com
Bᴜs Nᴏ: **1**

Luxurious Georgian style home just steps from Beach. Frommer recommended. TV, electric blankets, hairdryers, Tea/Coffee facilities in all rooms.

B&B	6	Ensuite	£20/£22.50	€25.39/€28.57	Dinner	-
B&B	-	Standard	-	-	Partial Board	-
Single Rate			£25.50/£35	€32.38/€44.44	Child reduction	25%

Galway 2km

Open: 1st January-20th December

Mrs Nora Hanniffy
ANNA REE HOUSE
49 Oaklands, Salthill,
Galway, Co Galway

Salthill

Tᴇʟ: **091 522583**

Modern home. Private parking. Rear of Church by Sacre Coeur Hotel. 5 mins walk Beach, Leisureland and Bus route. Electric blankets.

B&B	5	Ensuite	£19/£20	€24.13/€25.39	Dinner	-
B&B	1	Standard	£17/£17	€21.59	Partial Board	-
Single Rate			£23.50/£25.50	€29.84/€32.38	Child reduction	50%

Open: 1st February-1st November

Mrs Anne Lally
BAYVIEW
20 Seamount, Off Threadneedle
Road, Salthill, Galway Co Galway

Salthill

Tᴇʟ: **091 526008**
Bᴜs Nᴏ: **1**

Modern home. Lonely Planet recommended. TV, Electric blankets, Hairdryers, Tea/Coffee in all rooms. On bus route.

B&B	3	Ensuite	£20/£22.50	€25.39/€28.57	Dinner	-
B&B	-	Standard	-	-	Partial Board	-
Single Rate			£25.50/£30	€32.38/€38.09	Child reduction	50%

Galway 2km

Open: 1st April-31st October

Mrs Catherine Lydon
CARRAIG BEAG
1 Burren View Heights,
Knocknacarra Road, Salthill,
Galway, Co Galway

Salthill

Tᴇʟ: **091 521696**
Bᴜs Nᴏ: **2**

Luxurious brick house. Convenient to Beaches, Golf, Tennis. Ideal base for touring Connemara, Aran Islands etc. Recommended by "Best B&B's in Ireland" and Rick Steve's.

B&B	4	Ensuite	£20/£26	€25.39/€33.01	Dinner	-
B&B	-	Standard	-	-	Partial Board	-
Single Rate			£28/£40	€35.55/€50.79	Child reduction	33.3%

Galway 2km

Open: All Year Except Christmas

Mrs Mairead McGuire
WESTPOINT
**87 Threadneedle Road, Salthill,
Galway, Co Galway**

Salthill
TEL: **091 521026/582152** FAX: **091 582152**
EMAIL: westpointmac@netscape.net
BUS NO: **1, 2**

Purpose built family run B&B near Ardilan and Galway Bay Hotel. Quality assured & multi recommendations. Sea view. Parking. Bus route, Beach, Leisureland, Tennis & Golf.

B&B	6	Ensuite	£19/£25	€24.13/€31.74	Dinner £12.50
B&B	-	Standard	-		Partial Board -
Single Rate			£25.50/£28	€32.38/€35.55	Child reduction 25%

Galway 2km

Open: 1st January-20th December

Marian Mitchell
CHESTNUT LODGE
**35 Rockbarton Road,
Salthill, Co Galway**

Salthill
TEL: **091 529988**

Luxurious home beside Galway Bay and Beach. Golf Club, Tennis Club and Leisureland. Ideal for touring Connemara, Aran Islands and the Burren.

B&B	3	Ensuite	£19/£23	€24.13/€29.20	Dinner -
B&B	-	Standard	-		Partial Board -
Single Rate			£25.50/£28	€32.38/€35.55	Child reduction 25%

Galway 2km

Open: 1st April-31st September

John & Maureen Monaghan
MONTROSE HOUSE
**3 Monksfield, Salthill,
Galway, Co Galway**

Salthill
TEL: **091 525673**   FAX: **091 525673**
BUS NO: **1**

2 storey house in quiet area. Central to amenities. Tea/Coffee/Snack on arrival. On Bus route. Convenient Leisureland, Aquarium, Beach. 15 mins City Centre, excellent Restaurants & Pubs.

B&B	6	Ensuite	£19/£22	€24.13/€27.93	Dinner -
B&B	-	Standard	-		Partial Board -
Single Rate			£26/£28	€33.01/€35.55	Child reduction 50%

Galway 5km

Open: 1st January-15th December

Mrs Nora O'Malley
ST KIERAN'S
**33 Rockbarton Road, Salthill,
Galway, Co Galway**

Salthill
TEL: **091 523333**
EMAIL: michealomalley@hotmail.com

Family run home beside all amenities. Within walking distance of Beach, Leisureland, Golf, GAA and Tennis Club. Home cooking. Tea or Coffee on arrival.

B&B	3	Ensuite	£19/£19	€24.13	Dinner -
B&B	1	Standard	£17/£17	€21.59	Partial Board -
Single Rate			£23.50/£23.50	€29.84	Child reduction -

In Salthill

Open: 1st February-30th November

Mrs Ann O'Toole
CLYDAGH
**Knocknacarra Road, Salthill,
Galway, Co Galway**

Salthill
TEL: **091 524205**
BUS NO: **2**

Comfortable family home with private parking. Convenient to Beaches, Tennis, Golf. Bus route to City Centre. Ideal touring base for Connemara and Aran Island.

B&B	4	Ensuite	£19/£21	€24.13/€26.66	Dinner -
B&B	-	Standard	-		Partial Board -
Single Rate			£25.50/£25.50	€32.38	Child reduction 33.3%

Galway City 2km

Open: March-October

Mrs Nora Patten
LOCKERBIE
3 Rockbarton Green,
(Off Rockbarton Road),
Salthill, Galway, Co Galway

Salthill
TEL: 091 521434

Warm welcoming home in beautiful secluded surroundings, off Coast Road. Beside Bus stop Galway Bay, Golf. Ideal touring base for Connemara/Burren. Complimentary Tea/Coffee.

B&B	4	Ensuite	£19/£22.50	€24.13/€28.57	Dinner	-
B&B	-	Standard	-	-	Partial Board	-
Single Rate			£25.50/£25.50	€32.38	Child reduction	20%

Galway City 2km

Open: April-November

Mrs Ethna Regan
LISCARRA HOUSE
6 Seamount on Threadneedle Rd,
Salthill, Galway, Co Galway

Salthill
TEL: 091 521299
EMAIL: eregan@eircom.net
WEB: homepage.eircom.net/~gerregan
BUS NO: 1

Luxurious home just steps from Galway Bay, beside Beach, Tennis, Golf. TV, Tea/Coffee facilities, Electric blankets, Hairdryers all rooms. On bus route. R338.

B&B	4	Ensuite	£20/£22.50	€25.39/€28.57	Dinner	-
B&B	1	Standard	£18/£20	€22.86/€25.39	Partial Board	-
Single Rate			£25/£29	€31.74/€36.82	Child reduction	25%

Galway City 2km

Open: 1st March-30th November

Mrs Phil Waldron
CLUAIN ARD
86 Threadneedle Rd, Salthill,
Galway City, Co Galway

Salthill
TEL: 091 525333

Comfortable home in quiet cul-de-sac adjacent to Salthill, Leisureland, Tennis Club, Golf Club. Private parking. On Bus route.

B&B	4	Ensuite	£20/£22.50	€25.39/€28.57	Dinner	-
B&B	-	Standard	-	-	Partial Board	-
Single Rate			£25.50/£30	€32.38/€38.09	Child reduction	25%

Galway City 3km

Open: 1st March-31st October

Mrs Evelyn Wrynn
FENAGH HOUSE
11 Rockbarton Green,
Off Rockbarton Road, Salthill,
Galway, Co Galway

Salthill
TEL: 091 522835
EMAIL: ewrynn@eircom.net

Family home in tranquil setting beside Galway Bay. Ideal base for touring Connemara and the Burren. On bus route to City. Parking space.

B&B	3	Ensuite	£19/£23	€24.13/€29.20	Dinner	-
B&B	-	Standard	-	-	Partial Board	-
Single Rate			£26/£30	€33.01/€38.09	Child reduction	33.3%

Galway 1km

Open: 1st May-30th September

Mrs Georgianna Darby
MANDALAY BY THE SEA
10 Gentian/Blakes Hill,
Galway, Co Galway

Upper Salthill Gentian Hill Area
TEL: 091 524177　　FAX: 091 529952
EMAIL: mandalay@esatclear.ie

Luxurious balconied residence panoramic view of Galway Bay. Recommended ""Best B&B's in Ireland"", Lonely Planet and Hidden Places of Ireland. Off 336 Coast Rd. 2 miles from Galway City.

B&B	5	Ensuite	£19/£22	€24.13/€27.93	Dinner	-
B&B	1	Standard	£18/£20	€22.86/€25.39	Partial Board	-
Single Rate			£23.50/£28	€29.84/€35.55	Child reduction	25%

In Salthill

Open: All Year

Salthill 2km

Mrs Mary Duggan
KNOCKMOY HOUSE
7 Westbrook, Barna Road,
Galway, Co Galway

Upper Salthill
TEL: **091 590674**
BUS NO: **2**

Neo Georgian house overlooking Galway Bay. TV Lounge. Only 10 mins drive from Salthill, Golf, Tennis, Leisureland and Horse riding.

B&B	4	Ensuite	£19/£20	€24.13/€25.39	Dinner	-
B&B	-	Standard	-	-	Partial Board	-
Single Rate			£25.50/£25.50	€32.38	Child reduction	50%

Open: 15th March-31st October

Galway 1km

Mrs Christina Fahey
CASHELMARA LODGE
Knocknacarra Cross,
Salthill, Galway, Co Galway

Upper Salthill
TEL: **091 520020**
EMAIL: cashelmara@tinet.ie
BUS NO: **2**

New luxury accommodation overlooking Galway Bay. Beside Beach, Golf, Horseriding, Surfing, Tennis, Leisureland. Breakfast menu. Power Showers in all rooms.

B&B	4	Ensuite	£19/£25	€24.13/€31.74	Dinner	-
B&B	-	Standard	-	-	Partial Board	-
Single Rate			£25/£30	€31.74/€38.09	Child reduction	-

Open: 1st February-30th November

Salthill 1km

Michael & Celine Glynn
DRUMLIN VIEW
6 Cashelmara, Upper Salthill,
Galway, Co Galway

Upper Salthill
TEL: **091 529513**   FAX: **091 529513**
EMAIL: cglynn@iol.ie

Luxurious home, overlooking Galway Bay. Breakfast Menu. Home Baking. One of the finest Breakfasts in Ireland - "Brooklyn Spectator". Near Leisureland.

B&B	6	Ensuite	£20/£30	€25.39/€38.09	Dinner	-
B&B	-	Standard	-	-	Partial Board	-
Single Rate			£35/£40	€44.44/€50.79	Child reduction	25%

Open: All Year Except Christmas

Salthill 2km

Tom & Colette Keaveney
THE CONNAUGHT
Barna Road, Salthill,
Galway, Co Galway

Upper Salthill
TEL: **091 525865**   FAX: **091 525865**
EMAIL: tcconnaught@eircom.net
BUS NO: **2**

Luxurious family home, purpose built. All amenities close by. Touring base Connemara. Recommended "Best B&B's in Ireland/Guide de Routard. Home from home. Breakfast menu, Chef owner.

B&B	6	Ensuite	£19/£22	€24.13/€27.93	Dinner	-
B&B	-	Standard	-	-	Partial Board	-
Single Rate			£25.50/£28.50	€32.38/€36.19	Child reduction	25%

Open: 1st March-31st October

Salthill 2km

Mrs Caroline Larkin
KILBRACK HOUSE
2 Woodfield, Barna Road,
Galway, Co Galway

Upper Salthill
TEL: **091 590802**
EMAIL: kilbracklarkin@eircom.net
BUS NO: **2**

Luxurious home overlooking Galway Bay. Golf, Fishing, Horseriding, Leisureland, Aquarium, Tennis and good Restaurants nearby. Ideal touring base for Aran Islands.

B&B	6	Ensuite	£19/£25	€24.13/€31.74	Dinner	-
B&B	-	Standard	-	-	Partial Board	-
Single Rate			£25.50/£30	€32.38/€38.09	Child reduction	50%

Open: March-November

Salthill 2km

Ms Bernie Lavin
WOODVIEW HOUSE B&B
Cleann na Coille, Barna Road, Galway, Co Galway

Upper Salthill

Tel: **091 590755**   Fax: **091 590755**
Email: woodview@eircom.net
Web: www.galway.net/pages/woodview/

Warm welcoming home on Coast Road. Close to Salthill and Silverstrand Beach, Barna Woods, Rusheen Riding Centre, Leisureland, Golf Club and Restaurants.

B&B	4	Ensuite	£19/£25	€24.13/€31.74	Dinner	-
B&B	-	Standard	-	-	Partial Board	-
Single Rate			£25.50/£29	€32.38/€36.82	Child reduction	25%

Open: 1st January-20th December

Salthill 2km

David & Rita Lenihan
ATLANTIC SUNSET
Coast Road, Gentian Hill, Upper Salthill, Galway, Co Galway

Upper Salthill Gentian Hill Area

Tel: **091 521425**
Bus No: **2**

Luxurious comfortable home in scenic peaceful surroundings overlooking Galway Bay and Bird sanctuary. Award winning gardens 1998. Golf, Fishing, Beach, Leisureland closeby.

B&B	5	Ensuite	£19/£25	€24.13/€31.74	Dinner	-
B&B	-	Standard	-	-	Partial Board	-
Single Rate			-	-	Child reduction	50%

Open: 12th January-12th December

Salthill 2km

Mrs Teresa McDonagh
ARD MHUIRE
Knocknacarra Road, Upper Salthill, Galway, Co Galway

Upper Salthill

Tel: **091 522344**   Fax: **091 529629**
Email: teresa@ardmhuire.com
Web: www.ardmhuire.com

Attractive, comfortable home within walking distance of the Seaside. Close to Leisureland, Golf, Tennis, Fishing, Horse riding etc.

B&B	6	Ensuite	£19/£20	€24.13/€25.39	Dinner	-
B&B	-	Standard	-	-	Partial Board	-
Single Rate			£25.50/£25.50	€32.38	Child reduction	25%

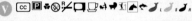

Open: 1st January-20th December

Galway 3km

Mrs Mary Meehan
SUMMERVILLE
4 Westbrook, Barna Rd, Galway, Co Galway

Upper Salthill

Tel: **091 590424**   Fax: **091 591026**
Email: meehanm@eircom.net
Bus No: **2**

Luxury balconied home with panoramic views of Galway Bay. Breakfast menu. TV, Hairdryers, Tea/Coffee all rooms. Near Beaches, Leisureland, Horse-riding, Golf, Woods.

B&B	4	Ensuite	£20	€25.39	Dinner	-
B&B	-	Standard	-	-	Partial Board	-
Single Rate			£25.50	€32.38	Child reduction	50%

Open: 1st May-30th September

Galway 2 km

Padraig and Maureen O'Donnell
SHAMROCK LODGE
4 Carragh Drive, Knocknacarra Road, Upper Salthill, Galway, Co Galway

Upper Salthill

Tel: **091 521429**   Fax: **091 521429**
Email: oods@eircom.net
Bus No: **2**

Overlooking Bay, Beach, Golf, Tennis, Leisureland, TV, Electric Blankets. Follow promenade, Golf Course, right at Spinnaker, 3rd left, 4th on right.

B&B	4	Ensuite	£19/£21	€24.13/€26.66	Dinner	-
B&B	-	Standard	-	-	Partial Board	-
Single Rate			£25.50/£25.50	€32.38	Child reduction	25%

Open: March-October

Galway 3km

Kevin & Maire O'Hare
ROSE VILLA
**10 Cashelmara,
Knocknacarra Cross,
Salthil, Co Galway**

Tel: **091 584200**   Fax: **091 584200**
Email: kevin.ohare@ireland.com

New luxury accommodation overlooking Galway Bay and Bird sanctuary. Close to Golf, Fishing, Horse Riding, Surfing, Leisureland. Ideal touring base.

B&B	4	Ensuite	£19/£25	€24.13/€31.74	Dinner -
B&B	-	Standard	-		Partial Board -
Single Rate			£25.50/£30	€32.38/€38.09	Child reduction 25%

Open: 1st January-23rd December

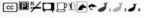

Salthill 1.5km

Bernie Power
FOUR WINDS LODGE
**Gentian Hill, Salthill,
Galway, Co Galway**

Tel: **091 526026**
Email: fourwindslodge@ireland.com
Web: www.galway.net/pages/fourwindslodge
Bus No: 2

Traditional home. Overlooking Galway Bay. Relax, enjoy breakfast in conservatory. Net access. Private gardens. First right after Statoil petrol after Golf Club.

B&B	4	Ensuite	£20/£30	€25.39/€38.09	Dinner -
B&B	-	Standard	-		Partial Board -
Single Rate			£25.50/£30	€32.38/€38.09	Child reduction 50%

Open: All Year Except Christmas

Mrs Patty Wheeler
WOODVILLE
**Barna Rd, Salthill,
Galway, Co Galway**

Tel: **091 524260**   Fax: **091 524260**
Email: woodville@esatclear.ie
Bus No: 2

Friendly home on Coast road overlooking Galway Bay. Ideal touring base. Beaches, 3 Golf Clubs, Tennis, Horseriding, Windsurfing, Canoeing. Bird santuary closeby.

B&B	4	Ensuite	£19/£25	€24.13/€31.74	Dinner -
B&B	-	Standard	-	-	Partial Board -
Single Rate			-	-	Child reduction 50%

Salthill 2km

Open: 1st March-31st October

In Gort

Mrs Kathleen O'Connor
THE ASHTREE
**Glenbrack, Galway Road,
Gort, Co Galway**

Tel: **091 631380**

Comfortable home on N18. Galway and Ennis 30 mins. The Burren, Coole Park, Thoorballylee and 18 hole Golf course nearby. Shannon Airport 1 hr.

B&B	3	Ensuite	£19/£19	€24.13	Dinner -
B&B	-	Standard	-		Partial Board -
Single Rate			£25.50/£25.50	€32.38	Child reduction 25%

Open: 1st April-31st October

Kinvara 4km

Mrs Maureen Fawle
HOLLYOAK
**Kinvara Road, Ballinderreen,
Kilcolgan, Co Galway**

Tel: **091 637165**

Spacious, warm, country home on N67 between Kinvara - Kilcolgan. Central Burren, Cliffs of Moher, Connemara. Banquets nightly in Dunguire Castle.

B&B	2	Ensuite	£19/£19	€24.13	Dinner -
B&B	2	Standard	£17/£17	€21.59	Partial Board -
Single Rate			£23.50/£25.50	€29.84/€32.38	Child reduction 25%

Open: 1st April-31st October

Kinvara 1.2km

Angela Larkin
BARN LODGE B&B
**Kinvara Road, Toureen,
Ballinderein, Kilcolgan,
Co Galway**

Kinvara
TEL: 091 637548

Country home situated on N67. 50 yards off main road between Kilcolgan, Ballindereen and Kinvara. Scenic route to Burren, Cliffs of Moher, Aran Islands. Banquets in Dungaire Castle.

B&B	4	Ensuite	£19/£19	€24.13	Dinner	-
B&B	-	Standard	-	-	Partial Board	-
Single Rate			£25.50/£25.50	€32.38	Child reduction	25%

Open: All Year Except Christmas

Kilcolgan 1km

Mrs Anne Kerins
CASTLEVIEW
**Weir Road, Kilcolgan,
Galway, Co Galway**

Kilcolgan Clarinbridge
TEL: 091 796172

"O'Sullivan B&B Guide" recommended. Tranquil, scenic surroundings. Galway 15km. Ideal touring base - Connemara & Burren. Excellent restaurants - walking distance.

B&B	2	Ensuite	£19	€24.13	Dinner	£12.50
B&B	1	Standard	£17	€21.59	Partial Board	-
Single Rate			£23.50	€29.84	Child reduction	33.3%

Open: February-November

Kilcolgan 1.3km

John & Detta Murphy
ASHGROVE
**Newtown, Kilcolgan,
Co Galway**

Kilcolgan
TEL: 091 796047
EMAIL: ashgrovebandb@eircom.net

Friendly comfortable home. Just off N18 Galway/Limerick rd, on N67 between Kilcolgan and Kinvara. Ideal touring base Burren/Connemara. Shannon Airport 1 hour drive.

B&B	3	Ensuite	£19/£19	€24.13	Dinner	-
B&B	-	Standard	-	-	Partial Board	-
Single Rate			£25.50/£25.50	€32.38	Child reduction	33.3%

Open: 1st April-30th September

Clifden 20km

Nancy Naughton
KYLEMORE HOUSE
**Kylemore, Connemara,
Co Galway**

Kylemore Connemara
TEL: 095 41143   FAX: 095 41143
EMAIL: kylemorehouse@eircom.net

Impressive Georgian house on the shores of Kylemore Lake. Ideal base walking. Spacious bedrooms. Home cooking. Horse riding, Beaches nearby. Recommended B&B Guide. On N59.

B&B	6	Ensuite	£20/£25	€25.39/€31.74	Dinner	£18
B&B	-	Standard	-	-	Partial Board	£250
Single Rate			£25.50/£35	€32.38/€44.44	Child reduction	-

Open: 1st April-1st November

In Leenane

Mrs Margaret Wallace
AVONDALE HOUSE
Leenane, Co Galway

Leenane Connemara Area
TEL: 095 42262

Friendly comfortable home in scenic area beside Village. Hillwalking, Adventure Centres, Angling, Pony Trekking, Restaurants in Village.

B&B	3	Ensuite	£19	€24.13	Dinner	-
B&B	-	Standard	-	-	Partial Board	-
Single Rate			-	-	Child reduction	25%

Open: 1st March-30th November

Loughrea 4km

Mrs Rose Plower
LA RIASC
Clostoken, Loughrea,
Co Galway

Loughrea
TEL: **091 841069**

Comfortable modern home, just off Dublin - Galway Road (N6). Galway side of Loughrea. Adjacent to award winning Restaurant "Meadow Court". Ideal touring base.

B&B	3	Ensuite	£19	€24.13	Dinner	-
B&B	1	Standard	£17	€21.59	Partial Board	-
Single Rate			£23.50/£25.50	€29.84/€32.38	Child reduction	25%

Open: 6th January-20th December

In Moycullen

Aine Mulkerrins
ARD IOSEF
Moycullen, Co Galway

Moycullen
TEL: **091 555149**

Friendly comfortable home on N59, 10km from Galway City. Fishing, Golf, Excellent Restaurants nearby. Breakfast menu. Ideal base for touring Connemara.

B&B	3	Ensuite	£20/£22	€25.39/€27.93	Dinner	-
B&B	1	Standard	£18/£20	€22.86/€25.39	Partial Board	-
Single Rate			£25.50/£26.50	€32.38/€33.65	Child reduction	25%

Open: 1st April-31st October

In Oranmore

Mary Carney
ARDFINNAN HOUSE
Maree Road, Oranmore,
Co Galway

Oranmore
TEL: **091 790749**

Comfortable accommodation, orthopaedic beds, home baking, 5 mins from Galway City. Close to Restaurants, Beaches, Golf, Parks, Sailing. Heritage facilities.

B&B	3	Ensuite	£19/£25	€24.13/€31.74	Dinner	£13.50
B&B	-	Standard	-	-	Partial Board	£195
Single Rate			£26.50/£26.50	€33.65	Child reduction	25%

Open: All Year

In Oranmore

Mrs Patricia Collins
CASTLE VIEW HOUSE
Galway Coast Road,
Oranmore, Co Galway

Oranmore
TEL: **091 794648**

Quiet country home, spacious bedrooms. Overlooking Galway Bay, Burren Mountains. Golf course and Horse riding nearby. Galway 7 mins drive.

B&B	4	Ensuite	£19/£19	€24.13	Dinner	-
B&B	-	Standard	-	-	Partial Board	-
Single Rate			-	-	Child reduction	25%

Open: All Year

Oranmore 1km

Mrs Mary Curran
BIRCHGROVE
Dublin Rd, Oranbeg,
Oranmore, Co Galway

Oranmore
TEL: **091 790238**
EMAIL: birchgrove@eircom.net
WEB: homepage.eircom.net/~birchgrove/

Comfortable modern bungalow off N6. Friendly relaxed atmosphere. Quality Restaurants/Pubs nearby. Ideal touring base. Quiet location. Galway 8 minutes.

B&B	3	Ensuite	£19/£19	€24.13	Dinner	£12.50
B&B	-	Standard	-	-	Partial Board	£185
Single Rate			£25.50	€32.38	Child reduction	33.3%

Open: All Year

Teresa Dundon
MILLBROOK
**Dublin Road, Oranmore,
Co Galway**

Oranmore
TEL: **091 794404**

Dormer bungalow on Dublin road, 5 mins walk from Oranmore Village. Sailing, Windsurfing, Golf nearby. Ideal touring base for Connemara, Burren.

B&B	3	Ensuite	£19/£20	€24.13/€25.39	Dinner	-
B&B	1	Standard	£17/£18	€21.59/€22.86	Partial Board	-
Single Rate			£25	€31.74	Child reduction	25%

In Oranmore

Open: April-October

Rose Mary Finlay
OCEAN VIEW
**Coast Road, Oranmore,
Co Galway**

Oranmore
TEL: **091 794040**   FAX: **091 794040**
EMAIL: oceanviewgalway@eircom.ie

Warm friendly comfortable home with spectacular views of Galway Bay, Mountains and Sunset. Breakfast menu. Home baking. Golf, Walking, Cycle, Sailing. Car Park.

B&B	3	Ensuite	£19/£25	€24.13/€31.74	Dinner	-
B&B	-	Standard	-	-	Partial Board	-
Single Rate			£25.50/£30	€32.38/€38.09	Child reduction	25%

Oranmore

Open: 1st January-23rd December

Geraldine & Seamus Grady
SHANLIN HOUSE
**Maree Road, Oranmore,
Co Galway**

Oranmore
TEL: **091 790381**   FAX: **091 790381**
EMAIL: ggrady@indigo.ie
WEB: www.shanlinhouse.com

Friendly Georgian home. Walk to Village, Pubs, Restaurants, Irish Music. 5 mins to Golf Courses, Rinville Park. Galway City 10km. Centrally located to tour Connemara, Burren.

B&B	4	Ensuite	£19/£25	€24.13/€31.74	Dinner	£15
B&B	-	Standard	-	-	Partial Board	-
Single Rate			£26/£26	€33.01	Child reduction	25%

In Oranmore

Open: All Year

Mrs Maureen Kelly
COOLIBAH HOUSE
**Dublin Road,
Oranmore, Co Galway**

Oranmore
TEL: **091 794996**

Comfortable modern home on N6, 100 mts East N18 & N6 roundabout. Ideal base for touring. Friendly and relaxing. 1km to Village.

B&B	3	Ensuite	£19	€24.13	Dinner	£12.50
B&B	-	Standard	-	-	Partial Board	-
Single Rate			£25.50	€32.38	Child reduction	25%

Oranmore 1km

Open: All Year Except Christmas

Mrs Kathleen McCarthy-Leyne
SON AMAR
**Coast Road, Oranmore,
Galway, Co Galway**

Oranmore
TEL: **091 794176**   FAX: **091 794176**

Georgian home, overlooking Galway Bay & Burren. SON AMAR offers peace, space, comfort in tranquil surroundings. A varied breakfast menu. Golf, Sailing, Walks, Horse Riding.

B&B	4	Ensuite	£19/£25	€24.13/€31.74	Dinner	-
B&B	2	Standard	-	-	Partial Board	-
Single Rate			£23.50/£25.50	€29.84/€32.38	Child reduction	25%

Oranmore 1km

Open: All Year

Oranmore 1km

Ms Marian McVicker
THE BIRCHES
10 Carrowmoneash,
Oranmore, Co Galway

Oranmore
TEL: **091 790394**
EMAIL: thebirches@eircom.net

Friendly family home. Quiet road off N6. Oranmore Lodge/Quality Hotels 200m.
Pubs/Restaurants in Village. Galway 8km, Airport 3km. Ideal touring/golf base.

				Dinner	-
B&B	4	Ensuite	£20/£25	€25.39/€31.74	
B&B	-	Standard	-	-	Partial Board	-
Single Rate			£26/£28	€33.01/€35.55	Child reduction	25%

Open: All Year Except Christmas

Oranmore 1km

Maureen Murphy
HILLVIEW
Moneymore, Oranmore,
Co Galway

Oranmore
TEL: **091 794341**

Dormer bungalow on N18. View of Clare hills. Ideal touring base for the Burren and Connemara.
18 hole Golf course nearby. Galway Airport 5km. Galway City 7km.

					Dinner	£12.50
B&B	3	Ensuite	£19/£19	€24.13		
B&B	1	Standard	£17/£17	€21.59	Partial Board	-
Single Rate			£25.50/£25.50	€32.38	Child reduction	25%

Open: 1st February-30th November

Oranmore 2km

Mrs Noeleen Murren
AVONDALE
Renville West, Oranmore,
Co Galway

Oranmore
TEL: **091 790527**
EMAIL: murrenwest@eircom.net

Spacious warm Georgian house. Large ensuite bedrooms. Quiet location. Leisure Park, Sailing and
Golf 1km. Close to excellent Restaurants. Galway City/ Airport 10km.

					Dinner	-
B&B	3	Ensuite	£20/£23	€25.39/€29.20		
B&B	-	Standard	-	-	Partial Board	-
Single Rate			£25.50/£28	€32.38/€35.55	Child reduction	25%

Open: 1st April-1st December

Oranmore 1km

Mrs Mary Noone
ASHBROOK HOUSE
Dublin Road, Oranmore,
Co Galway

Oranmore
TEL: **091 794196**   FAX: **091 794196**
EMAIL: mnoone@iol.ie
WEB: www.ashbrookhouse.com

Purpose built house 1 acre of landscaped gardens. Opposite Water Tower N6. Tea/Coffee, TV,
Hairdryer all rooms. Golf, Sailing, Horse Riding nearby. Ideal touring Cliffs of Moher, Connemara.

					Dinner	£15
B&B	4	Ensuite	£19/£25	€24.13/€31.74		
B&B	-	Standard	-	-	Partial Board	-
Single Rate			£26.50	€33.65	Child reduction	25%

Open: All Year

In Oughterard

Edwina Bunyan
THE WESTERN WAY
Camp Street, Oughterard,
Co Galway

Oughterard Connemara
TEL: **091 552475**
EMAIL: easgalmb@iol.ie

Old style spacious town residence in picturesque Oughterard. Relaxed atmosphere. Walk to top
class Restaurants and Pubs. Ideal base to tour Connemara.

					Dinner	-
B&B	2	Ensuite	£19/£19	€24.13		
B&B	1	Standard	£17/£17	€21.59	Partial Board	-
Single Rate			£28/£30	€35.55/€38.09	Child reduction	-

Open: 1st March-31st October

In Oughterard

Mrs Teresa Butler
CROSSRIVER
Glann Road, Oughterard,
Co Galway

Oughterard Connemara Area
Tel: 091 552676
Email: crossriver@clearvu.net

Superbly situated adjacent to Owen Riff River. 300 yards from Lough Corrib, famous for brown trout. Own boats available. 3 minutes walk from Village. Many first class Restaurants.

B&B	4	Ensuite	£19/£20	€24.13/€25.39	Dinner	-
B&B	2	Standard	£17/£17	€21.59	Partial Board	-
Single Rate			£25/£25	€31.74	Child reduction	50%

Open: 1st March-31th November

In Oughterard

Kathleen Dolly
WATERFALL LODGE
Oughterard,
Co Galway

Oughterard Connemara Area
Tel: 091 552168

Elegant period residence. Antique furnishings. Picturesque gardens. AA ♦♦♦♦ Quality award. Private Game Fishing. All bedrooms ensuite with colour TV.

B&B	6	Ensuite	£25/£25	€31.74	Dinner	-
B&B	-	Standard	-	-	Partial Board	-
Single Rate			£30/£30	€38.09	Child reduction	25%

Open: All Year Except Christmas

Oughterard 2km

Lal Faherty/Costelloe Family
LAKELAND COUNTRY HOUSE
Portacarron Bay, Oughterard,
Co Galway

Oughterard Connemara Area
Tel: 091 552121/552146 Fax: 091 552146
Email: mayfly@eircom.net

Lakeshore lodge with private gardens to Lake. Complete Angling/Boating facility on site. 5.mins drive from Village. Golfing, Walking. Off the N59, 2nd right after Golf Club sign.

B&B	8	Ensuite	£20/£20	€25.39	Dinner	£16
B&B	1	Standard	£18/£18	€22.86	Partial Board	£216
Single Rate			£26.50	€33.65	Child reduction	25%

Open: 15th January-15th December

In Oughterard

Ms Deirdre Forde
CAMILLAUN
Eighterard, Oughterard,
Co Galway

Oughterard Connemara Area
Tel: 091 552678   Fax: 091 552439
Email: camillaun@eircom.net
Web: http://homepage.eircom.net/~camillaunfishing

Riverside setting. Lake boats moored in garden. A short walk to the Village by pedestrian way. Turn at the Lake Hotel, down street over bridge, next right.

B&B	4	Ensuite	£19/£20	€24.13/€25.39	Dinner	-
B&B	-	Standard	-	-	Partial Board	-
Single Rate			£25.50	€32.38	Child reduction	25%

Open: 1st March-31st October

Carmel Geoghegan
RAILWAY LODGE
Canrower, Oughterard,
Co Galway

Oughterard Connemara Area
Tel: 091 552945
Email: railwaylodge@eircom.net
Bus No: 191

A real find! Delightful country home, individually decorated rooms. Antique furnishings. Relaxed atmosphere, enhanced by fine hospitality and good food.

B&B	3	Ensuite	£25	€31.74	Dinner	-
B&B	-	Standard	-	-	Partial Board	-
Single Rate			£30/£30	€38.09	Child reduction	-

Open: All Year Except Christmas

Mrs Brenda Joyce
THE SUNSET
Killola, Rosscahill,
Oughterard, Co Galway

Oughterard Connemara Area
TEL: 091 550146
EMAIL: thesunset@eircom.net

Modern country home in route N59. Ideal base for touring Connemara. Golfing, Fishing, Horse Riding available locally. Excellent home cooking.

B&B	3	Ensuite	£19/£20	€24.13/€25.39	Dinner	£17
B&B	1	Standard	£18/£19	€22.86/€24.13	Partial Board	-
Single Rate			£25/£25	€31.74	Child reduction	25%

Oughterard 4km

Open: 1st March-30th November

Ann Kelleher
RIVER WALK HOUSE
Riverside, Oughterard,
Co Galway

Oughterard Connemara Area
TEL: 091 552788　　　FAX: 091 557069
EMAIL: riverwalk@eircom.net

Comfortable friendly home in peaceful setting. Ideal base to tour Connemara and Aran Islands. 3 minutes walk to Oughterard Village. Fishing, Golf, Walking tours all nearby.

B&B	5	Ensuite	£19/£22	€24.13/€27.93	Dinner	-
B&B	-	Standard	-	-	Partial Board	-
Single Rate			£26/£28	€33.01/€35.55	Child reduction	25%

In Oughterard

Open: All Year

Mrs Dolores Leonard
FOREST HILL
Glann Road, Oughterard,
Co Galway

Oughterard Connemara Area
TEL: 091 552549
EMAIL: lakeshoreroad@eircom.net

Quiet. Peaceful country home. Surrounded by panoramic Connemara scenery. Ideal base for touring & walking. Very central for exploring Irish National Park, Kylemore Abbey & Ashford Castle.

B&B	6	Ensuite	£19/£19	€24.13	Dinner	£12.50
B&B	-	Standard	-	-	Partial Board	-
Single Rate			£25.50	€32.38	Child reduction	50%

Oughterard 4km

Open: 10th March-30th October

Mrs Mary Maloney
PINE GROVE
Glann Lakeshore, Hill of Doon
Road, Oughterard, Co Galway

Oughterard Connemara Area
TEL: 091 552101
EMAIL: annamal@gofree.indigo.ie

Quiet family home on "Western Way". Overlooking Lough Corrib. Turf fires, Fishing, Golfing, Horseriding & Hill Walks nearby.

B&B	3	Ensuite	£19	€24.13	Dinner	£16
B&B	1	Standard	£17	€21.59	Partial Board	-
Single Rate			£23.50/£23.50	€29.84	Child reduction	-

Oughterard 8km

Open: 1st April-30th October

Mrs Mary O'Halloran
LAKESIDE
Ardnasilla, Oughterard,
Co Galway

Oughterard Connemara Area
TEL: 091 552846　　　FAX: 091 552846

Superbly situated on the shores of Lough Corrib. Fishing, Boating, 18 hole Golf, Pitch & Putt, Aughnanure Castle 1km. Dillard Causin, Michele Erdvig Guides. First class Restaurants 4km.

B&B	4	Ensuite	£19/£21	€24.13/€26.66	Dinner	-
B&B	-	Standard	-	-	Partial Board	-
Single Rate			£25.50/£27	€32.38/€34.29	Child reduction	25%

Oughterard 4km

Open: 1st March-30th November

Miss Brid Tierney
GORTREVAGH HOUSE
Portacarron, Oughterard,
Co Galway

Oughterard Connemara Area
Tel: 091 552129

Old style charm, beside Golf Course, 10 mins from Lough Corrib. Tennis and Horse Riding nearby. Traditional cooking, speciality vegetarian.

B&B	2	Ensuite	£19	€24.13	Dinner	£12.50
B&B	3	Standard	£17	€21.59	Partial Board	-
Single Rate			£23.50	€29.84	Child reduction	25%

Oughterard 1km

Open: All Year Except Christmas

Mary & Tom Walsh
THE WATERFRONT
Corrib View, Oughterard,
Connemara, Co Galway

Oughterard Connemara Area
Tel: 091 552797   Fax: 091 552730
Email: waterfront@indigo.ie
Web: indigo.ie/~waterfnt/

Panoramic, Lakeside setting. Depart N59 at Golf course, towards Aughnanure Castle. Turn left, 0.5km. before the Castle towards Lake, drive along shore.

B&B	6	Ensuite	£19/£22	€24.13/€27.93	Dinner	-
B&B		Standard	-		Partial Board	-
Single Rate			£26/£28	€33.01/€35.55	Child reduction	25%

Oughterard 4km

Open: All Year Except Christmas

Sally Walsh
WOODSIDE LODGE
Killola, Ros,
Co Galway

Oughterard Connemara Area
Tel: 091 550123   Fax: 091 550123

Warm friendly family home. Peaceful Mountain and Lake surroundings. Ideal walking/touring base. Charming Oughterard Village, Fishing, Golf within 5km.

B&B	4	Ensuite	£19/£19	€24.13	Dinner	-
B&B		Standard	-		Partial Board	-
Single Rate			£25.50/£25.50	€32.38	Child reduction	50%

Oughterard 5km

Open: 1st May-15th September

Michael & Bridie Dolan
SHANNON VILLA
Bridge Road, Portumna,
Co Galway

Portumna
Tel: 0509 41269   Fax: 0509 41799
Email: shannonvilla@ireland.com

Delightful family home, total relaxation in our peaceful conservatory. Ideal for all leisure activities, Angling, Boating, Walks, Equestrian. Central tour base for Clonmacnois, Clonfert, Birr Castle.

B&B	4	Ensuite	£20/£22	€25.39/€27.93	Dinner	£18
B&B	1	Standard	£19/£21	€24.13/€26.66	Partial Board	£245
Single Rate			£25/£27	€31.74/€34.29	Child reduction	25%

In Portumna

Open: All Year

Mrs Elizabeth Ryan
AUVERGNE LODGE
Dominic Street, Portumna,
Co Galway

Portumna
Tel: 0509 41138   Fax: 0509 41138
Email: auvergnelodge@eircom.net

Warm friendly family home. Quiet area close to River Shannon, Lough Derg, Castle, Golf, Angling, Go Karting, Equestrian, Pubs, Restaurants, Hotel. TV, Tea/Coffee.

B&B	4	Ensuite	£19/£19	€24.13	Dinner	-
B&B		Standard	-		Partial Board	-
Single Rate			£25.50/£25.50	€32.38	Child reduction	50%

In Portumna

Open: All Year

Conneely Family
SUNNYMEADE
Tully, Renvyle,
Co Galway

Renvyle Connemara
TEL: **095 43491**   FAX: **095 43491**
EMAIL: sunny@eircom.net

Renvyle's longest established B&B. Deluxe accommodation, warm welcome, "Stress Free". Spectacular views of Atlantic Ocean. Walking, Horseriding, Bar, Food, Entertainment closeby.

B&B	4	Ensuite	£19	€24.13	Dinner	-
B&B	-	Standard	-	-	Partial Board	-
Single Rate			£25.50	€32.38	Child reduction	-

Clifden 19km

Open: 28th February-1st November

Mrs Noreen Conneely
SEA BREEZE
Gurteen, Renvyle,
Co Galway

Renvyle Connemara
TEL: **095 43489**   FAX: **095 43489**
EMAIL: seabreezebandbrenvyle@eircom.net
WEB: www.connemara.net/seabreeze

Luxury accommodation in scenic location. Convenient to Kylemore Abbey, Connemara National Park. Scuba Divewest, Oceans Alive, Golf, Fishing, Horse Riding nearby. Guest Conservatory.

B&B	3	Ensuite	£19/£20	€24.13/€25.39	Dinner	-
B&B	1	Standard	£17/£19	€21.59/€24.13	Partial Board	-
Single Rate			£23.50/£25.50	€29.84/€32.38	Child reduction	50%

Clifden 19km

Open: 1st January-20th December

Davin Family
OLDE CASTLE HOUSE
Curragh, Renvyle,
Connemara, Co Galway

Renvyle Connemara
TEL: **095 43460**

Traditional home situated in front of the sea beside 15th Century Renvyle Castle. Peaceful surroundings. House features in famous film Purple Taxi and Water Colour Challenge.

B&B	4	Ensuite	£19	€24.13	Dinner	£12.50
B&B	1	Standard	£17	€21.59	Partial Board	£190
Single Rate			£25	€31.74	Child reduction	-

Clifden 20km

Open: 15th March-26th November

Mr John Diamond
DIAMONDS CASTLE HOUSE B&B
Tully, Renvyle,
Co Galway

Renvyle Connemara
TEL: **095 43431**   FAX: **095 43431**
EMAIL: castlehouse@eircom.net

Recently renovated 19th Century house, oozing olde-worlde charm and character. Comfortable bedrooms with spacious ensuites and magnificent sea views.

B&B	4	Ensuite	£19/£19	€24.13	Dinner	-
B&B	-	Standard	-	-	Partial Board	-
Single Rate			£25.50/£25.50	€32.38	Child reduction	25%

Clifden 19km

Open: All Year

Mrs Monica Lydon
OCEAN LODGE
Renvyle,
Co Galway

Renvyle Connemara
TEL: **095 43481**   FAX: **095 43481**
EMAIL: oceanlodge@esatclear.ie

Luxury accommodation off N59. Ocean Views. Close to Kylemore Abbey, Connemara National Park, Scuba Dive West. Tea/Coffee in bedrooms. Panoramic ocean views.

B&B	5	Ensuite	£20/£24	€25.39/€30.47	Dinner	-
B&B	-	Standard	-	-	Partial Board	-
Single Rate			£25.50/£25.50	€32.38	Child reduction	25%

Tullycross 1.5km

Open: All Year

Spiddal 14km

Miss Sile Mullin
DERRYKYLE COUNTRY HOUSE
Casla/Costello,
Co Galway

Rossaveal
Tel: 091 572412

Quiet home, peaceful location. Warm atmosphere. Great base for touring Connemara and the Aran Islands. Sea and fresh water Angling nearby. Home baking.

B&B	2	Ensuite	£19	€24.13	Dinner	-
B&B	2	Standard	£17	€21.59	Partial Board	-
Single Rate			-	-	Child reduction	25%

Open: May-October

Catherine Burke
IVY ROCK HOUSE
Letterdyfe, Roundstone,
Co Galway

Roundstone Connemara Area
Tel: 095 35872   Fax: 095 35959
Email: ivyrockhouse@eircom.net

This newly refurbished Guesthouse overlooks the Sea and the Twelve Bens and is close to all amenities, Horseriding, Golf, Beaches.

B&B	5	Ensuite	£19/£20	€24.13/€25.39	Dinner	-
B&B	1	Standard	£19/£20	€24.13/€25.39	Partial Board	-
Single Rate			£28/£28	€35.55	Child reduction	25%

Open: 1st March-30th November

In Roundstone

Christina Lowry
ST. JOSEPH'S
Roundstone, Connemara,
Co Galway

Roundstone Connemara Area
Tel: 095 35865/35930 Fax: 095 35865
Email: christinalowry@eircom.net

Spacious, 19th Century town house overlooking Roundstone Harbour. Home from home. Repeat business. Traditional welcome. Bike shed, Hill, Beach & Island walks.

B&B	6	Ensuite	£19/£19.50	€24.13/€24.76	Dinner	-
B&B	-	Standard			Partial Board	-
Single Rate			£25.50/£30	€32.38/€38.09	Child reduction	50%

Open: January-8th December

In Roundstone

Linda Nee
RUSH LAKE HOUSE
Roundstone,
Co Galway

Roundstone Connemara Area
Tel: 095 35915   Fax: 095 35915

Peaceful setting overlooking Sea and Mountains, walking distance from Village. Friendly and relaxed atmosphere in a family run home.

B&B	4	Ensuite	£19/£20	€24.13/€25.39	Dinner	£14
B&B	-	Standard		-	Partial Board	£215
Single Rate			£25.50/£25.50	€32.38	Child reduction	25%

Open: 1st February-30th November

Spiddal 5.5km

Brian Clancy
SUAN NA MARA
Stripe, Furbo, Spiddal,
Co Galway

Spiddal Furbo
Tel: 091 591512   Fax: 091 591632
Web: www.suannamara.com

RAC ♦♦♦♦ Premier. Chef owned, evening dinner. Laundry service. Internet access. Bicyclehire. Gateway to Connemara, Aran Ferries. Beside Beach, Scenic walks. Route 336 West.

B&B	3	Ensuite	£22.50/£25	€28.57/€31.74	Dinner	£14.50
B&B	1	Standard	£22.50/£25	€28.57/€31.74	Partial Board	£250
Single Rate			£30/£32.50	€38.09/€41.27	Child reduction	25%

Open: All Year

Spiddal 3km

Mrs Alice Concannon
DUN LIOS
Park West, Spiddal,
Co Galway

Tel: **091 553165**
Email: concass@indigo.ie

Friendly family home with panoramic views of Galway Bay. Gateway to Connemara, Aran Islands. Restaurants, Traditional Music, Beach, Golf nearby. "Rough Guide" recommended.

B&B	4	Ensuite	£19/£20	€24.13/€25.39	Dinner	-
B&B	-	Standard	-	-	Partial Board	-
Single Rate			£25.50	€32.38	Child reduction	25%

Open: 1st May-31st October

Spiddal 5km

Mrs Maura Conneely
(Ni Chonghaile)
CALADHGEARR THATCH COTTAGE
Knock, Spiddal, Co Galway

Tel: **091 593124**
Email: cgthatchcot@ireland.com

Think old, friendly, traditional, find it in our thatch cottage, overlooking Galway Bay, on route 336 west of Spiddal Village. Recommended - Rough Guide to Ireland.

B&B	3	Ensuite	£20/£21	€25.39/€26.66	Dinner	-
B&B	-	Standard	-	-	Partial Board	-
Single Rate			£26/£27	€33.01/€34.29	Child reduction	25%

Open: 1st March-31st October

Spiddal 4km

Mrs Phil Conneely
CLUAIN BARRA
Knock, Inverin,
Co Galway

Tel: **091 593140**

Overlooking Clare Hills, Galway Bay, Aran Islands. Sandy Beaches, Aran Ferries and Inverin Airport nearby. Ideal for touring Connemara.

B&B	2	Ensuite	£19	€24.13	Dinner	-
B&B	1	Standard	£17	€21.59	Partial Board	-
Single Rate			£23.50/£25.50	€29.84/€32.38	Child reduction	33.3%

Open: 1st June-31st October

Spiddal 3km

Mrs Frances Cummins
(Ui Chuimin)
BRISEADH NA CARRAIGE
Pairc, Spiddal,
Co Galway

Tel: **091 553212**
Email: bnac@indigo.ie
Web: www.galwaybay.com

Guide du Routard recommended. Touring Connemara, Aran Islands, Galway Bay, Burren. Choice menu. Tea/Coffee arrival. Restaurants, Golf, Angling, Horse-riding, Beaches.

B&B	4	Ensuite	£19/£21	€24.13/€26.66	Dinner	-
B&B	-	Standard	-	-	Partial Board	-
Single Rate			-	-	Child reduction	25%

Open: All Year Except Christmas

In Spiddal

Mrs Barbara O'Malley-Curran
ARD AOIBHINN
Spiddal, Connemara,
Co Galway

Tel: **091 553179**   Fax: **091 553179**
Email: aoibhinn@gofree.indigo.ie

0.5km west Village. Multi Guidebook recommendations. Aran Ferry/Connemara/Burren. Tour bus pass door. Seafood Restaurants, Traditional music. Pubs, Bog. Seashore walks. AA ♦♦♦ award.

B&B	5	Ensuite	£19	€24.13	Dinner	-
B&B	-	Standard	-	-	Partial Board	-
Single Rate			£25.50/£25.50	€32.38	Child reduction	50%

Open: All Year

Spiddal 1.5km

Mrs Sarah Curran
SLIABH RUA HOUSE
Salahoona, Spiddal (R336), Galway, Co Galway

Spiddal Connemara
TEL: **091 553243**
EMAIL: sliabhrua@eircom.net

Seaside dormer home on scenic Coast Road, west of Spiddal. Spacious, relaxing, peaceful, ocean view, Cliffs of Moher, bog walks, Aran Ferries. Tour Connemara.

B&B	4	Ensuite	£19/£20	€24.13/€25.39	Dinner	-
B&B	-	Standard	-	-	Partial Board	-
Single Rate			£26/£30	€33.01/€38.09	Child reduction	-

Open: 13th April-29th October

Spiddal 1.5km

Patricia & William Farrell
IVERNA COTTAGE
Salahoona, Spiddal, Co Galway

Spiddal Connemara Area
TEL: **091 553762**

Recommended Sawdays " Special places to stay in Ireland". Welcome to join us here in spacious and interesting stone and wood cottage. Hope you love it too.

B&B	4	Ensuite	£19/£21	€24.13/€26.66	Dinner	-
B&B	-	Standard	-	-	Partial Board	-
Single Rate			£25.50/£35	€32.38/€44.44	Child reduction	33.3%

Open: 1st March-15th November

In Spiddal

Eamonn & Siobhan Feeney
TUAR BEAG
Spiddal, Co Galway

Spiddal Connemara Area
TEL: **091 553422**   FAX: **091 553010**
EMAIL: tuarbeagbandb@eircom.net
WEB: www.tuarbeag.com

Unique house built around 1831 thatched cottage. Bay view. Breakfast menu. Recommended Inside Ireland. Cooke/Rough guides. AA ◆◆◆◆ Award. West village R336.

B&B	6	Ensuite	£19/£21	€24.13/€26.66	Dinner	-
B&B	-	Standard	-	-	Partial Board	-
Single Rate			-	-	Child reduction	50%

Open: 1st February-15th November

Spiddal 1km

Mrs Moya Feeney
CALA 'N UISCE
Greenhill, Spiddal, Co Galway

Spiddal Connemara Area
TEL: **091 553324**   FAX: **091 553324**
EMAIL: moyafeeney@iolfree.ie

Dillard Causin recommended. Modern home on Seaward side of R336. Just west of Spiddal. Close to all amenities. Ideal for touring Connemara and Aran Islands.

B&B	6	Ensuite	£19/£20	€24.13/€25.39	Dinner	-
B&B	-	Standard	-	-	Partial Board	-
Single Rate			£26.50	€33.65	Child reduction	-

Open: 1st April-31st October

Spiddal 5km

Mrs Rita Feeney
ARD MHUIRBHI
Aille, Inverin, Spiddal, Co Galway

Spiddal Connemara Area
TEL: **091 593215**   FAX: **091 593215**
EMAIL: ardmhuirbhi@eircom.net

"Dillard Causin Guide" recommended. Spacious seaside accommodation on Coast Road R336. Superb views, peaceful location, family suites, electric blankets.

B&B	4	Ensuite	£19/£20	€24.13/€25.39	Dinner	-
B&B	1	Standard	£17/£17	€21.59	Partial Board	-
Single Rate			£23.50/£25.50	€29.84/€32.38	Child reduction	33.3%

Open: All Year except Christmas

Spiddal 1km

Vera Feeney
ARDMOR COUNTRY HOUSE
Greenhill, Spiddal,
Co Galway

Spiddal Connemara Area
TEL: **091 553145**   FAX: **091 553596**
EMAIL: ardmor@ireland.com
WEB: www.ardmorcountryhouse.com

Country home, superb views. Spacious rooms, comfort assured. Relaxed and friendly atmosphere. Breakfast awards. Recommended Frommer, Sullivan, Rough Guide. AA ♦♦♦♦ Selected.

B&B	7	Ensuite	£19/£22	€24.13/€27.93	Dinner	-
B&B	-	Standard	-	-	Partial Board	-
Single Rate			£25.50/£27	€32.38/€34.29	Child reduction	-

Open: February-December

Spiddal 2km

Mrs Sarah Flaherty
COIS CAOLAIRE
Ballintleva, Spiddal,
Co Galway

Spiddal Connemara Area
TEL: **091 553176**   FAX: **091 553624**
EMAIL: sarah-flaherty@hotmail.com

"Cead Mile Failte". Enjoy Irish hospitality in a family run home on the Coast R336 to Connemara. Scenic view of Galway Bay, Aran Island, Burren. Home Baking.

B&B	3	Ensuite	£19/£20	€24.13/€25.39	Dinner	£14
B&B	3	Standard	£17/£18	€21.59/€22.86	Partial Board	-
Single Rate			£25/£26	€31.74/€33.01	Child reduction	50%

Open: April-October

Ms Noreen Harte
AN CORRACH MOR
Coilleach, Spiddal,
Co Galway

Spiddal Connemara
TEL: **091 553735**   FAX: **091 553735**
EMAIL: noreenharte@eircom.net

High standard accommodation. Healthy eating option. Close to Sea. Ideal base for touring Connemara, Aran Islands, Burren. Close to Restaurants, Traditional Pubs, Golf, Country walks.

B&B	3	Ensuite	£19/£19.50	€24.13/€24.76	Dinner	-
B&B	-	Standard	-	-	Partial Board	-
Single Rate			£25.50	€32.38	Child reduction	25%

Open: All Year

Mary Joyce
ARD NA GREINE
Cre Dhulah, Spiddal,
Co Galway

Spiddal
TEL: **091 553039**
EMAIL: mjoyce81@hotmail.com

Modern friendly home, facing Atlantic. Near Restaurants, Pubs, Music, Bog walks, Golf, Beaches. Airport/Ferry for Aran Islands. Breakfast menu. TV, Laundry.

B&B	4	Ensuite	£19/£19	€24.13	Dinner	-
B&B	-	Standard	-	-	Partial Board	-
Single Rate			£25.50	€32.38	Child reduction	25%

Open: All Year Except Christmas

Spiddal 1.5km

Mrs Maureen Keady
(Ni Cheidigh)
COL-MAR HOUSE
Salahoona, Spiddal,
Co Galway

Spiddal Connemara
TEL: **091 553247**   FAX: **091 553247**

Peaceful country home. Set in private woods and colourful gardens. Warm hospitality, spacious, comfortable, relaxing. Guide du Routard, "Lonely Planets" recommended. 1.5km west Spiddal.

B&B	5	Ensuite	£19/£19	€24.13	Dinner	-
B&B	-	Standard	-	-	Partial Board	-
Single Rate			£25.50	€32.38	Child reduction	25%

Open: May-September

Mrs Patsy McCarthy
(MacCarthaigh)
SAILIN
Coill Rua, Spiddal, Co Galway

Spiddal Connemara Area
TEL: **091 553308**

Bungalow overlooking Galway Bay & Cliffs of Moher. 5 mins sandy beach. Ideal for touring Connemara & Aran Islands. Canoeing, Angling & Horse-riding.

B&B	3	Ensuite	£19	€24.13	Dinner	-
B&B	1	Standard	£17	€21.59	Partial Board	-
Single Rate			£23.50/£25.50	€29.84/€32.38	Child reduction	33.3%

Spiddal 2km

Open: 1st April-31st October

Mrs Peg O'Connor
RADHARC AN CHLAIR
Kellough, Spiddal,
Co Galway

Spiddal Connemara Area
TEL: **091 553267**
EMAIL: radharcanchlair@eircom.net

Bungalow tastefully decorated. Spacious rooms, overlooking Galway Bay, Aran Islands, Cliffs of Moher. Golf, beautiful Walks, Seafood Restaurants, Beaches, Touring Connemara.

B&B	4	Ensuite	£20	€25.39	Dinner	-
B&B	-	Standard	-	-	Partial Board	-
Single Rate			-	-	Child reduction	-

Spiddal 1.5km

Open: 1st May-1st November

Mrs Mary O'Dowd
RADHARC NA FARRAIGE
Moycullen Road, Spiddal,
Co Galway

Spiddal Connemara Area
TEL: **091 553434**

Home from home in quiet location overlooking Atlantic Ocean & Aran Islands. From Galway turn right in Village & travel 2km.

B&B	5	Ensuite	£19	€24.13	Dinner	-
B&B	1	Standard	£17	€21.59	Partial Board	-
Single Rate			£23.50/£25.50	€29.84/€32.38	Child reduction	25%

Spiddal 1.5km

Open: April-October

Mrs Mairead O'Flaherty
DUN-CHAOIN HOUSE
Cor-na Ron East, Inverin,
Co Galway

Spiddal Connemara Area
TEL: **091 593302**

Experience real comfort in a friendly, rural home, overlooking Galway Bay. Home-cooking, tranquil Bogwalks, Beaches. Aran Ferries, Airport nearby.

B&B	3	Ensuite	£19	€24.13	Dinner	£14
B&B	-	Standard	-	-	Partial Board	£185
Single Rate			£25.50	€32.38	Child reduction	25%

Spiddal 8km

Open: 1st June-30th September

Mrs Gabrielle Hurst
FOUR SEASONS
Carrowmoneen, Dublin Road,
Tuam, Co Galway

Tuam
TEL: **093 28375/25934** FAX: **093 25934**
EMAIL: ghurst@oceanfree.net

Spacious family residence in scenic, rural setting. Convenient for touring Galway, Connemara and Cong. Golf, Fishing and Horse-riding.

B&B	3	Ensuite	£19	€24.13	Dinner	-
B&B	-	Standard	-	-	Partial Board	-
Single Rate			£25.50	€32.38	Child reduction	-

Tuam 2km

Open: April-October

Mrs Josephine O'Connor
KILMORE HOUSE
**Galway Road, Tuam,
Co Galway**

Tuam

TEL: **093 28118/26525** FAX: **093 26525**
EMAIL: kilmorehouse@mail.com

Spacious modern residence on farm. Warm hospitality. Frommer recommended. Peaceful rural setting. Knock, Connemara and Galway convenient. Restaurants, Pubs nearby.

B&B	7	Ensuite	£19/£19	€24.13	Dinner	£14
B&B	-	Standard	-	-	Partial Board	£195
Single Rate			£25.50/£25.50	€32.38	Child reduction	25%

Tuam 1km

Open: All Year

Connemara National Park

Welcome to Mayo, "Ireland's best kept secret". Blue flag beaches, rivers, lakes and deep-sea fishing. Visitor attractions, great Golf courses, the most incredible Touring, Trekking and Walking countryside, but most of all the hospitality of the people of Mayo.

Mrs Margo Cannon
TEACH MWEEWILLIN
Currane, Achill,
Co Mayo

Achill Island

TEL: **098 45134**   FAX: **098 45225**
EMAIL: scannon@anu.ie

Hilltop house overlooking Achill Island. Mountain climbing, Sailing. Frommer Guide Recommended. Community Centre Area, has Geological, Historical and Botanical interests.

B&B	2	Ensuite	£19	€24.13	Dinner	£13.50
B&B	2	Standard	£17	€21.59	Partial Board	-
Single Rate			£23.50	€29.84	Child reduction	33.3%

Achill Sound 7km

Ⓥ

Open: 30th April-30th September

Michael G Lavelle
REALT NA MARA
Dooagh, Achill Island,
Co Mayo

Achill Island

TEL: **098 43005**   FAX: **098 43006**
EMAIL: mglavell@gofree.indigo.ie
WEB: www.dirl.com/mayorealtnamara.htm

On main road in Dooagh Village overlooking the Bay. New modern B&B. Family run with many facilities such as Snooker Room, Sauna, Gym, Jacuzzi, Laundry room, Drying.

B&B	6	Ensuite	£19/£25	€24.13/€31.74	Dinner	-
B&B	-	Standard	-	-	Partial Board	-
Single Rate			£25.50/£35	€32.38/€44.44	Child reduction	50%

Westport 55km

Ⓥ

Open: 1st March-30th November

Mrs Teresa McNamara
WEST COAST HOUSE
School Road, Dooagh,
Achill Island, Co Mayo

Achill Island

TEL: **098 43317**   FAX: **098 43317**
EMAIL: westcoast@anu.ie
WEB: www.dirl.com/mayo/westcoasthouse

AA ♦♦♦. Panoramic view, Tranquil setting. Orthopaedic beds. Hairdryer, Payphone, Breakfast menu, Drying room, Laundry service. Tours arranged. Fish Restaurant.

B&B	5	Ensuite	£19/£22	€24.13/€27.93	Dinner	£12.50
B&B	-	Standard	-	-	Partial Board	£185
Single Rate			£25.50/£28	€32.38/€35.55	Child reduction	25%

Keel 1km

Ⓥ

Open: 1st March-11th November

Mrs Frances Masterson
ROCKMOUNT
Achill Sound, Achill Island,
Co Mayo

Achill Island

TEL: **098 45272**

Frommer Guide recommended. Scenic surroundings, adjacent to Bus Stop, House of Prayer, Village, Sea, Mountains, Electric Blankets. Tea making facilities.

B&B	4	Ensuite	£19	€24.13	Dinner	-
B&B	2	Standard	£17	€21.59	Partial Board	-
Single Rate			£23.50/£25	€29.84/€31.74	Child reduction	-

In Achill Sound

Ⓥ

Open: 1st January-1st December

Achill Sound 1km

Mrs T Moran
WOODVIEW HOUSE
**Springvale, Achill Sound,
Co Mayo**

Achill Island
TEL: **098 45261**

Modern bungalow in quiet scenic surroundings with panoramic view of Sea and Mountains, 1km from House of Prayer.

B&B	3	Ensuite	£19	€24.13	Dinner	£12.50
B&B	3	Standard	£17	€21.59	Partial Board	-
Single Rate			£23.50	€29.84	Child reduction	-

Open: All Year Except Christmas

Achill Sound 3km

Mrs Ann Sweeney
FINNCORRY HOUSE
**Atlantic Drive, Bleanaskill Bay,
Achill Island, Co Mayo**

Achill Island
TEL: **098 45755**   FAX: **098 45755**
EMAIL: achill-island@hotmail.com
WEB: achill.mayo-ireland.ie/finncorry.htm

Relax, enjoy traditional hospitality in luxuriously appointed modern home. Peaceful setting overlooking Bleanaskill Bay. En-Suite for wheelchair, AA/RAC Approved-◆◆◆◆.

B&B	6	Ensuite	£19/£19	€24.13	Dinner	£14
B&B	-	Standard			Partial Board	-
Single Rate			£25.50/£25.50	€32.38	Child reduction	33.3%

Open: March-October

Geraldine Best
GLENEAGLE HOUSE
**Foxford Road, Ballina,
Co Mayo**

Ballina
TEL: **096 70228**

Dormer bungalow, a home of genuine welcome. 10 mins walk from Town. Rooms ensuite with TV, Tea and Coffee facilities. Ideal for Fishing and Golfing.

B&B	3	Ensuite	£19/£20	€24.13/€25.39	Dinner	-
B&B	-	Standard			Partial Board	-
Single Rate			£25.50/£26.50	€32.38/€33.65	Child reduction	25%

In Ballina

Open: 1st March-30th November

In Ballina

Mrs Josephine Corrigan
GREEN HILL
**Cathedral Close, Ballina,
Co Mayo**

Ballina
TEL: **096 22767**

Comfortable home in quiet location at rear of Cathedral, within walking distance of River Moy, Ridge Pool and Town Centre.

B&B	3	Ensuite	£19/£19	€24.13	Dinner	-
B&B	-	Standard	£17/£17	€21.59	Partial Board	-
Single Rate			£23.50/£25.50	€29.84/€32.38	Child reduction	33.3%

Open: 1st January-20th December

Ballina 1km

Mrs Noelle Curry
EVERGREEN
**Foxford Road, Ballina,
Co Mayo**

Ballina
TEL: **096 71343**
EMAIL: evergreen-curry@iol.ie
WEB: ballina.mayo-ireland.ie/evergreen.htm

Welcome to our comfortable bungalow in peaceful location walking distance of Town. Rooms ensuite with TV, Private car park.

B&B	4	Ensuite	£19/£19	€24.13	Dinner	-
B&B	1	Standard	£17/£18	€21.59/€22.86	Partial Board	-
Single Rate			-	-	Child reduction	50%

Open: All Year

In Ballina

Mrs Marie Dempsey	**Ballina**
WHITESTREAM HSE	TEL: **096 21582**
Foxford Rd (N26), Ballina, Co Mayo	EMAIL: whitestreamhse@iol.ie

Highly recommended. Spacious residence, extensive gardens. 10 mins walking distance of Town, Bus and Train. Beside famous River Moy.

B&B	6	Ensuite	£19/£21	€24.13/€26.66	Dinner	-
B&B	-	Standard	-	-	Partial Board	-
Single Rate			£25.50/£30	€32.38/€38.09	Child reduction	25%

Open: 6th January-22nd December

Ballina 6km

Ms Dolores Jordan	**Ballina**
RED RIVER LODGE	TEL: **096 22841**
Iceford, Quay Rd, Ballina, Co Mayo	EMAIL: redriverlodge@eircom.net
	WEB: http://homepage.eircom.net/~redriverlodge

Friendly country home on 1 acre gardens overlooking Moy Estuary on scenic Quay Road to Enniscrone. 3km from Quay Village. Recommended by International Guides.

B&B	4	Ensuite	£19	€24.13	Dinner	-
B&B	-	Standard	-	-	Partial Board	-
Single Rate			£25.50	€32.38	Child reduction	25%

Open: March-October

Ballina 3.5km

Agnes and Brendan McElvanna	**Ballina**
CLADDAGH HOUSE	TEL: **096 71670**
Sligo Rd, Ballina, Co Mayo	EMAIL: brenclad@eircom.net
	WEB: homepage.eircom.net/~clad

Modern home, excellent views. Comfortable and spacious. Guest TV Lounge, complimentary Tea/Coffee. Hospitality and friendly atmosphere. Full Fire Safety Certificate.

B&B	6	Ensuite	£19/£19	€24.13	Dinner	-
B&B	-	Standard	-		Partial Board	-
Single Rate			£25.50/£25.50	€32.38	Child reduction	33.3%

Open: 1st March-31st October

Ballina 1km

Mrs Carmel Murray	**Ballina**
ASHLEY HOUSE	TEL: **096 22799**
Ardoughan, Ballina, Co Mayo	EMAIL: ashleyhousebb@hotmail.com

Welcome to our highly recommended home off main Crossmolina Rd N59. All guests bedrooms ground floor. Award winning gardens. Walking distance to Town. Near Belleek Castle.

B&B	4	Ensuite	£19	€24.13	Dinner	-
B&B	-	Standard	-		Partial Board	-
Single Rate			£25.50	€32.38	Child reduction	33.3%

Open: All Year

Ballina 2km

Mary O'Dowd	**Ballina**
CNOC BREANDAIN	TEL: **096 22145**
Quay Road, Ballina, Co Mayo	EMAIL: nodowd@iol.ie

Country home overlooking Moy Estuary. Noted for hospitality. Many recommendations. Breakfast menu. 2km past Quay Village towards Enniscrone. Good restaurants nearby.

B&B	4	Ensuite	£19	€24.13	Dinner	-
B&B	-	Standard	-		Partial Board	-
Single Rate			£25.50	€32.38	Child reduction	33.3%

Open: 1st June-31st August

Mrs Breege Padden
QUIGNALEGAN HOUSE
**Quignalegan, Sligo Road,
Ballina, Co Mayo**

Ballina
TEL: **096 71644**   FAX: **096 71644**

Warm welcoming home. Convenient to Golf, Beach, Fishing, Horseriding, Country Walks. All rooms with Televisions, Hairdryers. Complimentary refreshments. Private parking.

B&B	6	Ensuite	£19	€24.13	Dinner -
B&B	-	Standard	-	-	Partial Board -
Single Rate			£25.50	€32.38	Child reduction 33.3%

Ballina 3km

Open: 1st March-31st October

Mrs Mary Reilly
BELVEDERE HOUSE,
**Foxford Rd, Ballina,
Co Mayo**

Ballina
TEL: **096 22004**

Modern Georgian style home on N26. Within walking distance from Town, Bus and Train. Ideal for Golf and Walking. Salmon Fishing on River Moy, Trout Fishing on Lough Conn.

B&B	4	Ensuite	£19	€24.13	Dinner -
B&B	-	Standard	-	-	Partial Board -
Single Rate			£25.50	€32.38	Child reduction 25%

In Ballina

Open: 1st January-20th December

Mrs Helen Smyth
ASHLEAM HOUSE
**Mount Falcon, Foxford Rd,
Ballina, Co Mayo**

Ballina
TEL: **096 22406**
EMAIL: helen.smyth@ireland.com

Country home, half way between Ballina and Foxford N26. Beside River Moy. Near Lough Conn. Noted for hospitality. Ideal as a base for touring. Golfing.

B&B	4	Ensuite	£19/£19	€24.13	Dinner -
B&B	2	Standard	£17/£17	€21.59	Partial Board -
Single Rate			£23.50/£25.50	€29.84/€32.38	Child reduction 25%

Ballina 4km

Open: 1st April-30th September

Mrs Breda Walsh
SUNCROFT
**3 Cathedral Close, Ballina,
Co Mayo**

Ballina
TEL: **096 21573**   FAX: **096 21573**
EMAIL: breda.suncroft@unison.ie

Town house in quiet location behind Cathedral. Town Centre and River Moy, Ridge Pool 300 mtrs. Le Guide De Routard recommended.

B&B	4	Ensuite	£19/£19	€24.13	Dinner -
B&B	1	Standard	£17/£18	€21.59/€22.86	Partial Board -
Single Rate			£26/£26	€33.01	Child reduction 33.3%

In Ballina

Open: 1st January-20th December

Martin & Breege Kavanagh
FRIARSQUARTER HOUSE
**Convent Road, Ballinrobe,
Co Mayo**

Ballinrobe
TEL: **092 41154**

Elegant house, period furnishings. Spacious gardens. Le Guide Du Routard recommended. 18 Champion Golf course. Touring Base. Connemara Knock N84.

B&B	3	Ensuite	£19/£19	€24.13	Dinner -
B&B	1	Standard	£18/£18	€22.86	Partial Board -
Single Rate			£25	€31.74	Child reduction 50%

In Ballinrobe

Open: All Year

Ballinrobe

Anne Mahon
RIVERSIDE HOUSE
**Cornmarket, Ballinrobe,
Co Mayo**

TEL: 092 41674
EMAIL: annmahon@iol.ie

Modern home in Lake District. Championship Golf Course, Scenic Walks. Easy driving distance Ashford Castle, Westport, Knock Shrine, Galway, Connemara, Fishing.

B&B	3	Ensuite	£19/£19	€24.13	Dinner	-
B&B	1	Standard	£17/£17	€21.59	Partial Board	-
Single Rate			£23.50/£25.50	€29.84/€32.38	Child reduction	50%

Ballinrobe

Open: 6th January-20th December

Ballycastle

Mrs Carmel Murphy
THE HAWTHORNS
**Belderrig, Ballina,
Co Mayo**

TEL: 096 43148   FAX: 096 43148
EMAIL: camurphy@indigo.ie

Enjoy warm friendly hospitality in the picturesque Village of Belderrig. Beside Sea/Fishing Port. Hill/Cliff Walking. Ceide Fields nearby.

B&B	2	Ensuite	£19/£19	€24.13	Dinner	£12.50
B&B	1	Standard	£17/£17	€21.59	Partial Board	£185
Single Rate			£23.50/£25.50	€29.84/€32.38	Child reduction	50%

Ballycastle 10km

Open: All Year

Ballyhaunis

Annette Fleming
EASCAI
**Lavallyroe, Clonfad,
Ballyhaunis, Co Mayo**

TEL: 0907 46040

Ideally situated on N83 for touring Galway, Westport, Sligo, Roscommon, all 1 hr drive. 18km from Knock, 25km from Knock Airport. Taxi service available.

B&B	4	Ensuite	£19/£20	€24.13/€25.39	Dinner	£12.50
B&B	-	Standard			Partial Board	£200
Single Rate			£25.50/£25.50	€32.38	Child reduction	25%

Ballyhaunis 8km

Open: All Year

Bangor Erris

Mrs Evelyn Cosgrove
HILLCREST HOUSE
**Main Street, Bangor Erris,
Ballina, Co Mayo**

TEL: 097 83494
EMAIL: hillcresthouse@eircom.net
WEB: homepage.eircom.net/~hillcresthouse

Visit Ceide Fields. Recommended B&B Guide to Ireland. Walkers, Drying room facilities. Off Bangor Trail and Western Way. Ideal for Fishing, Cycling storage. Afternoon tea on arrival.

B&B	2	Ensuite	£19/£20	€24.13/€25.39	Dinner	£12.50
B&B	2	Standard	£17/£18	€21.59/€22.86	Partial Board	£185
Single Rate			£23.50/£25	€29.84/€31.74	Child reduction	25%

Bangor Erris

Open: All Year

Belmullet Peninsula

Josephine Geraghty
BRU CHIANN LIR
**Tirrane, Clogher, Belmullet,
Ballina, Co Mayo**

TEL: 097 85741   FAX: 097 85741
EMAIL: bruclannlir@eircom.net

Visit this unspoilt Peninsula location. Surrounded by Sea, Boat trips/Angling arranged. Quiet Blue Flag Beaches, Walks, Golf, Birdlife. We have it all.

B&B	5	Ensuite	£19/£19	€24.13	Dinner	-
B&B	-	Standard			Partial Board	-
Single Rate			£25.50/£25.50	€32.38	Child reduction	25%

Belmullet 13km

Open: 1st May-30th September

Ms Mairin Maguire-Murphy
DROM CAOIN
Belmullet,
Co Mayo

Belmullet
TEL: **097 81195/82953** FAX: **097 81195**
EMAIL: dromcaoin@esatlink.com

Panoramic view of Blacksod Bay and Achill Island. AIB Best Food Award, Vegetarian option. Carne 18 hole Links, Sea Angling, Blue Flag Beaches, Ceide fields, Cycle storage, Drying room.

B&B	4	Ensuite	£20	€25.39	Dinner	£13.50
B&B	-	Standard	£26	-	Partial Board	-
Single Rate			£26	€33.01	Child reduction	33.3%

Belmullet 1km   **Open:** All Year

Anne Reilly
HIGHDRIFT
Haven View, Ballina Road,
Belmullet, Co Mayo

Belmullet
TEL: **097 81260**   FAX: **097 81260**

Quiet scenic surroundings overlooking the Atlantic and Broadhaven Bay. Turf fires. 5 mins walk to Town. Visit Mullet Peninsula and Ceide fields. Warm welcome.

B&B	3	Ensuite	£19/£19	€24.13	Dinner	£12.50
B&B	1	Standard	£17.50/£17.50	€22.22	Partial Board	-
Single Rate			£24/£24	€30.47	Child reduction	25%

Belmullet 1km      **Open:** 1st April-15th October

---

Mrs Bernie Collins
DRUMSHINNAGH HOUSE
Rahins, Newport Road,
Castlebar, Co Mayo

Castlebar
TEL: **094 24211**   FAX: **094 24211**
EMAIL: berniecollins@oceanfree.net

On Newport/Mulranny/Achill Island Road (R311). 300m off main road. Ideal for Touring, Fishing, Golfing. Boat & Wet room available.

B&B	4	Ensuite	£20	€25.39	Dinner	-
B&B	-	Standard	-	-	Partial Board	-
Single Rate			£25.50	€32.38	Child reduction	25%

Castlebar 3km      **Open:** 17th March-31st October

---

Mrs Maureen Daly
WOODVIEW LODGE
Breaffy (Breaghwy), Castlebar,
Co Mayo

Castlebar
TEL: **094 23985**   FAX: **094 23985**
EMAIL: woodviewlodge@eircom.net

Luxurious country home, quiet peaceful location. N60 on Claremorris Road opposite Breaffy House Hotel. Rooms ensuite, Tea/Coffee, TV, Hairdryers.

B&B	6	Ensuite	£19	€24.13	Dinner	-
B&B	-	Standard	-	-	Partial Board	-
Single Rate			£25.50	€32.38	Child reduction	25%

Castlebar 4km   **Open:** All Year

Mrs Breeda Flannelly
FORT-VILLA HOUSE
Moneen, Castlebar,
Co Mayo

Castlebar
TEL: **094 21002**   FAX: **094 26827**
EMAIL: flanprop@eircom.net

Old Georgian House, walking distance Town Centre. Touring centre. Outdoor activities, Fishing, Golf. Beside N5 roundabout. Rooms TV, Teasmaid. Friendly welcome.

B&B	5	Ensuite	£19	€24.13	Dinner	-
B&B	-	Standard	-	-	Partial Board	-
Single Rate			£25.50	€32.38	Child reduction	-

Castlebar 1km   **Open:** 1st April-1st October

Castlebar 4km

Mrs Ann Lavelle
HILLCREST
Westport Rd, Castlebar,
Co Mayo

Castlebar

TEL: **094 21554**
EMAIL: bandbhillcrest@tinet.ie

Highly recommended family home. 4km from Castlebar, 12km from Westport. Ideal location for touring Achill Island, Connemara, Clifden etc.

			£	€		
B&B	2	Ensuite	£19	€24.13	Dinner	-
B&B	1	Standard	£17	€21.59	Partial Board	-
Single Rate			£23.50/£25.50	€29.84/€32.38	Child reduction	-

Open: All Year

Castlebar 1km

Mrs Noreen McGinley
ASHLEIGH
Westport Rd N5,
Castlebar, Co Mayo

Castlebar

TEL: **094 24714**
EMAIL: ashleigh@iol.ie

Cosy, welcoming, award winning B&B. Guest TV lounge. TV, Electric Blankets, Hairdryers, Tea/Coffee all rooms. Breakfast Menu. Superb touring base. Friendly welcome.

			£	€		
B&B	4	Ensuite	£19	€24.13	Dinner	-
B&B	-	Standard	-	-	Partial Board	-
Single Rate			£25.50	€32.38	Child reduction	33.3%

Open: 14th January-14th December

Castlebar 6km

Mrs Kay McGrath
WINDERMERE HOUSE
Westport Road, Islandeady,
Castlebar, Co Mayo

Castlebar

TEL: **094 23329**
EMAIL: windermerehse@eircom.net

Luxurious spacious home. Bilberry Lake 1km. Home away from home. Brittany Ferries selected. Breakfast Menu. Trouser press, Hairdryers. Boat hire. Friendly and relaxed atmosphere.

			£	€		
B&B	3	Ensuite	£19/£19	€24.13	Dinner	£12.50
B&B	1	Standard	£17	€21.59	Partial Board	£185
Single Rate			-	-	Child reduction	-

Open: All Year

Castlebar 2km

Grainne McManus
BALLARD HOUSE
Aughaluskey, Windsor,
Castlebar, Co Mayo

Castlebar

TEL: **094 26125**   FAX: **094 26125**
EMAIL: ballardhouse@eircom.net

A warm welcome awaits you in our home. Peaceful country location off the Dublin Rd. N5. All home cooking. Ideal base for Golf, Fishing, Walking and Cycling.

			£	€		
B&B	2	Ensuite	£20/£20	€25.39	Dinner	-
B&B	-	Standard	£18/£18	€22.86	Partial Board	-
Single Rate			£23.50/£25.50	€29.84/€32.38	Child reduction	50%

Open: 17th March-30th November

Castlebar 1km

Rody and Mary McRandal
CARRAIG RUA
The Curragh, Castlebar,
Co Mayo

Castlebar

TEL: **094 22103**
EMAIL: mcrandal@iol.ie

Comfortable town house home, within walking distance of Town Centre and all amenities. Touring centre.

			£	€		
B&B	3	Ensuite	£19	€24.13	Dinner	-
B&B	-	Standard	-	-	Partial Board	-
Single Rate			£25.50	€32.38	Child reduction	25%

Open: All Year Except Christmas

In Castlebar

Monica Nealon
PRIMROSE COTTAGE B&B
**Pontoon Road, Castlebar,
Co Mayo**

Castlebar
Tel: **094 21247**

Dormer style home, Luxurious welcoming ambience. Customer focused. Guest lounge. Breakfast menu. On R310 scenic route. Knock Airport 30 mins. Touring base Mayo, Galway, Sligo.

B&B	2	Ensuite	£21/£21	€26.66	Dinner	-
B&B	1	Standard	£21/£21	€26.66	Partial Board	-
Single Rate			£26.50/£26.50	€33.65	Child reduction	-

Open: 1st January-18th December

In Castlebar

Mrs Eileen Pierce
FOUR WINDS
**Maryland, Breaffy Road,
Castlebar, Co Mayo**

Castlebar
Tel: **094 21767**   Fax: **094 21767**
Email: epierce_fourwinds@esatclear.ie

Spacious house. Quiet location. N60 walking distance Town. TV, Hairdryers in bedrooms. Convenient to Breaffy House Hotel, Train Station. Visit Knock Shrine. Ballintubber Abbey.

B&B	5	Ensuite	£19	€24.13	Dinner	-
B&B	-	Standard	-	-	Partial Board	-
Single Rate			£25.50	€32.38	Child reduction	50%

Open: 1st April-30th November

In Castlebar

Mrs Teresa Quinn
NEPHIN HOUSE
**Westport Road, Castlebar,
Co Mayo**

Castlebar
Tel: **094 23840**   Fax: **094 23840**
Email: quinnnephin@eircom.net

Comfortable home. Beside Westport road roundabout. Walking distance from Town. Travellers Friend Hotel, Hospital. TV, Tea/Coffee, Hairdryers in rooms. Ideal touring base.

B&B	3	Ensuite	£19/£19	€24.13	Dinner	-
B&B	-	Standard	-	-	Partial Board	-
Single Rate			£25.50	€32.38	Child reduction	25%

Open: 1st May-31st October

Castlebar 4km

Mrs Breege Scahill
MILLHILL HOUSE
**Westport Road, Castlebar,
Co Mayo**

Castlebar
Tel: **094 24279**
Email: millhill@eircom.net
Web: homepage.eircom.net/~millhill

Quality accommodation off main road. Easy to find. Take Westport road N5 from Castlebar. Sign on left. Convenient to Westport. Guest lounge, TV, Tea/Coffee facilities.

B&B	2	Ensuite	£19	€24.13	Dinner	-
B&B	1	Standard	£17	€21.59	Partial Board	-
Single Rate			£23.50/£25.50	€29.84/€32.38	Child reduction	50%

Open: May-October

Castlebar 2km

Mrs Bernadette Walsh
ROCKSBERRY B&B
**Westport Road, Castlebar,
Co Mayo**

Castlebar
Tel: **094 27254**   Fax: **094 27254**

Comfortable home on Castlebar/Westport road. Hairdryers, TV, Tea/Coffee in bedrooms. Boat hire for local Lakes.

B&B	3	Ensuite	£19/£19	€24.13	Dinner	-
B&B	-	Standard	-	-	Partial Board	-
Single Rate			£25.50/£25.50	€32.38	Child reduction	33.3%

Open: 1st February-30th November

Castlebar 1km

Mrs Nora Ward
DEVARD
Westport Road, Castlebar,
Co Mayo

Castlebar

TEL: **094 23462**   FAX: **094 23462**
EMAIL: devard@esatclear.ie
WEB: www.esatclear.ie/~devard

Bungalow on N5 Westport road, 2 doors from Spar Foodstore. Electric Blankets, Hairdryers, TV, Tea/Coffee in bedrooms. Award winning gardens.

B&B	5	Ensuite	£19/£19	€24.13	Dinner	-
B&B	-	Standard	-	-	Partial Board	-
Single Rate			£25.50/£25.50	€32.38	Child reduction	50%

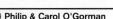

Open: All Year

Charlestown 1km

Philip & Carol O'Gorman
ASHFORT
Galway/Knock Road,
Charlestown, Co Mayo

Charlestown

TEL: **094 54706**   FAX: **094 55885**
EMAIL: ashfort@esatclear.ie

Spacious, comfortable home. Quiet, central location on routes N17/N5. Personal attention, Route planning, Genealogy guidance. Knock Airport 5 mins. Knock Shrine 20 min. Frommer Guide.

B&B	5	Ensuite	£19/£19	€24.13	Dinner	-
B&B	-	Standard	-	-	Partial Board	-
Single Rate			£25.50/£25.50	€32.38	Child reduction	25%

Open: 1st March-1st December

In Claremorris

Mrs Rita Cleary
CASA MIA
Ballyhaunis Road,
Claremorris, Co Mayo

Claremorris

TEL: **094 71405**

Situated Claremorris/Ballyhaunis Road N60. Convenient Knock Shrine, Airport, Ballintubber Abbey Riding School. 18 hole Golf Course.

B&B	2	Ensuite	£19	€24.13	Dinner	-
B&B	2	Standard	£17	€21.59	Partial Board	-
Single Rate			£23.50/£25	€29.84/€31.74	Child reduction	25%

Open: 1st February-30th November

Claremorris 5km

Pat & Carmel Conway
CONWAYS B&B
Coilmore,
Claremorris, Co Mayo

Claremorris

TEL: **094 71117**
EMAIL: coilmore@eircom.net

Set in mature secluded gardens on Ballyhaunis road N60. Close to Knock Shrine, Airport, Horse Riding, Golf, Swimming Pool. Home Baking. Welcome assured.

B&B	1	Ensuite	£19	€24.13	Dinner	-
B&B	2	Standard	£17	€21.59	Partial Board	-
Single Rate			£23.50	€29.84	Child reduction	33.3%

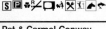

Open: 1st January-31st December

Cong 1km

Mrs Ann Coakley
HAZEL GROVE
Drumshiel, Cong,
Co Mayo

Cong Connemara Area

TEL: **092 46060**   FAX: **092 46060**
EMAIL: hazelgrovecong@eircom.net

Warm friendly home, peaceful area between Lakes Corrib/Mask. Panoramic view of Connemara Mountains. Historic area. Ideal touring base for Connemara/Mayo.

B&B	4	Ensuite	£19/£19	€24.13	Dinner	-
B&B	1	Standard	£17/£17	€21.59	Partial Board	-
Single Rate			£25.50/£25.50	€32.38	Child reduction	25%

Open: 1st February-30th November

Christina Dunleavy
ASHFIELD HOUSE
**Caherduff, Neale,
Ballinrobe, Co Mayo**

Cong
TEL: **092 46759**   FAX: **092 46759**
EMAIL: ashfield@mayo-ireland.ie

Tastefully decorated home; close to Ashford Castle, Cong Abbey, Quiet Man Heritage cottage, Golf courses. Convenient for Fishing on Lough Corrib/Mask.

B&B	3	Ensuite	£19/£20	€24.13 /€25.39	Dinner -
B&B	-	Standard		-	Partial Board -
Single Rate			£25.50	€32.38	Child reduction 25%

Cong 2km

Open: 1st March-31st October

Madge Gorman
DRINGEEN BAY B&B
**Cong,
Co Mayo**

Cong Connemara Area
TEL: **092 46103**
EMAIL: dringeenbay@eircom.net

Elegant home located off R345 Cong/Clonbur road. 300m from shore of Lough Mask. Scenic mountain views. Home baking. Forest walks, extensive gardens. Ideal base for touring Connemara.

B&B	2	Ensuite	£19/£19	€24.13	Dinner -
B&B	1	Standard	£17/£17	€21.59	Partial Board -
Single Rate			£23.50/£25.50	€29.84/€32.38	Child reduction 50%

Cong 3km

Open: 1st May-30th September

Mrs Ann Holian
VILLA PIO
**Gortacurra Cross,
Cong, Co Mayo**

Cong Connemara Area
TEL: **092 46403**   FAX: **092 46403**
EMAIL: villapiocong@hotmail.com

Situated off R334 near Lough Corrib. Boat/Engine Hire. Ideal for walkers, cyclists and touring Connemara. Quiet Man film location and Ashford Castle. Taxi Service.

B&B	2	Ensuite	£19	€24.13	Dinner -
B&B	1	Standard	£17	€21.59	Partial Board -
Single Rate			£25.50	€32.38	Child reduction 50%

Cong 3km

Open: All Year

Kathy O'Connor
DOLMEN HOUSE
**Drumsheel, Cong,
Co Mayo**

Cong
TEL: **092 46466**   FAX: **092 46466**

Luxurious new house overlooking Connemara Mountains. Excellent touring base. Paradise for Anglers, Walkers, Golfers. Sauna available.

B&B	5	Ensuite	£19/£20	€24.13/€25.39	Dinner -
B&B	-	Standard		-	Partial Board -
Single Rate			£24/£25	€30.47/€31.74	Child reduction 25%

In Cong

Open: All Year

Maureen Varley
ROCKLAWN HOUSE
**Drumshiel, Cong,
Co Mayo**

Cong
TEL: **092 46616**

Family home on banks of Cong Canal. Excellent walks, tours steeped in local history. Angling, Boat trips locally. Drying room, Homebaking. 2km from Cong.

B&B	4	Ensuite	£19	€24.13	Dinner -
B&B	-	Standard		-	Partial Board -
Single Rate			£25.50	€32.38	Child reduction 50%

Cong 2km

Open: 1st May-31st October

In Crossmolina

Mrs Nuala Gallagher-Matthews
LAKE VIEW HOUSE
Ballina Road, Crossmolina,
Co Mayo

Crossmolina
TEL: 096 31296
EMAIL: lakeviewhouse@oceanfree.net

Country home. Close to Lough Conn. Family Research/Archaeological Centres and Ceide Fields. Boat/Ghillie hire. Fishing arranged. Tea/Coffee facilities. Ideal touring base.

B&B	6	Ensuite	£19/£19	€24.13	Dinner	-
B&B	-	Standard	-	-	Partial Board	-
Single Rate			£25.50/£25.50	€32.38	Child reduction	33.3%

Open: 1st April-31st October

Crossmolina 3km

Mrs Nora Naughton
WOODVIEW HOUSE
Enniscoe, Castlehill,
Crossmolina, Co Mayo

Crossmolina
TEL: 096 31125
EMAIL: noranaughton@eircom.net
WEB: www.welcome.to/woodviewhouse

Country home, beside Lough Conn. Family Research Centre. Ceide fields close by. Fishing arranged. Boats/Ghille-Hire. Tea/Coffee facilities. 3km Pontoon/Castlebar Rd. Ground floor bedrooms.

B&B	4	Ensuite	£19/£19	€24.13	Dinner	-
B&B	2	Standard	£17/£17	€21.59	Partial Board	-
Single Rate			£25/£25	€31.74	Child reduction	25%

Open: 15th April-31st October

Killala 3km

Mrs Mary O'Hara
BEACH VIEW HOUSE
Ross, Killala,
Co Mayo

Killala
TEL: 096 32023

Bungalow on peninsula surrounded by award winning Beaches. Fishing, Walking, Historical interests. On route to Ceide Fields. 2km off R314 Northbound of Killala.

B&B	3	Ensuite	£19/£19	€24.13	Dinner	-
B&B	1	Standard	£17/£17	€21.59	Partial Board	-
Single Rate			£23.50/£25.50	€29.84/€32.38	Child reduction	33.3%

Open: All Year

In Kiltimagh

Mrs Mary Carney
HILLCREST
Kilkelly Rd, Kiltimagh,
Co Mayo

Kiltimagh
TEL: 094 81112
EMAIL: carneyandrea@eircom.net

Comfortable family home on spacious landscaped grounds. Ideal touring base for West of Ireland. 5 min drive Knock Shrine and Connaught Regional Airport.

B&B	6	Ensuite	£19/£19	€24.13	Dinner	-
B&B	-	Standard	-	-	Partial Board	-
Single Rate			£25.50	€32.38	Child reduction	25%

Open: All Year Except Christmas

Knock 1km

Maureen Carney and Family
BURREN
Kiltimagh Road, Knock,
Co Mayo

Knock
TEL: 094 88362   FAX: 094 88362

Modern family home on R323, west off N17, 1km from roundabout. All ground floor rooms. TV Lounge with Tea/Coffee making facilities. Private parking.

B&B	4	Ensuite	£19	€24.13	Dinner	-
B&B	-	Standard	-	-	Partial Board	-
Single Rate			£25.50	€32.38	Child reduction	33.3%

Open: 1st June-30th September

In Knock

Mrs Kathleen Carty
CARRAMORE HOUSE
**Airport Road, Knock,
Co Mayo**

Tel: **094 88149**   Fax: **094 88154**

Family home 500 metres from Shrine. Electric blankets, TV, Hairdryers, Complimentary Tea/Coffee. Routes planned. Guidance on Genealogy Tracing. Convenient to bus stop. Own parking lot.

B&B	6	Ensuite	£19	€24.13	Dinner	-
B&B		Standard	-	-	Partial Board	-
Single Rate			£25.50	€32.38	Child reduction	33.3%

Open: 17th March-31st October

Ms Mary Coyne
AISHLING HOUSE
**Ballyhaunis Road, Knock,
Co Mayo**

Tel: **094 88558**

Bright, spacious, warm and welcoming on N60. Private parking. Ideal touring West. Lakes, Golf, Horse riding. Beside Shrine. Convenient Airport.

B&B	5	Ensuite	£19	€24.13	Dinner	-
B&B	1	Standard	£17	€21.59	Partial Board	-
Single Rate			-	-	Child reduction	33.3%

Open: All Year

In Knock

Taffe Family
ESKERVILLE
**Claremorris Rd, Knock,
Co Mayo**

Tel: **094 88413**

Beige Dormer Bungalow situated on Claremorris/Galway Road. In Knock N17. Private Parking. Mature Gardens. Credit cards. Children welcome.

B&B	4	Ensuite	£19/£19	€24.13	Dinner	£12.50
B&B	1	Standard	£17/£17	€21.59	Partial Board	£185
Single Rate			£23.50/£25.50	€29.84/€32.38	Child reduction	25%

Open: All Year

In Louisburgh

Mrs Claire Kenny
SPRINGFIELD HOUSE
**Westport Rd, Louisburgh,
Co Mayo**

Tel: **098 66289**

On main Louisburgh/Westport Road (R335). Safe sandy Beaches, Sea & River Fishing. Ideal area for Walking, Mountain Climbing & Cycling.

B&B	3	Ensuite	£19	€24.13	Dinner	-
B&B	1	Standard	£17	€21.59	Partial Board	-
Single Rate			£25.50	€32.38	Child reduction	25%

Open: 1st January-30th November

In Louisburgh

Mrs Ann McNamara
WHITETHORNS
**Bunowen Road, Louisburgh,
Co Mayo**

Tel: **098 66062**

Bungalow in scenic location on Bunowen road off R335 at Roman Catholic Church, 5 minutes walk to Louisburgh. Safe sandy Beaches, Walking, Cycling, Fishing.

B&B	4	Ensuite	£19	€24.13	Dinner	-
B&B		Standard	-	-	Partial Board	-
Single Rate			£25.50	€32.38	Child reduction	25%

Open: 1st April-30th September

Louisburgh

Mrs Mary Sammin
THE THREE ARCHES
**Askelane, Louisburgh,
Co Mayo**

TEL: **098 66484**
EMAIL: 3arches@gofree.indigo.ie

Modern bungalow with panoramic view. Ideal touring centre for Clare Island. Croagh Patrick. Safe Sandy Beaches. Scenic Walks. Home Cooking.

B&B	2	Ensuite	£19	€24.13	Dinner	£14
B&B	2	Standard	£17	€21.59	Partial Board	£190
Single Rate			-	-	Child reduction	50%

Louisburgh 3km

Open: 1st May-30th September

Mulranny

Mrs Catherine Reilly
BREEZEMOUNT B&B
Mulranny, Co Mayo

TEL: **098 36145**   FAX: **098 36145**
EMAIL: kayjim@gofree.indigo.ie

Modern bungalow with panoramic view, opposite Croagh Patrick on Clew Bay, adjoining Golf Links. Ideal location for touring Achill Island.

B&B	4	Ensuite	£19	€24.13	Dinner	-
B&B	1	Standard	£17	€21.59	Partial Board	-
Single Rate			£25.50	€32.38	Child reduction	50%

Mulranny 1km

Open: All Year Except Christmas

Westport

John & Mary Cafferkey
HAZELBROOK
**Deerpark East, Newport Road,
Westport, Co Mayo**

TEL: **098 26865**
EMAIL: hazelbrookhouse@eircom.net

Modern home in a quiet residential area. 4 mins walk to Town Centre. Ideally situated for touring the West Coast. Reflexology and Massage available. Car park.

B&B	6	Ensuite	£19/£20	€24.13/€25.39	Dinner	-
B&B		Standard	-	-	Partial Board	-
Single Rate			£25.50/£30	-€32.38/€38.09	Child reduction	25%

In Westport

Open: All Year

Westport

Ann Cusack
ARD BAWN
**Leenane Road, Westport,
Co Mayo**

TEL: **098 26135**

Spacious tastefully decorated bungalow close to Westport on Leenane/Clifden Road (N59). 8 minutes walk to Town. Many recommendations, nice views.

B&B	3	Ensuite	£19	€24.13	Dinner	-
B&B	-	Standard	-	-	Partial Board	-
Single Rate			-	-	Child reduction	50%

In Westport

Open: 1st February-31st October

Westport

Mary & John Doherty
LUI-NA-GREINE
**Castlebar Road, Westport,
Co Mayo**

TEL: **098 25536**

Bungalow on N5 scenic area within walking distance of Town. Spacious gardens. Car park. Recommended "Guide to Ireland", "En Irlande".

B&B	4	Ensuite	£20/£20	€25.39	Dinner	-
B&B	2	Standard	£18/£18	€22.86	Partial Board	-
Single Rate			£25/£26	€31.74/€33.01	Child reduction	50%

Westport 1km

Open: 6th April-30th October

Brian & Michelle Durcan
INDIAN WELLS
**19 Knockranny Village,
Castlebar Road N5, Westport,
Co Mayo**

Westport
TEL: **098 28418**

Modern, spacious, colonial style house. 1km from Town Centre. In quiet, exclusive residential area, 400m off N5. All rooms ensuite.

B&B	4	Ensuite	£20/£20	€25.39	Dinner	-
B&B	-	Standard			Partial Board	-
Single Rate			£30/£35	€38.09/€44.44	Child reduction	-

Westport 1km

Open: 6th January-20th December

Mrs Vera English
HILLSIDE LODGE
**Castlebar Road, Westport,
Co Mayo**

Westport
TEL: **098 25668**
EMAIL: veraandjohn@unison.ie
WEB: www.homepage.eircom.net/~hillsidelodge

Warm welcoming family home just a short distance from Town. Ideal touring base for Achill, Connemara and Knock. Take N5 from Westport past Shell Garage on left.

B&B	2	Ensuite	£19/£19	€24.13	Dinner	-
B&B	1	Standard	£17/£17	€21.59	Partial Board	-
Single Rate			£23.50/£23.50	€29.84	Child reduction	**50%**

Westport 1km

Open: 1st February-30th December

Maureen & Peter Flynn
CEDAR LODGE
**Kings Hill, Newport Rd N59,
Westport, Co Mayo**

Westport
TEL: **098 25417**   FAX: **098 25417**
EMAIL: mflynn@esatclear.ie
WEB: homepage.eircom.net/~cedarlodgewestport

Welcoming peaceful bungalow, landscaped gardens (Award 1997). Irish hospitality. Great breakfast menu, 6 min walk Town, near Golf. Frommer, Routard, Rough Guide, Best B&B's Recommended.

B&B	4	Ensuite	£19/£20	€24.13/€25.39	Dinner	-
B&B	-	Standard			Partial Board	-
Single Rate			£25.50/£32	€32.38/€40.63	Child reduction	-

In Westport

Open: February-November

Mrs Angela Gavin
CARRABAUN HOUSE
**Carrabaun, Leenane Road,
Westport, Co Mayo**

Westport
TEL: **098 26196**   FAX: **098 28466**
EMAIL: carrabaun@anu.ie

New spacious period house. Panoramic views. Hairdryer, TV, Trouser Press, Tea/Coffee, Electric Blanket, Breakfast menu. Near Golfing, Pubs, Restaurants, N59.

B&B	6	Ensuite	£20/£20	€25.39	Dinner	-
B&B	-	Standard			Partial Board	-
Single Rate			£30/£30	€38.09	Child reduction	**25%**

Westport 1 km

Open: 1st January-21st December

Mrs Mary Churchill Gavin
HIGHGROVE
**Murrisk, Westport,
Co Mayo**

Westport
TEL: **098 64819**   FAX: **098 64819**
EMAIL: mgavin@unison.ie

On R335 from Westport in the foothills of Croagh Patrick and Famine monument. Restaurant etc. Quiet and Relaxing. A welcome awaits you. Westport 8km.

B&B	2	Ensuite	£19/£20	€24.13/€25.39	Dinner	-
B&B	2	Standard	£17/£18	€21.59/€22.86	Partial Board	-
Single Rate			£23.50	€29.84	Child reduction	**25%**

Westport 8km

Open: May-September

Mrs Maureen Geraghty
ST BRENDANS
Kilmeena, Westport,
Co Mayo

Westport
TEL: **098 41209**

Dormer type house, 3 guest bedrooms upstairs and 3 family rooms downstairs. Close to all amenities, Fishing. Ideal touring base.

				Dinner	-
B&B	3	Ensuite	£19	€24.13	
B&B	-	Standard	-	-	Partial Board	-
Single Rate			£25.50	€32.38	Child reduction	50%

S P R ⚡ ✗ 🍽 🚶 ➤ 🎣 ◀ ➤

Open: 15th April-30th September

In Westport

Mrs Bridget Gibbons
BROADLANDS
Quay Road, Westport,
Co Mayo

Westport
TEL: **098 27377**

Large bungalow, situated on the coast road to Louisburgh. Close to Town Centre, Westport Quay, Pubs & Restaurants.

				Dinner	-
B&B	5	Ensuite	£20/£20	€25.39	
B&B	-	Standard	-	-	Partial Board	-
Single Rate			£25.50/£30	€32.38/€38.09	Child reduction	-

cc P ⊗ ✗ ⚡ 🍽 🎣 ◀ ➤

Open: All Year

Westport 12km

Mrs Beatrice Gill
SEA BREEZE
Kilsallagh, Westport,
Co Mayo

Westport
TEL: **098 66548**
EMAIL: seabreeze@eircom.net
WEB: http://homepage.eircom.net/~beatricegill/

Comfortable, friendly home, breathtaking views. From Westport take R335 to avail of hospitality and delicious food. Close to Pubs, Restaurants, Croagh Patrick, Beach.

				Dinner	£15
B&B	3	Ensuite	£19/£20	€24.13/€25.39	
B&B	-	Standard	-	-	Partial Board	-
Single Rate			£25.50/£27.50	€32.38/€34.91	Child reduction	50%

cc P ⚡ ✗ 🚶 ➤ ✗ 🚶 🚲 ➤ J s J R

Open: 1st January-22nd December

In Westport

Mrs Nuala Hopkins
WOODSIDE
Golf Course Road, Westport,
Co Mayo

Westport
TEL: **098 26436**
EMAIL: nhopkins@eircom.net

Family run B&B. Built on historical site. 10 minutes walk Westport Town Centre. Private car park. Nearby Westport Championship Golf Course, Horse Riding.

				Dinner	-
B&B	6	Ensuite	£19/£20	€24.13/€25.39	
B&B	-	Standard	-	-	Partial Board	-
Single Rate			-	-	Child reduction	-

cc P ⊗ R ✗ ⚡ 🍽 ◀ ➤ J L s J R

Open: 16th March-31st October

Westport 1.5km

Mary Jordan
ROSMO HOUSE
Rosbeg, Westport,
Co Mayo

Westport
TEL: **098 25925**
EMAIL: rosmohouse@unison.ie

Purpose built house. Quiet location on T39/R335 Coast Road. Short distance Croagh Patrick, Harbour, Pubs, Restaurants. Satellite, TV/Video, Power showers, Tea/Coffee facilities. Car park.

				Dinner	-
B&B	4	Ensuite	£19/£20	€24.13/€25.39	
B&B	-	Standard	-	-	Partial Board	-
Single Rate			£25.50/£30	€32.38/€38.09	Child reduction	50%

cc P ⊗ ✗ ⚡ 🍽 🚶 🍽 ◀ ➤ J L s J R

Open: 1st May-1st November

David and Sara Kelly
QUAY WEST
**Quay Road, Westport,
Co Mayo**

In Westport

Purpose built house on T39/R335. Rooms Ensuite, Power Showers, Orthopaedic Beds. TV Lounge, Walking distance Town, Pubs, Restaurants.

				Dinner	-
B&B	6	Ensuite	£19/£22	€24.13/€27.93	
B&B	-	Standard		Partial Board	-
Single Rate			£25.50/£30	€32.38/€38.09	Child reduction	-

Open: All Year

Mary Kelly
BIRCHSIDE
**Streamstown, Belclare,
Westport, Co Mayo**

Westport 4.5km

New spacious house on T39/R335 Coast Road. Close to Beaches, Pubs, Restaurants. Panoramic views Croagh Patrick, Clew Bay. Private parking. Tea/Coffee facilities. 2km Quay.

					Dinner	-
B&B	2	Ensuite	£19/£20	€24.13/€25.39		
B&B	1	Standard	£17/£18	€21.59/€22.86	Partial Board	-
Single Rate			£25.50/£30	€32.38/€38.09	Child reduction	33.3%

Open: May-September

Robert & Sheila Kilkelly
ST ANTHONY'S
**Distillery Rd, Westport,
Co Mayo**

Westport
TEL: **098 28887**   FAX: **098 25172**
EMAIL: sk@achh.iol.ie
WEB: www.st_anthonys.com

In Westport

Enjoy a little luxury in an 1820 Built Town House. Private parking on one acre of grounds. Riverside. Tea/Coffee facilities. Two ensuites with Jacuzzi.

					Dinner	-
B&B	5	Ensuite	£20/£25	€25.39/€31.74		
B&B	-	Standard		-	Partial Board	-
Single Rate			£25/£30	€31.74/€38.09	Child reduction	-

Open: 1st January-24th December

Ronan & Eithne Larkin
AODHNAIT LODGE
**Rosbeg, Westport,
Co Mayo**

Westport
TEL: **098 25784**   FAX: **098 26258**
EMAIL: aodhnait@eircom.net
WEB: www.aodhnait.ie

Westport 3km

Quiet country home on the shores of Clew Bay. Ideal base for Mayo/Connemara. Walking distance of Harbour. Home baking, Breakfast menu. AA ◆◆◆◆. On R335.

					Dinner	-
B&B	4	Ensuite	£20/£23	€25.39/€29.20		
B&B	-	Standard		-	Partial Board	-
Single Rate			£27	€34.29	Child reduction	50%

Open: 6th January-18th December

Mrs Angela McDonagh
DOVEDALE
**Rampart Wood, Golf Course Rd,
Westport, Co Mayo**

Westport
TEL: **098 25154**   FAX: **098 25154**
EMAIL: dovedale@ireland.com

Westport 1km

Modern home set in woodland surroundings. Mature gardens. Private parking. 10 mins walk to Town Centre. Golf, Horse riding, Sailing. Route N59, Newport road 1km.

					Dinner	-
B&B	4	Ensuite	£19/£19	€24.13		
B&B	1	Standard	£18/£18	€22.86	Partial Board	-
Single Rate			£28/£28	€35.55	Child reduction	-

Open: 1st April-31th October

Westport 2km

Mrs Josephine McGreal
CEOL NA MARA
**Lower Quay, Westport,
Co Mayo**

Westport
TEL: **098 26969**   FAX: **098 26969**
EMAIL: kevinmcgreal@eircom.net

Town house located on Westports Quay close to award winning Pubs and Restaurants. Westport House .5km away. Private car park.

				Dinner	-
B&B	4	Ensuite	£19/£20	€24.13/€25.39	
B&B	-	Standard	-	-	Partial Board -
Single Rate			£25.50/£25.50	€32.38	Child reduction 50%

Open: 4th January-20th December

In Westport

Mrs Margaret Madigan
ADARE HOUSE
**Quay Road, Westport,
Co Mayo**

Westport
TEL: **098 26102**   FAX: **098 26202**
EMAIL: adarehouse@eircom.net

New house T39/R335. 7 minutes walk Town, Pubs, Restaurants. Panoramic views. Orthopaedic beds. Guest Lounge. Tea/Coffee facilities. Breakfast menu.

					Dinner	-
B&B	5	Ensuite	£19/£19	€24.13		
B&B	1	Standard	£17/£17	€21.59	Partial Board -
Single Rate			£25/£25.50	€31.74/€32.38	Child reduction 25%

Open: 1st January-20th December

Westport 1.5km

Mrs Mary Mitchell
CILLCOMAN LODGE
**Rosbeg, Westport,
Co Mayo**

Westport
TEL: **098 26379**
EMAIL: cillcomanlodge@eircom.net

Situated on Coast Road. Quiet location with parking facilities and garden. Guest TV lounge. Adjacent to Harbour, Pubs & Restaurants.

					Dinner	-
B&B	6	Ensuite	£19/£20	€24.13/€25.39		
B&B	-	Standard	-	-	Partial Board -
Single Rate			£25.50/£30	€32.38/€38.09	Child reduction 33.3%

Open: 1st April-31th October

Westport 1.5km

Mrs Ann O'Flaherty
GLENDERAN
**Rosbeg, Westport,
Co Mayo**

Westport
TEL: **098 26585**   FAX: **098 27352**
EMAIL: glenderan@anu.ie
WEB: www.anu.ie/glenderan/index.html

New house, quiet location beside Harbour. Walking distance Pubs/Restaurants. Satellite TV, Coffee/Tea, Hairdryers in bedrooms. Car Park. T39/R335. Past Quays Pub, 200 metres turn left.

					Dinner	-
B&B	4	Ensuite	£20	€25.39		
B&B	2	Standard	£18	€22.86	Partial Board -
Single Rate			£29	€36.82	Child reduction 50%

Open: 1st March-1st November

Westport 2km

Mrs Kay O'Malley
RIVERBANK HOUSE
**Rosbeg, Westport Harbour,
Co Mayo**

Westport
TEL: **098 25719**

Country peacefulness, on T39/R335. Walking distance Pubs/Restaurants, Home baking, Car Park, Tea/Coffee facilities. Recommended 300 best B&B Guide, AA ♦♦♦.

					Dinner	-
B&B	8	Ensuite	£20	€25.39		
B&B	-	Standard	-	-	Partial Board -
Single Rate			£25.50/£27	€32.38/€34.29	Child reduction 33.3%

Open: 1st April-31stOctober

Mrs Marian O'Malley
MOHER HOUSE
**Liscarney, Westport,
Co Mayo**

Westport
TEL: **098 21360**
EMAIL: moherhouse@unison.ie
WEB: homepage.eircom.net/~moherhouse

Country home on N59. Award winning garden '99. Breakfast, Dinner, Veg Menu. Home cooking. Afternoon Tea on arrival. Peat fire in lounge. Off Western Way. Walkers Best B&B. Pub transport.

B&B	3	Ensuite	£19/£20	€24.13/€25.39	Dinner	£12.50
B&B	1	Standard	£17/£18	€21.59/€22.86	Partial Board	£185
Single Rate			£23.50/£25.50	€29.84/€32.38	Child reduction	25%

Westport 8km

Open: 1st March-31st October

Mrs Mary O'Malley
ARD CAOIN
**The Quay, Westport,
Co Mayo**

Westport
TEL: **098 25492**
EMAIL: malley@cbn.ie

Adjacent to Westport House by the Harbour. Beside excellent Restaurants & Pubs. Private car park. Tea/Coffee, E-mail facilities. Fishing organised.

B&B	4	Ensuite	£19/£20	€24.13/€25.39	Dinner	-
B&B	-	Standard			Partial Board	-
Single Rate			£25.50/£30	€32.38/€38.09	Child reduction	50%

Westport 1.5km

Open: 1st April-31st October

Vincent & Catherine O'Reilly
EMANIA
**Castlebar Road, Sheeaune,
Westport, Co Mayo**

Westport
TEL: **098 26459/28751**
EMAIL: piaras@anu.ie

Country dwelling, own grounds. Private parking. Located on N5 Road between Westport and Castlebar. Friendly, hospitable atmosphere. Tea/Coffee on arrival.

B&B	2	Ensuite	£19/£19	€24.13	Dinner	£12.50
B&B	2	Standard	£17/£17	€21.59	Partial Board	£185
Single Rate			£23.50/£25.50	€29.84/€32.38	Child reduction	50%

Westport 1.3km

Open: 15th June-1st September

Mrs Catherine Owens
SEACREST HOUSE
**Claggan, Kilmeena,
Westport, Co Mayo**

Westport
TEL: **098 41631**

Mountain/sea views, breakfast menu, home baking, dinner on request. Beside Golf course. Excellent Fishing/Walking area. Signposted on N59.

B&B	4	Ensuite	£19	€24.13	Dinner	£14
B&B	2	Standard	£17	€21.59	Partial Board	-
Single Rate			£23.50/£25.50	€29.84/€32.38	Child reduction	25%

Westport 9km

Open: 15th April-31st September

Mrs Noreen Reddington
BROOKLODGE
**Deerpark East, Newport Rd,
Westport, Co Mayo**

Westport
TEL: **098 26654**

Modern home, quiet residential area. 5 minutes walk Town. Warm welcome, with Tea/Coffee on arrival. Recommended 400 Best B&B's Ireland.

B&B	2	Ensuite	£19	€24.13	Dinner	-
B&B	2	Standard	£17	€21.59	Partial Board	-
Single Rate			£25/£25.50	€31.74/€32.38	Child reduction	50%

Westport 1km

Open: 1st March-1st November

Julie & Aiden Redmond
HARMONY HEIGHTS
Kings Hill, Newport Road, Westport, Co Mayo

Westport
TEL: **098 25491**　　FAX: **094 22231**

Original family home-traditional Irish hospitality. Elevated bungalow with veranda, flowers/shrubs. Route 59. Third turn left from Newport Road Bridge.

B&B	2	Ensuite	£19	€24.13	Dinner	-
B&B	1	Standard	£17	€21.59	Partial Board	-
Single Rate			£23.50/£26	€29.84/€33.01	Child reduction	-

In Westport　　　　Open: 8th January-16th December

Mrs Michelle Reidy
WOODVILLE LODGE
Knockranny, Westport, Co Mayo

Westport
TEL: **098 27822**　　FAX: **098 27822**
EMAIL: mra@anu.ie
WEB: www.yeilding.com/woodville_lodge.htm

Woodville Lodge is very close to many fine Pubs and excellent Restaurants. An ideal location for touring Connemara and Achill Island. Breathtaking scenery.

B&B	4	Ensuite	£20/£22.50	€25.39/€28.57	Dinner	-
B&B	-	Standard	-	-	Partial Board	-
Single Rate			£30/£35	€38.09/€44.44	Child reduction	25%

In Westport　　　　Open: 1st January-22nd December

A Ruane
ANNA LODGE
6 Distillery Court, Westport, Co Mayo

Westport
TEL: **098 28219**
EMAIL: amcr@e-merge.ie

Welcoming new Town house set in a cul-de-sac surrounded by the magnificent original eighteenth Century Distillery walls.

B&B	3	Ensuite	£19/£19	€24.13	Dinner	-
B&B	-	Standard	-		Partial Board	-
Single Rate			£25.50/£25.50	€32.38	Child reduction	-

Westport　　　　Open: 1st March-31st October

Mrs Marie Ruane
WOODVIEW HOUSE
Buckwaria, Castlebar Rd N5 Westport, Co Mayo

Westport
TEL: **098 27879**
EMAIL: truane@iol.ie
WEB: www.woodviewhouse.com

New home, quiet location on own ground. Peaceful wooded area. Private parking. Award winning Gardens and House. .5km off N5. Walking distance of Town. Breakfast Menu.

B&B	6	Ensuite	£19/£21	€24.13/€26.66	Dinner	-
B&B	-	Standard	-	-	Partial Board	-
Single Rate			£30/£33	€38.09/€41.90	Child reduction	25%

Westport 1km　　　　Open: 1st February-30th November

Mrs Valerie Sammon
AILLMORE
Knockranny Village, Castlebar Rd, N5 Westport, Co Mayo

Westport
TEL: **098 27818**
EMAIL: vsammon@eircom.net
WEB: http://westport.mayo-ireland.ie/Aillmore.htm

Cosy, modern home in peaceful location. Just 15 mins walk to Town. Extensive Local/Irish history Library available. 500m off N5. Warm welcome assured.

B&B	4	Ensuite	£19/£20	€24.13/€25.39	Dinner	-
B&B	-	Standard	-	-	Partial Board	-
Single Rate			£30/£35	€38.09/€/44.44	Child reduction	50%

Westport 1km　　　　Open: All Year Except Christmas

Westport 1km

Christine Scahill
LURGAN HOUSE
**Carnalurgan, Westport,
Co Mayo**

Westport
TEL: **098 27126**   FAX: **098 27126**
EMAIL: lurganhouse@eircom.net

Georgian house N59/R335. Spacious bedrooms. Central to suggested driving tours. Close to Pubs/Restaurants/Sandy Beaches/Golf/Fishing/Croagh Patrick.

B&B	3	Ensuite	£19/£21	€24.13/€26.66	Dinner	-
B&B	1	Standard	£17/£17	€21.59	Partial Board	-
Single Rate			£25/£30	€31.74/€38.09	Child reduction	50%

Open: 1st March–31st October

In Westport

Mrs Rita Sheridan
ALTAMONT HOUSE
**Ballinrobe Road, Westport,
Co Mayo**

Westport
TEL: **098 25226**

Pre-famine (1848). Tastefully modernised home, 5 minutes walk from Town Centre. Interesting Garden for guests use. Recommended "300 Best B&B's Ireland"

B&B	5	Ensuite	£20/£20	€25.39	Dinner	-
B&B	3	Standard	£18/£18	€22.86	Partial Board	-
Single Rate			-	-	Child reduction	25%

Open: 1st March–1st November

Westport 5km

Aidan & Mary Walsh
EAGLE BROOK
**Knockrooskey, Westport,
Co Mayo**

Westport
TEL: **098 35347**
EMAIL: eaglebrook@eircom.net
WEB: homepage.eircom.net/~eaglebrook

Modern country home. Main Galway/Westport Road (R330). Adjacent to Ballintubber Abbey. Easy access to Croagh Patrick. Award winning garden with panoramic views.

B&B	2	Ensuite	£19/£19	€24.13	Dinner	-
B&B	2	Standard	£17/£17	€21.59	Partial Board	-
Single Rate			£23.50/£25.50	€29.84/€32.38	Child reduction	-

Open: 1st June–10th September

IRELAND AND THE ENVIRONMENT

Ireland is a beautiful country. Research has shown that people come to Ireland to meet the friendly local people and enjoy our unspoilt natural landscape. We try as much as we can to keep our country clean and "green" and we appreciate your co-operation in this matter.

We love to share this beauty with as many people as we can. Therefore it is in all our interests to maintain and enhance the natural splendour that Ireland is lucky enough to enjoy. Respect for natural amenities is essential in order to sustain this beautiful, unspoilt environment. By leaving the places we visit tidy we can all do our bit to help, thus ensuring that future generations will come to visit a naturally green Ireland too.

The county that gave Ireland its last High King and modern Ireland its first President.

Rich in wonderful landscape containing Rivers, Lakes, Mountains, Moorlands, Archaeological Features and Forest Park.

A fisherman's paradise, also numerous Golf Courses and other leisure activities.

Mrs Noreen Fayne
FAIRWAYS
Hodson Bay, Athlone,
Co Roscommon

Athlone
TEL: **0902 94492**

Dormer bungalow on N61 - 6km Athlone. 1km from Golf Club, Hodson Bay Hotel and Lough Ree - Mature Gardens - Extensive Parking.

B&B	3	Ensuite	£19/£20	€24.13/€25.39	Dinner —
B&B	-	Standard	-	-	Partial Board —
Single Rate			-	-	Child reduction 33.3%

Athlone 6km

Open: 1st March-30th November

Mrs Catherine Harney
REESIDE
Barrymore, Athlone,
Co Roscommon

Athlone
TEL: **0902 92051**
EMAIL: reeside@oceanfree.net

Country Home on four acres. Road N61, beside Lough Ree & River Shannon. Close to Hodson Bay Hotel, Athlone Golf Club. Luxury cruiser available for trips on Lough Ree.

B&B	4	Ensuite	£19	€24.13	Dinner —
B&B	-	Standard	-	-	Partial Board —
Single Rate			£25.50	€32.38	Child reduction 33.3%

Athlone 5km

Open: January-20th December

Mrs Teresa Hegarty
CASTLESIDE HOUSE
Kiltoom, Athlone,
Co Roscommon

Athlone
TEL: **0902 89195**   FAX: **0902 89195**
EMAIL: castleside@esatclear.ie

Quiet Country home adjacent Moyvannion Castle. Convenient to Lough Ree, Fishing, Boating, Water Sports, Golf, Hodson Bay Hotel, Horse Riding.

B&B	4	Ensuite	£20/£22.50	€25.39/€28.57	Dinner £12.50
B&B	1	Standard	-	-	Partial Board £185
Single Rate			£25.50/£28	€32.38/€35.55	Child reduction 33.3%

Athlone 7km

Open: All Year Except Christmas

Gerald & Eleanor Kelly
LOUGHREE LODGE
Kiltoom, Athlone,
Co Roscommon

Athlone
TEL: **0902 89214**   FAX: **0902 89349**
EMAIL: eleanorcousinskelly@hotmail.com

Spacious residence situated on beautiful landscaped gardens overlooking Lough Ree. On N61, 7km from Athlone. Relaxed friendly atmosphere.

B&B	4	Ensuite	£19/£19	€24.13	Dinner —
B&B	-	Standard	-		Partial Board —
Single Rate			£25.50/£25.50	€32.38	Child reduction 25%

Athlone 7km

Open: 1st March-31st October

Athlone 12km

Nora Ward
CARRICK VIEW
**Curraghboy, Athlone,
Co Roscommon**

TEL: **0902 88294**

Dormer bungalow in peaceful country surroundings 6km off N61. TV Lounge, Private parking. Ideal base for Touring, Golfing, Fishing. Hodson Bay 8km.

B&B	4	Ensuite	£19	€24.13	Dinner	-
B&B	-	Standard	-	-	Partial Board	-
Single Rate			£25.50	€32.38	Child reduction	50%

Open: 1st March-31st October

Boyle

Mary Cooney
CESH CORRAN
**Abbey Terrace, Sligo Rd
Boyle, Co Roscommon**

TEL: **079 62265**   FAX: **079 62265**
EMAIL: cooneym@iol.ie
WEB: www.iol.ie/~cooneym

A beautifully restored Edwardian town house on the old Dublin/Sligo road, overlooking historic Boyle Abbey. Private parking. Lough Key Forest Park 1 mile.

B&B	3	Ensuite	£20/£25	€25.39/€31.74	Dinner	-
B&B	-	Standard	-	-	Partial Board	-
Single Rate			£25.50/£25.50	€32.38	Child reduction	20%

Open: 1st January-24th December

Boyle 1km

Carmel & Martin Dolan
AVONLEA
**Carrick Road, Boyle,
Co Roscommon**

TEL: **079 62538**

Family run modern house on Carrick Road R294, off N4 Dublin/Sligo Road. Close to Forest Park Hotel, Boyle Abbey, King House, Walking route and Forest Park.

B&B	2	Ensuite	£19/£19	€24.13	Dinner	-
B&B	1	Standard	£17/£17	€21.59	Partial Board	-
Single Rate			£23.50/£25.50	€29.84/€32.38	Child reduction	25%

Open: All Year Except Christmas

Boyle 1km

Brenda McCormack
ROSDARRIG
**Dublin Road, Boyle,
Co Roscommon**

TEL: **079 62040**
EMAIL: rosdarrig@yahoo.co.uk

Modern home on edge of Town. Irish hospitality. Walk to Pubs/Restaurants. Views Curlew Mountains/surrounding farmland. Close to Boyle Abbey/Forest Park Hotel/Lakes/Forest Park.

B&B	5	Ensuite	£19	€24.13	Dinner	-
B&B	-	Standard	-	-	Partial Board	-
Single Rate			-	-	Child reduction	50%

Open: 1st March-30th November

Boyle 1km

Christina and Martin Mitchell
ABBEY HOUSE
**Boyle,
Co Roscommon**

TEL: **079 62385**   FAX: **079 62385**

Victorian house nestled between Boyle River and Abbey. Within walking distance of Town Centre and Forest Park. Large mature gardens.

B&B	5	Ensuite	£20	€25.39	Dinner	-
B&B	1	Standard	£18	€22.86	Partial Board	-
Single Rate			£25.50	€32.38	Child reduction	25%

Open: 1st March-31st October

Castlerea 1km

Mrs Rita Morgan
ARMCASHEL B&B
Knock Rd,
Castlerea, Co Roscommon

Castlerea
Tel: **0907 20117**

Modern spacious dormer bungalow on N60. Peaceful surroundings overlooking Clonalis Estate. Base for touring. Daily train to and from Dublin. Knock 25 mins. Galway 60 mins.

B&B	5	Ensuite	£19/£19	€24.13	Dinner	-
B&B	1	Standard	£17/£19	€21.59/€24.13	Partial Board	-
Single Rate			£23.50/£25	€29.84/€31.74	Child reduction	33.3%

Open: 10th January-21st December

In Rooskey Village

Mrs Carmel Davis
AVONDALE HOUSE
Rooskey, Carrick-on-Shannon,
Co Roscommon

Rooskey
Tel: **078 38095**
Email: avondalerooskey@eircom.net

Luxury two storey house family run. Highly recommended. Peaceful surroundings. Situated near river Shannon, Famine Museum 12km. Fishing nearby. Midway Dublin/Donegal.

B&B	4	Ensuite	£19/£19	€24.13	Dinner	£12.50
B&B	-	Standard	-	-	Partial Board	-
Single Rate			£25.50	€32.38	Child reduction	33.3%

Open: All Year Except Christmas

Roscommon 2km

Mrs Kathleen Carthy
HILLCREST HOUSE
Racecourse Road,
Roscommon,
Co Roscommon

Roscommon
Tel: **0903 25201**

Warm hospitality in a modern country house in scenic location. Ideal base for touring West and Midlands. Situated on the N60 beside Roscommon Racecourse.

B&B	4	Ensuite	£19/£19	€24.13	Dinner	-
B&B	-	Standard	-	-	Partial Board	-
Single Rate			£25.50/£25.50	€32.38	Child reduction	50%

Open: All Year

In Roscommon

Noelle Hynes
RIVERSIDE HOUSE
Riverside Avenue, Circular Road,
Roscommon Town,
Co Roscommon

Roscommon Town
Tel: **0903 26897**

Modern dormer bungalow set in mature grounds in Roscommon Town within walking distance of Golf Course, Castle and Museum.

B&B	2	Ensuite	£19	€24.13	Dinner	-
B&B	2	Standard	£17	€21.59	Partial Board	-
Single Rate			£23.50	€29.84	Child reduction	50%

Open: All Year

In Roscommon

Mrs Paula McNamara
THE GARDENS
The Walk, Roscommon,
Co Roscommon

Roscommon
Tel: **0903 26828**   Fax: **0903 26828**

Modern home, large gardens. Peaceful location, within walking distance of Town. Golf Course, Old Abbey and Castle nearby

B&B	4	Ensuite	£19	€24.13	Dinner	-
B&B	1	Standard	£17	€21.59	Partial Board	-
Single Rate			-	-	Child reduction	25%

Open: June-September

Strokestown 7km

Mrs Ans Clyne
LAKESHORE LODGE
Kilglass Lake, Clooneen,
Strokestown, Co Roscommon

Strokestown
TEL: **078 33966**   FAX: **078 33966**

Modern home with gardens to Kilglass Lake. Jetty, Angling boats. 7km Strokestown Park House-Famine museum. Dutch, French, German spoken. Ideal fishing base.

B&B	4	Ensuite	£19/£21	€24.13/€26.66	Dinner	£12.50
B&B	-	Standard	-	-	Partial Board	£220
Single Rate			£25.50/£27.50	€32.38/€34.91	Child reduction	-

Open: 1st April-31st October

Tulsk 3km

Mrs Kathleen Durkan
GORTNACRANNAGH
Elphin,
Co Roscommon

Tulsk
TEL: **078 35631**

Two-storey, pebble dashed house, quiet Country surroundings. Dining area within conservatory. Base for touring West, Midlands. 2 miles Tulsk, N61.

B&B	3	Ensuite	£19/£19	€24.13	Dinner	-
B&B	1	Standard	£17/£17	€21.59	Partial Board	-
Single Rate			£23.50/£25.50	€29.84/€32.38	Child reduction	25%

Open: 1st January-24th December

APPROVED ACCOMMODATION SIGNS

Approved Accommodation Signs
This sign will be displayed at most premises which are approved to Irish Tourist Board Standards.

Panneaux d'homologation des établissements
Ces panneaux sont affichés dans la plupart des établissements homologués selon les normes de l'Office du tourisme irlandais.

Plakette fúr Geprúfte Unterkunft
Diese Plaketten werden an den meisten Häusern angezeigt, die von auf die Einhaltung der Normen der irischen Fremdenverkehrsbehörde überprüft und zugelassen wurden.

Borden voor goedgekeurde accommodatie
Deze borden vindt u bij de meeste huizen die zijn goedgekeurd door voor de normen van de Ierse Toeristenbond.

Simbolo di sistemazione approvata
Questi simboli saranno esposti nella maggior parte delle case approvate (associazione dei Bed & Breakfast approvati per qualità), rispondenti agli standard dell'Ente del Turismo Irlandese.

Símbolo de alojamiento aprobado
Estos símbolos se muestran en los establecimientos que han sido aprobados por bajos los estandars de la Oficina de Turismo Irlandesa.

Skyltar för Godkänd logi
Dessa skyltar finns vid de flesta gästhus som har godkänts (Föreningen för kvalitetsgodkända gästhus AB), enligt irländska turisföreningens normer.

Heritage Island

is a group of the most prestigious heritage attractions in all of Ireland...

The centres range from historic houses, castles, monuments, museums, galleries, national parks, interpretative centres, gardens and theme parks.

Visitors can avail of big savings by displaying the *Heritage Island Explorer* coupon at the following attractions, which will entitle them to reduced admission, many two for one's and special offers...

Armagh • Armagh Planetarium **Cavan** • Belturbet Station • Cavan County Museum • Cavan Crystal Visitor Centre • Maudabawn Cultural Centre	**Clare** • Bunratty Castle and Folk Park • Clare County Museum • Craggaunowen	**Cork** • Cork City Gaol • Millstreet Country Park • Mizen Vision • Old Midleton Distillery **Donegal** • Donegal County Museum	**Down** • Castle Ward • Exploris Aquarium • Mount Stewart House and Gardens • Somme Heritage Centre • St. Patrick Centre	**Dublin** • Ceol - The Irish Traditional Music Centre • Dublinia • Guinness Hopstore • Hot Press Irish Music Hall of Fame
Dublin (continued) • ICON - Home of Baileys® in Ireland • James Joyce Centre • Old Jameson Distillery • St. Patrick's Cathedral • Trinity College Library and Dublin Experience	**Fermanagh** • Belleek Pottery Visitor Centre • Castle Coole	**Galway** • Galway Irish Crystal Heritage Centre • Kylemore Abbey and Gardens	**Kerry** • Crag Cave • Jeanie Johnston Visitor Shipyard • Kerry the Kingdom	**Kildare** • Irish National Stud, Japanese Gardens & St. Fiachra's Garden • Steam Museum
Limerick • Adare Heritage Centre • Hunt Museum, Limerick • King John's Castle • Limerick County Museum	**Louth** • County Museum, Dundalk • Millmount Museum	**Meath** • Kells Heritage Centre • Trim Visitor Centre **Monaghan** • Monaghan County Museum	**Offaly** • Birr Castle Demesne & Ireland's Historic Science Centre • Tullamore Dew Heritage Centre	**Roscommon** • Cruachán Ai Visitor Centre • King House • Lough Key Forest Park • Strokestown Park
Sligo • Drumcliffe Church and Visitor Centre • Michael Coleman Heritage Centre **Tipperary** • Brú Ború	**Waterford** • Waterford Crystal Visitor Centre • Waterford Treasures at the Granary and Reginald's Tower	**Westmeath** • Athlone Castle Visitor Centre • Belvedere House, Gardens and Park	**Wexford** • Irish National Heritage Park • National 1798 Visitor Centre	**Wicklow** • Avondale House • National Sealife Centre • Powerscourt House and Gardens • Russborough • Wicklow's Historic Gaol

Heritage Island members confirmed as at August 2000. Heritage Island can not accept responsibility for any errors or omissions.

For full details on centres, opening times, discounts and special offers see Heritage Island Touring Guide 2001 available at Tourist Information Centres, nationwide.

Heritage Island,
37 Main Street,
Donnybrook, Dublin 4.
Tel: + 353 1 260 0055
Fax: + 353 1 260 0058
E mail: heritage.island@indigo.ie
Web: www.heritageisland.com

CUT ALONG DOTTED LINE

HERITAGE ISLAND EXPLORER

Display this coupon at any Heritage Island Centre to qualify for reduced admission. Touring Guide available at Tourist Information Offices throughout Ireland, or contact www.heritageisland.com

Der Führer ist in acht geographische Regionen gegliedert, die wiederum in die einzelnen Grafschaften aufgeteilt sind (Karte der Regionen und Grafschaften s. S. 3). Die Regionen sind: **östliche Midlands, Nordwest, Nordirland, Dublin, Südost, Cork/Kerry, Shannon, Westirland.**

Buchungsverfahren

Es ist empfehlenswert, die erste und letzte Übernachtung immer im voraus zu buchen.

Verfügbarkeit von Zimmern in Dublin

In der Hochsaison - Mai bis Oktober - ist es schwierig, in Dublin Zimmer zu finden, wenn man Unterkunft nicht im voraus gebucht hat.
Wir empfehlen dringend, die Unterkunft weit im voraus zu buchen, wenn Sie die Hauptstadt während dieser Monate besuchen wollen.

Verlassen Sie sich nie darauf, dass Sie in Dublin kurzfristig Zimmer finden können. Reservieren Sie immer im voraus.

Weitere Reservierungen

Wenn Sie in Irland sind und bei der Suche nach weiterer Unterkunft Probleme auftreten, dann kontaktieren Sie eine beliebige Touristeninformationsstelle oder holen Sie sich Rat oder Hilfe bei Ihrem Gastgeber/Ihrer Gastgeberin in Town and Country Homes. Sie/Er wird Ihnen gerne bei der Buchung weiterer Übernachtungen helfen (zum Preis eines Telefongesprächs).

Buchungen mit Kreditkarte

Kreditkarten werden in Pensionen akzeptiert, die das [cc] Symbol anzeigen.

Telefonische Reservierungen können durch Angabe einer gültigen Kreditkartennummer garantiert werden.

Reisebürogutscheine

Bitte legen Sie Ihre Unterkunftsgutscheine bei Ihrer Ankunft vor. Die Gutscheine gelten nur in Häusern, die mit dem Symbol Ⓥ gekennzeichnet sind. Die Standardgutscheine beziehen sich auf Übernachtung und Frühstück in einem Zimmer ohne eigenes Bad. Der Zuschlag für ein Zimmer mit Bad/Waschgelegenheit beträgt maximal £2.00 pro Person bzw. sollte £5.00 für ein Zimmer, das von drei oder mehr Personen geteilt wird, nicht überschreiten.
"En-suite" Gutscheine beziehen sich auf ein Zimmer mit eigenem Bad. Eine zusätzliche Gebühr fällt nicht an.

Zuschlag für Dublin

In den Monaten Juli und August wird für die Stadt und die Grafschaft Dublin (Dublin City und County) ein Zimmerzuschlag in Höhe von

£5.00 auf Reisebürogutscheine erhoben. Die Gebühr ist direkt an den Vermieter zu zahlen und ist nicht in dem Zimmergutschein enthalten.

Stornierungsverfahren

Bitte erkundigen Sie sich bei der Buchung nach den Bedingungen für den Fall, daß Sie eine bestätigte Reservierung absagen müssen. Die Person, die die Buchung vornimmt, haftet für die vereinbarte Stornierungsgebühr.

Bitte benachrichtigen Sie die Pension so bald wie möglich telefonisch, wenn Sie Ihren Aufenthalt absagen müssen. Sollte die Absage oder Änderung einer Buchung so kurzfristig erfolgen, daß eine Neuvermietung nicht möglich ist, werden folgende Gebühren in Rechnung gestellt:
• **14 Tage:** keine Gebühr
• **24 Stunden bzw. bei Nichterscheinen:** 75% der Ü/F-kosten für die erste Übernachtung

Späte Ankunft

Bitte beachten Sie, daß eine spätere **Ankunft nach 18.00 Uhr ausdrücklich mit der Pension vereinbart werden muß.**

Anzahlungen in bar / mit Kreditkarte

Bei Vorausbuchungen wird man Sie möglicherweise um Angabe einer Scheck- oder Kreditkartennummer als Sicherheit für die Ankunft bitten. Bitte erkundigen Sie sich nach den Bedingungen.

Ankunft/Abreise:

Bitte teilen Sie mit, wenn Sie sehr früh ankommen.
• Zimmer verfügbar zwischen 14.00 und 18.00 Uhr
• Die Abreise sollte nicht später als 11.00 Uhr erfolgen
• Ankunft nach Möglichkeit vor 18.00 Uhr.

Kinderermäßigung

Ermäßigung wird gewährt, wenn Kinder das Zimmer der Eltern teilen oder wenn drei oder mehr Kinder ein Zimmer teilen. Ein oder zwei Kinder in einem separaten Zimmer zahlen den vollen Preis. Bitte fragen Sie bei der Reservierung, ob das Haus für Kinder geeignet ist.
In einigen Häusern stehen Kinderbetten 🛒 zur Verfügung, für die u. U. eine kleine Gebühr erhoben wird.

Abendmahlzeiten

Können im voraus gebucht werden, nach Möglichkeit vor 12 Uhr mittags.
Imbisse ☒ werden auf Anfrage serviert.

Haustiere

Mit Ausnahme von Blindenhunden sind Haustiere aus Hygienegründen nicht im Haus erlaubt.

Familienname

NAME DES TOWN UND
COUNTRY HAUSES

Anschrift

Region:

Tel: Fax:
Email:
Web:
Linienbusnr.:

Beschreibung des Town and Country Hauses

B&B	# Ensuite	Min£/Max£	Min€/Max€	Dinner	£
B&B	# Standard	Min£/Max£	Min€/Max€	Partial Board Min£/Max£	
	Single Rate	Min£/Max£	Min€/Max€	Nacllaß f.Kinder	%

Nächste Stadt/Ortschaft Entfernung in km

Symbole der Einrichtungen   **Geöffnet::**

B+B pps: Übern./Frühst. pro Person im
2-Bett-Zimmer.
Part Brd: Übern./Frühst., Abendessen
#: Anz. der Zimmer

Nacllaß f.Kinder, im Zimmer d. Eltern, od. drei
oder mehr Kinder in einem Zimmer
Sngl Rm: Einzelzimmer

Symbole:

	Kreditkarten werden akzeptiert		Babysitter, normalerweise bis 24.00 Uhr
	Für behinderte Personen und Helfer geeignet.		Kinderbett erhältlich
	Einzelzimmer		Imbißmöglichkeit
	Privatparkplatzg		Weinlizenz
	Gälisch wird gesprochen		Wandern
	Haustiere willkommen		Radfahren
	Nichtraucherhaus		Golfplatz in der Nähe.
	Nichtraucherschlafzimmer		Pferdereiten in der Nähe
	Fernsehgerät im Zimmer		Angeln
	Telefon mit Direktwahl im Zimmer	L	Angeln im Fluss im Umkreis von 15km.
	Tee /Kaffeezubereitungsmöglichkeit im Zimme	S	Angeln im See im Umkreis von 15km.
		R	Angeln im Meer im Umkreis von 15km.
			Reisebürogutscheine werden akzeptiert
			Reisebürogutscheine werden nicht akzeptiert

ehinderte Personen/Rollstuhlfahrer

Das National Rehabilitation Board (NRB) hat
Häuser auf ihre Eignung für behinderte Personen
und deren Helfer überprüft. Diese sind mit dem
Symbol ( ) gekennzeichnet.

omplimente und Kommentare

Beschwerden sollten vor der Abreise zunächst
an den Eigentümer des Hauses gerichtet
werden. Sollte dies bei Verdacht auf eine
überhöhte Berechnung zu keiner Einigung
führen, senden Sie Ihre Rechnung bitte an
**Customer Care, Town & Country Homes,
Belleek Road, Ballyshannon, Co. Donegal.**
Um den hohen Standard aufrecht zu erhalten, für
den unser Verband bekannt ist, sind uns Ihre
Anmerkungen über den Service allgemein und
über das Niveau, das Sie in den Häusern
vorgefunden haben, sehr willkommen. Ihre
konstruktive Kritik wird ernstgenommen und hilft

uns, unsere Leistungen laufend zu verbessern.

Fehler und Auslassungen

Die Information in dieser Broschüre wurde mit
der größten Sorgfalt unter Berücksichtigung der
irischen Verbraucherschutzgesetze zusammen-
gestellt. Town & Country Homes Association
übernimmt jedoch keine Gewähr für Fehler oder
Ungenauigkeiten, die in der uns zur Verfügung
gestellten Information enthalten sind oder für
Schäden und Enttäuschungen, die durch ein
Verlassen auf diese Information entstehen.
Fehler, die Town & Country Homes Association
zur Kenntnis gebracht werden, werden in der
nächsten Ausgabe berücksichtigt. Änderungen
können eintreten, wenn ein Haus nach
Drucklegung dieses Führers verkauft wird und
der Eigentümer wechselt.

Comment utiliser ce guide

Ce guide est divisé en huit régions géographiques subdivisées en comtés (voir la carte des régions et comtés page 3). Les régions sont les suivantes: **Midlands East (Centre-Est), North West (Nord-Ouest), Northern Ireland (Irlande du Nord), Dublin, South East (Sud-Est), Cork/Kerry, Shannon, Ireland West (Irlande Ouest).**

Réservations

Nous vous recommandons de toujours réserver l'avance votre hébergement de la première et de la dernière nuitée.

Disponibilité de chambres Dublin

En pleine saison touristique, de mai - septembre, il est difficile de trouver des chambres - Dublin ou dans l'agglomération de cette ville sans réservation préalable.

Lors d'un séjour dans la capitale au cours des mois d'été nous vous recommandons vivement de réserver votre hébergement longtemps - l'avance.

Ne comptez en aucun cas trouver des chambres - Dublin - la dernière minute. Réservez toujours - l'avance.

Réservations pour les nuitées suivantes

En cas de difficulté - trouver un hébergement lors d'un séjour en Irlande, contactez l'office de tourisme du lieu ou demandez l'aide de voitre húte/hútesse Town and Country Homes.
Moyennant le prix de la communication téléphonique, il/elle vous aidera - réserver l'hébergement de la ou des nuitée(s) suivante (s).

Réservations par carte de crédit

Les cartes de crédit sont acceptées par les établissements affichant le symbole [CC].

Les réservations téléphoniques sont confirmées sur simple communication de votre numéro de carte de crédit en cours de validité.

Supplément - Dublin:

Un supplément de 5 IEP par chambre est prélevé au cours des mois de juillet et d'août sur les bons d'agents de voyages pour la ville et le Comté de Dublin. Ce montant est à régler directement au fournisseur de l'hébergement et n'est pas compris dans le montant du bon.

Bons d'agents de voyage

Ceux-ci sont à présenter dès l'arrivée. Les bons ne sont acceptés que par les établissements affichant le symbole Ⓥ. Les bons standard assurent l'hébergement et le petit déjeuner en chambre sans salle de bain. Supplément pour salle de bain privée: maximum £2.00 par personne. Le supplément par chambre pour 3 ou plus ne doit pas dépasser £ 5.00 par chambre.
Les bons "en suite" concernent les chambres avec salle de bain, sans aucun supplément.

Annulations

Lors de la réservation renseignez-vous auprès de l'établissement sur ses conditions d'annulation. La personne effectuant la réservation devra régler les frais d'annulation convenus, dont la pénalité "Absence"ou, si la réservation n'a pas été honorée, une pénalité de 75% du tarif B&B pour la première nuit. Ces pénalités seront prélevées directement sur la carte de crédit.

Arrivées tardives

Arrivées tardives - soit après 18.00 heures - avec l'accord spécifique de l'établissement.

Arrivées/départs

Prévenir de toute arrivée en avance.
* Les chambres sont mises à disposition entre 14.00h et 18.00 h.
* Les chambres sont à libérer avant 11.00 heures.
* Les réservations sont à honorer avant 18.00 heures.

Réductions pour les enfants

Celle-ci est consentie lorsque les enfants partagent la chambre des parents ou lorsqu'une chambre est occupée par trois enfants ou plus. Le tarif normal s'applique lorsqu'un ou deux enfants occupent des chambres séparées. Veuillez vérifier lors de la réservation que l'établissement convient aux enfants. Certains établissements peuvent mettre des lits 🛏 d'enfant à votre disposition. Un léger supplément pourra être demandé.

Repas du soir

A réserver à l'avance, de préférence avant midi le même jour. Collations servies 🗙 sur demande dans certains établissements.

Animaux domestiques

A l'exception des chiens d'aveugle et pour des raisons d'hygiène, les animaux domestiques ne sont pas admis à l'intérieur des établissements.

Personnes handicapées et utilisateurs de chaises roulantes

Le National Rehabilitation Board (NRB) a approuvé un certain nombre d'établissements adaptés aux personnes handicapées accompagnées. Ceux-ci sont repérés par le symbole ♿.

414

Nom de famille
NOM DE L'ÉTABLISSEMENT
TOWN AND COUNTRY
Adresse

Région

TEL: FAX:
EMAIL:
WEB:
BUS N° :

Description de l'établissement Town and Country Home

B&B	# Ensuite	Min£/Max£	Min€/Max€	Dinner	£
B&B	# Standard	Min£/Max£	Min€/Max€	Partial Board Min£/Max£	
Single Rate		Min£/Max£	Min€/Max€	réduction pour les infants	%

Distance jusqu'à la ville la plus proche en km

Symboles équipements

OUVERTURE:

B+B PPS: chambre et petit déj. par personne partageant une chambre
PART BRD: Chambre, petit déj. et diner
#: Nbre Chambres

de réduction pour les infants % partageant la chambre des parents ou lorsque trois enfants ou plus partagent une chambre
SNGL RM: Chambre pour une personne

Symboles

CC	Cartes de crédit acceptées		🛏	Lits d'enfant disponibles
🧑‍🦽	Accès pour personnes handicapées accompagnées		🍴	Collations servies
S	Chambre unique		🍷	Licence vin
P	Parking privé		🚶	Randonnées pédestres
☘	On parle irlandais		🚲	Excursions á bicyclette
🐾	Animaux domestiques autorisés		⛳	Golf dans les environs
⊗	Interdiction de fumer dans l'établissement		🐴	Équitation dans les environs
R̸	Interdiction de fumer dans les chambres		🐟	Possibilité de pêche
📺	Télévision dans les chambres		🐟 L	Pêche en lac á moins de 15km.
☎	Téléphone direct dans les chambres		🐟 S	Pêche en mer á moins de 15km.
☕	Possibilité de faire thé/café dans les chambres		🐟 R	Pêche en riviére á moins de 15km.
👶	Baby-sitter, en principe jusqu'à minuit		V	Bons d'agents de voyage acceptés.
			X	Bons d'agents de voyage non acceptés

Compliments et commentaires

Les sujets de mécontentement doivent toujours être portés à l'attention du propriétaire avant le départ. Si vous ne pouvez obtenir satisfaction en cas de tarif jugé excessif, vous enverrez votre reçu accompagné de votre réclamation à l'adresse suivante : **Customer Care, Town & Country Homes, Belleek Road, Ballyshannon, Co. Donegal.**
Pour maintenir l'excellence qui fait notre réputation, vos commentaires sur le niveau général du service et la qualité des prestations sont les bienvenus. Toute critique constructive sera examinée attentivement afin d'assurer l'amélioration constante du service.

Erreurs et omissions

Nous avons fait tout notre possible pour veiller à l'exactitude de cette publication conformément aux lois irlandaises de protection du consommateur. La Town & Country Homes Association Ltd. n'accepte aucune responsabilité pour les erreurs ou omissions dans les documents fournis par ses membres pour inclusion dans cette publication, ni pour toute perte ou déception par rapport aux attentes suscitées par l'information contenue dans ladite publication. Si de telles erreurs ou omissions sont portées à notre attention, les éditions suivantes seront modifiées en conséquence. Des changements peuvent intervenir après mise sous presse lorsque les propriétés sont vendues et que les établissements changent de propriétaire.

La guía está dividida en ocho regiones geográficas que se encuentran subdivididas en condados (véase la página 3 para el mapa de regiones y condados). Las regiones son: **Región central este, Noroeste, Irlanda del Norte, Dublín, Sureste, Cork/Kerry, Shannon, Oeste de Irlanda.**

Procedimiento de reservas

Se recomienda reservar siempre con anticipación el alojamiento de la primera y última noche.

Disponibilidad de alojamiento en Dublín

A menos que se haya reservado con antelación, es difícil encontrar alojamiento en Dublín ciudad o en el condado de Dublín en plena temporada turística, de mayo a octubre.

Si se visita la capital durante estos meses, recomendamos firmemente hacer la reserva del alojamiento con mucha anticipación.

No confíe en encontrar habitaciones disponibles a corto plazo; haga siempre su reserva por anticipado

Reservas posteriores

En caso de que tenga problemas para encontrar alojamiento una vez se encuentre en Irlanda, póngase en contacto con cualquier Oficina de Turismo o pida consejo y ayuda al dueño o la dueña de la casa Town and Country Homes. Por el coste de una llamada telefónica el/ella le ayudará a hacer la reserva para la siguiente o siguientes noches. .

Reservas con tarjetas de crédito

Las casas con el símbolo cc aceptan tarjetas de crédito.

Se podrán garantizar las reservas realizadas mediante llamadas telefónicas indicando un número de tarjeta de crédito válido.

Vales de agencias de viaje

Le rogamos presente los vales a su llegada. Los vales sólo serán validos en aquellas casas que muestren el símbolo V. Los vales estándar cubren habitación en B&B sin servicio privado. Para elevarse a la categoría de habitaciones con baño privado (en suite) el recargo será de £2.00 por persona. El recargo máximo para 3 personas o más compartiendo no excederá de £5 por habitación.
Los vales en suite cubren la estancia en una habitación con instalaciones privadas completas. No se ha de pagar ningún recargo adicional.

Suplemento para Dublín

Se aplica un suplemento por habitación para la ciudad y el condado de Dublín de £5 los meses de julio y agosto en los vales de Agencias de

Viajes. Esto se paga directamente a la persona que proporciona el alojamiento y no está incluido en el vale.

Política de cancelaciones

Cuando se haya confirmado una reserva, le rogamos compruebe con le establecimiento al realizar la reserva la política de cancelaciones. La persona que realice la reserva es responsable del recargo por cancelación acordado, incluidos los recargos por "Sin aparecer" y si la reserva no se ha podido aprovechar, se deducirá un 75% de la tarjeta de crédito como recargo por no aparecer por la primera noche.

Llegadas después de las 6pm

Le rogamos que las llegadas tardías - **después de las 6pm se realizarán mediante Acuerdo especial con la casa.**

Depósitos en metálico/ depósitos mediante tarjeta de crédito

Para realizar reservas por adelantado, se le podrá pedir un número de cheque o tarjeta de crédito para garantizar la llegada. Compruebe Términos y Condiciones.

Horas de entrada/ salida

Le rogamos comunique llegadas tempranas.
- Las habitaciones están disponibles de 2pm a 6pm.
- La hora de salida no deberá realizarse más tarde de las 11am.
- Las reservas se deberán realizar antes de las 6pm. En caso de que vaya a llegar tarde, le rogamos confirme el mismo día de llegada con el/la anfitrión/a.

Descuento para niños

Se aplica cuando los niños comparten la habitación de los padres o cuando tres o más niños comparten una habitación. Se aplica la tarifa completa cuando uno o dos niños ocupan habitaciones separadas. Le rogamos compruebe que la casa es adecuada para niños cuando realice la reserva. En algunas casas se encuentran disponibles cunas 🛒 - puede haber un recargo nominal.

Cenas

Reserve con antelación preferiblemente antes de las 12 del medio día de ese mismo día.
Comidas ligeras disponibles ✕ a petición suya.

Animales domésticos

Con la excepción de perros-guías, por cuestiones de higiene, no se permite la entrada de animales domésticos en las casas.

Apellido
NOMBRE DE LA CIUDAD Y
DE LA CASA
Dirección

Descripción de la ciudad y de la Casa

Tel: Fax:
Email:
Web:
Autobus No:

B&B	# Ensuite	Min£/Max£	Min€/Max€	Dinner	£
B&B	# Standard	Min£/Max£	Min€/Max€	Partial Board Min£/Max£	
Single Rate		Min£/Max£	Min€/Max€	De descuento por niño	%

Distancia en kilómetros **a la
ciudad más cercana**

Símbolos de Instalaciones

Abierto:

B+B pps: Bed & Breakfast por persona
compartiendo
Part Brd: Bed & Breakfast, media pensión -
cena.-.
#: No de habitaciones

De descuento por niños % que comparten la
habitación de los padres o cuando tres o más
niños compartan una habitación
Sngl Rm: Habitación sencilla

Símbolos

- cc Se aceptan tarjetas de crédito
- Acceso a minusválidos con ayudante
- S Habitación sencilla
- P Aparcamiento privado fuera de la vía pública
- Se habla irlandé
- Animales domésticos permitidos
- Prohibido fumar en la casa
- Prohibido fumar en las habitaciones
- TV en las habitaciones
- Teléfono directo en las habitaciones
- Servicios para té/café en las habitaciones
- Canguro, normalmente hasta las 12 de la noche

- Cuna disponible
- Comidas ligeras disponibles
- Licencia para vinos
- recorridos a pie
- recorridos en bicicleta
- Posibilidad de practicar golf en las proximidades
- Posibilidad de practicar equitación en las proximidades
- Faciladades para la Pesca
- *L* Pesca en lago a una distancia menor de 15km.
- *S* Pesca en el mar a una distancia menor de 15km.
- *R* Pesca en rio a una distancia menor de 15km.
- Se aceptan vales de agencias de viaje
- No se aceptan vales de agencias de viaje

Personas con minusvalías/ usuarios de sillas de ruedas

El Consejo de Rehabilitación Nacional (National Rehabilitation Board "NRB") ha dado su aprobación a casas adecuadas para personas con minusvalías y sus ayudantes y éstas se encuentran en la lista bajo el símbolo.

Quejas y comentarios

Las reclamaciones se deberán hacer primero ante los propietarios de las casas antes de la salida. Si ésta no es atendida satisfactoriamente en el caso de que presuntamente le hubieran cobrado de más, deberá enviar el recibo junto con su queja a: **Customer Care, Town & Country Homes, Belleek Road, Ballyshannon, Co. Donegal.** Para mantener los altos estandars por los que se conoce a la Asociación, todos los comentarios sobre el nivel general de servicio y estandars que ha recibido serán bienvenidos y todas las críticas constructivas se tomarán seriamente en cuenta para asegurar la continua mejora de los servicios.

Errores y Omisiones

Se ha cuidado todo lo posible la exactitud de esta publicación conforme a las Leyes de Protección al Cliente de Irlanda. La Asociación de Casas de Ciudad y Campo Ltd. no puede aceptar responsabilidad por errores u omisiones de material facilitado para su inclusión en esta publicación o por cualquier pérdida o decepción causadas por dependencia de información incluida en ésta. Cuando se nos haga saber, se enmendarán futuras ediciones en consecuencia. Puede que ocurran ciertos cambios después de llevar este folleto a imprimir, como que se vendan propiedades o que las casas cambien depropietarios

Uso di questa guida

La guida è divisa in otto regioni geografiche che sono a loro volta suddivise in contee (vedi pagina 3 per mappa delle regioni e contee). Le regioni sono: **Centro Est, Nord Ovest, Irelanda del Nord, Dublino, Sud Est, Cork/Kerry, Shannon, Ovest.**

Modalità di prenotazione
Si consiglia sempre di prenotare in anticipo la prima e l'ultima notte del vostro soggiorno.

Camere disponibili a Dublino
In alta stagione turistica – da maggio a ottobre – è abbastanza difficile trovare camere disponibili a Dublino e nella sua contea a meno che non si abbia già prenotato.
Se si desidera visitare la capitale irlandese durante i mesi sopracitati, vi consigliamo di prenotare il vostro alloggio con notevole anticipo.

È bene ricordare che è quasi impossibile trovare a Dublino un alloggio disponibile all'ultimo minuto.
Onde evitare spiacevoli inconvenienti si consiglia di prenotare in anticipo.

Prenotazioni successive
Se dovessero sorgere dei problemi nel trovare un alloggio una volta in Irlanda, si prega di contattare qualsiasi ufficio turistico o cercare consiglio e assistenza tramite il personale del luogo dove si alloggia (Town and Country Homes). Costoro saranno in grado di aiutarvi a trovare una sistemazione per eventuali notti successive che si necessitano e per il modico costo di una semplice telefonata.

Prenotazioni con carta di credito
Si accettano carte di credito nelle case con il simbolo cc .

Le prenotazioni telefoniche possono essere garantite comunicando un numero di carta di credito valida.

Voucher delle agenzie di viaggio
Presentare il voucher al momento dell'arrivo. I voucher sono validi solo nelle case indicate con il simbolo. Normalmente i voucher includono pernottamento e prima colazione in camera senza servizi privati. Per le camere con servizi privati (en-suite) il supplemento massimo è di £2 per persona. Il supplemento massimo per tre o più persone in condivisione non dovrebbe superare £5 per camera.
I voucher "en-suite" includono una camera con servizi privati completi. Non è previsto nessun altro supplemento.

Supplemento Dublino
Un supplemento camera di £5 per la città e la contea di Dublino viene applicato per i mesi di luglio ed agosto sui vouchers delle Agenzie viaggi. Tale supplemento va pagato direttamente a chi fornisce la sistemazione e non è incluso nel voucher.

Prassi di annullamento
Una volta che la prenotazione è stata confermata, controllare la prassi di annullamento dei proprietari della casa al momento della prenotazione. La persona che effettua la prenotazione risponde della penale di annullamento convenuta, incluse le penali per "mancato arrivo" e se non ci si avvale della prenotazione una penale del 75% della tariffa per la prima notte per Mancato Arrivo verrà dedotta dalla carta di credito.

Arrivi a tarda ora
NB: arrivi dopo le **ore 18.00 solo previo accordo speciale con i proprietari della casa.**

Arrivo/Partenza:
Avvisare se si prevede di arrivare in anticipo.
* Le camere sono disponibili fra le 14.00 e le 18.00.
* Partenza: non oltre le 11.00.
* Le camere vanno occupate entro le 18.00.

Riduzione per bambini
Si applica se i bambini condividono la camera dei genitori o se tre o più bambini condividono la stessa camera. La tariffa intera si applica se uno o due bambini occupano una camera separata. Controllare al momento della prenotazione che la casa sia adatta ad ospitare bambini. In alcune case sono disponibili lettini: potrebbe esserci un addebito simbolico.

Pasti serali
Prenotare in anticipo preferibilmente non più tardi di mezzogiorno del giorno stesso. Spuntini disponibili su richiesta.

Animali domestici
Ad eccezione dei cani guida per ciechi, per motivi igienici, gli animali non sono ammessi nei locali.

Disabili/invalidi
Il National Rehabilitation Board (NRB: ente nazionale riabilitazione) ha approvato case attrezzate per l'accoglienza di disabili con accompagnatore, indicate con il simbolo.

Barra Codice Colore per ogni Regione

Nome della Famiglia
NOME DELLA CASA DI CITTÀ E CAMPAGNA
Indirizzo

Area

TEL: FAX:
EMAIL:
WEB:
AUTOBUS NO:

Descrizione della Casa di Città e Campagna

B&B	# Ensuite	Min£/Max£	Min€/Max€	Dinner	£
B&B	# Standard	Min£/Max£	Min€/Max€	Partial Board Min£/Max£
Single Rate		Min£/Max£	Min€/Max€	Riduzione per Bambini %

Città più vicina distanza in km

Simboli Servizi   **Aperto:**

B+B PPS: Pernottamento e Prima colazione per persona in condivisione
PART BRD: Pernottamento e Prima colazione, Pasto serale
#: No Camere

Riduzione per Bambini % in condivisione con i genitori o se tre o più bambini dividono una camera
SNGL RM: Camera Singola

Simboli

CC	Si accettano carte di credito
🦽	Accesso disabili con accompagnatore
S	Camera singola
P	Posto macchina privato
☘	Si parla irlandese
🐾	Sono ammessi animali domestici
⊗	Casa non fumatori
⚥	Camere non fumatori
▭	TV nelle camere
☎	Telefono diretto nelle camere
☕	Possibilità di preparare té/caffé in camera
👶	Babysitter, generalmente fino a mezzanotte

🛏	Lettino disponibile
✗	Spuntini disponibill
♀	Licenza vendita vini
🚶	Passeggiate
🚲	Giri in bicicletta
⛳	Possibilità di golf nelle vicinanze
🐴	Possibilità di equitazione nelle vicinanze
🐬	Attrezzature per la pesca.
🐟 L	Pesca lacustre nel raggio di 15km.
🐟 S	Pesca marina nel raggio di 15km.
🐟 R	Pesca fluviale nel raggio di 15km.
V	Si accettano voucher di agenzie di viaggio
✗	Non si accettano voucher di agenzie di viaggio

Complimenti e Commenti

Eventuali reclami vanno sempre portati all'attenzione del proprietario della casa prima della partenza. In caso di mancata soddisfazione nel caso di presunto eccesso di prezzo, inoltrare la ricevuta con il reclamo a: **Customer Care, Town & Country Homes, Belleek Road, Ballyshannon, Co. Donegal.**
Al fine di mantenere gli alti standard per i quali l'Associazione è rinomata, saranno apprezzati tutti i commenti sul livello generale del servizio e gli standard che avete incontrato. Tutte le critiche costruttive verranno prese in attenta considerazione per assicurare un continuo miglioramento del servizio.

Errori e Omissioni

È stata posta ogni cura per assicurare accuratezza in questa pubblicazione in conformità alle leggi irlandesi a tutela dei consumatori. La Town & Country Homes Association Ltd. non si assume alcuna responsabilità per eventuali errori o omissioni nel materiale fornito dai membri per questa pubblicazione, o per qualsiasi perdita o delusione risultanti dall'uso delle informazioni qui contenute. Nel caso questi siano portati alla nostra attenzione, le future edizioni verranno emendate di conseguenza. Potrebbero esserci cambiamenti dopo l'andata in stampa nel caso in cui le proprietà siano vendute e la casa cambi di proprietario.

Hoe u deze gids gebruikt

De gids is onderverdeeld in acht geografische streken die weer in graafschappen zijn onderverdeeld (zie pagina 2 voor een kaart van de streken en graafschappen). De streken zijn: **Centraal Ierland, het Noordwesten, Noord Ierland, Dublin, het Zuidoosten, Cork/Kerry, Shannon, West Ierland.**

Reserveren
U wordt geadviseerd de logies voor de eerste en laatste nacht altijd van tevoren te reserveren.

Beschikbaarheld kamers in Dublin
In de stad en het graafschap Dublin is het in het hoogseizoen (mei dot en met oktober) vaak moeilijk logies te binden, tenzij u van tevoren hebt gereserveerd. Als u de hoofdstad tijdns deze maanden bezockt, raden wij u sterk aan **vroeg te reserveren**. U kunt er niet op rekenen in Dublin op korte termijn logies te vinden. Reserveer altijd van te voren.

Voorwaarts reserveren
Indien u problemen ondervindt bij het zoeken naar logies terwijl u in Ierland bent, kunt u contact opnemen met een vreemdelingenbureau of de host/hostess van Town and Country Homes. Zij/hij helpt u vij het reserveren van logies voor ve volgende nacht(en) voor de prijs van een telefoongesprek.

Reservering voor de volgende nacht
Voor de prijs van een telefoontje helpt het huis u met de reservering voor de volgende nacht/nachten. Maak gebruik van deze service om teleurstelling te voorkomen.

Reserveringen met credit card
Credit cards worden geaccepteerd in huizen met het symbool `CC`
Telefoonreserveringen kunnen worden gegarandeerd door een geldig credit card nummer op te geven.

Bonnen van reisbureaus
Overhandig uw bon bij aankomst.
Bonnen zijn alleen geldig in huizen met het symbool
Standaard bonnen zijn geldig voor Bed & Breakfast in een kamer zonder privé-faciliteiten. Voor opwaardering tot een kamer met badkamer betaalt u een maximale toeslag van £2,00 per persoon.

De maximale toeslag voor 3 of meer personen op één kamer is nooit meer dan £5,00 per kamer. Bonnen voor kamers met badkamer zijn voor kamers met volledige privé-faciliteiten.
Geen extra kosten worden in rekening gebracht.

Toeslag in Dublin.
In de maanden juli en augustus wordt in de stad en het graafschap Dublin een kamertoeslag van £5 berekend. Deze toeslag dient rechtstreeks aan de verlener van de accommodatie te worden betaald en is niet bij de bon inbegrepen.

Annuleringen
Wij adviseren u bij boeken van een reservering de annuleringsregels van het huis te controleren. De persoon die de reservering heeft gemaakt, is verantwoordelijk voor de overeengekomen annuleringskosten, inclusief de onkosten indien een gast niet verschijnt. In het geval geen gebruik wordt gemaakt van een reservering wordt 75% van de kosten voor de eerste nacht van de Credit Card afgetrokken.

Late aankomst
Een late aankomst **(na 18.00 uur) dient speciaal met het huis afgesproken te worden.**

Aankomst / Vertrek
Een vroege aankomst graag vooraf meedelen
- Kamers worden tussen 14.00 en 18.00 uur beschikbaar gesteld
- Vertrek - niet later dan 11.00 uur
- Gereserveerde kamers dienen om 18.00 uur te zijn ingenomen.

Kinderkorting
Een kinderkorting is van toepassing indien kinderen de kamer met hun ouders delen of indien 3 of meer kinderen de kamer delen. Het volle tarief is van toepassing wanneer 1 of 2 kinderen aparte kamers innemen. Controleer bij de reservering dat het huis geschikt is voor kinderen. Wiegen zijn in sommige huizen beschikbaar - soms tegen een nominaal tarief.

Avondmaaltijden
Deze dienen vooraf te worden gereserveerd, liefst voor 12.00 uur op de betreffende dag.
Lichte maaltijden ☒ zijn op verzoek beschikbaar.

Huisdieren
In het belang van hygiëne worden huisdieren niet binnenshuis toegelaten, met uitzondering van blindengeleidehonden.

Balk met kleurencode voor iedere streek

Familjens namn
NAMN PÅ GÄSTHUS
Adress

Streek

TEL: FAX:
EMAIL:
WEB:
BUSNUMMER:

Beschrijving van Town & Country Home

B&B	# Ensuite	Min£/Max£	Min€/Max€	Dinner £
B&B	# Standard	Min£/Max£	Min€/Max€	Partial Board Min£/Max£
Single Rate		Min£/Max£	Min€/Max€	© %

Afstand naar dichtstbijzijnde stad
in kilometers

Faciliteiten

Öpen:

B+B PPS: Bed & Breakfast per persoon in dezelfde kamer
PART BRD: Bed & Breakfast, avondmaaltijd
#: Antal Kamers

Percentage korting voor kinderen die de kamer van ouders delen of waar drie of meer kinderen een kamer delen.
SNGL RM: Eenpersoonskamer

Symbolen

CC	Credit cards worden geaccepteerd
🦽	Toegang voor gehandicapten met helper
S	Eenpersoonskamer
P	Privé parkeerplaats
☘	Iers gesproken
🐾	Huisdieren toegestaan
🚭	Roken verboden in het huis
🚭	Roken verboden op de kamer
📺	TV op de kamer
☎	Telefoon op de kamer
☕	Thee- en koffiefaciliteiten op de kamer
👶	Babysitter, gewoonlijk tot middernacht
🛏	Wieg beschikbaar

✕	Lichte maaltijden zijn beschikbaar
🍷	Wijnvergunning
🚶	Wandelen
🚲	Fietsen
⛳	Golf in de omtrek
🐴	Paardrijden in de omtrek
🐟	Mogelijkheden voor hengelsport
🐋 *L*	Meer binnen15km.
🐋 *S*	Zee binnen 15km.
🐋 *R*	Rivier binnen 15km.
V	Cheques van reisbureaus worden geaccepteerd
✕	Cheques van reisbureaus worden niet geaccepteerd

Gehandicapten/rolstoelgebruikers
De nationale revalidatieraad (NRB) heeft huizen goedgekeurd die geschikt zijn voor gehandicapten met helper en deze zijn op de lijst herkenbaar aan het symbool 🦽

Complimenten en opmerkingen
Klachten dienen in de eerste instantie vóór vertrek te worden besproken met de eigenaar van de accommodatie. Wanneer de klacht niet naar uw tevredenheid wordt afgehandeld, dient u contact op te nemen met: **Customer Care, Town & Country Homes, Belleek Road, Ballyshannon, Co. Donegal.**
Om de hoge standaarden waar de Association bekend om staat, te handhaven, worden alle opmerkingen over het algemene niveau van service en de standaarden die u heeft ervaren zeer gewaardeerd. Alle nuttige kritiek wordt serieus genomen om de verbetering van onze service te kunnen voortzetten.

Fouten en omissies
Wij trachten nauwkeurigheid van deze publicatie te verzekeren en te voldoen aan de Ierse Wet Consumentenbescherming. De Town & Country Homes Association Ltd. aanvaart geen verantwoordelijkheid voor fouten of omissies in materiaal dat is geleverd door leden voor opname in deze publicatie of voor verlies of teleurstelling door afhankelijkheid van informatie in deze publicatie. Waar dit tot onze aandacht wordt gebracht, worden toekomstige uitgaven gewijzigd. Er kunnen zich wijzigingen voordoen na de druk van deze publicatie waar huizen zijn verkocht en het eigenaarschap van het huis wordt veranderd.

421

Denna guidebok har indelats i atta geografiska regioner, dessa regioner har sedan indelats i landskap (se sid. 2 för kartor för regionerna och landskapen). Regionerna är: **östra inlandet, Nordväst, Nord Irland, Dublin, Sydöst, Cork/Kerry, Shannon, västra Irland.**

Bokning

Vi rekommenderar att logi för första och sista natten alltid bokas i förväg. Logi i Dublin City och länet Dublin måste reserveras minst 2/3 veckor i förväg och längre i förväg för juni/juli och augusti. När ett resesällskap eller en resebyrå förhandsbokar logi för en kund kommer namnet på hemmet att stå på kupongen. Denna kupong gäller därför inte på något annat ställe.

Bokning kan göras genom:
- Resesällskap eller resebyrå
- Att ta direkt kontakt med individuella hem Ankomstsgaranti kan begäras, t ex handpenning eller kreditkortsnummer
- Turistinformationskontor över hela Irland hjälper dig med bokningar mot ett belopp på 3 irländska pund
- Bekräfta alltid bokningar skriftligen.

Förhandsbokning:

Värdar/värdinnor hjälper gärna till med förhandsbokningar av logi för gäster, för kostnaden av ett telefonsamtal. För att undvika besvikelse rekommenderar vi att denna service utnyttjas.

Bokning med kreditkort

Kreditkort accepteras på ställen som har symbolen [CC].
Telefonbokning kan garanteras genom att ett giltigt kreditkortsnummer uppges.

RESEBYRÅKUPONGER

Var vänlig att visa kupongerna vid ankomsten. Kuponger gäller endast på de gästhus som uppvisar ☺ symbolen. Standardkuponger täcker Bed and Breakfast med rum utan privat badrum. Önskas privat badrum tillkommer en extra kostnad på 2 pund per person. Den högsta avgiften är 5 pund per rum för 3 eller fler personer som delar ett rum. Det finns kuponger som täcker kostnaden för rum med privat badrum. Inga andra kostnader tillkommer.

Extra tillägg för Dublin:

Ett extra tillägg på 5 pund per rum gäller i juli och augusti för Dublin City och länet Dublin, med resebyråkupongerna. Detta tillägg betalas direkt till den som hyr ut rummen och är inte § medräknat i kupongerna.

AVBESTÄLLNINGSREGLER

Var vänlig kontrollera avbeställningsreglerna med hemmet när du bokar och bekräftar bokningen. Personen som gör bokningen är ansvarig för avbeställningsavgiften samt kostnaden för "utebliven ankomst" och om bokningen inte utnyttjas tillkommer en kostnad på 75% av avgiften för "utebliven ankomst" för första natten, denna kommer att dras av på kreditkortet.

Sen ankomst

Var vänlig observera att sen ankomst, efter kl. 18.00, måste bestämmas enligt specialavtal med hemmet.

In-/Utcheckning:

Var vänlig meddela om tidigankomst.
Rummen kan intagas mellan kl. 14.00 och 18.00.
Utcheckning måste göras innan kl. 11.00.
Bokade rum måste intagas före kl. 18.00.

RABATT FÖR BARN

Gäller där barn delar rum med föräldrar, eller om 3 eller fler barn delar ett rum.
Fullt pris när 1 eller 2 barn bor i separat rum.
Kontrollera att huset är lämpligt för barn när ni bokar.
Barnsängar finns ➡på vissa ställen och kan lånas för en liten avgift.

KVÄLLSMÅLTIDER

Beställs i förväg, helst före kl. 12.00 dagen ifråga.
Lätta måltider ☒ serveras efter önskemål.

SÄLLSKAPSDJUR

Förutom guidehundar för blinda tillåts inga djur inne i husen av hygieniska skäl.

RÖRELSEHINDRAD PERSON/ RULLSTOLSBUNDEN PERSON

Det irländska rehabiliteringsförbundet (NRB) har godkänt gästhus som är lämpliga för personer med handikapp och som har ressällskap, dessa gästhus är markerade med symbolen ♿ .

Familjens namn
NAMN PÅ GÄSTHUS
Adress

Beskrivning på gästhuset

Område

TEL: FAX:
EMAIL:
WEB:
BUS N° :

B&B	# Ensuite	Min£/Max£	Min€/Max€	Dinner	£
B&B	# Standard	Min£/Max£	Min€/Max€	Partial Board Min£/Max£	
Single Rate		Min£/Max£	Min€/Max€	Rabatt för barn	%

Avstånd i km till **närmsta stad** (V)

Symboler

B+B PPS: Bed & Breakfast per person som delar rum.
PART BRD: Bed & Breakfast och kvällsmåltid.
#: Antal Rum

Öppettider:

Rabatt för barn delar föräldrars rum eller om 3 eller fler barn delar ett rum
SNGL RM: Enkelrum

Symbolen

- **CC** Kreditkort accepteras
- 🦽 Åtkomst för handikappad person och medhjälpare
- **S** Enkelrum
- **P** Privat bilparkering på gård
- ☘ Irländsktalande
- 🐾 Sällskapsdjur tillåts
- ⊗ Rökfritt hus
- ⚥ Rökfritt rum
- 📺 TV finns i rummet
- ☎ Telefon med direktanslutning i rum
- ☕ Te och kaffe kan göras på rummet
- ♿ Åtkomst för handikappad person och medhjälpare

- 🛏 Barnsäng finns
- ✗ Lätta måltider serveras
- ⚕ Licens att servera vin
- 🚶 Vandring
- 🚲 Cykling
- ⛳ Golf finns i närheten
- 🐴 Hästridning finns i närheten
- 🐟 Allt för fisket.
- 🐟L Insjöfiske inom 15km.
- 🐟S Havsfiske inom 15km.
- 🐟R Flodfiske inom 15km.

- (V) Resebyråkuponger accepteras
- ⊗ Resebyråkuponger accepteras inte

KOMPLIMANGER OCH KLAGOMÅL

Eventuella klagomål ska lämnas till gästhusets ägare innan ni åker därifrån. Om inget resultat erhålls om det skulle gälla eventuellt överpris, skickar du kvittot med ditt klagomål till **Customer Care, Town & Country Homes, Belleek Road, Ballyshannon, Co. Donegal.** För att kunna behålla den höga standarden som föreningen är känd för, tar vi gärna emot alla kommentarer om den allmänna servicen och standarden så som du har upplevt den. Vi tar all konstruktiv kritik på allvar så att vi kan fortsätta förbättra servicen.

FEL ELLER UTELÄMNANDEN

Vi har gjort vårt bästa för att alla fakta i den här broschyren skall stämma, detta enligt den irländska konsumentskyddslagen. Föreningen för Town & Country Homes Ltd. kan dock inte hållas ansvarig för fel eller utelämnanden i material som inkommer från medlemmar för publicering i denna utgåva, eller för förlust eller besvikelse som orsakats till följd av informationen, men om en fel har uppkommit och detta meddelas till föreningen kommer framtida utgåvor följaktligen att korrigeras. Ändringar kan förekomma efter utgåvan gått i tryck i fall där hus har sålts eller bytt ägare.

このガイドの使い方

このガイドではアイルランドを 7 つの地理的な地域に分けて取り扱っています。その地域はさらに郡（地域、郡の地図は 3 ページを参照）に分かれます。7 つの地域は北西部、ダブリン、南東部、コーク/ケリー、シャノン地域、西部、東内陸部です。

予約手続き

時期を問わず初日と最終日の宿泊先を前もって予約することをお勧めします。

ダブリンにおける部屋の予約情況：観光客の多い 5 月から 10 月にかけて、ダブリン市とダブリン郡で部屋を見つけるのは、事前に予約がない限り非常に難しくなります。この時期にダブリンを訪れる場合は、すべての宿泊先について事前に予約することをぜひお勧めします。直前になってからダブリンで部屋を見つけるのは極めて困難です。必ず事前に予約してください。

事前予約：アイルランドご滞在中に宿泊施設を見つけることで問題が生じた場合は、いずれかの観光協会へご連絡するか、あるいはタウン・アンド・カントリー・ホーム従業員のアドバイスおよび援助を仰いでください。電話料金のみの費用で、引き続いてのご宿泊を予約するお手伝いをさせていただきます。

クレジットカードでの予約

クレジットカードは CC マークの付いた宿泊施設でご利用できます。

電話で予約する際は、予約を保証するために有効なクレジットカードのカード番号を求められることがあります。予約時に条件款約をご確認ください。

旅行代理店のクーポン

ご到着時にクーポンを提示してください。クーポンは Ⓥ マークの付いた宿泊施設においてのみ有効です。

スタンダード・クーポンは B&B のバスルームなしの部屋に対して使用できます。一人につき最高 2 ポンドお支払いいただければバスルーム付きの部屋をご利用になれます。一部屋を 3 人もしくはそれ以上の人数でご利用の場合は、一部屋につき加算料金が 5 ポンドを越えることはありません。

オン・スイート・クーポンはバスルーム付きの部屋に対して使用できます。加算料金はありません。

ダブリンでの加算料金：7、8 月のダブリン市とダブリン郡においては、旅行代理店のクーポンに一部屋につき 5 ポンドの追加料金が適用されます。これはクーポンには含まれていない金額ですので、宿泊施設で直接お支払いください。

予約取消しの方針

予約を取消す際は直ちに電話してください。
- 14 日前に予約を取消した場合 - 取消し料なし
- 24 時間前に予約を取消した場合/取消さなかった場合 - 1 泊目の B&B 料金の 75%

チェックイン／チェックアウト

到着が早くなる場合は連絡してください。
- チェックインは午後 2 時から 6 時のあいだ
- チェックアウトは午前 11 時まで
- 予約は午後 6 時まで受付け

市街地までの距離 km　Ⓥ

地域			
タウン・ホームまたはカントリー・ホーム名			
住所			
タウン・アンド・カントリー・ホームの説明			

地域
電話：
ファックス：
電子メール：
ホームページ：
バス番号：

地域ごとに色分けされています。

	最低£/最高£	最低 /最高	夕食 £
B&B バスルーム付客室数 #	最低£/最高£	最低 /最高	Partial Board 最低£/最高£
B&B バスルームなし客室数 #	最低£/最高£	最低 /最高	子供割引 %
Single Rate			

設備のマーク：　　　　　　　　　　　　　　　　オープン期間：

B+B：宿泊と朝食、合部屋 1 人あたりの料金　　　%：保護者の部屋に子供が滞在する場合、または
Partial Brd：7 泊分の宿泊、朝食、夕食の料金　　　3 人以上の子供が 1 部屋に滞在する場合の割引率
#：部屋数　　　　　　　　　　　　　　　　　　Single Rate：シングルルーム料金

マーク

CC	クレジットカード使用可	寝室禁煙		ハイキング
	助力者同伴で身体障害者利用可 NDA 承認	寝室にテレビあり		サイクリング
S	シングルルーム	寝室に直通電話あり		5km 以内にゴルフ場あり
P	個人駐車場あり	寝室に紅茶／コーヒー設備あり		5km 以内に乗馬場あり
	アイルランド語使用	ベビーシッターあり、通常夜 12 時まで		釣り施設
	ペット用施設あり	ベビーベッドあり		15km 以内に釣りのできる湖
	全建物禁煙	軽食あり		15km 以内に釣りのできる海
		ワイン営業免許あり		15km 以内に釣りのできる川

Area Index

Area Index

Area Index

Area Index

Reservation

You can make a reservation with our homes by any of the following methods:

1. **Telephone** the home direct.

2. **Fax** the home if individual B&B has a fax machine .

3. **Email** the home where there is an email address.

4. Contact the home in writing.

5. Contact the Town and Country Homes **on-line reservation** on our website, www.townandcountry.ie
    Refer to the site details on the home,
    and click on 'Make Reservation'.

Please refer to "Using this Guide" Page 6 for further information

Tel: 00353 7222222
Fax: 00353 7222207
Email: admin@townandcountry.ie
WAP: www.bandbireland.com
Web: www.townandcountry.ie

Nominate Your Favourite Home

Address
Of Sender

Date

Dear Town and Country Homes
I have had an amazing experience in one of your
homes recently. I stayed with

Name ....

Address ....
....
....
....

On ....Date ....

Comments ....
....
....
....

Yours sincerely

Signed

Nominate your favourite home and enter into our free draw for
1 weeks accommodation in any of our homes plus return flight for 2 passengers
from any of Aer Lingus scheduled flights. Flights kindly sponsored by Aer Lingus.

Your favourite home will be entered for the "Best Town and Country Home 2001."
Prize kindly sponsored by Waterford Crystal Visitor Centre.
Return this letter to:
Town and Country Homes Association,
Belleek Rd, Ballyshannon, Co. Donegal,
or you can fax on 00 353 72 22207.